Our Religions

Our Religions

Edited by
Arvind Sharma

HarperSanFrancisco
A Division of HarperCollins*Publishers*

For information address HarperCollins Publishers, 10 East 53rd Street, New York, NY 10022.

FIRST EDITION

Library of Congress Cataloging-in-Publication Data

Our religions / edited by Arvind Sharma.
p. cm.
Includes bibliographical references and index.
ISBN 0-06-067264-1 (alk. paper)
1. Religions. I. Sharma, Arvind.
BL80.2.087 1993
291—dc20 92-56128
CIP

93 94 95 96 97 RRD(H) 10 9 8 7 6 5 4 3 2 1

This edition is printed on acid-free paper that meets the American National Standards Institute Z39.48 Standard.

for Wilfred Cantwell Smith

Contents

Let us never forget that there exists no other religious reality than the faith of the believer. If we really want to understand religion, we must refer exclusively to the believer's testimony. What we believe, from our point of view, about the nature or value of other religions, is a reliable testimony to our own faith, or to our own understanding of religious faith; but if our opinion about another religion differs from the opinion and evaluation of the believers, then we are no longer talking about their religion. We have turned aside from historical reality, and are concerned only with ourselves.

W. B. Kristensen
Religionshistorisk studium
(translation by Eric J. Sharpe)

We meet on the mountain height of absolute respect for the religious convictions of each other . . .

Hon. Charles Carroll Bonney
Opening address, September 11, 1893
World's Parliament of Religions, Chicago

Acknowledgments

I would like to thank Mary Gerhart for relaying the proposal of this book to Bill Newell; Bill for recommending it to John Loudon; John for his enthusiastic support and supervision of the project from its very inception; and his staff, specially Karen Levine and Terri Goff, for bringing it to a swift and successful conclusion, in time to figure in the centennial celebration of the 1893 World's Parliament of Religions. For this happy coincidence one can only thank the stars.

To the eminent scholars who have contributed to this book I owe a special debt of gratitude; but it is a debt that can never be repaid and a sense of gratitude that lies too deep for words.

Arvind Sharma
Editor

Introduction

The world of religion is composed of the religions of the world, seven of which—Hinduism, Buddhism, Confucianism, Taoism, Judaism, Christianity, and Islam—are presented in the covers of this book. Perhaps no book on the religions of the world can be the final or ultimate one, but it can be unique. This is such a book.

It is unique in several ways. It is unique because each author belongs to the tradition he is writing about, he speaks not only *of* his tradition, but his standing in the field enables him also to speak *for* it. Furthermore, poised as he is at the cutting edge of the tradition as it encounters modernity, each author is able to address the contemporary issues the tradition faces in a way that has rarely ever been attempted earlier, much less accomplished. Finally, the fact that all these spokesmen who write about their traditions do so from within the arena of the academic study of religion as it has evolved in the West renders their contribution all the more unique.

Two ends of the spectrum have often been played against each other in the study of religion: that one who knows one religion knows none and that one who knows too many does not know any. This book focuses not at the ends but at the colorful band that lies between these two ends. As the reader explores this band, constituted by the religions of the world, he or she will have to decide whether the various religions of the world are hyphens that unite or dashes that divide, and in doing so will determine the grammar of religious discourse in times to come.

CHAPTER 1

Hinduism

Arvind Sharma

Defining Hinduism

Mahatma Gandhi is acknowledged, even by his critics, as the greatest Hindu of modern times. However, on the evening of January 30, 1948, he was shot to death by a fellow Hindu, Nathuram Godse, for acquiescing in the partition of the country into India and Pakistan. Godse bowed to Gandhi reverentially before shooting him to death, and Gandhi raised his hand in a gesture of forgiveness as he fell. In performing these surreal acts of spiritual chivalry, both acted as they did in the name and spirit of Hinduism. How are we to define a religion that embraces both the victim and the assassin?

Gandhi, Godse, and God: The Difficulty in Defining Hinduism

Time passes, but paradoxes persist. When Gandhi was killed by Godse's bullets, the last word heard to escape his lips was that of Rāma—one of the Hindu names for God. Almost half a century later, on December 6, 1992, militant Hindu activists demolished a 464-year-old mosque, virtually with their bare hands, to replace it with a temple dedicated to the same Rāma in whose name Gandhi had laid down his life for the cause of Hindu-Muslim unity. Many Hindu women fasted the day after Gandhi died in 1948, but in 1992 "many women volunteers were seen crying," presumably with joy, as the domes of the mosque began crumbling under persistent pounding and a crescendo built up with chants of "Jai Shrī Rāma" (Hail Lord Rāma).

Hinduism does not make it easy for its followers to define it in the best of times, and the journey from Hindu piety to Hindu militancy under the banner of the same god does not make it any easier.

What is true of the gods of Hinduism is also true of the Hindus. The Hindus, no less than their gods, are difficult to pin down. This aspect of Hinduism is best illustrated by the experience of the Muslim savant of the eleventh century, Alberuni, who wrote a masterly treatise on India known by the title of its English translation as "Alberuni's India." At several points he is constrained to observe: "The Hindus differ among themselves..." or that "some Hindus believe..." until, finally, he bluntly states that there is not one thing that one Hindu says that is not denied by another!

Can such a religion ever be defined? To begin to answer this question, let us first turn this minus into a plus and reflect on what the problem of defining Hinduism itself tells us about Hinduism.

What This Difficulty Reveals about the Nature of Hinduism

The problem of defining Hinduism has its positive side: It helps to reveal Hinduism's distinctive nature in several ways. First, it tells us that Hinduism has a special relationship with India. After all, most Hindus believe that Rāma, like them, was born in India. Second, it shows that Hindus share a special kind of relationship with all Indians. Thus Hinduism is inclusive—particularly in the Indian context. Hindus today are quite willing to accept Buddhists, Jainas, and Sikhs—members of some other faiths of Indian origin—as Hindus, although the Buddhists, Jainas, and Sikhs may demur. Hinduism tends to extend this attitude to the Indian followers of the faiths of even non-Indian origin—even though these may demur even more strongly. Pushed to its logical extreme, a Hindu can claim that one is most a Hindu when least a Hindu, that is, when one has dissolved one's Hindu particularity in Hinduism's all-embracing inclusiveness. Hinduism in this extreme formulation paradoxically becomes identical with its own negation! Such a Hindu is like anyone else—only more so. Some Hindus are indeed willing to go that far but most still remain tied to India with a sacred thread, however attenuated it might become. Third, the difficulties in defining Hinduism tell us that not only does Hinduism have ethnic roots and tends to be inclusive but also that, in its eagerness to be inclusive and in its tolerance of diversity within, it is willing to overlook contradictions and may even generate them.

Given such diversity, it seems as if Hinduism is constantly seeking some anchor for the floating mass of diverse beliefs and practices that it encompasses. It is as if the storm itself generates a center, not so much that a storm forms around a center—which is the more usual way in which religions grow. Several such centers have been suggested and may have functioned as such. In classical India, the Vedas—a body of revealed texts—came close to occupying that position; Alberuni suggests that belief in reincarnation might have played a similar role in medieval Hinduism; and adherence to caste and the acceptance of the sanctity of the priestly class of brahmins and/or of the cow have also been suggested as constituting such centers. But while indicative of Hinduism in their own ways, none of these features is definitive.[1] In this, Hinduism may be compared to a doughnut; it is the doughnut that defines the doughnut-hole and not the other way around. J. L. Brockington has suggested, given the fact that diversity is "part of the essence of Hinduism," that its "distinctiveness is only intelligible in terms of its history"[2] and that "it is a subconscious recognition of this diversity, which defies any simple definitions, that leads Hindus to appeal to their perceived origins in the Veda; it is a recognition that the unifying factor lies in their common history. The appeal to the Vedas permits both an affirmation of the supremacy of tradition and an implicit acceptance of the reality of adaptation."[3] The fact that the Hindus call their own tradition *sanātana dharma* or "immemorial tradition" supports such a view.[4]

Toward a Definition of Hinduism

Hinduism, therefore, is closely associated with the Vedas, or rather with the acceptance of the *notion* of their authority, for the actual knowledge of the Vedas, such as it existed, was, for vast periods of its history, confined to the male members of the priestly class. Most Hindus were either in fact or formally excluded from it. Indeed, the acceptance of Vedic authority is perhaps the sole formal test of orthodoxy in Hinduism. However, even the acceptance of Vedic authority is so nominal in Hinduism that the French Indologist Louis Renou compares it to the formal tipping of the hat. The fact that so much might occasionally be made of this nominal requirement, when push comes to shove, tells us how tenuously and sinuously Hinduism hangs together. Given its massive diversity, the *nominal* acceptance of Vedic authority plays a very *real* role in moments of identity crisis, for there is little else to hold on to. Yet even Vedic authority is periodically questioned in the history of Hinduism; rites and practices now accepted as Hindu may even be pre-Vedic; the Vedas question their own authority and some forms of Hindu salvation transcend the Vedas so much so that such a standard school of Hindu philosophy as Advaita Vedānta is sometimes classified as nonorthodox. Even criticism, indifference, or outright repudiation of the Vedas is tolerated, provided it is not accompanied by a self-conscious rejection of the community. While Hinduism acknowledges that there can be apostasy, the abandonment of the entire tradition itself, it is not so much upset by heresy, the abandonment of some part of the tradition. There can be a world of difference between being a Hindu and being an orthodox Hindu. A non-orthodox Hindu is not such an oxymoron in Hinduism as it might be in Christianity or Islam.

Thus, while no strict definition of Hinduism's essence is possible, it may be defined descriptively. Fundamentally, a Hindu may be identified as one who does not deny being one. The collectivity of the beliefs and practices of those who accept the designation constitutes Hinduism. It is a peculiarly Hindu phenomenon that Hinduism may be defined as the religion of the Hindus and that this definition should, however narrowly, escape tautology.

Hinduism in the World Today

Who Is a Hindu in Today's World?

On February 15, 1989, a passenger arrived in Montreal, Canada, from Dacca, Bangladesh, carrying a passport that identified its bearer as Kudrat Bari, a Muslim. While going through Canada immigration this passenger confessed that he was traveling on a false passport and that he was in fact a Hindu, Dhiren Biswas by name. He was entering Canada as a refugee to escape religious persecution in Bangladesh, where he belonged to the minority Hindu community. Bangladesh had renounced secularism and established Islam as the state religion of Bangladesh in 1988. The immigration officials refused to accept the fact that he was a Hindu, insisting that he was what the passport declared him to be—a Muslim. Refugee status was denied to him and he was deported to Bangladesh on July 29, 1989.

This incident, though minor in itself, highlights the issue: How does one establish that one is a Hindu? Indeed, who is a Hindu? And, once again, what is Hinduism?

The steps that Dhiren Biswas took in his vain bid to establish his identity as a Hindu are revealing. He took four steps to establish it:

1. He secured a certificate from a doctor stating that he had not undergone circumcision, compulsory for Muslims;
2. He got another Hindu who had known him in Bangladesh to vouch that he was a Hindu and also to specify his caste;
3. He had himself interviewed by me, and I certified that to the best of my knowledge he was a Hindu; and
4. He had another certificate prepared by the temple priest of the Hindu Mission in Montreal stating that he had attended temple services and received *prasāda* (food partaken by devotees after it has been consecrated in worship).

Each step taken by Dhiren Biswas, alias Kudrat Bari, to establish the fact that he was a Hindu is revealing. Each step successively reveals that it is easier to *recognize, identify, certify,* or *observe* who is a Hindu than to define one.

The crucial point can now be made. Had Dhiren Biswas arrived from India rather than Bangladesh, he would have been readily identified as a Hindu, for 95 percent of the Hindus of the world live in India, over 80 percent of whose population is Hindu. A person coming from India is presumed to be a Hindu just as a person coming from Israel is presumed to be a Jew. In other words, Hinduism, at least to begin with, is an ethnic religion.

Hinduism as an Ethnic Religion: Hinduism in India

Hinduism in India today must first be viewed in relation to other religions represented in India. One striking statistical feature in this connection is the *proportionate* decline in the number of Hindus to the rest of the population. The British introduced the decennial census in India in 1880. Since then the proportion of the Hindus to the rest of the population of British India has been steadily declining. For British India the figures for the percentage of Hindus as a component of the overall population are as follows: 75.09 percent in 1881, 74.24 percent in 1891, 72.87 percent in 1901; 71.68 percent in 1911; 70.73 percent in 1921; 70.67 percent in 1931; and 69.46 percent in 1941.[5]

The trend has continued in independent India. After the division of India into a predominantly Hindu India and a predominantly Muslim Pakistan, the proportionate figures for Hindus were bound to be higher in independent India. But the proportion of the Hindus to the total population continues to decline, though at a declining rate: 84.98 percent in 1951; 83.50 percent in 1961; 82.72 percent in 1971;[6] and 82.64 percent in 1981.[7]

This is a very disturbing trend in terms of Hindu self-identity, and some of the recent political developments in India can be attributed to this anxiety. The anxiety is not unfounded. The population of Hindus in the former state of Travancore, now part of the state of Kerala in south India, fell from 83.0 percent in 1816 to 61.6 percent in 1931.[8] For, as will become apparent later from an overview of the history of Hinduism, Hinduism is not a fixed entity.

In the history of Hinduism, religious manifestations that the Hindus did not originally identify themselves with, for example, the religion of the Indus Valley of the third millennium B.C.E., were subsequently absorbed. Similarly, philosophical movements that did not identify themselves with the Hindu tradition—at least with the orthodox philosophical tradition—such as the atomists (called the Vaiśeṣikas) or the metaphysical dualists (followers of Sāṅkhya) proceeded to do so in due course. Thus the identity of the Hindu tradition is to some extent a variable; groups can fall in line or fall out of line. Sikhism is an interesting example of a tradition that is currently distancing itself from Hinduism.

This fluidity which characterizes Hindu identity has become a major problem for Hinduism in India today, because membership of the Hindu community is primarily a matter of self-definition. This is perhaps true for religious identity in every religion, but it is particularly so with Hinduism.

This self-identity has been rendered problematical by the Constitution of India in several ways.

1. The Constitution declares India as a secular state. Normally this would preclude governmental interference in matters of religion. However, the government has exercised this right very selectively; it has selected Hinduism for major state intervention on the assumption that, because the Hindus constitute an overwhelming majority of the population, the Indian Parliament can in effect function as a Hindu Parliament.

2. Simultaneously with thus interfering with Hindu institutions, it has safeguarded minority rights for religions other than Hinduism and even extended them through legislative measures.

3. The situation described under the first point is partly the consequence of the government's desire to reform Hinduism because it possesses no central governing body. It is, for instance, under this belief that reverse discrimination in favor of untouchables is enshrined in the Constitution. However, although untouchability is a peculiarly Hindu institution, the government, for electoral ends, sometimes extends the protection even to non-Hindus who can establish an untouchable background. Untouchables were a class of people whose touch was considered polluting by caste Hindus. They were victims of what might be called a form of religious apartheid, and the kind of discrimination blacks have suffered in the United States. A similar development has occurred recently in relation to reservation for backward castes. This has serious implications for Hindu self-identity.

4. In some states of India, such as Kerala and West Bengal, avowedly Marxist governments have been elected to office, and some Hindu organizations, such as the Rāmakrishna Mission, which most modern Hindus regard as representative of mainline Hinduism, have been forced to seek "minority religion" status and declare themselves non-Hindu to protect themselves from state intervention.

At the moment, therefore, Hinduism as an ethnic religion in India is in a crisis. Over the past two hundred years it gradually achieved a *reformist* and *pan-Indian* identity over and above its division into castes and sects and an *inclusive* identity that welcomed interaction with other Indian religions. Although the framers of the Indian Constitution intended to maintain this thrust, the actual consequence of the legal document they produced seems to have been the reverse. The implications of this situation are examined in greater detail under "The Religious Consequences of Freedom" later in the chapter.

Hinduism as a Universal Religion: Hinduism Outside India

Despite its ethnic moorings, Hinduism possesses a universalizing core within it. This has manifested itself in the periodic geographical expansion of Hinduism beyond India's borders, which was already under way before the beginning of the Common Era. This early expansion of Hinduism beyond the borders of India, primarily into Southeast Asia, was part of the process that accounts for its spread throughout India itself, after its early appearance in northwest India. The only surviving example of this expansion is Bali in Indonesia, although at one time virtually the whole of Southeast Asia felt its influence. The eclipse of Hinduism in India after the Muslim conquest also saw the waning of its influence overseas where, as in India, it yielded much ground to Islam.

The second geographical expansion of Hinduism was tied to the coattails of the British Empire. Hindus emigrated as indentured laborers to Malaya, Mauritius, Trinidad, and the Fiji Islands. In Trinidad, the Hindu tradition survives and provides grist to the literary mills of expatriate Indo-Anglican authors like V. S. Naipaul. But it is vibrantly alive in the other regions, for example, in the Fiji Islands, despite serious political setbacks in recent years.

The third geographical expansion of Hinduism was also made possible by the British presence in India, but it happened through Hindu initiative and therefore is unique. The most significant event in this connection is the address delivered by Swami Vivekānanda, as a young monk from India, at the World's Parliament of Religions in 1893 and the lectures that followed, in which he is said to have created modern Hinduism. That is, he offered a formulation of Hinduism that most English-educated Hindus came to regard as normative. This Hinduism is philosophical, spiritual, and experiential. It is based on the texts called the *Upaniṣads* or the final sections of the Vedas. It is also tolerant and accepts all other religions as true. Its significance is well illustrated by the provocative and exaggerated, but suggestive, title of one of the books in which the event is described: *Hinduism Invades America!*

Such an invasion has occurred, but it has been only a friendly one, so that many Hindu practices have spread like gentle ripples across the Western world. The widespread cultivation of *yoga* conjures up images of men and women in exotic postures. This branch of yoga (called *Haṭha Yoga*) focuses on the body, but the yoga of the mind (called *Rāja Yoga*) has proved equally popular, after undergoing a glamorous phase during which Transcendental Meditation was patronized by the Beatles. The famous text on yoga assigned to the fifth century and attributed to Patañjali, known as the *Yogasūtra* (I.2), defines the aim of this form of yoga as the cessation of all mental fluctuations. Hindu beliefs such as those of reincarnation and *karma* are also gaining acceptance. Recent surveys indicate that almost a quarter of the Western world now believes in reincarnation. The figure is even higher among blacks in America and in Europe in general. The Hindu idea of religious life as a journey undertaken through a variety of paths also dovetails with the religious pluralism of the modern West and provides it with a spiritual underpinning. These spiritual beliefs and practices have become so much a part of the religious landscape of the Western world that, by contrast with the very visible presence of Hare Kṛṣṇas dancing in the streets, they constitute Hinduism's invisible presence in the West.

The Relationship Between the Ethnic and the Universal

The interplay between the ethnic and the universal elements of Hinduism is illustrated by the Hindu Marriage and Divorce Act of 1955. This was perhaps the first time since India gained independence in 1947 that the government of India was called upon to define a Hindu, at least for legal purposes, as it had to specify the people to whom the Act applied. This Act was designed to consolidate and reform Hindu personal law relating to marriage. It defined a Hindu as a person who belongs to either of the two categories, A or B. All persons who were Indian citizens but were not "Muslim, Christian, Parsee or Jew" belonged to category A, while all those who were not Indian citizens "but claimed to be Hindu by religion" belonged to category B, and Hindus = A + B!

The Hindu Marriage and Divorce Act of 1955 offered a dual definition of Hinduism: an ethnic definition and a universal one. For an Indian citizen, it offered an ethnic definition; for one not an Indian citizen, it offered a universalistic definition—"one who is Hindu *by religion*." This distinction arises because Hinduism has undergone a creedal formulation over the past few centuries; thus, anyone anywhere in the world can now claim to be a Hindu if he or she accepts any of its many creedal formulations—the most popular ones being some form of Vedānta, though devotional movements and groups founded around charismatic gurus have also been gaining in popularity. This has given rise within Hinduism to a tension between its ethnic and its universal components.

We must distinguish here between ideological and communitarian universalism. Hinduism has always tended to be ideologically universalistic, in the sense of possessing a certain hospitable predisposition toward accepting approaches to the ultimate that may differ from its own. It has been slower in accommodating "outside" groups within its fold, though its history attests to considerable assimilation even along these lines by resort to legal or pious fictions. For example, numerous neo-Hindus and even non-Hindu visitors are allowed in some shrines. On the other hand, even a prime minister of India, Mrs. Gandhi, was refused entry into the temple at Puri because her husband was a Zoroastrian and not a Hindu! The ethnic and universal aspects of Hinduism thus together constitute the paradoxical axes of Hindu pluralism, keeping the map of Hinduism, as it were, forever on the drawing board of history. When Hinduism faced the challenge of the universalizing religions of Buddhism and Jainism, it fought fire with fire, with its own brand of universal devotionalism. When it could not match the militant and expansionist universalism of Islam with its own, it retreated into the confines of ethnicity (though without forsaking its universalizing potential). When subsequently it faced the challenge of an imperializing and universalizing Christianity, it countered it by developing both a Hindu nationalism on the one hand and by propagating a universalizing version of Hinduism on the other. It is also in the context of such challenges that, however reluctantly, Hindus have had to face the vexing question of either defining themselves or allowing themselves to be defined by others. These two vectors have not always coincided.

Hinduism's Contribution to Contemporary Religious Life

Hinduism may be difficult to define in theoretical terms or to confine to one part of the world in geographical terms, notwithstanding its strong links with India; but its contribution to the religious heritage of humanity is not in doubt. In many ways it is like any other religion. The Hindus, like the followers of any other religion, work, worship, pray, and seek well-being in this world and the next for themselves and their families and friends. The stereotype of the Hindu gazing at his navel with his leg twisted around his neck is hopelessly out of date. It never resembled the life of the average Hindu any more than a phone number resembles either the phone itself or the person whose number it is.

The fact that Hinduism is not as exotic as it might have been imagined to be does not mean that it has nothing to offer to stir our imagination. Its recognition of the use of the body as a vehicle of salvation as against an exclusive preoccupation with the mind or the spirit and its acceptance of multiple paths to reality as a philosophical grounding to religious plurality have already been anticipated as constituting fresh religious perspectives. Its bolder insights include two sensational claims: a metaphysical one—that the seeker is none other than the sought, and a practical one—that one may perform action without seeking the fruits thereof. Both these insights are disconcertingly counterintuitive and perhaps for that very reason so tantalizing. What can be more obvious than the fact that we are different from one another, and from God? Yet flying in the face of our daily experience of differences all around us, the nondualistic form of Hinduism boldly proclaims: "That thou art," as Uddālaka Āruṇi taught his son Śvetaketu (*Chāndogya Upaniṣad* VI.13.1–3):

> 1. *"Place this salt in the water. In the morning come unto me."*
> *Then he did so.*
> *Then he said to him: "That salt you placed in the water last evening—please bring it hither."*
> *Then he grasped for it, but did not find it, as it was completely dissolved.*
> 2. *"Please take a sip of it from this end," said he. "How is it?"*
> *"Salt."*
> *"Take a sip from the middle," said he. "How is it?"*
> *"Salt."*
> *"Take a sip from the end," said he. "How is it?"*
> *"Salt."*
> *"Set it aside. Then come unto me."*
> *He did so, saying, "It is always the same."*
> *Then he said to him: "Verily, indeed, my dear, you do not perceive Being here. Verily, indeed, it is here.*
> 3. *That which is the finest essence—this whole world has that as its soul. That is Reality. That is Ātman (Soul). That art thou, Śvetaketu."*[9]

Similarly, action without motivation, on the face of it, seems as impossible to think of as fire without fuel. Yet in the famous Hindu text, the *Bhagavadgītā*, Kṛṣṇa, who is God incarnate, instructs his dear friend and devotee, Arjuna, to perform actions without concern for the fruits one hopes to secure through them. He is tersely told (II.47):

> Action alone is within your control, it never extends to the fruits. Be not attached to the fruits of action nor be attached to inaction.

Paradoxically, this allows the mind, freed from anxiety, to concentrate on the means with undivided attention, and the probability of the goal being reached is thereby increased. However, pragmatic considerations apart, in Hinduism, God, like Lord Nelson, expects every man and woman to do his or her duty precisely because it is his or her duty. The God of Hinduism "cares for the adverb rather than the verb."

Contemporary Forms of Hinduism

Crucial to an understanding of the many contemporary forms of Hinduism is the realization that, despite the various changes associated with the modern world, the "saints still remain, however, as they have always been, the generating centers of Hindu religion."[10] That is, it is the contemporary saints who identify for Hindus at large or "generate" the form of Hinduism most relevant for the time. Mahatma Gandhi provides an excellent example here, as do the other figures dealt with later.

In Hinduism, even the systems of philosophy are either rooted in the experience of a saint or of many saints or seers. Hindu pluralism means that Hinduism can be all things to all human beings. But an individual is bound to ask, What is it to me? So all forms of Hinduism are based on an analysis of the individual human personality. This is in keeping with its concept of universality, which implies plurality rather than uniformity or isomorphic equality in Hinduism.

A human being is analyzed in two main ways in Hindu thought—vertically and horizontally. Vertically, one may divide the human being into two—into a dichotomy of body/soul or matter/mind. Horizontally, one may divide the human personality into the three elements of knowing, feeling, and willing. If the previous dichotomy is combined with this trichotomy, one obtains the five major forms of contemporary Hinduism, indeed of all Hinduism, as we shall see later. These forms are known as yogas. The word yoga, which is cognate with the English word yoke, means "to join." The word is used in Hinduism both in a specific and in a general sense. Sometimes it is used specifically to refer to a school of philosophy and a codified system or technique of relating human beings to God known as Rāja Yoga and called yoga for short. The word can also be used to designate not just one but any system, or even approach, that leads to the union of the human with the divine. Unless otherwise specified, the word will be used in this chapter in this latter and more comprehensive sense. It is a technique that unites human beings with God. Alternatively, the yogas are called *mārgas*, or paths—paths leading to the same goal, that of realization. The various yogas correspond to the different dimensions of human personality as follows:

Body	Haṭha Yoga
Mind	Rāja Yoga
Knowing	Jñāna Yoga
Feeling	Bhakti Yoga
Willing	Karma Yoga

There are connections among these yogas and also areas of overlap, for they cover the same spiritual terrain. But they are sufficiently distinguished to be spoken of separately. Although in modern Hinduism all five yogas, and many more, are represented, the main contemporary forms of Hinduism have crystallized around the yogas of Jñāna, Bhakti, and Karma. These terms may be comprehensively rendered into English as absolutistic Hinduism, theistic Hinduism, and activistic Hinduism. Each of the main forms of yoga is exemplified in modern Hinduism by a remarkable figure: Ramaṇa Maharshi, Rāmakrishna Paramahaṁsa, and Mahatma Gandhi.

Ramaṇa Maharshi and Absolutistic Hinduism

Absolutistic Hinduism believes in ultimate reality as an Absolute and is closely associated with the form of Hindu thought known as Advaita Vedānta. It is the preeminent form of intellectual Hinduism in our times. About three-fourths of Hindu intellectuals subscribe to this form of Hinduism in one way or another.

The main exponent of this form of Hinduism in modern times was Ramaṇa Maharshi (1879–1950). To a certain extent the biographies of Hindu saints provide clues to the form of Hinduism associated with them. Ramaṇa, while yet in his teens, underwent a spontaneous mystical experience; as a result of it, he finally left his home and spent the rest of his life on what is known as the hill of the holy beacon, from which he never descended. The form of spirituality he represented is characterized by both internal and external renunciation of a most austere kind, which leads to the realization of one's identity with the Absolute or Godhead. This form of Hinduism has consistently maintained that if we probe deep within ourselves, we will find that we are the ultimate reality itself, and the best way of discovering our true identity is by persistently asking, Who am I?, using the phrase virtually like a koan. The successful culmination of this quest leads to the realization that we ourselves, in reality, are the ultimate ground of the universe on which the drama of creation is being enacted, like a movie on a screen. We are like the screen but have wrongly identified with the characters on it; because of this wrong identification, we seem to undergo the experiences of the characters with whom we have identified—the empirical selves.

Absolutism is an ancient tradition within Hinduism, but what makes Ramaṇa a contemporary representative of it is the directness of his approach, embodied in his method of self-inquiry. It is based on the astonishing claim that a state of consciousness exists that is entirely free of thoughts but that, unlike deep sleep, is characterized by full awareness. It is without any characteristics—for that would imply the presence of thought—but that does not mean that it is characterless; it is sheer bliss, not in the sense that one might taste sugar as something sweet, but in the sense that sugar is compacted of sweetness. The experience of this state of consciousness is uniquely liberative.

In traditional Hinduism, the attainment of such a state was associated with scriptural studies, austere practices, renunciation of the world, celibacy, and a host of other forbidding requirements. Ramaṇa dismissed all of these as essentially insignificant and dissociated his teachings so completely from traditional baggage that he even gained many Western followers. He was often criticized for not doing anything for the world, to which he responded cryptically: "You are the world." When further reproached, he compared his apparent inactivity to the deceptive motionlessness of a top spinning at high speed.

This form of absolutistic Hinduism has never been very popular; yet, it has always been extremely influential and continues to be so in modern Hinduism. What makes it different in modern times is its universalistic and pragmatic formulation.

Rāmakrishna Paramahaṁsa and Theistic Hinduism

Various forms of theistic Hinduism are more popular. The major Hindu figure who experimented, with dazzling versatility, not only with various forms of Hindu theism but also with Islam and Christianity was Rāmakrishna (1836–1886). He loved God as the Lord "on whom everything is strung like pearls on a thread" (*Bhagavadgītā* VII.7); and the Goddess as Mother who always loves the child, even if the child is not devoted to her. His devotional intensity was such that he began menstruating when he adopted the mode of a female worshiper toward God.

The mission founded by his disciple Vivekānanda, and named after Rāmakrishna, is a major manifestation of modern Hinduism. Rāmakrishna was remarkable in that he combined a vindication of all the forms of traditional Hinduism[11] with such a catholicity of outlook that scholars have criticized his followers for representing him as less tolerant than he really was,[12] when even his allegedly compromised position itself seems tolerant in the extreme! It is as if, before Rāmakrishna, in the somewhat discredited Hinduism of the eighteenth century, all possibilities were indiscriminately admitted and none finally confirmed; in Rāmakrishna all possibilities were convincingly vindicated and new ones not merely admitted but accredited. According to Huston Smith, Rāmakrishna's teachings on the essential unity of the great religions "comprise Hinduism's finest voice on this topic."[13]

Mahatma Gandhi and Activistic Hinduism

If Ramaṇa is the exemplar of the path of knowledge as a form of modern Hinduism and Rāmakrishna that of devotion, Mahatma Gandhi is the exemplar of the path of action. Dramatic testimony to this effect comes from an encounter Gandhi had with a group of Hindus in 1948 who had been assaulted in the wake of Hindu-Muslim riots but had managed to make their escape and survive the massacre:

> Reports of the massacre had sent a chill of horror through India. They told Gandhi what had happened in mounting excitement and anger, and at last one of them, an old man, said angrily: "Why do you not take a rest? You have done enough harm! You have ruined us utterly! You ought to leave us now and take up your abode in the Himalayas!"
>
> "My Himalayas are here," Gandhi replied in a harsh voice. "To remove your sufferings and to die in your service is for me like going to the Himalayas."
>
> He had rarely been attacked so vehemently, and was taken aback.
>
> "You may be a great Mahatma, but what is it to us?" the old man went on. "Leave us alone! Forget us! Go away!"
>
> He was a powerfully built man and spoke in commanding tones. His vigor and anger compelled attention. There were about forty of these survivors, men and women, some of them with wounds, all bearing marks of great suffering. For a moment it crossed Gandhi's mind that the old man who spoke so violently was not a refugee but someone who was using the refugees for his own purpose; it was an unworthy thought, he quickly dismissed it, and talked to them quietly and simply.
>
> "Shall I go away at your bidding?" he asked. "Whom shall I listen to? Some ask me to stay, others tell me to go away. Some reprove and revile me, others extol me. What am I to do? I do what God commands me to do."
>
> The old man said: "It is God who is speaking to you through us. We are beside ourselves with grief."
>
> "My grief is no less than yours," Gandhi replied, and gradually he was able to pacify them.
>
> The incident disturbed him and he described it at length at his prayer meeting, saying that he would like nothing better than to go to the Himalayas, but that was not where he expected to find his peace. "I seek my peace amid disorders," he said, as years before he had said: "I seek my peace in the storm."[14]

The form of Hinduism Gandhi represented has remained the dominant form of modern Hinduism for most of this century. It involves active service as a path of God-realization. It is characterized by nonviolence, courage, faith in God, truth, ecumenism, self-sacrifice, social service, and a whole constellation of similar virtues pursued for the good of all or *sarvodaya*—to use Gandhi's expression. For most Hindus Gandhi formulated normative Hinduism for this century. He carried the social aspects of the other paths mentioned earlier to their logical conclusion. Consider untouchability. Ramaṇa never observed untouchability; Rāmakrishna went a step further and once cleaned a lavatory with his beard to overcome any prejudice on this account; Gandhi not only questioned its propriety, at the precocious age of twelve, face to face with his parents whom he highly esteemed, but also spent a lifetime campaigning against it. Again, consider worldly activity. Ramaṇa never left the hill of the holy beacon, claiming that his mere presence provided sufficient leaven for changing society; Rāmakrishna, who used to lapse into ecstasies frequently, barely left Calcutta except on a few occasions; Gandhi was continually moving through the country and even the world. Ramaṇa evinced little interest in social service. Rāmakrishna wondered in jest whether, if one met God, one would commend himself to him by saying: "I built a canal." But Gandhi's whole life was spent in active social service. Ramaṇa was single and celibate, Rāmakrishna was married and celibate, Gandhi was married and made a transition from monogamy to celibacy, but the role he played in the emancipation of women far exceeded that of either Ramaṇa or Rāmakrishna.

New Religious Movements in Hinduism

Gandhi represents an interesting point of transition, for although perhaps India alone could have produced him, India alone cannot explain him. Many Western ideas and ideals were insinuated into Hinduism through Gandhi. But while India cannot explain Gandhi, Hinduism can. For Hinduism has been known for its ability to assimilate new forms of thought and practice. Where there is much, there is always room for more. Yet Hinduism has a knack of enlarging the menu simultaneously with restricting the diet. The new religious movements in Hinduism reflect the continuation of this trend. They increasingly incorporate new elements of Western life, including consumerism, but within the lived reality of their own movements, they lay down a fairly clear life-style. Once again we witness the interplay of Hindu pluralism with Hindu pragmatism, whether it be in the Sai Baba movement; the Hare Kṛṣṇa movement; Transcendental Meditation; or any other movement with Hindu genes. They are, however, bound to represent one of the yogas or a combination thereof. The perfection they seek may be sought, apart from Haṭha Yoga, "either by psychic control (*Rāja-yoga*), or philosophy (*Jñāna-yoga*) or worship (*Bhakti-yoga*), or work (*Karma-yoga*) or any combination of these."[15] Some modern Hindus, perhaps significantly if overconfidently, claim that "this, indeed, is the whole of religion,"[16] subsuming Christianity and Islam under the path of devotion.[17]

Before leaving this topic, it must not only be recognized but also emphasized that the various forms of yoga, far from being mutually exclusive, are mutually complementary. What has enabled us to make a one-to-one identification of knowledge, devotion, and action is the predominance of that form in the religious life of Ramaṇa, Rāmakrishna, and Gandhi, respectively, rather than the absence of the other yogas. As the yogas are not mutually exclusive, all have to be accommodated in any comprehensive formulation of each. The models in the past achieved this result through a vertical or hierarchical synthesis. According to this method, sometimes called the ladder approach, the yogas were enumerated successively as leading from one to the other, culminating in the yoga of one's preference. Modern Hinduism, when it does not lapse into the earlier pattern, prefers to perceive the yogas on a horizontal rather than a vertical plane. According to this approach, sometimes called the wheel approach, all the yogas are to be considered on par like the spokes of a wheel; one may still understandably prefer one yoga over others but only in the sense of "first among equals." One may still prefer one color over another, even when they all constitute the same band of light.

Yogic techniques, however, are not the only way to achieve salvation in Hinduism. An ancient verse of unknown antiquity proclaims:

> These two in this world transcend the solar orb (attain liberation): the renunciant absorbed in yoga and one who sheds his body in the field of battle.

Can the singlepointedness of the sword secure salvation as well as the singlepointedness of the mind can? It might seem a moot point to us, but the militant tradition in Hinduism has had no doubt on this score.

Militant Hinduism

Mahatma Gandhi, a pacifist, was a great activistic Hindu leader, perhaps the greatest this century has produced. But we must now consider that he was shot to death by a fellow Hindu, who has now increasingly come to represent a new type of activistic Hinduism—militant Hinduism. It was customary until recently to dismiss Gandhi's assassin, Nathuram Godse (1910–1949), as a fanatic and as one opposed to the vigorous reform for Hinduism that Gandhi represented.[18] Recent developments in India reveal the shallowness of this assessment. It would be fatal not to recognize the role of partition in this context. It has not been sufficiently emphasized in current discourse that the demolition of the mosque in 1992 is a direct, if delayed, consequence of the partition in 1947.[19]

Godse killed Gandhi out of a resentment and anger felt at the partition of the country in 1947 by almost every Hindu. His target was wrong, but his aim was right. The partition of India was a tragedy for almost all Hindus; Godse only intensified the tragedy by making Gandhi also its victim. His own commitment to an undivided India is dramatized by the fact that, though Gandhi's ashes were immersed in the sacred rivers of India, Godse's ashes have been preserved, in accordance with his will, to be immersed in the Indus River *after* what is now Pakistan has once again become part of Mother India. Moreover, by killing Gandhi, Godse was signaling to the Hindus that Gandhi's nonviolence had failed to prevent partition. However, the medium obstructed the message; Gandhi's martyrdom loomed larger in the Indian imagination than his failure—until recently.

Is it possible to reconcile the diametrically opposed forms of Hinduism represented by Gandhi and Godse? Perhaps. "In those awful moments of life when the soul stands facing a great wrong and is torn with anguish and indignation the Kṣatriya [the warrior] exclaims: 'now you shan't do that; I'll kill you,' and the true Brahmin [the saint] will say, 'do not do that; I would rather die.'"[20] Although Gandhi was a *vaiśya* or belonged to the merchant class in the Hindu caste system, in life he actually acted like a brahmin, by preferring to die rather than kill to resolve a crisis. Godse, although a brahmin by birth, acted like a *kṣatriya* in killing Gandhi.

The militant tradition in Hinduism represents the *kṣatriya*, or warrior, strand within it. When Gandhi was in London, one of his compatriots there was V. D. Savarkar (1883–1966), who later was tried but acquitted in the Gandhi murder conspiracy case. Savarkar and Gandhi disagreed even then on the proper means of evicting the British and dealing with the Muslims, just as Bal Gangadhar Tilak, whom the British regarded as the "father of the Indian unrest," and Gandhi were to differ later on their interpretation of the *Bhagavadgītā*, the popular text of modern Hinduism that Tilak did much to popularize. Tilak and Gandhi agreed that it advocated activism, but for Tilak this included martial activism, an interpretation Gandhi avoided by regarding the text's martial setting as allegorical in nature. In the 1930s Gandhi actually almost lost control of the Congress to Subhas Chandra Bose, who advocated the violent overthrow of the British. Gandhi prevailed, but only by obscuring the militant strand in Hinduism. The British had disarmed India so completely that, idealism apart, Gandhian methods alone proved practicable. However, the Hindu militant tradition was kept alive by organizations such as the "National Volunteer Corps," known by its Indian initials as the RSS, founded in 1925. The Hindu tradition avoids but does not exclude violence. Even Gandhi preferred violence to cowardice. Let us consider the test case of facing a robber. Gandhi pointed out that although ideally people should allow themselves to be robbed rather than resist, "such forbearance can only be exercised out of strength and not out of weakness. Till that power is acquired they must be prepared to resist the wrongdoer by force" for violence may be an evil "but cowardice is worse than violence."[21]

In conclusion, we must return to the central fact of the increasing predominance of the universalizing tendency within Hinduism in its modern incarnation. The advocates of both nonviolence and violence share a surprising convergence in this respect. "Hinduism was once defined by Gandhi as 'search after truth through non-violent means.' It may be said that this is no definition of Hinduism, since the statement would be true of every religion. But this is exactly what Hinduism claims, *viz.*, that the truth of every religion is the same."[22] Now listen to V. D. Savarkar: "Equally certain it is that whenever the Hindus come to hold such a position whence they could dictate terms to the whole world—these terms cannot be very different from which [the] *Gītā* dictates or the Buddha lays down. *A Hindu is most intensely so, when he ceases to be a Hindu*..." (emphasis added).[23]

The Structure of Hinduism

The Spiritual Superstructure

In the preceding discussion three eminent figures—Ramaṇa, Rāmakrishna, and Gandhi—were used as emblematic of the main forms of contemporary Hinduism. If we take Ramaṇa as indicative of the path of knowledge, Rāmakrishna that of devotion, and Gandhi that of action, then the three figures, who are *formative* of modern Hinduism, represent religious orientations that may be characterized in Hindu terms as *jñāna* (knowledge), *bhakti* (devotion), and *karma* (action), each of which represents a characteristic *form* of Hinduism itself. These three terms and the concepts they embody are like pivots on which virtually the whole Hindu universe of discourse can be wheeled around. A simple illustration of this is provided by how all that has been said previously can be related to these three paths or yogas and how all that is going to be said can be brought in relation to these. For instance, the difficulty of defining Hinduism in a profoundly psychological rather than historical sense stems from the doctrine of yogas or mārgas. The word mārga means a path and is particularly suggestive as it resonates with the Vedic word *adhvaryu*, the priest who was in charge of "ways and means" at a sacrifice, and the medieval word *pantha*, the spiritual track left by a medieval mystic. They allude to the fact that Hinduism is basically an array of techniques for establishing linkages between the human world and the transcendental world beyond it. Such linkages provide a key to understanding Hinduism. The realm to which the human being is linked is accepted as salvifically potent as well as plural, so that several concepts of the "other" can be explored.

An analogy might help. Suppose we wish to travel from New York to San Francisco. We are in New York and know precisely where we are. But if we have never been to San Francisco, then we cannot be as sure about it as we are about New York. The goal appears vague and elusive. But it is not on that account unreal. Even contradictory statements about it will not prove its unreality—just as you could say simultaneously that San Francisco is hilly, and that it has a seashore, and both the statements would be true. To vacation in San Francisco, we will have to travel to it by following a certain route. If the situation is examined minutely, it will soon become obvious that each individual traveler will adopt a route *unique to the person*. Even if the two travelers leave for San Francisco from the same building, the *exact* route they will follow will still differ. As Hinduism tries to map such a widely and uniquely traveled territory, is it any wonder that the map will never quite fit the reality, however faithfully it may try to reflect it? And if we take into full account this passion for spiritual cartography which animates Hinduism, it is also easy to see why not only must there be as many Hinduisms as there are Hindus but also as many Hinduisms as there are non-Hindus, if, from the Hindu point of view, the non-Hindus are headed toward the same realm and are really fellow-travelers.

You could, of course, take the view that allowing a personal, virtually monogrammed route for each individual perhaps carries the point too far and that, although all individuals in a sense do follow their own routes, there are really only three basic modes of traveling to San Francisco—you can drive, fly, or take the train. This same statement may now be transferred to the condition of the individual who possesses three basic psychological modes—knowing, feeling, and willing. Thus, although all individuals are unique—from which it follows that the individual paths which they follow are unique and helps explain why the problems of defining Hinduism are unique—these three psychological modes are common to all human beings, which makes it possible to address them all, though each is unique. The fact that all human beings can thus be addressed is the foundation of the universalism of Hinduism, just as the uniqueness of each is the philosophical basis of its ethnicity, when castes coalesce to constitute a distinct unit of distinct individuals. We can now see how the creative interplay of the universal and the ethnic in Hinduism constitutes the two ends of the axle—the axle on which the wheel of Hinduism comes rolling down to us through the corridors of time.

It only requires a little imagination, if any at all, to identify knowing with jñāna, feeling with bhakti, and willing with karma, while realizing at the same time that they represent special forms of knowing, feeling, and willing. Each of these three main modalities of relating the human to the divine was exemplified in the lives of Ramaṇa, Rāmakrishna, and Gandhi.

The concept of yoga, or alternatively that of mārga or path, is thus structurally central to Hinduism, and when reinforced with the metaphor of journeying, renders many other dimensions of Hinduism more accessible. For instance, in Hinduism such journeying is typically visualized as not involving just one life but several lives. Thus emerges the idea of *saṁsāra*, the cosmic process of beings dying and being reborn, a doctrine confined to the initiate in Pythagoreanism but common knowledge in Hinduism. The concept also includes the individual's involvement in saṁsāra as one journeys on in the cosmos—either aimlessly or with the aim of breaking into the other realm. The search for a principle that explains the experiences that befall one in this process suggests the doctrine of karma, which states that actions produce consequences commensurate with their moral quality, which may fructify over several lives. The individual involved in such a cosmic process is called the *jīva*, a ripple in the cosmic ocean of saṁsāra.

At some point in this journeying, the jīva concludes that traveling hopefully is no longer to be preferred to arriving and seeks to be freed from his or her wanderings. Then the jīva wishes to take another route, one that will not keep one perpetually en route but will carry one to a divine destination and will bring one's journey to a felicitous conclusion. It is at this point that, instead of merely trying to walk to San Francisco from New York, in vague hope, the jīva decides to travel by a proper route. Again, the exact route the jīva takes will depend on the unique configuration of his or her personality, but because knowing, feeling, and willing are universal traits, it will broadly be oriented to one of these. The truth is that the jīva is destined to reach the supernal goal but has been temporarily distracted from it. This ability of the universe around us to seduce us away from the divine is called *māyā*, a term philosophically freighted with all sorts of connotations. To take a detour to Disneyland on our way from New York to San Francisco and to forget that we were really headed for San Francisco would represent the working of *māyā*. To be freed of this infatuation and to reach San Francisco would be tantamount to *mokṣa*, or the attainment of liberation. The attainment of mokṣa or liberation, both in its widest connotation as freedom from finitude and its narrower connotation as freedom from rebirth, is the summum bonum of Hinduism. Such a liberated person is said to walk away from the snares of the world like a lion emerging from a cage.

Just as there are different friends and hosts we may plan to visit in San Francisco, there are various deities of Hinduism, each with his or her own palatial mansion—a world in itself—comparable to the residences of our affluent friends. For example, we may visit the governor, who presides over the city like Viṣṇu, the preserver god of Hinduism. Or we may choose to meet the architect, still alive, who first designed San Francisco, just as the creator-god Brahmā designed the universe. We may meet a friend whom we have come to regard as the presiding deity of feminism, who calls herself Śakti (the divine feminine principle). Or we may decide to stay with our friend, the ecological prophet, who has promised to destroy the polluted city when its time has come, like Śiva, the Hindu god of destruction. Thus we may sojourn in the city not just of God, but of Goddess, and not just of gods but goddesses too. The relationships we may enjoy with our friends, parents, and so on in San Francisco are analogous to the relationships that may be enjoyed in the company of gods or goddesses—once their realms have been reached by the path of devotion, or bhakti, which can itself take the form of the love of a friend, devoted servant, lover, mother, father, son, beloved, and so on.

Or perhaps we came to San Francisco to pursue higher studies, to know more. The way we experience the city will now differ. We may even have traveled on student discounts—following, as it were, the path of jñāna. The Reality, in this scenario, which we will encounter in the realm of realization—a reality called *brahman* in Hindu thought—will be knowledge pure and simple, devoid of any other qualifications. Unlike our more gregarious friends who encountered the reality of San Francisco through persons, our own experience of it will now be dominated by a knowledge of principles. Our friends will know the same reality—the same San Francisco as qualified by persons with attributes of their own or in the Hindu idiom, as *saguṇa brahman* or *Īśvara* (God)—while we would know it as devoid of this element, as knowledge pure and simple, or *nirguṇa brahman* (Absolute) in the diction of Hindu thought.

But suppose we were not satisfied either with devotion or with knowledge; we came to San Francisco neither to hobnob with friends nor to learn progressive ideas—but to set up a computer business. We will then experience San Francisco in a unique way—as active entrepreneurs. We would experience the dynamic reality of San Francisco-as-brahman, with the quality of being in active relation to the world.

This metaphorical exploration discloses the essential structure of Hinduism, for at its heart lies the metaphor of the yogas or mārgas. Or to be more bold, *you* lie at the heart of Hinduism, and in your triple dispositions of knowing, feeling, and willing, the Hindu world lies concealed. The yogas or mārgas affect the experience of reality, but it must never be forgotten that it is the same reality, the same San Francisco, that is being experienced.

Even more than being characteristic of the experience *of* reality, the yogas or mārgas are paths *to* the attainment of reality. Knowing, feeling, and willing may be as different from one another as traveling by air, by car, or by train. Yet they all lead one to the Real just as planes, cars, and trains all lead one to San Francisco. However, in order not to be misunderstood, or perhaps trivialized, the metaphor also needs to be refined. The way Reality is known through jñāna involves an experiential and intuitive kind of knowledge, rather than mere intellectual knowledge. Similarly, the love or devotion signified by bhakti involves a profound and intimate love, which can be as close as the bond between lovers but which is untainted by carnality. The path characterized by action or karma is not one of ordinary karma, or action fueled by worldly desires, for that only leads to further journeying in saṁsāra, but is the kind of action that is concerned with "the roots and not with the fruits" of action: It is rooted in egolessness.

The Underlying Social Structure

The individual may have spiritual goals but society, of which he or she is a part, also has its claims. Hinduism provides a structure, predictably less individualistic and more communal, for meeting these claims consistently with the spiritual life. If the comprehensive superstructure of Hinduism is spiritually characterized by the three yogas, its social structure is equally comprehensively characterized by three doctrines: the doctrine of the *varṇas*; the doctrine of the *āśramas*; and the doctrine of the *puruṣārthas*. These constitute the base of the pyramid on which, it can be said, the higher you go, the closer you are to heaven.

Hinduism as a religious system uses these building blocks sometimes in very standard and sometimes in creative ways to keep the system meaningful to the Hindus as social beings. To the primordial question, What should I do?, Hinduism provides four answers, in keeping with its pluralism. This is known as the doctrine of the four goals of life (*puruṣārthas*). Hinduism accepts four valid goals of human endeavor: (1) the leading of a moral life; (2) the earning of wealth; (3) the enjoyment of the pleasures of the senses; and (4) the seeking of liberation. They are known as *dharma, artha, kāma*, and *mokṣa*, respectively. Thus Hinduism embraces a pluralism of ends as well as means at all levels, and therein lies another secret of its universalism. To the question, When should I do what?, Hinduism answers: Learn the principles of morality and vocation in the first twenty-five years of your life, earn wealth and enjoy sensuous pleasures in the next twenty-five years. Thereafter lead a virtuous and pious life in a hermitage for another twenty-five years, and then seek liberation. These four quarters which compose the century of one's life are known as stages of life (āśramas)—as those of the celibate student (*brahmacārī*), householder (*gṛhastha*), hermit (*vānaprastha*), and renunciant (*sannyāsī*).

To the question, Who should do what in a functionally differentiated society?, Hinduism answers: One should follow the vocation of the family one is born into. These vocations can broadly be grouped into four: the priest or more generally the intellectual (*brāhmaṇa*); the warrior and administrator (*kṣatriya*); the farmer and trader (*vaiśya*); and the laborer (*śūdra*). The birth ascription of vocation is justified by the doctrine of karma and rebirth, for as a Hindu, one is not born, one is reborn; one is not just accidentally born into a family belonging to a vocational group, one is reborn into it as a result of that universal accounting system called karma. It is possible though that Balinese Hinduism represents the original concept of varṇas. In the history of Hinduism, the doctrine of varṇas appears *before* the doctrine of karma. This raises the suspicion that the doctrine of karma may have provided a postfacto rationalization for a birth-oriented division of society that was already in place when the doctrine of karma became widespread. On the other hand, "In Bali *varna* is simply occupation. A businessman is a vaiśya, a teacher a brahmin, an employee a sudra and so on. No inferior or superior stature is attached, and if one switches profession—say from teacher to shopkeeper—one changes caste from brahmin to vaiśya."[24] Once again one senses in these interpretations of varṇa the coexistence of the ethnic and the universal elements in Hinduism, as also when numerous smaller social and/or ethnic units called *jātis* are ideologically encompassed within the more universal categories of the four varṇas. One's karma then determines one's dharma or code of conduct.

The best way I know to convey the exact semantic flavor of the term dharma, especially *sva-dharma* or one's own unique social and spiritual duty, is through a Rabbinic account. "Said Rabbi Zusya: 'In the world to come I shall not be asked, why were you not Moses?' I shall be asked, 'Why were you not Zusya?'" If karma is the great metaphysical organizing principle of Hinduism, dharma is its moral and sociological counterpart. It is better to consider it a *sociological* rather than *social* counterpart, because one is dealing here with idealized constructions or an ideology that is part and parcel of a religious system. The ideology does its best to explain and interpret historical and societal facts, which never fully corresponded to it. An ideology is, after all, not a mirror of reality, but rather an intentional distortion. "Yet it may reveal reality better than a mirror, because the essential components stand out." If the myths of the Vedas regulate cosmos, the ideology of the Hindu law books called *smṛtis* regulate Hindu society.

Dharma is an essential conceptual component of the smṛtis. It is the fixed star on the horizon, the guiding principle one identifies as one's own specific duty as a member of a particular class (varṇa); in a particular stage (āśrama) of life; and in pursuing a particular goal (puruṣārtha) consistently with one's humanity (*sādhāraṇa dharma*) as expressed in universal values such as charity, purity, and so on. One is exhorted to practice virtue or dharma in its sublimest sense, as if death's hand were already in one's hair! The harmonization of the universal with the unique in the human being epitomizes Hinduism's pursuit of perfection. This attempt to harmonize the universal with the unique in the human being is but a variation of a similar and larger agenda identified earlier—the attempt to harmonize the ethnic with the universal dimension within Hinduism. The pursuit of these agendas has generated and continues to generate a great variety of life-styles and an immense body of literature around Hinduism. We turn next to an examination of this material.

Sacred Life and Literature in Hinduism

The corpus of sacred literature in Hinduism is as large as that of any major religious tradition, but it is distinguished by the fact that the body of literature to which the term revelation may be applied within it is perhaps the largest among the religions of the world. Its relationship to other traditional bodies of sacred literature within Hinduism also tends to be more fluid.

Śruti

This primary category of literature in Hinduism, denoted by the word *śruti* or "that which is heard," may refer to either its divine "audition" or "vision," or to the fact that this revealed text both was and is ideally transmitted orally, though it has also been reduced to writing in modern times. Alternatively, it is called the Vedas, the plural form referring to its four divisions into the *ṚgVeda*, the *YajurVeda*, the *SāmaVeda*, and the *AtharvaVeda*; the singular form Veda refers to them as a collectivity.

The Vedas are not a book but a library and cover an enormous mass of material, all of which has the status of revelation in theory. Each is in turn divisible into four parts: *Saṁhitā* or *Mantra* (devotional hymns); *Brāhmaṇas* (priestly texts; the same word otherwise means a priest); *Āraṇyakas* (forest-books); and *Upaniṣads* (esoteric philosophical texts). The last and end parts, also called Vedānta (Veda + *anta* [end]) and consisting of the *Upaniṣads*, came to be generally regarded in the tradition as revelation par excellence, by a process of informal consensus rather than a formal decision typical of Hinduism, which tends to be definitional without being definitive.

The Vedas, by virtue of their historical priority and canonical primacy, play a very significant role in Hinduism but in unsuspecting ways. Most of later Hinduism, inasmuch as it may be assessed in Vedic terms, is really Vedantic rather than Vedic, because it was the *Upaniṣads* that really came to matter. As noted earlier, although the Veda was recognized as revelation by the Hindus, very few Hindus knew its actual contents. Nevertheless, the acceptance of Vedic authority became the criterion of Hindu orthodoxy, much the same way as swearing by the Constitution for Americans represents loyalty to the country, even though they may have never read the Constitution. The Vedas, for the tradition as a whole then, functioned as a symbol of the tradition and as the ultimate rather than the proximate basis of its beliefs and practices, for anything not inconsistent with the Vedas was considered admissible as Hindu. This negative criterion for orthodox inclusion once again attests to Hinduism's reluctance to limit itself. Indeed the Vedic seer proclaims:

> The earth is the mother, and I
> the son of the earth.
> (*AtharvaVeda* XII.1.12)

Smṛti

If the Vedas represent revelation, *smṛti* represents tradition. The word literally means "that which is remembered," although ironically it was the Vedas that were memorized. The Vedas, according to the dominant orthodox view, have no human author; by contrast, a smṛti, or a work of tradition, is a work whose author can be remembered. These works grew out of aphoristic mnemonic devices called *sūtras*, or threads, which were meant to be memorized by those who had the heart to learn them. These threads were then spun out into smṛtis. The word possesses both a restricted and an extended meaning. It can be restricted to apply to law books regulating the social, political, economic, and personal conduct of Hindus or extended to embrace virtually all forms of sacred writings of human origin. In a restricted sense, it will only apply to the material covered in this section; in an extended sense it could be used to cover all the succeeding sections.

A masterly survey of smṛti literature in the sense of law books was carried out by Professor P. V. Kane in his multivolume work, *A History of Dharmaśāstra*, and may be usefully consulted. In this section, it will suffice to identify the role of smṛtis. They may be considered prescriptive, if one is legally inclined, and suggestive, if one is liberally disposed within the Hindu milieu, although their passion for classification baffles modern readers. A "method" may, however, underlie the "madness." Marriage is classified as being of eight kinds. A deep compassion perhaps underlies this classification, which is so exhaustive that it is virtually impossible for anyone to be born out of wedlock!

The śruti deals with eternal truths pertaining to dharma and mokṣa, or morality and salvation. If the Vedānta is particularly concerned with explicating the latter, the smṛtis elaborate the former, especially in a sociopolitical setting. Although moral truths are eternal, their actual application is subject to temporal modification. Hence the view that different dharmas, or norms of conduct, are appropriate for different ages (*yugas*), and these are embodied in different smṛtis, of which at least twenty are listed. The pride of place among them is enjoyed by the *Manusmṛti* or *Mānavadharmaśāstra*, popularly known as the laws or institutes of Manu. To convert nature into culture, the smṛtis prescribed sixteen sacraments (*saṁskāras*) for those entitled to them, out of which now only those of marriage and obsequies are universally observed. The two are connected. Great emphasis has been placed traditionally in Hinduism on having a son, because the last rites were most efficaciously performed by one—a curiously Hindu way, Freud might say, of conjoining eros with thanatos. A special sacrament, comparable to the Bar Mitzvah or Confirmation, is the Investiture ceremony, wherein, upon being invested with the sacred thread, a male member of the three higher varṇas became a twice-born and was initiated into Vedic studies. Subsequently such initiation became virtually restricted to the priestly class, with the consequence that resentment against Brahmanical dominance in some parts of India has taken the form of forcible clipping of the cord. The ceremony seems to be going out of favor, if not vogue, in our more egalitarian age: Gandhi discarded his own sacred thread in protest against its denial to others.[25] Even the varṇa system itself, inasmuch as it was interpreted, especially by the higher castes, as conferring privileges rather than prescribing duties, has also been remolded somewhat in the crucible of the freedom struggle. B. G. Tilak (1856–1920) suggested that the privileges of brahmins should be conferred on all those who were jailed by the British during the struggle against the Raj, and when on Tilak's death his relatives objected to Gandhi, a non-Brahmin, being his pallbearer, Gandhi rejoined: "a public worker has no caste."

The principle that though moral laws are eternal, their actual application is mutable is important for understanding Hinduism. It allows room for both flexibility and rationalization. Levirate, or the custom by which a dead man's brother had to marry the widow, was once permitted within Hinduism (as in Judaism) and was subsequently discontinued. Some of the provisions of the smṛtis are suggestive of an ecological awareness along with that of generational continuity. The Five Daily Sacrifices included offerings to the gods, the seers, the ancestors, guests, and animals, the last being seen as having "rights but no duties." The verse, however, that begs pardon of the earth as one steps on it when getting up from the bed in the morning probably overdoes it. Nevertheless, there is a widespread feeling among some Hindus that the ancient smṛtis are dated, almost hopelessly so. The famous Hindu preacher Swami Vivekānanda (1863–1902) thought that the time was ripe for the preparation of a new smṛti more appropriate for our times. That role has now been taken over by the legislature in independent India. A famous text proclaims (*Āpastamba Dharma Sūtra* I.7.20.6): "Righteousness and unrighteousness do not show themselves to us in bodily form and say 'here we are.'" Norms of conduct do not fall like rain from the sky; they are established by the exemplary conduct of the virtuous. It is hoped that such people get elected to the legislatures.

Itihāsa

The śruti lays down the eternal law in bold letters. The smṛti works out the fine print, and from time to time great sages and kings exemplify dharma or normative conduct by their own example in red letters. Some of them were, or at least came to be looked upon as, incarnations of God. Their divine histories are referred to as the *Itihāsas*—a term now specially applied to two texts. One of them deals with the life and deeds of Rāma and is known as the *Rāmāyaṇa* (The Deeds of Rāma). This epic is so popular, especially in northern India, that the word Rāma—the last word uttered by Mahatma Gandhi—is virtually a synonym for God. The other great epic is the *Mahābhārata* (The Great War of the Bharata Tribe), closely associated with Kṛṣṇa. It deals with the fratricidal struggle for the throne in the royal family of the Bharatas, and its theme has become better known in the West with its stage adaptation by Peter Brook. Embedded in the *Mahābhārata* is the popular Hindu text, the *Bhagavadgītā*.

The *Rāmāyaṇa,* in about twenty-four thousand verses, narrates the adventures of Rāma from his birth and childhood through his exile, the abduction of his wife by a demon and her recovery after a titanic struggle during this period of exile, and then his triumphant return to Ayodhyā, the capital, which ushers in a golden age. Rāmarājya, or the Rule of Rāma, has become both the material and moral equivalent of the Kingdom of God on earth in Hinduism. The events of the epic are regularly enacted with great fanfare. The companion epic, the *Mahābhārata,* recounts in close to one hundred thousand verses the struggle of the Kauravas and their cousins, the Pāṇḍavas, for the royal throne, a struggle in which the Pāṇḍavas emerge successful with the help of Kṛṣṇa, who like Rāma of the other epic, is an incarnation of Viṣṇu. Though summarized here with brutal brevity, the main narrative contains many twists and turns, and the epic as a whole is really a storehouse of information about the Hindu world. What is more, it is fully aware of this and contains the encyclopedic boast that what is found here may be found elsewhere, but what is not found here will be found nowhere (18.5.38)! The two epics are grand narratives and like all grand narratives transport one to another realm.

Recent TV series based on these epics were so sensationally popular in India that the country almost came to a halt at the time they were screened. They are, however, more than just good or riveting stories. Both epics tackle issues of proper moral conduct. While the *Rāmāyaṇa* essentially endorses a formal ethics (never tell a lie), the *Mahābhārata* inclines more toward a teleological ethics (such a lapse may be permitted in the larger interest). The difference between the two may be illustrated by the standard case in which one witnesses an intended victim, chased by a would-be assassin, disappear in the streets. Should one tell the truth or tell a lie to save the person's life when questioned? Formal ethics would require a correct answer; teleological ethics would permit an incorrect one to save a life.

The epics are vitally concerned with questions of right and wrong, and the emphasis throughout is on morality. The lament of the putative author of the *Mahābhārata*, Vyāsa, has not gone unnoticed, though his advice may have gone unheeded:

> I proclaim with upraised hands in vain. From Righteousness flow wealth and happiness; why are you not righteous? (18.5.49)

Purāṇas

The gods, it is said, love the cryptic and are averse to the obvious (*Bṛhadāraṇyaka Upaniṣad* IV.2.2) but the *Purāṇas* leave nothing to the imagination. They not only tell it like it is but also tell on the gods like the press corps after the House of Windsor. The *Purāṇas* are less concerned with deeds of men and more with those of godlike men or gods and their repetitive, if occasionally regenerative, encounters with demons. Hinduism seems to lack a single, formal principle of evil, like Satan in the Western religions or Māra in Buddhism, thereby inviting the criticism that it is soft on evil, which it tends to regard as "dirt in the wrong place." Moreover, one is not evil, one commits evil. By contrast, God is visualized in three forms, as constituting the trinity (*trimūrti*) of Brahmā, Viṣṇu, and Śiva, corresponding to the three cosmic functions of emanation (or creation), preservation, and consummation (or destruction). Somewhat unaccountably, the worship of Brahmā ceased to be popular, but that of Viṣṇu and Śiva caught on.

The *Purāṇas,* eighteen in number, represent a form of popular—some would say popularized—Hinduism, combining ascetic and erotic elements and the sacred and the profane with the same unpredictability with which they are encountered in real life. One of the best known among them is the *Bhāgavata Purāṇa*, which deals with the early life of Kṛṣṇa, who appears in the *Mahābhārata* as an adult.

The *Purāṇas* are significant in that they present and represent popular religion. One section of the *Mārkaṇḍeya Purāṇa,* the *Devī Māhātmya,* or the Glory of the Goddess, is a prime example of feminine theology in Hinduism. If the smṛtis deal with humans, then the *Purāṇas* deal with divine beings, God or gods, in relation to themselves and to the universe. These repositories of legends and mythologies also contain accounts that sanctify the life of the cosmos, just as the sacraments sanctify the life of the individual. The difference in scale involves a difference in kind. God, as Viṣṇu, incarnates himself, in a docetic manner, to save or salvage the universe, even dignifying forms of animal life with his presence. Christianity subscribes to the doctrine of one incarnation only, Judaism and Islam to none, Hinduism to many. Though numerous, ten incarnations of God are singled out for special mention—as fish, tortoise, boar, man-lion, dwarf, axe-wielding Rāma, bow-wielding Rāma, Buddha, Kṛṣṇa, and one yet to arrive apocalyptically—the Kalkī, who embodies, as it were, Hinduism's nostalgia for the future!

Tantras

These texts, also called *Āgama,* deal with the cultic aspect of Hinduism. These cults center on the worship of the Sun, Viṣṇu, Śiva, Śakti, Gaṇeśa, and Kumāra. The sun-god is believed to be an early representation of Viṣṇu, and Ganeśa and Kumāra are the two sons of Śiva. Gaṇeśa recently figured in the popular television show "The Simpsons," entertaining evidence of Hinduism's cultic penetration of the West.

More generally, the three main cultic traditions of Hinduism are Vaiṣṇava (devoted to Viṣṇu), Śaiva (devoted to Śiva), and Śākta (devoted to Śakti). The Śaivas recognize 28 *Āgamas,* the Śāktas 77. There are several Vaiṣṇava *Tantras,* called the *Pāñcarātra,* of which 215 separate texts are mentioned.

Sometimes the word *tantra* is applied specifically to the Śākta *Āgamas.* Some of these cultic practices are antinomian in nature—whether practiced literally (by the so-called "left-handed" followers) or metaphorically (by the "right-handed" ones). The word Tāntrika has acquired the connotation of sexual mysticism in the popular imagination. Though not without some basis, its Hindu context is invariably one of cultic ritual or meditation. The basic tenet of this form of Tantra was to overcome an appetite not by abstention but through overindulgence, as a form of spiritual homeopathy to treat the dis-ease of life. It involved the use of mystical circles (*maṇḍalas*) and centers (*cakras*). Liberation is secured once the latter, seven in number and plotted along the astral spine, have been successively pierced by the spiritual energy—hitherto lying dormant at the base of the spine and called the *Kuṇḍalinī.* But it first has to be aroused from its coiled state and made upwardly mobile like a sperm.

Āgama literature is particularly significant in that it lays down rules for the construction of temples, and the installation and worship of images. The Vedas are essentially aniconic and rely on chanting as a mode of worship; by the time of the *Tantras*, beginning from around the fifth century, Hinduism had fully incorporated image worship and had turned audiovisual. The same process is represented in the use of *mantra* (acoustic triggers or verbal cues) and *yantra* (mystic diagrams) in the *Tantras*. Postures (*āsana*) and gestures (*mudrā*) of the deities were also considered mysteriously potent. Standard Hinduism relies heavily on homologies for system-building. These are often overt, though sometimes covert. In the *Tantras* the ratio is reversed. Hidden or occult connections predominate, enhancing its reputation for esotericism. According to the *Tantras*, if the search for reality is going to be really comprehensive, the physical body with all its parts and passions cannot be excluded from it. The *Tantras* harness passion and imagination for salvation. They proclaim the axiom: "one rises by what one falls," perhaps a sacralized version of the otherwise sexist Woody Allen aphorism: "a fallen woman is easy to pick up."

Darśana Literature

This body of literature in Hinduism pertains to the six acceptable schools of Hindu philosophy: Nyāya (logical realism); Vaiśeṣika (atomistic pluralism); Sāṅkhya (ontological dualism); Yoga (meditational self-realization); Mīmāṁsā (Vedic ritualism); and Vedānta (philosophical systems based on the Upaniṣads). All these schools (except Sāṅkhya) have their own foundational texts consisting of aphoristic statements that were commented upon by a succession of scholars. These scholars cannot be accused of lacking chutzpa. One of them reminded God, upon finding the doors of the shrine closed, that when the atheistic Buddhists come again, "your fate will lie in my hands."

The most significant of these schools, the Vedānta, utilizes not only the *Upaniṣads* but also an aphoristic summary of them called the *Brahmasūtra* as a second primary text. These two along with the *Bhagavadgītā* are collectively known as *Prasthāna-traya*, a term translated as the triple canon or, perhaps more suggestively, as the three points of departure. An overwhelming desire to know that by knowing which "the unknowable becomes known" (*Chāndogya Upaniṣad* VI.1.3) undergirds the vast intellectual enterprise of Vedānta.

Bhakti Literature in Regional Languages

The language of the literature hitherto described is Sanskrit. The eclipse of Hinduism after Islamic rule over India was followed by the emergence of the various regional languages of India, somewhat in the manner in which

Latin was replaced by modern European languages during the Reformation. Tamil had already provided the lead even prior to Muslim rule in this respect. The regional languages of India became the vehicle for the expression of religious and moral sentiment.

> To instance but a few, the *Tēvāram* and the *Tiruvācakam* are well-known among the hymns of the Śaiva saints of South India; the Vaiṣṇavas have correspondingly the *Divyaprabandham* and other devotional songs; the Caitanya movement and the songs of Tagore are responsible for the enrichment of Bengali devotional literature; the songs of Kabīr, the *Abhaṅgas* of the Mahārāṣṭra saints, the *Rāmayaṇa* of Tulasi Dās are all outpourings of God-intoxicated souls. If the essentials of Hinduism have found a place, difficult to dislodge, in the homes of even the lowliest and the last in this vast country, it is not a little due to these devotional poems in the languages of the people. To all of them the name "Veda" may be given, for has not the Veda itself declared that the Vedas are many, unending (*anantā vai vedāḥ*)?[26]

Modern Hinduism and the Bhagavadgītā

It is a striking fact of modern Hinduism that almost all major works in it have been written in English with some exceptions, of which B. G. Tilak's commentary on the *Bhagavadgītā*, written in Marathi, and the *Satyārtha Prakāśa* (The Light of Truth) of Swami Dayānanda Sarasvatī (1824–1883), written in Hindi, are eminent examples. This is not to say that the works of a Rammohun Roy (1772/74–1833) or a Radhakrishnan (1888–1975) or even a Gandhi are acceptable as part of the sacred literature of Hinduism, though one must wonder whether the writings of Śrī Aurobindo (1872–1950) may not indeed gain that status some day. What is even more significant about neo-Hinduism in the context of the sacred literature of Hinduism is another fact: the acceptance of the *Bhagavadgītā* (*Gītā* for short) as the primary scripture of Hinduism. It was always an important scripture in Hinduism, but since Tilak wrote his commentary on it in the 1920s, it has grown in stature to acquire the rank of the most significant text of modern Hinduism, with the consequence that any Hindu leader or scholar worth his or her salt has felt compelled to comment on it in one manner or another.

Connections

This mass of religious literature in Hinduism, though enormous, is intimately connected with life through a series of connections, correspondences, and resemblances. The *Bhagavadgītā* explores the three dimensions of religious experience—those of jñāna, bhakti, and karma—subtly, simultaneously, and perhaps inextricably. The Hindu tradition has been debating for centuries which of the yogas it ultimately espouses. The four Vedas have been aligned on occasion even with the four varṇas; and the fourfold division of the Vedas with the four stages of life (āśramas). Connections have been made within the sacred corpus itself in that the *Mahābhārata* is known as the fifth Veda, and the *Divyaprabandham* as the Tamil Veda because of its language. The various accounts of the deeds of the glorious ancestors and the gods, recounted in the *Itihāsas* and the *Purāṇas,* are depicted in art through the canons laid down in the *Āgamas.* The gods and goddesses are venerated domestically in shrines and publicly in temples, sometimes through the worship of images and at other times through imagery symbolic of them, the *liṅga* and the *śālagrāma* being prominent among such miniature representations. The former is a stone sacred to Śiva. Its shape is suggestive of a phallic association, although its exclusive identification as a phallic symbol is a modern "phallacy." The śālagrāma is a special kind of stone sacred to Viṣṇu. Such miniature symbols represent the portable spirituality of Hinduism.

The deeds of the gods and cultural heroes are celebrated through festivals that are held at regular intervals, which regularly sanctify intervals of time just as the holy places and the temples sanctify points in space. These facilitate the mythopoeic appropriation of the tradition. Among the holy places, Kāśī (the City of Light), otherwise known as Benares or Vārāṇasī, occupies the pride of place and comes close to being the Vatican of Hinduism. It contains numerous temples dedicated to the various gods, the one dedicated to Śiva being particularly renowned. If I choose to refer next to the modern Lakṣmīnārāyaṇa Temple at Delhi, it is because it is so characteristic of our times, with shrines dedicated to Lao Tzu, Confucius, and to our earth—to recognize whose organic unity, modern human beings had to go out in space. As a concession to the blandishments of tourism, one might also mention the complex of temples around Khajuraho with their erotic friezes—perhaps the most successful religious commercials in the history of humanity.

Hinduism brings people to itself in curious and sometimes even dramatic ways. For example, the brilliant Festival of Lights, or Dīpāvalī, is preceded by the spectacular festivities of Durgā Pūjā (Worship of the Goddess), which lasts for nine nights at the end of which the image of the Goddess is carried around in a grand procession called a *yātrā,* for its immersion. The spectacle of a procession is a scene often repeated on appropriate occasions around many a temple in India, with the temple deity occupying the place of honor. The best-known car procession is the one performed at the temple of Jagannātha at Puri, which generated the English loan-word "juggernaut" to convey a sense of the relentless crush that characterizes the scenes of religious enthusiasm witnessed on the occasion. It is characteristic of Hinduism that the lighting of lamps celebrates simultaneously the aerial return of Rāma to his capital city after vanquishing the demons as narrated in the *Rāmāyaṇa*, the slaying of a demon by the Goddess riding gloriously on a lion, and the annual reprieve of a demon who was banished to the netherworld but is nostalgically allowed to return to his kingdom on earth for that one night. The thousand points of light that illumine this festival are shimmering invocations of the Upaniṣadic prayer, "Lead me from darkness to light" (*Bṛhadāraṇyaka Upaniṣad* I.3.28), on a massive scale.

A calendar of Hindu festivals and a map of sacred places in Hinduism should properly conclude this section, though festivities know no bounds even if bound to certain points in time. The sacred realm is ultimately a territory without a map, and all the more adventurous for that, the Hindus assure us. Art also became the handmaiden of religion. As an example, consider the impressive and detailed portrayal of the figure of Śiva as Naṭarāja or the cosmic dancer representing either salvation in motion (for all eternity) or salvation frozen (in a moment). If one looks closely at the flowing tassels of the dancing Śiva, one espies a miniature maiden resting therein. This is none other than the sacred river Gaṅgā, which follows a celestial as well as terrestrial course. In its latter manifestation it emerges from the Himalayas on the plains of the north at Haridwar (Gateway to God) and commingles with the visible Yamunā and the invisible Sarasvatī at the Confluence (*saṅgama*) at Prayāga (present-day Allahabad), where famous religious gatherings are held (as at other holy places) at astrologically determined periodic intervals, the accounts of whose origins can be traced to the *Purāṇas*.

Like the Ganges, many rivers holy to the Hindus have their source in the Himalayas, and many centers of pilgrimage are situated amid its serrated peaks. The Himalayas serve as a celestial abode of many of the gods and goddesses of Hinduism and constitute the theater of divine drama. They dominate not merely the physical but also the spiritual landscape of India to such an extent that a famous poet has described them as the frozen laughter of Śiva. Peals of this laughter, however, can be heard all over the country from Kashmir to Cape Camorin, for every elevated range of India partakes of some of its divinity, just as every river comes to share, through a series of correlations and correspondences developed through the tales and the fables in the literature just discussed, the holiness of the river Ganges, and every holy place the sanctity of Kāśī.

The History of Hinduism: An Overview

Hinduism, like Shintō, has no historical founder. In this it resembles Judaism more than either Christianity or Islam, inasmuch as Judaism may be looked upon as founded by a series of prophets, Abraham and Moses being prominent among them, rather than by a single prophet. Yet, unlike Judaism, it does not accord superior status to the prophecy of a single figure like Moses. This feature of Hinduism is closely connected with its essential nature. It has been suggested that the lack of a historical founder indicates an absence of a sense of history. Hinduism in this respect would then be unique among the ethnic religions as both Judaism and Shinto mock such a generalization. But the suggestion is partly true. Hindus do not always attach the same theological value to historical events as do the religions of the West. The Hindus pull a switch here: They derive theological value from converting history into myth. By converting historical strifes into mythical struggles, the past is prevented from becoming an enemy of the present. Although such dehistoricization may occasionally serve some historical purpose, it is mainly used in the tradition with soteriological and metaphysical intent. A practicing Hindu, worshiping in his or her shrine, is perhaps as oblivious to the history of his or her religion as a scientist working in a laboratory is to the history of science. Spiritual truths may be revealed at a point in cosmic history, but they are themselves acosmic and transhistorical.

Such is the formal nature of revelation in Hinduism. Such revelations, moreover, are received not by one person but by a community of seers or *ṛṣis*, who are not so much individuals as types. Nevertheless, as members of a religious tradition, the Hindus have tried to make sense of history, like other people, by dividing it into ages, albeit mythical. One of these, it is claimed with startling precision, commenced on February 18, 3102 B.C.E. However, even in terms of sober history, it is difficult to assign a definite beginning to Hinduism. Three beginnings can be assigned to it. If the term is used to denote the beliefs and practices of all those people who now consider themselves Hindus, then Hinduism might turn out to be older than civilization, as Negrito and proto-Australoid elements can be identified even in present-day Hinduism. If Hinduism appears uncivilized at times, it is because it is older than civilization. If Hinduism is identified with the Vedas, its beginning may be placed around 1500 B.C.E. Some scholars, however, prefer to distinguish between Vedism and Hinduism—confining the latter term to the kind of religion that arose in response to the challenge posed by Buddhism and Jainism to Vedism.[27] Then Hinduism may properly be said to have emerged between the sixth and fourth centuries B.C.E. In any case, the long history of Hinduism is perhaps best presented by dividing it into convenient periods.

The Pre-Vedic Period

Although Hinduism is often identified with different degrees of affiliation with the Vedas, several of its features are regarded as pre-Vedic by historians. The first human inhabitants of India were the Negrito, who survive in parts of south India and the Andaman Islands. Ideas about the path of the dead to paradise guarded by an avenging demon have been traced to them. They were followed by the proto-Australoids, who introduced the use of the phases of the moon to designate the days of the Hindu calendar called *tithis*. Dravidian-speaking Near Eastern peoples represent the next wave of immigration, and if their identification with the peoples of the Indus Valley is correct, then several elements in Hinduism—such as the popular rite of *pūjā* or worship of images, the worship of proto-Śiva and Mother Goddess and of zoomorphic deities, the sanctity accorded to the *pīpal* tree (ficus religiosa), and the obsession with ablutions within Hinduism—may be traceable to this period.

The Vedic Period (ca. 1500 B.C.E.–ca. 300 B.C.E.)

The next wave of people to enter India are said to be the Aryans—a pastoral and nomadic people who ultimately conquered the Punjab and then spread their influence over the rest of the country. Their religious practices already contained Indo-European and Indo-Iranian elements.

The two main gods to which the hymns of the ṚgVeda are addressed are Indra and Agni, and this helps provide a clue to their religion. Indra, in his cosmic aspect, is the liberator of the waters; in his terrestrial aspect he is a martial hero who leads the fair-skinned Aryans (*āryavarṇa*) to victory over the dark-skinned non-Aryans (*dāsavarṇa*). Agni, or fire, refers to the domestic sphere, where it was piously maintained. A third major god is Soma, the deity of an exhilarating drink. There are numerous other deities assigned to the celestial, the atmospheric, and the terrestrial spheres. Varuṇa, an impressive deity, is assigned to the celestial, Indra to the atmospheric, and fire to the terrestrial sphere. Various other gods and goddesses included the sun, dawn, and so on. The religion of the ṚgVeda consisted of offerings made to the various gods, often poured into the fire to be carried to the gods in their heavenly abodes. The role of ritual in Vedism cannot be underestimated. It has been surmised that the survival of the present Vedic texts out of a much larger mass of material may be primarily if not entirely due to its use in ritual. Nor can one fail to recognize the mythic dimension. Whether the gods symbolize the activities and the phenomena of the universe or whether these phenomena and the activities symbolize the gods, or both, some other underlying reality is an issue that must be left to future scholars to determine.

With the growth of ritual, branches (*śākhās*) began to emerge, foreshadowing the subdivision of the tradition into schools, cults, sects, and so on in the course of its subsequent history. Gradually the ritual became more complicated as sacrifice assumed centrality in the ritual—fostering the belief that the very existence of the cosmos depended on the performance of the sacrificial ritual. This attitude dominates the *Brāhmaṇas*, or priestly texts. By around 800 B.C.E., however, this commitment to ritualism was called into question by people who retired to the forest to reflect on the significance of ritual. These reflections, contained in the *Āraṇyakas*, soon gave rise to deeper questions about the meaning of life and the nature of ultimate reality. This quest found its expression in the *Upaniṣads* (800 B.C.E. onward) and gave rise to a religious philosophy that is an active force in Hindu life to this day. The esoteric nature of the doctrines led to the veneration of the guru, which has characterized much of the later history of Hinduism.

The Classical Period (ca. 300 B.C.E.–ca. 1000)

The revolt against Vedic sacrificial ritual took two forms: internal and external. The *Upaniṣads*, while criticizing the previous tradition, still located themselves within it, but by the sixth century B.C.E. two major movements had arisen in India that placed themselves outside the pale of Vedic orthodoxy—the Buddhist and the Jaina. It was in the context of the challenge posed by these traditions that Hinduism defined itself. These movements rejected the Vedic tradition, commitment to worldly goals and life, and the institutions of caste and stages of life, at least in part, if not entirely. Hinduism formulated itself in the face of this challenge, by asserting the validity of the Vedas and the institutions of varṇa and āśrama. In the beginning, the Jaina and Buddhist movements gained in strength. The preponderance of epigraphic and archaeological evidence from the second century B.C.E. to the second century C.E. seems to indicate that the tide was running in favor of Buddhism, and a large number of foreigners, who were invading India around the time, were also converting to it.

For reasons difficult to identify clearly at this stage, gradually the tide turned. The establishment of the Gupta dynasty in the north around 300 C.E. seemed to signal the successful resurgence of Hinduism. By the time of Harṣa in the seventh century, it had made further gains, and by the tenth century, Hinduism had successfully reestablished itself as the dominant religion on the subcontinent.

The evidence of foreign travelers to India testifies to this. When Fa-hsien visited India in the fourth century, Buddhism was flourishing, but signs of Hindu revival were evident. By the time Hsüan-tsang visited India in the seventh century, the evidence of further decline of Buddhism was clear, as is also obvious from the account of I-ching who followed him. Incidentally, Hsüan-tsang asked for a quotation from the ṚgVeda to be sent to him after his return to China, and a Sanskrit translation of the

Tao Te Ching was also commissioned by a Hindu king at that time. This testifies to a vibrant interaction between Hinduism and Buddhism and India and China during this period, but by the time Alberuni decided to write his treatise on India in the eleventh century, India had once again become Hindu India, though not for long. The Hindu revival during this classical period is associated with a revival of Vedic consciousness, graphically portrayed by the gigantic image of the boar incarnation of Viṣṇu, who is represented as rescuing the earth from the abysmal depths into which it had fallen along with the Vedas.

The Medieval Period (ca. 1000–ca. 1800)

The main feature of this period consists of the fact that Islam provided the basic context for the development of Hinduism as a "text." The patron of Alberuni, Mahmūd of Ghazni, led seventeen successful raids into India and overcame Hindu resistance with surprising ease. He was more interested in sacking cities than in building an empire, at which his successors were more successful. In 1192 the major Rajput ruler of the north was defeated and killed by Muhammad Ghūrī, and by 1200 the so-called Slave dynasty had established Muslim rule over north India, destined to last until 1858.

Hinduism had been successful, until the arrival of Islam, in accommodating, if not absorbing, all challenges to it in the form of external aggression and internal dissension. It failed to perform this feat in the case of Islam and was profoundly affected by this circumstance. During this period, with the political line of resistance having collapsed, a social line of defense was set up in the form of a rigidified caste system and social ostracism of the Muslims. This coincided with the leadership of the community passing into the hands of the priests, who perhaps lacked the imagination to adopt any other strategy. At the same time, Islam exerted a dual influence. On the one hand it encouraged conversion, which, unlike the case of Indonesia, seemed to involve a virtually total repudiation of the ancestral religion. On the other, it encouraged monotheistic and egalitarian tendencies among those Hindus who were willing to follow its example but were unwilling to go all the way, and numerous movements that attempted to bridge the gap between the two arose. The movements associated with the names of Kabīr (fifteenth century?), Nānak (fifteenth century), Dādū (sixteenth century), and so on naturally come to mind. There was some interaction between mystical Islam and Hinduism, but the main body of Hinduism retreated into a protective shell and, basically in the grip of political despair, turned for spiritual solace to God. The anomie experienced by society found expression in the proliferation of Sannyāsīs, or renunciants. *Sannyāsa* became a form of escapism, as

Nānak clearly saw. The Hindu extremity was God's opportunity, and especially around the sixteenth century, the north witnessed an efflorescence of devotional poetry truly sensational in quality, a movement of which Sūrdās, Tulsīdās, Mīrābāī, and a host of other poet-saints are representative figures. The movement of Caitanya (fifteenth century), which emphasized public chanting, seems to have been an attempt to prevent Hinduism from becoming merely a religion of home and hearth, given the public dominance of Islam. The devotional movement is characterized by heavy popular emphasis on the salvific potency of the name of God—first primarily that of Kṛṣṇa (with his consort Rādhā) and then also of Rāma, culminating in the paradoxical claim that the name of God is even greater than God himself, thus making *japa*, or the murmur of God's name, a pervasive practice. It was Bhakti in Hinduism that is said to have asymptotically approached Ṣūfī developments in Indian Islam. This Bhakti, or the devotional movement, was a palliative but not a cure, and it is said to have come from the south where the devotees of Viṣṇu (Āḻvārs) and Śiva (Nāyaṉārs) had already elevated it to great heights by the ninth century. It is to the south that we now turn.

The Islamic penetration of the south began with the sack of Deogiri by Malik Kāfūr in 1307. However, the manner in which the south reacted to this was interesting and different. It must be noted that all the three major movements of Vedānta—represented by Śaṅkara (ninth century), Rāmānuja (twelfth century), and Madhva (thirteenth century)—arose in the south, and although the last two were theistic, they were also Vedantic and not merely devotional. The south displayed greater vigor and vitality, not merely religiously but also politically. The Vijayanagar Empire (fourteenth–seventeenth centuries), though it was also ultimately overrun by the Muslims, proved a bulwark against Islam for centuries.

Even the devotional movement in Mahārāṣṭra took two forms: the Vārakarī and the Dhārakarī. To the latter, which was activistic as well as devotional, belonged Rāmdās, the preceptor of Śivājī, under whose leadership the Marathas became a political force and may well have replaced Muslim rule, but for the British. The former is associated with the name of poet-saints whose names are household words in western India: Jñāneśvara (thirteenth century), Nāmadev (fourteenth century), and Tukārām (seventeenth century). The Bhakti movement spread all over the country, producing poet-saints like Śaṅkaradeva in Assam and Purandaradāsa in Karṇāṭaka (sixteenth century). The whole period, beginning from the tenth and especially from the twelfth to the eighteenth centuries, is characterized by a proliferation of sects that visibly distinguish themselves by such means as manner of dress, marks on the forehead, and so on. It seems as if Hindu theology, like Hindu society and polity, was subjected to a process of fission by its encounter with Islam. Both the sects and the castes are too numerous to enumerate but, though thus frayed, the fabric of Hinduism was not rent apart. The overarching concepts of varṇa and bhakti enabled their successful accommodation within Hinduism. Curiously enough, nonsectarian Advaita Vedānta seems to have had a limiting effect on sectarian proliferation both before the tenth and after the eighteenth centuries.

Throughout this period, often, though not always, the Vedic heritage was used as a legitimizing influence both politically and religiously. The two main Hindu political movements that achieved reasonable success during this period were the Vijayanagar Empire in the south, and the Marathas in the west (apart from the Sikhs in the Punjab). During the Vijayanagar Empire, Vedic learning underwent a revival, and the best-known Hindu commentary on the ṚgVeda, by Sāyaṇa, dates from that period. Similarly, Śivājī (1627–1680) was crowned with Vedic ritual and proclaimed himself as the protector of the Vedas. The devotional poetry of the period centers around Rāma and Kṛṣṇa, who are incarnations of Viṣṇu. Although the popularity of these gods was devotional and had little to do with the Vedas, their theology was Vedic in the sense that the incarnations occurred to protect the dharma of the Vedas.

It was also around this period that the sanctity of the cow became widely accepted as symbolic of Hinduism. This raises an interesting point. In the Vedic period, beef-eating was not taboo. A Vedic sage, when asked whether he believed in eating beef, is said to have replied: "Only if it is tender." There is even some literary evidence from the south that this taboo was not widespread prior to the Islamic presence. Obviously the content of the Vedas was now secondary to its role as a symbol of Hinduism, and far more significant than the fact that the Vedic Hindus may have been beef-eaters was the symbolic representation of the Veda as a cow. It is also a striking fact that the Sikh *Ādi Granth* is modeled on the ṚgVeda, so that the Sikh movement, although on the outskirts of Hinduism, was not beyond its influence.

The sanctity of the cow deserves further discussion. It appears so irrational to the Western beef-eater, but it was an article of faith that was upheld in common by the Hindus of the south and the north and even by the Sikhs. It seems that just as the rather vague veneration in which the Vedas were held crystallized into a dogma of Vedic infallibility under the pressure of attacks by the Buddhists, the Jainas, and the materialists at the philosophical level, the vague veneration of the cow—signs of which are also evident in the Vedic times and which were perhaps reinforced by its pastoral and agricultural usefulness—crystallized into a living symbol of Hinduism at the popular level in the encounter between Hinduism and Islam. How deeply ingrained this became in the Hindu mind can be gauged from an incident mentioned by Alberuni. He writes that the Shah of Kabul indicated his willingness to embrace Islam if that would not involve him in homosexuality and beef-eating. It is worth remarking that the cow is ritually slaughtered by the Muslims in India but not in other parts of the Islamic world on the occasion of ʿĪd al-Aḍḥā, which on that account is actually called Baqar ʿĪd (Cow Feast) in India.[28]

Because non-Hindus find the sacred cow syndrome hard to grasp, an analogy might help. Canadians, like citizens of all nations, respect their flag. But if the Americans across the border started burning the Canadian flag to spite Canadians and assert their military dominance, against which the Canadians could not retaliate, then the Canadian sentiment toward the flag would become far more charged than it is. It would then appear irrational to an outsider that the Canadians would hold a piece of cloth in such sacred esteem. The sanctity of the cow in Hinduism can hardly be explained through zoolatry. There is hardly a temple to be found dedicated to the cow (as distinguished from the bull). It is our strong suspicion that the explanation is historical. As late as 1947–1948, the conversion of the Hindus to Islam during the rioting in the Punjab involved the forced eating of beef.

Although the medieval period of Hinduism is characterized by devotion to the Hindu gods and the veneration of the cow, which seem to have little to do directly with the Vedas, the tradition seems to have remained subliminally anchored in the Vedas. Small wonder then that when Dārā Shukūh wished to establish a rapprochement between Hinduism and Islam in the seventeenth century, he undertook to translate the *Upaniṣads* into Persian. Europe first became acquainted with ancient Hindu thought in modern times through a Latin translation of this text.

The Modern Period (ca. 1800–1947)

As the British started supplanting native rulers all over the country and established their paramountcy over India, Hinduism faced a qualitatively different situation. For the Hindus the threat from Islam somewhat abated with the coming of British rule, but Christianity posed a new religious threat, albeit a milder one in comparison with Islam. At the same time, Hinduism now faced a new kind of threat—religious not in nature but in consequence: the threat from science, secularism, and humanitarianism, although the latter came cloaked in Christian guise. It was under Western initiative above all that a very significant development took place. Ancient Hindu learning was rediscovered and along with it the Vedas. The impact of this on the Hindu mind can be gauged from the fact that even such a nationalist as Swami Vivekānanda speculated that Max Mueller, who edited the ṚgVeda in modern times, was perhaps a reincarnation of Sāyaṇa of the Vijayanagar Empire!

Although a host of factors must be taken into account to explain the revival of Hinduism in the post-1800 period, from the point of Hinduism as a religious system, one must recognize the role of the Vedas in the process.

It was the issue of the Vedas and Vedic authority that came to the fore. The first major Hindu reformer, Raja Rammohun Roy, sought to justify non-idolatrous monotheism on the basis of Vedānta. Around 1830, he founded an association called the Brāhmo Samāj in Bengal to further his cause. A major rift developed in this organization on the issue of Vedic infallibility in the mid-nineteenth century. By the late nineteenth century Swami Dayānanda Sarasvatī had founded the Ārya Samāj, which swore by Vedic infallibility, at the other end of India, in Bombay.

Toward the end of the nineteenth century and into the twentieth, one witnesses a reversal of an earlier process. It was suggested earlier that it was under pressure from Buddhists, Jainas, and materialists that the Hindu tradition hardened its stance from one of vague veneration of the Vedas as its sacred heritage to the deliberate affirmation that they were uniquely authoritative. In modern times, however, although once again under pressure from modern, rational, reformist, and Christian sources, it did not react the same way. It exalted religious experience above religious authority and yet, while it no longer clung to Vedic authority, it was discreet enough not to throw the baby away with the bath water. Rāmakrishna was sometimes dismissive of the Vedas[29] while utilizing them as a symbol; and though Vivekānanda also on occasion poured scorn on Vedic infatuation on the part of the Hindus by lamenting that "if I take certain passages of the Vedas, and if I juggle the text and give it the most impossible meaning... all the imbeciles will follow me in a crowd," he did not hesitate to cite them in his discourses. Almost all the major religious figures of modern Hinduism—such as B. G. Tilak (1856–1920), R. Tagore (1861–1941), Aurobindo Ghose (1872–1950), and Mahatma Gandhi (1869–1948)—drew inspiration, though not their authority, from the Vedas, and even the retiring Ramaṇa Maharshi had them recited regularly. A very striking statement in this context was made by Mahatma Gandhi when he declared in his journal, *Harijan*, on January 30, 1937 (by a curious coincidence, on the very day he was to be assassinated eleven years later):

> I have now come to the final conclusion that if all the *Upaniṣads* and all the other scriptures happened all of a sudden to be reduced to ashes and if only the first verse of the *Īśopaniṣad* were left intact in the memory of the Hindus, Hinduism would survive for ever.

This famous verse may first be paraphrased as follows: "1. God is all: the entire universe is an expression of him. 2. Joy is not in hoarding but in giving. Attachment to finite and perishing things is evil, and is the cause of sorrow. Renunciation of attachment is the highest good."[30] Now we are ready for its translation:

> God dwells in whatever moves in this moving world. Enjoy it by having renounced it; covet not, whose wealth (do you think) is it?

The Old and the New

One can thus trace the destiny of Hinduism with the Veda first as its integrating, then its organizing, and then its legitimizing principle. At the same time, one must never overlook the fact that though the Vedas may be said, in some sense, to constitute the center of Hinduism, they do not constitute its core. That core belongs to Realization. A Hindu may not denounce the Veda, but he or she can renounce the Veda. It is in this razor-thin margin of difference between the center and the core that the synchronic and diachronic in Hinduism intersect. It is this path "sharp as a razor's edge" (*Kaṭha Upaniṣad* I.3.14) which the tradition has somehow traversed down the ages. This becomes obvious if one asks the clarifying question, How does the structure of Hinduism relate to its history?

The history of Hinduism, with the sacred thread of the Vedas running through its labyrinthine annals, like Ariadne's, also illustrates its structure, for its history can itself be interpreted in terms of its structure by the variation of a theme introduced earlier. The *Saṁhitā* portion of the Vedas can be seen as representing henotheistic bhakti, the *Brāhmaṇas* karma as ritual action, and the *Āraṇyakas* and the *Upaniṣads* again bhakti and jñāna, respectively, so that the three yogas can account as well for Vedism as Hinduism. The period from the sixth century B.C.E. to the tenth century C.E. was, in very broad terms, dominated by jñāna, from the eleventh to the seventeenth centuries by bhakti, and from the eighteenth century to the present day by karma. Thus periods of history through time, no less than people at a point in time, may be characterized, even organized, according to the scheme of tripartite yoga. For one mighty endeavor underlies all the categories of literature of Hinduism and all its periods of history: to transmute—by the alchemy of its arcane processes such as sublimation, redefinition, absorption, substitution, institution of correspondences, and so on and a whole battery of such techniques—a mass (*sarvam*) into a whole (*viśvam*); a chaos into a cosmos and if not into a universe then, at least, into a universe of shared discourse called Hinduism.

How Does Hinduism Work?

The first thing to realize before discussing how Hinduism works is that it works—to the astonishment of the Hindus themselves as much as the outsiders. After all, a religion that, like Judaism, has survived for virtually three thousand years must be doing something right.

How Hinduism Works

How, then, does Hinduism work? Perhaps the way Hinduism works is best explained first through an analogy and then by examples. The working of the American political system provides a good analogy. The Hindu way of life is the religious counterpart of a democracy. In a democracy people are free to choose their own leader, their way of life, and so on; in Hinduism, which possesses no established church, one is pretty much free to do as one chooses in the realm of one's spiritual life. However, just as political freedom does not mean that one can run through traffic lights, spiritual freedom does not mean that one can blithely disregard conventional norms on which social life is predicated. These norms can change, but the basic postulate of political and religious liberty remains unchallenged. Colloquial wisdom has it that in a democracy one is free to swing one's arms any way one likes so long as they do not hit somebody else's nose. (Whether you are free to hit your own nose is less of an issue but can become one.) Similarly, in Hinduism, you are free to formulate your own sacrality so long as it is not transgressive of others. In a democracy you choose your own human representatives; in Hinduism you choose your own representatives of the divine. In a democracy you may or may not cast your vote, in Hinduism you may or may not believe in one god or none.

What are the limits to the freedom democracy confers on us as a system? The only real limit entertained within a democratic system, apart from public order, decency, and so on, in the exercise of rights, is that no party can be allowed to function in a way that will subvert the system itself, and even here democracy tends to be indulgent. It allows the Communist party—avowedly antagonistic to democracy until very recent times—to function so long as it will not indulge in armed insurrection or advocate overthrow of the state. The problems democracy faces in dealing with communism illustrate effectively the difficulties Hinduism has in dealing with the Semitic religious tradition, especially as represented by Islam and Christianity. Democracy confers political freedom, and by that very mandate, it should allow the Communist party to function freely, which it in fact does to a certain extent. But inasmuch as the Party is opposed to the very freedom that a democracy cherishes, it creates a profound dilemma for a democracy. If a democracy forbids a Communist party from functioning, it compromises its commitment to freedom; but if it allows it to function, and the party is successful, it will undermine the very basis of that very freedom and the whole democratic structure and process. Most democracies make the following compromise: They allow the Communist party to function but somehow prevent it from subverting the democratic institutions themselves. The exclusiveness of Islam and Christianity poses a similar threat to the basic premise of Hinduism, namely, that of theological freedom, which, if replaced by the theological dogma of either Islam or Christianity or even communism (if it is viewed as a religion), will mean the end of Hinduism itself. In facing these religions, Hinduism faces the same dilemma a democracy faces in dealing with communism—and it is experimenting with a similar compromise in present-day India.

To understand how Hinduism works as a religious system, one needs to understand how democracy works as a political system. Democracy is a process: a process by which different people are elected to office and previous policies are changed, often reversed. Hinduism, too, is a process: Forms of worship change and so do social institutions and policies connected with them. At one time levirate was allowed, now it is not; at one time Sati (the practice of widow self-immolation on the husband's funeral pyre) was permitted, now it is banned. Just as in the United States, up to a point, slavery was seen as consistent with democracy, and after a point the position was reversed, untouchability was accepted up to a point as part of Hinduism and then legally abolished in 1950, amid a chorus of "Victory to Mahatma Gandhi."

Although it is true that democracy functions as a system and it is the system that is the key, not the result, still this system is anchored in the Constitution of the United States. What is Hinduism anchored in? Before the question is answered, it must be clarified that the democratic system is not so much anchored in the Constitution as in the concept of *constitutional authority*, for not only can the Constitution be amended, it is *interpreted* by the Supreme Court and such interpretations can vary over time. The Hindu counterpart to constitutional authority is Vedic authority; and the Hindu counterpart to the Constitution is the Veda. But we must probe deeper to discover the true springs of both American democracy and Hinduism. The American Constitution did not fall from heaven like manna, nor was it repatriated by the United Kingdom as in the case of Canada. The Constitution is a document that the *Americans gave to themselves*. However closely it may be allied to the American people, it cannot be identified with them. Hence, the real locus of the American democracy is the Americans, although its focus is the Constitution. Similarly, the real locus of Hinduism is the Hindus; its focus is the Veda.

Under the American Constitution any American citizen can be elected president of the United States—in principle. The difference from a Leninist Communist state may be recognized, where only a member of the Party can become a head of the state. Just as anyone can run for office in the United States, any Hindu can become a spiritual leader. Any Hindu could not, until recently, become a sacramental *priest*, only a brahmin could; but any Hindu could become a Sādhu or a Swami, that is, a spiritual figure. This distinction, reminiscent of Weber's distinction between priest and prophet, means that just as anyone can run for public office in America, anyone can become a saint or spiritual leader in Hinduism.

We have now identified two key elements that simultaneously unlock the arcane working of both the American political system and the Hindu religious system: the exercise of freedom and the exercise of initiative. The principles of freedom and initiative in theory are accompanied by two phenomena in practice: assimilation and tolerance. America is the great melting pot in which various ethnic identities get dissolved. This is true—but up to a point. Politicians are still concerned with the Jewish vote, the Hispanic vote, the Italian vote, the black vote, and so on. In Hinduism the counterpart to these political constituencies are the sects and castes, with this difference; the Hindu pattern may be compared more to a mosaic than a melting pot.

How Does a Tripartite System Work?

The American political system consists of three branches: the executive, the legislative, and the judicial. It is in the interaction of these that the drama of government is played out. Similarly, the tripartite system of yogas in Hinduism—jñāna, bhakti, and karma—constitutes the three legs of the Hindu tripod. The American system is said to be one of checks and balances. The three yogas operate in a similar way. Bhakti rescues the dispassion of jñāna from degenerating into callous indifference; jñāna rescues bhakti from the toils of irrational emotionalism; karma rescues both from a self-absorbed neglect of society. And jñāna and bhakti prevent activity from being tainted by egocentricity on the path of karma. Moreover, even within *one* component of the American political system, checks and balances are in place. Consider the legislative component: It is bicameral, consisting of a House of Representatives and a Senate. Similarly in Hinduism, even within one yoga there are checks and balances. When unilateral devotion to one's dharma in activistic Hinduism begins to invite exploitation by others, the militant version of activistic Hinduism emerges as a corrective.

To pursue the parallel even further: Just as the American government deals with an issue as it emerges in terms of its configuration and constellates the three branches accordingly, Hinduism acts in a similar way when faced with a situation or a challenge. It met the challenge of the gnostic religions of Buddhism and Jainism by bringing jñāna to the fore; the challenge of Islam, subsequent to its military failure, with bhakti (as when the executive requires help from the judiciary); and the challenge of activistic Christianity with karma. How it will face other issues and challenges remains to be seen.

The Political Experience of Hinduism

The Religious Consequences of Victory

Apart from the undeciphered seals of the Indus Valley culture (ca. third millennium B.C.E.) the earliest texts that deal with Hinduism are the Vedas. These texts describe a military conflict between a people, who called themselves Aryans, against the Dasyus, who have been variously identified as demons, Dravidians, indigenous tribals, or residents of an urban civilization of the Indus Valley. The Vedas record the victory gained by the Aryans over their rivals with the help of their war-god Indra, to whom over one-fourth of the hymns of the ṚgVeda, the earliest of their sacred texts, is dedicated, although numerous other gods are also mentioned, often as allies of Indra. After their victory, the Aryans faced a situation similar to the one faced by the Hebrews after their victories in Canaan: what attitude to adopt toward the beliefs and practices of the conquered peoples.

It seems that the Aryans adopted the attitude of religious magnanimity in political victory. The religious consequence of victory was the gradual integration of the beliefs and practices of the conquerors and the conquered, so that ultimately the two became indistinguishable, to the point where scholars wonder who really conquered whom. It is almost like the appropriation of the Greek pantheon by the Romans. In any case, while some hymns of the Vedas portray the conflict—sometimes quite savage, not merely between the Aryans and the Dasyus but sometimes among the Aryans themselves—the other hymns are more conciliatory in tone. Thus, while some of the ṚgVeda hymns pour scorn on the Dasyus as those who do not share the gods and the observances of the Aryans, another hymn contains the famous dictum: "The real is one, sages call it variously" (I.164.46).

This struck a note that reverberates throughout the history of Hinduism. Synthesis of beliefs and practices is virtually an ingrained tendency within Hinduism. This is the natural correlate of pluralism, which is tolerated and even encouraged.

The absorption of the worship of Śiva within Hinduism illustrates this tendency. Many scholars are of the view that Śiva was a pre-Aryan god who was worshiped by the people the Aryans conquered. After the conquest he seems to have gone through a phase of being a non-Aryan god, from having been a pre-Aryan one, and was excluded from sacrificial ritual characteristic of the Vedic religion. The story of Dakṣa, of Śiva's marriage to his daughter, her self-immolation at Śiva's exclusion from the sacrifice, and the subsequent desecration of the sacrifice by Śiva's hordes are said to represent the struggle and opposition involved in the process of the final assimilation of Śiva into the Hindu pantheon, with the result that he is one of the two chief gods of present-day Hinduism.

Assimilation in theology, however, was also accompanied by functional differentiation. Early in the history of Hinduism the roles of the priest and the king came to be clearly distinguished. This must be regarded as a very significant development, when we observe that such differentiation of roles is not a characteristic feature in the religious history of ancient Egypt and Mesopotamia among the dead religions and in the case of Judaism and, to a certain extent, Islam, among the living traditions. The differentiation of the role of the priest and the king is an early version of the separation of the church and the state, though in an embryonic form. The Aryans were Indo-Europeans who had arrived, according to a widely accepted view, at a tripartite view of society, which they imported into India. With the conquered people constituting the fourth layer, it could well be that the historical foundation of the caste system had by now been laid.

In the subsequent history of Hinduism this pattern was repeated many times until about 1000 C.E. Foreign hordes entered India and established their kingdoms, but in due course they were absorbed in the religious mosaic of India. Their gods were absorbed in the Hindu pantheon and they themselves in the Hindu social system as a caste. This process finally received the imprimatur of tradition when Hindu political power was successfully reasserted, often by the very people who had now become Hindus. Even internal religious upheavals were similarly managed by the system. After the virtual establishment of Buddhism as the state religion by Aśoka in the fourth century B.C.E., a Hindu dynasty (the Śuṅga) replaced the dynasty to which he belonged, and later Hindu kings like Harṣa (seventh century) paid homage to the Buddha as also to Sūrya (the sun god) and Śiva. It was also around this time that Buddha was accepted as an incarnation of Viṣṇu. It seems that once external invasions had been successfully weathered by native Hindu dynasties, a similar process of assimilation set in. A remarkable example of this is provided by the column dedicated to Viṣṇu erected by the Greek ambassador Heliodorus, who represented King Antialkidas at the court of the Indian King Bhagabhadra, in the second century B.C.E. near Besnagar in central India.

In other words, the political experience of Hinduism, so long as it was ultimately victorious in militarily overcoming the challenges to it from both within and outside India, was one of religious assimilation in its broadest senses—the gods were assimilated within the Hindu pantheon and the people within the Hindu community. Hindu pluralism figured in this process as both cause and consequence. The fact that this process took place gradually and without bloodshed is probably due to the implicit separation of church and state in the division of the sacred and secular realms between the brahmin and the kṣatriya, or the priest and the warrior. This may have been part of a deal in which the kṣatriya accepted the ritual superiority of the brahmin who conceded temporal sovereignty to the kṣatriya. One may note that just as the kṣatriya preserved the security of the society as a whole and not just his own, the brahmin was the custodian of the sanctity of the society as a whole and not just his own.

The Religious Consequences of Defeat

The conquest of India by the Muslims and the establishment of an Islamic state has been alluded to. It was an unprecedented experience for the Hindus. The fact that any religion would use the state apparatus as an instrument of its propagation is an experience that Hinduism has difficulty in handling even to this day. Moreover, during this long period of Muslim Rule (ca. 1000–1858), the Hindus squandered many chances of regaining control over their political destiny and somehow always managed to snatch defeat from the jaws of victory, so that the Hindus had to face the religious consequences of not just defeat but also demoralization. There are some parallels with the Jewish experience. There was the destruction not of the Temple but of temples, and a kind of Hindu diaspora. Thus Alberuni: "Hindu sciences have retired far away from those parts of the country conquered by us, and have fled to places where our hands cannot yet reach, to Kashmir, Benares and other places."[31]

But there was one marked contrast between the Hindu and Jewish experiences. While the Jews were scattered from their homeland, the Hindus were subdued in their own homeland. Their experience in terms of geography might have been different, but the "geography" of their experience—a wasteland of suffering—seems to have been similar. Just as the leadership of the Jewish community, with the loss of political control over its destiny, passed from royalty and priesthood into the hands of the rabbis, the effective leadership of the Hindu community virtually passed into the hands of the priests from that of the kings. In a manner somewhat similar to the way the rabbis protected Judaism by safeguarding Jewish law, the highly sacerdotal character of medieval Hinduism perhaps substituted for its political failure and served as its defense mechanism. It protected Hinduism, however, by virtually petrifying it. In contrast to the Hindus, the Jews had a strong sense of political destiny. One senses similar stirrings in the rise of the worship of Rāma, especially in the north (a more martial figure than Kṛṣṇa in the popular imagination), which may be connected with the subliminal need for a militant response felt by the Hindus. However, the dominant mood in the north was one of demoralization with the replacement of the Hindu rule by the Muslim. Hindu learning centered on Sanskrit received a setback, and the vacuum was filled at the political level by Persian but at the popular level by the rise of numerous regional languages to prominence. The literature of these languages in this period is highly devotional in nature—and of such remarkable merit that it evokes the finest aesthetic and devotional responses to this day. At the same time, one must wonder if it is not the plaintive cry of the nightingale in captivity, howsoever alluring. "Wherever there is ruin there is hope for treasure"—in this case it was literary.

South India emerged as the citadel of Hinduism after the north had been overrun by the Muslims. In the south, the Vijayanagar Empire (fourteenth–seventeenth centuries), although it also finally succumbed to Muslim pressure, held it at bay for a sufficiently long period of time to prevent such fissures in the body politic arising in the south as led to the formation of Pakistan and Bangladesh in the north.[32]

By the beginning of the nineteenth century, the British had established themselves in India with sufficient firmness to permit missionary activity within their realm. The victory of the British, and by proxy of Christianity, produced its own chain of consequences. Inasmuch as in Bengal and some other parts of India the British had replaced Muslim rule, the new dispensation was welcomed by the Hindus, who took avidly to Western learning. They turned out to be more selective in their acceptance of Christianity, but here too the religious consequences of military and political defeat were far-reaching. Christian missionaries brought the printing press to India with the revolutionary result that texts which for centuries had been the exclusive preserve of the brahmins could be bought and read (often in translation) on the roadside. This silent revolution transformed Hinduism, and, coupled with the spread of British education over India, enabled the consolidation of Hindu identity in an unprecedented manner. The fact that Hindus from different parts of India by and large use English as their language of religious, though not sacerdotal discourse (which continues to be Sanskrit), is a major and perhaps unforeseen consequence of military defeat at the hands of the English.

The fact that the British had defeated both the Hindus and the Muslims and now ruled over both could have created an interesting consequence—uniting the two communities in a common cause against the British/Christian enemy. The mutiny against the British in 1857–1858 and the Gandhian movement in its early phase raised such hopes, but they were never realized, for the country was partitioned along religious lines in 1947. For the Hindus this partition represented the religious consequence of *two* defeats—at the hands of the Muslims as well as the Christians.

On the whole it can be said that Hinduism fared better in its encounter with Christianity than in its clash with Islam. Islamic rule over the Hindus was longer (approximately seven hundred years) and more successful in the sense that a quarter of the Hindu population was converted to Islam.

Christian rule, compromised by the rise of secularism to a certain extent, was shorter in duration (two hundred years) and less successful in the sense that only about 3 percent of Hindus converted to Christianity. But what it achieved ideologically was almost as significant for Hinduism as what it could not achieve numerically. Although the Hindu response to Islam led to many remarkable developments, they were still confined to a medieval framework. The Britisher was the middle man and Christianity the midwife—to alter the metaphor—in transforming Hinduism from a religion of the medieval world into a religion of the modern world.

One major religious consequence of the Christian presence in India as a result of military defeat of the Hindus (as represented by the British victory over the Marathas in the region around Bombay) was the projection of the *Bhagavadgītā* as the central scripture of modern Hinduism within a century. One would have expected such a development within Hinduism when it faced the people with the book—the Muslims—but it was curiously delayed until the encounter with another people of the book—the Christians, unless one were to argue that the Rāmāyaṇa of Tulsīdās played a similar role in north India in medieval times. Scholars have expressed surprise at the sudden and successful emergence of the *Bhagavadgītā* early in the twentieth century as *the* scripture of Hinduism. Although the fact that the *Bhagavadgītā* had always been an important scripture should not be overlooked, its widespread acceptance as *the* scripture of Hinduism in modern times certainly seems to have been influenced by the example of the Bible in relation to Christianity. Its martial context was also not irrelevant for a subject people trying to throw off the British yoke.

The Religious Consequences of Freedom

The context of the *Bhagavadgītā* is martial, but the actual struggle through which India regained its political independence was essentially nonviolent—conducted as it was under the leadership of Mahatma Gandhi. This struggle, after the failure of an armed insurrection to dislodge the British in 1857–1858, really began in earnest around 1905 and picked up momentum after 1920 when Mahatma Gandhi emerged as its preeminent leader.

It is important to consider the background of this movement to assess its religious consequences. The movement was aimed at unifying all Indians—irrespective of their religious backgrounds—against the British. The British could hope to retain control over India only by preventing such unification. To this end the British, while ostensibly maintaining a secular stance, embarked on a policy of keeping the Hindus and the Muslims from coming together, as these two constituted the major religious groups. The British also tried to prevent the Hindus from presenting a unified front as well by trying to separate the untouchables into a distinct group. They succeeded in dividing the Hindus and the Muslims but failed in dividing the Hindus.

The religious consequences of freedom represent the working out of all of these forces.

1. One religious consequence of freedom gained on August 15, 1947, was the partition of the country into India and Pakistan on religious grounds. In other words, it was clear that the Hindus and the Muslims had failed to develop a modus vivendi even in the face of a common enemy.

2. While Pakistan was conceptually created as a homeland for Indian Muslims, India was not visualized as the homeland of the Hindus. The opposition then, at least as perceived by the leaders of India, was *not* between a Muslim Pakistan and a Hindu India but between a "theocratic" Pakistan and a secular India. Thus India, unlike Nepal, is not a Hindu state.

3. India's commitment to secularism was the result of the convergence of two distinct outlooks represented respectively by Gandhi and Nehru. Gandhi held all religions to be equally valid and therefore wanted a secular state on religious grounds. Nehru believed that religion as such was a reactionary force with which a modern nation-state should dissociate itself. In other words, he was secular on secular grounds. The net result was that both reinforced the secular element in national life though in different ways. This development was further facilitated by the pluralistic nature of Hinduism.

4. However, Indian secularism did not possess as firm a wall of separation between the church and the state as in the United States, ironically because Hinduism does not possess a church. The state had to step in to take control of Hindu affairs at the national level by default, and spearheaded many reforms, such as the Hindu Marriage and Divorce Act already referred to. The management of Hindu endowments is also supervised by the state. It should be remembered that the British in India were not fully secular—and that the Anglican Church in part was funded through the public exchequer. However, while the British departure from secularism was conformist, the Indian departure was reformist.[33]

The religious consequences of freedom, therefore, were manifold and the Hindus are still living with them. The antipathy between the Muslims and the Hindus that accompanied partition remains unabated and has involved India in three wars with Pakistan—the last one, in 1971, resulting in the dismemberment of the old Pakistan into Pakistan and Bangladesh.

The fact, however, that after experimenting with secularism for some years under Indian inspiration, Bangladesh declared itself as an Islamic state in 1988 indicates that the gulf between secularity and theocracy remains to be bridged in Pakistan and Bangladesh and may even be widening in India itself. It raises the question, Can India remain a secular state when the Indian subcontinent is not? Hindu political identity, which had so far remained submerged in the sea of an Indian identity, is beginning to surface like a giant whale with unpredictable consequences. As Hindu political self-definition is essentially reactive, it reflects the Hindu response to reinforced Muslim and Sikh identities within India. This must be considered an unforeseen religious consequence of freedom, which was ushered in with the expectation that a secular Indian national identity would gradually replace all subnational identities based on religion, language, and so on.

The religious consequences of freedom, therefore, are also significant for Hinduism in terms of what they mean for the non-Hindus, reinforcing our earlier point that there are not only as many Hinduisms as there are Hindus but also as many Hinduisms as there are non-Hindus. While the government did not feel any scruples in modifying Hindu practices through legislation, it was extremely solicitous of the minorities. Such was the political legacy of the Independence Movement in which Hindu political identity was kept muted to encourage the growth of Indian nationalism by making the minorities feel secure. The bridge is now becoming a barrier. According to Article 30 of the Indian Constitution: "(1) All minorities, whether based on religion or language, shall have the right to establish and administer educational institutions of their choice. (2) The State shall not, in granting aid to educational institutions, discriminate against any educational institution on the ground that it is under the management of a minority, whether based on religion or language." This article actually confers *more* rights on the non-Hindu minorities compared to the Hindu majority. This explains a strange quirk of history, that denominations of Hinduism, supposedly the religion of the majority, have sought and secured protection under these provisions from interference by the state in running their educational institutions, in those states of India where non-Hindu or anti-Hindu parties have gained political power, sometimes by claiming that they are *not* Hindu! The Ārya Samāj won the status of a minority religion first in Bihar, and then in the Punjab in 1971, where Sikhs tended to win political power. The Ramakrishna Mission won a similar recognition in 1987 in West Bengal with a Marxist government in power.

Hindu Tolerance and Hindu Fundamentalism

This uneven nature of the Indian Constitution, which functions with political checks in dealing with minorities and without them in dealing with the Hindus, was already identified by Donald Eugene Smith in 1963 as potentially problematical in the secular context.[34] The working of the Constitution has justified the fears. The government has retreated from the directive of framing a uniform civil code for all Indians as required by Article 44 of the Constitution, by exempting the Muslim community on grounds of protection of minority rights on the one hand, while on the other, its interference with Hindu practices, sometimes well-intentioned, as symbolized by enactments against the glorification of Sati passed in 1987–1988, continues unabated and feeds the feeling that Indian secularism is increasingly being directed *against* Hinduism. This has produced the first stirrings of Hindu militancy in independent India.

Essential to Hindu fundamentalism (or more appropriately Hindu nationalism) is the belief that "the Hindu majority is a persecuted majority," and that India's minorities have "acquired privileges beyond their due."[35] This observation, made by a foreign journalist after he had been punched and had his spectacles stomped upon the previous day, represents a perception shared by many Hindus, although its accuracy could be questioned. But in politics, perception is reality. The grievances of the Hindus found a focus in the agitation against a mosque that was built, according to the Hindus, on the very spot where Lord Rāma was born and, furthermore, after demolishing a temple, by the Moghul Emperor Bābar in 1528 after his successful invasion of India. The attempt to build a temple on the site led, in 1990, to the largest mass movement in India since Independence. At its height, more people were detained by the police than during the course of the Salt March and the Quit India movements *combined*—the two major movements launched by Mahatma Gandhi against the British. At one time the number of policemen in Ayodhyā exceeded the total population of the town itself. The seismic implications of such a mass movement became evident to all when two years later, in 1992, a throng estimated at 300,000 stormed the mosque and reduced it to rubble. This razing of the mosque was both an awesome and awful event—it was awesome in that no one really thought the Hindus *could* have done it; it was awful inasmuch as one must wonder whether the Hindus *should* have done it.

The Hindu militants, by demolishing the Muslim mosque in Ayodhyā on December 6, 1992, crossed the Rubicon, perhaps without realizing it. Unless the current trends are reversed, secularism and democracy are now on a collision course in India.

Hitherto the Hindu self-perception of being a tolerant religion had, by and large, kept the militant tendencies in check. Hinduism has enjoyed and cultivated this reputation for tolerance and even insisted at times that it is not merely a characteristic of it but constitutive of it. For if two Hindus have little in common, then it is the mutual tolerance of this diversity that allows them to participate in the membership of the same community. Hitherto

Hindus had projected this attitude toward religious pluralism internal to and *within* Hinduism, toward religious pluralism *outside* of Hinduism as represented, for instance, by Islam and Christianity. This tolerance of intolerance, however, has now flipped, it seems, into the intolerance of the intolerance of other religions.

This section of the chapter must be concluded with a clarification to avoid a serious misunderstanding. The acceptance of the warrior-ethic in Hinduism must be clearly distinguished from the rise of fundamentalism in modern times, although it cannot be separated from it. The martial component is an element in the *structure* of Hinduism, but the rise of Hindu fundamentalism that we are witnessing now is a new *historical* development. The division of the country into India and Pakistan was no doubt accompanied by a communal conflagration, but the "flames which reduced the Mahatma's body to ashes" also "proved to be the last flicker of the conflagration." For a decade after his death there was no major religious disturbance in either India or Pakistan. The new Hindu fundamentalism has placed not Gandhi but his assassin Godse on the pedestal, but that shift seems to have occurred as a consequence of the anti-Hindu character Indian secularism acquired at the hands of the Indian state *after* the martyrdom of Mahatma Gandhi. If the current pressures continue, Hindus will increasingly view religious tolerance as a *right* that one Hindu extends automatically to another Hindu *within* Hinduism, but as a *privilege* that must be earned by those outside Hinduism on clearly defined terms.

What We Learn about Religion from the Study of Hinduism

Is There Such a Thing as Hinduism?

It should be clear by now that Hinduism is not a thing, it is a process. Or one might say that the process is the thing. Hinduism may be usefully looked upon as a method. A method should not be confused with its results. Consider the scientific method characterized by observation, experimentation, and hypothesis-testing. The same method produced such divergent results as Newtonian and Einsteinian physics. But it was the *same* method that produced these different results, and science includes *both* the method and the results. Hinduism may be viewed similarly. It is a method for the discovery of spiritual truths, and its long history is a record of such discoveries, however uneven in quality. It is instructive to extend this way of looking at a religion, namely Hinduism, to looking at religion itself. Religion itself is a method of engaging the ultimate; the various religions are various methods of doing so; their histories are a record of the results of these efforts. Such an approach prevents us from adopting a static or essentialist approach to a religion; it enables us to look at it in dynamic and existential terms.

As Many Hinduisms as Hindus

Because of its conscious acceptance of diversity, Hinduism makes one aware of the unconscious presence of diversity in the phenomenon of religion itself. For instance, is it not true to say, disconcerting though it might appear at first, that there are as many Christianities as Christians? That is, every Christian appropriates Christianity in his or her own way, and in a way somewhat different from the way it is appropriated by another. Even for people who follow the same religious tradition, the precise *meaning* it possesses for the individual followers can differ, even if it might be more broadly capable of being associated with the person's age, income, education, and so on. The specific spiritual nuance it possesses for an individual is unique and not identical with that of a fellow-believer, even if the difference might be so subtle as to be apparently indistinguishable. But then chocolate, honey, and candy all taste sweet, yet the flavors still differ. Another way of gaining the same insight in the study of religion would be to ask ourselves: Do we personally believe in all the things that have been believed or practiced in the history of our religion or even as it is practiced now? We may choose to belong to a tradition but we are invariably selective, in range or emphasis, in our appropriation of it.

Hinduism, like all religions, recognizes the primacy of truth, but it also more explicitly recognizes the role of temperament in seeking it. It takes these differences into account in two ways: in allowing people a remarkably free hand in choosing the kind of god they might want to worship and in the spiritual method they might consider appropriate for such worship, though whether one is eligible for a particular mode of worship (*adhikārin*) is not totally disregarded. The presence of image worship within Hinduism is a further recognition of the role of difference in religious approaches. It reminds us that just as we think in mental images, and often in different mental images, some may prefer to contemplate visible images and often different visible images. The concept of "the chosen people" is thus turned, in the plastic hands of Hinduism, into the "choosing people"—Hindus choose the gods they worship. For instance, some might choose to worship god as male, some as female. Hindu polytheism is an expression of Hindu pluralism. But although there may be as many Hinduisms as there are Hindus, there is only one Reality. Reality has many names and faces, but it is one. A Hindu sage Yājñavalkya (ca. eighth century B.C.E.) makes this explicit in a dialogue with Vidagdha Śākalya.

> Then Vidagdha Śākalya questioned him. "How many gods are there, Yājñavalkya?"
>
> He answered in accord with the following *Nivid* (invocationary formula): "As many as are mentioned in the *Nivid* of the Hymn to All the Gods, namely, three hundred and three, and three thousand and three [=3306]."
>
> "Yes," said he, "but just how many gods are there, Yājñavalkya?"
> "Thirty-three."
> "Yes," said he, "but just how many gods are there, Yājñavalkya?"
> "Six."
> "Yes," said he, "but just how many gods are there, Yājñavalkya?"
> "Three."
> "Yes," said he, "but just how many gods are there, Yājñavalkya?"
> "Two."
> "Yes," said he, "but just how many gods are there, Yājñavalkya?"
> "One and a half."
> "Yes," said he, "but just how many gods are there, Yājñavalkya?"
> "One."[36]

The role of temperament in the study of religion can take curious forms. For instance, although there are differences in degrees, there is a similarity in kind in that liberals and conservatives are found across the board in the various religions of the world. Similarly, it seems that various kinds of mystical experience: introvertive and extrovertive, ecstatic and instatic, or personal and impersonal—also cut across traditions. The relationship of works and grace in relation to God also falls in this category. The distinction is quaintly labeled cat-logic and monkey-logic. A cat carries its young around entirely by itself—this denotes reliance on God through faith alone. The young of the monkey, however, cling to the mother as she leaps from branch to branch—this illustrates the cooperation of human endeavor with grace. (I have not been able to come up with an example of marsupial logic despite prolonged sojourn in Australia.)

As Many Hinduisms as Non-Hindus

The history of Hinduism is one of progressive assimilation—it is at least characterized by a constant effort in that direction. Thus Hinduism is a result of assimilating a number of traditions that, to begin with, lay outside its pale. At the time the early Aryans entered India, more or less around the same time the Hebrews entered Canaan, they frowned upon several religious practices as un-Aryan. Within a few centuries they had become part and parcel of Hinduism. Then around the sixth century B.C.E., India, especially north India, witnessed a tremendous religious ferment—out of which arose Buddhism and Jainism. Over the next several centuries, Buddhism (and much of Jainism) was absorbed into Hinduism in India. Buddha became an incarnation of the Hindu god Viṣṇu. When Mahatma Gandhi left for England at the age of eighteen, he was administered the triple vows of abstention from meat, wine, and sex. These vows were administered to the Hindu Gandhi by a Jaina monk. In the case of Islam and Christianity, Hinduism could not perform, or at least has not yet performed, any spectacular feat of assimilation, but it has been profoundly influenced by both these traditions. Thus non-Hindus, in this oblique way, have contributed as much to Hinduism as the Hindus. It seems that Hinduism only represents a special case of a more general phenomenon in the study of religion—that a tradition is as much a product of the forces it encounters as of the forces internal to it. Christianity appropriated the entire scripture of another tradition, namely Judaism, and Islam appropriated virtually the entire Judeo-Christian prophetic heritage, recognizing Muḥammad as the last representative of it. Thus the process is not unique to Hinduism: What is unique is the absence of any absolute claim to finality alongside such assimilation.

Two Types of Religion

By exploring the unique, or at least distinctive, features of a particular religion, one also gains insight into the phenomenon of religion itself—as one might of the whole from the part. One also gains insight as much by recognizing differences as by recognizing similarities. We examined the somewhat ambiguous relationship between the Vedas and Hinduism and suggested that it was the togetherness of the people that found its expression in the affiliation with the Vedas. By contrast, Christianity and Islam grew *around* a core—if Hinduism is a circumference seeking a center, then they are like circumferences radiating from a center. Thus the followers of Jesus Christ became Christians or of the Buddha, Buddhists. The founder comes first, as Muḥammad with the Qur'ān in the case of Islam. By contrast with the Vedas, which were revealed over centuries, the Qur'ān was revealed over twenty-two years. This suggests a distinction between two types of religions: one in which a common core emerges from the togetherness of a community (e.g., Hinduism, Judaism, primal religions) and another in which a community coalesces around a common core (e.g., Christianity, Buddhism, Islam). Hinduism tries to present itself as a (perfect ?) model of this first kind of religion, as distinguished from the religions of the second type, which try to present themselves as models of a perfect religion.

The type of universalism associated with each also differs. The first type of religion regards religion per se as something universal, the other type wants to make its own brand of religion universal. Language provides a helpful analogy here. The term universal language may either mean that language is a universal phenomenon or that one language, say English, is spoken by everyone all over the world. The first type of religions interprets universalism in the first sense and is potentially tolerant. The second type of religions interprets universalism in the second sense and tends to be potentially hegemonistic. Because of the potential presence of these two forms of universalism within it, Hinduism is led into the belief that, through the magic of tolerance, it can draw a charmed circle and claim that even if not everything can be drawn within it, nothing at the same time may remain outside of it, even if it means that it forever hovers on the dim circumference of the circle. Nothing is excluded, although it may temporarily remain unincluded. In its enthusiasm for universalism of one kind or another, or both, Hinduism seems to forget what it should know, that though even extremes can meet, sometimes even similarities can divide.

Hinduism in the Study of Religion

The Distinction Between Text and Symbol

The role of the Vedas or rather Vedic authority in the study of Hinduism is often alluded to in this chapter. A closer examination of this point helps to identify the nuances that the study of Hinduism can introduce in the study of religion. I almost imperceptibly tried to sneak past you two expressions as synonymous that are really not so: the Vedas and Vedic authority. One could accept the Vedas as a part of one's religious heritage and yet reject their authority as something to be accepted uncritically. In other words, acceptance of the Vedas need not imply the acceptance of their authority. In dealing with the religions of the West—Judaism, Christianity, and Islam—the distinction between accepting the text and accepting its authority is not normally drawn and becomes relevant perhaps only in modern times. The study of Hinduism indicates how the relationship between a tradition and its revealed texts can be calibrated in different ways. The Vedic period in itself covers a period of almost a thousand years, and obviously the texts produced during this period could become formally authoritative only after a closure of some kind had been applied. Well, such a closure was never *formally* applied by contrast with the sacred Scriptures of the religions of the West. An *Upaniṣad* purportedly appended to the *AtharvaVeda* as late as the sixteenth or seventeenth century, significantly bearing the title *Allopaniṣad,* represents an attempt to synthesize Hinduism and Islam. Thus Hinduism leaves open the possibility that somehow the idea of a revealed text can be harmonized with the notion of a progressive revelation, making the contradictory complementary.

This loose though definite association with a scripture can also be noted in an earlier period. The Hindus existed prior to the Vedas, just as the Christians existed prior to the New Testament. After all, the Christian canon was formulated some three centuries after the time of Jesus. The contrast in this case with Islam is clear—the religion here commences with the scripture, the first revelation of the Qur'ān. If Hinduism is to be traced back to the Indus Valley culture of the third millennium B.C.E. or to an even anterior date, then any legitimation of its beliefs and practices must be considered retrospective. Another aspect needs to be considered as well: that the emphasis on Vedic authority in Hinduism seems to have been not so much a spontaneous development within it as a response—a stiffening of attitude—in the face of Buddhist, Jaina, and materialist attacks on it. In Buddhist literature one finds the word Veda used for revealed texts of both Hindu *and* other ascetics as well. To that extent the assertion of its authoritative character coincided with that of any revelation, at least at the time. Finally, when Hindu texts of a general nature on Hindu philosophy were composed, they often cited chapter and verse to substantiate what would appear to be a rather startling claim: that materialist, Buddhist, and Jaina schools of thought were also based on the Vedas, testifying to Hinduism's voracious appetite for comprehensiveness, and its aspiration to constitute a single textual community, if possible, within which religious groups could reconcile their differences and achieve liberation as well.

These facts, which by themselves seem isolated and disparate, begin to fall into place once Hinduism is viewed as a religious system that is inclusive and encyclopedic. Various ways were devised to encompass as many beliefs and practices as possible within Hinduism, but the ultimate maneuver was the evolution of the concept of the Veda as symbolic of spiritual authority. Thus one finds saints and religious innovators freely prefacing or concluding their own statements with the claim: "thus say the Vedas." It is of course possible to get away with this sort of thing when one is dealing with a corpus that was never formally closed and grew over several centuries, in a culture in which the term Veda as the "fifth" Veda, or as Tamil Veda, could be applied to any corpus of literature that invited sanctity. That such textual elasticity can be combined with claims to textual authority suggests that the notion of what anthropologists call "working definitions" may have been applied in a religiously operational manner in relation to sacred texts. In a more minor way, the fact that the Vedas were transmitted orally for centuries must alter the literal understanding of the category of "scripture" in the study of religion and upgrade the assessment of other sacred oral traditions, as, for instance, those found in Africa.

The Distinction Between Theory and Practice

The idea of Vedic authority continues to be suggestive. When it is said that the Vedas are the authoritative scriptures of Hinduism, one tends to form the impression that they enunciate a set of firmly laid down doctrines. In practice, however, the situation turns out to be otherwise, because of the place assigned to reflection within the tradition, for "even in the doctrines based upon revelation, the ultimate appeal in them may not be to reason; but, at the same time, they do not signify a blind reliance on untested and unsupported authority. They may consequently be taken as *rationalistic in practice, though not in theory*."[37] In the study of Hindu philosophy, one runs into this phenomenon time and again. The school of Advaita Vedānta, for instance, is dogmatic in theory but "if Advaita is dogmatic, the dogma is there only to be transcended"[38] so that it again ceases to be so in practice, as *mediate* knowledge, such as that imparted by the Vedas, cannot be equated with *immediate* realization. Here the pragmatic pole of Hinduism comes to the fore, just as the encyclopedic pole assumed prominence in the previous section.

It is true that all religious traditions have a gap between theory and practice. It is also true that in all religious systems, the paradigmatic formulation does not always coincide with the pragmatic reality. All this is as true of Hinduism as of other religious traditions viewed as systems; what is remarkable about Hinduism is that the primacy of practice is part of the paradigm itself. Troy Wilson Organ observes:

> In India today it is not unusual to find a person who denies he is a Hindu but who acts in a manner which others associate with Hinduism. I recall an occasion in India in which a dinner companion who, after assuring me he had completely deserted Hinduism, carefully removed a fly from his glass of water, placed it on the floor, and then observed, "I think it will be all right now." I could not refrain from reminding my friend that his act revealed more about his religion than his words.[39]

Similarly, a fresh Hindu convert to Christianity was baffled when asked not to visit the temple of Kālī any longer because he had now converted to Christianity and wondered whether he had to give up his dharma now that he had become a Christian. In other words, he was wondering aloud whether he had to abandon Hinduism in practice just because he had given it up in theory, a position he found apparently incomprehensible.

The Distinction Between Authority and Power

This emphasis on praxis in Hinduism tends to divorce authority from power. For instance, according to the hierarchy of the caste system, religious authority lies with the brahmins, the priestly class who possess the charisma of office, so to say, in Weberian terms. But charismatic authority in Hinduism is tied more to the practice of virtue, with the result that two of the pivotal figures in modern Hinduism, Vivekānanda and Gandhi, did not belong to that caste—the former was śūdra and the latter vaiśya—and both wielded far greater power in the community than the priests themselves, who are accorded necessary but not necessarily high esteem. This is also true of earlier phases of Hinduism. Even those who had hereditary authority could only convert it into power through the example of a virtuous life.

How Could Anarchy Function?

But how exactly does the pragmatic centering of Hinduism allow it to function amid an apparently anarchical encyclopedism that even Hindus, once outside India, find as shocking as the Western observer? One such Indian gives vent to this frustration in such strong language that only his own ethnic background saves him from the charge of being congenitally hostile to Hinduism. He writes:

> The so-called Hinduism is a rolling conference of conceptual spaces, all of them facing all, and all of them requiring all. Each claims loyalty to the *śrutis*, each showing how its claims are decisively true, and charging the rival schools with perpetuating the confusion of tongue in the *dharmakṣetra* [the field of religion]. . . . A lay Hindu . . . is a living contradiction, unsynthetic and logically incomplete to any and all. "Synthetic unity" has never existed in Hinduism, neither in conceptual space nor in lived time. Hinduism is a moving form of life whose predicament is to be incomplete to its own logics; it is a history of contradictions in flesh, fortunately demanding that their resolution be constantly postponed.[40]

David M. Knipe puts a positive spin on this: ". . . the curious result of the endless experimentation of Hindu tradition is that true innovation is virtually impossible."[41] S. Radhakrishnan tried to impart an even more positive spin to this state of affairs when he said years ago: "What is built for ever is for ever building."[42] Small wonder, then, that Hinduism should be to India what comparative religion is to the world.

This is of course the great danger; that in wanting to be all things to all human beings, Hinduism might be found wanting by all, precisely because it wants to be all things to all. Hinduism is able to convert the contradiction into a paradox through its pragmatism—by claiming that for everyone the *next* step is clear, even if the *distant* horizon presents a spectacle of spiraling galactic confusion. The techniques of conflict resolution are thus commonplace in Hinduism. Should one live in the world or renounce it? Well, it allows for both living in and renouncing the world. One may first live in the world and then renounce it, in accordance with the doctrine of the four stages of life. Like "staging," that is, reducing conflicting courses of action to harmonious stages, "simultanization" is also a typical Hindu strategy. Thus one can simultaneously live in the world *physically*, but renounce the world *mentally* in accordance with the precepts of the *Bhagavadgītā*. Should one worship Viṣṇu or Śiva? One may worship either Viṣṇu or Śiva or first one and then the other, or both simultaneously as in the icon of Harihara—half of which is Viṣṇu and half Śiva.

Interiorization is another favorite Hindu technique. Thus, if a ritual cannot be performed externally, such as a huge sacrifice, it may be performed mentally with equal efficacy. Other techniques include substitution (without suppression), for example, replacing animals with vegetables in sacrifice; hyphenation (without elimination), for example, combining two systems of philosophy into one as in Nyāya-Vaiśeṣika; equivalence (without ambivalence), for example, between the Vedas and other sacred texts; ambiguousness (without disingenuousness), for example, is the ultimate reality (*Brahman*) with or without attributes (*saguṇa* or *nirguṇa*); correspondence (without preponderance) as between the microcosm and the macrocosm, and so on. The enumeration of these techniques would require a book and this is a chapter.

The point, however, concerns not the actual strategies so much as the approach that gives rise to these strategies and underlies them: that each individual can find his or her own golden thread in the tangled skein of Hinduism's mass of beliefs and practices; and that thread, though it might appear as fine as yarn, is as strong as steel in guiding one to one's spiritual destiny. For instance, Hinduism helped Joseph Campbell by encouraging him to "follow his bliss." He says:

> Now I came to this idea of bliss because in Sanskrit, which is the great spiritual language in the world, there are three terms that represent the brink, the jumping-off place to the ocean of transcendence: *Sat, Chit, Ananda*. The word "*Sat*" means being. "*Chit*" means consciousness. "*Ananda*" means bliss or rapture. I thought, "I don't know whether my consciousness is proper consciousness or not; I don't know whether what I know of my being is my proper being or not; but I do know where my rapture is. So let me hang on to rapture, and that will bring me both my consciousness and my being. I think it worked." [43]

Recommended Reading

A. L. Basham. *The Wonder That Was India*. New York: Grove Press, 1954. The best general introduction to Hinduism located within the larger matrix of Indian culture and civilization.

Abbe Dubois. *Hindu Manners, Customs and Ceremonies*. Translated by Henry K. Beauchamp. Oxford: Oxford University Press, 1906. An eyewitness account of Hinduism in south India as seen by a French Jesuit in the eighteenth century—a pivotal period in relation to modern Hinduism.

Ainslie T. Embree, ed. *Alberuni's India*. New York: W. W. Norton & Co., 1971. An abridged version of E. C. Sachau's translation of Alberuni's book on India and Hinduism. Presents Hinduism as seen by an eleventh-century Muslim savant—a century that constitutes a turning point in the history of Hinduism.

Thomas J. Hopkins. *The Hindu Religious Tradition*. Encino, CA: Dickenson Publishing Company, 1971. A well-knit and integrated account of the historical evolution of the tradition.

Klaus K. Klostermaier. *A Survey of Hinduism*. Albany: State University of New York Press, 1989. An excellent comprehensive overview of the tradition, which takes contemporary developments into full account.

David M. Knipe. *Hinduism: Experiments in the Sacred*. San Francisco: HarperSanFrancisco, 1991. A clear, concise, and compact introduction to the tradition, which does not neglect the contemporary dimension.

T. M. P. Mahadevan. *Outlines of Hinduism*. Bombay: Chetana, 1971. An excellent foil to Hopkins's book in which the tradition is treated diachronically; Mahadevan presents it synchronically.

S. Radhakrishnan. *The Hindu View of Life*. New York: Macmillan, 1927. The material for this book was originally delivered in a series of lectures at Manchester College in 1926. Surprisingly, it remains to this day perhaps the most felicitous introduction to Hinduism for a Western audience.

Louis Renou. *The Nature of Hinduism*. Translated by Patrick Evans. New York: Walker and Company, 1951. A comprehensive and eminently readable account of the tradition as a whole.

———. *The Religions of India*. University of London: Athlone Press, 1953. The first 110 pages constitute a succinct introduction to Hinduism, which is erudite without being recondite.

———, ed. *Hinduism*. New York: George Braziller, 1962. A rich sampling of the textual sources, with a lucid introduction to the tradition as a whole and brief introductory notes on the excerpted material.

Notes

1. See J. L. Brockington, *The Sacred Thread: Hinduism in Its Continuity and Diversity* (Edinburgh: Edinburgh University Press, 1981), 1–7.
2. Brockington, *The Sacred Thread,* 2.
3. Brockington, *The Sacred Thread,* 7.
4. M. Hiriyanna, *Essentials of Indian Philosophy* (London: Allen & Unwin, 1949), 45.
5. Kingsley Davis, *The Population of India and Pakistan* (New York: Russell & Russell, 1951), 178.
6. P. J. Bhattacharjee and G. N. Shastri, *Population in India* (New Delhi: Vikas Publishing, 1974), 64.
7. *Census of India 1981,* Series 1, India, Paper 3 of 1984 (New Delhi: Office of the Registrar General, 1984), x.
8. See *Economic and Political Weekly,* February 13, 1993, 289.
9. Robert Ernest Hume, trans., *The Thirteen Principal Upanishads* (London: Oxford University Press, 1968), 248.
10. Thomas J. Hopkins, *The Hindu Religious Tradition* (Belmont, CA: Dickenson Publishing Company, 1971), 139.
11. See Claude Alan Stark, *God of All* (Cape Cod, MA: Claude Stark, 1974).
12. Walter G. Neevel, Jr., "The Transformation of Śrī Rāmakrishna," in *Hinduism: New Essays in the History of Religions,* ed. Bardwell L. Smith (Leiden: E. J. Brill, 1976), 76.
13. Huston Smith, *The World's Religions* (San Francisco: HarperSanFrancisco, 1991), 73.
14. Robert Payne, *The Life and Death of Mahatma Gandhi* (New York: E. P. Dutton & Co., 1969), 578.
15. Swami Nirvedananda, *Hinduism at a Glance* (Calcutta: Ramakrishna Mission, 1969), 225.
16. Swami Nirvedananda, *Hinduism at a Glance,* 225.
17. Swami Nirvedananda, *Hinduism at a Glance,* 89 n. 1.
18. A. L. Basham, "Hinduism," in *The Concise Encyclopedia of Living Faiths,* ed. R. C. Zaehner (Boston: Beacon Press, 1959), 259.
19. Reservations have been expressed as to whether the disputed structure at Ayodhyā can be properly referred to as a mosque; see *News India,* January 22, 1993, 4.
20. S. Radhakrishnan, *The Hindu View of Life* (New York: Macmillan, 1927), 84.
21. See Arvind Sharma, "Fearlessness (Abhaya) as a Fundamental Category in Gandhian Thought and Practice," *South Asia* 8, no. 1 (June 1987): 39.
22. T. M. P. Mahadevan, *Outlines of Hinduism* (Bombay: Chetana, 1971), 227.
23. Wm. Theodore de Bary, ed., *Sources of Indian Tradition* (New York and London: Columbia University Press, 1958), vol. 2, p. 335.
24. *Hinduism Today* 14, no. 12 (December 1992): 26.

25. However, see David M. Knipe, "Hinduism: Experiments in the Sacred," in *Religious Traditions of the World*, ed. H. Byron Earhart (San Francisco: HarperSanFrancisco, 1993), 829.
26. Mahadevan, *Outlines of Hinduism*, 39. The source of the text cited is *Taittirīya Brāhmaṇa Kāṭhaka*, I, xi, 4.
27. Louis Renou, ed., *Hinduism* (New York: George Braziller, 1962), 18–19.
28. See Annemarie Schimmel, "Islamic Religious Year," in *The Encyclopedia of Religion*, ed. Mircea Eliade (New York: Macmillan, 1987), vol. 7, p. 456.
29. Louis Renou, *The Destiny of the Veda in India*, ed. and trans. Dev Raj Chanana (Delhi: Motilal Banarsidass, 1965), 61.
30. Mahadevan, *Outlines of Hinduism*, 27.
31. E. C. Sachau, ed. and trans., *Alberuni's India* (London: Truebner, 1888), vol. 1, p. 22.
32. K. A. Nilakanta Sastri, *A History of South India from Prehistoric Times to the Fall of the Vijayanagar* (Oxford University Press, 1955), 297.
33. The following provisions of the Indian Constitution (1950) are relevant in this context:

    Article 25(1)

    Subject to public order, morality and health and to other provisions of this Part, all persons are equally entitled to freedom of conscience and the right freely to profess, practice and propagate religion.

    Article 25(2)

    Nothing in this Article shall effect the operation of any existing law or prevent the State from making any law—

    a. regulating or restricting any economic, financial, political and other secular activity which may be associated with religious practice;

    b. providing for social welfare and reform or the throwing open of Hindu religious institutions of a public character to all classes and sections of India.
34. Donald Eugene Smith, *India as a Secular State* (Princeton: Princeton University Press, 1963), 496–497.
35. Edward A. Gargan, "Peril to the Indian State: A Defiant Hindu Fervor," *The New York Times*, December 8, 1992, A16.
36. Hume, *The Thirteen Principal Upanishads*, 119–120.
37. Hiriyanna, *Essentials of Indian Philosophy*, 129.
38. Hiriyanna, *Essentials of Indian Philosophy*, 173.
39. Troy Wilson Organ, *Hinduism: Its Historical Development* (Woodbury, NY: Barron's Educational Series, 1974), 2.
40. Bibhuti S. Yadav, as cited in Klaus Klostermaier, *A Survey of Hinduism* (Albany: State University of New York Press, 1989), 4.
41. Knipe, "Hinduism," 832.
42. Radhakrishnan, *The Hindu View of Life*, 17.
43. Joseph Campbell, *The Power of Myth* (with Bill Moyers), ed. Betty Sue Flowers (New York: Doubleday, 1988), 120.

CHAPTER 2

Buddhism

Masao Abe

What Is Buddhism?

In the American presidential election held in November 1988, the Republican candidate, George Bush, defeated the Democratic candidate, Michael Dukakis. Although it was Michael Dukakis who was ultimately nominated as the Democratic candidate, at one stage in the nomination process the governor of New York, Mario Cuomo, was deemed a serious contender. Throughout this phase of the nomination campaign, however, Mario Cuomo kept denying that he would run. Yet the more strenuously he denied his intention, the more of an issue his likely candidacy became, leading a political analyst to comment: "*Cuomo is very Zen. He runs by not running!*" Who would have thought half a century ago that a Buddhist term from Japan would enter the political discourse of the United States of America?

The Diversity of Buddhism[1]

And yet, if one examines the word *Zen* itself closely, one should not be surprised. The English language adopted the word, of course, from Japanese. The Japanese form itself, however, is an adaptation from the Chinese (*ch'an*). The Chinese form, in turn, is an adaptation of the Sanskrit (*dhyāna*). And the Sanskrit is a reappropriation from the Pali form (*jhāna*), which goes back to the Vedic Sanskrit form (dhyāna) again, the same as in classical Sanskrit. The word means meditation or meditative trance.

What is in a name? There is quite a lot in this one. In its journey through time this word, *Zen*, has spanned more than three thousand years; in its journey through space it has traveled from the foothills of the Himalayas to the highrises of Manhattan after passing through the deserts of central Asia, the ricefields of China, and the monasteries of Japan. The net of Buddhism has been flung far and wide in time and space—like the net of Indra (the king of the gods), to use one of its famous metaphors—with a shining gem studded at each point of the intersection of its lines. Each intersection represents a facet of the teaching in a different part of the world. Let us now, for a moment, turn our gaze from the net to the network of which Buddhism consists. A net *is* a network: Each part of the net is related to all and all to each. Each gem of the net is reflected in every other gem and these gems in turn are again reflected in one another ad infinitum. This illustrates a crucial Buddhist doctrine: the interpenetration of a concatenation of causes and conditions apart from which there is nothing (read *no-thing*).

Now let us turn our gaze from the network to the ocean over which a net is typically cast. This vast body of water which the ocean represents washes many shores and contains numerous currents within it, but every bit of it, every sip of it, contains the same saline flavor. The Buddha, the historical founder of Buddhism as we know it, declared: "As the great ocean has but one flavor, the taste of salt, so does the Doctrine and the Discipline of the Buddha have but one flavor—the flavor of emancipation" (*Aṅguttara-Nikāya*, VIII.II.ix). Although an ocean may have one flavor, it touches many diverse land masses. Or to use a more modern example, Coca-Cola may have one flavor, but it comes in many bottles with labels in different languages.

What impresses the Buddhist no less than the non-Buddhist is the striking diversity represented by Buddhism in comparison to the other major missionary religions of the world such as Christianity and Islam. At the heart of Christianity is a person—Jesus Christ. At the heart of Islam is a text—the Qur'ān; at the heart of Buddhism is a story—that of Buddha's realization. The Christians carried the figure of Jesus Christ to the far corners of the globe and the Muslims did the same with the message of God as delivered to the prophet Muḥammad. But for almost five hundred years before the Christians got into the act and two thousand years before the Muslims followed suit, the Buddhists were already out there offering the gift of *dharma*—the teachings of Buddhism—to whoever was willing to accept it, in their own language, and in their own culture. Unlike the Christians, the Buddhists did not have a definitive physical event such as the Crucifixion and the Resurrection of Jesus Christ to talk about. Rather, they talked of an elusive if enchanting experience called *Nirvāṇa*. Unlike the Muslims, the Buddhists did not have a fixed canon in one language. The Buddha, right from the beginning, allowed his followers to record his teachings in their own languages. Thus Buddhism, in comparison with Christianity and Islam, allowed much greater scope for expansion and even proliferation in the realm of both doctrine and scripture from its very inception. This greater latitude, combined with a longer historical record in relation to Christianity and Islam, naturally enabled Buddhism to assume forms more diverse than those assumed by these two religions.

Skillful Means

The diversity displayed by Buddhism is not an accident. It represents the operation of a conscious factor in the history of Buddhism. This factor is represented by the Buddhist doctrine of *upāya-kauśalya*, often translated as "skill in means" or "skillful means" and sometimes referred to only as *upāya*. According to this doctrine, the teachings of Buddhism should be preached in consonance with the spiritual, moral, and intellectual level of the audience; Buddhism must speak to its condition. In the beginning, this doctrine was primarily applied to individuals, as in the moving story about a young girl named Kisā Gotamī. ("Kisā," which means "the lean one," may even have been a nickname suggested by her thinness.) Kisā got married and in due course had a son; in the patriarchal but matrifocal society of the times her status within the family immediately rose. Unfortunately, her son died when he was just old enough to run about, leaving her distraught with grief. Kisā Gotamī placed the dead child on her shoulder and went from house to house asking for a medicine to revive him. "And people said, 'she has gone mad.'" One sympathetic person sent her to the Buddha as the only person who might be able to help her. Buddha promised to revive her son through a ritual, the performance of which required a handful of mustard seeds—but the seeds had to come from a house where no one had ever died. Kisā Gotamī ran to the village but soon discovered that there was no house to be found in which no one had ever died. In this way the Buddha made her realize that mortality was an inevitable feature of the human condition, that even a Lazarus, once raised from the dead, had to die again. She cremated the dead child, came back to the Buddha, and asked to be ordained. The verses she uttered upon attaining enlightenment are part of the Buddhist canon.

Buddhism applied this principle of skillful means not just to individuals but to whole cultures. To the Hindu elite it presented its teaching in Sanskrit, to the Chinese in Chinese. In Tibet, where the pre-Buddhist religion of Bön contained magical features, it presented itself in a magical guise. In South Asia it accommodated itself to the popular worship of spirits. One is therefore entitled to ask, How does one draw the line between adaptability and opportunism? Because one's actions are to be judged by one's intentions, one doesn't; for underlying all these bewildering adaptations to local conditions was a single aspiration: to share with everyone the gift of dharma, the teachings of the Buddha—a gift not to be excelled.

Defining Buddhism

Given the diversity of Buddhism, which is consciously espoused, one is naturally led to ask, What holds this vast system of diverse beliefs and practices together? Let us stretch-test some of the threads that are said to hold the fabric of Buddhism together.

THE TRIPLE REFUGE

The Buddhist profession of faith is known as the Triple Refuge (*triśaraṇa*), which came later to be known as the Three Jewels (*triratna*) and even as the "Three Treasures." It constitutes the basic profession of faith in Buddhism, and every Buddhist, monastic and lay, man and woman, repeats it to this day. It runs as follows: "I go for refuge to the Buddha; I go for refuge to the Doctrine [*Dharma*]; I go for refuge to the Community [*Saṅgha*]." One formally becomes a Buddhist by reciting the Triple Refuge three times.

It would be tempting to regard this as the unifying core of Buddhism and to define Buddhism as the religion of the followers of the Buddha. In Tibet, however, a fourth profession—going for refuge to the Lama (teacher)—was added. Even the first profession remains somewhat ambiguous in view of the ineffability of the postmortem state of the Buddha. In later Buddhism, which allowed for a plurality of Buddhas, the profession seems to lose the pristine clarity of seeking refuge in the one historical Gautama Buddha. However, strictly speaking, Buddhism is older than the triple profession, just as Islam is older than the *shahādah* (which is really a composite of two halves that occur separately in the Qur'ān and proclaim: "There is no god but God and Muḥammad is His messenger") and Christianity is older than the Apostles' Creed ("I believe in God the Father Almighty, Maker of heaven and earth: And in Jesus Christ, his only Son, our Lord: . . ."). Originally a monk was admitted to the Buddhist Community simply by being addressed by the Buddha thus: "Come, O Monk! . . ."

THE FIGURE OF THE BUDDHA

It would be equally tempting to argue that as there was no Buddhism before the Buddha, and as all Buddhism ultimately appeals to the authority of the Buddha, here we have the thread that is spun into the warp and woof of Buddhism. Strictly speaking, though, Buddha is one in a series, as much a type as a person. There have been Buddhas before him and there will be Buddhas after him. In fact we already know the personal name of the next Buddha: Maitreya. Even if this is disregarded as a later development in imitation of Central Asian messianism or perhaps as an influence of Jainism (a rival religion that allowed for a series of twenty-four holy figures called *tīrthaṅkaras* comparable to the Buddha), we have to contend with the fact that the word Buddha is not a name but a title, and that the title means "the enlightened one." In other words, when we speak of Gautama Buddha we must realize that the Buddha minus enlightenment is just an ordinary person, who could not have founded Buddhism; the appeal to the authority of the Buddha is an appeal to the enlightenment of the Buddha. Even the insights of Buddhism in its earliest forms were considered to exist independently of the Buddha. The texts proclaim this boldly, even proudly, as when it is declared in the part of the canon of early Buddhism known as *Aṅguttara-Nikāya,* a text from which was also cited earlier: "whether there be the appearance or non-appearance of a Buddha, this causal law of nature, this orderly fixing of things prevails, namely that all phenomena are devoid of self (or substantiality)" (III.14.134).

THE FOUR GREAT TRUTHS

Is there some other unifying strand within Buddhism? It could be maintained that it is provided by the Four Great Truths of Buddhism enunciated by the Buddha in the very first sermon delivered at Sārnāth near Banaras. The tradition itself recognizes that something sensational happened then; it celebrates the momentousness of the event by referring to the sermon as the Turning of the Wheel of Law, as if something mighty had now been set in motion. After his enlightenment, the Buddha could have decided not to preach. In the nomenclature of Buddhism he could have decided to remain a private Buddha (*Pratyeka-Buddha*), and the world would have been deprived of the religious tradition now called Buddhism. Hence the significance of his decision to preach, and hence too the significance of the first sermon. The first sermon is so quintessentially Buddhist that it must be summarized here: It enunciates the Four Noble Truths that are accepted by all Buddhists.

The first noble truth preached by the Buddha is that of the existence of suffering, a fact that becomes painfully obvious at the time of birth and death, in sickness and old age, through association with the unpleasant and dissociation from the pleasant, that is, when we feel frustrated and attacked. The second noble truth identifies the cause of suffering as desire, whether for pleasures, for life, or even for death. The third noble truth directs attention to the fact that if suffering has a cause then it can be removed by removing the cause; the fourth great truth supplies a detailed blueprint of the life-style to follow to remove the cause. This eight-point program is technically known as the Eightfold Path consisting of: right view; right aspiration; right speech; right action; right livelihood; right effort; right mindfulness; and right meditation. The tradition explains what is meant by *right* in each case. For instance, right speech means avoiding harsh, mendacious, frivolous, or malicious talk. The Eightfold Path leads to Nirvāṇa, the summum bonum of Buddhism, which involves the cessation of all suffering.

And yet to identify the Four Noble Truths with Buddhism would amount to destroying Buddhism in the name of Buddhism, for even these Truths were merely meant to serve as *provisional* teaching, to be regarded as a raft that is discarded once one has reached the shore.

DHARMA AND DHARMAS

We are again, in typically Buddhist fashion, brought back to experience. To the extent that we can identify this experience, we can pinpoint Buddhism; we can indicate the primal point out of which the ever-expanding universe of Buddhism has emerged. It seems to us that this core, as is already implied in the first sermon, lies in the doctrine of *Anattā* or *Śūnyatā* or *Anātmavāda*, or in the doctrine of the absence of Self. It is the realization of "No-Self" that constitutes enlightenment or realization. Walpola Sri Rahula, a well-known exponent and an adherent of the Theravāda tradition, remarks: "Buddhism stands unique in the history of human thought in denying the existence of such a Soul, Self, or *Ātman*. According to the teaching of the Buddha, the idea of self is an imaginary, false belief which has no corresponding reality, and it produces harmful thoughts of 'me' and 'mine,' selfish desire, craving, attachment, hatred, ill-will, conceit, pride, egoism, and other defilements, impurities and problems."[2] Edward Conze elaborates: "The specific contribution of Buddhism to religious thought lies in its insistence on the doctrine of *'not-self'* (*an-attā in Pali, an-ātman in Sanskrit*). The belief in a 'self' is considered by all Buddhists as an indispensable condition to the emergence of suffering. We conjure up such ideas as 'I' and 'mine,' and many most undesirable states result."[3]

Conze illustrates his point with the help of a very common experience—that of a toothache. "If there is a tooth, and there is decay in that tooth, this is a process in the tooth, and in the nerve attached to it. If now my 'I' reaches out to the tooth, convinces itself that this is 'my' tooth—and it sometimes does not seem to need very much convincing—and believes that what happens to the tooth is bound to affect *me*, a certain disturbance of thought is likely to result. The Buddhist sees it like this: Here is the idea of 'I,' a mere figment of the imagination, with nothing real to correspond to it."[4]

This becomes clear when one examines the words Buddhists use to describe what we in English have taken to calling Buddhism. The Buddhists, from right after Buddha's death, grouped his teaching under the headings of *Vinaya* (Discipline) and Dharma (Doctrine). Hence they were alternatively called the *Buddha-Śāsana* or the Instructions of the Buddha and the *Buddha-Vacana* or the Words of the Buddha. But if asked to refer to this totality, the Buddhists simply use the word dharma (Pali: *dhamma*), which has at least four different connotations. We must clearly distinguish among these if we are to define Buddhism properly, if briefly and somewhat cryptically, as dharma. Dharma can mean, among other things, the Absolute truth; right conduct; and doctrine. These three senses of the word Buddhism more or less shares with other religions of Indian origin. Yet a wholly unique fourth sense is imparted when Buddhism uses the word to refer to the ultimate constituents of experience, the way atomic and subatomic particles have come to be regarded as the ultimate constituents of matter in modern physics. "A *'dharma'* is an impersonal event, which belongs to no person or individual, but just goes along on its own objective way, and it was regarded as a most praiseworthy achievement on the part of a Buddhist monk if he succeeded in accounting to himself for the contents of mind with the help of these impersonal dharmas, of which tradition provided him with definite lists, without ever bringing in the nebulous and pernicious word 'I.' No other religion has included anything like this in the mental training of its adherents, and the originality of Buddhism is to be found largely in what it has to say about these elusive dharmas."[5] Dharmas may be elusive, but they are ultimate, even if ultimately elusive. "There is no term in Buddhist terminology wider than *dhamma*. It includes not only the conditioned things and states, but also the non-conditioned, the Absolute, Nirvāṇa. There is nothing in the universe or outside, good or bad, conditioned or non-conditioned, relative or absolute, which is not included in this term."[6] By combining the first and the fourth senses of the word dharma, we may describe Buddhism as a religious system that defines dharma in terms of dharmas.

What Do We Learn about Religion from the Study of Buddhism?

Buddhism as Orthodoxy

Buddhism stands in such stark contrast to the concepts associated with the word *religion* in the West that what we *un*learn about religion in the study of Buddhism becomes far more significant than what we learn about it in the study of religion. One brought up in the West, for example, takes it for granted that religion involves the concepts of God, prophets, and revelation. The great religions of the West—Judaism, Christianity, and Islam—all believe in one God even though they may have different views regarding this "one God"; in prophets, even if they debate who may and may not be accepted as one; and in revelation, even though they may not agree which is the "true" one. Though they might differ as to the contents of these concepts, they do not differ as to what the structure of religion is supposed to be in terms of these concepts. If we use the word *orthodoxy* to signify belief in such a construct on the part of the religions of the West, then, in a word, Buddhism "deconstructs." Buddhism does not believe in God, but it does believe in gods. These gods, however, are beings who have achieved a special status in the cosmic bureaucracy and there is nothing special about them, except that they performed exceptionally virtuous acts in their past lives, thereby accumulating exceptionally good karma.

With God out of the picture, ideas of prophecy and revelation also have to be abandoned, or at least radically altered, if they are to be applied to

Buddhism. Buddha is a teacher rather than a prophet, and what he says constitutes teaching rather than revelation. Thus the words of the Buddha may be compared to the Torah, since the word denotes "Teaching," but the parallel must cease here as these teachings in Buddhism are those of a human being who speaks not for God but of his own experience. Curiously enough, Buddhism, though philosophically opposed to *mono*theism, is not practically opposed to theism, inasmuch as theistic beliefs may be conducive to leading a good moral life. Buddhism even concedes that some teachers may indeed speak of gods (and even of revelation) so long as only moral excellence is claimed for them, and not the attributes of creatorship, omniscience, and omnipotence. In other words, Buddhism rejects the metaphysical attributes of God while accepting the moral attributes. As for revelation, statements thus made may be considered worthwhile unless dogmatically asserted to be immune from critical examination.

Buddhism thus connects the idea of "right belief" or orthodoxy not merely with its truth but also with its usefulness or value. It might be insisted that it has its own form of "right belief," which constitutes the first step of the noble Eightfold Path. But such belief is only provisional, as we saw earlier, to be subsequently abandoned like a raft once the river has been crossed, thereby celebrating its own dispensability. Buddhism offers teachings (or instruction); it does not proclaim dogmas.

Buddhism as Orthopraxy

It could be claimed that though Buddhism dispenses with orthodoxy in the acknowledged sense of the word, it replaces orthodoxy with orthopraxy. It replaces the right word with the right deed, so that in the beginning was the deed, not the word.

There is an element of truth in this assessment, since conduct counts for more than belief in Buddhism, which is in contrast to both Western religion and philosophy. Typically, adherence to a religion like Judaism or Christianity takes the form, primarily, of acceptance of its dogma; this is less true of Judaism where religious identity takes a more communal rather than dogmatic form. But compared to Judaism, conduct in Buddhism possesses a more individualistic dimension, even within the context of the Buddhist community. In Western religions, this gap between doctrine and practice is at least deplored; in the case of Western philosophy it is simply ignored. Such an attitude just wouldn't do in Buddhism.

It is true, then, that the scales are tipped in favor of orthopraxy as compared to orthodoxy in Buddhism. But this becomes increasingly less true in a formal sense as the history of Buddhism unfolds. For instance, the monastic ideal dominated the Theravāda form of Buddhism to the point that, around the beginning of the Common Era, the belief that being a monk was a sine qua non for realization gained widespread acceptance; if perchance a householder attained Nirvāṇa, he or she was to immediately enter the monastic order or else would die. In the Mahāyāna form of Buddhism, however, the monk, as representing orthopraxy, ceased to possess any inherent advantage over the householder, a position illustrated by the text called *Vimalakīrtinirdeśa*. In this text, the householder Vimalakīrti humbles well-known monks in philosophical encounters to such a degree that they were reluctant to go to his bedside to inquire about his well-being when he was ill, lest they be humiliated again. Now available only in Chinese and Tibetan, the text was extremely popular in China, and scenes from it are often depicted in Buddhist art and architecture. With the development of antinomian Buddhism in some forms of Tantra, the earlier concept of orthopraxy itself, in the sense of adherence to the Eightfold Path, came to be questioned. Finally, in the form of Buddhism known as Zen one encounters cases of scandalous rather than pious behavior!

Defining Religion as a Soteriological System: Two Types of Religions

What we learn about religion from the study of Buddhism boils down to this: A religion that is essentially a system of salvation from individuated existence can wreak havoc with the more usual categories in the study of religion. It is, of course, true that all religious systems possess a soteriological component, along with dimensions of myth, ritual, and so on. But in most of these systems salvation is regarded as a postmortem state, so that all the other dimensions of the religion serve as pillars that uphold the system as a whole. Buddhism, however, emphasizes salvation here and now; it calls itself a "Come and See for Yourself" religion, so that all its other dimensions are bent toward this overarching purpose. It is in the light of this unique aspect of Buddhism that much of what has been said in this and the previous section must be understood.

Once the primacy of premortem salvation in Buddhism as a soteriological system (rather than as a religious system of which soteriology is a part) is recognized, elements that originally seemed glib or bizarre appear in a new perspective. For instance, the famous Buddhist emperor of India, Aśoka (273–236 B.C.E.), declared in one of his edicts: "Whatever is Buddha-said is well-said." When Buddhism reached China this saying had been dialectically metamorphosed into: "Whatever is well-said is Buddha-said." In a word, Buddhism is a living repudiation of the genetic fallacy that the (soteriological) value of a statement derives from its source. Rather, the statement derives its value irrespective of source, from the help it renders in attaining enlightenment. Similarly, the various transformations of Buddhism can be seen in the same light. It will be recalled that in Buddhism desire is identified as the cause of suffering. For desire to exist, the following must exist: someone who desires; something that is desired; and a relationship between the two—that of attachment. Buddhism, by denying the reality of a permanent substratum anywhere, tries to undermine this framework by emphasizing that: *Really* there is no one who desires. Then it presses the point further by pointing out that: *Really* nothing exists on its own *to* be worthy of being an object of desire. Tantra focuses on the magical or illusory nature of the relationship between the subject and the object so that the relationship dissolves in mist, whereas Zen refuses to fall into the trap of making any formulation whatsoever and nips the whole illusionary process in the bud.

Once Buddhism is viewed as a soteriological system, other elements associated with it as a religion become clear. "A soteriological doctrine like Buddhism becomes a 'philosophy' when its intellectual content is explained to outsiders," and it becomes a "religion" if it is adopted by a state or a society, where it must play other roles, even though these must ultimately subserve the soteriological system.

A residual sense of puzzlement might still persist. How can a system that ultimately denies the existence of either a person or a thing continue to exist? Is the formulation of such a system itself not a recipe for self-destruction? It is, but as an end, not as a means.

A simple example may clarify the matter. Suppose that the teacher of an evening class at a university enters the classroom and finds a note addressed to her marked "confidential," which informs her that "No class should be held today." Let us now first examine the form and then the content of this message. The teacher receives this message on a slip of paper. Is the message identical with the slip of paper? It is not, as the message could have been conveyed orally. However, let us ask again: Is there any other way in which the teacher can, in *her* situation at that moment, have access to the message, other than through a piece of paper? The answer is no, because the office is closed and the building is empty. The slip of paper is not identical with the message and yet is necessary—in fact the only available means for its delivery. In this sense Buddhism as a religious system constitutes the form; it may not be the only form, but it is the indispensable form to be dispensed with ultimately.

Now we turn to the content of the message. Because of the message, the teacher dismisses the class. Now was the content of the message consistent with this development? Yes. The class is dismissed. We noted earlier, however, that the form was not identical with the content but, rather, conveyed it. The slip of paper that bore the inscription "No class should be held today" is still lying on the desk, where the teacher left it after leaving the room with her students, for the sake of the teacher who is going to take the class in the next hour and must dismiss his class too by reading the same note.

Buddhism is that religious system which keeps relaying its self-eliminating soteriology. Alternatively, it is that soteriological system which keeps echoing its message, with each echo giving rise to a new one as it goes out of existence itself through the corridors of time in the resonating chambers of the Buddha, the Dharma, and the Saṅgha.

To describe Buddhism as a soteriological system is not to deny it as a historical system but to recognize the fact that both these statements are really alternative statements of the same fact. A Buddhist accepts the fact of the absence of the Self and aims at the extinction of the Self *while* functioning as a dynamic organism. What is true of the Buddhist is also true of Buddhism. It will become apparent from the subsequent sections that:

> Throughout its history, Buddhism has the unity of an *organism*, in that each new development takes place in continuity from the previous one. Nothing could look more different from a tadpole than a frog, and yet they are stages of the same animal, and evolve continuously from each other. The Buddhist capacity for metamorphosis must astound those who only see the end-products separated by long intervals of time, as different as chrysalis and butterfly. In fact they are connected by many gradations, which lead from one to the other, and which only close study can detect. There is in Buddhism really no innovation, but what seems so is in fact a subtle adaptation of pre-existing ideas. Great attention has always been paid to continuous doctrinal development, and to the proper transmission of the teachings.[7]

But this unity is the unity not of a rock but of a river. In other words, it is a continuity rather than a unity. It is not Buddhism that evolves; the evolution is Buddhism. It is not the river that flows, the flow is the river; and there is no riverbed—the flow is therefore "empty." This is how the continuity of Buddhism as a system is coterminous with its teleology as a system—that of Emptiness—for "all Buddhists have had one and the same *aim*, which is the 'extinction of self,' the dying out of separate individuality, and their teachings and practices have generally tended to foster such easily recognisable spiritual *virtues* as serenity, detachment, consideration and tenderness for others. In the scriptures, the dharma has been compared to a *taste*. The word of the Buddha is there defined as that which has the taste of peace, the taste of emancipation, the taste of Nirvāṇa. It is, of course, a peculiarity of tastes that they are not easily described and must elude those who refuse actually to taste them for themselves."[8]

Buddhism in the World Today

The Geography and Demography of Buddhism

Buddhists constitute approximately 6 percent of the population of the globe according to the data available for 1988. South Asia and East Asia represent areas of maximum concentration, although Buddhists are also represented in Latin America, Europe, North America, and the former USSR in smaller numbers. They are minimally represented in Africa and Oceania.

The situation was quite different at the beginning of this century. In 1900, forms of Mahāyāna Buddhism could credibly be asserted as major religions of China, Tibet, Korea, Mongolia, and to some extent Japan, and most of Southeast Asia could be said to follow some form of Theravāda Buddhism, as it does to this day. Thus virtually the whole of Asia, with the major exception of India and Indonesia, could have been characterized as Buddhist, and Buddhists would well have accounted for more than 30 percent of the world's population.

The political upheavals of this century have not been favorable for Buddhism. The loss of China and Tibet to communism on the one hand and of Mongolia on the other reduced the number of its adherents sharply. In Japan it continues to be a vital force, notwithstanding the revival of Shinto, but in South Korea it has lost ground to Christianity, which is now the major religion in terms of adherents; in North Korea it has yielded to communism.

On the other hand, Buddhism has made a much more powerful impact on the West through Zen and Tibetan Buddhism than might have been expected. Some see in the movement of Tibetan Buddhism to the West the fulfillment of a prophecy made by Padmasambhava (eighth century), who is credited with having first introduced it into Tibet on a firm basis.

Buddhism and Communism

The relative ease with which communism replaced Buddhism in China has induced considerable introspection among students of Buddhism and comparative religion. As the interaction between the two continues, somewhat violently in Tibet, more unobtrusively in Mongolia, and intermittently in Śrī Laṅkā, two questions arise: How is Buddhism as a whole to be related to communism? and How are the two distinct forms of Buddhism—Theravāda and Mahāyāna—to be related to communism?

Buddhism and communism offer points of both convergence and contrast, though in general the contrastive elements would probably appear more significant. The convergence occurs because both Buddhism and communism are atheistic and seem to have a similar, though not identical, view of the nature of the relationship between matter and mind. Communism is alternatively known as scientific materialism because it regards mental consciousness as an epiphenomenon of matter. Buddhism, especially early Buddhism, emphasizes the mutual dependence of mind and matter. In fact, the Buddha is believed to have said that if one had to choose between identifying human personality with mind or matter, then matter might be a better choice. The material body is a relatively stable entity while mental consciousness changes from moment to moment.

The Buddhist view on property, especially as owned by the Saṅgha, is also communitarian and potentially communistic. The difference is one of attitude and scale. Mao's commune and a Zen monastery were not as apart as might appear at first sight. Moreover, communism tries to apply the concept of public ownership on a national scale. The recent collapse of communism in the former USSR raises the question of whether such change in scale invariably involves shifts in values as well, which carry it beyond the Buddhist system of values.

Despite such metaphysical and organizational similarities, however, and a recognition of economic factors as forces in themselves, the two systems diverge in their view about the nature and destiny of human beings. The Communist doctrine of blanket egalitarianism, denial of postmortem existence, and primacy of materialism comes in conflict with the Buddhist recognition of temperamental differences among individuals, the doctrine of karma and rebirth, and the goal of doing away with desires. The Marxist idea of confrontation between the classes does not sit well with the general Buddhist preference for concord and harmony.

The success of communism in China in the face of Mahāyāna Buddhism has aroused the suspicion that Mahāyāna Buddhism for some reason may be particularly vulnerable to communism. R. C. Zaehner suggests that the identification of Nirvāṇa and *saṁsāra* in Mahāyāna Buddhism, an identity that is explained in detail later in this chapter under the heading "Identity of Saṁsāra and Nirvāṇa," in the "Emptiness" section, paved the way for the triumph of saṁsāra over Nirvāṇa in China; that is to say, the triumph of communism over Buddhism.[9]

Buddhism and Science

The discovery of a nontheistic religion like Buddhism by the scientific and secular West, which was in the process of freeing itself from the trammels of theism, led to its projection as a rational and scientific religion consistent with modern science. Even when allowance is made for a certain measure of overenthusiasm displayed by both the Buddhists and their modern scientific admirers in the matter, it still seems possible to maintain that the worldview of Buddhism, among all the major religions of the world, may be more in harmony with science than that of any other religion. The reasons for holding such a view are the following:

1. The Buddhist attitude toward reality is open-minded rather than dogmatic;
2. Buddhism tends to favor a naturalistic rather than a supernaturalistic view of the universe;
3. The Buddha arrived at Nirvāṇa through a process of experimentation analogous to that of modern science; and
4. Certain specifically Buddhist views such as those of time, space, and matter have been confirmed by, or are at least consistent with, those of modern science.

It is further argued that even if such were not the case, the Buddhist doctrine of skillful means combined with the undogmatic nature of Buddhism provides enough room for accommodation with the scientific culture of the West, of the kind achieved, for example, with the cultures of China or Japan in the past.

Yet our identification of Buddhism as a soteriological system raises some interesting points in this context. Let us consider only two here, one historical and the other philosophical. Let us assume that modern atomic physics has disclosed a world as much characterized by "emptiness" as the Buddhist worldview. Despite more than two centuries of scientific progress, however, this has not, with the possible exception of Hume, led to the analogous development in psychology that the human personality is also "empty," as the Buddhists claim. Moreover, in the Buddhist case the doctrine of the emptiness of the person achieved philosophical maturity first and was *succeeded* by the doctrine of the emptiness of the universe with which science *begins*. The search for an explanation as to why the process of discovering the emptiness of the universe did not lead to postulating the emptiness of the person in modern science—that is, in reverse in comparison to Buddhism—provides an interesting clue. In Buddhism it is consistently maintained that the whole is not greater than the sum of the parts: That is why there is no soul *over and above* the sum of the various elements constitutive of the human personality. It is, however, the consistent experience of modern science that the whole *can* be greater than the sum of the parts, as when two gases—hydrogen and oxygen—come together and produce water. Water possesses the quality of liquidity, which does not belong to either of the gases.

The Buddhist point of view differs from that of modern science in that it aims at exposing the tendency of language to talk of dynamic "processes" as if they are static "things." For instance, we say: "The water of the river is flowing." But in reality there is no "river" that flows; the flow is the river. By saying that the "river flows," we first convert the flowing body of water into a fixed "entity" called river, which does not exist as a fixed entity, and then proceed to compound the error by making the act of flowing an attribute of this really nonexistent entity.

The Many Forms of Buddhism

The Doctrinal Forms of Buddhism: Theravāda, Mahāyāna, Tantra, and Zen

THERAVĀDA

To begin with, Buddhism was one of the many "new religious movements" that arose in the wake of the breakdown of the Vedic sacrificial religion around the sixth century B.C.E. It is because it was adopted by Aśoka as virtually the state religion in the third century B.C.E. that you are reading this chapter today. Numerous other movements of the same period became obsolete rejects in due course through the benign neglect of history, but its espousal by Aśoka placed Buddhism in the forefront of Indian religious history. Scholars are not quite certain as to exactly what doctrinal forms Buddhism possessed prior to this period. Aśoka's son Mahinda, however, became a monk and carried one brand of Buddhism to Śrī Laṅkā. According to tradition, he was accompanied by his sister, who carried with her a sapling of the tree under which the Buddha had attained enlightenment. Of the many formulations of early Buddhism, the one that survived is the one that was transplanted in Śrī Laṅkā. Thus the earliest doctrinal form of Buddhism with which we are now most familiar owes its survival to an accident of history: It is the sole surviving formulation out of many, which numbered eighteen according to tradition and close to thirty according to modern historians.

The Buddha preached in all probability in a language called Ardhamāgadhī, the language of the region he was born in, which was then known as Magadha and is now known as Bihar. However, right from the beginning his followers began to record his teachings in their own language, and so the various sects alluded to above came to possess their canon in a different language. The Dharmaguptakas, a relatively obscure sect, kept it in Gāndhārī (the language then spoken in the region around modern Kandahar), the more popular Sarvāstivādins kept it in Sanskrit, and the best known, the Theravādins, whose views we shall be discussing, kept it in Pali—the language in all probability of the region around Ujjain in western India.

The teachings of the Buddha, however preserved, are associated with the word Nirvāṇa. Thus the Buddha claimed that the holy life was lived "for the plunge into Nirvāṇa, for going beyond to Nirvāṇa, and for culminating in Nirvāṇa." Thus if the doctrine of early Buddhism were to be summarized in one word, it would be Nirvāṇa.

When asked to describe the nirvāṇic state, however, the Buddha answered with silence, for it was beyond verbal description. But although beyond the range of words, it was not beyond the range of experience. Although the experience could not be described, the consequence of having undergone it was quite manifest: freedom from suffering (*duḥkha*; Pali: *dukkha*). Indeed, we could alternatively condense what the Buddha taught into two clauses: of suffering, and the cessation of suffering. These two clauses, when elaborated into four, constitute the basic formulation of Buddhism, the Four Noble Truths—already described—which may briefly be referred to as the truth of:

1. the existence of suffering (*dukkha*);
2. the arising of suffering (*samudaya*);
3. the cessation of suffering (*nirodha*); and
4. the way leading to that cessation (*mārga*; Pali: *magga*).

In a famous dialogue with a disciple, Māluṅkyaputta, Buddha was plied with metaphysical questions regarding the size and origin of the universe, and so on. The Buddha refused to answer them on the ground that they did not lead to Nirvāṇa. Once he grabbed a fistful of leaves from a tree and compared what he had told the monks to the sheaf of leaves in his hand and what he had not told them to the foliage on the tree. And then he explained that "of what I have known I have told only a little because what I have not told you... is not useful... does not lead to Nirvāṇa."

One is thus thrown back onto the Four Noble Truths. The doctrinal form that Theravāda Buddhism finally assumed took the following shape. One could be a lay disciple of the Buddha, which involved accepting the Three Refuges and the five *śīlas* or rules of moral conduct; namely, abstention from killing, lying, stealing, sexual misconduct, and intoxicants. As a lay follower, one earned religious merit by observing these and catering to the needs of the Community. This resulted in propitious rebirths. If, however, one wished to break the chain of rebirths forever and break out into the freedom of Nirvāṇa, this was best attempted by becoming a monk, for a monk's life is untrammeled by the obstructions that professional and domestic life present to a single-minded quest for salvation. In modern parlance it amounts to the difference between being a part-time student and a full-time student. As a novitiate one took five additional vows to the ones mentioned above, which involved abstention from eating after midday, partaking in secular amusements, using perfumes, and so on, sleeping on luxurious beds, and accepting money. On the more formal side, the monk accepted the 227 rules of the Monastic Order known as the *pātimokkha* (Sanskrit: *prātimokṣa*), which were recited fortnightly in order for the monks to confess any breach thereof. As a monk, one's possessions were minimal (three robes, one girdle, one alms bowl, one razor, one needle, one water strainer), and the property of the Order was held communally.

On the spiritual side, with more time and energy at his or her disposal, the monk or nun could quickly progress right through the steps of the Eightfold Path to the last two—those of right-mindfulness and right meditation. These are discussed in detail in the texts. Right meditation consisted of several stages of which three schemes are encountered—a fourfold one, an eightfold one, and a ninefold one. In terms of the last scheme, the unique contribution of the Buddha lay in reaching the ninth, as the other eight had been experienced by his contemporaries. It was in this last—called *saññā-vedayita-nirodha*—that consciousness becomes "completely void." These states of absorption could be quite profound. Once Buddha walked through a thunderstorm oblivious of it, though it caused considerable damage all around him.

The approach to Nirvāṇa progressively involved four stages of sanctification, known as the *sotāpanna* (stream-entrant); the *sakadāgāmī* (once-returner); the *anāgāmī* (never-returner); and the *arahant*, who had achieved Nirvāṇa. The "stream-entrant" had entered the stream that was ultimately to carry him or her to Nirvāṇa in the course of not more than seven lives. The "once-returner" was destined to one more human birth prior to attaining Nirvāṇa. The "never-returner" would no more have to be reborn in the human condition but would achieve Nirvāṇa after being reborn in a celestial realm. The Arahant or *Arhat* has made it—as an Arhat "one had accomplished whatever was to be accomplished." An Arhat would never be reborn and nothing could be predicated of what became of him or her after death, for one was now "immeasurable, unfathomable like the ocean."

This form of doctrinal Buddhism, however, came to be questioned as the normative formulation of Buddhism at the Second Council held at Vaisālī a hundred years after the death of the Buddha. The First Council is widely believed to have been held, after Buddha's death, at Rājagṛha, at which Upāli had recited the rules laid down by the Buddha as he recalled them, and Ānanda had recited the Sermons. These recitations provided the nucleus of the canon, which was transmitted orally. At the Second Council a split developed of which several versions are extant. If these accounts are viewed in conjunction, they suggest that the breach may have had both doctrinal and disciplinary bases. The seceding group was known as the Mahāsāṅghikas or those of the Great Assembly. The nomenclature seems to imply a group with broader sympathies, involving perhaps a closer contact with the laity, in contrast to the perhaps somewhat confining monasticism of the Theravādins. In any case, the Mahāsāṅghikas, who were also inclined to transfigure the Buddha into a superhuman being, seem to have set forces in motion that culminated in the emergence of Mahāyāna as a form of Buddhism by the first century B.C.E.

MAHĀYĀNA

The Mahāyāna was a self-conscious movement, as its very designation suggests. Just as the Muslims developed self-consciously as a distinct community, much more so than the early Christians, the Mahāyāna developed as a movement distinct from the earlier sects with far greater self-consciousness than the earlier Buddhist movements. It deliberately designated itself as the Mahāyāna, or the Great Vehicle, by way of contrast with the earlier forms of Buddhism, which were called Hīnayāna (Small or Inferior Vehicle). On what, then, precisely, did its claim to greatness rest?

The Buddhist philosopher Asaṅga (fourth century) noted the following points of greatness to establish its superiority:

1. it accepted the teaching of not one but all the Buddhas;
2. it aimed at the salvation of *all* sentient beings;
3. it taught the emptiness not only of an individual's personality but also of all dharmas;
4. it regarded the activity of all Bodhisattvas and not just Buddhas as salvific; and
5. it advocated the ideal not of Arhathood but of Buddhahood itself.

Before one could become a Buddha, however, one had to be a *Bodhisattva,* a sentient being who has resolved to become a Buddha. The ultimate stage of sanctification in Theravāda Buddhism was represented by Arhathood. This Arhat ideal was replaced by the Bodhisattva ideal in Mahāyāna Buddhism. Who, then, is a Bodhisattva?

Buddhism has always believed that though in principle the potentiality of becoming a Buddha lay dormant in every sentient being, its actualization is an achievement of such breathtaking magnitude that it cannot possibly be accomplished within a single lifetime. The founder of Buddhism, Gautama Buddha, in a previous aeon, took the vow to become a Buddha, then spent several lives perfecting the moral and mental skills necessary to accomplish his vow. His achievement of Buddhahood marked the culmination of an effort sustained over several aeons, perhaps even involving intergalactic sojourns in several parts of the universe. During the period that extended between undertaking the vow to become a Buddha and its actual accomplishment—however gigantic the interval may be—the Buddha is referred to as a Bodhisattva or a Buddha-to-be. The word means one whose entire essence is bent on attaining enlightenment.

To fully appreciate the doctrinal point involved here one needs to ask two questions: What is the difference between an Arhat and a Buddha? and What is the difference between an Arhat and a Bodhisattva?

A Buddha achieves enlightenment on his or her own, by his or her own efforts, unaided, while the Arhat achieves enlightenment through the guidance of the Buddha. This point needs to be understood carefully. Early Buddhism is full of statements such as: "One is one's own refuge, who else could be the refuge?" Buddha's valedictory exhortation to his disciples is well known in both its renderings: "Be islands unto yourselves" or "Be lamps unto yourselves." Does this not mean that the Arhat, like the Buddha, makes it on his or her own? Yes, but with the benefit of the Buddha or his teachings as the guide; the Buddha himself made it entirely on his own, unaided. As the Buddha proclaimed to the wandering Upaka in his first postenlightenment encounter with a human being: "I have no teacher" (curiously, when Buddha then went on to claim he was "enlightened" Upaka merely said: "Maybe" and went his way!). In the Pali canon, the Arhats are called *buddhānubuddha*, that is, those who became enlightened in the wake of Buddha's enlightenment, as distinguished from the Buddha who became enlightened on his own.

But if an Arhat has achieved enlightenment while a Bodhisattva is still striving toward it, is the Arhat not a notch above the Bodhisattva? How could the Mahāyāna possibly claim that the Bodhisattva ideal is superior to that of the Arhat?

The key to the answer lies in the fact that whereas the Arhat had only his or her own enlightenment in mind, the Bodhisattva vows to achieve enlightenment not only for him- or herself but also for the sake of all sentient beings. It is the universality of the Bodhisattva's aspiration that is contrasted with the Arhat's more personal inspiration. Once again the point needs to be understood carefully. An Arhat may also, during his or her postnirvāṇic ministry, lead many other sentient beings to Nirvāṇa, just like the Bodhisattva. The crucial difference between the two lies in the nature of the *intention* underlying the original resolve to secure enlightenment. This is particularly significant in Buddhism in which intention is closely associated with the concept of *karma*. The following statement of the Buddha is often cited on the point: "O monks, it is volition [*cetanā*] that I call *karma*. Having willed one acts through body, speech and mind."

The Bodhisattva is typically described as a being who stands on the threshold of Nirvāṇa but postpones entry into it, because once one finally enters Nirvāṇa, one is of no more use to other sentient beings, for individuality has no place in Nirvāṇa. Such is the Bodhisattva's surpassing compassion, however, that the Bodhisattva puts off his or her own Nirvāṇa so that others may enter it. It is as if a group leader were to locate a lost building and, to make sure that all the students in his or her custody found a safe haven there, were not to enter until all the students in his or her charge had first entered it. A complicating consideration could, however, arise at this point: How could one who is not yet fully enlightened lead others to enlightenment?

This consideration was accommodated in several ways. It was pointed out that being a Bodhisattva is as good as having arrived. It also led to the evolution of three models of the Bodhisattva: the Bodhisattva as king, the Bodhisattva as helmsman, and the Bodhisattva as shepherd. A king is first crowned and then looks after the welfare of the subjects. According to this model, a Bodhisattva first achieved his own enlightenment and then guided others to it. A helmsman alights from the boat along with the passengers. A Bodhisattva of this type attained enlightenment simultaneously with the followers. A shepherd goads the sheep inside the stockade first and then enters it, locking the door. Bodhisattvas of this type made sure that those in their flock achieved Buddhahood before they achieved it for themselves.

Ultimately, however, such considerations led to a revision of the concept of the Buddha itself, who was identified with the Absolute. This eternal Buddha was ever present everywhere in the cosmos within everything as its Buddha-nature. As the Buddha, in this understanding, was identical with Emptiness, it is to an analysis of this doctrine that we must now turn.

To grasp the doctrine of Emptiness, it is necessary to form a correct idea of the Buddhist view of the arising of suffering. According to Buddhism, desire is part of a nexus of factors whose relationship is described as *pratītya-samutpāda*, or dependent coorigination, a concept that is explained with the help of the following stylized formula: When this is, that is; this arising, that arises; when this is not, that is not; this ceasing, that ceases. If this concept is now applied to a human being, all the constituents of whose being—body, sensations, perceptions, volitions, and acts of consciousness—are in a state of flux, then with respect to this person, indeed any person, "One thing disappears, conditioning the appearance of the next in a series of cause and effect. There is no unchanging substance in them. There is nothing behind them that can be called a permanent Self (*Ātman*), individuality, or anything that can in reality be called 'I.' Every one will agree that neither matter, nor sensation, nor perception, nor any one of those mental activities, nor consciousness can really be called 'I.' But when these five physical and mental aggregates which are interdependent are working together in combination as a physio-psychological machine, we get the idea of 'I.' But this is only a false idea...."[10]

Thus the individual could be viewed as empty when put under the microscope of pratītya-samutpāda. Early Buddhism also regarded the external universe as *anitya* (impermanent), as *anātma* (lacking in permanent substratum), and as *duḥkha* (characterized by suffering), "whether the Buddhas arise or do not arise," to declare this to be the case. It also viewed the operations of the external universe no less than that of human personality as characterized by pratītya-samutpāda. Yet in early Buddhism, though the emptiness of the individual was asserted, the same was not asserted of the universe. The question arises: If the individual no less than the universe is characterized as *anitya, anātma,* and *duḥkha,* by pratītya-samutpāda, and is empty as well, and the external universe is equally characterized by these features, why is the universe also not "empty"?

The early Buddhist answer to the above question was negative because of its concept of dharma. In this context the word does not mean morality or doctrine. It is used here in a special and technical sense. The early Buddhists believed that though "existence did not consist of a primary substance, whether material or spiritual," it consisted of "a number of elements" or dharmas. They are "not things but elements of things" that actually *exist.* Though the exact nature of the existence was a matter of debate, they may be described "as flashes of reality."

Mahāyāna Buddhism took the position that if one examined the issue closely, the dharmas also were empty like the individual, inasmuch as they were also characterized by pratītya-samutpāda, and were ever in flux, with the preceding accounting for the succeeding ad infinitum. Thus both the individual and the world were empty. Nāgārjuna (second century) put the matter in a nutshell. It is his doctrine of Emptiness that became central to subsequent developments in Buddhism and is explained in detail later in this chapter under "Emptiness."

Issues such as these gave rise to philosophical disputation within Mahāyāna, but the doctrine of Emptiness also created the climate for a third major doctrinal development in the history of Buddhism.

TANTRA

To appreciate this development one must consider the implications the concept of emptiness has for the nature of reality. The doctrine of Emptiness is, as is obvious, highly subversive of our commonsense notions of reality. This subversion, however, created room for the creation of a new option, which was exercised by Tantra. If, on closer inspection, it turns out that the so-called *objective* world is empty, and my *subjective* world of dreams and fantasies has no reality and is thus empty, then the possibility of life in a new dimension is generated. I can, with equal validity, now choose between living in the *objective* world and living in the *subjective* world, as both are ultimately empty or illusory. And I may prefer to live in my subjective world either because it is more easily manipulated by me in accordance with my worldly wishes or because I can manipulate it more easily and effectively to achieve my spiritual goals or ends. The ideal type in this form of Buddhism was no longer the Arhat or the Bodhisattva but the Siddha—the adept in these manipulative techniques. In the end, Tantra is essentially a soteriological manipulation of the subjective world. If it is remembered that many Tantrika practices were esoteric and that leading a monastic life involved withdrawal from the world of "objective" reality anyway, the phenomenon of Tantra begins to appear less puzzling. Some of these practices, especially the ones containing sexual elements—either by way of symbolic or ritual practice—have been criticized as perverted. But another perspective can be presented when Tantra is seen as a doctrinal development lineally connected with Theravāda and Mahāyāna Buddhism.

> Since it is obviously wrong to conceive the impermanent as permanent, one might well believe that it is right to regard the impermanent as impermanent. In the Hīnayāna this inference had indeed been intended. But, so the Mahāyāna argues, it would be clearly untrue to attribute impermanence, ill, etc., to Emptiness, or to dharmas which are empty of own-being, or to dharmas of which the own-being has never been produced. Both permanence and impermanence are misconceptions indicative of perversity. "Since there is thus nothing that is not a perverted view, in relation to what could there be a perversion?" The implication here is that correlative terms give sense only in relation to one another, and that one of the pair alone and by itself can neither exist nor be conceived. In other words, in a universe where there is *only* perversion there can be no perversion at all, at least by way of an attested fact.[11]

The earliest pre-Mahāyāna form of Buddhism that has come down to us is the Theravāda. And it can be seen as undergoing three cycles of development: an early cycle in which it was one of many sects; a second cycle in which it was transplanted to South Asia and took root; and a third cycle of its consolidation in the medieval period. Similarly, three cycles can also be identified in relation to the Mahāyāna: the first cycle representing proto-Mahāyāna developments in India; a second cycle representing its full-fledged emergence in India, dramatized by the conversion of Vasubandhu (who as a pre-Mahāyānist composed the still venerated *Abhidharma Kośa*, or *The Treasury of Higher Subtleties*, before being converted by his brother Asaṅga in the fourth century); and a third cycle representing the diffusion of Mahāyānist modes of thought outside India.

It is possible to describe the doctrinal development of Tantra similarly in three cycles. The first cycle is represented by Mantrayāna, which essentially represents the accommodation of the magical elements in the tradition; the second by Vajrayāna, when this material is systematized in terms of Buddhist categories in which magical procedures are refined into "the art of living which enables us to utilize each activity of body, speech and mind as an aid on the path to liberation." This is followed by a third cycle, the Sahajayāna, when all this paraphernalia is shed and a spiritual supernaturalism yields to a simple but salvific naturalism. From this to Zen is but a step.

ZEN

The fourth major doctrinal formulation is Zen and it also seems to go through a triple cycle. Its first phase is represented by its development in India; the second by its development in China once it was established there as Ch'an; and the third phase by its development in Japan. We saw earlier how, once the principle of the emptiness of the human personality had been introduced, the inner logic of Buddhism extended it to the universe, then to the manipulation of the universe, and then to the abandonment of such manipulation as itself empty. If there is really nothing, then all that is needed is the experiential recognition of this sheer simplicity. The sheer simplicity of the situation also suggests its immediacy—with the corollary that realization can come in an instant. That realization could thus be instantaneous was not instantly realized in the Buddhist tradition, although instances of such realization are found scattered as far back as the Psalms of the Elders in the Pali canon. It was in the hands of Zen that it received due recognition, when it was grasped that if the mind is the main obstacle to realization and the pride of the mind is its rationality, then by undermining such rationality by, for example, bewildering it with a constant mental impasse in the form of a *koan* or confronting it with the immobilizing enigma of an ever-existing realization, the Gordian knot did not have to be untangled, it could be cut. Small wonder then that Zen sums itself up in these words:

A special transmission outside of doctrines
Not setting up the written word as an authority
Pointing directly at the heart of man
Seeing one's nature and becoming a Buddha

The Canonical Forms of Buddhism: The Tripiṭaka, the Mahāyāna Sūtras, Tantra, and Zen Texts

The doctrines discussed in the previous sections are derived from texts in which they have been propounded. These texts are voluminous. "Make no mistake, the volume is colossal. Just the collection of Chinese translations of the Prajna Sutras takes up four volumes of the most recent Taishō edition of the Buddhist canon, each volume about the size of a copy of the *Encyclopedia Britannica,* and numbering about a thousand pages. The English translation of the *Lotus Sutra* runs to about two hundred fifty printed pages. As for the *Avatamsaka,* the original Sanskrit version is said to consist of about one hundred thousand stanzas of four lines each, and one of the Chinese translations, which is more correctly an abridgement of the original, has eighty chapters, or about four hundred fifty printed pages in the Taishō edition."[12] The sacred literature of Buddhism, like that of Hinduism, is immense; but whereas Hinduism entertains, like Islam, the concept of a sacred language—Sanskrit (even though in Hinduism various languages are employed in sacred discourse)—Buddhism from its very inception avoided exclusive or even primary association with one language. In one famous dialogue, although the exact meaning of it is disputed, the Buddha is believed to have allowed the monks to preserve his teachings in their own languages. Hence while Hinduism may be described as multilingual, Buddhism is polyglot. The comparison with Christianity is happier in the sense that at the heart of both Christianity and Buddhism lies a story and a story can be told in any language. In the case of Christianity, it is the story of the divine passion of a person and in the case of Buddhism the story of the enlightenment of a person; but both are stories, and the words themselves are not as important as in Hinduism and Islam, for instance. It is the salvific tale that is all-important—told in any language. But even here there is a dissimilarity, for "unlike the Christians, the Buddhists had no small, portable, definitive though extremely ambiguous gospel, recognized and accepted by all. In consequence they had some difficulties in arriving at a criterion of the authenticity of the sacred text," with "resulting embarrassments."[13]

THE TRIPIṬAKA

Early Buddhism is saved from this embarrassment by the providential hand of history. We know that pre-Mahāyāna Buddhism possessed several distinct sects. It is also known that these sects or schools had their own canons, which were preserved in their own languages. However, it is the canon of the Theravāda school that alone has survived intact and is now available to us, in the language called Pali. The canon is known as the *Tripiṭaka* or the "three baskets." It has been suggested that it came to be so called because the long strips of prepared palm-leaf on which the texts were written were originally stored in baskets, after the canon had been committed to writing during the time of King Vaṭṭagāmaṇī (89–77 B.C.E.) in Śrī Laṅkā. However, the word *piṭakasampadā*—in the sense of the "authority of the sacred texts"—appears in the Pali canon itself in relation to Brahmanical lore. The early suggestion of T. W. Rhys Davids that the word *piṭaka*, or basket, denoted transmission of material, the way building material is passed on along a line of workers, rather than an article of storage thus gains in credibility.

The nucleus of the canon is said to go back to the recitation, by Upāli and Ānanda respectively, of the rules (Vinaya) and the Sermons (*Sutta*) at the gathering where they were approved by five hundred Arhats, with the sole exception of Purāṇa, who preferred to remember Buddha's words as he himself recalled them. This corpus gradually grew in size and by the time it was committed to writing, after a lapse of several centuries after the death of the Buddha, it had achieved a formidable dimension. We shall discover that by contrast with the Mahāyāna canon, it is fairly well organized. It could well be the case that other sources, now lost, preserved the buzzing, blooming, and confounding vitality of the original movement more faithfully, whereas the Pali canon represents a systematic redaction of the materials, the compilers of which had the gift to know what to omit.

The canon consists of three parts called baskets (piṭakas); these are known as the *Vinaya Piṭaka*, the *Sutta Piṭaka*, and the *Abhidhamma Piṭaka*.

The *Vinaya Piṭaka* deals with the 227 rules of the Monastic Order with additional rules for nuns and recounts in detail the exact circumstances in which the rules came to be promulgated, indicating the ad hoc nature of the process. For instance, one rule lays down that a nun shall reveal the contents of her begging bowl when asked by a monk to do so. The origin of the rule lies in the attempt of a nun to smuggle an aborted fetus out of a home concealed in the begging bowl. According to some scholars, at least some of these accounts may represent postfacto rationalizations of existing rules.

The *Sutta Piṭaka* (Sanskrit: *Sūtrapiṭaka*) is the largest of the three and is subdivided into five *Nikāyas* or groups. These are the *Dīgha-Nikāya* (a collection of long sermons); the *Majjhima-Nikāya* (a collection of medium-length sermons); the *Saṁyutta-Nikāya* (a collection of connected sayings); the *Aṅguttara-Nikāya* (a collection of graduated pronouncements in groups of two to eleven items); and the *Khuddaka-Nikāya* (or minor anthology).

It is the *Khuddaka-Nikāya*—the minor collection—that ironically contains some of the more significant sections of the corpus. To mention only five: It contains the *Jātakas* or 547 stories of Buddha's past lives; the *Dhammapada* or verses on dharma, virtually the Buddhist gospel; the *Theragāthā* or psalms of the elder monks and the *Therīgāthā* or psalms of the elder nuns and the *Sutta-Nipāta* or collected discourses. On linguistic grounds, the *Sutta-Nipāta* is believed to represent the oldest stratum of the canon wherein Buddhist egalitarianism already makes its appearance in contrast to Hindu hierarchicalism in the following verses: "For worms, serpents, fish, birds, and animals there are marks that constitute their own species. There is difference in creatures endowed with bodies, but amongst human beings this is not the case; the differences among human beings are nominal only" (*Sutta-Nipāta*: 602–611). It also contains a description of Nirvāṇa, which was paradigmatic in later discussions of it (1074, 1075) and which ends with the statement:

> When all conditions are removed,
> All ways of telling also are removed.

The third part of the canon—the *Abhidhamma* (Sanskrit: *Abhidharma*)—emerged later. It consisted of an effort to specify and categorize the various dharmas or ultimate constituents of experience to which reality is reduced in Buddhism and of which the Theravādins counted 174. It is here that Buddhist sectarian differences in the pre-Mahāyāna period took their sharpest form, some even contesting the authenticity of the *Abhidhamma* as a canonical category itself, with others content to differ over specific contents.

The authoritative commentary on these works was written by Buddhaghosa in the fifth century. In keeping with the triadic approach of this section, the names of the three major commentators of the Pali canon may be mentioned—Buddhadatta, Buddhaghosa, and Dhammapāla. They translated the old Sinhalese commentaries into Pali, and all three ironically were non-Śrī Laṅkan. Among them, Buddhaghosa is specially known for his *Visuddhimagga*, a compendium of the entire canon, as it were, and a work widely venerated in the Theravāda tradition.

THE MAHĀYĀNA SŪTRAS

It is extremely difficult to make a systematic presentation of the Mahāyāna canon. It is a fact worth noting at the outset that the Vinaya rules basically remained unaltered with the spread of Buddhism. As against the 227 rules of the Pali canon, the Chinese consists of 250 and the Tibetan has 253. The major changes in Buddhism occurred in the realm of doctrine, and though they were not without consequences for the role of the Community, the structure of the Community by and large remained identifiable—even when in Japan monks started marrying to show their faith in the saving grace of the Buddha called Amitābha.

Doctrinal diversity, however, found its expression in a crop of fresh *sūtras*, but the Mahāyāna canon was not systematized the way the Theravāda was, although several catholic Chinese sects, such as the T'ien-t'ai and the Hua-yen, made remarkable efforts in this direction. So one might say that several attempts were made at systematization—in India, China, Tibet, and Japan, for instance—with the result that one is left again without a system, because there are too many. The simplest approach might be to begin identifying what came to be known as the nine dharmas, the word dharma now denoting not merely a doctrine but a doctrinal text. These nine dharmas, also known as Vaipulya Sūtras, or Elaboration of the Doctrines, again seem to represent a traditional formalized number. By retaining the number and altering the enumeration to suit our needs, the method might still be usefully employed.

1. *Saddharma-Puṇḍarīka* (second century C.E.), or the Lotus of the True Law, is one of the most popular, significant, and characteristic of the Mahāyāna Sūtras. For some schools of Mahāyāna in China and Japan, it represented the acme of Buddha's teaching. It is placed around 200 C.E., as it came to be translated into Chinese from around 250 C.E. onward, and represents the Buddha as an eternal reality whose earthly manifestation was merely a device to lead people to salvation. It has been said that if for the early disciples of Jesus Christ the miracle was that one who dwelt among them should have been the Son of God, the marvel for St. Paul was that the Son of God should have come down and chosen to live among humans. If for the Theravāda Buddhists the marvel was that a human being—one like them—could become a Buddha, the marvel for the Mahāyāna Buddhists was that the supramundane Buddha should have descended—or condescended—to appear as a human being. This spirit pervades the Lotus of the True Law, which also considers all the teachings of Buddhism—*Hīnayāna, Mahāyāna,* and other *yānas*—to be united in one single vehicle (*ekayāna*), just as it reduces the multiplicity of the Bodhisattvas and the Buddhas to the one eternal Buddha.

2. The body of literature called the *Prajñāpāramitā Sūtras* (second century C.E.), or the Perfection of Wisdom, represents a genre in itself, of which the *Aṣṭasāhasrikā-Prajñā-Pāramitā-Sūtra* or the Perfection of Wisdom in eight thousand verses may be taken as representative. The text is usually placed in the second century when the doctrine of Emptiness, which it expounds, began to catch on. Sūtras of 100,000; 25,000; and 18,000 verses are also known. The famous *Vajracchedikā* or Diamond Sūtra and the *Hṛdaya-Sūtra* or Heart Sūtra represent condensations of such sūtras. The former concludes by comparing all activities to "a dream, a phantasm, a bubble, a shadow, a drop of dew or a flash of lightning."

3. As the title of *Laṅkāvatāra-Sūtra* (third century C.E.), or the Sūtra of Descent to Laṅkā, suggests, the teachings of this sūtra are believed to have been expounded by the Buddha on a visit to Śrī Laṅkā at the invitation of Rāvaṇa. It was translated into Chinese in the fifth century and is highly regarded for its exposition of Buddhist idealism.

4. *Kāraṇḍavyūha-Sūtra* (third century C.E.), or the Sūtra of the Manifestation of Karaṇḍa, is a sūtra devoted expressly to one Bodhisattva, perhaps the most popular, Avalokiteśvara by name, who became a female figure in China (Kwan-Yin) and Japan (Kannon). The sex change is variously explained as the result of assimilation with a goddess figure

or the identification of compassion, the main quality of the Bodhisattva, with the feminine principle. In any case, not only do the Bodhisattvas transcend sex-specific identifications, but they also can assume any form they choose. The famous and precious mantra, *Om maṇi padme hūṃ* (the jewel is in the lotus), is his/her gift to humanity.

5. *Sukhāvatīvyūha-Sūtra* (first century C.E.), or the Array of the Happy Land, is devoted to celebrating the glory of the Buddha Amitābha who according to the sūtra has created a pure land (by contrast with the impure universe) where those with faith will be reborn.

6. *Samādhirāja-Sūtra* (fifth century C.E.), or the Sūtra of King of Meditations, deals with the art of meditation in which a Buddha instructs a Bodhisattva on how to attain enlightenment through meditations countless as sand.

7. *Suvarṇaprabhāsa-Sūtra* (ca. fifth century C.E.), or the Sūtra of the Golden Light, was another popular sūtra that reflects the popular dimension of Mahāyāna teaching, combining the doctrine of Emptiness with magical elements.

8. *Avataṁsaka-Sūtra* (second century C.E.), or the Garland Sūtra, emphasizes the interrelatedness of all phenomena and the interpenetration of the Absolute with all phenomena. According to both the T'ien-t'ai and the Hua-yen Schools, this sūtra was preached by the Buddha immediately after enlightenment. In its final form it incorporated the *Daśabhūmika* and the *Gaṇḍavyūha Sūtras*. *Daśabhūmika-Sūtra* (fourth century C.E.) describes the ten stages of Bodhisattvahood. In early Buddhism, the accomplishment of Buddhahood on the part of the Buddha involved the perfecting of six virtues, of which wisdom or *prajñā* was the coping stone, hence the significance of the *Prajñāpāramitā Sūtras*. In Mahāyāna Buddhism, however, as early as 400 C.E., for by then this text had been translated into Chinese, the Bodhisattva's career came to span ten stations. After the sixth, one became a "celestial" Bodhisattva who could engage in the task of leading others to salvation. *Gaṇḍavyūha-Sūtra* (second century C.E.), or the Sūtra of the Splendid Manifestations of Dimensions, focuses on the Bodhisattva Mañjuśrī, as it relates the attainment of Buddhahood by the youth Sudhana. "The *sūtra* also stresses the interconnectedness of each individual being and the whole universe; it asserts that the altruistic spirit of benevolence or compassion is the fundamental principle of Mahāyāna."[14]

9. *Mahāratnakūṭa* (fifth century C.E.), or the Pinnacle of Jewels, is a collection of forty-nine sūtras, each of which stands alone but all of which taken together are said to constitute a comprehensive expression of the dharma.[15]

Mahāyāna literature, in addition to sūtras, also includes many śāstras. The Mahāyāna distinction between sūtras and śāstras is somewhat in line with the distinction in Hinduism between śruti and smṛti—the former representing "revealed" texts; the latter representing works of human authors.[16]

TANTRA

The Pali canon purports to record Buddha's own words. The Mahāyāna canon claims to report the sermons of the Buddhas and Bodhisattvas, and, however dubious the claim may appear, it at least shows an attempt to acknowledge the authority of Buddhas or Buddhas-to-be. Tantrika literature betrays no such anxiety, although a few texts are ascribed to the historical Buddha. Unlike the Mahāyāna, Tantra literature tends to be esoteric rather than exoteric, but like the Mahāyāna texts, Tantrika texts have also been severally classified. The safest course to follow, therefore, would be to enumerate a few leading ones, bearing in mind the distinction between left-handed and right-handed Tantra, the former taking the repudiation of conventional morality literally and the latter figuratively. Among the earliest and best-known left-handed Tantra texts are the *Guhyasamāja-Tantra*, or the Treatise of the Secret Society, and the *Hevajra-Tantra*, or the Treatise of the Buddha Hevajra. Tantrika literature is still being identified and systematized, but it is interesting that its categorization sometimes utilizes the categories of *kriyā tantras*, *caryā tantras*, *yoga tantras*, and *anuttara tantras*, which resemble the Hindu stages of Tantrika progression described as *caryā* (external care of temple, etc.), *kriyā* (performance of ritual), *yoga* (meditation), and *jñāna* (knowledge). The two Tantras mentioned earlier belong to the *anuttara tantra* class, as does the *Kālacakra-Tantra*, or the Treatise on the Wheel of Time, where the Buddha is cast in the role of the creator. This Tantra serves as an example of a right-handed Tantra text.

The Tantra school emphasized the role of the occult in religious life to the point that it used deliberately opaque language (*sandhyā* or *sandhā bhāṣā*), the true meaning of which could only be revealed by the master to the disciple. Although it is true that, according to the Theravāda tradition, the Buddha disclaimed having the "closed fist" of the teacher, even in Theravāda Buddhism, monks were forbidden from teaching "the scripture word by word to an unordained person"; this trend achieved unforeseen extensions in Tantra.

ZEN TEXTS

In Theravāda Buddhism at least the text was settled, if not as open to all as the general egalitarianism of Buddhism would suggest; in Mahāyāna

Buddhism the texts were almost too many to cope with; in Tantra they receded out of general reach into esoteric circles; in Zen their value itself was called into question. Sometimes the texts are kept close to the lavatory in the monasteries, which should tell us something. Soto Zen is less radical in its rejection of texts than Rinzai Zen, but despite such biblioclasm, some texts are venerated, like the *Platform Sūtra* of the sixth Chinese patriarch Hui-neng (638–713), who is said to have attained enlightenment on listening to a recitation of the Diamond Sūtra. It is interesting that another sūtra respected in Zen circles, the *Śūraṅgama-Sūtra*, although a putative translation from a Sanskrit original, exists only in Chinese. In a sense Zen falls into the prajñā (or insight) tradition of Buddhism, and it has been remarked that it is the manner in which Zen uses Mahāyāna Sūtras, rather than the texts' scholastic content, that sets it apart. D. T. Suzuki notes that the *Prajñāpāramitāhṛdaya-Sūtra* is "daily recited in the Zen monasteries." Zen, of course, has its own collections of koans, a famous one being the *Wu-men-kuan* (The Gateless Gate), as well as the texts of the Zen masters themselves, such as Dogen's *Shōbōgenzō* (The Treasury of the Right Dharma Eye) or Hakuin's *Orategama* (Embossed Teakettle).

Conclusion

Attempts were made to collect and organize this mass of literature into an ordered whole. The Chinese catalog, dated 518 C.E., lists 2,113 works of which 276 are extant. A well-known collection of the Buddhist corpus as a whole, with its codification in the *Kanjur* (a collection of sūtras) and the *Tanjur* (a collection of śāstras), was made in Tibet in the thirteenth and fourteenth centuries, respectively, and printed for the first time in Peking in 1411. The Japanese *Taishō Issaikyō* (1924–1929), referred to earlier, contains 2,184 works in 55 volumes of about 1,000 pages each. The unity of this vast corpus of the literature of Buddhism is perhaps best identified with the help of a metaphor—that of taste. The metaphor of taste is helpful here for it is this intangible taste that, according to a leading Buddhist scholar, really unifies the vast and diverse corpus of Buddhism. He writes: "Furthermore, all Buddhist writings have a *flavor* of their own, and for thirty years I have not ceased marvelling at its presence in each one of them. The Scriptures themselves compare the Dharma to a taste, saying that the Buddha's words are those which have the taste of peace, the taste of emancipation, the taste of Nirvāṇa. Tastes can unfortunately not be described, and even the greatest poet could not tell the taste of a peach and say how it differs from that of an apple. Those who refuse to taste the Scriptures for themselves are therefore at a serious disadvantage in their appreciation of the unity which underlies all forms of Buddhism."[17]

The Structure of Buddhism: The Wheel of Dharma

The triple confession of faith in Buddhism—of seeking refuge in the Buddha, the Dharma, and the Saṅgha—reveals the basic triadic structure of Buddhism. Each confession is capable of further elaboration in a way that coincides with the development of the various forms of Buddhism discussed in the previous section.

The Buddha

Buddhism as we know it traces itself to a historical founder, Gautama Buddha, whose given name was Siddhārtha. Gautama or Gotama was his eponym and the Buddha an honorific that means "enlightened," that is, "one who has awoken to the nature and meaning of life."

The date of the Buddha is a matter of controversy, as may be judged from the range of chronological speculation about the century in which he lived: from the tenth century B.C.E. according to some Chinese sects, to the fourth century B.C.E. by some Japanese calculations. Most scholars so far, however, have been content to place him in the sixth century B.C.E. and, more precisely, date his life as extending from 563 to 483 B.C.E. This consensual reckoning is adopted in this chapter.

The life of the Buddha can be presented in at least three broad versions: human, superhuman, and suprahuman.

The earliest details of the life of the Buddha can be gathered from the Pali canon—that is, from the material contained in the *Vinaya Piṭaka* and the *Sutta Piṭaka*—from the episodic accounts narrating the circumstances in which the rules of the Monastic Order were framed according to the *Vinaya Piṭaka*, and from biographical and autobiographical references contained in the *Sutta Piṭaka*.

The biography of the "historical" Buddha thus revealed is easily summarized. He was born a prince. His father ruled a kingdom on the border of modern India and Nepal. His given name was Siddhārtha. He was married at the age of sixteen to Gopā, or Yaśodharā and had a son named Rāhula, but he renounced the world at the age of twenty-nine. Six years of vigorous quest lead to enlightenment at the age of thirty-five under a tree in Bodh Gayā. Thereafter he became an itinerant monk. His public ministry lasted for forty-five years, during the course of which he founded a Monastic

Order of monks and nuns. He died at the age of eighty at Kusinārā in modern Uttar Pradesh in India.[18]

This human version of the life of the Buddha actually also contains many marvelous features already in the earliest accounts. With the passage of time it underwent further edifying embellishment, with the result that within a few centuries of his death, the Buddha had captured the imagination of his followers as a superhuman being. This is evident from the three main biographies, or more properly hagiographies, available to us: the *Mahāvastu*, or the Great Story (second century C.E.); the *Lalitavistara*, or the Extended Narration of the Sports (of the Future Buddha) (second century C.E.); and the *Buddhacarita*, or the Deeds of the Buddha, ascribed to Aśvaghoṣa (first century C.E.) and composed in the classical epic style. These texts include some traditional material, such as the Buddha's triumph over Māra, the Buddhist counterpart of Satan, and elaborate on it or incorporate new material such as his prodigious and precocious intellectual gifts as a student.

The suprahuman version of the life of the Buddha does not regard him as a human being at all. This version emerged around the fourth century B.C.E. under the influence of the doctrine that there was an ever-existent eternal Buddha who had merely assumed the form of the human Buddha and carried out a celestial charade as an exercise in skill in means to lead people to salvation as described in the *Lotus Sūtra*.

An examination of how the life of the Buddha has been treated within Buddhism discloses that several approaches toward it were adopted. The following six approaches deserve special mention.

1. According to one approach the details of the life and person of the Buddha are inconsequential. There might as well not even have been such a person. What is important is that we possess a body of saving doctrine to which his name has been tagged, from which it might as well be clipped, for what is of supreme importance is the doctrine. This, in our view, is the real import of the violently iconoclastic Zen saying: "If you meet the Buddha, kill him." This attitude finds expression early in Buddhism. Buddha himself discouraged personal adoration as a distraction from salvific practice, as when he asked Vakkhali: "What do you see in this vile body of mine?" Later, in the *Milindapañha*, when the Greek King Menander (Sanskrit: Milinda) asks a Buddhist monk to adduce proof for the historical existence of the Buddha, he is blithely told that none is needed—all that matters is that a body of doctrine which passes under the name of the Buddha exists and its saving property alone is our concern.

2. Another approach emphasizes not Buddha's dispensability but his humanity. This approach may have some ancient antecedents, as when

the divinization of the Buddha was resisted by some Buddhist sects less disposed in that direction, by asking the telling questions: "Was he not born at Lumbinī? Did he not attain enlightenment under the Bodhi tree? Did he not set the wheel of law rolling at Banaras? Did he not pass away at Kusinārā?" Over the past century, such a presentation of the life of the Buddha has gained much vogue. A parallel here is suggested by the life of Muḥammad, who is now considered human in every respect except one—that he became the conduit of God's revelation, the Qur'ān constituting his "sole miracle." Similarly, Buddha is now considered human in every respect except for his unique experience of Nirvāṇa. But unlike Muḥammad, who is the last of his kind, Buddha in a sense is the first. All human beings have within themselves the potential to become a Buddha, if they so will and endeavor. We can call the Buddha a human being par excellence: "He was so perfect in his 'human-ness' that he came to be regarded later in popular religion almost as 'super-human.'"[19]

3. Early Buddhism, however, attached as much importance to Buddha's previous life as to his present one. The fact that the Buddha was a Bodhisattva or a Buddha-to-be before he became a Buddha is not lost sight of. It is as if under popular pressure the "present" life of the Buddha began to be pressed out to cover his premortem and postmortem existences as well. The extension of the Buddha's life in the premortem direction is evident in the development of the 547 Jātaka tales, which deal with the previous lives of the Buddha. The flavor of a Jātaka story may be savored with the help of an example, after a word of explanation.

Once a human being resolves to become a Buddha, a set of virtues must be perfected before that goal can be achieved, and several lives may be involved in the process. An original tradition listed six such virtues, called *pārāmitās,* usually translated as perfections: charity (*dāna*); edifying conduct (*śīla*); patience (*kṣānti*); vigor (*vīrya*); concentration (*samādhi*); and insight (*prajñā*). The list was finally extended to ten in Buddhism, to include skill in means (*upāya-kauśalya*); resolution (*praṇidhāna*); strength (*bala*); and knowledge (*jñāna*). The following Jātaka story displays the Bodhisattva perfecting the virtue of charity. While roaming in the forest with his fellow princes in a past life the Bodhisattva came upon a tigress who had just given birth to cubs, was too weak to even stir as a result, and was about to perish from hunger. To perfect the virtue of charity, "The friendly prince then threw himself down in front of the tigress. But she did nothing to him. The Bodhisattva noticed that she was too weak to move. As a merciful man he had taken no sword with him. He therefore cut his throat with a sharp piece of bamboo, and fell down near the tigress. She noticed the Bodhisattva's body all covered with blood, and in no time ate up all the flesh and blood, leaving only the bones."[20]

Our modern taste might find the ideological excess exhibited by the Bodhisattva repelling despite its altruism, but the Buddhists would see in it another attempt at a moral assertion, through self-sacrifice, of the ontological doctrine that there is in fact no Self to sacrifice.

4. In later Buddhism, this interest in the previous lives of the Buddha was retained, but metaphysical interest now focused on the postmortem state of the Buddha. Early Buddhism had refused to answer or even ask the question of the postmortem existence of the Buddha as not "fitting the case" (just as the question, In which direction does the fire go—east, west, north, or south—upon being blown out? does not fit the case). Mahāyāna Buddhism, however, had developed what came to be known as the *trikāya* doctrine, or the doctrine of the three bodies, by the fourth century. According to this formulation, the Buddha possessed three bodies: a body of essence (*dharma-kāya*); a body of communal enjoyment (*saṁbhoga-kāya*); and a manifest body (*nirmāṇa-kāya*).

The dharma-kāya or Buddha's body of essence was what the Buddha really was, is, and will always be: an eternal and cosmic reality identical with everything. The other two bodies are emanations from this body. The second body came in handy to explain the origin of the vast corpus of literature Mahāyāna Buddhism had developed, which could only be attributed to the "historical" Buddha by straining credibility to the breaking point. These sūtras, by this device, were made "Buddhonymous" as it were, instead of being left anonymous or pseudonymous. It was believed that they were sermons delivered by the Buddha or the Buddha-to-be at celestial gatherings of the elect, when they enjoyed the bliss of his presence. The nirmāṇa-kāya was a phantom conjured up by the Buddha to playact the drama of being born, renouncing the world, achieving salvation, and leading others to it, whereas in fact Buddha had achieved his realization ages ago.

5. In later Buddhism the universe came to be peopled by a plurality of Buddhas. Such a development had already occurred *temporally* in Theravāda Buddhism. The figures of the Buddha-to-be Maitreya, and a past Buddha Dīpaṅkara, following whose example the present Buddha, aeons ago, resolved to become a Buddha, are clearly mentioned in early Buddhism. Originally the historical Buddha was one of a series of seven, which was extended to twenty-four—with Buddha being the twenty-fifth, preceded by Dīpaṅkara. Subsequent series exceed the half-century mark, then the century mark. In Mahāyāna Buddhism, however, the concept was also extended *spatially* so that several Buddhas could exist simultaneously, busying themselves with the noble task of

guiding all sentient beings to salvation. They were also spatially organized, somewhat like the *lokapālas* or guardians of the various directions in Hinduism, and had their own "heavens" in the ten directions.

6. Various further developments pertaining to the concept of the Buddha took place in Tantrika Buddhism as well, but of greater interest is the relationship that came to be established between a Buddha and a Bodhisattva. The development of Tantrism in Tibet illustrates this point well. The extension of the career of the Bodhisattva to cover ten rather than six pāramitās has been alluded to. After perfecting the sixth pāramitā, that of prajñā (insight), the Bodhisattva stands face to face with enlightenment but decides to continue in the universe for the sake of others, thereby becoming what has been called a "celestial" Bodhisattva. Avalokiteśvara is one such Bodhisattva, who is the protective deity of Tibet. The emergence of a set of new Buddhas has already been alluded to—Amitābha being one of them. Now Avalokiteśvara as a Bodhisattva has Amitābha as "his spiritual sire," whose image he wears in his crown. But of even greater interest is the development of the reincarnatory ideas around the Bodhisattva Avalokiteśvara, of whom it was claimed that he would appear thirteen times to rule over Lhasa in succession—the succeeding births to be identified by special signs. These ideas were developed within the Yellow Church of Tibet in the fifteenth century.

Hand in hand with an altered concept of the Buddha went an altered concept of seeking refuge in the Buddha. The proper attitude one adopted toward the Buddha in the triple profession was that of faith or *śraddhā*. In the first approach to the Buddha identified earlier, faith has little role to play as such, as the entire emphasis is made to rest on the teaching: Faith in the teaching takes the place of faith in the teacher. In the second approach identified, in which the Buddha is viewed as a human being, faith in the teacher means little more than faith pending realization, for in Buddhism as a soteriological system the emphasis has always been on the "question of knowing and seeing, and not that of believing. The teaching of the Buddha is qualified as *ehi-passika*, inviting you to 'come and see' and not to come and believe."[21]

However, once we get past the purely personal or historical notions of the Buddha and view him in the broader perspective of Buddhism as a whole, the concept of faith rapidly begins to change to that of devotion. But the change was gradual. For instance, one of the issues that arose in Buddhism after Buddha's passing away was the following: If the Buddha or other Arhats have passed into Nirvāṇa, then how could worship at the *stūpas*, or tumuli, enshrining their relics produce any result at all? The answer offered was that the results are a consequence of the faith of the believer and were not personal responses to the worship as such by the Buddhist sages. It is clear, however, that such an argument was not required in the case of the Bodhisattvas who had *not* passed into Nirvāṇa but were already present in the universe, ever so full of compassion and ready to respond to the prayers of the faithful. The same would apply to the *dharma-kāya* of the Buddha, and to the multiple Buddhas who were really only its manifestations.

This altered conception of faith was also accompanied by an altered conception of karma. In Theravāda Buddhism, despite some exceptions, karma was not considered transferable. Everyone was heir to their own karma, good or evil. It was, however, also a part of the Theravāda view of karma that the concept was closely tied to intention or volition. Thus the view emerged in Mahāyāna Buddhism that by an act of resolution it was possible to transfer karma to someone else or to take over someone else's karma. This doctrine, which is known as *parivarta*, particularly applied to the Bodhisattvas and the Buddhas who had over the aeons stored up vast reservoirs of good karma and who, filled with compassion, were willing to transfer it to those who petitioned them. Moreover, out of compassion they were prepared to take on themselves the evil karma of others.

Thus while in Theravāda Buddhism the word *śraddhā* (Pali: *saddhā*) meant confidence in the teaching of the Buddha, which was a matter of progressive self-realization, in Mahāyāna it changed to faith in the sense of *bhakti* or devotion through which one became the recipient of the karmic grace of a Buddha or Bodhisattva. The emergence of the Pure Land schools can thus be genetically located in the changing concepts of the Buddha and the changing modes of seeking refuge. According to these schools, one completely gave up relying on one's effort to achieve salvation and relied entirely on the grace of the Buddha. Such reliance on the Buddha is in direct opposition to the Theravāda tradition, according to which the Buddha's dying words were: "strive for your salvation with diligence." In this form of Mahāyāna, associated particularly with devotion to the Amitābha Buddha, otherwise known as Amida, one did not strive for salvation at all but left it to Amida to save one. At first it was thought that one might at least constantly repeat Amida's name. This was eventually taken as indicative of a lack of faith in the compassionate grace of Amida by Shinran and his followers, and saying his name only once was deemed enough. Finally, faith was even given an acoustic interpretation. As in the mysticism of the name in medieval Hinduism, the sound of "Amida" by itself was considered salvifically potent.

The Dharma

The Buddha was the source of the Dharma at one level, but at another level the Dharma was the source of the Buddha. To resolve this paradox one must once again refer to the different senses in which the word dharma can be used in Buddhism. When it is said that the Buddha is the source of the Dharma, what is meant is that the teachings of Buddhism (dharma = doctrine) can be traced back to the Buddha. When the statement is reversed and it is claimed that the Dharma is the source of the Buddha, what is meant is that Buddhas appear in the universe at regular intervals in keeping with certain cosmic laws (dharma = law). We are fortunately living in one such interval. Be that as it may, the Buddhas show us the path to the supreme Dharma or realization (dharma = Nirvāṇa) through the practice of Dharma or morality (dharma = moral conduct), enabling us to grasp the significance of the dharmas or the constituents of the universe correctly. These various connotations of the word enable us to make the following convoluted statement: that Dharma revealed by Dharma guides us with Dharma through a proper understanding of dharmas to Dharma. Translation: Doctrines revealed by the cosmic laws in accordance with which Buddhas appear enable one to lead the life that leads one to grasp the true nature of things as they are (*yathābhūtam*), thus enabling one to achieve Nirvāṇa.

In the rest of this section, for the sake of consistency, the word dharma will be used in the sense of doctrine, as it is in the course of this doctrinal exposition that the other connotations of the word appear and gain cogency.

The basic teaching of the Buddha is said to consist of the Four Great Truths. Just as a physician identifies the symptoms of a disease, offers a diagnosis, suggests a cure, and prescribes a treatment, the Buddha identified the symptoms of the disease of life itself, offered a diagnosis, suggested a cure, and prescribed a course of treatment. The First Great Truth identifies the symptoms. It is known as the truth of the existence of suffering (dukkha): "birth is sorrow, age is sorrow, disease is sorrow, contact with the unpleasant is sorrow, separation from the pleasant is sorrow, every wish unfulfilled is sorrow—in short all the five components of individuality are sorrow." These five components of individuality are identified as the body, feelings, perceptions, emotions and volitions, and acts of consciousness. All these are said to represent suffering because they are continually changing, and to be liable to change entails being liable to suffering.

How then do we come to acquire these components of individuality? The Second Noble Truth provides the answer: It is the desire for existence, for annihilation, and for sense pleasures that causes us to be reborn and assume a life-form, which, as we saw earlier, inescapably involves suffering. It should be noted that the Buddhists do not admit that individuality contains any permanent element such as the soul; thus, when an individual is reborn, no soul passes from one body to another as in Hinduism. Rather, the process is similar to the way a series of echoes is produced. Just as one echo, in ceasing to exist, gives rise to another, so also one psychophysical organism (comprising the five components of individuality) in ceasing to be gives rise to another. The cause underlying this arising is desire, hence the Second Noble Truth is known as the truth of the arising (*samudaya*) of suffering. Thus suffering has a cause. However, since it is logical to assume that the effect would cease if the cause ceases, we are led to the Third Noble Truth—the truth of the cessation (*nirodha*) of suffering.

How is the cessation of suffering to be brought about? The answer to this question leads us to the Fourth Noble Truth, known as the *middle* path or the Eightfold Path. Both these terms as used for the path reveal the structure of Buddha's teaching.

Let us first focus on the Fourth Great Truth understood as the middle path. In this sense the word has two clear connotations in the teachings of the Buddha, a moral one and a metaphysical one. The moral connotation is clearly stated in the first sermon delivered at the Deer Park itself, when the Buddha prescribes a middle path for his followers; middle, that is, because it avoids the two extremes of overindulgence and self-mortification. One can hear an echo of Buddha's own life in this—as a prince he had led a life of indulgence, as an ascetic of mortification—and did not gain the ultimate end through either but rather by leading a life that avoided these extremes.

Metaphysically the Buddha had struggled with two doctrines: one which held that the Self and the universe are eternal (*sassatavāda*) and the other which held that neither was so (*ucchedavāda*). The Buddha identified the correct approach as one that steers the middle course between eternalism and annihilationism. For according to the Buddha it is not correct to say that the constituents of the universe are eternal, because the universe is obviously changing all the time, a fact confirmed by even a cursory observation. However, neither is it possible to say that the constituents are annihilated, for in ceasing to be they at the same time give rise to another set of causes and conditions. This view of the Buddha is otherwise known as that of pratītya-samutpāda (Pali: *paṭicca-samuppāda*).

The moral understanding of the middle way essentially remains the same through the history of Buddhism, as manifested in the rules of the Monastic Order (Vinaya) and even more so in the prātimokṣa (Pali: *pātimokkha*) contained therein. The prātimokṣa showed a remarkable constancy even in comparison to the rest of the Vinaya. The *Vinaya Piṭaka,* through all the elaborations of doctrine and proliferations of sects in Buddhism, displayed in turn far greater stability as a whole in comparison to the *Sutta Piṭaka* and this in turn was relatively more consistent and stable when compared with the third part of the canon, the *Abhidharma* (Pali: *Abhidhamma*).

The evolution of the understanding of the middle way in its philosophical or metaphysical sense provides a clue to a series of successive developments within Buddhism that might otherwise remain opaque.

The Theravāda movement of Buddhism understood the doctrine of the middle way—understood as pratītya-samutpāda—as essentially applying to the individual and explaining the individual's bondage to saṁsāra or the process of rebirth. The explanation took the form of a chain of causation consisting of twelve elements explained in direct order (*anuloma*) as follows: Ignorance (*avidyā*) causes volitional actions (*saṁskāras*), which cause acts of consciousness (*vijñāna*), which cause mind and body to appear (*nāma-rūpa*), which are the cause of the six sense-organs (*ṣaḍāyatana*). These cause contact (*sparśa*) with sense objects, which cause sensation (*vedanā*), which causes desire (*tṛṣṇā*); which causes grasping (*upādāna*), which in its own turn results in the desire for continuing existence (*bhava*), which is the cause of birth (*janma*). Birth in turn causes old age and death (*jarā-maraṇa*).

In the popular account of the life of the Buddha, he is believed to have beheld four signs prior to renouncing the world: a sick man, an old man, a dead man, and a monk—symbolizing the decrepitude of aging, the pathology of sickness, the phobia of death, and in the monk, the hope of transcending them. If traumatized by these experiences the Buddha renounced the world to find an answer to the question of suffering in life and death, then here we finally have the answer formulated for us, which could also be read in the reverse order (*pratiloma*) as follows: "old age and death" are caused by "birth," which is caused by "becoming"... and so on. There is, however, also a third perspective from which this causal nexus can be viewed—that of the process of rebirth. According to this interpretation of these twelve factors (*nidānas*), the first two belong to past existence, the next eight to the present, and the last two to future birth.

Thus the process of saṁsāra can be explained in terms of the middle way understood philosophically, the way out of which is also provided by the middle way understood morally. It is clear that there is an opposition here between saṁsāra and Nirvāṇa: One is in saṁsāra and in the end one steps out of it and attains Nirvāṇa by following the middle way or the Eightfold Path.

In Mahāyāna Buddhism the doctrine of the middle way was interpreted in a revolutionary way so as to eliminate the distinction between saṁsāra and Nirvāṇa. This point is explained in detail later under "Identity of Saṁsāra and Nirvāṇa."

The Saṅgha

It is vital to the proper understanding of Buddhism that the real *witness* to Buddhism is the Saṅgha, just as the Catholic church is the witness to Christianity in Catholicism. The most telling fact that confirms this view is the following: When we say that Buddhism disappeared from India, what we really mean is that the Buddhist Community is no more to be found in India, not that people there do not revere the Buddha or accept many of his doctrines.

The Buddhist Saṅgha plays a key role in the structure of Buddhism in relation to society and polity, despite its limited numbers, because it constitutes an elite corps. The proportion of the monks to the population varied with place and time. In the seventh century, Hsüan-tsang estimated that India had 520,000 monks, of which 80,000 belonged to Mahāyāna. In the fifth century, Śrī Laṅkā had 60,000 monks, according to Fa-hsien. In the same century China is believed to have had around 77,000 monks and nuns, the figure rising to 2,000,000 in the sixth century. Śrī Laṅkā had only about 8,000 monks left when Buddhist fortunes were at a low ebb in the nineteenth century, but the situation has since improved. In Tibet, prior to the Chinese occupation, a third of the male population is believed to have lived in monasteries, and in the heyday of Buddhism in Mongolia, the monasteries absorbed almost 45 percent of the population. But Thailand leads the world today in the size of the Saṅgha, which had around 250,000 members in 1959. Korea had 7,000 monks in 1947.

The latest figures available for some of the representative Buddhist countries are presented below in the form of a table, in which the figures for Śrī Laṅkā are an approximation.

Country	*Year*	*Monks*	*Nuns*
Japan	1989	64,809	48,490
Korea	1983	14,206	6,549
Thailand	1985	338,441	11,928
Burma	1990	143,072	23,017
Śrī Laṅkā	1992	30,000	3,000

It is also worth noting that in the Buddhist Community of North America there are at least as many women lay followers as men.[22]

The discussion of the Saṅgha as a structural element in Buddhism may be divided into three parts: its own structure; its structural relationship with society; and its structural relationship with polity.

The Buddhist Saṅgha is essentially a decentralized body. Even a handful of monks can start a chapter on their own, and they do not have to technically owe allegiance to any external authority. After his death, Buddha did not appoint a successor or any machinery for regulating the various chapters, except for the rules of the Vinaya. The existence of a monastic order, however, clearly demarcates it from the laity, without whose support the Order could not exist. The order, then, is seen as existing in a symbiotic relationship with the laity. The laity provides for the needs of the order, however minimal, and the order looks after both the spiritual and material welfare of the laity. The administering to spiritual welfare is obvious through sermons and so on, but it was also a matter of popular belief in Asia that the monks possessed occult powers that affected the material well-being of the region. As an extreme example, one may cite the fact that on occasion the monks accompanied the army in Śrī Laṅkā, as the sight of Bhikkhus was "both a blessing and a protection." Though the distinction between the laity and the order was clear, it did not mean that the laity were totally outside the soteriological ambience of Buddhism. They could take the five vows instead of the ten for the monk, and for limited periods even observe the eight vows. Moreover, apart from the triple confession being common to all Buddhists—ordained or lay—the laity could earn merit and secure a better rebirth both in material and spiritual terms by serving the order. The construction and worship of relics was another way in which popular religiosity could be expressed; architectural remains from all over Asia attest to this. Three terms are significant in this connection: the stūpa, the *dagoba,* and the *pagoda.* The stūpa was a commemorative mound enshrining a relic; the dāgoba (Sanskrit: *dhātu-garbha*) referred to a stūpa distinguished by a spire while the pagoda, said to have evolved from the Chinese watchtower, was a storied structure. All are venerated.

Pilgrimages remained a major mode of religious participation for the monks, laity, and royalty alike. The following account of the Chinese monk Fa-hsien's visit to such a site in the fourth century evokes the sentiments associated with such pilgrimages before the world became a global village.

> When Fā-hien and Tao-ching first arrived at the Jetavana monastery, and thought how the World-honoured one had formerly resided there for twenty-five years, painful reflections arose in their minds. Born in a borderland, along with their like-minded friends, they had travelled through so many kingdoms; some of those friends had returned (to their own land), and some had (died), proving the impermanence and uncertainty of life; and to-day they saw the place where Buddha had lived now unoccupied by him. They were melancholy through their pain of heart, and the crowd of monks came out, and asked them from what kingdom they were come. "We are come," they replied, "from the land of Han." "Strange," said the monks with a sigh, "that men of a border country should be able to come here in search of our Law!" Then they said to one another, "During all the time that we, preceptors and monks, have succeeded to one another, we have never seen men of Han, followers of our system, arrive here."[23]

Numerous visits by the devout are attested to while king Aśoka had memorials erected at all the four main places sanctified by the Buddha story: where he was born (the Lumbinī Garden); where he achieved enlightenment (Bodh Gayā); where he preached the first sermon (Sārnāth); and where he passed away (Kusinārā). Aśoka commemorated his visit to the birthplace of the Buddha with the following inscription:

> By his sacred and gracious Majesty the King, consecrated 20 years, coming in person, was worshipped this spot, inasmuch as here was born the Buddha Sakyamuni. A stone bearing a figure was caused to be constructed and a pillar of stone also set up, to show that the Blessed One was born here.[24]

Because the Buddhist Saṅgha was not an ecclesiastical organization, it was open to the influence of the state, benign or malign, to a degree and extent that would not have been possible had it possessed its own structure. The state had to intervene at times to regulate the affairs of the church. Several patterns of relationship may be identified here: 1. mutual noninterference; 2. the assertion of autonomy vis-à-vis the state; 3. assertion of state authority vis-à-vis the Saṅgha, either through regulation or persecution; and 4. identification of the two.

The survey of the history of Buddhism discloses that all four were actualized in history.

1. Mutual noninterference: This was the pattern prior to the adoption of Buddhism virtually as a state religion by Aśoka;
2. Assertion of autonomy is represented by Hui-yüan's successful protest in the fifth century against monks having to bow to the Emperor during the period of the Chin dynasty;
3. The assertion of state authority over the Saṅgha in terms of support, regulation, or persecution is exemplified by the experience of Buddhism under the T'ang dynasty in China; and
4. The identification of the two is illustrated by the case of Lamaism in Tibet; the virtual fusion of the two in Korea (550–664); and by the northern Wei Empire of China, especially during 460–464.

In this last case, T'an-yao had five gigantic figures of the Buddha carved at Yün-kang, which were identified with the five emperors of the dynasty who were regarded as contemporary manifestations of the Buddha. To take a more modern example, the King of Thailand still appoints the Saṅgharāja or the Head of the Order.

The Buddhist Saṅgha was a vital presence in many cultures in the context of both society and polity, which often involved it in certain kinds of tension that had to be contained or resolved. This is most immediately apparent in the political sphere from the instances mentioned above; it was equally so in the social sphere, where the question of its relationship with the laity has always needed defining—as with the political authorities—and was defined in different ways. The Saṅgha had to mediate between being too far removed from the laity and being too closely involved with it, just as in the case of the political powers-that-be. In its own way it has been guided by the middle way here, interpreted in a dynamic sense, with movement in one direction often being corrected by movement in another.

One might thus contrast the eremitic ideal of living alone like "the horn of a rhinoceros" in early Buddhism with the laicization of the monastic order in Jodō Shinshū, in which the priests get married and lead a householder's life in order not to set themselves apart consciously—for Amida's grace, like rain and sunshine, falls on all alike. Nevertheless, these extreme examples apart, a more common phenomenon was an attempt at the assertion of the monastic ideal whenever it tended to be compromised by laicization or politicization. In Śrī Laṅkā, for instance, in the ninth century, the *paṃśukūlikas* revived the tradition of "from rags to robes," as opposed to the "rags to riches" approach of the settled monasteries. Similarly, when some monks became so prone to settling down as to be called city-dwellers (*grāmavāsī*), a movement toward living in the forests was initiated by other monks. When the monastic isolation of Theravāda started appearing excessive, on the other hand, Mahāyāna, with its greater concern for the laity, appeared as a corrective movement.

Even when the Saṅgha was founded it had to face problems of self-definition in Buddha's own lifetime. It is well known that Buddha permitted the ordination of nuns only hesitatingly and that some residue of resentment survived even its establishment, as is indicated by the charge brought against Ānanda for having influenced the Buddha's judgment in this matter. The trends within the Saṅgha can be epitomized in three words: accommodation, expansion, and purification. The introduction of women into the order was an accommodation, which also characterized its spread in the various cultures outside India. Expansion was the concomitant of accommodation and required occasional purification. The activities of Atīśa (eleventh century) and Tsoṅ-kha-pa (fifteenth century) in Tibet are well known in this connection. Similarly, the Lu-tsung or Vinaya school in China (sixth century) and the Ritsu or *Vinaya Piṭaka* school in Japan (eighth century) tried to retain an emphasis on monastic discipline.

Each major phase of development in Buddhism involved some monastic modification. For instance, the Theravāda movement was constantly on guard against the dilution of the monastic ideal and resisted change. There was resistance to compromises and subsequent attempts at modification toward earlier ideals, when such compromises occurred. However, the Mahāyāna signaled not only a change in attitude toward the laity but also introduced de facto changes in the monastic order, the most significant of which was perhaps the relaxation of the rule against keeping medicines. Tantra seemed to alter the basic ethos of the Saṅgha itself by developing cultic rules for closed groups and by inculcating a new morality, which from the earlier standpoint amounted to immorality. Finally, under Ch'an, a new set of rules was developed by Po-chang (720–814), the most significant feature of which was represented by the motto: "A day without work—a day without eating." Thus doctrinal, canonical, and monastic developments within Buddhism went hand in hand.

For Whom the Wheel Rolls? The Telos of the Structure

The three refuges—the Buddha, the Dharma, and the Saṅgha—help us not only to explain the structure of Buddhism but also the changes it underwent. To carry the architectonic metaphor further: If the formal cause of a building is its concept, the material cause the substances involved in making it, and the efficient cause the architect, then one might identify the Dharma as the formal cause, the Saṅgha as the material cause, and the Buddha as the efficient cause of the edifice of Buddhism. But what about the final cause? Whatever it might be in the case of the building, in the case of Buddhism it is Nirvāṇa. In a sense, a house is a very appropriate metaphor for Nirvāṇa, which consists of the realization of Emptiness, for it is precisely the emptiness of a house, the emptiness within its walls, which makes it habitable—which makes it a house!

Emptiness

The Meaning of Emptiness

The ultimate reality in Buddhism is not God, or Being, or Substance; it is *Śūnyatā,* which is often translated as "Emptiness." Why does Buddhism take "emptiness" as the ultimate reality? What does Buddhism indicate by the term "emptiness"? To understand the real meaning of "emptiness," one must begin by emptying one's mind of the negative connotations the word has in the English language. In this regard the etymological explanation of the term Śūnyatā will be helpful. As Garma C. C. Chang discusses in his book *The Buddhist Teaching of Totality: The Philosophy of Hwa Yen Buddhism:*

> . . . Śūnyatā is a combination of the stem *śūnya,* "void or empty," and a participle suffix, *tā,* here rendered as "ness." Śūnyatā is therefore translated as "Voidness or Emptiness." It is believed that *śūnya* was originally derived from the root *svi,* "to swell," and *śūnya* implies "relating to the swollen." As the proverb says, "A swollen head is an empty head," so something which looks swollen or inflated outside is usually hollow or empty inside. Śūnyatā suggests therefore that although things in the phenomenal world appear to be real and substantial outside, they are actually tenuous and empty within. They are not real but only appear

> to be real. Śūnyatā denotes the absence of any kind of self, or selfhood. All things are empty in that they lack a subsisting entity or self-being (Svabhāva).[25]

This is the connotation of the term Śūnyatā. The realization that "although things in the phenomenal world appear to be real and substantial outside, they are actually tenuous and empty within" was intuitively realized in *Prajñāpāramitā* literature and was logically or philosophically formulated by Nāgārjuna, especially in his important writing, *Mūlamadhyamakakārikās.*[26] The basic purport of *Prajñāpāramitā Sūtra* and *Mūlamadhyamakakārikās* is that if a phenomenal thing is real as *svabhāva* (self-being or self-existent thing), then we cannot understand the world of causality and change in terms of arising and ceasing—which we are, in fact, constantly experiencing. Accordingly, the phenomenal thing does not exist as svabhāva. In terms of a self-existing thing, the phenomenal thing is empty.

The Buddhists believe that to be called "substantial or real" a thing must be able to exist on its own. However, if we look at the universe, we find that everything in it exists only in relation to something else. A son is a son only in relation to the father; and a father similarly in relation to the son. Fatherhood does not exist on its own but only in relation to something else. The Buddhists use the word svabhāva to denote existence on its own, that is, nondependent existence, which alone, according to them, qualifies as true or genuine existence. But if everything in the world depends on something else for being what it is, then nothing in the universe can be said to possess svabhāva or genuine self-existence; hence it is empty. For instance, we are familiar with the phenomenon of fire. We also know that fire requires fuel to burn. However, can fire ever exist without fuel? It cannot. And can fuel exist without fire? We may be tempted to say yes, but Buddhism asks us to pause for a moment before we do so. A log of wood cannot qualify as *fuel* if the phenomenon of fire did not exist. A log of wood would then remain merely a log of wood—it is the possibility of using it for fire that makes it into fuel. Hence it possesses no svabhāva or self-nature as fuel.

Through these examples of Nāgārjuna, we are led to a definition of svabhāva. That is: Svabhāva is that which is self-existing because it is not something that is produced dependently by something else. It is an enduring, permanent being without change, birth, and death. Svabhāva is a singular being without partition. In short, svabhāva in Nāgārjuna's sense is a self-existing, enduring, singular substance. Such a self-existing svabhāva is nothing but a substantialization or reification of the concept and does not exist anywhere outside of the realm of thinking and language. In our daily lives the role of language is so great that people easily reify or substantialize the word or concept as if there is an enduring, unchanging reality corresponding to the word or concept. In other words, people often apply the universality and constancy implied in the meaning of a word to the object. Especially those who have entered into the realm of metaphysics constructed through reification of concepts think that the self-existing svabhāva is truth, while the realm of fact is merely phenomenal. In the days of Nāgārjuna, various forms of metaphysics of language, such as that of the Abhidharma philosophy, were prevailing. The *Prajñāpāramitā Sūtra* and *Mūlamadhyamakakārikās* were composed to break through such an attachment to metaphysics.

Concept, Language, and Reality

Let me explain this issue further by citing from our daily experience. People of America are used to calling California the "West Coast"; thus, they often think that California is an entity called "the West Coast," or a substance corresponding to the notion of "West Coast." However, although California may be called the West Coast from the viewpoint of Washington, D.C., New York, or Boston, West Coast is merely a relative notion, not a self-existing entity. If we look at California from the point of view of Hawaii or Japan, California is not the west coast but the east coast. Again, if we look at California from the point of view of British Columbia, California is not the west coast but the south coast. East and west, south and north—all are relative notions without enduring reality. There is neither absolute east nor absolute west; neither absolute south nor absolute north. Such a notion of absolute east or absolute west is simply a human conceptual construction; it is not real. Rather, it is nonsubstantial and empty. This is easily understood. Exactly the same understanding can be applied to the notion of right and left, high and low, big and small, and so on. There can be no absolute right, absolute high, or absolute big in reality.

However, when we move to the notions of good and evil, true and false, or beauty and ugliness, the situation is not so simple. Many philosophies and religions talk about the absolute good (for instance, the Supreme Good, or summum bonum) and absolute evil (original sin and eternal punishment). This is because, unlike the notions of east and west, high and low, big and small—which refer to the physical, objective, value-free dimension—the notions of good and evil, true and false, and beauty and ugliness denote the existential, subjective, value-oriented dimension. They are situated not merely in the ontic, or ontological, dimension (a dimension concerning how something *is*) but also in the axiological dimension (a dimension concerning how something *ought* to be). Due to this axiological nature, the notions of good and evil, true and false, and beauty and ugliness inevitably lead us to the notion of absolute good, absolute evil, absolute truth, absolute falsehood, and so forth. Thus people believe, for instance, in the notion of absolute good as the enduring, unchangeable, and universal reality, and they take it to be the ultimate goal of their ethical life. However, Buddhism, particularly Nāgārjuna and his Mādhyamika philosophy, insists that such a notion of absolute good (and similar notions) is not unchangeable or enduring, but nonsubstantial and empty. This is because in the axiological dimension, the notion of absolute good, for instance, is nothing but a reification, or substantialization of the notion of good. To begin with, the very distinction of good and evil is, to Nāgārjuna, nothing but a reification or substantialization of a human concept that is devoid of reality. In short, all value judgments are, after all, unreal human conceptual constructions.

In Nāgārjuna all value judgments arise from *vikalpa*, human thinking, which is a discriminating, bifurcating, and dualistic way of thinking. To him, this vikalpa is the source of human suffering because people are attached to it and grasp discriminating and dualistic thoughts as true and real. If we are free from vikalpa and awaken to the emptiness of dualistic discrimination, then we are emancipated from suffering through the realization of Śūnyatā. In the *Mūlamadhyamakakārikās*, chapter 18, Nāgārjuna[27] states the following:

> On account of the destruction of pain (*kleśa*) of action there is release; for pains of action exist for him who constructs them. These pains result from phenomenal extension (*prapañca*); but this phenomenal extension comes to a stop by emptiness. (18:5)
>
> When the domain of thought has been dissipated, "that which can be stated" is dissipated. Those things which are unoriginated and not terminated, like *nirvāṇa*, constitute the Truth (*dharmatā*). (18:7)
>
> "Not caused by something," "peaceful," "not elaborated by discursive thought," "indeterminate," "undifferentiated"; such are the characteristics of true reality (*tattva*). (18:9)

Prapañca, here translated as phenomenal extension and discursive thought, originally indicated diversity or plurality including complex development of thinking and language. To Nāgārjuna, prapañca implies verbal pluralism or fiction of language. Vikalpa arises from prapañca because human thinking is nothing but a fiction unrelated to reality. The process of human knowledge based on language is a perversion. It is necessary for us to retrogress from attachment to thinking and judgment to the realm of nondiscursive intuition. In so doing we face reality prior to language. This is the realm of "emptiness." Emptiness indicates the reality of the world in intuition apart from language; therefore, there is emancipation from suffering caused by attachment to discrimination. Accordingly, Emptiness is not only a philosophical notion, it is also a religious and soteriological one.

Reification in the Religious Dimension

Earlier in this section we saw the problem of reification and substantialization of human concepts in the ontic, or ontological, dimension and in the axiological dimension as well. Also, it was suggested that we must be liberated from such reification of human concepts through awakening to the nonsubstantial emptiness of phenomenal things to realize true reality.

Exactly the same issue is involved when we move from the realm of ethics to the realm of religion. In the axiological realm, or the value-oriented realm—such as good and evil, truth and falsehood, beauty and ugliness—the criteria for value judgments are crucial. Therefore, a value judgment and its criteria are easily reified, or substantialized. However, the realm of religion is beyond such value judgment because it is based on the unconditional love of God or the unlimited compassion of Buddha, which are supported by the divine will of God or supreme wisdom. Unlike the realm of ethics (good and evil), the realm of learning (the true and the false), and the realm of aesthetics (the beautiful and the ugly), the realm of religion is free from the reification or substantialization of value judgments. For instance, in Christianity Jesus says, "I have not come to call respectable people, but outcasts" (Matt. 9:13, *Good News Bible*). In Buddhism, Shinran (1173–1262) emphasized the unconditional compassion of Amida Buddha. He declared, "Even a good person is saved in the Pure Land. How much more so is an evil person."[28]

Thus, in both Christianity and Buddhism, value judgment is not only transcended, but it is also reversed. However, if we go a step further, we see a significant difference between Christianity and Buddhism in regard to value judgment and the understanding of ultimate reality. In Christianity, although all human-made value judgments (including wisdom in the sense of the Greeks) are transcended by God, God himself is believed to be the "only wise God" (Rom. 16:27) and the "judge of all" (Heb. 12:23). Indeed, God, the ultimate reality in Christianity, is believed to be the Supreme Good beyond the duality of good and evil and the source of all value judgments. The will of God is believed to be self-existing. By contrast, in Buddhism the ultimate reality, Nirvāṇa, is not the supreme good or the judge of all, but that which is *neither* good *nor* evil. This is because in Buddhism the ultimate reality is to be realized as nondual by *completely* overcoming all duality.

It is clear that the Christian notion of God is not merely transcendent. In terms of *homoousia*, God is fully immanent and fully transcendent in the incarnation of Jesus Christ. However, this paradoxical identity of immanence and transcendence, the human and the divine (both truly human and truly God), is realized without the clear realization of *neither* immanent *nor* transcendent, *neither* human *nor* divine. The paradoxical identity is realized somewhat objectively without the negation of negation, that is, absolute negation. Hence, although through faith in Jesus Christ a Christian *participates in* the death and resurrection of Jesus Christ, he or she does not become *identical* with God except in some forms of Christian mysticism. In this sense the Christian notion of God is fundamentally transcendent and is not completely free from reification and substantialization. Here I am using the terms reification and substantialization in a special sense. It is definitely clear that the Christian notion of God is not a reification or substantialization of the divine—especially in the Trinitarian notion of God, which is dialectical, reciprocal, and necessarily understood in terms of Father, Son, and Spirit. However, are this Trinitarian God and the human self completely reciprocal; are this Trinitarian God and each and every nonhuman creature also completely reciprocal?[29]

On the other hand, Buddhism clearly realizes the possibility of reification and substantialization in the religious dimension. In the first place, when Buddhism transcends the axiological dimension, it overcomes all duality completely and attains a nondualistic position. This means that both ends of duality, for instance good and evil, are equally overcome through the double negation of the two ends—i.e., good and evil. This double negation of both ends of duality does not entail the supreme good, but that which is neither good nor evil. This is the reason why in Buddhism ultimate reality is not God as the supreme good, but Emptiness, which is neither good nor evil.

The preceding is the first important difference between Christianity and Buddhism. This difference derives from the fact that Buddhism *completely* overcomes the duality of value judgment in the axiological dimension through the negation of negation, and thus reaches the religious dimension, which is entirely free from even the notion of absolute good. Christianity, however, transcends value judgment in the axiological dimension, not necessarily through the realization of negation of negation; that is, not through completely overcoming duality itself, but by moving toward the extreme point of the good.

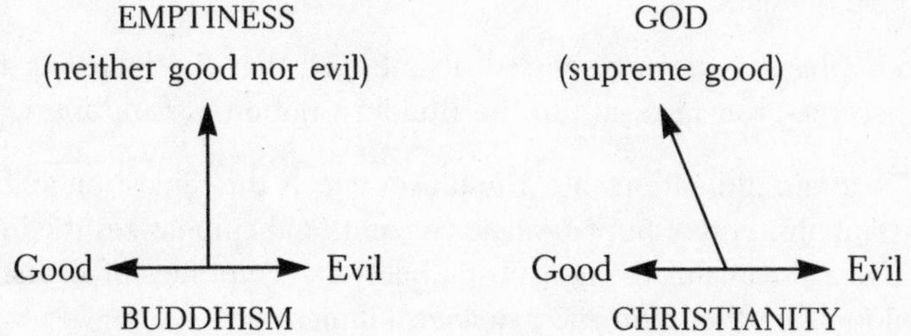

Again, this difference takes place because, in Buddhism, the nonsubstantiality and emptiness of the notion of good and evil are clearly realized, and reification and substantialization of any sort are carefully rejected; whereas, in Christianity, the nonsubstantiality and emptiness of the notion of good are not categorically recognized due to Christianity's emphasis on divine justice. And, when the notion of good is absolutized, some reification and substantialization are inevitable. Here we must notice how crucial the realization of nonsubstantiality and emptiness of the notion of good is, even when it is absolutized, for us to attain ultimate reality by going beyond any possible reification and substantialization.

Self-emptying of Emptiness

The second important difference between Christianity and Buddhism concerning ultimate reality is as follows. In Buddhism, Emptiness as ultimate reality must be emptied. However important Emptiness may be, if it is represented and we attach ourselves to it as "emptiness," it is not true Emptiness. In Nāgārjuna's *Mūlamadhyamakakārikā*, emptiness that is dimly perceived is likened to a snake wrongly grasped, or (magical) knowledge incorrectly applied.[30] Emptiness that is objectified and conceptualized must be emptied. The self-negation, or self-emptying, of Emptiness is essential for the authentic realization of Emptiness. By contrast, in Christianity the *kenosis* (self-emptying) of Christ is emphasized (Phil. 2:5–8), but not necessarily the *kenosis* of God.[31]

Christian theology generally states that the Son of God became a human being without God ceasing to be God. In his book *Does God Exist?* Hans Küng says:

> The distinction of the Son of God from God the Father, his obedience and subordination to the Father, is of course upheld everywhere in the New Testament. The Father is "greater" than he is and there are things that are known only to the Father and not to him. Neither is there any mention anywhere in the New Testament of the incarnation of God himself.[32]

From what has been discussed, it is hoped that the following three points become clear in regard to the Buddhist notion of Emptiness.

1. To attain ultimate reality, Buddhism rejects the reification and substantialization of human-made concepts and emphasizes the importance of realizing the nonsubstantiality and emptiness of all dualistic notions in the ontic and axiological dimensions.

2. Thus, ultimate reality in Buddhism is not God, Being, or Substance; rather, it is "Emptiness," which is freed from any reification and substantialization in the religious dimension.
3. This Emptiness itself must be emptied by rejecting any attachment to emptiness. True Emptiness is not a static state of everything's nonsubstantiality, but rather a dynamic function of emptying everything, including itself.

When Buddhism declares that everything without exception is empty, these three points are implied.

Emptiness and Dependent Coorigination[33]

The notion of Emptiness is not nihilistic. It has a positive and affirmative aspect. What is ultimately negated in the teaching of Emptiness is the Self (Ātman) and any self-substantiated entity (svabhāva). Through the negation of the Self and the self-substantiated entity, true reality manifests itself. Although negation is an essential factor of Mādhyamika philosophy, if it is a mere negation, Mādhyamika philosophy would be nihilistic. It is the law of dependent coorigination (pratītya-samutpāda) that manifests itself through the negation of Ātman and svabhāva, that is, through the realization of the emptiness of everything. In Nāgārjuna, emptiness and dependent coorigination are synonymous. This is why he states in the *Mūlamadhyamakakārikās*, chapter 24,[34] that:

> The "originating dependently" we call "emptiness"; this apprehension, i.e., taking into account [all other things], is the understanding of the middle way. (24:18)
>
> Since there is no *dharma* whatever originating independently, no *dharma* whatever exists which is not empty. (24:19)

Indeed, it is the central task for Mādhyamika philosophy to penetrate into the truth of dependent coorigination.

Dependent coorigination presents the fundamental standpoint of early Buddhism and is its most basic teaching. Historically speaking, the teaching of dependent coorigination has been continually maintained from early Buddhism to Mādhyamika. In this process of development, contrary to the Hīnayāna interpretation of dependent coorigination, which had been stereotyped, Mādhyamika philosophy revived the original dynamic nature of dependent coorigination on the basis of the full realization of Emptiness. Although the teaching of dependent coorigination indicates causality (i.e., a causal relationship from cause to effect), the dependent coorigination as understood by Nāgārjuna does not signify a process from a self-existing cause to a self-existing effect. As he states in *Kārikās* 24:19, "there is no *dharma* whatever originating independently, no *dharma* whatever exists which is not empty." Both the dharma called the cause and the dharma called the effect are equally devoid of a self-existent entity. We know that fuel is the cause of fire and fire the effect of fuel. Let us now ask the further question, Which came first, fire or fuel? If we say fire came first, we face the logical absurdity of fire burning without "fuel." If we say fuel came first, we face the logical absurdity of identifying a cause without knowing about the effect. If we say they appeared together, then all fuels will have to be simultaneously on fire. In Nāgārjuna, dependent coorigination in the true sense is realized when the self-existent entity of each and every thing is completely negated and realized to be empty.

In the first chapter of the *Mūlamadhyamikakārikās*, which may be entitled "An Analysis of Conditioning Causes (*pratyaya*),"[35] Nāgārjuna states:

> Never are any existing things found to originate from themselves, from something else, from both, or from no cause. (1:1)

However, this statement does not deny "originating." Fire does empirically "originate" in fuel. Rather, it denies the existence of any self-substantiated entity. In other words, that statement simply indicates the function of originating dependently without any independent entity. Thus we come to know that in Nāgārjuna, the realization of Emptiness is inseparably connected with the law of dependent coorigination.

The Two Truths Theory

In Mādhyamika philosophy, this identity of emptiness and dependent coorigination is always linked with the two truths theory.[36] You might respond to what has been said above with bafflement and complain that all this philosophizing runs counter to your daily experience of life. No amount of theory can refute the fact that you actually use fuel and fire to barbecue. It is the nature of the fire to cook (however, can it cook itself?), and you enjoy your steak, despite all this talk about both fuel and fire being empty.

The Buddhists do not deny that our everyday ideas of things such as fire and fuel possess practical efficacy. All they say is that they cannot stand philosophical scrutiny. We see the sun rise every morning. The astronomer sees it rise too, but the astronomer knows that this experience will not bear scientific scrutiny because the sun is a fixed star. It cannot rise. It only appears to rise because of the rotation of the earth. Thus we are operating at two levels: From the pragmatic viewpoint, we see the sun rise and also say the sun rises, but from an astronomical viewpoint we deny that this happens.

The Buddhists similarly speak of two levels of truth: the conventional and the ultimate. Conventionally, the sun rises; really, it does not. Conventionally, objects exist; really, they are empty.

Dependent coorigination, before or without the realization of Emptiness, indicates the worldly, conventional truth of birth and death transmigration—that is, the realm of saṁsāra. Speaking from the standpoint of ultimate truth, this realm of transmigration, or saṁsāra, is the realm of suffering based on ignorance. However, in our everyday life, the notion of dependent coorigination, as understood in terms of causality and transmigration, is useful and true conventionally. Speaking from the worldly, or conventional, standpoint, saṁsāra is not merely unreal but includes conventional truth. But the process of saṁsāra (however conventionally true it may be) is rooted in fundamental ignorance and full of suffering, because the causal relationship is understood there without the realization of Emptiness. Thus, it is necessary to overcome ignorance in order to awaken to wisdom; it is essential to be emancipated from transmigration to attain Nirvāṇa—a blissful freedom from birth and death.

This is why Buddhism emphasizes not abiding in saṁsāra, or being attached to the realm of transmigration. In this detachment, the trans-saṁsāric realm is opened up, and ultimate truth is fully realized. However, this does not entail the denial of dependent coorigination; rather, the notion of dependent coorigination is restored in a higher dimension. If ultimate truth is simply distinguished from conventional truth, and the goal of Buddhist life is taken to be beyond mundane life, then it is not the *true* realization of ultimate truth. For this kind of ultimate truth still stands in a relative relationship to conventional truth and is nothing but an extension from conventional truth. Ultimate truth is not merely transcendent, apart from mundane life. Without attaching to the distinction between ultimate and conventional truth, ultimate truth encompasses mundane life and validates its conventional meaning. The two truths theory is not intended merely to be a refutation of worldly, or conventional, truth in favor of ultimate truth, but rather, it indicates the dynamic structure and interrelationship of the two truths.[37]

Identity of Saṁsāra and Nirvāṇa

The identity of emptiness and dependent coorigination and the dynamic interrelation between the two truths in Mādhyamika philosophy are realized fully and religiously in the Mahāyāna teaching of "Saṁsāra-as-it-is is Nirvāṇa."[38]

The goal of Buddhist life is Nirvāṇa, which is to be attained by overcoming saṁsāra. To be emancipated from suffering, one should not be attached to saṁsāra. "Throughout its long history, however, Mahāyāna Buddhism has always emphasized 'Do not abide in Nirvāṇa' as much as 'Do not abide in *saṁsāra*.' If one abides in so-called Nirvāṇa by transcending *saṁsāra*, it must be said that one is not yet free from attachment, an attachment to Nirvāṇa, and is confined by the discrimination between Nirvāṇa and *saṁsāra*."[39] One is still "selfish because that person loftily abides in his or her own 'enlightenment' apart from the sufferings of other *saṁsāra* bound sentient beings. True selflessness and compassion can be realized only by transcending Nirvāṇa to return to and work in the midst of sufferings of the ever-changing world."[40] "Therefore, Nirvāṇa in the Mahāyāna sense, while transcending saṁsāra, is nothing but the realization of *saṁsāra* as *saṁsāra*, no more no less, through the complete returning to *saṁsāra* itself. This is why, in Mahāyāna Buddhism, it is often said of true Nirvāṇa that, '*saṁsāra* as-it-is is Nirvāṇa.'" Nirvāṇa is the real "source of *prajñā* (wisdom) because it is entirely free from the discriminating mind and thus is able to see everything in its uniqueness and distinctiveness without any sense of attachment. It is also the source of *karuṇā* (compassion) because it is unselfishly concerned with the salvation of all others in *saṁsāra* through one's own returning to *saṁsāra*."[41] Thus, Mahāyāna Buddhism emphasizes "not abiding in *saṁsāra* for the sake of wisdom; not abiding in Nirvāṇa to fulfil compassion." This complete no-abiding and free moving from saṁsāra to Nirvāṇa, from Nirvāṇa to saṁsāra is the true Nirvāṇa in the Mahāyāna sense. And this is the soteriological meaning of "Emptiness."[42]

How Buddhism Works

The Importance of the Saṅgha

In the study of Buddhism, the analysis of its monastic institutions seems dull and pale when compared with the charismatic glamour of Buddha's life or the panoramic grandeur of his teachings as they unfold through the ages. But just as the foundation of a building almost invisibly supports the grand superstructure, it is the Saṅgha that sustains Buddhism. So long as the Saṅgha functions, Buddhism works; when the Saṅgha falls, Buddhism collapses.

The role of the Saṅgha in the context of Buddhism is, of course, apparent even to a casual observer. In fact it is quite visible, whether it be in the orange robes of the monks in Śrī Laṅkā, the mauve robes of those in Tibet, the dark brown robes of those in Vietnam, or the black robes of the Zen monks in Japan. But what tends to get overlooked is the Saṅgha's crucial role in sustaining Buddhism as a religious system. To gain a full appreciation of what is involved here, the following points need to be borne in mind.

1. Buddhism was the first major religious tradition in history (with the possible exception of the Jainas, a sect of ancient India) to institutionalize monasticism. Wandering religious mendicants were known in India as far back as the Ṛgvedic period, but it was the Buddha who organized a regular community of monks. It was a major development in the history of religious ideas and one that, like all useful innovations, caught on rapidly causing other religions to follow suit. Although eremitic asceticism had become part of Hinduism by the time Buddhism arose, Buddha's contribution lay in providing it with a cenobitic dimension.[43]

2. Many scholars have made observations to the effect that "the continuity of the monastic organization has been the only constant factor in Buddhist history" or that "what unifying element there is in Buddhism, Mahāyāna and non-Mahāyāna, is provided by the monks and their adherence to the monastic rule." This is an observation so elementary in its nature that it risks being overlooked on account of its obviousness. Buddhism is not designed to function as a religious system without a monastic order—even if the monks themselves decide to lead the life of householders, as in some Pure Land sects.

3. When the Buddha predicted the decline of Buddhism, the main emphasis in the description rested on the decline of the Saṅgha, so that first "monks will not be able to practise analytical insights,"[44] then proper conduct will disappear with "the breaking of the moral habit by the last monk or on the extinction of his life,"[45] and so on.

4. When the Buddha died he did not appoint a successor. The *Mahāparinibbāna Sutta* (VI.1) contains the decisive proclamation: "The Doctrine and Discipline, Ānanda, which I have taught and enjoined upon you is to be your teacher when I am gone." According to J. Kashyap, "within the lifetime of the Buddha, the rules governing the *saṅgha*—not only for the individual but also for the community as a whole—had been so framed and the conduct so perfectly outlined, that there was no need to have a supreme chief, or so to say, a Buddhist pope, after the passing away of the master." Kashyap also regards the Buddhist Saṅgha as "the earliest monastic institution governed by perfect democratic principles which continues to this day."[46] Even after a certain element of exaggeration is allowed for, it is clear that the Buddha did have sufficient confidence in the Saṅgha as a communal body to dispense with the role of a personal leader after him. History, by and large, has justified that confidence.

5. It is clear from the accounts of the Buddhist pilgrims, especially Buddhist pilgrims to India, that often monks who followed *different* sects or systems resided in the *same* monastery side by side. "In theory a monastery could happily contain monks espousing quite different doctrines so long as they *behaved* in the same way—crucially, so long as they adhered to the same monastic code."[47]

6. The heinousness associated with causing a split in the Saṅgha is also an indication of the significance attached to it as the structural foundation of Buddhism. The reasons for the split also often have more to do with differences regarding rules than differences regarding doctrines.

7. It may be argued that the laity always comprised a sizable number of Buddhists. It, however, always took its moral cues, if not its code, from the monks and was never disjoined from the Saṅgha. In fact, technically it constitutes part of it. It seems clear, therefore, that "in spite of considerable diversity in Buddhism there is a relative unity and stability in the moral code and in particular in the order of monks (and, in Mahāyāna countries, nuns)."[48]

8. The Buddhist use of skillful means was alluded to earlier. It might justly be asked: What, if anything, prevented "skillful means" from degenerating into rank opportunism or mere laxity? The crux of the matter here was to chart a middle way between the Scylla of moral laxity and the Charbydis of arbitrary doctrinal speculation. In the matter of doctrinal speculation there "was one factor which limited and restrained the 'skill in means' of these men, and that was the fact that before they wrote their books their minds had been remoulded and disciplined by many years of meditation on traditional lines."[49] In the matter of moral laxity, one can now understand why Tantra has so often been blamed—fairly or unfairly—for Buddhism's decline in India. The persistence of the Vinaya sects and the periodical purifications of the monastic order may reflect a recognition of the crucial significance of the Saṅgha as well.

It must be constantly borne in mind that the Buddhist Saṅgha is regularly described as *Cātuddisa Bhikkhu-Saṅgha* or the Saṅgha of the Four Quarters. It never forsook its claims to universality either in terms of admission or in terms of mission, despite the fact that it consisted of many separate and self-contained communities and of self-governing colonies of monks and nuns. In a very vital sense, the Saṅgha through history has been an extended presence of the Buddha, just as the Christian church is of Jesus Christ. Religions retain a semblance of unity through their doctrinal and historical variety by acknowledging the shared source of authority, which for the Buddhists was represented by the Buddha, the Dharma, and the

Saṅgha. In Buddha's lifetime, that sequence represented the actual order; after the Buddha the order still held, but in reverse.

The Importance of Skillful Means

It is quite clear then that Buddhism works through the exercise of skillful means by the Saṅgha as a corporate body and by its individual members.[50] "The foundation of Buddhism is compassion; its door is convenience."

Four patterns of the exercise of such skillful means by the Saṅgha can be identified for each of the four main faces, facets, or phases of Buddhism we have singled out for a closer look: Theravāda, Mahāyāna, Tantra, and Zen.

In Theravāda Buddhism, though the Arhat ideal was in the forefront of the tradition, we find the Arhats employing skillful means. One must keep in mind that skillful means and compassion were always closely associated. For instance, when one Arhat, Pūrṇa, wanted to go to a somewhat rude frontier area known as Śroṇāparānta to propagate Buddhism, the Buddha warned him that he might be abused, struck, beaten up, and even killed—in that order. It was when the Arhat replied that if abused he would be thankful the inhabitants did not strike him, if struck he would be thankful that they did not beat him up, and so on, that the Buddha permitted him to preach among them.[51]

Mahāyāna Buddhism placed the Bodhisattva ideal in the foreground. There too the Bodhisattva is described as practicing skillful means, to the extent that in one case a Bodhisattva forsakes celibacy cultivated over "four billion two hundred million years" to not disappoint a passionate admirer. He yields to passion out of compassion.[52]

Tantra gave pride of place to the *Siddha*. The Siddha practices his skillful means by taking a personal interest in the spiritual development of his pupil, as Mar-pa did in the case of Mi-la-ras-pa or Milarepa (1040–1123), when he forced him to labor for twelve years to overcome the evil karma of practicing sorcery.[53]

In Zen Buddhism, the *Roshi* is the ideal type who embodies sudden enlightenment and employs skillful means to provoke it in the disciples. "Zen created the method (*upāya*) of 'direct pointing' in order to escape from this vicious circle [of abstract thought], in order to thrust the real immediately in our notice. When reading a difficult book it is of no help to think, 'I *should* concentrate,' for one thinks about concentration instead of what the book has to say, likewise, in studying or practising Zen it is of no help to think about Zen."[54] Alan Watts relates how "Professor Irving Lee, of Northwestern University, used to hold up a matchbox before a class, asking 'What is this?' The students would usually drop squarely into the trap and say, 'A matchbox!' At this the professor would say, 'No, no! It's *this*—' throwing the matchbox at the class, and adding, '*Matchbox* is a noise, is *this* a noise?'"[55] Zen is replete with such applications of skillful means.

The Saṅgha and Skillful Means

In the previous section, various instances of the application of skillful means at the individual level were provided, and this is indeed one way and one level at which we can see how Buddhism works. Buddhism as a religious system works at a corporate level through the application of upāya by the Saṅgha to a whole society or culture. This is done through an elite corps constantly reorganizing itself and devising new skills to deliver the message of the Buddha in different times and climes. The movement is always toward Nirvāṇa, which is achieved by ridding one at the moral level of selfishness, and at a profounder level of a perceptual error of belief in Self, of which selfishness is a psychological expression. The work began with the Theravāda tradition and was continued by Mahāyāna, which called itself "great because it comprises such a wealth of *upāya*, or methods for the realization of *Nirvāṇa*. These methods range from the sophisticated dialectic of Nāgārjuna, whose object is to free the mind from all fixed conceptions, to the Sukhāvatī or Pure Land doctrine of liberation through faith in the power of Amitābha, the Buddha of Boundless Light, who is said to have attained his awakening many aeons before the time of Gautama. They include even the Tantric Buddhism of Medieval India,"[56] and the Way of Zen.

The Saṅgha and the Doctrine of "No-Self"

Not only does Buddhism work through the Saṅgha, utilizing skillful means to ultimately lead one to the doctrine of No-Self and through it to emancipation, but also the Saṅgha might itself be a product of this doctrine. Many religions in ancient India observed the practice of settling down at one place for the duration of the rainy season (*āvāsa*), but none of these except Buddhism developed the institution of the monastery or *vihāra*. Although why this should have happened is not clear, the suggestion is worth considering that "the characteristically Buddhist doctrine of selflessness (*anatta*) may have had, on its reverse side, an emphasis on a wider community of being where the notion of *anatta* could be strengthened, and where a common life could be enjoyed which reduced need for personal possessions and hence personal identity to a minimum."[57]

Buddhism in the Study of Religion

Buddhism as a Missionary Religion

By one account, the religions of the world can be divided into two categories: missionary religions and nonmissionary religions. Three religious traditions can be unambiguously placed in the category of missionary religions: Buddhism, Christianity, and Islam. As missionary religions, each one of these came into contact with many different local and national cultures, and mutual interaction between these international religions and the various national cultures they spread over was inevitable. Although all the three missionary religions have accommodated themselves to the national cultures in which they found themselves, these three religions defined their missionary roles in slightly different ways. These self-definitions affected their patterns of accommodation with national cultures.

By developing a hint provided by Max Weber (1864–1920), a famous sociologist of religion, we can distinguish between emissary, promissory, and commissary missionary activity, depending on the degree of pressure with which the obligation to convert others is felt by those belonging to the tradition. It is clear that, on this reckoning, Buddhism would fall into the emissary category, Christianity would fall into the promissory category, and Islam into the commissary, if the distinction among the three is drawn as follows. Emissary missionary activity involves establishing a presence and minimizing the differences between one's own religion and the religion one encounters while retaining one's commitment to one's own tradition. Promissory missionary activity involves not merely establishing a presence but also promising more to the proselyte; it also involves emphasizing the differences between one's religion and those of others. Commissary missionary activity places the followers of a religion under a commission to convert and maximizes its difference from other religions.

This typology creates room for the suggestion that with whichever cultural tradition Buddhism interacted as a religious tradition, because of its emissary character, it assumed a national form to a far greater extent than missionary religions of the promissory or commissary types. This suggestion may be examined in light of the view that Buddhism underwent more or less five clearly defined stages as it spread outside India to other countries, especially to the north. The first stage was marked by the translation of Buddhist texts into the languages of the cultures involved. This laid the foundation for the second stage when Buddhist thought had to be brought into meaningful relationship with systems of thought already prevalent in the culture. The third stage marked an attempt to retain the Indian connection as Buddhist thought was assimilated to the local condition. Then came the "fourth phase, which is perhaps the most important of all, and normally took 600 years to reach. A truly Chinese, Japanese, Tibetan Buddhism, which no longer did violence to the national character, asserted itself—in China with the Ch'an sect, in Japan in the Kamakura period, in Tibet with the Kahgyudpas and Gelugpas."[58] This was usually followed by a period of decay or inertia.

As it underwent these phases, however, Buddhism went through a cycle of sorts. It started as a cult, then became a sect, then a denomination, then a church, and then a sect again (or even a cult) as a variation of a theme with which the sociologist Ernst Troeltsch (1865–1923) has made us familiar. This process, however, was not as colorless as it might seem, and Buddhism acquired its own particular hue in the different countries and cultures where it made itself at home. These hues may be identified with broad strokes.

Buddhism has acquired a characteristically different hue in the various parts of the world where it has established itself. In *Śrī Laṅkā,* for instance, it has become strongly tinged with Sinhalese nationalism, to the extent that when an emperor mourned the loss of life involved in repelling an invasion, he was told by the Saṅgha that no injury or loss of life was involved except for the injury accidentally caused to some monks in the course of the campaign. In *Burma* it has taken a conservative hue and has preserved the ancient tradition of holding Buddhist councils. The Sixth Great Council was held in Rangoon in 1956. Indeed, of all the Theravāda countries, Burma is said to preserve the tradition in its purest form. In *Thailand* the institution of temporary ordination of monks has become well established, which is also allowed in Burma but not permitted in Śrī Laṅkā. Thailand is also distinguished by possessing the largest number of monks and novices among the Theravāda countries and by the insistence that the King must be Buddhist. *Cambodia* seesawed between Hinduism and Buddhism and then between Buddhism of the Mahāyāna and Theravāda varieties. *Vietnam* ultimately became as much if not more Confucian than Mahāyāna in its orientation.

In other parts of Asia a similar pattern can be identified. If in Śrī Laṅkā Buddhism became an ally of nationalism, under Nichiren (1222–1282) in *Japan* it almost became a form of expansionism. The sect he founded aimed at spreading true Buddhism from Japan all over the world, thus presenting us with "a uniquely Japanese form of Buddhism, having no prototype in China." In *China,* Buddhism became one of the Three Teachings—a very different mode of accommodation—with the understanding that Taoism provided the model for relating to the natural realm, Confucianism to the human realm, and Buddhism to the transcendental realm.

Buddhism and the Dialogue of World Religions

The various ways in which Buddhism adjusted to its host cultures are a tribute to its "skill in means" or, in more modern idiom, to its ability to engage in constructive dialogue with other religions and cultures. The subject of dialogue is moving into the forefront in the study of religion, and in this respect the study of Buddhism acquires special significance. For above all, Buddhist thought emphasizes the interrelatedness of everything and thus provides a philosophical grounding for dialogue. It not only prepares us in this manner philosophically to engage in dialogue, but it also prepares us practically to face the consequences of dialogue. The dialogical interaction of religions invariably, if imperceptibly, involves change. Any encounter, however subtly, changes both the parties involved; by emphasizing the fact that "there is nothing which changes, change is the thing," Buddhism prepares us mentally to be ready for such change. It is perhaps not an accident that the two religions which have been most effectively engaging in dialogue in recent times are Buddhism and Christianity—two traditions with prolonged experience of functioning in religiously plural environments. Buddhism, however, has tended to feel more at ease with such plurality, and its contribution to dialogue is the attitude that it brings to it. A leading living exponent of the tradition, the eminent Buddhist leader of Thailand, Buddhadāsa, represents this attitude, which may be illustrated through the example of water. He points out that at one stage one can distinguish between different kinds of water such as rainwater, ditchwater, well water, underground water, and so on. However, if the pollutants from the water are removed or its location overlooked, these differences disappear and all of them can equally be called water. If one proceeds further along this course, pure water itself turns out to be two parts hydrogen and one part oxygen. "Hydrogen and oxygen are not water. The substance we have been calling water has disappeared. It is void, empty."[59] David C. Chappell uses this simile to point out that Buddhadāsa distinguishes among three levels in terms of which religious pluralism may be understood: 1. conventional distinctions, 2. shared essence, and 3. voidness. According to him it is the identification of the second level which separates Buddhadāsa from the nondualists who see no difference whatever among religions.

We noted the distinction drawn in Mahāyāna Buddhism between two levels of truth. "It is this intermediate stage between conventional truth and the highest truth that is Buddhadāsa's contribution to our quest for a Buddhist attitude toward other religions. At this level, the distinctions between religions are seen as temporary, partial, and secondary in comparison to the more important understanding of the kinship between different religious people. This provides the most complete approach to other religions ever articulated by a Buddhist and provides a basis for differentiation, for parity and collaboration, and for transcendence. Accordingly, we who work in the field of interreligious study and dialogue are deeply indebted to Venerable Bhikkhu Buddhadāsa for his clear leadership in our new world of religious pluralism."[60]

To the process of dialogue in a world characterized by religious pluralism Buddhism brings two rare commodities: a passion for realization and compassion for all living beings, which can blend in an unexpectedly edifying manner. This becomes clear from an incident recounted by Edward Conze:

> Once I had lunch with a Mongol Lama, and tried to get him vegetarian food. He declared that it was quite unnecessary, "We Mongol monks always eat meat, because there is nothing else." So I said, "Well, I only thought of the *Vinaya*," meaning the monastic disciplinary code. But he rejoined at once, "Yes, we know that by habitually eating meat we act against the ordinances of the Lord Buddha. As a result of our sin we may well be reborn in hell. But it is our duty to bring the dharma to the Mongol people, and so we just have to take the consequences as they come."[61]

Should the Mongols be deprived of heaven (read Nirvāṇa) just because one will go to hell?

Recommended Reading

Masao Abe. *Zen and Western Thought*. Honolulu: University of Hawaii Press, 1985. A modern introduction to Zen.

Kenneth K. S. Ch'en. *Buddhism: The Light of Asia*. Woodbury, NY: Barron's Educational Series, 1968. A remarkably lucid exposition of Buddhism in general as religion and culture.

Edward Conze. *Buddhism: Its Essence and Development*. New York: Harper & Brothers, 1959. A valuable survey of Buddhism especially in terms of doctrinal developments.

———. *A Short History of Buddhism*. Bombay: Chetana. 1960. A comprehensive and incisive survey of Buddhism as a historical phenomenon.

———. "Buddhism: The Mahāyāna." In *The Concise Encyclopedia of Living Faiths*, edited by R. C. Zaehner. Boston: Beacon Press, 1959. The best short single introduction to Mahāyāna Buddhism without going into its philosophical complexities.

Roger J. Corless. *The Vision of Buddhism: The Space Under the Tree*. New York: Paragon House, 1989. An engaging introduction to a vast tradition that presents Buddhism as a process of "transformation disguised as information."

Keiji Nishitani. *Religion and Nothingness.* Translated by Jan van Bragt. Berkeley: University of California Press, 1982. A pioneering work by a renowned philosopher on the larger implications of the doctrine of Emptiness.

Walpola Sri Rahula, *What the Buddha Taught* (revised edition). New York: Grove Press, 1974. The best single introduction to the key concepts of Theravāda Buddhism.

Edward J. Thomas. *The Life of Buddha as Legend and History.* London: Routledge & Kegan Paul, 1949. The life of the Buddha presented in its changing perceptions within Buddhism in the light of critical scholarship.

———. *The History of Buddhist Thought.* New York: Barnes & Noble, 1971. A standard and useful account of the history of Buddhist thought.

Paul Williams. *Mahāyāna Buddhism: The Doctrinal Foundations.* London and New York: Routledge, 1989. A sophisticated attempt at tackling the formidable task of charting the intellectual currents of Mahāyāna Buddhism.

Notes

1. I would like to thank the editor for his cooperation in the preparation of this chapter apart from the section on Emptiness.
2. See Walpola Sri Rahula, *What the Buddha Taught* (New York: Grove Press, 1974), 51.
3. Edward Conze, *Buddhism: Its Essence and Development* (New York: Harper & Brothers, 1959), 18.
4. Conze, *Buddhism.*
5. Rahula, *What the Buddha Taught,* 26.
6. Rahula, *What the Buddha Taught,* 58.
7. Conze, *A Short History of Buddhism,* xi–xii.
8. Conze, *A Short History of Buddhism,* xi. Some words have been cited in the lowercase.
9. R. C. Zaehner, ed., *The Concise Encyclopedia of Living Faiths* (Boston: Beacon Press, 1959), 416.
10. Rahula, *What the Buddha Taught,* 26.
11. Edward Conze, *Buddhist Thought in India; Three Phases of Buddhist Philosophy* (Ann Arbor: University of Michigan Press, 1967), 206.
12. Kenneth K. S. Ch'en, *Buddhism: The Light of Asia* (Woodbury, NY: Barron's Educational Series, 1968), 234.
13. Conze, *Buddhist Thought in India,* 30.
14. Nakamura Hajime, "Mahāyāna Buddhism," in *The Encyclopedia of Religion,* ed. Mircea Eliade (New York: Macmillan, 1987), vol. 2, p. 464.
15. For the sake of completeness the following texts may also be mentioned:
    1. *Vimalakīrtinirdeśa* (first century C.E.), or the Instructions of Vimalakīrtī, glorifies a householder as a Bodhisattva.

2. *Mahāparinirvāṇa-Sūtra* (fourth century C.E.) (to be distinguished from the *Mahāparinibbānasutta* in Pali) is remarkable for its willingness to talk of Buddha-nature in terms of Self, albeit as a concession.
3. *Tathāgatagarbha-Sūtra* (third century C.E.) deals with the question of Buddha-nature.
4. *Śrīmālādevīsiṁhanāda-Sūtra* (third century C.E.), or the Sūtra of the Lion's Roar of Śrīmālā, deals with the *dharmakāya* with which the *tathāgatagarbha* is identified. This last term, which means the "womb of the Buddhas," was another formulation of the ultimate in Mahāyāna Buddhism.
5. *Sandhinirmocana-Sūtra* (fourth century C.E.), or the Sūtra of Emancipation from the Connection (of rebirth), which claims to represent the final teaching of the Buddha, deals with the question of *ālayavijñāna* or substratum consciousness (often translated as storehouse consciousness), to explain both the continuity of the subject and the multiplicity of objects in the context of Buddhist idealism.
6. *Śūraṅgamasamādhi-Sūtra* (second century C.E.) deals with the figure of the Bodhisattva Mañjuśrī like the *Aṅgulimālīya-Sūtra* and *Mañjuśrīparinirvāṇa-Sūtra.*
7. *Śūraṅgama-Sūtra* (fourth century C.E.), found only in Chinese, deals with various techniques of meditation and their relative merits.

16. Among these the better known are:
1. *Mahāyānaśraddhotpāda* (first century C.E.), or Awakening of Faith in the Great Vehicle, sometimes ascribed to Aśvaghoṣa but found only in the Chinese version and, according to some scholars, also composed as a putative translation at a later date.
2. *Madhyamakakārikās* (second century C.E.), or aphorisms on the Mādhyamika System, composed by Nāgārjuna, in which Emptiness, a fundamental doctrine in Mahāyāna Buddhism, is philosophically expounded.
3. *Mahāyānasaṅgraha* (fourth century C.E.), or Acceptance of the Great Vehicle, composed by Asaṅga.
4. *Vijñaptimātratā* (fourth century C.E.), or Ideation Only, by Asaṅga's brother Vasubandhu, expounding the view that external objects are mental representations.
5. *Abhisamayālaṅkāra* (fourth century C.E.), or the Memorial Verses on Reunion (with the Absolute), ascribed to Matsyendranātha and particularly favored in Tibet, which offers a summary of the *Aṣṭasāhasrikā.*
6. *Yogācārabhūmiśāstra* (fourth century C.E.), or The Treatise on Stages of Yogācāra, said to have been recited by Maitreya himself to help Asaṅga convince people of the truth of the doctrine of Void, which also charts the course of a Bodhisattva's career.

17. Edward Conze, "Buddhism: The Mahāyāna," in *The Concise Encyclopedia of Living Faiths,* ed. R. C. Zaehner (Boston: Beacon Press, 1959), 308.
18. Rahula, *What the Buddha Taught,* xv–xvi.
19. Rahula, *What the Buddha Taught,* 1.
20. Edward Conze, trans., *Buddhist Scriptures* (Harmondsworth: Penguin Books, 1959), 26.

21. Rahula, *What the Buddha Taught*, 9.
22. Information kindly provided by Richard P. Hayes, Jérôme Ducor, H. L. Senaviratna, Rita M. Gross, and the Embassy of Myanmar in Washington, D.C.
23. James Legge, trans., *A Record of Buddhist Kingdoms* (New York: Dover Publications, 1965; first published 1886), 57–58.
24. Ch'en, *Buddhism: The Light of Asia*, 28.
25. See Garma C. C. Chang, *The Buddhist Teaching of Totality: The Philosophy of Hwa Yen Buddhism* (University Park and London: Pennsylvania State University Press, 1971), 60. Please note that in the following pages the famous treatise of Nāgārjuna, otherwise cited as *Mūlamadhyamakakārikā* or *Mūlamadhyamakakārikāḥ*, has also been referred to as *Mūlamadhyamakakārikās*, that is, in the English plural.
26. In the fifteenth chapter of *Mūlamadhyamakakārikās*, Nāgārjuna examines *svabhāva* as follows:

    The production of a self-existent thing by a conditioning cause is not possible, [For] being produced through dependence on a cause, a self-existent thing would be "something which is produced" (kṛtaka). (15-1)

    How, indeed, will a self-existent thing become "something which is produced"? Certainly, a self-existent thing [by definition] is "not-produced" and is independent of anything else. (15-2)

    If there would be an existent thing by its own nature, there could not be "non-existence" of that [thing]. (15-8)

    [An opponent asks:] If there is no basic self-nature, of what will there be "otherness"? [Nāgārjuna answers:] If there is basic self-nature, of what will there be "otherness"? (15-9)

    See Frederick J. Streng, *Emptiness: A Study in Religious Meaning* (Nashville: Abingdon Press, 1967), 199–200.
27. Streng, *Emptiness*, 204.
28. *The Tannisho* (Kyoto: Ryukoku Translation Center, 1966), 22.
29. See J. Cobb and C. Ives, eds. *The Emptying God: A Buddhist-Jewish-Christian Conversation* (New York: Orbis Press, 1990), 162–169.
30. *Mūlamadhyamakakārikā* (24-11). See Streng, *Emptiness*, 213.
31. Cobb and Ives, *The Emptying God*, 9.
32. Cobb and Ives, *The Emptying God*, 14. See also Hans Küng, *Does God Exist?* (Garden City, NY: Doubleday, 1980), 684–685.
33. In the last two subsections the author is indebted to Nagao Gadjin, *Chukan to Yuishiki* (Tokyo: Iwanami, 1978), 6–21; G. Nagao, *The Fundamental Standpoint of Mādhyamika Philosophy*, trans. John Keenan (New York: SUNY, 1989) and Yuichi Kajiyama, *Kū no Ronri* (Tokyo: Kadokawa, 1980).
34. Streng, *Emptiness*, 213.
35. Streng, *Emptiness*, 183.
36. Mādhyamika philosophy recognizes two levels of reality: the conventional (*samvṛti*) and the ultimate (*paramārtha*). As Gadjin Nagao explains:

    The two terms, worldly convention and ultimate meaning, correspond respectively to the ideas of the worldly (*laukika*) and the world transcendent, or that which is beyond the world (*lokottara*). The world of ordinary, everyday consciousness is here referred to as the worldly, which includes not only the biological world but also the human world of culture and society. The higher, transcendent world is regarded as a religious, numinous world, and ultimate meaning is established as a negation of the everyday world, beyond it and transcendent to it.

See Gadjin Nagao, *The Fundamental Standpoint of Mādhyamika Philosophy* (Albany: State University of New York Press, 1989), 23.

37. This dynamic interrelationship of the two truths is explained by Nagao as follows (*The Fundamental Standpoint of Mādhyamika Philosophy,* 31, with adaptation):

 Each of these two truths is useful, and as such true: each is true, and as such useful. The two truths are simultaneously dependently cooriginating and empty. Indeed it was in virtue of insight into the two truths that Nāgārjuna was able to identify emptiness with dependent coorigination. Put conversely, emptiness is not simply the silence of ultimate meaning, but is also the actual functioning of worldly conventions; dependent coorigination is not simply conventional, but is the dependent coorigination of awakening to ultimate meaning.

38. Masao Abe, *Zen and Western Thought* (Honolulu: University of Hawaii Press, 1985), 178 (with adaptation).
39. Abe, *Zen and Western Thought.*
40. Abe, *Zen and Western Thought,* 49 (with adaptation).
41. Abe, *Zen and Western Thought,* 178 (with adaptation).
42. See also Cobb and Ives, *The Emptying God,* 29–33.
43. See Sukumar Dutt, *Early Buddhist Monachism* (New York: Asia Publishing House, 1960), 12.
44. Edward Conze, ed., *Buddhist Texts Through the Ages* (New York: Philosophical Library, 1954), 47.
45. Conze, *Buddhist Texts Through the Ages,* 48.
46. Bhikkhu J. Kashyap, "Origin and Expansion of Buddhism" in Kenneth W. Morgan, ed., *The Path of the Buddha* (New York: The Ronald Press Company, 1956), 35. Some words cited in the lowercase.
47. Paul Williams, *Mahāyāna Buddhism: The Doctrinal Foundations* (London and New York: Routledge, 1989), 4.
48. Williams, *Mahāyāna Buddhism,* 6.
49. Conze, *A Short History of Buddhism,* 46.
50. Conze, "Buddhism: The Mahāyāna," 307–308.
51. Conze, *Buddhism,* 71. Italics dispensed with.
52. Garma C. C. Chang, ed., *A Treasury of Mahāyāna Sūtras* (University Park and London: Pennsylvania State University Press, 1983), 433.
53. W. Y. Evans-Wentz, ed. *Tibet's Great Yogi Milarepa,* 2d ed. (New York: Oxford University Press, 1951), 130–131.
54. Alan Watts, *The Way of Zen* (New York: Vintage Books, 1957), 127.
55. Watts, *The Way of Zen,* 130.
56. Watts, *The Way of Zen,* 59.
57. T. O. Ling, "Saṅgh," in *A Dictionary of Comparative Religion,* ed. S. G. F. Brandon (New York: Macmillan, 1970), 555, with some words cited in the lowercase.
58. Conze, *A Short History of Buddhism,* 46.

59. Donald K. Swearer, ed., *Me and Mine: Selected Essays of Bhikkhu Buddhadāsa* (Albany: State University of New York Press, 1989), 147.
60. David C. Chappell, "Six Buddhist Attitudes Towards Other Religions," in *Radical Conservatism: Buddhism in the Contemporary World,* ed. Sulak Sivaraksa et al. (Bangkok: Thai Inter-Religious Commission for Development, 1990), 551–552.
61. Conze, "Buddhism: The Mahāyāna," 307–308.

CHAPTER 3

Confucianism

Tu Wei-ming

What Is the Confucian Way?

There is something ethically elevating about Jesus Christ's exhortation to turn the other cheek: It appeals to the streak of self-effacing idealism in many of us. We believe that this unilateral altruism symbolizes a higher virtue than simply the revengeful "eye for an eye and tooth for a tooth." It might come as a surprise that another response is possible, no less noble, but characterized by lofty pragmatism rather than sheer idealism. When Confucius was asked: "Should one not return malice with kindness?" he replied, "If you return malice with kindness, what will you return kindness with? Therefore, return malice with uprightness (justice), but return kindness with kindness."[1] Perhaps, for us, the more intriguing ethical principle was advocated by Mencius: "The great man (a profoundly moral person) need not keep his word nor does he necessarily see his action through to the end. He aims only at what is right."[2] We are about to embark on the study of an ethico-religious tradition that so delicately shifts the moral focus from abstract principles to lived realities that it challenges many of our familiar categories in the comparative study of ethics and religion.

Defining Confucian Spirituality

Are we isolated individuals, or do we live as a center of interpersonal relationships? Is moral self-knowledge necessary for personal growth? Can any society prosper or endure without developing a basic sense of duty and responsibility among its members? Should our pluralistic society deliberately cultivate shared values and a common ground of human understanding? As we become acutely aware of our earth's vulnerability and increasingly wary of our own fate as an "endangered species," what are the critical spiritual questions we must ask?

The fundamental concern of the Confucian tradition is learning to be human. The focus is not on the human in contrast with nature or with Heaven but the human that seeks harmony with nature and mutuality with Heaven. Indeed, learning to be human, in the Confucian perspective, entails a broadening and deepening process that acknowledges the interconnectedness of all the modalities of existence defining the human condition. Through an ever-expanding network of relationships encompassing the family, community, nation, world, and beyond, the Confucian seeks to realize humanity in its all-embracing fullness. This process of inclusion helps deepen our self-knowledge at the same time through a ceaseless effort to make our body healthy, our mind-and-heart alert, our soul pure, and our spirit brilliant. Self-cultivation is an end in itself and its primary purpose is self-realization.

A defining characteristic of Confucian humanism is faith in the creative transformation of our human condition as a communal act and as a dialogical response to Heaven. This involves the integration of four dimensions of humanity: self, community, nature, and Heaven. An exploration of Confucian spirituality must take the following into consideration: the self as creative transformation; the community as a necessary vehicle for human flourishing; nature as the proper home for our form of life; and Heaven as the source of ultimate self-realization.

Self as Creative Transformation

Confucius made it explicit that learning is for the sake of the self rather than for the sake of others.[3] On the surface, this seems to imply a sense of individuality fundamentally different from the conventional view of the primacy of the group in Confucian ethics. However, the Confucian insistence on learning for the sake of the self is predicated on the conviction that self-cultivation is an end in itself rather than a means to an end. Those who are committed to the cultivation of their personal life for its own sake can create inner resources for self-realization unimaginable to those who view self-cultivation merely as a tool for external goals such as social advancement and political success. Although we are obligated to assume social responsibility and participate in political affairs, it is self-cultivation, as the root, securely grounding us in our lifeworld that enables us to participate in society and politics as independent moral agents rather than pawns in a game of power relationships. If we do not take self-realization seriously, we may easily allow ourselves to be defined by power and wealth totally external to our inner resources and our personal sense of worth.

For the Confucians, a personal sense of worth is vitally important, because their commitment to improving the world from within compels them to take the status quo as the point of departure for their spiritual journey. If they do not subscribe to the thesis that learning is primarily for self-improvement, the demand for social service will undermine the integrity of self-cultivation as a noble end in itself. Therefore, learning as character-building is for the sake of self-realization. The self so conceived is an open system involved in continuous transformation; it is never a static structure. The idea of the self as a discrete entity, isolated from the world, is diametrically opposed to the Confucian self as an open, dynamic, and transformative process.

The Confucian self, rooted in personal worth, seeks to generate its inner resources for self-transformation. Self-transformation, the result of self-cultivation, signifies a process of self-realization. However, since the idea of selfhood devoid of communication with the outside world is alien to the Confucian tradition, Confucian self-transformation does not take the form of searching exclusively for one's own inner spirituality. Rather, in the Confucian perspective, authentic self-transformation involves tapping spiritual resources from the cumulative symbolic tradition (culture), the sympathetic resonance of society, the vital energy of nature, and the creative power of Heaven.

Community as a Necessary Vehicle for Human Flourishing

A distinctive feature of the Confucian spiritual orientation is the view that the human community is an integral part of our quest for self-realization. The idea of cutting loose from our primordial ties—ethnicity, gender, language, land, and other intractable realities of life—as a precondition for our salvation is not even a rejected possibility in the Confucian tradition. Confucians are profoundly aware that we are embedded in this world and that our spiritual journey must begin at home here and now. Although the sense of embeddedness may impose a structural limitation on the range of possibility we can realistically envision in our spiritual self-transformation, it does not inhibit us from shaping the form of life most appropriate to our human condition. The Confucian proposal that we begin our spiritual journey at home is based on the strong belief that our self, far from being an isolated individuality, is experientially and practically a center of relationships. As a center of relationships, it constantly enters into communication with a variety of human beings. The significance of the other for our self-cultivation is evident, because we rarely cultivate ourselves in isolation. It is through constant human interaction that we gradually learn to appreciate our selfhood as a transformative process. Indeed, our feelings, thoughts, and ideas are not necessarily our private properties. While they are intensely personal, they need not be private; they are often better thought of as shareable public goods. The willingness to share empowers us to generate a dynamic process of interchange, first with members of our family and, then, with our neighborhood community, and beyond.[4]

This broadening process is central to the Confucian project of self-cultivation. As the opening statement of the Confucian classic, the *Great Learning*, states:

> The ancients who wished to illuminate "brilliant virtue" all under Heaven first governed their states. Wishing to govern their states, they first regulated their families. Wishing to regulate their families, they first cultivated their personal lives. Wishing to cultivate their personal

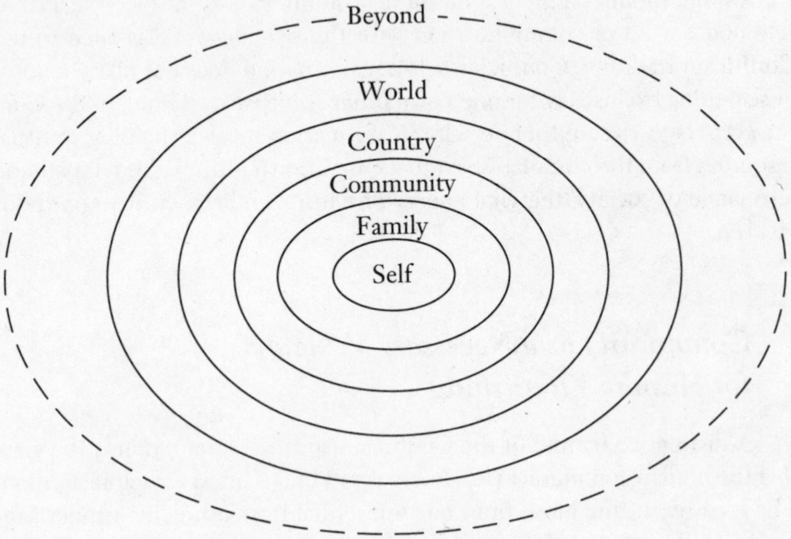

lives, they first rectified their hearts and minds. Wishing to rectify their hearts and minds, they first authenticated their intentions. Wishing to authenticate their intentions, they first refined their knowledge. The refinement of knowledge lay in the study of things. For only when things are studied is knowledge refined; only when knowledge is refined are intentions authentic; only when intentions are authentic are hearts and minds rectified; only when hearts and minds are rectified are personal lives cultivated; only when personal lives are cultivated are families regulated; only when families are regulated are states governed; only when states are governed is there peace all under Heaven. Therefore, from the Son of Heaven to the common people, all, without exception, must take self-cultivation as the root.[5]

This statement suggests not only a broadening but also a deepening process. The way that the community is "embodied" in our self-transformation implies a continuous interplay between an inclusive process and a penetrating awareness. The assumption is that the more we broaden ourselves to involve others, the more we are capable of deepening our self-awareness; our persistence in deepening our self-awareness is the basis for our fruitful interaction with an ever-expanding network of human-relatedness.

Nature as Home

The Confucian ideal of human flourishing is, strictly speaking, not anthropological and is certainly not anthropocentric. Men, or rather human beings, are not the measure of all things. Such an idea strikes the Confucians as parochial. The proper measure for humanity is cosmological as well as anthropological; indeed it is "anthropocosmic." In the order of things, nature provides not only sustenance for life but also an inspiration for sustainable life. Implicit in the course of nature—the alternations of day and night and the changes of the four seasons—is a lesson in the enduring pattern of transformation: regularity, balance, and harmony.

Human civilization through time has endured natural calamities such as floods and hurricanes, but, despite the hardships of survival, the Confucians find nature a hospitable environment for our existence. They feel fortunate to have been blessed with "Heaven's timeliness and Earth's efficaciousness" and with the "wind and water," essentially wholesome for good health. Nature is revered for its generosity and its grandeur. Its awe-inspiring presence enables us to appreciate the fecundity and sanctity of our "home":

> The sky before us is only this bright, shining mass; but when viewed in its unlimited extent, the sun, moon, stars, and constellations are suspended in it and all things are covered by it. The earth before us is but a handful of soil; but in its breadth and depth, it sustains mountains like Hua and Yüeh without feeling their weight, contains the rivers and seas without letting them leak away, and sustains all things. The mountain before us is but a fistful of straw; but in all the vastness of its size, grass and trees grow upon it, birds and beasts dwell on it, and stores of precious things [minerals] are discovered in it. The water before us is but a spoonful of liquid, but in all its unfathomable depth, the monsters, dragons, fishes, and turtles are produced in them, and wealth becomes abundant because of it.[6]

This sense of nature as home empowers the Confucians to find ultimate meaning in ordinary human existence, to cultivate a regularized, balanced, and harmonious life-style, and to regard what many other religions refer to as "secular" as "sacred."[7]

Heaven as the Source of Ultimate Self-transformation

Although radical transcendence, such as conceptualizing God as the "wholly other," is absent in Confucian symbolism, Heaven as a source for moral creativity, meaning of life, and ultimate self-transformation features prominently throughout the Confucian tradition. In this sense, all major Confucian thinkers are profoundly religious. Their ways of being religious are significantly different from those in organized religions such as Christianity, Buddhism, or Islam, but their reverence for life, commitment to work, and dedication to ultimate self-transformation are based on a calling comparable in intensity of feeling and seriousness of purpose to any of the great world religions.

The Confucian calling presupposes that Heaven is omniscient and omnipresent, if not omnipotent. What we do here and now as human beings has implications for ourselves, for our human community, for nature, and for Heaven. We need not appropriate the Way of Heaven by departing from where we are here and now, but since the Way of Heaven is right here, near at hand, and inseparable from our ordinary daily existence, what we do in the confines of our home is not only anthropologically but also cosmologically significant. If we properly nurture our human way, we will never be estranged from the Way of Heaven. Indeed, as we learn to appreciate the richness of ordinary daily existence, we understand that the great mystery of life is inherent in our common experience of living, as if the secret code of the Way of Heaven is embedded in the human way.

However, our internal organic connectedness with the transcendent through our own personal experience makes us aware of our inadequacy as well as strength because we are charged with the awesome responsibility of realizing Heaven's Way through our humble human endeavors. The deepest meaning of humanity lies in its authentic manifestation as the guardian of nature and the cocreator of the cosmos:

> Only those who are absolutely sincere can fully develop their nature. If they can fully develop their nature, they can fully develop the nature of others. If they can fully develop the nature of others, they can then fully develop the nature of things. If they can fully develop the nature of things, they can then assist in the transforming and nourishing process of Heaven and Earth. If they can assist in the transforming and nourishing process of Heaven and Earth, they can thus form a trinity with Heaven and Earth.[8]

It is humanly possible to assist in the transforming and nourishing process of Heaven and Earth; it is authentically human to form a trinity with Heaven and Earth; and it is our categorical imperative to respond to Heaven's calling to serve as the guardian of nature and the cocreator of the cosmos.

The Formation of the Confucian Tradition[9]

Confucianism as an East Asian Way of Life

Confucianism is a worldview, a social ethic, a political ideology, a scholarly tradition, and a way of life. Although Confucianism is often grouped together with Buddhism, Christianity, Hinduism, Islam, Judaism, and Taoism as a major historical religion, it is neither an institutionalized religion nor a worship-centered religion. Yet, it has exerted profound influence on East Asian political culture as well as on East Asian spiritual life. Since Confucianism has made such an indelible mark on the government, society, education, and family of East Asia, the Sinic world (including industrial and socialist East Asia—Japan, South Korea, Taiwan, Hong Kong, Singapore, mainland China, North Korea, and Vietnam) has been characterized as "Confucian." Whether or not this is adequate, it is beyond dispute that Confucian ethical and spiritual values have served, for well over twenty-five hundred years, as the source of inspiration as well as the court of appeal for human interaction at all levels—between individuals, communities, and nations in the Sinic world.

Confucianism was not an organized missionary tradition, but by the first century B.C.E., it had spread to those East Asian countries under the influence of Chinese literate culture. The age of Confucianism, in the centuries following the Confucian revival of Sung times (960–1279 C.E.), embraced Chosŏn dynasty Korea and the Late Le dynasty in Vietnam since the fifteenth century and Tokugawa Japan since the seventeenth century. Prior to the advent of Western powers in East Asia in the mid-nineteenth century, the Confucian persuasion was so predominant in the art of governance, the form and content of elite education, and the moral discourse of the populace that China, Korea, and Japan were all distinctively "Confucian" states. We may add that East Asian communities in Southeast Asia and throughout the world have also been under Confucian influence.

The story of Confucianism does not begin with Confucius (Latinized form of K'ung-fu-tzu, Master K'ung; 551–479 B.C.E.). The Chinese term, *Ju-chia*, which is inadequately rendered as Confucianism, literally means the "family of scholars," signifying a genealogy, a school, or a tradition of learning. Confucius was not the founder of Confucianism in the sense that Buddha was the founder of Buddhism and Christ was the founder of Christianity. However, although Confucius failed to live up to the highest Confucian ideal, "inner sageliness and outer kingliness," he has been honored as the foremost teacher, a timely sage, and the true embodiment of the Confucian Way.

Confucianism is a historical phenomenon. The emergence of the Confucian tradition as a way of life, its elevation to the status of a state cult, its decline as a moral persuasion, its continuous influence in society, its revival as a living faith, its metamorphosis into a political ideology, its response to the Western impact, and its modern transformation can all be analyzed as integral parts of East Asian history. The Confucians do not have an esoteric interpretation of their past that is fundamentally different from the historical narrative. Indeed, a distinctive feature of Confucianism is its expressed intention to regard the everyday human world as profoundly spiritual. By regarding "the secular as sacred," the Confucians try to refashion the world from within according to their cultural ideal of the unity between the human community and Heaven. As a major ethical and spiritual tradition, Confucianism emerged in ancient China originally as a tiny stream among several currents of thought. It gradually grew in strength to become the dominant intellectual force. The period of 550 to 200 B.C.E., historically known as the age of the "hundred philosophers," was a golden age in classical Chinese thought. The four main competing intellectual schools—Confucianism, Taoism, Moism, and Legalism—offered substantially different responses to the decline and fall of the glorious Chou civilization, an elaborate "feudal" ritual system that had provided economic well-being, political order, social stability, and cultural elegance in China proper for several centuries. These schools vigorously contended in their attempt to propose the best solutions to the problems of their day, each trying to bring order to chaos and give meaning to life under constant threat of brutal warfare.

The Taoists, who developed a philosophy of nature and freedom, advocated a total rejection of human civilization, which they believed to be the source of spiritual pollution. The Moists were concerned about the aggressiveness of hegemonic states, the wastefulness of the aristocratic style of life, and pervasive injustice. They organized themselves into military units to bring about love and peace through self-sacrifice. The Legalists accepted the inevitable disintegration of the "feudal" ritual system and allied themselves with the centers of power. The Confucians opted for a long-term solution to the collapse of the Chou dynasty through commitment to education as character-building. They believed that one could attain true nobility through self-cultivation and inner enlightenment. Their ideal humanity (sagehood) and their practical model (the profound person) were represented not only by prophets and philosophers but also teachers and statesmen. This combination of theory and practice endowed them with spiritual vision and political mission and enabled them to form a fellowship of those who shared a common faith and creed.

For several centuries, Confucius was counted as one of the major Chinese philosophers and Confucianism as one of the schools in the Chinese world of thought. It took a few generations of persistent effort by the followers of Confucius to establish the "scholarly tradition" advocated by Confucius as the dominant intellectual force in China. However, several centuries had elapsed before the establishment of Confucian teaching as the official ideology of imperial China. Even then, Confucianism never existed as an exclusive orthodoxy of the state. The attempt to promote Confucianism as the state ideology in the second century B.C.E. at the expense of other schools was short-lived, though successful. Rather, it was the gradual expansion of the Confucian cultural movement into different layers of an alien despotic polity and various echelons of society that empowered the tradition to become truly influential. The carriers of the Confucian tradition were the scholars who, by self-definition, were men of action as well as ideas. Through their efforts, the Confucian persuasion penetrated virtually all dimensions of life in traditional China and, by implication, the Sinic world at large.

As a viable way of life for so many for so long, Confucianism has been viewed both as a philosophy and as a religion. As an all-encompassing humanism that neither denies nor slights Heaven, it is not only the faith and creed of Chinese scholars but also a way of life in East Asia. Indeed, Confucianism is so deeply ingrained in the fabric of Sinic societies and politics that Confucian ethics is often taken for granted as self-evident. East Asians may profess themselves to be Shintoists, Taoists, Buddhists, Muslims, or Christians, but seldom do they cease to be Confucians.

Historical Context

Confucius considered himself a "transmitter" rather than a "creator"; he consciously tried to reanimate the old to attain the new. He proposed that we retrieve the meaning of the past by breathing vitality into seemingly outmoded rituals. Confucius' love of antiquity was motivated by his strong desire to understand why certain rituals, such as the ancestral cult, reverence for Heaven, and the mourning ceremonies, survived for centuries. His journey into the past was a search for roots—the roots of humanity's deepest needs for belonging and communication. He had faith in the cumulative culture. The fact that traditional ways had declined did not diminish their great potential for innovation in the future. Confucius' sense of history was so strong that he saw himself as a conservationist responsible for the continuity of the cultural values and the social norms that had worked so well for the Chou civilization.

The scholarly tradition envisioned by Confucius can be traced back to the sage-kings of antiquity. Although the earliest dynasty confirmed by archaeology to date is the Shang dynasty (ca. twenty-third century B.C.E.), the history that Confucius claimed to have been relevant was much earlier. Confucius may have initiated a cultural process known in the West as Confucianism, but he and those who followed him considered themselves part of a tradition, later identified by Chinese historians as the Ju-chia, "scholarly tradition," which had its origins two millennia previously when, legend has it, the sage-kings Yao and Shun formed a moral community by their exemplary teaching.

Confucius may have made reference to the golden age of Yao and Shun as the "great harmony," but his hero was the Duke of Chou (d. 1094 B.C.E.), who was said to have helped to consolidate and refine the "feudal" ritual system, thus enabling the Chou dynasty to survive in relative peace and prosperity for more than five centuries. Inspired by the statesmanship of the Duke, Confucius' lifelong dream was to be in a position where he could emulate the Duke by putting into practice the political ideas, the humane government (*jen-cheng*), that he had learned from the ancient sage-kings. Although Confucius was never given a chance to put his political ideals into practice, his conception of politics as moral persuasion became a defining characteristic of East Asian political culture.

The idea of Heaven, unique in Chou cosmology, was compatible with the concept of the Lord-on-High in the Shang dynasty. The Lord-on-High may have referred to the progenitor of the Shang royal lineage, thus enabling the Shang kings to claim their position as divine descendants as the emperors of Japan later did. Heaven to the Chou kings, however, was a much more generalized anthropomorphic God. They believed that the Mandate of Heaven (the functional equivalent of the will of the Lord-on-High) was not constant and that there was no guarantee that the descendants of the Chou royal house would be entrusted with kingship, a lesson they learned from their successful conquest of the Shang dynasty. Had the Mandate of Heaven been fixed, they may have reasoned among themselves, they could not have dislodged it from the Shang kings. The very fact that the Shang dynasty had lost its Mandate unequivocally indicated that Heaven might look for other criteria for bestowing its Mandate. This may have been the justification for the thesis: "Heaven sees with the eyes of the people. Heaven hears with the ears of the people."[10] The virtues of the kings, in other words, were essential for the maintenance of their power and authority. Confucius and his followers never failed to underscore the point that virtue, the result of moral self-cultivation, is an inseparable dimension of political leadership.

This emphasis on benevolent rulership, as attested to in the pronouncements of numerous bronze inscriptions, was both a reaction to the collapse of the Shang dynasty and an affirmation of a deep-rooted worldview. Although the Chou military conquest, which may have occurred in 1046 B.C.E.,[11] was the immediate cause of the downfall of the Shang dynasty, the Chou conquerors strongly believed that the last Shang king lost the Mandate of Heaven because of his debauchery. Since the Mandate of Heaven was never wedded to a particular lineage and since the only guarantee for the preservation of the Mandate was the ruler's superior performance, the Chou kings were anxious to retain the trust of the people. The rhetoric of benevolent rulership was also predicated on the belief that, since one is intimately connected with one's ancestral line (which, for the royal household, extends to virtually all members of the nobility), one acts on behalf of a community. The mutuality between Heaven and the human community further demands that the kings, as sons of Heaven, conduct themselves in the spirit of filial piety, not only toward their own ancestors but toward Heaven as well. The Confucian idea of the state as an enlarged family may have been genetically derived from this historical experience in Chou feudalism, but the ethical justification that rulers, like parents, must assume full responsibility for the well-being of the people is predicated on the Confucian conception that politics is primarily moral persuasion. Partly because of the vitality of the "feudal" ritual system and partly because of the strength of the royal household itself, the Chou kings were able to control their kingdom for several centuries, but in 771 B.C.E. they were forced to move their capital eastward to present-day Lo-yang to avoid barbarian attacks from central Asia. The real power then passed into the hands of feudal lords. However, the surviving line of the Chou kings continued to be recognized in name, enabling them to exercise some measure of symbolic control. The "feudal" ritual system was based on blood ties, marriage alliances, and old covenants as well as newly negotiated contracts. It was an elaborate system of mutual dependence. The use of cultural values and social norms for the maintenance of inter-state as well as domestic order was premised on a shared political vision: Authority lies in universal kingship, which is heavily invested with ethical and religious power by the Mandate of Heaven. Organic social solidarity was achieved not by legal constraint but by ritual observance. It is important to note that the Confucian predilection for family-centered social ethics, informed by ritual behavior and the Confucian aversion against impersonal social control through law, continues to influence East Asian societies to this date.

Ironically, by Confucius' time, the "feudal" ritual system had been so fundamentally undermined that political crises precipitated a profound sense of moral decline. The center of symbolic control could no longer keep the Chou ritual system from total disintegration. Archaeological and textual evidence shows that the period witnessed both unprecedented economic growth (e.g., the use of iron for agricultural implements, the availability of metallic coinage, commercialization, and urbanization) and a loosening of the kinship bonds of rigidly stratified society. Both contributed to a major restructuring of the political system. The Confucian concern for stability was, therefore, a response to the disintegration of order. However, by responding to the social chaos, what Confucius offered was much more fundamental than the expedient means of restoring orderliness. He opted to raise the ultimate question of how to learn to be human. In so doing he attempted to reformulate and revitalize institutions that had been critical to political stability and social order for centuries: the family, the school, the local community, the state, and the kingdom. Confucius did not accept the status quo, which held that wealth and power spoke the loudest. He felt that virtue, both as a personal quality and as a requirement for leadership, was essential for individual dignity, communal solidarity, and political order.

The Life of Confucius

If the English-speaking community were to choose one word to characterize the Chinese way of life for the last two thousand years, the word would be *Confucian*. It is assumed that no other person in Chinese history has so profoundly influenced the thoughts and actions of his people. He was a teacher of humanity, a transmitter of culture, an interpreter of history, and a molder of the Chinese mind. Considering Confucius' tremendous importance, his life seems starkly undramatic, or, as a Chinese expression has it, "plain and real." The plainness and reality of Confucius' life, however, illustrate the fact that his humanity was not a revealed truth but an expression of self-cultivation, the result of a unceasing effort on the part of an individual human being to shape his own destiny. What Confucius exemplifies to intellectuals is faith in the possibility of ordinary human beings to become awe-inspiring sages and worthies; but even to the commoners, the belief that one can become successful, even prominent, through self-effort, is not merely an imagined possibility but a practicable idea. The insistence that human beings are teachable, improvable, and indeed perfectible—through personal and communal endeavor—is deeply rooted in the Chinese mentality.

Although the facts about Confucius' life are scanty, they provide us with an unusually precise time frame and historical context. Confucius was born in the twenty-second year of the reign of Duke Hsiang of Lu (551 B.C.E.). The traditional claim that he was born on the twenty-seventh day of the eighth lunar month has been generally accepted by historians, thus September 28 is widely observed in East Asia as Confucius' birthday. It is an official holiday, "Teachers' Day," in Taiwan, a day of cultural celebration in mainland China, Hong Kong, Singapore, and more recently in California. Confucius was born in Ch'ü-fu in the small feudal state of Lu (now Shantung Province), which was noted for its preservation of the ritual and music of the Chou civilization. His family name was K'ung and his personal name Ch'iu, but he is referred to as either "K'ung Tzu" or "K'ung Fu-tzu" ("Master K'ung") throughout Chinese history. The adjectival "Confucian," conveniently derived from the Latinized "Confucius," is not a meaningful term in Chinese; nor is the term "Confucianism," which was coined in eighteenth-century Europe.

Confucius' ancestors were probably members of the aristocracy who had become poverty-stricken commoners by the time of his birth. His father died when he was only three years old. Instructed first by his mother and then by a host of other teachers, Confucius distinguished himself as an indefatigable student in his teens. Thus, Confucius inadvertently initiated a great tradition in East Asian education: the exemplary teaching, often through oral transmission, of the mother. The centrality of the mother as an educator in Confucian learning is widely recognized but seldom analyzed. Confucius recalled toward the end of his life that his heart became set upon learning at fifteen. A historical account notes that, even though he was already known as an informed young scholar, he inquired about everything on a visit to the Grand Temple. Confucius' inquisitiveness made it clear to his followers that one of the highest virtues in Confucian ethics is love of learning.

Confucius served in minor government posts, managing stables and keeping books for granaries, before he married a woman of similar background when he was nineteen. It appears that he may have already acquired a reputation as a multitalented scholar. He had just turned twenty when he named his newborn son "Carp," allegedly after a gift from the Lu King. Confucius' mastery of the six arts—ritual, music, archery, charioteering, calligraphy, and arithmetic—and his familiarity with classical traditions, notably poetry and history, helped him to start a brilliant teaching career in his thirties. The combination of learning and teaching enabled Confucius to shape the life of a scholar as both the recipient and transmitter of a cultural tradition.

We do not know who Confucius' teachers were. There is an obviously apocryphal story that he sought instruction on ritual from the Taoist master, Lao Tzu, but it is well known that he made a conscientious effort to find the right masters to teach him, among other things, ritual and music. Confucius is known as the first private teacher in China, for he was instrumental in establishing the art of teaching as a vocation, even as a way of life. Before Confucius, aristocratic families had hired tutors to educate their sons, and government officials had instructed their subordinates in administrative and bureaucratic matters, but he was the first person to devote his whole life to learning and teaching for the purpose of transforming and improving society. All human beings, he believed, could benefit from self-cultivation. He inaugurated a humanities program for potential leaders, opened the doors of education to all, and defined learning not merely as the acquisition of knowledge but also as character-building. The spiritual value of this seemingly secular humanistic enterprise lies in its implicit faith that ultimate self-transformation in ordinary human existence is not only possible but practicable.

For the historical Confucius, the primary function of education was to provide the proper training for the profound person ("nobleman," *chün-tzu*). Such training is essentially a process that involves constant self-improvement and continuous social interaction. Although he emphatically noted that the purpose of learning is self-knowledge and self-realization, he found public service a natural consequence of true education. Confucius confronted learned hermits whose life-style and spiritual orientation challenged the validity of his desire to serve the world; he resisted the temptation to "herd with birds and beasts" by living apart from the human community and opted instead to try to transform the world from within. For decades, Confucius was actively involved in the political arena, attempting to put his humanist ideas into practice through governmental channels. Through praxis, Confucius demonstrated his commitment to the meaningfulness of this world and his faith that the Way would eventually prevail in the social and political realities of his time. Instead of creating a spiritual sanctuary outside the lived experience of his society, he tried to "sacralize" the human community by forming a fellowship of the like-minded. This existential choice, a fidelity to the human community as it was constituted, was profoundly consequential for the emerging religious landscape in East Asia.

In his late forties and early fifties, Confucius served first as a magistrate, then as an assistant minister of public works, and eventually as the minister of justice in the state of Lu. It is likely that he accompanied King Lu as his chief minister on one of his diplomatic missions. Confucius' political career was, however, brief. His loyalty to the king alienated him from those holding power at the time, the Three Chi families, and his moral rectitude did not sit well with those in the king's inner circle who enraptured the king with sensuous delights. At fifty-six, when he realized that his superiors were uninterested in his policies, he left the country in an attempt to find another feudal state that would accept his service.

Despite his political frustration, he was accompanied by a growing circle of students. His self-imposed exile lasted almost thirteen years, and his reputation as a man of vision and mission spread. A guardian of a border post once characterized him as the "wooden tongue for a bell" of the age, delivering Heaven's prophetic note to awaken the people.[12] Indeed, Confucius was perceived as the heroic conscience who knew that he might not succeed but, fired by a righteous passion, continuously did the best he could. At the age of sixty-seven, he returned home to teach and to preserve his cherished classical traditions by writing and editing. He died in 479 B.C.E. at the age of seventy-three. According to the *Records of the Historian*, seventy-two of his students had mastered the "six arts," and those who claimed to be his followers at that time numbered three thousand. Confucius once remarked that at seventy he could follow the dictates of his heart without transgressing the boundaries of right.[13] This ability to attain perfect harmony between what he is and what he ought to be has served as a lofty measure for transforming unrefined impulses into elegantly cultivated aesthetic expressions of the self for centuries of Confucian followers to emulate.

The First Epoch of the Confucian Way

According to Han Fei Tzu (d. 233 B.C.E.), shortly after Confucius' death his followers split into eight distinct schools, each of which claimed to be the legitimate heir to the Confucian legacy. Presumably each school was associated with or inspired by one or more of Confucius' disciples. Although the conflicting interpretations of the Master's message may have resulted in the parting of the Way, it seems to have engendered a new intellectual dynamism. Confucians did not dominate the world of thought in China in the fifth century B.C.E. among the disputers of the Way, but they seem to have developed the richest cultural and spiritual resources for setting the agenda for the intellectual discourse. Already, Confucius' intimate disciples, the mystic Yen Hui, the faithful Tseng Tzu, the talented Tzu Kung, the erudite Tzu-hsia, and others generated a great deal of enthusiasm among the second generation of his students. Even though it was not at all clear at the time that the Confucian tradition would eventually emerge as the most powerful persuasion in Chinese history, it was well on its way to becoming a prominent voice. Nevertheless, it would take several generations of persistent effort to enable the Confucian persuasion to prevail.

Mencius (?371–289 B.C.E.) complained that the world of thought in the early Warring States period (403–222 B.C.E.) was dominated by the collectivism of Mo Tzu and the individualism of Yang Chu (440–360 B.C.E.). Judging from the historical situation a century after Confucius' death, the disintegration of the Chou "feudal" ritual system and the rise of powerful hegemonic states clearly show that the Confucian attempt to moralize politics was met with cynicism and ridicule and that wealth and power spoke the loudest. Those who attracted more attention at that time were the hermits (the early Taoists), who left the mundane world to create a spiritual sanctuary in nature and lead a contemplative life, and the realists (the proto-Legalists), who attempted to influence the political process by assisting ambitious kings to gain wealth and power. The Confucians refused to leave the political stage to cultivate their inner tranquillity in the wilderness, for they could not bear the thought of abandoning the human community. Nor would they identify themselves with the interests of a ruling minority, because their social consciousness impelled them to serve as the conscience of the people. They were in a dilemma. They wanted to be actively involved in politics, but they could not accept the status quo as the legitimate arena in which authority and power were exercised. They were disgusted with power politics, but they could not detach themselves from affairs of the state. In short, they were *in* but not *of* the world; they could not leave the world, nor could they effectively change it.

Mencius: The Paradigmatic Confucian Intellectual

Mencius is known as the self-styled transmitter of the Confucian Way. Educated first by his mother (further enhancing the importance of the mother as an educator in the Confucian tradition) and then allegedly by a student of Confucius' grandson, Mencius brilliantly performed his role as a social critic, a moral philosopher, and a political activist. He devoted himself to the task of cultivating a class of scholar-officials who were not directly involved in agriculture, industry, and commerce but were vital to the proper functioning of the state and, more importantly, to the well-being of the people. In his sophisticated argument against the physiocrats (those who advocated the supremacy of agriculture), he intelligently employed the idea of the "division of labor" to defend those who "labor with their minds," and observed that "service" is as important as "productivity."[14] For him, Confucians could serve the vital interests of the state as scholars—not by becoming bureaucratic functionaries but by assuming the responsibility of teaching the ruling minority "humane government" (*jen-cheng*) and the kingly way (*wang-tao*). In his dealing with feudal lords, Mencius conducted himself not merely as political adviser but also as a teacher of kings. He made it explicit that a real "profound person" could not be corrupted by wealth, subdued by power, or affected by poverty.[15]

What Mencius advocated, then, was the role and function of an "organic intellectual" (who is organically linked to the world but intellectually committed to its fundamental moral reconstitution) dedicated to the preservation and enlargement of the Confucian Way. Intent on putting the Confucian belief that the Way can be enlarged by human effort into social practice, Mencius created a cultural space and a political arena for the organic intellectual. He reinterpreted the idea of the "great man" in terms of the knight and guardian of the Way rather than a subservient minister. He showed contempt for those who wielded tremendous power and influence through political manipulation; he condemned them for their inability to live up to the real calling of the Mandate of Heaven, for they, in the last analysis, served the ambitions of kings in a manner comparable to an obedient concubine. In contrast, he noted that the true great man dwells in humanity and walks the path of righteousness for the sake of the Way.[16] Thus, Mencius redefined the Confucian scholar as a knight and guardian of the Way. True to the Confucian spirit, he perceived that the carrier of the Way was an organic intellectual who performed the sacred mission of maintaining the meaning structure of society by becoming directly involved in politics as a moral exemplar.

To articulate the relationship between Confucian moral idealism and the concrete social and political realities of his time, Mencius criticized as impractical the prevailing ideologies of Mo Tzu's collectivism and Yang Chu's individualism. Mo Tzu advocated "universal love," but Mencius contended that the result of the Moist admonition to treat a stranger as intimately as one's own father would be to treat one's own father as indifferently as a stranger. Yang Chu, on the other hand, advocated the primacy of the self. Mencius contended that excessive attention to self-interest would lead to political disorder. Indeed, in Moist collectivism, "fatherhood" cannot be established, and in Yang Chu's individualism, "kingship" cannot be established.[17] Since regulation of the family is the basis of social stability and governance of the state is the foundation of universal peace, neither Moist collectivism nor Yangist individualism is politically feasible for bringing true benefit to the people.

Mencius's strategy for social reform was to change the language of profit, self-interest, wealth, and power into a moral discourse with emphasis on rightness, public-spiritedness, welfare, and exemplary authority. Mencius was not arguing against profit. Rather, he implored the feudal lords to opt for the great benefit that would sustain their own profit, self-interest, wealth, and power from a long-term perspective. He urged them to look beyond the horizon of their palaces and to cultivate a common bond with their ministers, officers, clerks, and the seemingly undifferentiated masses. Only then, he contended, would they be able to sustain their rulership or even maintain their livelihood for years to come. He encouraged them to extend their benevolence because it was crucial even for the protection of their own families.

Mencius's appeal to that which is common to all people as a mechanism of governance was predicated on his strong "populist" sense that the people are more important than the state, and the state is more important than the king;[18] the ruler who does not act in accordance with the kingly way is unfit. In a telling application of the Confucian principle of the "rectification of names," Mencius concluded that an unfit ruler should be criticized, rehabilitated, or, as a last resort, deposed.[19] Since Heaven wills that the well-being of the people be maintained and that the ruler be held responsible for it, revolution—or, literally, "to change the Mandate"—in severe cases is not only justifiable but highly desirable.

Mencius's "populist" conception of politics is predicated on his philosophical vision that human beings are perfectible through self-effort and that human nature is basically good. While he acknowledged biological and environmental factors in shaping the human condition, he insisted that we become moral primarily by willing to be so. According to Mencius, willing entails the transformative moral act, because our natural propensity to be good is automatically activated whenever we decide to bring it up to our conscious attention. As an illustration, Mencius built his idea of the humane government on the assertion that every human being is capable of commiseration:

> No man is devoid of a heart-mind sensitive to the suffering of others. Such a sensitive heart-mind was possessed by the Former Kings and this manifested itself in humane government. With such a sensitive heart-mind behind humane government, it was as easy to rule the world as rolling it on your palm.[20]

Mencius continued to observe that each human being is endowed with four feelings: commiseration, shame, modesty, and a sense of right and wrong. These feelings, like fire starting up or a spring coming through, serve as the bases for cultivating the four cardinal virtues: humanity, rightness, ritual, and wisdom. The message is that we become moral not because we are told we must be good but because our nature, the depth-dimension of humanity, spontaneously expresses itself as goodness.

Mencius maintained that we all have the inner spiritual resources to deepen our self-awareness and broaden our networks of communal participation. Biological and environmental constraints notwithstanding, we always have the freedom and the ability to refine and enlarge our Heaven-endowed nobility (our "great body"). While Mencius realistically accepted the proposition that, in regard to instinctual demands for appetite and sex, human beings are little different from other animals, he insisted that we could enlarge the tiny difference (the uniqueness of being human) and transform ourselves into true exemplars of authentic humanity by focusing on the "four beginnings."[21]

Mencius's idea of degrees of excellence in character-building vividly illustrates this continuous refinement and enlargement of our selfhood:

> Those who command our liking are called good (*shan*).
> Those who are sincere with themselves are called true (*hsin*).
> Those who are sufficient and real are called beautiful (*mei*).
> Those whose sufficiency and reality shine forth are called great (*ta*).
> Those whose greatness transforms itself are called sagely (*sheng*).
> Those whose sageliness is beyond our comprehension are called spiritual (*shen*).[22]

Furthermore, Mencius asserted that if we fully realize the potential in our hearts and minds, we will understand our nature; and by understanding our nature, we will know Heaven.[23] This profound faith in the human capacity for self-knowledge and for understanding Heaven by tapping spiritual resources from within enabled Mencius to add an "anthropocosmic" dimension to the Confucian project. Learning to be fully human, in this Mencian perspective, entails the cultivation of human sensitivity to embody the whole universe as one's lived experience:

> All the ten thousand things are there in me. There is no greater joy for me than to find, on self-examination, that I am true to myself. Try your best to treat others as you would wish to be treated yourself, and you will find that this is the shortest way to humanity.[24]

The Confucian scholar, as envisioned by Mencius, is an exemplary teacher, a political leader, a meaning-making thinker, and an organic intellectual.

Hsün Tzu: The Transmitter of Confucian Scholarship

If Mencius brought Confucian moral idealism to fruition, Hsün Tzu (fl. 298–238 B.C.E.) conscientiously transformed the Confucian project into a realistic and systematic inquiry into the human condition with special reference to ritual and authority. Widely acknowledged as the most eminent of the notable scholars who congregated in Chi-hsia, the capital of the wealthy and powerful Ch'i state in the mid-third century B.C.E., Hsün Tzu distinguished himself in erudition, intellectual sophistication, logic, empiricism, practical-mindedness, and argumentation. His critique of the so-called "twelve philosophers" gave an overview of the intellectual scene of his time. His penetrating insights into the shortcomings of virtually all the major currents of thought propounded by his fellow thinkers helped to establish the Confucian school as a forceful political and social persuasion.

His ability to incorporate insights from his contemporaries to formulate a synthetic vision of self and society significantly broadened the Confucian discourse. His principal adversary, however, was Mencius, and he vigorously attacked Mencius's view that human nature is good as naive moral optimism.

True to the Confucian (and, for that matter, Mencian) spirit, Hsün Tzu underscored the centrality of self-cultivation. He outlined the process of Confucian education—from learning to become a profound person to emulating sagehood and from studying poetry to practicing ritual—as a ceaseless endeavor to accumulate knowledge, skills, insight, and wisdom. He believed that unless social constraints were well articulated, human beings were prone to make excessive demands to satisfy their passions, which would inevitably undermine social solidarity, the precondition for human flourishing. For him, the most serious flaw in the Mencian commitment to the goodness of human nature obviates the need for ritual and authority for the maintenance of organic social solidarity. By stressing that human nature is evil, Hsün Tzu singled out the cognitive function of the mind (human rationality) as the basis for morality. We become moral by voluntarily harnessing our desires and passions to act in accordance with societal norms.

Like Mencius, Hsün Tzu believed in the perfectibility of all human beings through self-cultivation, in humanity and rightness as cardinal virtues, in humane government as the kingly way, in social harmony, and in education. His view of how all this could actually come about, however, was significantly different from Mencius's. The Confucian project, as shaped by Hsün Tzu, defines learning as socialization. Authorities such as ancient sages and worthies, the classical tradition, conventional norms, teachers, governmental rules and regulations, and political officers are all important resources for transforming human nature. A cultured person is by definition a fully socialized participant of the human community who has successfully sublimated his or her instinctual demands to further the public good.

Hsün Tzu's tough-minded stance on law, order, authority, and ritual seems precariously close to the Legalist policy of social conformity, which was designed exclusively for the benefit of the ruler. His insistence on objective standards of behavior may have provided the ideological basis for the rise of authoritarianism, which resulted in the dictatorship of the Ch'in (221–206 B.C.E.). As a matter of fact, two of the most influential Legalists, the theoretician Han Fei (d. 233 B.C.E.), from the state of Han, and the Ch'in minister Li Ssu (d. 208 B.C.E.), were his pupils. Yet, Hsün Tzu was instrumental in the continuation of the Confucian project as a scholarly enterprise. He would not have subscribed to the Legalist strategy of enhancing the power of the state at the expense of cultural diversity in society. His naturalistic interpretation of Heaven, his sophisticated understanding of culture, his insightful observations on the epistemological aspect of the mind and the social function of language, his emphasis on moral reasoning and the art of argumentation, his belief in progress, and his interest in political institutions so significantly enriched the Confucian heritage that he was revered by Confucians as the paradigmatic scholar for more than three centuries.

Mencius and Hsün Tzu deepened and broadened the Confucian project to such an extent that the Master's views on human nature and the Way of Heaven, which were rarely understood by his immediate disciples, became fully expounded into a coherent "anthropocosmic" vision. Learning to be human, in light of Mencius's and Hsün Tzu's interpretations, encompasses the whole process of transforming our biological reality into an aesthetic expression of the self. The rich vocabulary of self-cultivation—the ritualization of the body, the nourishment of the heart-and-mind, the purification of the soul, and the refinement of the spirit—integrated with the equally sophisticated language of the art of "managing the world" (*ching-shih*) provided two inseparable dimensions to the Confucian project: "inner sagehood and outer kingliness."

The Confucianization of Politics

The short-lived dictatorship of the Ch'in marked a brief triumph for Legalism, but in the early years of the Western Han (206 B.C.E.–8 C.E.), the Legalist practice of the absolute power of the emperor, complete subjugation of the peripheral states to the central government, total uniformity of thought, and ruthless enforcement of law was replaced by the Taoist practice of reconciliation and noninterference. This practice has been commonly known throughout history as the Huang Lao method, which refers to the art of rulership attributed to the Yellow Emperor (Huang Ti) and the mysterious "founder" of Taoism, Lao Tzu. A few Confucian thinkers, such as Lu Chia and Chia I, made important policy recommendations. Even before the emergence of Tung Chung-shu (ca. 179–ca. 104 B.C.E.) the Confucian persuasion was heard in the Han court, and the incipient tendencies to build an empire on Confucian principles became more and more evident. Actually the gradual Confucianization of Han politics began soon after the founding of the dynasty. Both the decision of the founding fathers to allow the reinstitution of the feudal system and the first emperor's implementation of elaborate court ritual enabled Han Confucians to become instrumental in shaping the basic structure of the government. The imperial decision to redress the cultural damage inflicted through the book-burning fiasco of the Ch'in by retrieving lost classics through extensive research and oral transmission indicated a deliberate effort to make the Confucian tradition an integral part of the emerging political ideology.

By the time of the reign of the Martial Emperor (Wu Ti, 141–87 B.C.E.), who was by temperament a Legalist despot, the Confucian persuasion was deeply entrenched in the central bureaucracy. Confucian influence was evident in the clear separation of the court and the government (which was often under the leadership of a scholarly prime minister), in the process of recruiting officials through the dual mechanism of recommendation and selection, in the family-centered social structure, in the agriculture-based economy, and in the educational network. Confucian ideas were also firmly established in the legal system as ritual became increasingly important in governing behavior, defining social relationships, and adjudicating civil disputes. Yet it was not until the prime minister, Kung-sun Hung (d. 121 B.C.E.), persuaded the Martial Emperor to formally announce that the *Ju* School alone would receive state sponsorship, that Confucianism became an officially recognized imperial ideology and state cult.

As a result, the Confucian classics became the core curriculum for all levels of education. In 136 B.C.E., the Martial Emperor set up five Erudites of the Five Classics at court and in 124 B.C.E. assigned fifty official students to study with them, thus creating a de facto imperial university. By 50 B.C.E., the student enrollment at the university had grown to an impressive three thousand, and by 1 C.E. a hundred men a year were entering government service through the examinations administered by the state. In short, those with a Confucian education began to staff the bureaucracy. In 58 C.E. all government schools were required to make sacrifices to Confucius, and in 175 C.E. the court had the approved version of the classics, which had been determined by scholarly conferences and research teams under imperial auspices for several decades, carved on large stone tablets. These steles were erected in the capital and are today well preserved in the national museum of Hsi-an. This act of committing to permanence and to public display the precise content of the sacred scriptures symbolizes the completion of the formation of the classical Confucian tradition.

The establishment of Confucianism as the official ideology of the Han dynasty was often hailed as the triumph of the teachings of Confucius, Mencius, and Hsün Tzu in Chinese intellectual history. In the perspective of Confucian spirituality, the triumph was, at best, a mixed blessing. Prior to the Han dynasty, there had never been the functional equivalent of rendering things that are God's to God and things that are Caesar's to Caesar in the Confucian tradition, but, true Confucians always maintained a critical stance toward the status quo. It is a gross mistake, as in Max Weber's *Religion of China*, to characterize the Confucian life-orientation as "adjustment to the world."[25] The Confucian commitment to transforming the world from within was a double-edged sword: While they accepted the improvability of the state of affairs and thus respected the status quo as a point of departure, they demanded, often without compromise, a fundamental restructuring of the existing power relationships, if they could no longer maintain the well-being of the people.

However, as the official ideology reflecting the vested interests of the ruling minority, Han Confucianism manifested itself primarily as a path of profit and emolument. This of course does not imply that the Confucian Way of humanity and rightness was totally relegated to the background. Actually, the disputers of the Way in Han political culture focused their attention on two conflicting paths: the authentic Confucian quest for self-cultivation and social responsibility and the politicized Confucian goal of social advancement at the expense of self-cultivation. Indeed, once those who were seasoned in Confucian learning also became politically prominent, the range of possibilities between political manipulation and moral rectitude was quite extensive. The ambiguity of mixing them in a variety of ways became a fact of life.

Tung Chung-shu: Mutuality Between Heaven and Humanity

Like the Grand Historian Ssu-ma Ch'ien, Tung Chung-shu (ca. 179–ca. 104 B.C.E.) took the Confucian classic, the *Spring and Autumn Annals*, absolutely seriously. However, his own work, *Luxuriant Gems of the Spring and Autumn Annals*, is far from being a book of historical judgment. It is also a metaphysical treatise in the spirit of the *Book of Change*. A man extraordinarily dedicated to learning (he is said to have been so absorbed in his studies that for three years he did not even glance at the garden in front of him) and staunchly committed to moral idealism (one of his often-quoted dicta is "rectifying rightness without scheming for profit; enlightening the Way without calculating efficaciousness"[26]), Tung was instrumental in developing a characteristically Han interpretation of the Confucian project.

Despite the Martial Emperor's pronouncement that Confucianism alone would receive imperial sponsorship, Taoists, Yin-Yang Cosmologists, Moists, Legalists, shamanists, mediums, healers, magicians, geomancers, and others contributed to the cosmological thinking of the Han cultural elite. Tung himself was a beneficiary of this intellectual syncretism, for he freely tapped the spiritual resources of his time in formulating his own worldview. His theory of the correspondence between humanity and nature, which involves a forced analogy between the four seasons, twelve months, and 366 days in a year and the four limbs, twelve sections (three in each limb), and 366 bones in the human body, is predicated on an organismic vision in which all modalities of being are interconnected in a complex network of relationships. The moral to draw from this metaphysics of consanguinity is that human actions have cosmic consequences.

Tung's inquiries into the meaning of the "five phases" (metal, wood, water, fire, and earth), into the correspondence between humans and the numerical categories of Heaven, and into the sympathetic activation of things of the same kind—as well as his studies of cardinal Confucian values such as humanity, rightness, ritual, wisdom, and faithfulness—enabled him to develop an elaborate worldview integrating Confucian ethics with naturalistic cosmology. What Tung accomplished was not merely a "theological" justification of the emperor as the "Son of Heaven." Rather, his theory of mutual responsiveness between Heaven and humanity provided Confucian scholars with a higher law to judge the conduct of the ruler. As a matter of fact, his rhetoric of "portents of catastrophes and anomalies," which asserted that floods, droughts, earthquakes, comets, eclipses, and even benign but unusual natural phenomena such as "growing beards on women" are celestial signs warning against rulers' wicked deeds, later acted as an effective deterrent to the whims and excesses of the monarchs. Tung offered the Confucian intellectuals an interpretive power with far-reaching political implications.

Tung's mode of thought reflects the scholarly penchant for prognostication, divination, and numerological speculation that was prevalent during his time. Known as adherents of the "New Text" school, these scholars based their arguments on the reconstructed classical texts written in the "new script" of the Han and were intensely interested in exploring the "subtle words and great meanings" of the classics as a means of influencing politics. The usurpation of Wang Mang (9–23) was in part occasioned by the popular demand of the Confucian literati that a change in the Mandate of Heaven was inevitable.

Despite Tung's immense popularity, his worldview was not universally accepted by Han Confucian scholars. A reaction in favor of a more rational and moralistic approach to the Confucian classics, known as the "Old Text" school, had already become entrenched before the fall of the Western Han. An alternative worldview was presented by Yang Hsiüng (ca. 53 B.C.E.–18 C.E.) in the *Model Sayings*, a collection of moralistic aphorisms in the style of the *Analects* and the *Classic of the Great Mystery*, which elaborated a cosmological speculation in the style of the *Book of Change*. The "Old Text" school, claiming its own recensions of authentic classical texts allegedly rediscovered during the Han period and written in an "old" script before the Ch'in unification, was widely accepted in the Eastern Han (25–220). As the institutions of the Erudites and the imperial university expanded in the Eastern Han, the study of the classics became more refined and elaborate. Confucian scholasticism, like its counterparts in Talmudic and biblical studies, became highly professionalized, to the extent that its vitality as a moral discourse was sapped.

Nevertheless, Confucian ethics continued to exert great influence on government, schools, and society at large. Toward the end of the Han, virtually every educated male adult was seasoned in Confucian classics. Confucius' role as the patron saint of education was firmly established, and all public schools throughout the land offered regular sacrifices to him. Confucian temples sprang up throughout the country. The imperial courts continued to honor Confucius from age to age; a Confucian shrine eventually stood in every one of the two thousand counties. As a result, the teacher, along with Heaven, Earth, the emperor, and parents, became one of the most respected authorities in traditional China.

The deification of Confucius notwithstanding, the image of Confucius as a teacher who, through personal example of ceaseless learning, distinguished himself as the most honored man under Heaven persisted. Confucius, the man and the myth, exercised a great deal of symbolic power in Chinese society without ever losing his humanness. The efficaciousness of even the mythologized Confucius lies in its moral transformation.

Confucian Ethics in the Age of Buddhism and Taoism

Incompetent rulership, faction-ridden bureaucracy, a mismanaged tax structure, and the domination of eunuch power toward the end of the Eastern Han prompted widespread protests by the imperial university students. The court's high-handed policy sanctioning the imprisonment and execution of thousands of students and their official sympathizers in 169 put a temporary stop to the intellectual revolt, but a large-scale rebellion followed as a downward economic spiral made the peasant's life unbearable. The peasant rebellion, led by Confucian scholars as well as Taoist religious leaders of faith-healing sects, combined with open insurrections of the military brought down the Han dynasty and thus put an end to the first Chinese empire. With the breakdown of the imperial Han system, which was not unlike the decline and fall of the Roman Empire, "barbarians" invaded from the north. The northern China plains were fought over, despoiled, and controlled by rival tribes, and a succession of states was established in the south. This period of disunity, from the early third to the late sixth century, marked the apparent decline of Confucianism, the upsurge of Neo-Taoism, and the spread of Buddhism.

The prominence of the Taoist and Buddhist persuasions among the cultural elite and the populace in general, however, did not mean that the dynamism of the Confucian tradition was spent. In fact, Confucian ethics was virtually inseparable from the moral fabric of Chinese society, and Confucius continued to be universally honored as the paradigmatic sage. The outstanding Taoist thinker, Wang Pi (226–249), argued that Confucius, by not speculating on the nature of the Tao, had a better experiential understanding of it than Lao Tzu himself. The Confucian classics remained the foundation of all literate culture, and sophisticated commentaries continued to be produced throughout the age. Confucian values never ceased to dominate in such political institutions as the central bureaucracy, the recruitment of officials, and local governance. The political forms of life were distinctively Confucian as well. When a "barbarian" state adopted a Sinicization policy, as was the case in the Northern Wei (386–535), it was by and large Confucian in character. In the south, systematic attempts were made to strengthen family ties by establishing clan rules, genealogical trees, and ancestral rituals based on Confucian ethics. Although Confucianism was no longer the official ideology, it was embraced as the rule of conduct by prominent families, local elites, and occasionally conquest dynasties. The reunification of China by the Sui (581–618) and the restoration of lasting peace and prosperity by the T'ang (618–907) gave a powerful stimulus to the revival of Confucian learning. The publication of a definitive, official edition of the Five Classics, with elaborate commentaries and subcommentaries, and the implementation of Confucian rituals at all levels of governmental practice (including the compilation of the famous T'ang legal code) were two outstanding examples of Confucianism in practice. An examination system was established based on literary competence. It made the mastery of Confucian classics a prerequisite for political success and was, therefore, perhaps the single most important institutional innovation in defining elite culture in Confucian terms.

Nevertheless, the intellectual and spiritual scene of the T'ang was dominated by Buddhism and, to a lesser degree, by Taoism. The philosophical originality of the dynasty was mainly represented by monk-scholars such as Chi-tsang (549–623), Hsüan-tsang (596–664), and Chih-i (538–597). An unintended consequence in the development of Confucian thought in this context was the prominent rise of some of the most metaphysically significant Confucian texts, notably *Chung-yung (Doctrine of the Mean)* and *I-chuan (The Great Commentary of the Book of Change)*, which appealed to some Buddhist and Taoist thinkers. A sign of a possible Confucian turn in the T'ang was Li Ao's (d. ca. 844) essay on "Returning to Nature," which foreshadowed some salient features of Sung (960–1279) Confucian thought. However, the most influential precursor of a Confucian revival was Han Yü (768–824). A great essayist, he attacked Buddhism with telling effectiveness from the perspectives of social ethics and cultural identity. He discussed and provoked interest in the question of what actually constitutes the Confucian Way. The issue of *Tao-t'ung*, the transmission of the Way or the authentic method to repossess the Way, has stimulated much discussion in the Confucian tradition since the eleventh century.

In the political arena, the style of governance exemplified by T'ang T'ai-tsung, arguably the most cosmopolitan, intelligent, and broad-minded emperor in Chinese history, was characteristically Confucian. The *Chen-kuan cheng-yao* (*The Essentials of Government in the Chen-kuan Reign, 626–647*), supposedly a veritable record of his rulership, is, to this date, an often-cited text for enlightened leadership. It must be noted, however, that the despotic mechanisms of control had been so deeply ingrained in Chinese political culture at this time that emperorship was taken for granted as the only legitimate form of government. As a result, scholar-officials who were selected through competitive examinations and staffed the bureaucracy became the de facto carriers of the Confucian Way, a far cry from the Mencian idea of an organic intellectual as the knight and guardian of the Way. Still, some ministers in T'ai-tsung's court, notably the senior statesman Wei Chen, commanded such an awe-inspiring presence in front of the monarch that they continued to evoke the Mencius-like spirit of personal dignity and political responsibility. To them, the Confucian idea of following the Way rather than the monarch was a practicable morality rather than a mere imagined possibility.

Confucius and his two major followers, Mencius and Hsün Tzu, initiated the first epoch of Confucian humanism. By the first century B.C.E., at the height of the Former Han dynasty (206 B.C.E. to 8 C.E.), the Confucian tradition had become the dominant intellectual force in moral education, political ideology, and social ethics in China. It is important to note, however, that while Confucianism was the orthodoxy defining the life orientation of the cultural elite, it coexisted with many other currents of thought—Taoism, Legalism, Yin-Yang Cosmology, theories of the Five Phases, and a variety of folk beliefs in the Chinese philosophical and religious landscape. Indeed, a distinctive feature of Confucian humanism is its inclusiveness, symbolizing a deliberate effort to accommodate seemingly incompatible systems of ideas in a correlative worldview, as in Tung Chung-shu's anthropocosmic syncretism. Still, the first epoch of Confucian humanism tapered off by the third century, even though Confucian influence in government institution, social organization, and cultural production persisted. Surely, Confucian humanism further developed in the age of Buddhism and Taoism, but the truly impressive Confucian revival occurred in the eleventh century. The emergence of what is often referred to in English as Neo-Confucianism signals the second epoch of Confucian humanism.

The Second Epoch of the Confucian Way

The Buddhist conquest of China and the Chinese transformation of Buddhism, a process that comprised the introduction, domestication, growth, and appropriation of a distinctly Indian form of spirituality, lasted for at least six centuries. Since Buddhist ideas were introduced to China via Taoist categories and since the development of the Taoist religion benefited from modeling itself on Buddhist institutions and practices, the spiritual dynamic in medieval China was characterized by Buddhist and Taoist values. Against this background, the reemergence of Confucianism as the leading intellectual force involved both a creative response to the Buddhist and Taoist challenge and an imaginative reinterpretation and reappropriation of classical Confucian insights. Furthermore, after the collapse of the T'ang Empire, the grave threats to the survival of Chinese culture from the Khitans, the Jurchens, and later the Mongols prompted the literati to protect their common heritage by deepening their communal critical self-awareness. To enrich their personal knowledge and preserve China as a civilization-state, they explored the symbolic and spiritual resources that made Confucianism a living tradition.

The Anthropocosmic Vision

The Sung dynasty (960–1279) was militarily weak and geographically much smaller than the T'ang in size, but its cultural splendor and economic prosperity were unprecedented in Chinese history. The Sung "commercial revolution" produced social patterns that included flourishing markets, densely populated urban centers, elaborate communication networks, theatrical performances, literary groups, and popular religions. These patterns remained in many ways unchanged into the nineteenth century, prompting Sinologists, notably Naito Torajirō, to characterize this period as the beginning of "modern" China. Indeed, technological advances in agriculture, textiles, lacquer, porcelain, printing, maritime trade, and weaponry in the Sung were unrivaled anywhere in the world, demonstrating that China at the time excelled not only in the fine arts but also in hard sciences. The decline of the aristocracy, the widespread availability of printed books, the democratization of education, and the full implementation of the examination system produced a new social class—the gentry—which was noted for its literary proficiency, social consciousness, and political participation. The outstanding members of this class, such as the classicists Hu Yüan (993–1059) and Sun Fu (992–1057), the reformers Fan Chung-yen (989–1052) and Wang An-shih (1021–1086), the writer-officials Ou-yang Hsiu (1007–1072) and Su Shih (1036–1101), the statesman-historian Ssu-ma Kuang (1018–1086), and the metaphysician Shao Yüng (1011–1077), contributed to the revival of the Confucian persuasion in, respectively, education, politics, literature, history, and cosmology. Collectively, they influenced the development of a literatus style, which was a way of life informed by Confucian ethics.

Nevertheless, the Confucian revival, understood in traditional historiography as the establishment of the lineage of the "Learning of the Tao" (*Tao-hsüeh*), can be traced through a line of thinkers from Chou Tun-i (1017–1073), via Chang Tsai (1020–1077), Ch'eng Hao (1032–1085), and Ch'eng I (1033–1107), to the great synthesizer, Chu Hsi (1130–1200). These thinkers developed an inclusive humanist vision that integrated personal self-cultivation with social ethics and moral metaphysics with a holistic philosophy of life. In the eyes of the Sung literati, this new philosophy authentically reanimated classical Confucian insights and successfully applied these insights to the concerns of their own age.

CHOU TUN-I

Chou Tun-i ingeniously articulated the relationship between the "great transformation" of the cosmos and the moral development of the person. In his cosmology, humanity, as the recipient of the highest excellence from Heaven, is itself a center of "anthropocosmic" creativity. He developed this all-embracing humanism by a thought-provoking interpretation of the Taoist diagram of the Great Ultimate (*t'ai-chi*) from the perspective of Confucian metaphysics as embodied in the *Book of Change*:

> When the reality of the Ultimate of Non-being and the essence of yin, yang, and the Five Phases come into mysterious union, integration ensues. *Ch'ien* (Heaven) constitutes the male element, and *k'un* (Earth) constitutes the female element. The interaction of these two vital forces engenders and transforms the myriad things. The myriad things produce and reproduce, resulting in an unending transformation.
>
> Human beings alone receive (the Five Phases) in their highest excellence, and therefore they are most sentient. Their physical forms appear, and their spirit gives rise to consciousness. The five moral principles of their nature (humanity, rightness, propriety, wisdom, and faithfulness) are aroused by, and react to, the external world and engage in activity; good and evil are distinguished; and human affairs take place.[27]

This cosmogonic vision seeks to establish the uniquely Sinic idea of trinity: Heaven, Earth, and Humanity. Human beings, so conceived, are knights and guardians of the Way because the values needed to assist and nourish the transforming process of Heaven and Earth are inherently embodied in human nature.

Human beings are, by definition, spiritual beings. The numinous quality of being human is vividly depicted in the idea of sagehood. Chou Tun-i portrays the sage as the living embodiment of three "anthropocosmic" characteristics: *cheng* (sincerity), *shen* (spirituality), and *chi* (incipient activation). *Cheng,* which can also be rendered as authenticity and reality, connotes a sense of genuineness. Since sages, like Heaven and Earth, are completely true to human nature, which is endowed with the highest excellence of the cosmic vital forces, they are always in a state of tranquillity without any need of self-expression. As sincerity is defined as "the state of absolute quiet and inactivity,"[28] the sage, by embodying sincerity, manifests authentic, real, and genuine humanity without motion or activity. Yet, sagehood is also the foundation of the five constant virtues and the source of all activities. This is based on the belief that although the sages are always in a state of tranquillity, they, like the spirit, "when acted on, immediately penetrate all things."[29] Sagehood as responsiveness must be redefined in spiritual terms; it is not only sincerity but also the wondrous ability to interact with things that characterizes the modus operandi of the sage. The

Confucian sage who is endowed with the virtues of humanity, rightness, propriety, wisdom, and faithfulness differs from the Taoist holy man who forever dwells in a state of nonaction in one subtle but vital area: moral creativity. While the holy man transcends any differentiation, including the difference between right and wrong, the sage must move deftly in the intricacies of human affairs. This need to navigate the path of self-realization in the density of human-relatedness enables the Confucian sage to acquire an insight into *chi* (incipient activation): "an originating power, an inward spring of activity, an emergence not yet visible, a critical point at which one's direction toward good or evil is set."[30]

Obviously, the sage who is sincere, spiritual, and incipiently activating reveals a quality of moral creativity comparable in subtlety, if not in grandeur, to the transforming and nourishing process of Heaven and Earth.

Indeed, the human world inspired by Heaven-endowed virtues is a moral community imbued with numinous qualities:

> The virtue of loving is called humanity, that of doing what is proper is called rightness, that of putting things in order is called propriety, that of penetration is called wisdom, and that of abiding by one's commitments is called faithfulness. Those who are in accord with their nature are sages. Those who return to their nature and adhere to it are worthies. And those whose subtle emanation cannot be seen and whose [goodness] is abundant and all-pervasive without limit are humans of the spirit.[31]

It is important to note that, far from being a utopian vision of what human society ought to be but never is, Chou's meditation on the *Book of Change* was intended to serve as a guide for action. Surely, it was not merely a manual for proper conduct. It was, however, thought to contain feasible and practical recommendations for fellow Confucians, including those who served in the government. It should be noted that virtually all major Confucian thinkers were scholar-officials, men with extensive practical experience. Indeed, Chou Tun-i envisioned his conversation partners to be fellow scholar-officials who had to deal with bureaucratic routine on a daily basis. This lofty idea that human nature is conferred by Heaven, combined with a pragmatic concern for its actual implementation in ordinary daily living, gives the Confucian project a particular contour that crosses boundaries between self and society, sacred and profane, the human world and the Way of Heaven, and political affairs and religious concerns.

CHANG TSAI

Implicit in this is a profound sense of human rootedness in the order of things. We are here for a reason and we know it: If we fully realize our humanity, we fulfill not only the "anthropological" responsibility of enabling our community, indeed our species, to flourish but also the "cosmological" charge to be the knights and guardians of the Mandate of Heaven. This is the precise reason that while the Way does not enlarge us, we can enlarge the Way through our human effort. Chang Tsai's (1020–1077) article of faith, as pronounced in the *Western Inscription*, is a Confucian declaration of faith, a profoundly religious articulation of the meaning of being human:

> Heaven is my father and Earth is my mother, and even such a small creature as I finds an intimate place in their midst.
>
> Therefore that which fills the universe I regard as my body and that which directs the universe I consider as my nature.
>
> All people are my brothers and sisters, and all things are my companions.... Even those who are tired, infirm, crippled, or sick; those who have no brothers or children, wives or husbands, are all my brothers [and sisters] who are in distress and have no one to turn to.
>
> When the time comes, to keep him from harm—this is the care of a son. To rejoice in Heaven and to have no anxiety—this is filial piety at its purest.
>
> ...
>
> One who knows the principles of transformation will skillfully carry forward the undertakings [of Heaven and Earth], and one who penetrates spirit to the highest degree will skillfully carry out their will.
>
> Do nothing shameful in the recesses of your own house and thus bring no dishonor to them. Preserve your mind and nourish your nature and thus (serve them) with untiring effort.
>
> ...
>
> Wealth, honor, blessing, and benefits are meant for the enrichment of my life, while poverty, humble station, and sorrow are meant to help me to fulfillment.
>
> In life I follow and serve [Heaven and Earth]. In death I will be at peace.[32]

This moving characterization of human beings as filial children of Heaven and Earth identifies the human home as conterminous with the cosmos, but the vastness of this imagined community paradoxically produces an experience of intimacy devoid of the sense of estrangement and alienation characteristic of modern existentialism. However, this seemingly naive romantic assertion about human consanguinity with Heaven and Earth is grounded in an experiential understanding of the authentic human possibility of building a wholesome relationship with the cosmos, which, as the great transformation, provides the primordial source for our existence.

In Chang Tsai's cosmological thinking, the vital energy (*ch'i*) is omnipresent. It provides a "material" as well as a "spiritual" link for us to be organismically united with Heaven, Earth, and the myriad things. We find an intimate niche in the universe because we are, in essence, made of the same stuff as animals, plants, rocks, and dust. Our sense of home, rather than estrangement, is therefore a reflection of our true feeling that we naturally and realistically belong here:

> The integration and disintegration of vital energy is to the Great Vacuity as the freezing and melting of ice in water. If we realize that the Great Vacuity is identical with vital energy, we know that there is no such thing as non-being. Therefore, when discussing the ultimate problems of the nature of things and the Way of Heaven, the sages limit themselves to the marvelous changes and transformation of yin and yang and the Five Phases (of Metal, Wood, Water, Fire, and Earth). The doctrine of those superficial and mistaken philosophers who draw the distinction between being and non-being is not the way to investigate principle to the utmost.[33]

Indeed, since we come into being as the result of the same great transformation that gives rise to Heaven, Earth, and the myriad things, it is natural to our humanness that we feel at home in the company of those sharing the same vital energy:

> From the Great Vacuity, there is Heaven. From the transformation of vital energy, there is the Way. In the unity of the Great Vacuity and vital energy, there is nature (of human beings and things). And in the unity of the nature of consciousness, there is the mind-and-heart.[34]

However, Chang Tsai was not a "materialist" but a teacher of enlightenment, sincerity, and ultimate self-transformation; true to the spirit of Chou Tun-i, his overall concern was how human beings who embody the finest essences of the vital energy in the cosmos realize themselves by emulating the examples of sages and worthies. His dictum, "the oneness of the principle and the multiplicity of its manifestations,"[35] was as much a moral prescription as a cosmological insight. Its purpose was not only to provide a picture of what we could become but also to offer a guidance for what we ought to do:

> By enlarging our heart-minds, we can enter into all the things in the world [to examine and understand their principles]. As long as anything is not yet entered into, there is still something outside our heart-minds. The heart-minds of ordinary people are limited to the narrowness of what is seen and what is heard. The sages, however, fully develop their nature and do not allow what is seen or heard to fetter their heart-minds. They regard everything in the world to be their own selves. This

> is why Mencius said that if we exert our heart-minds to the utmost, we can know nature and Heaven. Heaven is so vast that there is nothing outside of it. Therefore the heart-mind that leaves something outside is not capable of uniting itself with the heart-mind of Heaven. Knowledge coming from seeing and hearing is knowledge obtained through contact with things. It is not knowledge obtained through our moral nature. Knowledge obtained through our moral nature does not originate from seeing or hearing.[36]

CH'ENG HAO AND CH'ENG I

The idea that the capacity to embody the cosmos is intrinsic to the sensitivity of our heart-minds is vividly depicted in Ch'eng Hao's (1032–1085) holistic humanist vision:

> A book on medicine describes paralysis of the four limbs as absence of humanity (*jen*). This is an excellent description. Persons who embody humanity regard Heaven, Earth, and the myriad things as one body. To them there is nothing that is not themselves. Since they have recognized all things as themselves, can there be any limit to their humanity? If things are not part of the self, naturally they have nothing to do with it. As in the case of the paralysis of the four limbs, the vital energy no longer penetrates them and, as a result, they are no longer part of the self.[37]

This theme of mutuality of Heaven and humanity, consanguinity among human beings, and harmony between the human community and nature was brought to fruition in Ch'eng Hao's definition of humanity as "forming one body with all things."[38] To him, the presence of the Heavenly Principle (*T'ien-li*) in all things and in human nature enables the human heart-mind to purify itself in a spirit of reverence. In a religious perspective, the centrality of spiritual self-transformation became even more enhanced and the idea of humanity as defined by commiseration and cosmic connectedness was still more eloquently and systematically expressed in the subsequent developments of Confucian thought. Ch'eng I (1033–1107), following his brother's lead, formulated the famous dictum: "self cultivation requires reverence; the pursuit of learning depends on the extension of knowledge."[39] However, by making special reference to the "investigation of things" (*ko-wu*), he raised doubts about the appropriateness of his brother's exclusive focus on the inner illumination of the heart-mind in Confucian self-cultivation. The learning of the heart-mind as advocated by Ch'eng Hao and the learning of the principle as advocated by Ch'eng I became two distinct modes of thought in Sung Confucianism.

CHU HSI

Chu Hsi (1130–1200), clearly following Ch'eng I's School of Principle and implicitly rejecting Ch'eng Hao's School of Mind, developed a pattern of interpreting and transmitting the Confucian Way that would define the Confucian project for centuries—not only for the Chinese, but for the Koreans and Japanese as well. If, as quite a few scholars have advocated, Confucianism symbolizes a distinct form of East Asian spirituality, the type of Confucianism they are referring to was shaped by Chu Hsi. Master Chu virtually reconstituted the Confucian tradition, giving it new meaning, new structure, and new texture. Through conscientious appropriation and systematic interpretation, he developed a type of new Confucianism. This school is known as Neo-Confucianism in the West but often referred to as the Learning of the Principle (*Li-hsüeh*) in modern China.

A textual note is appropriate at this juncture. Within the Five Classics, which had become the sacred books of Confucian education since the Han dynasty, the *Doctrine of the Mean* and the *Great Learning*—two chapters in the *Book of Rites*—were often studied as independent treatises. Together with the *Analects* and *Mencius*, these chapters had been included in the core curriculum of Confucian education for centuries before Chu Hsi's birth. However, by putting them in a particular sequence—the *Great Learning*, the *Analects*, *Mencius*, and the *Doctrine of the Mean*—and by synthesizing their commentaries, interpreting them as a coherent humanistic vision, and calling them the Four Books, Master Chu fundamentally restructured the priority of the Confucian scriptural tradition by placing the Four Books above the Five Classics.[40] The Four Books became the central texts for both primary education and civil service examinations in traditional China from the fourteenth century on. Thus, they have exerted far greater influence on Chinese life and thought in the last six hundred years than any other scripture.

As an interpreter and transmitter of the Confucian Way, Chu Hsi identified the early Sung masters who, both as his own spiritual fathers and as true bearers of the sagely teaching, rightly belonged to the authentic lineage of Confucius and Mencius. His judgment, later widely accepted by governments in East Asia, was based principally on these philosophical insights. The select four, Chou Tun-i, Chang Tsai, and the Ch'eng brothers, were Chu Hsi's cultural heroes. Shao Yüng and Ssu-ma Kuang were originally on this august list, but Chu Hsi apparently changed his mind, perhaps because of Shao's excessive metaphysical speculation and Ssu-ma's obsession with historical facts.

Up until Chu Hsi's time, the idea of self-cultivation in the Confucian thinking of the Sung masters was characterized by a few ambiguous, though fruitful, concepts: the Great Ultimate, principle, vital energy, nature, mind, and humanity. Master Chu defined the process of the "investigation of things" as a rigorous discipline of the mind to probe the underlying principle in things so that vital energy can be transformed and enlightened humanity (as manifestation of nature and the Great Ultimate) realized. Accordingly, he recommended a twofold method of study: to cultivate a sense of reverence and to pursue extensive knowledge. This combination of morality and wisdom made his pedagogy an inclusive approach to humanist education. Book reading, quiet sitting, ritual practice, physical exercise, calligraphy, arithmetic, and empirical observation all have a place in his pedagogical program. Chu Hsi reestablished the White Deer Grotto in present-day Kiangsi as an academy. It became the intellectual center of his age and provided an instructional model for all schools in East Asia for generations to come.

Chu Hsi's "anthropocosmic vision" is elegantly presented in his famous "Treatise on Humanity":

> The moral qualities of the heart-mind of Heaven and Earth are four: origination, flourish, advantage, and firmness. And the principle of origination unites and controls them all. In their operation they constitute the course of the four seasons, and the vital energy of the spring permeates all. Therefore in the human heart-mind there are four moral qualities—namely humanity (*jen*), rightness (*i*), propriety (*li*), and wisdom (*chih*)—and humanity embraces them all. In their emanation and function, they constitute the feeling of love, respect, being right, and discrimination between right and wrong—and the feeling of commiseration pervades them all.
>
> . . .
>
> [Humanity] as constituting the Way (Tao) consists of the fact that the heart-mind of Heaven and Earth to produce things is present in everything. Before feelings are aroused, this substance is already existent in its completeness. After feelings are aroused, its function is infinite. If we can truly practice love and preserve it, then we have in it the spring of all virtues and the root of all good deeds. This is why in the teachings of the Confucian school, the student is always urged to exert anxious and unceasing effort in the pursuit of humanity.[41]

Chu Hsi and those he identified as his spiritual teachers believed that learning to be human is not only an anthropological commitment but also a cosmological enterprise. Indeed, unless we transcend our anthropocentric predicament, we cannot appreciate the true import of humanity.

LU HSIANG-SHAN

Chu Hsi was considered the preeminent Confucian scholar in Sung China, but his interpretation of self-cultivation as necessary for apprehending the Confucian Way was seriously challenged by his contemporary, Lu

Hsiang-shan (1139–1193). Claiming that he appropriated the true wisdom of Confucian teaching by reading Mencius, Lu criticized Chu Hsi's theory of the "investigation of things" as a form of fragmented and ineffective empiricism. Instead, he advocated a return to Mencian moral idealism by insisting that the establishment of the "great body" is the primary precondition for self-realization. For him, the learning of the heart-mind as a quest for self-knowledge provided the basis upon which the investigation of things assumed its proper significance. Lu's face-to-face confrontation with Master Chu in the famous meeting at the Goose Lake Temple in 1175 further convinced him that the Confucian project as Chu Hsi had shaped it was not Mencian. Although Lu's challenge remained a minority position for some time, his learning of the mind later became a major intellectual force in Ming China (1368–1644) and Tokugawa Japan (1600–1867).

A distinctive feature of Lu Hsiang-shan's holistic "anthropocosmic" insight is the sense of immediacy in forming an organismic unity with the cosmos, crossing boundaries of time and space, in our self-understanding:

> The four directions plus upward and downward constitute the spatial continuum (*yü*). What has gone by in the past and what is to come in the future constitute the temporal continuum (*chou*). The universe (these continua) is my heart-mind, and my heart-mind is the universe. Sages appeared tens of thousands of generations ago. They shared this heart-mind; they shared this principle. Sages will appear tens of thousands of generations to come. They will share this heart-mind; they will share this principle. Over the four seas sages appear. They share this mind; they share this principle.[42]

Lu's unequivocal assertion that "the affairs of the universe (*yü-chou*) are my own affairs; my own affairs are affairs of the universe"[43] may appear to be an unbridled romantic statement about forming one body with the universe. Implicit in this seemingly idealist faith, however, is a moral imperative:

> This principle existing throughout the universe is hidden from nothing and nothing can escape from it. Heaven and Earth are what they are because they follow this principle without partiality. Human beings coexist with Heaven and Earth as the three ultimates. How can we be selfish and disobey principle? Mencius said, "First build up the nobler part (the 'great body') of your nature then the inferior part cannot overcome it." It is because we fail to build up the nobler part of our nature that it is overcome by the inferior part. In consequence we violate principle and become different from Heaven and Earth.[44]

Therefore, by maintaining that "the universe has never separated itself from human beings, human beings separate themselves from the universe,"[45] Lu Hsiang-shan reenacted Chang Tsai's faith that we are blessed by Heaven and Earth with an "intimate place" in the cosmos and that we ought to overcome our self-imposed partiality and make ourselves worthy members of our home.

Forming One Body with All Things

For approximately 150 years, from the time the Sung court moved its capital to the south and reestablished itself there in 1127, northern China was ruled by three conquest dynasties, Liao (947–1125), Hsi-hsia (990–1227), and Chin (1115–1234). Although the bureaucracies and political cultures of both Liao and Hsi-hsia were under Confucian influence, no discernible intellectual developments helped to further the Confucian tradition. The situation in the Jurchen Chin dynasty was entirely different. Despite the paucity of information about the Confucian renaissance in the southern Sung, the Chin scholar-officials continued the classical, artistic, literary, and historiographic traditions of the north and developed a richly textured cultural form of their own. Chao Ping-wen's (1159–1232) combination of literary talent and moral concerns and Wang Jo-hsü's (1172–1248) productive scholarship in classics and history—as depicted in Yüan Hao-wen's (1190–1259) biographic sketches and preserved in their collected works—compared well with the high standards set by their counterparts in the south.

As the Mongols reunited China in 1279, the intellectual dynamism of the south profoundly affected the northern style of scholarship. The harsh treatment of scholars by the conquering Yüan (Mongol) dynasty (1271–1368) seriously damaged the well-being of the scholarly community and the prestige of the scholar-official class. Nevertheless, outstanding Confucian thinkers emerged throughout the period. Some opted to purify themselves so that they could repossess the Way for the future; some decided to engage themselves in politics to put their teaching into practice.

HSÜ HENG

Hsü Heng (1209–1281) took the practical approach. He was appointed by Khubilai, the Great Khan in Marco Polo's *Description of the World*, to be president of the Imperial Academy and was respected as the leading scholar in the court. Hsü conscientiously and meticulously introduced Chu Hsi's teaching to the Mongols. He assumed personal responsibility for educating the sons of Mongol nobility to become qualified teachers of Confucian classics. His erudition and skills in medicine, legal affairs, military science, arithmetic, astronomy, and irrigation enabled him to function as an informed adviser to the conquering dynasty. He set the tone for the eventual success of the Confucianization of Yüan bureaucracy. In fact, it was the Yüan court that first officially adopted the Four Books as the basis of the civil service examination, a practice religiously observed until 1905. Thanks to Hsü Heng, Chu Hsi's teaching prevailed in the Mongol conquest, but the shape of the Confucian project envisioned by Master Chu was significantly simplified.

LIU YIN AND WU CHENG

The hermit-scholar Liu Yin (1249–1293), on the other hand, allegedly refused Khubilai's summons in order to maintain the dignity of the Confucian Way. To him, education was for self-realization. Loyal to the Chin culture in which he was reared and faithful to the Confucian Way that he had learned from the Sung masters, Liu Yin rigorously applied philological methods to classical studies and strongly advocated the importance of history. However, true to Chu Hsi's spirit, he took seriously the idea of the investigation of things and put a great deal of emphasis on the learning of the mind.[46] Liu Yin's contemporary, Wu Cheng (1249–1333), further developed the learning of the mind. He fully acknowledged the contribution of Lu Hsiang-shan to the Confucian tradition, even though he was an admirer of Hsü Heng and considered himself a follower of Chu Hsi. Wu assigned himself the challenging task of harmonizing the differences between Chu and Lu. As a result, he reoriented Chu's balanced approach to morality and wisdom to accommodate Lu's existential concern for self-knowledge. This prepared the way for the revival of Lu's learning of the mind in the Ming (1368–1644).

WANG YANG-MING

The thought of the first outstanding Ming Confucian scholar, Hsüeh Hsüan (1389–1464), already reveals the turn toward moral subjectivity. Although Hsüeh was a devoted follower of Chu Hsi, his *Records of Reading* clearly shows that he considered the cultivation of "heart-mind and nature" to be particularly important. Two other early Ming scholars, Wu Yü-pi (1391–1469) and Ch'en Hsien-chang (1428–1500), helped to define Confucian education for those who studied the classics as not simply preparing for examinations but as learning of the "body and heart-mind." They cleared the way for Wang Yang-ming (1472–1529), the most influential Confucian thinker after Chu Hsi.

Wang Yang-ming allied himself with Lu Hsiang-shan's learning of the heart-mind, as a critique of the excessive attention to philological details characteristic of Chu Hsi's followers. He advocated the precept of "uniting thought and action." By focusing on the transformative power of the will, he inspired a whole generation of Confucian students to return to the moral idealism of Mencius. His own personal example of combining teaching with bureaucratic routine, administrative responsibility, and leadership in military campaigns demonstrated that he was a man of deeds. Yet, despite his competence in practical affairs, his primary concern was moral education, which he felt had to be grounded on the "original substance" of the mind. He later identified this as the "primordial awareness" (*liang-chih*), a consciousness and conscience of the good that every human being possesses. He further suggested that "primordial awareness," as the Heavenly Principle, underlies all beings from the highest forms of spirituality to grass, wood, bricks, and stone. Because the universe consists of vital energy informed by "primordial awareness," it is a dynamic process rather than a static structure. Human beings must learn to regard Heaven and Earth and the myriad things as one body by extending their consciousness and conscience of the good to embrace an ever-expanding network of relationships. In his brilliant inquiry on the *Great Learning,* Wang Yang-ming gives a nuanced articulation of how this all-encompassing human-heartedness actually reveals itself in different modalities of being without losing sight of its integrity as true feeling of commiseration:

> The great man [for our purpose, it should be read in the gender neutral sense of a broadly minded "profound person"] regards Heaven, Earth, and the myriad things as one body. He regards the world as one family and the country as one person. As to those who made a cleavage between objects and distinguish between the self and others, they are small men.
>
> That the great man can regard Heaven, Earth, and the myriad things as one body is not because he deliberately wants to do so, but because it is natural to the humane nature of his heart-mind that he do so. Forming one body with Heaven, Earth, and the myriad things is not only true of the great man. Even the heart-mind of the small man is no different. Only he himself makes it small. Therefore when he sees a child about to fall into a well, he cannot help a feeling of alarm and commiseration. This shows that his humanity forms one body with the child. It may be objected that the child belongs to the same species. Again, when he observes the pitiful cries and frightened appearance of birds and animals about to be slaughtered, he cannot help feeling an "inability to bear" their suffering. This shows his humanity forms one body with birds and animals. It may be objected that birds and animals are sentient beings as he is. But when he sees plants broken and destroyed, he cannot help a feeling of pity. This shows his humanity forms one body with plants. It may be said that plants are living things as he is. Yet, even if he sees tiles and stones shattered and crushed, he

> cannot help a feeling of regret. This shows that his humanity forms one body with tiles and stones. This means that even the heart-mind of the small man necessarily has the humanity that forms one body with all. Such a heart-mind is rooted in the Heaven-endowed nature, and is naturally intelligent, clear, and not beclouded. For this reason it is called the "brilliant virtue."[47]

The "brilliant virtue" inherent in human nature, as the ontological basis for self-realization, enables all human beings, great or small, "to restore the condition of forming one body with Heaven, Earth, and the myriad things, a condition that is originally so, that is all." Indeed, "[i]t is not that outside the original substance something can be added,"[48] for we are empowered, by nature of our humanity, to form a spiritual communion with virtually all modalities of being in a comprehensive and yet appropriately differentiated way.

Wang Yang-ming's "dynamic idealism," as Wing-tsit Chan characterizes it,[49] set the Confucian agenda for several generations in China. His followers, such as the conscientious communitarian Wang Chi (1497–1582), who devoted his long life to building a community of the like-minded, and the radical individualist Li Chih (1527–1602), who proposed to reduce all human relationships to friendship, broadened the Confucian project to accommodate a variety of life-styles. Among Wang's critics, Liu Tsung-chou (1578–1645) was one of the most thoughtful. His *Human Schemata (Jen-p'u)* offers a rigorous phenomenological description of human errors as a corrective to Wang Yang-ming's moral optimism. Liu's student, Huang Tsung-hsi (1610–1695), compiled a comprehensive biographic history of Ming Confucians based on Liu's outlines. One of Huang's intellectual rivals, Ku Yen-wu (1613–1682), also a critic of Wang Yang-ming, excelled in the study of political institutions, ancient phonology, and classical philology. Although Ku was well known in his time and honored as the patron saint of "evidential learning" in the eighteenth century, his contemporary, Wang Fu-chih (1619–1692), largely unknown to his contemporary scholar-officials, was discovered two hundred years later as one of the most sophisticated original minds in Confucian philosophy. His extensive writings on metaphysics, history, and the classics have made him one of the most revered creative thinkers in Chinese intellectual history.

Sagely Learning in East Asia

Among all the dynasties, Chinese and foreign, the long-lived Chosŏn (Yi) in Korea (1392–1910) was undoubtedly the most thoroughly Confucianized. Since the fifteenth century, when the aristocracy (*yangban*) defined itself as the carrier of Confucian values, the penetration of Confucian persuasion in court politics and in elite culture has been unprecedented. The Confucian tradition's vitality, as manifested in political behavior, legal practice, ancestral veneration, genealogy, village schools, and student activism, is still widely felt in South Korea.

The single most important Korean Confucian, Yi T'oegye (1501–1570), helped shape the particular character of Chosŏn Confucianism through his creative interpretation of Chu Hsi's teaching. Critically aware of the philosophical turn engineered by Wang Yang-ming, T'oegye transmitted the Chu Hsi legacy as a response to the advocates of the learning of the mind. As a result, he made Chosŏn Confucianism at least as much a true heir to Sung learning as Ming Confucianism was. Indeed, his *Discourse on the Ten Sagely Diagrams*, as an instructional aid for educating the king, offers a succinct depiction of all the major concepts in Sung learning. His exchange of letters with Ki Taesung (1527–1572) in the famous Four-Seven debate, which discussed the relationship between Mencius's *four* basic human feelings (commiseration, shame, modesty, and a sense of right and wrong) and the *seven* emotions (joy, anger, sorrow, happiness, love, desire, and hatred), raised the level of Confucian dialogue to a new height in intellectual sophistication. Yi Yulgok's (1536–1584) challenge to T'oegye's representation of Chu Hsi's Confucian project, following Master Chu's thought, significantly enriched the repertoire of the Learning of the Principle. The leadership of the central government, combined with the numerous academies set up by aristocratic families and institutions such as the community compact system and the village schools, made the Learning of the Principle not only a political ideology but also a common creed in Korea.

Master T'oegye's *Ten Diagrams of Sagely Learning*, originally intended as an instruction manual for the king's moral education, is a most insightful and informative synopsis of the essential precepts of Confucian teaching.[50] The Confucian religious project, as T'oegye understood it, is centered around a profound sense of reverence: for the self, for the human community, for nature, and for Heaven. Through "elementary learning," we acquire the intimate knowledge of ritual to guide our conduct. We learn to stand, sit, talk, and walk properly not only to show our respect to those around us but also to cultivate a sense of reverence for the routines in our ordinary daily life. As we grow up, we learn to appreciate the values embedded in our basic human relationships: love between parent and child, proper sequence among siblings, mutual responsibility between husband and wife, trust among friends, and rightness in politics. Indeed, society ought to be a fiduciary community based on the spirit of reciprocity. Such a universal principle of considerateness is also extended to nature. Since our human flourishing, in thought and practice, is not the imposition of the anthropocentric view of the universe, it prohibits us from arrogantly asserting that humans are the measure of all things. Indeed, our respect for the sanctity of the earth enables us to continuously try to harmonize with nature. Still, in the ultimate sense, even though Mencius assured us that we can know Heaven through realizing the full potential of our heart-minds and understanding our human nature, we are in awe of the Mandate of Heaven. Our sense of reverence toward Heaven is a constitutive part of our self-cultivation.

Chu Hsi's teaching, as interpreted by T'oegye, was introduced by Yamazaki Ansai (1618–1682) to the Japanese intellectual community. A distinctive feature of Yamazaki's thought was his re-presentation of native Shintoism in Confucian terminology. The diversity and vitality of Japanese Confucianism was further evidenced in the appropriation of Wang Yang-ming's dynamic idealism by the samurai-scholars, notably Kumazawa Banzan (1619–1691). However, it is in Ogyū Sorai's (1666–1728) determination to return to pre-Confucian sources to rediscover the original basis of Confucian teaching that one finds a true exemplification of the independent-mindedness of Japanese Confucians. Indeed, Ogyū's brand of "ancient learning," with particular emphasis on philological exactitude, foreshadowed a similar scholarly movement in China by at least a generation. Although Tokugawa Japan was never as Confucianized as Yi Korea had been, virtually every educated person in Japanese society was exposed to the Four Books by the end of the seventeenth century.

The Confucianization of Chinese society reached its apex during the Ch'ing dynasty (1644–1912) when China was again ruled by a conquering (Manchu) dynasty. The Ch'ing emperors outshone their counterparts in the Ming in presenting themselves as exemplars of Confucian kingship. They consciously and ingeniously transformed Confucian teaching into a political ideology; indeed, a mechanism of symbolic control. Jealously guarding their imperial prerogative as the ultimate interpreters of Confucian truth, they substantially undermined the ability of scholars to transmit the Confucian Way by imposing harsh measures such as a literary inquisition. Understandably, Ku Yen-wu's classical scholarship, rather than his insights on political reform, inspired the eighteenth-century scholars devoted to "evidential learning" with emphasis on textual analysis, etymology, and philological research. Tai Chen (1723–1777), the most philosophically minded philologist among them, couched his brilliant critique of Sung learning in his commentary on *The Meanings of Terms in the Book of Mencius*. Tai Chen was one of the eminent scholars appointed by the Ch'ien-lung Emperor in 1773 to compile an imperial manuscript library. This massive scholarly attempt, *The Complete Library of the Four Treasures,* symbolized the grandiose plan of the Manchu court to give an account of all the important works of the four branches of learning—the classics, history, philosophy, and literature—in Confucian culture. The project comprised more than 36,000 volumes with comments on about 10,230 titles, employed as many as 15,000 copyists, and lasted for twenty years. Ch'ien-lung and the learned scholars around him may have enclosed their cultural heritage in a definitive form, but the Confucian tradition was yet to encounter its most serious threat, which was to come in the form of European expansionism.

Core Values as Embodied in Confucian Sacred Texts

The Analects *as the Embodiment of Confucian Ideas*

The *Analects* (*Lun-yü*), the most revered sacred scripture in the Confucian tradition, was probably compiled by the second generation of Confucius' disciples. Based primarily on the Master's sayings, preserved in both oral and written transmissions, it captures the Confucian spirit in form and content the same way that the Platonic dialogues underscore Socratic pedagogy. Since Confucius is widely seen as a mere commonsense moralizer who gave practical advice to students in everyday situations, the *Analects* has often been viewed by the critical modern reader as a collection of unrelated conversations randomly put together. If we approach the *Analects* as a sacred scripture that is centered around a sagely personality and intended for those who wanted to revive and reanimate a historical moment or a sacred time, we come close to understanding why it has been revered in China for centuries. The *Analects* is a communal memory, a literary device of those who considered themselves beneficiaries of the Confucian Way. It is used to continue the memory and to transmit the form of life as a living tradition. These digested statements centering around Confucius do not seem to have been compiled to present an argument or to record an event but to offer an invitation to readers to take part in an ongoing conversation. Dialogue is used to show Confucius in thought and action—not as an isolated individual, but as a center of relationships. The sayings of the *Analects* reveal the inner person of Confucius—his ambitions, his fears, his joys, his commitments, and, above all, his self-image. Confucians for centuries learned to reenact the awe-inspiring ritual of participating in a conversation with Confucius through the *Analects*.

One of Confucius' most significant personal descriptions is a short autobiographic account of his own spiritual development found in the *Analects*:

> At fifteen I set my heart on learning; at thirty I firmly took my stand; at forty I came to be free from doubts; at fifty I understood the Decree of Heaven; at sixty my ear was attuned; at seventy I followed my heart's desire without overstepping the line.[51]

Confucius' life as a student and teacher exemplified the Confucian idea that education is a ceaseless process of self-realization. When one of his students reportedly had difficulty describing him, Confucius came to his aid: "Why did you not simply say something to this effect: he is the sort of man who forgets to eat when he engages himself in vigorous pursuit of learning, who is so full of joy that he forgets his worries and who does not notice that old age is coming on?"[52]

Confucius was deeply concerned that the culture (*wen*) he cherished was not being transmitted and that the learning (*hsüeh*) he propounded was not being instructed. However, his strong sense of mission never interfered with his ability to silently remember what had been imparted to him, to learn without flagging and to teach without growing weary.[53] He made strenuous demands on himself: "It is these things that cause me concern: failure to cultivate virtue, failure to go deeply into what I have learned, inability to move up to what I have heard to be right, and inability to reform myself when I have defects."[54] What he demanded of his students was the willingness to learn: "I do not enlighten anyone who is not eager to learn, nor encourage anyone who is not anxious to put his ideas into words."[55]

The community that Confucius created through his inspiring personality was a scholarly fellowship of like-minded men of different ages and backgrounds from different states. They were attracted to Confucius because they shared his vision and took part in varying degrees in his mission to bring moral order to an increasingly fragmented polity. This mission was difficult and even dangerous. The Master himself suffered from joblessness, homelessness, starvation and, occasionally, life-threatening violence. Yet, his faith in the survivability of the culture that he cherished and the workability of his approach to teaching was so steadfast that he convinced his followers as well as himself that Heaven was on their side. When Confucius' life was threatened in K'uang, he said:

> Since the death of King Wen [founder of the Chou dynasty], does not the mission of culture (*wen*) rest here in me? If Heaven intends this culture to be destroyed, those who come after me will not be able to have any part of it. If Heaven does not intend this culture to be destroyed, then what can the men of K'uang do to me?[56]

This expression of self-confidence was totally devoid of presumptuousness in Confucius' self-image. Indeed, he made it explicit that he was far from attaining sagehood and that all he really excelled in was "love of learning."[57] To him, learning not only broadened his knowledge and deepened his self-awareness but also defined who he was. He frankly acknowledged that he was not born of knowledge[58] and that he did not belong to the class of men who could innovate without possessing knowledge.[59] Rather, he reported that he used his ears widely and followed what was good in what he had heard and used his eyes widely and retained what he had seen in his mind. He considered his learning "a lower level of knowledge."[60] This level of knowledge, which is attainable through self-effort rather than divine inspiration, is presumably accessible to the majority of the human community. In this sense, Confucius was neither a prophet with privileged access to the divine nor a philosopher who has already seen the truth, but a teacher of humanity who is an advanced fellow traveler on the way to self-realization.

As a teacher of humanity, Confucius stated his ambition in terms of human care: "To bring comfort to the old, to have trust in friends, and to cherish the young."[61] Confucius' vision of the way to develop a moral community began with a holistic reflection on the human condition. Instead of dwelling on abstract ideas such as the state of nature, he sought to understand the actual situation of a given time and use that as a point of departure. His aim was to restore trust in government and to transform society into a moral community by cultivating a sense of human caring in politics and society. To achieve that aim, the creation of a scholarly community, the fellowship of *chün-tzu* (profound persons), was essential. In the words of Confucius' disciple, Tseng Tzu, the truly profound person "must be broad-minded and resolute, for his burden is heavy and his road is long. He takes humanity as his burden. Is that not heavy? Only with death does his road come to an end. Is that not long?"[62] However, the fellowship of *chün-tzu*, as moral vanguards of society, did not seek to establish a radically different order. Its mission was to reformulate and revitalize those institutions which were believed to have maintained social solidarity and enabled people to live in harmony and prosperity for centuries. An obvious example was the role and function of the family.

It is related in the *Analects* that when Confucius was asked why he did not take part in government, he responded by citing a passage from an ancient classic, the *Book of Documents*, "Simply by being a good son and friendly to his brothers a man can exert an influence upon government!", to show that one's personal conduct is politically significant.[63] This is grounded in the Confucian conviction that the self-cultivation of each person is the root of social order and that social order is the basis for political stability and universal peace. This assertion that family ethics is politically efficacious must be seen in the context of the Confucian conception of politics as "rectification" (*cheng*). The rulers are supposed to be ethical exemplars who govern by moral leadership and exemplary teaching rather than force. The government's responsibility is not only to provide food and security but also to educate the people. Law and punishment are the minimum requirements for order; social harmony can only be attained by virtue through ritual performance. To perform ritual is to take part in a communal act to promote mutual understanding.

One of the fundamental Confucian values that ensures the integrity of ritual performance is filial piety. Confucius sees filial piety as the first step toward moral excellence. The way to enhance personal dignity and identity is not to alienate ourselves from the family but to cultivate our genuine feelings for our parents and siblings. To learn to embody the family in our hearts and minds is to enable ourselves to move beyond self-centeredness, or, to borrow from modern psychology, to transform the enclosed private ego into an open self. Indeed, the cardinal Confucian virtue (humanity) is the result of self-cultivation. The first test for our self-cultivation is our ability to cultivate meaningful relationships with our family members. Filial piety does not demand unconditional submissiveness to parental authority but recognition of and reverence for our source of life.

The purpose of filial piety, as the Greeks would have it, is "human flourishing" for both parent and child. Confucians see it as an essential way of learning to be human. They are fond of applying the family metaphor to the community, the country, and the universe. They prefer to address the emperor as the son of Heaven, the king as ruler-father, and the magistrate as the "father-mother official," because they assume that implicit in the family-centered nomenclature is a political vision. When Confucius responded that taking care of family affairs is itself active participation in politics, he already made it clear that family ethics is not merely a private concern, for the public good is realized by and through it.

In response to his best disciple, Yen Hui, Confucius defined humanity as "conquer yourself and return to ritual."[64] This interplay between inner spiritual self-transformation (the Master is said to have freed himself from four things: "opinionatedness, dogmatism, obstinacy, and egoism"[65]) and social participation enabled Confucius to be "loyal" (*chung*) to himself and "considerate" (*shu*) of others.[66] Confucius' legacy, laden with profound ethical implications, is captured by his "plain and real" appreciation of learning to be human as a communal enterprise.

The Mencian Idea of the Five Relationships

The reference to the "five relationships" in the *Book of Mencius* occurs in the context of an elaborate debate with a radical physiocrat who advocated that "[t]o earn his keep a good and wise ruler shares the work of tilling the land with his people."[67] Mencius, in arguing against the proposition that ruling the empire must be combined with the work of tilling the land, invokes the principle of the division of labor. Having established the claim that a hundred different crafts made by potters, blacksmiths, hat-makers, or weavers are necessary for society, Mencius advocates his famous thesis: "There are those who use their minds and there are those who use their muscles. The former govern; the latter are governed. Those who govern are supported by those who are governed."[68] The thesis, sustained by the principle of mutuality, specifies a pattern of interaction between two groups of people: those who are in the "service sector" and those who are producers. Mencius's initial response to the physiocratic challenge is that potters, blacksmiths, hat-makers, and weavers are, like farmers, producers. He further states that those who are not directly involved in productivity but who use their minds (the ruling minority) are vital to the well-being of the community.

For example, the Sage-King Yao did not have the leisure to plough fields, for he was duty-bound to make the security of the empire and the livelihood of the people his primary concerns. His success in restoring the human community after the Flood was due to his ability to appoint the right officers to share responsibility for bringing order to the empire and food to the people. Yet, although order and food provided the minimum condition for human survival, they were not enough for human flourishing:

> Hou Chi [the minister in charge of agriculture] taught the people how to farm and grow the five kinds of grain. When these ripened, the people multiplied. This is the way of the common people: once they have a full belly and warm clothes on their back they degenerate to the level of animals if they are allowed to lead idle lives, without education and discipline.[69]

Human flourishing beyond the basic needs for physical comfort was the reason that the virtues of the "five relationships" were introduced. Thus, Mencius continues:

> This gave the sage King further cause for concern, and so he appointed Hsieh as the Minister of Education whose duty was to teach the people human relationships: love between father and son, duty between ruler and subject, distinction between husband and wife, precedence of the old over the young, and faith between friends.[70]

The context in which Mencius introduced the "five relationships" suggests that the purpose of education is to combat idleness after a measure of economic affluence is secured. This helps us to understand that the virtues governing the relationships are prescriptive as well as demonstrative.

FATHER-SON

Love between father and son is intended to show that the proper relationship between them is mutual affection rather than one-way obedience; it also offers a guidance for those who fail to live up to the norm specified for such a relationship. Since affection between mother and son is more natural than that between father and son, love as a virtue can perform a compensatory function in harmonizing this transgenerational relationship. The ritual of fathers exchanging sons for instruction, for fear that formal education conducted at home by fathers might damage parental love, was often practiced in traditional Confucian families. The Mencian advice is pertinent here:

> Kung-sun Ch'ou said, "Why does a gentleman not take on the teaching of his own sons?" "Because in the nature of things," said Mencius, "it will not work. A teacher necessarily resorts to correction, and if correction produces no effect, it will end by losing his temper. When this happens, father and son will hurt each other instead. 'You teach me by correcting me, but you yourself are not correct.' So father and son hurt each other, and it is bad that such a thing should happen. In antiquity people taught one another's sons. Father and son should not demand goodness from each other. To do so will estrange them, and there is nothing more inauspicious than estrangement between father and son."[71]

RULER-MINISTER

Similarly, duty between ruler and subject is an acknowledgment of the danger of organizing this single most important political relationship in terms of personal profit. The principle of duty (*i*), or more appropriately, righteousness, is sharply contrasted with profit (*li*) for both moral and pragmatic reasons. Mencius observes that the main cause of conflict in the political arena is the abandonment of righteousness as the raison d'être for the ruling minority to enjoy privilege and status without involving themselves in productive labor. Any attempt to profit unjustly or abuse their power in this way in fact makes their legitimate claim to leadership suspect. Their ability to govern is undermined and the public sphere over which they reign becomes privatized.

Mencius recommends the restoration of trust between ruler and subject as the precondition for reestablishing this vitally important relationship. Obviously, love between father and son and duty (or righteousness) between ruler and subject are not transferable, but the spirit of mutuality underlies both of them. In the case of the ruler-subject relationship, Mencius unequivocally states that the prince must earn the support of his ministers. Indeed, their attitude toward him depends on how he treats them:

> If a prince treats his ministers as his hands and feet, they will treat him as their belly and heart. If he treats them as his horses and hounds, they will treat him as a mere fellow-countryman. If he treats them as mud and weeds, they will treat him as an enemy.[72]

Although love between father and son can serve as a standard of inspiration for duty between ruler and subject, the affection rooted in "flesh and blood" is radically different from the calling engendered by the division of labor in society. Such a division not only recognizes the contribution of those who produce but also sanctifies the role of those who labor with their minds as leaders, governors, and servants of the public sphere. However, intent on applying the virtues of the family as the microcosm of the world to the empire as a whole, Mencius insists:

> There is a common expression, "The Empire, the state, the family." The Empire has its basis in the state, the state in the family, and the family in one's own self.[73]

What Mencius advocates here is the fundamental principle of extending the self to the family, the state, the world, and beyond. By implication, love between father and son is politically significant and duty between ruler and subject is, in spirit, an extension of the family ethic. This may have been the reason that in Confucian political culture love between father and son often served as an analogy for duty between ruler and subject, even though the difference, as Mencius originally detects it, is enormous.

HUSBAND-WIFE

If age features prominently in the father-son relationship and position in the ruler-subject relationship, gender defines the husband-wife relationship. Although age and position are not irrelevant in the husband-wife relationship, they are subsumed under the category of "distinction" (*pieh*). It has often been assumed that, by stressing the importance of distinction in such a relationship, the Confucians deliberately undermine romantic love in the conjugal relationship. Quite a number of scholars have noted that the value of duty looms so large in Confucian family ethics that the role of the wife must be preceded by that of the daughter-in-law. If children are involved, the role of the mother should also take precedence over that of the wife.

Nevertheless, the value of distinction in governing the husband-wife relationship is also based on the principle of mutuality. The underlying spirit is not dominance but division of labor. Occasionally commentators cite the etymological origin of the word *ch'i* (first tone, "wife") as *ch'i* (second tone, "equal") to support the view that the wife is the husband's equal.

Surely, in a male-dominated society, equality between husband and wife as we understand it is out of the question, but the Mencian idea of distinction is in accord with the Confucian vision of the "Age of Great Unity" when "men have their tasks and women their hearths." Although the idea of the wife, rather than the husband, as the homemaker is being challenged today, the division of labor between husband and wife in a collaborative effort to raise a family is still widely recognized as a necessity, if not a virtue.

In a prescriptive sense, love and affection between husband and wife are taken for granted. The focus is then on the precautionary measures pertinent to such a relationship for the purpose of human flourishing. As the dangers of estrangement between father and son and alienation between ruler and minister must be overcome to make their relationships mutually fruitful, the danger of excessive indulgence between husband and wife is a cause for concern. Conjugal intimacy may breed nepotism, which, in turn, may lead to social irresponsibility, if the interests of the nuclear family supersede concerns for other family members and the larger community.

OLD-YOUNG

"Precedence of the old over the young" governs more than sibling relationships. It underscores age as a factor in organizing human relationships. The word *precedence* (*hsü*) also means order and sequence. Age is thus an ordering and sequencing principle. A distinctive feature of Confucian ethics is to accept seniority as a value in setting up social hierarchy. However, age alone does not automatically give one status. The unexamined assertion that Confucians respect the old loses much of its persuasion in the light of the Master's harsh words to an unmannerly old man of his acquaintance: "In youth, not humble as befits a junior; in manhood, doing nothing worthy of being handed down. And merely to live on, getting older and older, is to be a useless pest."[74]

The Confucian commitment to personal moral growth through self-effort justifies the condemnation of those who fail to realize their own potential. The aforementioned Yüan Jang, who prompted Confucius not only to use harsh words but to "hit him on the shank with his staff,"[75] seems to have consistently squandered his time and energy. However, to the Confucians, age normally embodies experience and wisdom and, therefore, commands respect. Mencius notes with pride the legacy bequeathed by Tseng Tzu, one of the most revered disciples of Confucius:

> There are three things which are acknowledged by the world to be exalted: rank, age and virtue. At court, rank is supreme; in the village, age; but for assisting the world and ruling over the people it is virtue.[76]

Undoubtedly, in the Confucian order of things, virtue takes precedence over rank and age. However, as pragmatists and realists, the Confucians are acutely aware of the necessity of hierarchy in establishing stability and harmony in society. Tseng Tzu's strategy of using age and virtue in his confrontation with rank is characteristic of the Confucian approach to political power:

> How can a man, on the strength of the possession of one of these, treat the other two with arrogance? Hence a prince who is to achieve great things must have subjects he does not summon. If he wants to consult them, he goes to them. If he does not honor virtue and delight in the Way in such a manner, he is not worthy of being helped towards the achievements of great things.... Today there are many states, all equal in size and virtue, none being able to dominate the others. This is simply because the rulers are given to employing those they can teach rather than those from whom they can learn.[77]

"Precedence of the old over the young" is thus a deliberate attempt to build an ethic on a biological reality. The reason that "filial piety" (*hsiao*) and "brotherly love" (*t'i*) are considered "roots" (*pen*) for realizing full humanity is partly due to the Confucian belief that moral self-cultivation begins with the recognition that biological bonding provides an authentic opportunity for personal realization. The duty-consciousness generated by the acknowledgment that we are beneficiaries of our parents and older siblings and that our well-being is inseparable from theirs is not one-way obedience. Rather, it is a response to a debt that one can never repay and an awareness that the willingness to assume responsibility for paying that debt is morally exhilarating. Of course, such an ethic has many complex dimensions. The legend of the Sage-King Shun, who had a heartless father and a scheming half-brother, amply illustrates the difficulty when the desired spirit of mutuality is absent.[78] We need not unpack the whole legend here. Suffice it to say that the Confucians are aware of the ambiguity and paradox involved in assigning great value to generation and age in the attempt to harmonize interpersonal relationships at home.

FRIEND-FRIEND

Friendship, based on neither rank nor age, is the paradigmatic expression of the spirit of mutuality. Hierarchy may have been a dominant theme in Confucian ethics, but it is certainly inapplicable to "faith between friends." The centrality of friendship in moral exhortation provides a basis for the teacher-disciple relationship, which, in turn, offers a model for Confucian self-understanding in reference to the ruler.

The case of Tseng Tzu, mentioned earlier, is instructive here. By claiming that both virtue and age were on his side, Tseng Tzu made it explicit to the king that he would not be summoned like an ordinary subject to the court; however, if the king was willing to learn, he would give frank advice. Fully informed by this sense of dignity, independence, and autonomy, Mencius also conducted himself as a senior friend and teacher to the kings he encountered. Thus, he confronted the ruler with his candid assessment of the lack of moral leadership in officialdom, embarrassed the ruler with his sharp criticism of the miserable state of affairs, and even startled the ruler with the likelihood of revolution. A trusted friend, in this sense, is a critic, a teacher, and a fellow traveler on the Way. Faith or trust (*hsin*) between friends is sustained by a lasting commitment to mutual flourishing rather than by the temporary comfort of sharing food and drink. Consistent with Confucian ethics, a well-known Chinese proverb states that the "friendship" between shallow people is as sweet as honey, but friendship between profound persons is as plain as water.

We can examine the five primary human relationships in the perspective of Confucian self-cultivation as a communal act. The implications are:

1. Confucians, by stressing the centrality of self-cultivation, do not undermine the corporate effort that is required for the family, the community, the state, and the world to become humane or fully human.

2. Indeed, the interchange between the self, as an open system in a dynamic process of "embodying" an ever-expanding network of human relatedness, and society, as a fiduciary community, constantly reenacts the ritual of actively participating in mutual exhortation. This interchange defines the Confucian project of self-realization in terms of personal and communal self-transcendence.

3. As the self overcomes egoism to become authentically human, the family must overcome nepotism to become authentically human. By analogy, the community must overcome parochialism, the state must overcome ethnocentrism, and the world must overcome anthropocentrism to become authentically human. In light of Confucian inclusive humanism, the transformed self individually and corporately transcends egoism, nepotism, parochialism, ethnocentrism, and anthropocentrism for it to "form one body with Heaven, Earth and the myriad things."[79]

Our purpose in presenting an inquiry into the "five relationships" from the perspective of self-cultivation philosophy is to show that, although the underlying structure of the "five relationships" suggests a strong concern for social ethics, the psychocultural roots that sustain the persuasive power of these relationships in Confucian moral education are deeply grounded in an "anthropocosmic" vision.

Confucian Critique of the "Three Bonds"

In the modern egalitarian and liberal perspective, the least appealing legacy of Confucian ethics is the so-called "three bonds" (*san-kang*); namely, the authority of the ruler over the minister, the father over the son, and the husband over the wife. Chinese intellectuals' iconoclastic attacks on the Confucian establishment in the first decades of the twentieth century have given the impression that the rationale for the bonds was motivated by an authoritarian impulse to dominate the subservient, the young, and the female. Based on this perception, the three bonds have been depicted as three forms of bondage and Confucian ethics has been condemned as despotic, autocratic, patriarchal, gerontocratic, and male-chauvinistic.

Historically, the idea of the three bonds emerged in Confucian literature relatively late, almost four centuries after Mencius first advocated the virtues of the "five relationships."[80] The systematic efforts, under imperial patronage, of the Han dynasty (206 B.C.E.–220 C.E.) scholar-officials to transform Confucian ethics into a political ideology was instrumental in promoting the three bonds as an integral part of the core curriculum for moral education. Ironically, the first textual evidence of the idea occurs in the *Han Fei Tzu*, the Legalist classic: "The minister serves the king, the son serves the father, and the wife serves the husband. If the three are followed, the world will be in peace; if the three are violated, the world will be in chaos."[81] Obviously, the Han ideologists, like the Legalists, were mainly concerned about the functional utility of the three bonds as a mechanism of symbolic control for the primary purpose of social stability. The perception that regularizing these cardinal relationships helps maintain political order is not incompatible with the Confucian idea that basic dyadic relationships, private as well as public, are the foundation of a fiduciary community, but the fixed hierarchy encompassed in the ideology of the three bonds is detrimental to human flourishing. Indeed, the three bonds drastically altered the Mencian intention by relegating the spirit of mutuality to the background.

Obviously, the three bonds, based on dominance/subservience, underscore the hierarchical relationship as an inviolable principle for maintaining social order. The primary concern is not the well-being of the individual persons involved in these dyadic relationships, but the particular pattern of social stability that results from these rigidly prescribed rules of conduct.

The centrality of the father-son relationship in providing the basic structure of justification for the three bonds has the advantage of adding persuasive power to the political authority of the ruler and the husband. In a hierarchic and patriarchal society, it must seem convincing that the ruler or the husband, like the father, should be the interpreter, the executor, and the judge of the moral code, for he assumes full responsibility for the stability and harmony of society. Position and gender, like age, are conceived as natural patterns of the social landscape. If the inferior challenges the superior or the wife dominates the husband, the moral fabric of society will be damaged. Once this line of reasoning (or, in our modern perspective, unreasoning) is accepted, the minister has no recourse but to demonstrate unquestioned loyalty as a defining characteristic of his being. Similarly, as the male-centered perspective becomes pervasive, position and age can both be subsumed under the category of gender: Since the female under no circumstances should assume a dominating role, she must practice the art of "following"—as a daughter, she follows her father; as a wife, she follows her husband; and as a mother, she follows her son.[82]

The value of obedience, specifically practiced by the son, the minister, and the wife looms large in the ideology of the three bonds. This politicization of Confucian ethics fundamentally restructures the five relationships, making them the "legalist" mechanism of symbolic control rather than the interpersonal base for the realization of the Mencian idea of a fiduciary community. I use the word *legalist* to describe the three bonds both to note their apparent origin and to stress their coercive nature. However, the politicized Confucian implementation of the three bonds is much more demanding than their legalist origin and nature may suggest. When Han Fei Tzu pronounced that "if the minister serves the king, the son serves the father, and the wife serves the husband," then "the world will be in peace," he may have been simply making a descriptive statement concerning an ordered society in behavioral terms, but the politicized Confucian idea of the three bonds demands not only correct conduct, but also right attitude; indeed, orthodox belief. The logic of the three bonds seems distinctly Confucian in character. Of course the word *Confucian* here has taken on a new meaning. It is no longer the teachings of Confucius and his disciples, who were politically powerless but spiritually influential proponents of the Way of the Sage-Kings. Rather, the Confucians who propounded the logic of the three bonds were prominent scholars of the Han court who, as shapers of an emerging political ideology defined by Confucian categories, were invited by the emperor to reach a national consensus on the vital cosmological and ethical issues confronting the state. Needless to say, the ethics of the three bonds as an integral part of this politicized Confucian mechanism of symbolic control is a far cry from the Mencian idea of the five relationships.

The Five Classics as Five Visions

As a transmitter, Confucius responded creatively to the symbolic resources of his own culture. He injected new meanings and dynamism into the ritual system, language, and the whole symbolic structure that comprised Chou culture. In doing so, Confucius helped formulate five important visions that became the classical Confucian Way. The first vision is poetic (and by inference artistic and musical) whereby a human being is conceived as one who is constantly involved in an internal resonance between the self and other human beings, and between the self and the transmitted culture. Poetry refines human feelings and sentiments into artistic expressions of humanity. To understand poetry is to have access to these collective feelings. The ability to respond to the world in a poetic sense is considered essential to the development of the person. As noted in the *Analects*, when children become excited by poetry, they are already well on the way toward understanding themselves, especially their inner feelings.

A second important vision in Confucianism is the social vision. Ritual, in the Confucian context, is closely related to the social vision of human communication. Ritual is not the concern for external form; rather, ritual is a concern for both verbal and nonverbal communication within the human community. Children must be taught ritual behavior, because adult behavior, after all, derives from habits learned as children. An important part of ritual is timeliness, in that different behavior is called for in different social settings and circumstances.

A third vision is historical. A society is not created simply by contractual relationships of interested parties. Society, or culture, comes into being through a very long and strenuous process of collective effort. Every human society has a collective memory. The ability to relate to that collective memory is also the ability to identify one's self.

Confucianism also includes a political vision. We are expected to participate in the polity of which we are a part. We humans are political beings in the sense that we should be responsive to and responsible for the collective enterprise of the community as a whole. This is part of the reason that Confucians never created a spiritual sanctuary totally outside this world. In the Confucian tradition, there is no church, no temple, and no shrine that is actually or symbolically removed from the political or social arenas of ordinary human life. However, although the Confucians were in the world, they never simply submitted themselves to the status quo; nor did they merely adjust themselves to the world. In fact, the tension and conflict between what the Confucians conceived as the political ideal and the actual state of the political order has always been acute, and their continuous struggle to bridge the gap often endangered their personal well-being with tragic consequences for their families.

The fifth Confucian vision is metaphysical, based on the conviction that all modalities of being in the universe are interconnected. Joseph Needham characterizes this as the organismic unity of Chinese cosmological thinking.[83] Confucians believe that all modalities of being—human beings, nature, and the spiritual world—are internally interconnected. This metaphysical (one might call it ecological) vision enables the Confucians to advocate the importance of both the realization of the person in the human community and the unity of humanity and Heaven.

If we take these five visions holistically, we cannot subscribe to the reductionist ideas of humans as simply tool-users, language-bearers, or political animals. Rather, human beings combine all five dimensions: they are simultaneously poetic, social, political, historical, and metaphysical beings.

The Five Classics can be described in terms of the five visions: metaphysical, political, poetic, social, and historical. The metaphysical vision, symbolized by the *Book of Change* (*I Ching*), combines divinatory art with numerological technique and ethical insight. According to the philosophy of change, the cosmos is a great transformation occasioned by the constant interaction of two complementary as well as conflicting vital energies, *yin* and *yang*. The universe, which resulted from this great transformation, always exhibits organismic unity and dynamism. The profound person, inspired by the harmony and creativity of the universe, must emulate the highest ideal of the "unity of man and Heaven" through ceaseless self-exertion.

The political vision, symbolized by the *Book of Documents* (*Shu Ching*), addresses the kingly way by delineating the ethical foundation for a humane government. The legendary Three Emperors (Yao, Shun, and Yü) all ruled by virtue. Their sagacity, filial piety, and hard work enabled them to create a political culture based on responsibility and trust. Through exemplary teaching, they encouraged people to enter into a "covenant" with them so that social harmony could be achieved without punishment or coercion. Even in the Three Dynasties (Hsia, Shang, and Chou), moral authority, as ritualized power, was sufficient to maintain political order. The human continuum, from the undifferentiated masses, via the enlightened people and the nobility, to the sage-king, formed an organic unity as an integral part of the great cosmic transformation.

The poetic vision, symbolized by the *Book of Poetry* (*Shih Ching*), underscores the Confucian value of common human feelings. The majority of the verses express emotions and sentiments of persons and communities from all echelons of society. The internal resonance or basic rhythm of the poetic world characterized by the Book is mutual responsiveness. The tone as a whole is honest rather than earnest and evocative rather than expressive.

The social vision, symbolized by the *Book of Rites* (*Li Chi*), defines society not as an adversarial system based on contractual relationships but as a community of trust with emphasis on communication. The society organized by the four functional occupations—the scholar, farmer, artisan, and merchant—is, in the true sense of the word, a cooperation. As a contributing member of the cooperation, each person is obligated to recognize the existence of others and to serve the public good. By the principle of "the rectification of names," it is the king's duty to act kingly and the father's duty to act fatherly. If the king or father fails to behave properly, he cannot expect his minister or son to act in accordance with ritual. It is in this sense that a chapter in the *Rites*, entitled the *Great Learning*, must be regarded: "From the Son of Heaven to the commoner, all must regard self-cultivation as the root."[84] This pervasive "duty-consciousness" features prominently in all Confucian literature on ritual.

The historical vision, symbolized by the *Spring and Autumn Annals* (*Ch'un-ch'iu*), emphasizes the significance of collective memory for communal self-identification. Historical consciousness is a defining characteristic of Confucian thought. By defining himself as a transmitter and as a lover of antiquity, Confucius made it explicit that a sense of history is not only desirable but also necessary for self-knowledge. Confucius' emphasis on the importance of history was in a way his reappropriation of the ancient wisdom that reanimating the old is the best way to attain the new. Confucius may not have authored the *Spring and Autumn Annals*, but it seems likely that he applied moral judgment to political events in China proper from the eighth century to the fifth century B.C.E. In this unprecedented political criticism, he assumed a godlike role in evaluating politics by assigning ultimate "praise and blame" in history to the most powerful and influential political actors of the period. This practice inspired not only the innovative style of the Grand Historian, Ssu-ma Ch'ien (d. ca. 85 B.C.E.), but was widely employed by others writing dynastic histories in imperial China.

The Five Classics as five visions—metaphysical, political, poetic, social, and historical—provide a holistic context for the development of Confucian scholarship as a comprehensive inquiry in the humanities.

A defining characteristic of Confucian humanism is its multiperspective view of the human condition. This nonreductionist approach is predicated on the strong conviction that human beings are more than rational beings, political animals, tool users, or language manipulators; they are endowed with rich resources of self-transformation and they come into being through a long and strenuous process. Indeed, the core values embodied in the Confucian sacred texts suggest a subtly textured and finely layered appreciation of the meaning of being human; while we are embedded in our human-relatedness, our ultimate concern is the continuous self-transformation of our body and mind so that, through our sociality, we realize ourselves as witnesses of the Mandate of Heaven.

Salient Features of the Confucian Spiritual Orientation

Informed by the two major epochs of the Confucian tradition and the core values embodied in the Confucian sacred texts, we may wonder what significance this distinctively Confucian spiritual orientation really has for students in the comparative study of religion. It should be obvious that some of the conceptual apparatuses widely employed in religious studies are inadequate in dealing with the Confucian tradition. Virtually all familiar exclusive dichotomies have lost their explanatory power: spirit/matter, body/mind, sacred/profane, creator/creature, and transcendence/immanence. We need to develop a new method, formulate a new procedure, and cultivate new symbolic resources to meet the challenge.

A simple, if not simple-minded, way out is to exclude the Confucian tradition from a comparative study of religion. While it is neat to confine ourselves to the spirit, the life of the mind, the sacred world, the power of the creator, and the transcendent dimension in our religious discourse, the picture emerging from such discussions is likely to be one-sided. A much more exciting intellectual enterprise is to explore the spirituality of matter, the embodiment of the mind, the possibility of regarding the secular as sacred, the creative and transformative potential in humanity, and the meaning of immanent transcendence. Still, the provocativeness of the Confucian spiritual orientation lies in its "religiosity," rather than in its humanness, this-worldliness, and immanence.

Learning to Be Human

What distinguishes the Confucian approach to human flourishing is its emphasis on education—education as a form of learning, particularly "learning for the sake of oneself." Learning is conceived by the Confucians as a continuous holistic process of character-building. The process involves an existential commitment to the task of self-realization through the conscientious cultivation of the "great body." This involves a continuing—an unceasing—process of self-learning for the purpose of acquiring self-knowledge. Self-reflection and personal introspective examination are constantly practiced as part of the daily routine. The Confucian self, in this sense, is not a static structure but a dynamic ever-changing process.

The case of the seventeenth-century Confucian teacher Sun Ch'i-feng (1584–1675) is illuminating. His continuous self-reflexivity enabled him to detect lapses in word and deed at eighty-nine when he celebrated his ninetieth birthday. With a touch of humor, he even remarked in front of his students that only after he had turned eighty did he realize his childishness in his seventies. The Confucian definition of an adult (a mature person) is someone who has taken the "becoming process" seriously and is, therefore, well on his or her way to maturity. However, since the process of learning to be human is ceaseless, maturing never ends. We can sharpen our understanding of this dimension of the Confucian project by applying this insight to the life history of Confucius himself. Before Confucius died at the age of seventy-three, he had remarked that he "could follow the dictates of my heart without overstepping the boundaries of right" at seventy.[85] This total harmony between what one is and what one ought to be has been identified by later Confucians as an awe-inspiring attainment: the fusion of necessity with spontaneity. We can raise the counterfactual question: Had Confucius enjoyed the longevity of the Buddha and lived to the ripe old age of eighty, would he have been involved in further self-improvement? Despite the strong belief that what Confucius had attained symbolizes the highest stage of human maturation, the consensus among Confucian followers is that, of course, if he had lived longer, he would have continued his unceasing efforts to learn and improve himself so that he could provide further richness and nuances to his life. Such a question seems out of place in either the Christian or Buddhist context.

We may summarize the Confucian paradox as follows: Ontologically every human being is inevitably a sage, and existentially no human being can ever become a sage. To put it in personal terms, I am not what I ought to be, but the resources for me to learn what I ought to be are embedded in the very structure of what I am. This paradox, that every person is a potential sage while actually the process of learning to be a sage is never-ending, forms the context in which the Confucian Way is to be pursued.

This-Worldliness

Another salient feature of the Confucian spiritual orientation is the commitment to the intrinsic reasonableness and meaningfulness of this world here and now. Nevertheless, this commitment, far from being an adjustment to the world or an acceptance of the status quo, is motivated by a steadfast determination to transform the world from within. The perception that what the world is falls short of what it ought to be enables the Confucian to maintain a critical distance from the established economic interests, political power, and social hierarchy of the time. The existential decision not to take flight from the world but to immerse oneself in the economic, political, and social affairs of the time compels the Confucian to continuously interact with those in power and wrestle with "mundane" issues of the "secular" order. With a strong sense of moral responsibility and often with a profound sense of human tragedy as well, true Confucians, like Confucius, do what they realistically know cannot be done. A fruitful way of approaching this vitally important and often misunderstood dimension of Confucian spirituality is to examine, in some detail, how Confucius actually defined himself in such matters. Whether Confucius was "a prosaic and parochial moralizer" and his collected conversations, the *Analects*, fragmentary and commonsensical or "a thinker with an imaginative vision of man equal in its grandeur to any [major philosophical or religious tradition]"[86] depends on our assessment of this particular aspect of the Confucian legacy.

Confucius' self-understanding may serve as a starting point for our exploration. He characterized himself as a fellow human being with a Heaven-ordained mission to transmit the Way as an inexhaustible student and a tireless teacher. A fellow human being specifies Confucius' humanness as an irreducible reality of his existence. The following exchange in the *Analects* clearly shows his existential choice to participate in the human fellowship, even though the thought of detaching himself from the world was not only a real possibility but also a persistent temptation:

> Ch'ang-shu and Chieh-ni were cultivating their fields together. Confucius was passing that way and told [his disciple] Tzu-lu to ask them where the river could be forded. Ch'ang-shu said, "Who is the one holding the reins in the carriage?" Tzu-lu said, "It is K'ung Ch'iu [Confucius' given name]." "Is he the K'ung Ch'iu of Lu [Confucius' native state]?" "Yes." "Then he already knows where the river can be forded!" Tzu-lu asked Chieh-ni. Chieh-ni said, "Who are you sir?" Tzu-lu replied, "I am Chung-yu [given name of Tzu-lu]." "Are you a follower of K'ung Ch'iu of Lu?" "Yes." Chieh-ni said, "The whole world is swept as though by a torrential flood. Who can change it? As for you, instead of following one who flies from this man or that man, is it not better to follow those who flee the world all together?" And with that he went on covering the seed without stopping. Tzu-lu went to Confucius and told him about the conversation. Confucius was lost in thought for a while and said, "One cannot herd with birds and beasts. If I do not associate with humankind, with whom shall I associate? If the Way prevailed in the world, there would be no need for me to change it."[87]

This exchange vividly portrays the encounter of two significantly different approaches to life. The hermits Ch'ang-chu and Chieh-ni opted to abdicate their social responsibility and "flee the world all together." While it would perhaps be inaccurate to characterize them as Taoists, their challenge to Confucius was unmistakably Taoistic. Confucius seems to have accepted their assessment of the objective conditions of their day: "the whole world is swept away as though by a torrential flood." He himself characterized the situation this way: "The phoenix does not come; the river chart does not emerge."[88] Yet, his personal decision about how to confront the disorders of his day differed radically from most men. The Taoists endeavored to cultivate their own piece of "pure land" so that they could enjoy a personal sense of tranquillity and unity with nature. They perceived with an ironic detachment people like Confucius who made desperate, and always abortive, attempts to right the wrongs of the world. They themselves, not unlike Thomas More with his utopian view of the mundane world, determined that politics had degenerated to the point of no return. To them, Confucius' "fleeing from this man or that man," which obviously referred to his frustrations with this or that ruler, was an exercise in futility.

The decision of Ch'ang-chu and Chieh-ni to sever their relationship with humankind was laden with far-reaching ethical and spiritual implications. In their view, the only hope for personal fulfillment in an age of disorder was to ignore the world's problems and "tend one's own garden." Ch'ang-chu's seemingly sarcastic remark that Confucius already knew where the river could be forded signifies, in a deeper sense, that the river, the "torrential flood that is sweeping the whole world," is too dangerous to be forded at all. Chieh-ni's rhetorical question to Tzu-lu—"Is it not better to follow those who flee the world all together?"—can best be understood as a warning, indeed, as an invitation. In fact, Chieh-ni's question was ominous, for Tzu-lu later lost his life in a political struggle.

Confucius knew what his Taoist critics had opted to do, or more appropriately, what they had chosen to become. The Taoist choice actually appealed to him as a highly desirable style of life. Confucius himself once expressed a wish "to go and live among the nine wild tribes of the east"[89] and jokingly stated that if the Way did not prevail, he would "get upon a raft, and float about on the sea."[90] Confucius' fascination with music, his sensitivity to nature, and his delight in the simple pleasures of life[91] can all be cited to show that he was not, by temperament, out of tune with the Taoist vision. But for Confucius, it was precisely the nature of the times—the turmoil and disorder—that called for political engagement rather than detachment. There is pathos in his lamentation, "If the Way prevailed in the world, there would be no need for me to change it." His audacious personal assumption of the moral responsibility to change the world, to "repossess the Way,"[92] aroused much excitement, and also much suspicion, on the part of many people. A brief encounter with the "Madman of Ch'u" was not untypical:

> *Chieh Yü, the Madman of Ch'u, went past Confucius, singing,*
> *Phoenix, oh phoenix!*
> *How thy virtue has declined!*
> *What is past is beyond help,*
> *What is to come is not yet lost.*
> *Give up, give up!*
> *Perilous is the lot of those in office today.*
>
> Confucius got down from his carriage with the intention of speaking with him, but the Madman avoided him by hurrying off, and in the end Confucius was unable to speak with him.[93]

The Madman of Ch'u was obviously impressed by the dangerous nature of Confucius' self-assigned mission. Others were equally impressed by its apparent impracticality:

> When Tzu-lu was stopping at the Stone Gate for the night, the gate keeper asked him, "Where are you from?" Tzu-lu said, "From Confucius." "Oh, is he the one who knows that it cannot be done and still does it?"[94]

In other words, in the awkward but accurate translation of James Legge, he "knows the impractical nature of the times, and yet he will be doing in them,"[95] because his sense of mission urges him on.

The seemingly contradictory description of Confucius' critical awareness of the impracticality of putting his Way into practice, and his self-conscious resoluteness to carry it out with all his heart, perceptively captures the spirit of the Confucian project. By inextricably linking his own fortune with the whole world, even though he realistically understood that he could do very little to prevent the world from being swept away by a torrential flood, he still chose to do the best he could to show the Way of avoiding such an impending disaster. This may have been an exercise in futility, especially if we apply pragmatic criteria to assess his success in the political arena. However, despite pessimistic talk about a world beyond redemption, Confucius' faith in the transformability and perfectibility of human nature was never in question. However bleak the immediate situation may have appeared to him, he believed the Way could still prevail in society, and even in politics, through education. In any case, he saw the great task of "repossessing the Way" as a Heaven-ordained moral imperative and a spiritual calling, not to be denied whatever the odds.

Transcendence in Immanence

We should also note that, despite Confucius' this-worldly spiritual orientation, he was not exclusively concerned with the improvement of the secular order. To characterize Confucius as a social reformer is deceptively simplistic. The Confucian project has a transcendent dimension. The idea that the human Way is sanctioned by Heaven implies that Confucian this-worldliness is profoundly religious. The religiousness of Confucius' mission as a "social reformer" is exemplified in a passage in the *Analects* about a border guard at Yi, in the state of Wei:

> The border official of Yi requested an audience, saying, "I have never been denied an audience by any nobleman who has come to this place." The followers presented him. When he came out, he said, "What worry have you, gentlemen, about the loss of office. The empire has long been without the Way. Heaven is about to use your Master as the wooden tongue for a bell [to rouse the empire]."[96]

Suggestively, Confucius himself interpreted his own mission in transcendent terms. Once when Huan T'ui, the Minister of War in the state of Sung, attempted to kill him, he commented on the incident with unusual self-assurance: "Heaven is author of the virtue that is in me. What can Huan T'ui do to me?"[97] This seemingly presumptuous self-description signifies a deep-rooted commitment to the Way as a Heaven-ordained mission:

> When under siege in K'uang, the Master said, "With King Wen dead, is not culture (*wen*) invested here in me? If Heaven intends this culture to be destroyed, those who come after me will not be able to have any part of it. If Heaven does not intend this culture to be destroyed, then what can the men of K'uang do to me?"[98]

It would be misleading, however, if the transcendent dimension of the Confucian project were interpreted to mean that the course of culture, or the Way, would eventually prevail on its own. Confucius made it explicit: "It is the human that can make the Way great, and not the Way that can make the human great."[99] At the same time, as a mere human mortal, he also realized how difficult it was to live up to the demands of the Way of Heaven, and he was the first to admit his own shortcomings in this regard:

> There are four things in the Way of the profound person, none of which I have been able to do. To serve my father as I would expect my son to serve me: that I have not been able to do. To serve my ruler as I would expect my ministers to serve me: that I have not been able to do. To serve my elder brothers as I would expect my younger brothers to serve me: that I have not been able to do. To be the first to treat friends as I would expect my friends to treat me: that I have not been able to do.[100]

The tension and conflict between his sense of mission—that he was entrusted by Heaven to transmit the Way—and his sense of deficiency "in practicing the ordinary virtues and in the exercise of care in ordinary conversation"[101] generated a dynamism in Confucius' "earnest and genuine" effort to learn fully to be human. This dynamism made him an inexhaustible student and an untiring teacher: "To remember silently [what I have learned], to learn untiringly, and to teach others without being wearied—that is just natural to me."[102] What drew people to this teacher was a quiet charisma embodied in his daily interactions with students. There was no prophetic claim of privileged access to the divine. Nor was there any suggestion of noble birth or superior native intelligence. Yet, he aroused the devotion of his followers with the magic quality of his sincerity and authenticity:

> Shu-sun Wu-shu made defamatory remarks about Chung-ni [Confucius]. Tzu-kung said, "He is simply wasting his time. Chung-ni cannot be defamed. In other cases, men of excellence are like hills which one can climb over. Chung-ni is like the sun and the moon which one has no way of climbing over. Even if someone wanted to cut himself off from them, how could this detract from the sun and the moon? It would merely serve the more to show that he did not know his own measure."[103]

What inspired such devotion and confidence in his followers? Certainly they seem to have been heartened by his vision of the transcendent embedded in the practical living of ordinary daily existence. Moreover the commonness, humility, and reverence with which he approached life along with his burning conviction that steady improvement in human life is both a possibility and a necessity seem to have inspired many of them. Confucius may have failed as a potential statesman or as a practical social reformer. As an inspiring witness to the possibilities of human life, however, he certainly lived up to the calling of a fellow human being with a Heaven-ordained mission to transmit the Way, as an inexhaustible student and an untiring teacher.

Human-Relatedness

The personality of Confucius symbolizes a deep faith in the intrinsic worth of humanity. We may well ask ourselves whether such a seemingly naive faith can still be relevant to our problem-riddled world of the late twentieth century. To be sure, we are today constantly threatened by annihilation as a result of human wickedness, or, if you will, sinfulness. But in the Confucian view, the human condition can be improved and society can be transformed because human nature is forever improvable. This is a sense of duty that springs from the knowledge that we are irrevocably embedded in life on this earth. If we do not care for our home here, there is no other home to escape to. There is not even an afterlife to anticipate if we fail to live our lives morally, meaningfully, and fully on this earth here and now. Confucius asks that we take ourselves, and our lives here and now, absolutely seriously. We learn to be human neither to please the world nor to meet the expectations of our parents, but for the sake of ourselves as improvable human beings.

At the same time, since we are not isolated individuals, we should not choose to be loners. Robinson Crusoe's life of isolation is exhilarating to many of us not because of his solitude and independence, but because he demonstrated hope and perseverance. Confucians may think highly of these admirable human qualities, but they strongly believe that the dignity, autonomy, and independence of the person need not be based on individualism. To define our personhood or our selfhood through human fellowship (with others) does not undermine our individuality but instead recognizes the self-evident truth that human beings reach their highest potential through communication and communal participation with other human beings. Confucian humanism advocates that the world is redeemable through human effort, and that we can fully realize ourselves (or attain ultimate salvation) by self-cultivation. The Confucian view of personal development can be visualized as an open-ended series of concentric circles, because the Confucian idea of the self is not built on the idea of individuality as the core of the person (unlike the Judeo-Christian sense of the soul or the Hindu sense of *ātman*). Rather, in Confucianism, the self is always understood as the center of relationships. This open-ended series of concentric circles points to an ever-extending horizon. A person's growth and development should never be viewed as a lonely struggle, for it involves participation in a large context of human-relatedness. Moreover, this process of learning to be human is not simply the development of the self in relation to one's family, neighborhood, community, or state; it is also a deepening process of self-knowledge and self-understanding.

The point of departure for building a moral life through Confucian education is first to discipline the body. The six arts that constitute Confucian education—ritual, music, marksmanship, horsemanship, calligraphy, and mathematics—can all be understood as forms of training the body. Teaching young children, often beginning at the age of eight, to learn how to handle their bodies is not a trivial matter. In the case of ritual, it is extremely complicated (and important) to teach children the proper way to walk, to use their hands, to sit, and to answer simple questions. This ritualization of the body in which youngsters eventually learn the ritual language to express themselves enables them to participate in the larger human community and to communicate meaningfully through their bodily movements as well as words and ideas.

The notion of *shen-chiao*, often translated as "exemplary teaching," literally means "body teaching"—teaching through the example of the body rather than simply teaching by words. The teachers, through personal exemplification, induce the students to emulate them as standards of inspiration rather than mechanistic models. The Confucian *Analects* contains many interesting examples of this kind. The modern reader may find it difficult to appreciate some of the descriptions of how Confucius presented gifts, taught, ate, visited a temple, or how he performed simple mundane acts. These may seem to many to be conventional descriptions of ordinary behavior, but the message of the *Analects*, especially to those who are attuned to listen, is to present Confucius as a living person in the context of human-relatedness and in the process of ritualizing his own body.

Confucius' concern with ritual, with "learning to be human," and with "repossessing and transmitting the Way," suggests a critical awareness that cultural creativity necessarily involves accepting certain aspects of the past to emulate in the present. Creating something out of nothing is not the paradigm of creativity for the Confucian. Rather, creativity in the cultural arena entails interpretive brilliance. It is in this sense that Confucius characterized himself as a transmitter rather than the creator of a tradition. Though Confucius was not the founder of the *Ju* tradition, he revived and reinvigorated it, through his personal hermeneutic act, to the extent that, at least in the English-speaking community, the *Ju* tradition is synonymous with the Confucian Way. In this sense, Confucius is more like Moses than either Christ or Buddha.

The Modern Transformation of the Confucian Tradition: The Dynamics of the Family

As we have already noted, the dichotomy of sacred and profane is quite alien to the Confucian tradition. It is misleading to characterize Confucian humanism as "secular." Since Confucians believe that the meaning of human existence is realized in ordinary daily "practical living," they not only regard the secular as sacred but experience Heaven through the knowledge of the human heart-and-mind. The transcendent dimension of the Confucian project, far from being the "wholly other," is intimately connected with human nature. Strictly speaking, since human nature is endowed by Heaven, and since the heart-and-mind is the defining characteristic of human nature, full realization of the heart-and-mind naturally leads to personal knowledge of human nature. This, in turn, enriches personal knowledge of Heaven.

The attempted integration of transcendence and immanence in the Confucian project impels us to characterize the Confucian vision not only as anthropological but also as cosmological. Indeed, we insist on characterizing the Confucian vision as anthropocosmic, signifying the mutuality and unity of humanity and Heaven. A logical consequence of this vision is the inseparability of ethics and religiosity. One's moral responsibility is not complete if it is not extended to Heaven. This sense of mission to make the world safer and more livable, to improve the quality of life, and to transform society into a moral community is not only humanistic; it is deeply spiritual.

In the Confucian order of things, the corollary of this transcendent dimension is that the Way of Heaven is immanent in human affairs. Our aspiration to know Heaven and our longing to be united with Heaven are grounded in our obligations to our fellow human beings. Personal salvation, unless it involves one's family, society, country, and the whole world, is analogous to the situation of the hermit who has fled the world, one-sided and of limited significance. Realistically, we as individuals may not be able to go far beyond our immediate environment in fostering improvement in the human condition. Even the greatest of Confucian cultural heroes and role models, like the sage emperors Yao and Shun, could not confer benefits on the people and bring salvation to all, as Confucius himself noted. Yet, he went on to emphasize that salvation is necessarily communal:

> A man of humanity, wishing to establish his character, also establishes the character of others, and wishing to enlarge himself, also helps others to enlarge themselves. To be able to take the analogy near at hand (for understanding others) may be called the method of realizing humanity.[104]

The significance of the other in realizing one's own humanity suggests that Confucian sagehood, as a center of relationships, is an open system. Confucius' idea of "learning for the sake of oneself" signifies a process of deepening self-awareness for the sake of broadening one's human-relatedness. Confucius' assertion that "Heaven produced the virtue that is within me" is not a particularistic claim. In the Confucian tradition, it can very well be universalized to mean that the Heaven-endowed "brilliant virtue" (*ming-te*) is inherent in each of us as our authentic human nature. Furthermore, Confucius' self-definition as a transmitter of the Way is also universalizable. All reflective human beings are, in a sense, cultural transmitters. The transmission of the Way is a collaborative enterprise, a collective effort.

To make ourselves worthy partners in such a noble task, the Confucian would ask us to cultivate our sensitivity to the basic feelings that undergird our common humanity, to train ourselves to assume political responsibility and leadership in affairs of state, to master the grammar of action that defines a civilized society, to nurture a profound sense of history, and to open ourselves up to the higher level of learning so that we can truly know the Mandate of Heaven. Confucian education, including self-cultivation and the study of the Confucian classics, is the vehicle by which one learns to pursue the path of humanity holistically. In the Confucian tradition, human beings are not merely rational animals; they are aesthetic, political, social, historical, and metaphysical beings all in one integrated whole. To repossess the Way means to continue this holistic humanist vision. Understandably, to transmit the Way requires constant learning. A true Confucian is always a student and, as a corollary, an exemplary teacher.

An intriguing issue for the Confucian student-teacher is the modern transformation of the Confucian family, which amounts to a microcosmic reexamination of the entire Confucian project. We maintain that the Confucian perception of the family, even in the perspective of a pluralistic modern society, is neither a romantic nor sentimental assertion about human-relatedness, but a vitally important insight into the perennial human condition, laden with far-reaching ethical and religious implications. In fact, we further maintain that family, as the Confucians conceive of it, has great validity for our world today. Yet, common sense reminds us, even in the highest cultural aspirations, there is an inherent barbarism lurking behind the scene. In other words, any great tradition, once crystallized and concretized in a particular social and political institution, may assume many negative shades of meaning. With this cautionary note, let us offer a modern perspective on the psychocultural dynamics of the Confucian family.

If we characterize the Confucian family in terms of the three bonds as they evolved into a highly politicized method of symbolic control, we must wonder why and how such an oppressive system, which totally undermines the weak, the young, and the female, has managed to survive for so long. On the other hand, if we naively believe that the Confucian family as it actually existed as a social unit throughout imperial China was the embodiment of the Mencian idea of mutuality, we must be perplexed by the wave after wave of iconoclastic attacks against traditional Chinese culture, focusing on the Confucian family, since the May Fourth Movement in China in 1919. The psychocultural dynamics of the Confucian family lies in the complex interaction between the authoritarianism of the three bonds and the benevolence of the five relationships. It may appear to be too simple, if not simple-minded, to characterize the three bonds as authoritarian and the five relationships as benevolent. Such a dichotomy seems to imply that while the three bonds, as a politicized Confucian ideology of control, are detrimental to human flourishing, the five relationships informed by the Mencian idea of self-cultivation are not only compatible with but also essential to personal growth. On a purely theoretical level, there is a measure of truth in this dichotomous thinking. After all, the institution of the three bonds was a deliberate attempt to utilize Confucian values for the maintenance of a specific social order. Mencius surely would not have approved of the political act of converting the moral education of the five relationships to the ideological control of the three bonds. Surely, it is misleading to define the Mencian intent of the five relationships with the logic of the three bonds, but a sophisticated understanding of the three bonds must also involve an adequate appreciation of the Mencian conception of the five relationships. In other words, while we should not misinterpret the five relationships because of the social consequences of the three bonds, we must bear in mind that the five relationships served as an ideological background for the three bonds.

From our modern point of view, the three bonds are callously exploitative, primarily based on power and domination, and hardly redeemable as family ethics. Paradoxically, however, the three principles (hierarchy, age, and gender) inherent in the "bonds" are fully recognized by the Confucians as constitutive part of the human condition. To be sure, equality as a social ideal looms large in Confucian culture, but, contrary to Taoist relativism and Moist universalism, Confucians accept the concrete living human being differentiated by hierarchy, age, and gender as an irreducible reality. This insistence that the person embedded in a given set of human relationships is to be taken as the point of departure in any ethical reflection makes the Confucians sensitive, susceptible, and vulnerable to the status quo. Even though this does not at all mean that the Confucians uncritically accept existing power relationships, they are, as Max Weber has pointed out, prone to "adjustment to" rather than "transformation of" the world.[105] As a result, Confucian ethics is more likely than, for example, Protestant ethics, to be politicized. Understandably, the family has been perceived by the Confucian state to be a vitally important political unit.

The secularity of Confucian ethics in dealing with the mundane affairs of the world gives it a particular contour significantly different from those of the other major ethico-religious traditions (e.g., Christianity, Islam, and Buddhism). The Confucian life orientation, being this-worldly, takes political authority seriously as an essential factor for the maintenance of social order. Confucians consider the respect for authority an important virtue, even though they are often highly critical of the existing power relationships. This is predicated on the Confucian emphasis on duty-consciousness, which is more demanding of the leadership (including the ruling minority and the cultural elite) than of the general populace. The rationale is that self-imposed discipline as a life-style of personal cultivation is a prerequisite for moral and political leadership. A clear manifestation of this life-style is the practice of frugality; the precarious livelihood of the farmer rather than the conspicuous consumption of the merchant serves as the basis for social ethics. It was not an accident that the Confucian intellectual considered that the farmer, rather than the merchant, embodied the desired philosophy of life.

Historically the question of whether the traditional Chinese state was transformed, in symbol if not in reality, into an expanded family or whether the family had become an instrument of the state need not concern us here. The characterization of the emperor as the "king-father" and local officials, such as the magistrates, as the "father-mother officers," however, seems to indicate that the Confucian attempt to give a familial dimension to the political discourse was not inconsequential. An obvious result of this Confucianization (some might prefer "ritualization") of Chinese politics has been to make the political arena inseparable from the ethical realm. What one does in the seemingly private confine of one's home becomes politically significant; moreover, a confirmed Confucian, whether in office or in retirement, considers the affairs of the state to be as relevant and immediate as family affairs. Ethics that govern family relationships automatically have far-reaching social and political implications. Although the pattern of domination underlying the three bonds has lost much of its persuasive power, the significance of hierarchy, age, and gender in family ethics remains important.

If we take a more differentiated view of authority as manifested in the three bonds, we notice that the ruler's authority over the minister is fundamentally different from the father's authority over the son. Since the principle that governs the ruler-minister relationship is righteousness, it is not only permissible but also imperative that the minister remonstrate with the ruler for the well-being of the state. Indeed, the minister can choose to sever his relationship with the ruler by resigning or attempt to rectify the relationship by organizing a joint effort (often with the approval of the imperial clansmen) to have the ruler removed. The very fact that such incidents occurred in the Han dynasty when the three bonds reigned as supreme values indicates that the Confucian idea of justice was put into practice as a guiding principle for political action. The authority of the ruler over the minister, which is informed by righteousness, is, far from being absolute authority, at its best a respect for hierarchy for the sake of political stability and bureaucratic efficiency.

The authority of the father over the son, on the other hand, is based on an irreversible biological linkage. The respect for age (normally a symbol of experience and wisdom) is characteristically Confucian, but as I have already noted earlier, age itself does not necessarily command respect. The Confucian concern for human flourishing as a continuous process of self-realization impels the father as well as the son to engage himself in personal cultivation. The ideal father-son relationship is nourished by affection, but the son's cultivated sense of veneration serves as a basis for his tender care for the aging father. The fruitful mutuality between father and son is more frequently realized in the power of the adult son to provide for the dependent father than in the authority of the father to discipline the young son.

Radically different from the ruler's authority over the minister, the father's authority is neither external nor contractual. It grows out of the son's increasing awareness of indebtedness. Indeed, despite well-established legal constraints in traditional China, the father's authority, like ritualized power, must be recognized—indeed actively enacted upon— by the son to make it efficacious. The case of the Sage-King Shun amply demonstrates that the authority of his undeserving father lies solely in Shun's unquestioned filial piety. If we fail to understand the voluntary participation of the son (I am tempted to say, "the power of the son") in maintaining the authority of the father, we cannot adequately grasp the grammar of action defining the father-son relationship.

The authority of the husband over the wife, which resulted from blatantly patriarchal conditioning, has no redeeming feature. Yet, authority here means something different from either authority derived from status as in the ruler-minister relationship or authority derived from age as in the father-son relationship. The husband-wife relationship is contractual and, therefore, revocable. The Confucians acknowledge divorce as an unhappy eventuality in some marriages. There is no unworldly sanction against divorce. Confucius himself is said to have divorced (or separated from his wife three times). Rules for or against divorce are specific and based on social conventions designed to preserve family harmony.

It is not true that the Confucian wife is "owned" by the husband like a piece of property. The wife's status is not only determined by her husband's position but also by her own family's prominence. By implication, her long-term fate is inevitably intertwined with the economic and political conditions of her children, both sons and daughters. In the domestic arena, the husband's influence may prevail, especially in extraordinary situations when vital decisions are made, such as the selection of tutors for sons' education, but the wife usually wields actual power on a daily basis. We do not have to go to popular literature to confirm the fact that even though husbands always have formal control, the wives have numerous informal ways of doing what they consider appropriate or, at the very least, ways of making their wishes known. With a strong emphasis on family harmony as a social value, and even a political asset, the Confucian husband is well disposed to exercise the art of compromise in domestic affairs.

The Confucian wife is known for her forbearance. However, her patient restraint, far from being a sign of weakness, is often a demonstration of inner strength. Though her purposiveness may appear to be covertly and subtly manipulative, she has both power and legitimacy to ensure that her vision of the proper way to maintain the well-being of the family prevails; for the wife, in idea if not in practice, is not subservient to the husband but is his equal. The authority of the husband, like that of the ruler or the father, must be recognized to make it efficacious. The spirit of mutuality is evident here.

The husband depends as much on the wife to handle his domestic affairs as the wife depends on the husband to enhance her public status.

In short, the three bonds as they both reflect and shape the particular mentality characterized by despotic, gerontocratic, and patriarchal tendencies are not to be confused with the five relationships. Yet, to the extent that the three bonds were deliberate attempts to put the idea of the five relationships into practice, they exhibited a version of Confucian values in action. Although the ideals governing the five relationships as Mencius conceived of them may have been realized only on rare occasions throughout Chinese history, they were actually put into practice in the formation of Confucian family ethics. However, the three bonds, as they assumed canonical status in defining the modus operandi of the Confucian family, influenced the view of basic human relationships in traditional China. As long as the supremacy of the three bonds is primarily motivated by the political aim of social control, their contribution to human flourishing is at most a mixed blessing, if not outright negative. However, the psychocultural dynamic of the Confucian family lies neither in the authoritarianism of the three bonds nor in the benevolence of the five relationships but in the complex interaction of the two—namely, in the particular pattern of authority informed by hierarchy, age, and gender.

The ills of the Confucian family as characterized by the authoritarianism of the three bonds have been thoroughly exposed by some of the most brilliant and influential minds in modern China. Pa Chin's novel, *The Family*,[106] representative of the intellectual mentality of the May Fourth generation, poignantly reminds us that the Confucian idea of "home," in the perspective of contemporary consciousness informed by Western liberal democratic ideas, is actually a "prison house" denying the basic rights of the individual and enslaving the creative energy of the young. Indeed, Confucian family ethics as depicted by the indignant pen of Lu Hsün with telling effectiveness is no more than "ritual teaching" (*li-chiao*) that, instead of humanizing the world, contains the subtle message of cannibalism, or, in his graphic phrase: "Eat people!"[107] The slogan, "Down with Confucius and Sons!" is directed against the feudal past in general and the Confucian family in particular. Understandably, many social scientists have concluded that, both in theory and practice, the decline of the Confucian family is inevitable. For the first few decades of the twentieth century, the survivability of the Confucian family looked bleak. As recently as the 1970s, when the process of modernization was perceived as the linear progression and dissemination of Westernization, if not Americanization, the Confucian family was widely critiqued in academic circles as the single most important cultural factor inhibiting the development of the Sinic world. The incompatibility of Confucian humanism in general and the Confucian family in particular with modernization was taken for granted.

The rhetorical situation has drastically changed, as the rise of Japan and subsequently the Four Dragons (South Korea, Taiwan, Hong Kong, and Singapore) as the most dynamic area of sustained economic growth since World War II demands a cultural as well as an institutional explanation. The need to reassess the Confucian role in East Asian modernity has become compelling. Peter Berger observes in an essay addressing the issue:

> For several years now the so-called post-Confucian hypothesis has enjoyed a certain vogue. It is essentially simple: both Japan and the newly industrialized countries of East Asia belong to the broad area of influence of Sinitic civilization, and there can be no doubt that Confucianism has been a very powerful force in all of them. The hypothesis is that the key variable in explaining the economic performance of these countries is Confucian ethics—or post-Confucian ethics, in the sense that the moral values in question are now relatively detached from the Confucian tradition proper and have become more widely diffused. Historical evidence on the spread of Confucian education and ideology is very relevant to this hypothesis, but equally important is empirical research into the sway of Confucian-derived values in the lives of ordinary people, many of whom have never read a Confucian classic and have little education, Confucian or other. Robert Bellah has coined the happy phrase "bourgeois Confucianism" to distinguish this from the "high" Confucianism of the Mandarin elite of traditional China. The work currently being done by S. G. Redding and his associates at the University of Hong Kong on the norms of Chinese entrepreneurs is informed by precisely this point of view.[108]

Having outlined the "Confucian hypothesis," Berger offers his own opinion on the matter:

> I'm strongly inclined to believe that, as evidence continues to come in, this hypothesis will be supported. It is inconceivable to me that at least some of the Confucian-derived values intended by the hypothesis—a positive attitude to the affairs of this world, a sustained lifestyle of discipline and self-cultivation, respect for authority, frugality, and overriding concern for stable family life—should not be relevant to the work ethic and the overall social attitudes of the region. At the same time, I strongly suspect that Confucianism is by no means the only cultural and religious factor in play. Other factors will have to be explored.[109]

Consequently, the role of the Confucian family in making a positive contribution to the economic development and social stability of these dynamic areas in the Pacific Rim has gradually been recognized. The perennial issues engendered by the authoritarianism of the three bonds and the benevolence of the five relationships are still readily visible in East Asia. Either the corporate spirit of industrial East Asia or the feudal ghost of Communist East Asia is infused with a strong dose of Confucian familism. The East Asian strength in maintaining social stability and the East Asian weakness in developing a full-fledged democracy are both intimately intertwined with Confucian ethics. The great subtlety in honoring age and the blatant insensitivity in deprecating gender equally reflect an East Asian mentality with deep Confucian roots. Families imbued with Confucian values are perhaps still the single most important social institution in imparting ways of learning to be human in East Asian societies. Whether or not we are witnessing the revitalization of the Confucian family, a sophisticated appreciation of East Asian culture past and present demands that we understand its psychocultural dynamics.[110]

The Third Epoch of the Confucian Way

The original Confucian intention, as envisioned by Confucius and Mencius is, simply put, to cultivate ourselves and bring peace and comfort to others. This commonsense approach to self-realization, predicated on the idea of the self as a center of relationships, society as a fiduciary community, and Heaven as immanent transcendence, evolved into a comprehensive way of life, an inclusive humanism with profound religious significance. But like any great ethico-religious system, Confucianism has been put to many different uses over many centuries. In addition to being an idealistic ethic of transcendent humanism, Confucianism also came to be identified with state power, with authoritarian relationships, and with rigid and steep social hierarchies. Thus Confucianism became identified with the political status quo not only in China but also elsewhere in East Asia, especially in Korea, Japan, and Vietnam. The Western arrival in China in the nineteenth century coincided with the decline of the Chinese political system and the decay of many of its central institutions. As Chinese intellectuals saw their land endure one humiliation after another at the hands of foreigners in the nineteenth and early twentieth centuries, they came to believe that Chinese civilization itself had broken down and failed its own people. As Confucianism was so closely identified with the central values of the civilization, Confucianism came under severe attack as the chief villain responsible for all the ills of Chinese life, including political despotism, social disintegration, economic backwardness, poverty, disease, starvation, and even footbinding and opium addiction.

Since the 1920s, China has witnessed and experienced repeated waves of anti-Confucian campaigns. Joseph Levenson of the University of California at Berkeley in his influential and thought-provoking trilogy, *Confucian China and Its Modern Fate,* directly states that the decline of the Confucian tradition had been an irreversible tendency in the 1950s.[111] Intellectual attempts to revitalize it were at best passively traditionalistic; often they could be easily stigmatized as sentimentally conservative or viciously reactionary. Levenson's trilogy raises some serious questions about the survivability of Confucianism, as China was being confronted with such other options as liberty, democracy, and science from the West. Mary Wright of Yale University in her more focused scholarly monograph, *The Last Stand of Chinese Conservatism,* tells the story of a major reform, an effort led by the best minds of the government to restructure Confucian institutions and to mobilize traditional Confucian values to fight against the encroachment of the West in the nineteenth century. These men, widely known as the conscientious scholar-officials of the T'ung-chih Restoration, failed to turn the tide, and Mary Wright concluded from their failure that Confucianism is incompatible with the modern world.[112]

Many brilliant Chinese thinkers, under the influence of Western education, believed that the Confucian emphasis on authority had become oppressive in elevating the past over the present, families over individuals, rulers over subjects, male over female, and old over young. To them, Confucianism was mainly responsible for inhibiting creativity and destroying individual initiative and freedom in China's desperate attempt to modernize; there was no salvific or liberating potential in the Confucian project. Ritual appeared not as a positive process of learning to be human but rather as an artificial set of externally imposed rules, outmoded and hypocritical.

Such a hostile portrayal of Confucianism, though begun as a totalistic iconoclastic attack on traditional Chinese culture by a handful of articulate Western-minded intellectuals, soon became a powerful intellectual current. Moreover, the anti-Confucian movement became powerfully intertwined with an emergent Chinese nationalism in the 1920s and 1930s. The leader and main beneficiary of the nationalist and anti-Confucian movement was the Chinese Communist Party (CCP), which unified China under Communist rule in 1949. The CCP was determined, among other things, to rid China of her feudal past characterized by the three bonds of the Confucian tradition. Paradoxically, however, the determination of the CCP leadership to develop an indigenous ideology in the form of Sinicized Marxism to fight against imperialism and bourgeois capitalism opened a cultural space for Confucian values and folk ideas to play a significant role in the Chinese style of socialism. Yet, it is important to note that the Confucian elements in the Chinese socialist ideology were seldom acknowledged, and, ironically, outmoded Confucian rituals and practices often were uncritically accepted by

CCP leaders as the Chinese ways of doing things. Mao Tse-tung's thought, officially proclaimed by the CCP as the Sinicized Marxism-Leninism par excellence, was vehemently anti-Confucian. Mao and his followers were determined to supplant the Confucian legacy with a new culture as a true guide for China's modernization. Their efforts culminated in the Great Proletarian Cultural Revolution of the late 1960s and early 1970s. Many personal tragedies occurred during the Cultural Revolution as the nation was swept up in a great frenzy of political struggles, which led to chaos and the breakdown of political order and the destruction of the moral fabric of the entire society. It is one of the ironies of the modern world that the many atrocities committed in the name of Mao and Marx during the Cultural Revolution led to a great revulsion against Maoist policies and have today helped to raise the stature of Confucianism in China to perhaps its highest point in the twentieth century.

Surely, the CCP is not about to abdicate power to restore a "Confucian system," but many of its leaders now recognize that Confucianism has made many valuable contributions to Chinese life, that many of the ills of the old order were separable from and even diametrically opposed to Confucian teaching, and that China today still has much to gain and much to learn from its own cultural heritage.

Through the tumultuous revolutions of modern Chinese history, Confucianism has in a sense been liberated from the trappings of power, the imperial political system, and the oppressive authoritarianism that so offended the Chinese intellectuals of the May Fourth Movement. As a result, today is a particularly opportune time to examine the ethico-religious ideals of the Confucian heritage. Confucian studies are once again being revitalized in China, Confucius' birthplace is now a popular tourist site, and annual sacrifices are being performed to commemorate the sage's birth (September 28).

In the last two decades a number of other East Asian cities and states (including Japan, South Korea, Taiwan, Singapore, and Hong Kong) have dramatically demonstrated that there is no necessary incompatibility between the Confucian tradition and Western-style modern transformation. Industrialized East Asia has recently enjoyed the world's most rapid and sustained economic growth. Such growth rates have been attained not through the repudiation of the East Asian Confucian heritage, but through creative transformation of spiritual resources inherent in the Confucian tradition. Thus, throughout East Asia, the Confucian vision, deeply rooted in twenty-five hundred years of history, takes an active role in the modernizing process. As a result, the Confucian tradition is itself being revitalized. Few scholars doubt that, as a major spiritual heritage in human civilization, the Confucian tradition remains a vital force that can touch our hearts, stimulate our minds, and enrich our lives, even in the late twentieth century. Whether or not there will be a "third epoch" of the Confucian Way is also on the agenda for exploration.[113]

Contemporary Relevance

The question of a third epoch of Confucian humanism has been addressed by three generations of New Confucian thinkers since the May Fourth Movement. The lifelong work of seminal minds such as Hsiüng Shih-li (1883–1968), Liang Shu-ming (1893–1988), Chang Chün-mai [Carsun Chang] (1886–1969), T'ang Chün-i (1909–1978), Hsü Fu-kuan (1903–1982), and Mou Tsung-san (1909–) clearly demonstrates that Levenson may have been misled by the discredited thesis that modernization, defined in terms of secularism, scientism, and professionalism, is incompatible with either tradition or religion; and Mary Wright may have been misled by a Eurocentric mentality specifying that Westernization is an inevitable consequence of modernization. The challenge to the New Confucians is how a revitalized Confucian humanism might answer questions that the Enlightenment mentality has raised regarding the strengths and limitations of market economy, democratic polity, and rights-centered society; the tension between equality and liberty; the negative effects of science and technology; the unintended consequences of individualism and the Faustian drive to know, to explore, to subdue, and to conquer; the conflict between individualist capitalism and collectivist socialism; the dynamism and exploitation of an adversary system; the exportability of Western (and, by implication, American) styles of life; and the universalizability of cherished "modern" values such as human rights, self-interest, privacy, and due process of law.

The geopolitical context in which these issues are raised is often referred to as the "Sinic World." Specifically, it involves both industrial and socialist East Asia. By industrial East Asia, we mean Japan and the Four Mini-Dragons (South Korea, Taiwan, Hong Kong, and, for cultural and ethnic reasons, Singapore); by socialist East Asia, we mean the People's Republic of China (PRC), North Korea, and, for cultural and historical reasons, Vietnam. The Sinic World or East Asia is also marked by rice, chopsticks, and *Han-tzu* (*Kanji*, the written characters), signifying that the area shares, in addition to the Confucian heritage, the same staple food, a manner of eating, and a medium of communication. However, in characterizing East Asia as Confucian, we by no means undermine its religious, ethnic, and cultural diversity. The presence of Mahāyāna Buddhism throughout East Asia, Taoism and folk traditions in China, shamanism and Christianity in Korea, and Shintō and new religions in Japan is vitally important for any adequate appreciation of the complex East Asian religious landscape. Still, beyond dispute, since Confucian culture has been pivotal in shaping East Asian education both for the elite and the general public, government both in theory and practice, and symbolic expression both written and oral for centuries prior to the impact of the modern West, the designation of East Asia as "Confucian" in the ethico-religious sense is comparable in validity to employing "Christian," "Islamic," "Hindu," and "Buddhist" in identifying regions such as Europe, the Middle East, India, or Southeast Asia. Notwithstanding the crudeness and inadequacy of such denotations, they give us a sense of the life-orientation, which can be otherwise easily relegated to the background as a residual category.

Confucian East Asia (for comprehensiveness we should also include East Asian communities in Southeast Asia, North America, Europe, and other parts of the world) is well on its way to challenging the monopoly of wealth and power by the modern West (Western Europe and North America). In terms of international trade, it is at least comparable in economic strength to the European Economic Community (EEC) and North American Free Trade Agreement (NAFTA) countries. Besides, as the most vibrant economic area in the global community, the PRC is no longer a "sleeping lion," but a newly awakened regional power roaring for recognition. It is inconceivable that the new world order will be forged without the active participation of Confucian East Asia. For nationalist reasons alone, the revival of the Confucian discourse seems inevitable. Already, in the English-speaking mass media, the Confucian challenge to the liberal democratic West has been frequently mentioned as a new phenomenon in the emerging political culture of the world.[114]

The Confucian Form of Life

Whether or not there is a distinctive Confucian model of development, the rise of industrial East Asia suggests the advent of a form of modernity significantly different from that in Western Europe and North America. The strength of the countries comprising Confucian East Asia (besides Japan and the Four Mini-Dragons, the PRC, Vietnam, and likely North Korea all seem to fit the "model") is twofold: They have thoroughly domesticated the kind of Western expertise or "know-how" that is instrumental in international competition; and they have successfully mobilized indigenous resources in developing political leadership and social cohesiveness congenial to economic growth. In the terminology of military strategy, they have outmaneuvered their competitors because of superior self-knowledge and knowledge of others. This ability to cultivate self-knowledge and gain knowledge of others is the result of many factors. Historically the East Asian intellectuals have studied the West for more than a century. They have been devoted students of Dutch, English, French, German, and American learning. Indeed, a defining characteristic of an East Asian intellectual is his or her privileged access to Western learning through firsthand experience. The psychology of uncertainty, marginality, and alienation in a volatile geopolitical situation demands that they be constantly alert and ingeniously flexible. Since they have limited cultivable land and intense population pressure, the human factor is central to their overall development strategy. What they have shown is that culture matters, that values people cherish or unconsciously uphold provide guidance for their actions, that the motivational structure of people is not only relevant but also crucial to their economic ethics, and that the life-orientation of a society makes a difference in the economic behavior of its people. The so-called Confucian hypothesis is, therefore, predicated on the conviction that the role of culture is a necessary background for understanding the economic dynamics of Confucian East Asia.

Although the eminent structural-functional sociologist Talcott Parsons insisted that individualism is inevitably and intrinsically linked to modernity,[115] the actual development experience in Confucian East Asia suggests that a communalism based on an ever-expanding network of relationships is equally, if not more, compatible with modernity. In light of the East Asian development model, the Confucian form of life as an imagined community, if not a realized society, differs from the modern West in several critical areas in political economy:

1. The fundamental faith of Confucian societies lies in the improvability of the human condition through personal self-cultivation as a communal act. Self-interest is always a cherished value and mutual aid in family, neighborhood, school, and office is often taken for granted.

2. Since the person in the Confucian perception is not an isolated individual but a center of relationships, the emphasis on self-reliance underscores the necessity and desirability of locating one's own niche in a network of human-relatedness.

3. Family cohesion is the glue for "organic" social solidarity. Even though voluntary associations provide the institutional infrastructure for a vibrant economy, a cohesive family system ensures a disciplined and reliable work force. The Confucians believe that regulated and flourishing families (both nuclear and extended) provide the root for social stability and political order.

4. Primary and secondary education is intended for character-building as well as for the acquisition of practical knowledge. The commitment to education is more than the recognition of its utility in modern economy; it is an articulation of East Asian "civil religion." The Confucians offer a long-term perspective on human development: It may take ten years to cultivate a tree, but to cultivate a person requires a century.

5. Law, especially the penal code, is necessary for maintaining order, but the glue that binds the society together is *li* (propriety, ritual, or civilized mode of conduct). A sense of duty, rather than a demand for rights, features prominently in Confucian social ethics.

6. The exemplary leadership of the government or, more broadly, the political elite is as important as the "invisible hand" of the market for enhancing economic productivity. Although the Confucians advocate noninterference in the commercial sector, they strongly urge government to assume full responsibility for the well-being of society as a whole.

7. The Confucian commitment to self-cultivation, family cohesiveness, social stability, political order, and world peace is predicated on an anthropocosmic vision that regards the secular world as sacred. Intent on transforming the system from within, the Confucian life-orientation takes the existential human condition of the concrete, living person as its point of departure. The ultimate meaning of life is realized through ordinary practical living. This pragmatic idealism enables Confucian societies to creatively transform the world without appeal to any form of radical transcendence. The apparent lack of exclusive claim to ultimate truth is a reflection of a strong and pervasive conviction that the Way is pluralistic and that religious tolerance is a natural outcome of the negatively stated golden rule: "Do not do to others what you would not want others to do to you."

These Confucian perspectives on the core values in political economy suggest not only a less individualistic, less self-interested, less adversarial, and less legalistic approach to modernity but also an authentic possibility of a thoroughly modern form of life significantly different from that in the modern West. Indeed, it is neither individualist capitalism nor collectivist socialism but a humanism that has accepted market economy without undermining the leadership, especially the moral responsibility, of the central government and rejected class struggle without abandoning the principle of equality. As industrial East Asian countries begin to fully democratize by developing their unique style of civil societies, they are well on their way to navigating a middle course between capitalism and socialism.

Future Prospects

If we use the metaphor of a flowing stream to envision the development of the Confucian tradition, we see that its source in the state of Lu was tiny. In the first epoch of the Confucian way, the small brooks of Chu and Ssu gradually expanded to become the mighty river that defined the life-orientation of the Chinese for centuries. Despite its apparent decline as the result of the disintegration of the unified Han Empire, foreign conquests, and the Buddhist conquest of the Chinese mind, the river re-emerged from a subterraneous reservoir in the second epoch of the Confucian Way to become, in the words of Professor Shimada Kenji of Kyoto University, a manifestation of East Asian spirituality. After more than a century of total disorientation, not to mention paucity in creative transformation, if there is an authentic possibility of a third epoch of the Confucian Way, it cannot afford to remain Chinese or East Asian; it must flow beyond the Sinic world to receive the sustenance for its continuous vitality.

In concluding, we may draw some inspiration from the vivid image of the Yellow River flowing into the blue sea, symbolizing, to the radical Westernizers in the PRC in the 1980s, that China must allow her outmoded feudal culture to be forever drowned in the advanced civilizations of Western Europe and North America. Yet, as the Yellow River cannot be expected to flow directly into the Atlantic, it must first encounter the powerful currents of the Pacific. The cunning of history may show that the Confucian intellectual effervescence on the periphery of the Sinic world is particularly efficacious for its flourishing abroad and its eventual return to the mother country. The third epoch of the Confucian Way may have been initiated in Peking, but it is in Hong Kong, Taipei, Kyoto, and Seoul that it has truly endured. With a view toward the future, for the sake of its spiritual enrichment and intellectual empowerment, it seems well advised that the agenda for the journey home includes excursions to such places as New York, Paris, Cairo, and Madras.

A New Confucian articulation of faith, as inspired by Confucius, Mencius, Tung Chung-shu, Chu Hsi, Wang Yang-ming, and the New Confucians, may take the modern West as its point of departure. This Confucian perspective on the meaning of life states:

> Copernicus decentered the earth, Darwin relativized the godlike image of man, Marx exploded the ideology of social harmony, and Freud complicated our conscious life. They have redefined humanity for the modern age. Yet they have also empowered us, with communal, critical self-awareness, to renew our faith in the ancient Confucian wisdom that the globe is the center of our universe and the only home for us and that we are the guardians of the good earth, the trustees of the Mandate of Heaven that enjoins us to make our bodies healthy, our hearts sensitive, our minds alert, our souls refined, and our spirits brilliant.
>
> We are here because embedded in our human nature is the secret code for Heaven's self-realization. Heaven is certainly omnipresent, may even be omniscient, but is most likely not omnipotent. It needs

our active participation to realize its own truth. We are Heaven's partners, indeed cocreators. We serve Heaven with common sense, the lack of which nowadays has brought us to the brink of self-destruction. Since we help Heaven to realize itself through our self-discovery and self-understanding in day-to-day living, the ultimate meaning of life is found in our ordinary, human existence.[116]

Recommended Reading

Wing-tsit Chan, trans. and comp. *A Source Book in Chinese Philosophy.* Princeton: Princeton University Press, 1973. A comprehensive attempt to make some of the essential texts in Chinese thought accessible to the English-speaking intellectual community.

Julia Ching. *Confucianism and Christianity: A Comparative Study.* New York: Kodansga International, 1977. A contemporary attempt at Confucian-Christian dialogue.

Wm. T. de Bary. *The Liberal Tradition in China.* New York: Columbia University Press, 1983. Explores a dimension of Confucian humanism from the perspective of liberal education.

Benjamin A. Elman. *From Philosophy to Philology.* Cambridge, MA: Harvard University Press, 1985. A pioneering effort to describe the critical transformation of Confucian scholarship in the eighteenth century.

Herbert Fingarette. *Confucius—The Secular as Sacred.* New York: Harper & Row, 1972. A thought-provoking discussion of ritual not only for reasons of its historical significance but also for its contemporary significance.

Daniel K. Gardner. *Chu Hsi and the Ta-hsüeh: Neo-Confucian Reflection on the Confucian Canon.* Stanford: Stanford University Press, 1986. Presents a careful Sinological analysis of Master Chu's interpretive strategy to make the *Great Learning* a central document in Confucian education.

A. C. Graham. *Disputers of the Tao.* La Salle, IL: Open Court, 1989. Situates the Confucian project in the context of the general history of Chinese thought during its formative period.

David Hall and Roger Ames. *Thinking Through Confucius.* Albany: State University of New York Press, 1987. Introduces Confucian ethics to contemporary philosophical discourse.

Hsiao Kung-ch'üan. *A Modern China and a New World: K'ang Yu-wei, Reform and Utopia, 1858–1927.* Seattle: Washington University Press, 1975. A masterly account of a major modern Confucian thinker in the context of China's creative response to the challenge of the modern West.

Joseph R. Levenson. *Confucian China and Its Modern Fate: A Trilogy.* Berkeley: University of California Press, 1968. A seminal essay on the modern transformation of Confucian humanism.

Thomas Metzger. *Escape from Predicament: Neo-Confucianism and China's Evolving Political Culture*. New York: Columbia University Press, 1977. A thoughtful critique of Max Weber's interpretation of the role of Confucian ethics in China's modern transformation.

Donald Munro. *The Concept of Man in Early China*. Stanford: Stanford University Press, 1969. A balanced account of approaches to human nature in classical Chinese thought.

Benjamin I. Schwartz. *The World of Thought in Ancient China*. Cambridge, MA: Harvard University Press, 1985. Offers a comparative civilizational perspective on Confucian teaching.

Lee H. Yearly. *Mencius and Aquinas: Theories of Virtue and Conceptions of Courage*. Albany: State University of New York Press, 1990. An original contribution to the comparative philosophy of religions that effectively presents Mencius as a thinker with an imaginative vision of the human condition.

Notes

1. *Analects*, 14:34.
2. *Mencius*, IVB:11. See *Mencius*, trans. D. C. Lau, 2 vols. (Hong Kong: The Chinese University Press, 1984), I, p. 163.
3. *Analects*, 14:24.
4. Tu Wei-ming, "Embodying the Universe: A Note on Confucian Self-Realization," in *Confucian Thought: Selfhood as Creative Transformation* (Albany: State University of New York Press, 1991), 175.
5. *The Great Learning*, chap. 1. Cf. Daniel K. Gardner, *Chu Hsi and the Ta-hsüeh: Neo-Confucian Reflection on the Confucian Canon* (Cambridge, MA: Council on East Asian Studies, Harvard University, 1986), 88–94.
6. *The Doctrine of the Mean*, chap. 26. See *A Source Book in Chinese Philosophy*, trans. and comp. Wing-tsit Chan (Princeton: Princeton University Press, 1973), 109. For *tien*, "sky" rather than "heaven" is used in this translation.
7. An expression borrowed from Herbert Fingarette, *Confucius—The Secular as Sacred* (New York: Harper & Row, 1972).
8. *Doctrine of the Mean*, chap 22. See *A Source Book*, 107–108. Singular pronouns ("he") have been replaced by the plural ("they") in this translation.
9. The historical material in the sections "The Formation of the Confucian Tradition" and "The First Epoch of the Confucian Way" is drawn from (1) my contribution to "Confucius and Confucianism" in *Encyclopaedia Britannica, Macropaedia* (15th ed., 1988), vol. 16, pp. 653–662; (2) my essay on "Confucianism in an Historical Perspective," IEAP Occasional Paper and Monograph Series 15 (Singapore: Institute of East Asian Philosophies, 1989); and (3) my paper on the "Confucian Tradition in Chinese History" in *Heritage of China: Contemporary Perspectives on Chinese Civilization*, ed. Paul S. Ropp (Berkeley: University of California Press, 1990), 112–137. I have made substantial revision

and enlargement of my previous work to underscore the religious dimension of Confucian humanism.

10. *Mencius*, 5A:5; Lau, *Mencius*, II, p. 191.
11. Professor David Nivison claims that the conquest occurred in 1045 B.C.E. in "The Dates of Western Chou," *Harvard Journal of Asiatic Studies* 43, no. 2 (December 1983): 564. Subsequently, based on new evidence, he changed the dating to 1046 B.C.E.
12. *Analects*, 3:24.
13. *Analects*, 2:4.
14. *Mencius*, IIIA:4.
15. *Mencius*, IIIB:2.
16. *Mencius*, IIIB:2.
17. *Mencius*, IIIB:9.
18. *Mencius*, VIIB:14.
19. *Mencius*, IB:8.
20. *Mencius*, IIA:6. Cf. Lau, *Mencius*, I, p. 67.
21. *Mencius*, 4B:19.
22. *Mencius*, VIIB:25. Cf. Lau, *Mencius*, II, p. 297.
23. *Mencius*, VIIA:1
24. *Mencius*, VIIA:4. See Lau, *Mencius*, II, p. 265. For *jen*, "humanity" rather than "benevolence" is used in this translation.
25. Max Weber, *The Religion of China: Confucianism and Taoism*, trans. Hans H. Gerth (New York: Free Press, 1968), 235.
26. The statement is found in Tung's biography in the *Han-shu* (History of the Former Han Dynasty).
27. A *Source Book*, 463. For *wu-hsing*, "five phases" rather than "five elements" and for *i*, "rightness" rather than "righteousness" are used in this translation.
28. A *Source Book*, "Sagehood," 467.
29. A *Source Book*, 467.
30. A *Source Book*, 467.
31. A *Source Book*, 466, with minor modifications.
32. Chang Tsai, "The Western Inscription," A *Source Book*, 497–498.
33. A *Source Book*, 503–504. For *wu-hsing*, "five phases" rather than "five elements" is used in this translation.
34. A *Source Book*, 504. For *ch'i*, "vital energy" rather than "material force" and for *hsin*, "heart-and-mind" rather than "mind" are used in this translation.
35. Attributed to him by Chu Hsi and others. See A *Source Book*, 498–500.
36. A *Source Book*, 515, with minor modifications.
37. *Erh-Ch'eng i-shu* (Surviving Works of Masters Ch'eng I and Ch'eng Hao), 2A:2a–b. See A *Source Book*, 530. For *ch'i*, "vital energy" rather than "vital force" is used in this translation.
38. "On Understanding of the Nature of Jen (Humanity)," in *Erh-Ch'eng i-shu*, 2A:3a–b. See A *Source Book*, 523–524.
39. *Erh-Ch'eng i-shu*, 18:5b. See A *Source Book*, 562. For *ching*, "reverence" rather than "seriousness" is used in this translation.
40. Gardner, *Chu Hsi and the Ta-hsueh*, 5–16.
41. "A Treatise on Humanity," in *Chu Tzu wen-chi* (Collection of Literary Works of Chu Hsi), 67:20a. See A *Source Book*, 294. For *ch'i*, "vital energy" rather than

"material force," for *hsin*, "heart-mind" rather than "mind," and for *i*, "rightness" rather than "righteousness" are used in this translation.

42. *Hsiang-shan ch'üan-chi* (The Complete Works of Lu Hsiang-shan), 22:5a. See A *Source Book*, 579–580. For *hsin*, "heart-mind" rather than "mind" is used in this translation.
43. *Hsiang-shan ch'üan-chi*, 22:5a. See A *Source Book*, 580.
44. *Hsiang-shan ch'üan-chi*, 11:1a. See A *Source Book*, 578–579.
45. *Hsiang-shan ch'üan-chi*, 34:5b. See A *Source Book*, 582.
46. Tu Wei-ming, "Towards an Understanding of Liu Yin's Confucian Eremitism," in Tu Wei-ming, *Way, Learning, and Politics: Essays on the Confucian Intellectual* (Singapore: Institute of East Asian Philosophies, 1989), 57–92.
47. "Inquiry on the Great Learning," in *Instructions for Practical Living and Other Neo-Confucian Writings by Wang Yang-ming*, trans. Wing-tsit Chan (New York: Columbia University Press, preface 1962), 272. For *ming-te*, "brilliant virtue" rather than "clear character" is used in this translation.
48. *Instructions for Practical Living*, 273.
49. A *Source Book*, 654.
50. Michael C. Kalton, *To Become a Sage: Ten Diagrams on Sage Learning by Yi T'oegye* (New York: Columbia University Press, 1988).
51. *Analects*, 2:4. See Lau, trans., *Confucius: The Analects* (Harmondsworth: Penguin Classic, 1979), 63.
52. *Analects*, 7:19. Cf. Lau, *Confucius*, 88.
53. *Analects*, 7:2.
54. *Analects*, 7:3. See Lau, *Confucius*, 86.
55. *Analects*, 7:8. See Lau, *Confucius*, 96, with minor modifications.
56. *Analects*, 9:5.
57. *Analects*, 5:28.
58. *Analects*, 7:20.
59. *Analects*, 7:28
60. *Analects*, 7:28.
61. *Analects*, 5:26. See Lau, *Confucius*, 80. For *an*, "comfort" rather than "peace" is used in this translation.
62. *Analects*, 8:7. Cf. Lau, *Confucius*, 93.
63. *Analects*, 2:21.
64. *Analects*, 12:1.
65. *Analects*, 9:4.
66. *Analects*, 4:15.
67. *Mencius*, IIIA:4. See Lau, *Mencius*, I, p. 103.
68. *Mencius*, IIIA:4; Lau, *Mencius*, I, p. 105. For *chih*, "govern" and "governed" rather than "rule" and "ruled" are used in this translation.
69. *Mencius*, IIIA:4; Lau, *Mencius*, I, p. 107.
70. *Mencius*, IIIA:4; Lau, *Mencius*, I, p. 107.
71. *Mencius*, IVA:18; Lau, *Mencius*, I , pp. 150–157.
72. *Mencius*, IVB:3; Lau, *Mencius*, I, p. 159.
73. *Mencius*, IVA:5; Lau, *Mencius*, I, p. 141.
74. *Analects*, 14:46. For this translation, see *The Analects of Confucius*, trans. Arthur Waley (reprint; London: George Allen & Unwin, 1938, New York: Random House), 192.

75. *Analects*, 14:46.
76. *Mencius*, IIB:2; Lau, *Mencius*, I, p. 75.
77. *Mencius*, IIB:2; Lau, *Mencius*, I, p. 77.
78. *Mencius*, VA:2.
79. *Mencius*, VIIA:4.
80. In A.D. 75, an imperial conference was organized to settle some of the vital cosmological and ethical issues confronting the official ideology of the Han dynasty. It is in the record of that conference, commonly known as *Discussions in the White Tiger Hall* (*Po-hu t'ung*), that reference is made to the "three bonds." See the chapter on "San-kan liu-chi" ("Three bonds and six principles") in *Po-hu t'ung*, chap. 29. For the precise reference see No. 2 of the *Harvard-Yenching Institute Sinological Index Series* (Index to *Po Hu Tung*), authorized reprint (Taipei: Chinese Materials and Research Aids Service Center, 1966), 7/29/11a–b.
81. See the "Chung-hsiao" ("Loyalty and Filial Piety") chapter of the *Han Fei Tzu*. For the precise reference, see *Han Fei Tzu suo-yin* (Index to *Han Fei Tzu*), comps. Chou Chung-ling, Shih Shao-shih, and Hsü Wei-liang (Peking: Chung-hua Book Co., 1982), chap. 51, p. 863.
82. This is clearly stated in the "Chia-ch'u" ("Marriage") chapter of the *Po-hu t'ung*. See *Po-hu t'ung*, the Pao-ching-t'ang ts'ung-shu (Peking: Chih-li Book Co., 1923), chuan 9, chap. 40, pp. 1a–11b.
83. Joseph Needham, "History of Scientific Thought," in *Science and Civilization in China* (Cambridge: Cambridge University Press, 1956), vol. II, p. 412.
84. *The Great Learning*, chap. 1.
85. *Analects*, 2:4.
86. Fingarette, *Confucius*, vii.
87. *Analects*, 18:6. For this translation, see *A Source Book*, 48. While Chan translates *wu-jan* as "ruefully," in this particular case I follow D. C. Lau in rendering it as "lost in thought for a while." See Lau, *Confucius*, 150. James Legge renders the same expression as "with a sigh." See Legge, trans., *The Chinese Classics* (Oxford: Clarendon Press, 1883), vol. I, p. 334.
88. *Analects*, 9:8. The arrival of the phoenix and the emergence of the river chart were considered the auspicious signs of a peaceful age.
89. *Analects*, 9:13. See Legge, *The Chinese Classics*, 221.
90. *Analects*, 5:6. See Legge, *The Chinese Classics*, 174.
91. For some outstanding examples of this, see *Analects*, 7:13, 6:21, and 7:15.
92. An expression used by William T. de Bary in conceptualizing the idea of *tao-t'ung* in the Confucian tradition. See his *The Liberal Tradition in China* (Hong Kong: The Chinese University Press and New York: Columbia University Press, 1983), 9.
93. *Analects*, 18:5. See Lau, *Confucius*, 149–150.
94. *Analects*, 14:41.
95. Legge, *The Chinese Classics*, 290. D. C. Lau is more explicit in his rendering of the same passage: "Is that the K'ung who keeps working towards a goal the realization of which he knows to be hopeless?" See Lau, *Confucius*, 130. It should be noted that in Lau's translation, this saying is classified as XIV:38 instead of 14:41.
96. *Analects*, 3:24. See Lau, *Confucius*, 71.

97. *Analects*, 7:23. See Lau, *Confucius*, 89.
98. *Analects*, 9:5. See Lau, *Confucius*, 96.
99. *Analects*, 15:28. See *A Source Book*, 44.
100. *The Doctrine of the Mean* (*Chung-yung*), chap. 13. See *A Source Book*, 101. For a brief discussion on this, see Tu Wei-ming, *Centrality and Commonality: An Essay on Chung-yung* (Honolulu: University Press of Hawaii, 1976), 37–45.
101. *The Doctrine of the Mean*, chap. 13. See *A Source Book*, 101.
102. *Analects*, 7:2. See *A Source Book*, 31.
103. *Analects*, 19:24. See Lau, *Confucius*, 156.
104. *Analects*, 6:28. See *A Source Book*, 31.
105. Weber, *The Religion of China*, 226–249.
106. Pa Chin (Li Fei-kan, 1905–), *The Family*, trans. Sidney Shapiro (Peking: Foreign Languages Press, 1958).
107. Lu Hsün (1881–1936), *A Madman's Diary*, in *The Complete Stories of Lu Xun*, trans. Yang Xianyi and Gladys Yang (Bloomington: Indiana University Press and Peking: Foreign Languages Press, 1981), 4.
108. Peter Berger, "An East Asian Development Model?" in *In Search of an East Asian Development Model*, eds. Peter Berger and Hsin-huang Michael Hsiao (New Brunswick, NJ: Transaction Books, 1988), 7.
109. Berger, "An East Asian Development Model?," 7–8.
110. For a preliminary exploration of this issue, see Tu Wei-ming, "A Confucian Perspective on the Rise of Industrial East Asia," *Bulletin of the American Academy of Arts and Sciences* 17, no. 1 (October 1988): 32–50.
111. Joseph R. Levenson, *Confucian China and Its Modern Fate: A Trilogy* (Berkeley: University of California, 1968).
112. Mary Wright, *The Last Stand of Chinese Conservatism: The T'ung-chih Restoration, 1862–1874* (Stanford: Stanford University Press, 1957).
113. Tu Wei-ming, "Towards a Third Epoch of Confucian Humanism," in *Confucianism: Dynamics of a Tradition* (New York: Macmillan, 1986), 3–21, 188–192.
114. Tu Wei-ming, "The Search for Roots in Industrial East Asia: The Case of the Confucian Revival," in *Fundamentalisms Observed*, eds. Martin E. Marty and R. Scott Appleby (Chicago: University of Chicago Press, 1991), 740–781.
115. Talcott Parsons, *The System of Modern Societies* (Englewood Cliffs, NJ: Prentice-Hall, 1971), 114ff.
116. Tu Wei-ming, *Life Magazine*, December 1988.

CHAPTER 4

Taoism

Liu Xiaogan

Defining Taoism

A news item a few years ago in *The New York Times* took the academic world by surprise. Harper & Row had acquired the rights to an English version of a Chinese classic, for which they had paid the highest amount ever for a work of its kind. Moreover, the author, poet Stephen Mitchell, did not even know Chinese.

This classic of five thousand characters was none other than the *Tao Te Ching*, or *Lao Tzu*, a text essential to understanding the tradition you will be reading more about in this chapter. The circumstances of Mitchell's publication reveal that the text, in its size and style, exemplifies a philosophy of economy and universality that extended to the terms of the translation itself. In keeping with Taoist principles, less was shown to be more, and the medium once again turned out to be the message! In this case, however, a message was also delivered through the medium, which is of great relevance to the modern world.

The rapid progress of civilization and technology has brought humankind such innovations as computers, highways, jet airliners, spaceships, and nuclear power, but also problems of ecological crisis and spiritual perplexity. These problems of modernity may outweigh their advantages. If Lao Tzu were to instruct us in the solving of these problems, he would remind us that two thousand years ago he predicted the consequences we are now facing. Indeed, if we had adopted Lao Tzu's doctrine, the crises in modern society would be much less severe.

More and more people know of Lao Tzu, and some people even know that he is the author of the *Tao Te Ching* and the first thinker of Taoism. The more one knows about Taoism, however, the more difficult it is to define it.

What Is Taoism?

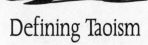

Literally, the word *Taoism* indicates a school that focuses on the significance of the *Tao*, the Way. But most scholars who have talked about the Tao, and the different Chinese schools such as Confucianism and Legalism, have used the word *Tao* in various ways. Even individual Taoists offer different explanations of the Tao. This is a common phenomenon: The more popular a doctrine is, the vaguer its meaning becomes. Although we cannot explain the specific meaning of Taoism by the word *Tao*, we can say that the concept of the Tao has a higher position in the Taoist system than in other philosophical or religious systems, and that the Tao is the most significant concept of the philosophical systems of Lao Tzu and Chuang Tzu. In addition, the word *Tao* imparts a unique meaning to the Taoist system by the emphasis it places on the central importance of metaphysics.

Some concepts may be purely theoretical, designed without regard for facts or events, while other concepts pertain more directly to complicated phenomena or events. Taoism is one of the latter concepts. In available Chinese classical literature, the earliest appearance of the word *Taoism* (Tao Chia) is in *Historical Records (Shi Chi),* the first official history written by Ssu-ma Ch'ien (145–86? B.C.E.), about four hundred years after the age of Lao Tzu. According to Ssu-ma Ch'ien, Taoism was to be equated with the Huang Lao school, which was named after Huang Ti (Yellow Emperor), the earliest legendary king and common ancestor of Chinese peoples, and Lao Tzu. The Huang Lao school emerged in the fourth to the third century B.C.E., in the middle Warring States period, becoming fashionable in the second century B.C.E., during the former Han dynasty. However, since then the meaning of the word Taoism has become complicated. In the third century C.E., when another Taoist branch (*Hsüan Hsüeh,* mystical learning) was flourishing, Taoism was associated with Lao Tzu and Chuang Tzu rather than the Yellow Emperor. This indicated that the Taoist school had changed from being a social and political theory into an individual and spiritual teaching. The word Taoism was also used to indicate the religious movement distinguished by the pursuit of immortality, which claimed Lao Tzu as its founder.

Modern Chinese scholars recognize two forms of Taoism: Taoist philosophy (*Tao Chia*) and Taoist religion (*Tao Chiao*). Taoist philosophy competed with Confucianism and Legalism from the fifth century through the second century B.C. (the Warring States and the beginning of the former Han period). Taoist religion is that unique Chinese organized indigenous movement which was included, together with Buddhism and Confucianism after the third century C.E., among the "three teachings." For most Chinese scholars, Confucianism played an important religious role in premodern China, but Confucianism, unlike Taoism, was not an institutionalized religion possessing its own church and clergy.

TAO CHIA

In contemporary China, most scholars believe that philosophical Taoism was started by Lao Tzu in the sixth century B.C.E. and developed in the second century B.C.E. It includes the Chuang Tzu school and the Huang Lao school, and perhaps the school of *Hsüan Hsüeh* as well. The essential doctrine of early Taoism is that the Tao is the unique source of the universe and determines all things; that everything in the world is composed of positive and negative parts; that opposites always transform into each other; and that people should take no unnatural action (*wu-wei*) but follow the natural law.

TAO CHIAO

Religious Taoism possesses some specific features, which originated in the second century C.E. (late Han dynasty) and have continued into contemporary China. Although influenced by Buddhism, religious Taoism represents an indigenous Chinese religion among the religions of modern China—Buddhism, Confucianism, Islam, Catholicism, and Protestantism. Its polytheistic system includes worship of both gods and ancestors. In its popular forms it is represented by a pantheon of gods, spirits, and ghosts, and it has absorbed almost every ancient practice known to the Chinese people, such as offering sacrifices to ancestors, praying for favorable weather, and dispelling evil spirits.[1] Unlike other religions, religious Taoism is not concerned with life after death. It seems that Taoism is unique among the religions of China in that it almost wholly pursues longevity and physical immortality. Hence, it has some secular characteristics. In many Chinese folk stories, Taoist gods—especially female immortals—descend to the mortal world to communicate with laypeople and, occasionally, to marry and live a worldly life.

In contemporary China there are basically two main sects of religious Taoism: the Orthodox Unity (*Cheng-i*) sect, which originated from the Five Pecks of Rice Sect (*Wu-tou-mi Tao*), founded by Chang Tao Ling in the later Han dynasty (25–220 C.E.), and the Complete Purity Sect (*Ch'uan Chen*), which was founded by Wang Che (Wang Ch'ung Yang, 1113–1169), a reformist Taoist in the Chin dynasty (1115–1234), and his apprentice, Ch'iu Chu-chi (1148–1227). The former is more prominent in Taiwan and the latter in mainland China. Like Buddhist monks, priests of the Complete Purity Sect live in monasteries and convents, wear robes, and have a restricted diet, whereas priests of the Orthodox Unity sect are allowed to eat a regular diet, are not forced to cover their hair or leave home, and are commonly known as the "Taoist priests living at homes."

Taoists

Who are Taoists? Theoretically, the term *Taoists* suggests diverse groups—the people who practice philosophical Taoism, those who believe in religious Taoism, the Taoist clergy—but, practically, it is difficult to specify who, in fact, are Taoists, as the term Taoist may denote as much of an attitude as a person.

Next to Confucianism, the most important and influential native philosophy of the Chinese has undoubtedly been that of the Taoist school. No other doctrine of the ancient period except Confucianism has for so long maintained its vigor and appeal to the Chinese mind.[2] For Chinese intellectuals, Taoist philosophy is a significant way of seeking spiritual freedom and escape from misfortune and social pressure. Some of the officials out of political favor ease their depression and recover their mental balance by reading and talking about Taoist philosophy. Writers and painters, both ancient and modern, draw much inspiration from Taoist romanticism and find much in it that appeals to their imagination. The new generation in contemporary China has also discovered the concepts of individualism and liberty in Taoist writings.

Even Mao Tse-Tung, the most important Marxist politician in modern China, adopted some essential elements of Taoist philosophy. For example, during the early Anti-Japanese War period (1937–1945), he published a famous paper, "On Protracted War," in which he expressed his belief that the weaker Chinese people would defeat the well-armed Japanese Imperialists through a long-drawn-out struggle. This belief partly came from Lao Tzu's proposition that eventually weakness will defeat strength and softness overcome hardness. In the reconstruction period of China in the mid 1950s, Mao published an article, "On the Ten Important Relationships," in which he emphasized that to increase military force, more attention must be paid to civil construction; and to develop heavy industry, some priority should be given to the development of light industry. These proposals represented the application of Lao Tzu's methodology; that is, to realize a certain end, one has to start with its opposite, the reverse means. Unfortunately, Mao himself forgot the spirit of his article, and two years later launched the pan-national campaigns such as the Great Leap Forward and the Masses Steel-Making Movement, urging students, peasants, clerks, officials, and housewives to make steel all over the country, intending to produce as much steel as the United Kingdom and the United States. Such mass movements brought China to the brink of disaster: Countless tons of coal and wood were burned up and thousands of articles made of iron were rendered useless. During this period at least 20 million people died of famine.

Although Taoist philosophy has influenced the lives of the Chinese people, especially of intellectuals, it is not the first choice as an overall system, especially by those in power. Taoist philosophy is basically anti-traditional and a guide for the weak caught up in social competition. It is, therefore, more attractive to those who do not have fortune on their side than to those who strive to retain their fortune and success. In over two thousand years, only one branch of Taoist philosophy has become the main current of political life—the Huang Lao school, in the early half of the second century B.C.E. (former Han dynasty). In modern China, few people consider themselves to be philosophical Taoists, although there is much interest in Taoist philosophy and Taoist classics.

In the case of religious Taoism, the situation is somewhat different. The members of the Taoist clergy certainly declare themselves Taoists. The monks and nuns of the Complete Purity (*Ch'uan Chen*) sect wear the robe and leggings of ancient times and wear their hair long and tied in a knot. They also have special Taoist caps and Taoist shoes. Lay believers in Taoism, however, are not easy to identify, and there are many reasons why the statistical count of Taoists is much lower than the number of people who hold certain Taoist beliefs and take part in Taoist services. For example, religion in China is generally woven into the broad fabric of family and social life, with the exception of religious professionals who live apart in monasteries. In Chinese culture, religious traditions are not clearly distinct from moral practices, philosophical doctrines, social customs, and folklore. In fact, there was not even a specific word in Chinese for "religion" until modern times, when one was coined to match the Western term. Laypeople in China do not usually belong to an institutionalized sect, nor do their religious lives have anything to do with accepting articles of faith.

Taoism, as an inherent and "locally born and bred" religion in China, absorbed many folk beliefs and customs during its formation, and in its maturity continues to interact with folk religious activities. Taoism has adopted so many classics and ideas of different schools that the *Taoist Canon* is a great encyclopedia of Chinese indigenous culture. People are even at times unaware that the religious services they attend are Taoist.

Since the antitraditional May Fourth movement in 1919, Taoist religion, along with other religions, has been attacked by intellectuals from the point of view of science and democracy. For example, Liang Ch'i-ch'ao, an early twentieth-century reformer, once wrote that Taoism was a great humiliation and that its activities have not benefited the nation at all.[3] Today, some people identify Taoist religion with superstition on account of its association with the use of alchemical and magical recipes for achieving this-worldly or other-worldly ends.

After 1949, when the People's Republic of China was established, many Taoist priests became peasants to work to support themselves, and many temples were closed or destroyed. According to a recent estimate, there are about three thousand Taoist priests and nuns in mainland China and an unknown number of Taoist followers.[4] However, the Taoist temples are popular on festival days; for example, 110,000 worshipers and holiday visitors jammed the Taoist temple in Guang-chou city on Lantern Festival Day in 1985.[5] The Mount Wu-tang Center receives seven hundred thousand pilgrims a year. Still, though its influence is clearly broad, most people do not wish to be labeled as Taoist believers. In China, Taoist religion is more important as a part of cultural tradition than as an organized religion.

Taoist Religion in Modern China

Interest in Taoist religion has declined in modern China. For example, in Ch'eng Tu, the capital city of Ssu Ch'uan Province, of more than one hundred Taoist temples before the "Great Cultural Revolution" (1966–1976), only one remains, and now only four large temples in the entire province remain open to the public. There were more than one thousand monks and nuns in former times and five hundred around 1949, but now only a few dozen remain, most of them young novices who study under older monks and nuns. In Fu-chien Province, the government statistics for all religions show no Taoist believers, and, in contrast to Buddhism's 9,675, only 79 priests and nuns.[6]

Although Taoism has lost most of its popular appeal as China's native religion, Taoist influence has not disappeared and is recovering somewhat. One hundred Taoist monasteries and temples were open in the middle 1980s, with about twenty Taoist temples training young priests, each temple having approximately twenty young Taoists. In Beijing, the White Cloud Temple has held several courses since 1982, with forty male students in attendance each year. In 1988 a special half-year course for female students was held. In Shanghai, a three-year Taoist course with thirty-one students was launched in 1986. Young men and women from all over the country traveled to the Taoist sacred mountains to embrace Taoist monastic life, but the temples were forced to turn them away because of government quotas. To be candidates for the Taoist clergy, people must meet the following criteria: They must be willing volunteers, have family approval, be unmarried, and be under the age of thirty, with a senior high school education.

Although the number of temples has decreased, under the socialist system local governments have helped to restore temples as historical relics. For example, Peking's White Cloud Temple was renovated at a cost of 1 million *yuan* (then about U.S. $358,000) by 1984.[7] However, most temples do not get the same treatment. They are neither private property, nor state-owned, nor a collective enterprise like a factory. Taoist temples follow the government policy of self-support. Generally they have two kinds of income-producing projects: production and services. Some large temples produce wine, soda water, and tea, and offer services to visitors and tourists. They also receive donations.

Because religious Taoism has declined, its doctrines have not undergone extensive development. But its religious practices and doctrines have undergone some changes in a socialist society. For example, monks or nuns declare that they are serving the people and helping the socialist system, and their rank and salaries are comparable to those in official service. Moreover, Taoists have also developed a new understanding of immortality. According to a famous abbot, Taoists now believe: "Burn yourself and go to heaven," which doesn't mean that you should burn yourself while alive or that you must have your body burnt after death. It means that if your body is consumed by the fire of your religious zeal, your soul will go to heaven, and you will become an immortal. That is the first principle of Taoism.[8] Contemporary Taoists also have abolished some regulations, taboos, and commandments, although strictly observing the Taoist discipline, including routine work in a monastery or convent. Some young Taoist students are required to study English; a few have read English books with great interest and have found intimations of the Tao in contemporary Western philosophy and in quantum mechanics. The young priests also declare that whatever they do as Taoists is for the public and not for the individual.[9] It is possible that the young generation will create a new image of Taoism in China.

The greatest influence of Taoism in current China is found in daily life or popular culture. *Ch'i-kung,* which has become very popular in the last decade, is a traditional Chinese art of self-exercise and therapy that draws most of its resources from Taoist scriptures or Taoist experience, although Buddhism and Confucianism have also contributed to it. Another influential aspect of Taoism is martial arts (*wu-shu* or *kung-fu*). Some young people are drawn to Taoism through romantic images of Taoist priests and heroes who, like Oriental Robin Hoods, defeat legions of bandits with their martial arts skills as immortalized in movies and popular novels.[10] The various arts and secret methods of longevity tapped from Taoist tradition are also of interest to senior citizens, and varied recipes for health and cures continue to be adopted by more and more people. Taoist tradition has thus permeated worldly life.

Generally speaking, Taoism has its strongest influence in the southern rural areas of China. Elsewhere, Taoist religion is alive wherever traditional Chinese culture survives—in Taiwan, Hong Kong, Singapore, Indonesia, Thailand, and Hawaii, and in Western cities, such as New York, San Francisco, Vancouver, and Toronto—because Taoist tradition is woven into the very fabric of Chinese culture. The strongest Taoist tradition is found in Taiwan. Its establishment in the island was contemporaneous with the great emigration from the opposite mainland Fu Chien Province in the seventeenth and eighteenth centuries. In 1938, the Japanese governor-general of Taiwan launched a campaign, which was resisted in various ways by the Taiwanese people, to abolish indigenous Chinese temples and shrines on the island.[11] The Japanese plan failed after the end of World War II.[12] In 1949, the sixty-third celestial master, Chang En-p'u, moved to Taiwan from the mainland and gave new impetus to the religion. There Taoism, particularly the Orthodox Unity (*Cheng-i*) Taoism, may still be observed in its traditional setting, distinct from the manifestations of popular religion that surround it. Since the 1960s Taoism has enjoyed a renaissance in Taiwan, and much work is being done in the areas of temple building and restoration. It has been reported that there are more than four thousand Taoist temples in Taiwan, and that most of them belong to the *Cheng-i* sect.

Taoist Philosophy and Religion

Chinese counterparts of the English words *religion* and *philosophy* did not exist until early in this century, so the differences between Taoist philosophy and Taoist religion are not very relevant in premodern China. Since the English word Taoism was created in the early nineteenth century, it cannot reflect the difference between religious and philosophical Taoism. Prior to 1950, the majority of the Sinologists believed that philosophical and religious Taoism were incompatible. Since 1950, chiefly due to the work of French scholars Marcel Granet and Henri Maspero and their students, many Sinologists have realized that these two groups may be viewed as belonging to a common tradition.[13] Nonetheless, Chinese scholars have divided the two so clearly that few study their relationship.

There are certain connections between Taoist philosophy and religion. For example, Taoist philosophers were both thought of as the founders of Taoist religion and revered as gods in its polytheistic system. The earliest Taoist religious book, the *Classic of the Great Peace* (*T'ai-p'ing Ching*), and other classics were claimed to have been originally handed down by Lao Tzu. To compete with Buddhism, later Taoists even said that Lao Tzu had been the instructor of Śākyamuni. Many noble titles were also conferred on Lao Tzu, such as the "Saint Ancestor Great Tao Mysterious Primary Emperor." Clearly Lao Tzu was considered a divinity in the Taoist religion, as were other Taoist philosophers such as Chuang Tzu and Lieh Tzu.

The classics of Taoist philosophers were also revered as sacred texts of the Taoist religion. The title "Great Upper Mysterious Primary Emperor Tao Te True Classic" was conferred on *Tao Te Ching (Lao Tzu)*; on *Chuang Tzu* that of "Southern Chinese True Classic"; on *Lieh Tzu* that of "Vacant Empty Ultimate Virtue True Classic"; and on *Wen Tzu* that of "Mastering of the Mystery True Classic." Taoist religion also borrowed many concepts and ideas from Taoist philosophy, such as the *Tao*, material or vital force (*ch'i*), heaven (*t'ien*), individual power (*te*), spontaneity (*tzu-jan*), nonaction (*wu-wei*), sitting and forgetting (*tso-wang*), and pure person (*chen-jen*). In Taoist religious texts, such as the *Classic of the Great Peace, The Master Who Embraces Simplicity* (*Pao P'u Tzu*), and later books, words or ideas cited from *Lao Tzu* or *Chuang Tzu* can be found frequently.

However, a comprehensive investigation of Taoist religion reveals that it is possible to overemphasize the connections between Taoist religion and philosophy. Some religious Taoists do not regard Taoist philosophers as the most important thinkers or gods. There are many historical figures, legendary heroes, ancient and contemporary emperors, scholars, and generals woven into the polytheistic system of Taoist religion. The more the Taoist religion matured, in fact, the lower was the position given to Taoist philosophers as gods in the religious system. In the first century, before the formal establishment of Taoist religion, sacrifices were offered to Lao Tzu, together with the Yellow Emperor and the Buddha. By the sixth century, a classic of the Taoist religion, *Chen Ling Wei Yeh T'u*, ranked Lao Tzu on the fourth level among gods classified into seven levels. Later he was regarded as the third of the "three pure gods" (*san-ch'ing*) of the Taoist religion. When the *Taoist Canon* was divided into three main parts according to their relative significance, all of the Taoist philosophers' books were classified as belonging to the third part.

There is a fundamental reason why religious Taoists no longer regard philosophical Taoists as important in their system: Taoist philosophers concentrate on spiritual transcendence, whereas religious Taoists seek physical immortality. In fact, religious Taoism moves in a direction opposite to that of philosophical Taoism. Taoist philosophers do not think it necessary for people to pursue a long life. Lao Tzu's *Tao Te Ching* says in chapter 13: "The reason I have great trouble is that I have a body. When I no longer have a body, what trouble have I?" And it says in chapter 75: "It is only those who do not seek after life who are wiser in valuing life."[14] Chuang Tzu said: "The True Man of ancient times knew nothing of loving life, knew nothing of hating death." "Life and death are fated—constant as the succession of dark and dawn. . . . Man can do nothing about it."[15] Clearly, the founders of philosophical Taoism held that people cannot and should not choose between life and death. Rather, instead of having a desire for either, people should transcend the difference between them. No Taoist philosopher focuses on the ideas of longevity and immortality, although there are vague references to long life in the *Tao Te Ching* and *Chuang Tzu*. The transcendent attitude of Taoist philosophy toward life and death is simply the reflection of philosophical Taoism's main principle; that is, following nature and taking no unnatural action (tzu-jan and wu-wei). By contrast, Taoist religion regards the possibility and importance of immortality as its cardinal principle.

Philosophical and religious Taoism also are different in their attitudes toward society's rulers. Philosophical Taoism is antitraditional and transcends common values. Both Lao Tzu and Chuang Tzu criticized rulers and the political and moral theory of Confucianism. Both believe that society would be much better off without any ruler, law, or morality. Religious Taoists, however, respect the sovereigns and Confucianism. For example, the religious Taoist Ko Hung (283–343) said, "The people who want to be immortals must have loyalty for the ruler and filial piety for parents . . . as the basic principle,"[16] and he wrote the "outer chapters" to develop Confucianism. K'ou Ch'ien Chih, another important religious Taoist, said that a Taoist should also learn Confucianism and help the emperor to govern the world. The no-sovereignists, one branch of Chuang Tzu's followers, attacked any kind of ruler, whether benevolent or cruel. Ko Hung wrote a special essay,

"Interrogating Pao," in the *Pao P'u Tzu,* to refute them. Taoist religion pays much more attention to the present and to practical interests than Taoist philosophy. In general, philosophical Taoism is more individualistic and critical than Taoist religion, while the latter is more social and practical than the former. Hence, religious Taoists, when they employed the terms of Taoist philosophy—such as Tao, te, and wu-wei, for example—provided these terms with meanings of their own.

Lao Tzu and the Origin of Taoism

Most Chinese scholars think that Lao Tzu is the first important Taoist, although there are different opinions about his date and identity. According to Ssu-ma Ch'ien's biography of Lao Tzu in the *Historical Records (Shih Chi)* in the late second century B.C.E., Lao Tzu was a senior contemporary of Confucius, who lived in the sixth century B.C.E. According to my latest investigation based on the comparisons of verse style in the *Tao Te Ching* and *The Classic of Songs,* what Ssu-ma Ch'ien said is plausible unless new discoveries compel a revision of the conclusion.[17]

According to Ssu-ma Ch'ien, Lao Tzu's family name was Li, his given name was Erh, and he was also known as Tan. Lao means old and Tzu is a title of respect for gentlemen in ancient China. Thus Lao Tzu literally means "the old master." He was a native of the state of Ch'u in the southern part of the present Honan Province and was reputed to have instructed Confucius in ceremonies. It is also said that, after living in Chou for a long time and perceiving its imminent downfall, Lao Tzu made a decision to leave for the west. At Han-ku Pass, he was detained by a gatekeeper named Yin Hsi, who asked Lao Tzu to write a book for him before leaving to be a recluse. Thus Lao Tzu drafted two chapters to record the significance of the *Tao* (the Way) and *Te* (individual power) in about five thousand characters, which are named after him. This piece of writing also came to be known as the *Tao Te Ching* in later times. The *Lao Tzu* or *Tao Te Ching* is essential for the analysis of Lao Tzu's philosophy, although it is possible that some words or sentences were added by later editors or writers.

Taoist Metaphysics

Lao Tzu developed the first brief system of metaphysics in Chinese intellectual history, which concentrates on the concept of Tao. Tao literally means a "way" and is often extended to imply a political or moral principle by which different schools express various ideas. However, Lao Tzu attributed a totally new meaning to Tao or the Way. He regarded it as the general source of the universe; thus, his Tao is a metaphysical concept. It is impossible to find any exact word to represent or define Lao Tzu's Tao in modern languages, even modern Chinese.

We can, however, give some description of the Tao. Tao is the unique origin of the world: "Tao produced the One, the One produced the Two, the Two produced the Three, and the Three produced the ten thousand things" (chapter 42).[18] Tao is the prime source, the One is the primordial being, or the Chaos; the Two indicates *yin* (the negative or the feminine) and *yang* (the positive or the masculine); the Three are yin, yang, and their unity. Despite various explanations of One, Two, and Three, this is basically the Chinese version of creation.

Tao determines all things, or everything depends on it: "The great Way is broad, reaching left as well as right. Myriad creatures depend on it for life yet it does not turn away from them" (chapter 34); "Myriad creatures all revere the Way" (chapter 51). Lao Tzu strongly believed that the Tao is universal and that everything will develop or transform perfectly according to Tao. It also, therefore, includes the way of universal process and the highest principle. This is Lao Tzu's simple ontology.

Tao is mysterious: "We look at it and do not see it... We listen to it and do not hear it.... We touch it and do not find it... These three cannot be further inquired into, and hence merge into one. Going up high, it is not bright, and coming down low, it is not dark. Infinite and boundless, it cannot be given any name" (chapter 14). We cannot understand Tao by our senses or our reason, but it is a real being. Tao is beyond the capacity of ordinary knowledge and the human intellect, but people can reach or gain Tao by intuition: "The pursuit of learning is to increase day after day. The pursuit of Tao is to decrease day after day" (chapter 48). "One may see Tao of Heaven without looking through the windows" (chapter 47). Realizing Tao requires very different skills than those adopted by average people for common cognition.

The Tao functions spontaneously, without any will or purpose: "Man models himself on earth, Earth on heaven, Heaven on Tao, and Tao on spontaneity" (chapter 25). Tao "accomplishes its task, but does not claim credit for it. It clothes and feeds all things but does not claim to be master over them. Always without desires, it may be called the small. All things come to it and it does not master them; hence it may be called the Great" (chapter 34). Tao functions totally through natural processes and emerges from natural processes, hence it is not like a Creator who creates the world through will and purpose. According to Confucianism, Tao is a general principle of politics and morality and Te is individual virtue or character. However, for

Lao Tzu, Tao is the ultimate reality and the general principle of the universe, and Te is the localization of Tao. Te is what a thing or a person gets when it or he or she comes into being and is the foundation of its functioning according to Tao. Hence, Te is the individual principle of everything and everybody.

Lao Tzu's Methodology

Lao Tzu's philosophy is antitraditional, and his methodology is extraordinary and significant. Lao Tzu declares that everything contains opposite sides, and each side depends on the other: "Being and non-being produce each other; Difficult and easy complete each other; Long and short contrast each other. . . . Front and back follow each other. Therefore the sage manages affairs without action (*wu-wei*), and spreads doctrines without words" (chapter 2). The theory that opposite sides always transform into each other is the philosophical foundation of Lao Tzu's methodology, and also that of wu-wei, its key concept. The awareness that opposites convert into each other gave rise to the Chinese aphorism: "Calamity is that upon which happiness depends; happiness is that in which calamity is latent."

In *Lao Tzu*, there are about seventy concepts of things in pairs, such as good and evil, long and short, bright and dark, full and empty, lead and follow, strong and weak, beauty and ugliness, difficult and easy, favor and disgrace, superior and inferior, hasty and tranquil, glory and humility, masculine and feminine, contract and expand, increase and decrease, offensive and defensive, advance and retreat, auspicious and inauspicious, being and nonbeing. Most of them can be summed up as activity versus passivity, toughness versus softness, competition versus forbearance. Among all of these antitheses, Lao Tzu preferred the latter as more beneficial than the former and believed that people benefit much more from the latter. He advocates: "knowing the male (the active force) but keeping to the female (the passive force)," "knowing the white but keeping to the black," "knowing glory but keeping to humility" (chapter 28). Because it is easy to move or fall from a favorable position, you had better keep to the point you dislike. Here are some clearer examples of Lao Tzu's method: "In order to contract, it is necessary first to expand. In order to weaken, it is necessary first to strengthen. In order to destroy, it is necessary first to promote. In order to grasp, it is necessary first to give" (chapter 36). Lao Tzu says that to accomplish anything, it is necessary to start with the opposite of what is sought. To sum up, the essence of Lao Tzu's methodology is to begin the pursuit of an end from a point diametrically opposed to it.

The reverse position can be summarized as wu-wei. In Chinese, wu-wei literally means "no behavior" or "doing nothing." But no one advocates absolute nonaction. Wu-wei is, rather, a concept or idea that is used to negate or restrict human action. In other words, wu-wei means the cancellation or limitation of human behavior, particularly social activities. There are a number of gradations in the Taoist theories of wu-wei: wu-wei as nonbehavior or doing nothing; wu-wei as taking as little action as possible; wu-wei as taking action spontaneously; wu-wei as a passive or pliable attitude toward society; wu-wei as waiting for the spontaneous transformation of things; and wu-wei as taking action according to objective conditions and the nature of things, namely, acting naturally. Although it is not possible to express the complexity of these meanings in one word, "nonaction" may be used as a convenient code.

Lao Tzu believed that wu-wei can lead to a peaceful and harmonious society. He said: "The more cunning and skill man possesses, the more vicious things will appear. The more laws and orders are made prominent, the more thieves and robbers there will be. Therefore the sage says: I take no action and the people of themselves are transformed.... I engage in no activity and the people of themselves become prosperous" (chapter 57). The opposite of wu-wei is *yu-wei*, or taking action. Here cunning and skill, laws and orders belong to yu-wei, which causes vicious actions, thieves, and robbers; in contrast, wu-wei brings prosperity, harmony, and peace. About wu-wei, Lao Tzu coined a famous phrase: *Wu-wei erh wu-pu-wei*—"do nothing and nothing is left undone." He said: "No action is undertaken, and yet nothing is left undone. An empire is often brought to one who undertakes no activity. If one undertakes activity, he is not qualified to win the empire" (chapter 48). Lao Tzu advocated wu-wei because he really believed that it is only by wu-wei that people can reach any ideal state of affairs.

Wu-wei indicates the special values of passivity, yielding, and quietude, which are beneficial and suitable especially for unfortunate or weak people. Only wu-wei can help weak people conquer the opponent and become strong. This is the benefit of wu-wei. Lao Tzu said: "The softest things in the world overcome the hardest things in the world.... Through this I know the advantage of taking no action" (chapter 43). He also argues: "There is nothing softer and weaker than water. And yet there is nothing better for attacking hard and strong things.... All the world knows that the weak overcomes the strong and the soft overcomes the hard. But none can practice it" (chapter 78). Water, dripping constantly, wears holes in stone; water on the shore grinds rock and transforms it into sand or dust. In human society, strong countries can easily launch a war, but weaker countries often win the war in the end. This is the plain truth—that suppleness can overcome hardness—but as it is easy to forget and difficult to maintain, Lao Tzu asserts it repeatedly.

Another important concept related to wu-wei is *tzu-jan*: "spontaneity" or "being natural." The Tao is natural, and all things in the world should develop spontaneously. Unnatural effort must finally fail. The belief that the universe and social life will develop spontaneously is the foundation of the theory of wu-wei, as well as of Taoist philosophy. As a modern interpretation, the criteria of tzu-jan would include an internal motivation of things, the smooth development of things without sharp turn or discontinuance, and the transformation of things without strife and conflict.

Taoist Views of Society and Politics

Lao Tzu established the foundations of the social and political traditions of Taoism. The Taoist ideal society is a primitive community with a natural, harmonious, and simple life and exists without war and competition. Lao Tzu said: "Let there be a small country with a low population.... Let the people value their lives highly and not migrate far.... Let them relish their food, enjoy their clothing, be content with their homes, and delight in their customs. Though neighboring communities overlook one another and the crowing of cocks and barking of dogs can be heard, yet the people there may grow old and die without ever visiting one another." This is a beautiful picture of Taoist life in a primitive agrarian society, which is filled with a peaceful, joyful, and satisfied atmosphere.

The picture is also a criticism of contemporary society. Lao Tzu condemned the ruler: "The people starve because the ruler eats too much tax-grain.... They are difficult to rule because their ruler does too many things.... The people take death lightly because their ruler strives for life too vigorously." In the philosophical Taoist view, the sovereign is the source of misfortune and turmoil. In China, Taoist philosophy is the main intellectual resource of unorthodoxy and criticism.

The Transformation of Taoist Philosophy

The earliest biography of Chuang Tzu is also provided by Ssu-ma Ch'ien in the *Historical Records*. It is, with only approximately 245 characters, the only credible material about Chuang Tzu's identity and life. As with other ancient figures, there are arguments about Chuang Tzu's life and writings, though relatively less than those about Lao Tzu. According to the *Historical Records*, his last name was Chuang, given name Chou, and Tzu is the respected title of "master." Thus Chuang Tzu means "Master Chuang." He was a native of a place called Meng in a small state named Sung, near the border between present-day Honan and Shantung Provinces; he was born later than 369 and died before 286 B.C.E.[19]—during the middle of the Warring States period—and he once served as an officer in charge of a royal lacquer garden, which may have been his highest position. It was said that King Wei of Ch'u, having heard his name, once sent messengers with gifts to invite him to his state, promising to make him chief minister. Chuang Tzu, however, merely laughed and said to them: "Go away, do not defile me.... I prefer the enjoyment of my free will."[20]

Chuang Tzu was a great philosopher as well as a great writer. He is the most important source of Chinese romanticism and humor. It was said that Chuang Tzu wrote a book with more than one hundred thousand characters and fifty-two chapters. Today, however, the only available version of *Chuang Tzu* consists of approximately seventy thousand characters and thirty-three chapters, and it is clearly written by both Chuang Tzu and his followers. Hence the authorship of *Chuang Tzu* may be attributed both to Chuang Tzu and to a school named after him.

The present edition of *Chuang Tzu* is divided into three parts: Inner Chapters, Outer Chapters, and Miscellaneous Chapters. Scholars in China take various positions about the authors and dates of these chapters. According to my textual analysis of *Chuang Tzu*, the Inner Chapters were basically written by Chuang Tzu, and the Outer and Miscellaneous Chapters were written by his followers. The Outer and Miscellaneous Chapters can be classified into three groups according to their characteristic thought: the expositors of Chuang Tzu, the no-sovereignists among Chuang Tzu's followers, and the Huang Lao scholars among Chuang Tzu's followers. Quite a few scholars continue to raise traditional questions about *Chuang Tzu* and argue that certain chapters of *Chuang Tzu* were written by early Han dynasty scholars. Yet more than 40 percent of its chapters—including the Inner, Outer, and Miscellaneous Chapters—are quoted by *Han Fei Tzu* and *Lü Shih Ch'un Ch'iu*, which had been completed before the Ch'in (221–207 B.C.E.) dynasty. We have every reason to believe, therefore, that *Chuang Tzu* was completed before the Han dynasty.[21]

Chuang Tzu's Philosophy of Life

Chuang Tzu received the concept of Tao from Lao Tzu and gives a clearer expression of it: "Tao has its reality and its signs but is without action or form.... It is its own source, its own root. Before Heaven and earth existed it had already been there since ancient times" (chapter 6).[22] This is the most precise description of the ultimate reality of Taoism and is the first concept of Chuang Tzu's Tao.

However, Chuang Tzu develops a new concept of Tao in chapter 2: "What is Tao hidden by, that we have true and false? What are words hidden by, that we have right and wrong? How can Tao go away and not exist? How can words exist and not be acceptable? Tao is hidden by little accomplishments, and words are hidden by vain show. Therefore there are the rights and wrongs among Confucians and Moists." Tao here, just like words, can be hidden and can even disappear under the influence of human behavior. This understanding is very different from the Tao mentioned previously that is the reality of the universe, its own source, and which remains uninfluenced by other things. Thus the other concept of Chuang Tzu is that the Tao is the highest spiritual state and is a subjective experience.

Tao as a spiritual state represents Chuang Tzu's ideal of life. It is an ideal state of mind completely devoid of reflection of the mundane world: "The man in ancient time, his knowledge had reached the ultimate. What is the ultimate? Someone thought there had not yet begun to be things.... The next thought there were things but there had not yet begun to be borders. The next thought there were borders but they had not yet begun to distinguish the right and the wrong. The lighting up of right and wrong is the reason why Tao is injured. The reason why the Tao is injured is the reason why love becomes complete" (chapter 2). In Chuang Tzu's view, the highest state of mind is total detachment, without any perception of the world or distinction between things. Any differentiation, value judgment, or emotional tendency will injure the Tao, or the highest state of mind. In other words, Chuang Tzu's ideal state of spirit is characterized by no-mind and no-feeling. This Tao is also the state of mind of one who has reached the Tao as ultimate reality or has realized the union with Tao or the universe.

Chuang Tzu describes some approaches to achieve such a state of mind. One is *hsin-chai* ("heart-fast"); that is, the fasting of the mind, which means emptying the mind so that Tao will move into the emptiness. Another is *tso-wang* ("sitting and forgetting"), which indicates that with sitting down and forgetting everything, including one's limbs and body, perception and intellect, one makes oneself identical with the Tao. Another is *wai-wu* ("detaching from things"): By observing tranquil self-cultivation for three days, one will forget the mundane world; in seven days, one will forget everything; in nine days, one will forget one's life. Then one is able suddenly to break through from the world of darkness to the coming of daylight. Then one can see the Ultimate—namely, the Tao—and be timeless, without past and present, beyond living and dying. One forgets all the world, forgets everything, forgets one's life and step by step has no ideas, senses, feelings, wishes, intentions, and so on. No consciousness of the mundane world remains, but only the experience of the primordial Universe or the Tao.

The person who truly realizes the union with Tao or the universe can also reach another stage: free and easy wandering, which characterizes Chuang Tzu's philosophy of life. In his first chapter, Chuang Tzu describes how the (spiritual person) "climbs up on the vapor of the clouds, rides a flying dragon, and roams beyond the world," or "mounts on the truth of heaven and earth, rides the six changes of the weather, and travels into the infinite." How does the person wander or travel? Not by really riding clouds in the sky, but by traversing the spiritual realm with the mind. As Chuang Tzu said: "Just go along with things and let mind move freely."[23] Chuang Tzu's free and easy wandering means that one's mind is free to travel in one's realm of fancy after detachment from the practical world. Therefore, free and easy wandering is neither the journey of immortals in heaven (as in later Taoist religious teachings) nor the common imagination related to mundane life. It is purely personal and spiritual freedom and is based on obedience to destiny and circumstance. On the one hand, Chuang Tzu is passive in adjusting to surroundings in earthly life; on the other, however, he is active in pursuing personal freedom in the spiritual realm.

Chuang Tzu's attitude toward death and life is based on his theory that both life and death are one phase of the movement of ch'i in the universe. Ch'i literally means "air," "vapor," or something similar in modern Chinese, but it is used broadly and variously. In ancient Chinese, ch'i is a basic concept of Chinese thought with different meanings: In addition to air, vapor, breath, it indicates the fundamental substance of nature and living beings, as well as life force. Generally speaking, ch'i indicates matter, which is continuous, energetic, and dynamic. Sometimes it is translated as "material force" or "vital force." According to the account in chapter 18, when Chuang Tzu's wife died and one of his friends came to convey his condolences, Chuang Tzu was sitting and singing. The friend criticized him, and Chuang Tzu said: "When she first died, how could I not grieve like anyone else? But looking back, at the beginning she had no life; not only no life but also no body; not only no body, but also no *ch'i*. In the midst of the jumble of wonder and mystery a change took place and there is *ch'i*, then another change and there is her body, then another change again and there is her life. All things are in transformation. Now there has been another change and she has died. It is just like the progression of spring, summer, fall, and winter. Now she is going to lie down peacefully in a vast room. If I were to follow after her crying and sobbing, it would show that I do not understand anything about fate. So I stopped."[24] Ch'i is the foundation of body and life, which are just a phase of the circulation of ch'i. In the Taoist view, everything is composed of ch'i and will return to ch'i, therefore people should not fear death and cling to life. Ch'i is somehow mysterious in terms of science, but it is an important and useful concept in

Chinese culture, including traditional medicine, the practice of acupuncture, and the ch'i kung exercise. In Taoist religion, ch'i is an essential concept in the theory of immortality.

Chuang Tzu's Methodology

Chuang Tzu is the most important skeptic in Chinese intellectual history. He taught that people cannot attain full cognition of the world because of the limitations in life. He said: "Your life has a limit but knowledge has none. If you use what is limited to pursue what has no limit, you will be in danger. If you understand this and still strive for knowledge, you will be in danger for certain!" (chapter 3). Chuang Tzu also emphasizes that everything depends on other things, which depend still on others, and so on—hence people cannot reach certain knowledge. He illustrated this with a fable: The Penumbra said to the Shadow: "A little while ago you were walking and now you're standing still; a little while ago you were sitting and now you're standing up. Why this lack of independent action?" The Shadow answered: "Do I have to wait for something before I can be like this? Does what I wait for also have to wait for something before it can be like this? Am I waiting for the scales of a snake or the wings of a cicada? How do I know why it is so? How do I know why it isn't so?" (chapter 2).[25] Shadow's answer, which expresses Chuang Tzu's idea that people cannot know the truth in the chain of phenomena and so should give up the pursuit of ordinary knowledge, raises difficult questions.

Chuang Tzu also claimed that people cannot reach the truth because there is no certain standard of what is right. For example, if a man sleeps in a damp place, his back aches and he ends up half paralyzed, but is this true of a loach (a fish that lives in mud)? If he lives in a tree, he is terrified and shakes with fright, but is this true of a monkey? Of these three creatures, then, which one knows the proper place to live? Men eat meat, deer eat grass, centipedes find snakes tasty, and hawks relish mice. Of these four, which knows what is the proper food? Therefore, people cannot tell what is right or wrong, and all arguments about good or evil are insignificant. Chuang Tzu was not interested in value judgments; rather, his purpose was to move toward the ultimate destination—transcendent freedom, which is identical with Tao.

Chuang Tzu's methodology is characterized by his unique theory of the equality of all things. He argues: "Everything is That, and everything is also This. People do not know that they themselves are That, but only know that they themselves are This. So I say, That comes out of This, and This depends on That—which is to say that This and That give birth to each other. But where there is birth there must be death; where there is death there must be birth. Where there is acceptability there must be unacceptability; where there is unacceptability there must be acceptability. When you follow right you would find that you follow wrong, and when you follow wrong you would find that you follow right.... This is That, and That is also This. That is a pair of right and wrong, and This is also a pair of right and wrong. Are there really That and This? Are there really not That and This? A state in which That and This no longer find their opposites is called the hinge of the Tao. The hinge can keep in the center of a circle and respond to everything endlessly" (chapter 2).[26] Chuang Tzu points out that the opposites are relative. That and This, right and wrong, birth and death, unacceptability and acceptability—all of these opposites always depend on each other, convert into each other. This is an excellent expression of dialectics. However, the next step is the recognition that there are no differences between the opposites, and that people should consider That and This, right and wrong, to be the same. People can then move beyond the struggle between That and This, right and wrong, as they stand in the center of the circle of conflict and respond indifferently without any inadequacy. This is an important stage in transcending the empirical world and reaching the end, which is union with Tao.

Chuang Tzu's Followers

The authors of chapters 17 through 27 and chapter 31 of the *Chuang Tzu*, or the expositors among Chuang Tzu's disciples,[27] basically interpreted their master's teachings rather than expounding their own ideas, but they also developed some new elements. For example, they created a foundation for the Taoist theory of human nature. There was much discussion at that time about whether human nature was naturally good or evil. Mencius, the second founder of Confucianism, insisted that human nature was fundamentally good and different from animals, while another great Confucian scholar, Hsun Tzu, asserted that human nature was inherently evil because everyone wants to eat good food and take more rest. A philosopher, Kao Tzu, insisted that the nature of people when born is neither good nor evil, but could become either, depending on what they learn. In contrast to other philosophers, the expositors of Chuang Tzu's school developed a theory that human nature is beyond good and evil. They held that the inborn nature of humankind is naturally perfect and that any change in it, whether good or evil, represents loss of the original nature.

The disciples carry on the idea of no-mind and no-emotion from Chuang Tzu but direct it toward creative work instead of transcendent freedom. They were convinced that the creation of extraordinary art required an exceptional state of mind, which meant that the artist should concentrate on nothing but the natural conception of the object she or he will create. They tell a story about the sculptor Ch'ing who created a bell stand that looked demonic and ghostly and amazed everyone who saw it. When he was asked for his secret, he replied that when he was going to make a bell stand, he first made sure to fast to still the heart. After fasting three days, he was no longer concerned about congratulation and reward or honors and payment. After fasting five days, he became oblivious to any blame or praise, skill or clumsiness. After fasting seven days, he became so intent that he forgot he had a body and four limbs. Only then was he able to go into the mountain forest and observe the nature of the wood as Heaven makes it grow. The aptitude of the body had attained its peak; and only then did he have a complete vision of the bell stand, only then did he put his hand to it. "So I join what is Heaven's to what is Heaven's." Chuang Tzu's disciples thus extended his doctrine of spiritual freedom into the realm of aesthetics. Their theory has had great influence on literary and artistic creation.

The no-sovereignists among Chuang Tzu's followers[28] adopted and expanded his theory of equalizing all things to condemn any kind of ruler. In ancient China, they asserted, Yao was an example of the good sovereign, and Chieh was an example of the bad sovereign. But the no-sovereignists argued that Yao made people excited so that there was no calm, while Chieh made people suffer so that there was no contentment. Both excitement and suffering change people's plain nature; therefore, the management of both Yao and Chieh should be rejected. The no-sovereignists claimed that the best society had no ruler and that the best way to manage the world is to leave people alone, because people should live absolutely freely and peacefully without any control. Whereas Chuang Tzu tended toward escape from the everyday world, the no-sovereignists pursued utopia within secular society.

Like most Taoists, the key concept of the no-sovereignists was the primary nature of the human, but this led them in the direction of political criticism. They argued that the way for the trainer to manage horses is against the natural life of horses and totally destroys the nature of horses. The trainer therefore sins against the horses. For the same reason, the potter and carpenter destroy the nature of clay and wood, and they are deservedly criticized. The managers of the world ruin the true nature of people, although every ruler would like to say that he greatly benefits them.

The Huang Lao School

The Huang Lao school started in the fourth century B.C.E. (the middle Warring States period) and flourished in the second century B.C.E. (the former Han dynasty). The word *Huang* comes from Huang-Ti, the legendary

Yellow Emperor and the word *Lao* from Lao Tzu, which reveals the school as indeed a branch of Taoism. It seems that the Huang Lao school is a combination of the Huang school and Lao doctrine. The Huang school, however, cannot be found in Chinese history. According to the bibliographical catalog in *Han Shu* (the *History of the Former Han Dynasty*), books bearing Huang Ti's name were classified into twelve categories: Taoism, Yin Yang school, storytellers, military, astronomy, calendar, *wu hsing* (five elemental operational qualities), divination, medicine, immortals, and the art of sexual intercourse, to name a few. Although many authors named their works after Huang Ti's name, there was no school specifically so called. Basically, "Huang Lao school" is just a name for Taoism in the Han dynasty.

Some books and scholars are related to Huang Lao scholarship, such as *Guan Tzu, Chuang Tzu,* Shen Pu-hai, Shen Tao, *The Silk Manuscript of the Huang Lao School, He Guan Tzu, Lü Shi Ch'un Ch'iu,* and *Huai Nan Tzu.* None of these is authoritative for the Huang Lao school. Some scholars argue that *The Silk Manuscript of the Huang Lao School,* a group of texts discovered and named in 1973, is a reliable classic of the school, but it seems too legalistic. Since the only reliable statement about the school is found in the comments of Ssu-ma Ch'ien in the *Historical Records,* we can conclude that in *Chuang Tzu,* the seven chapters—12 through 16, 33, and chapter 11 except session 1—are typical works of Huang Lao thought.[29]

Unlike Lao Tzu and Chuang Tzu, the most remarkable feature of the Huang Lao school is convergence: "following the great smoothness of the Yin Yang School, adopting the advantage of Confucianism and Mohism, applying the essence of Logicians and Legalism."[30] Huang Lao scholars absorbed elements from other schools while retaining basic conceptions and ideas of Taoism. They arranged fundamental principles of each school into a new system beginning with Taoism, followed by Confucianism, then Legalism, and ending with Mohism. For example, they declared: "The men of old who made clear the great Tao, first made Heaven clear, and the morality and virtue were next... Goodwill and Duty were next... inquiry and inspection were next... judging right or wrong was next: and when judging right or wrong was clear, reward and punishment were next."[31] Tao is the essential concept of Taoism, morality and virtue are basic conceptions of Confucianism, and reward and punishment are key elements of Legalism. The school preferred convergence to divergence and held that to make differences come together is profound.

Influenced by Confucianism and Legalism, the Huang Lao school acknowledged the difference between lord and subjects. The school's scholars argued that ministers must deal with details while the sovereign does nothing. Lao Tzu and Chuang Tzu believed that a sovereign should do nothing, and that as long as he ruled in that way, the world would be better off. But neither addressed the question of whether or not society is required to act when its ruler does nothing. Huang Lao scholars added "taking action"—namely, management by ministers—to the nonaction of the sovereign, so that the theory of wu-wei becomes a potential doctrine of operational politics.

Both Lao Tzu and Chuang Tzu declared that people should follow nature by nonaction. However, with the mutual influence between individual schools, Huang Lao scholars created a new method of following nature: "to advance following timeliness; to transform according to environment; then you can institute custom and conduct your career without inappropriateness."[32] They argued that nothing is better than traveling by boat on water, and nothing is better than traveling by cart on land. If you push a boat on the ground because it can move fast on water, you cannot march far, and may even die trying. The difference between ancient and modern is just like that of land and water. To hope to employ the policy of one state in another state is just like pushing a boat on land; you will certainly achieve nothing even if you work very hard, and you yourself will be hurt.[33] The difference between water and land is a distinction of objective situations, and that of boat and cart is of alternative means. People's choices must be consistent with circumstances. Thus, to follow nature generally in Lao Tzu and Chuang Tzu becomes for the Huang Lao scholars a specific principle to obey timeliness. No matter how developed modern society is, people still must act consistently with time and circumstance to succeed in their undertakings.

The *Huai Nan Tzu* is the most important book of the Huang Lao school in Han China. The early part of the former Han dynasty (ca. second century B.C.E.) was a time of peace, as some sovereigns attempted to follow Taoist theory by lessening taxes and reducing forced labor. Taoism, which had primarily been a guide for the thought and conduct of individuals, now also became a basis for government practice. At the same time, the conflicts between philosophical schools lessened, and they borrowed increasingly from each other. The *Huai Nan Tzu* reflects those new tendencies and presented some new ideas. Here is an example: "The way of a sovereign is not to keep doing something, but to refrain from much action. What is the so-called *wu-wei*? In his position, the knowledgeable causes no trouble; the brave never inflicts pain upon his people; the benevolent does not fret over his people."[34] The author of this passage argues that the ruler should neither use his sovereign position nor follow personal preference as an impetus for action. As long as these basic rules are observed, the ruler can do anything. However, according to this theory, the sovereign should be a symbol of power and society rather than a person who has the privilege to control or change the natural status of human life.

In fact, some authors of the *Huai Nan Tzu* develop a totally new sense of the meaning of wu-wei. Wu-wei is now based on people's will and the laws of the state. In the political system constructed by the authors, the will of the people is superior to the law, the law is superior to the ruler, the ruler is superior to the bureaucracy, and the bureaucracy, in turn, governs the people. Its formulation is almost modern. Another important development occurs in the explanation of "doing nothing but nothing left undone" (*wu-wei erh wu-pu-wei*): "(The sage) indifferently takes no action, and yet there is nothing left undone.... What is so called *wu-wei* (doing nothing) means that one should take no action before natural development; what is so called *wu-pu-wei* (nothing left undone) means that one should take action according to the development of things themselves."[35] In Lao Tzu's philosophy, the idea that nothing is left undone implied the outcome and advantage of doing nothing. But for the *Huai Nan Tzu*, "doing nothing" and "nothing is left undone" are no longer two phases of approach and sequence but the same thing—namely, conditional behavior. The condition is "to take no action before things happen," or "to take action according to the development of things themselves." Hence, both nonaction and "nothing is left undone" are results of particular human actions. Therefore wu-wei was converted from nonaction to a certain type of action.

Here is another detailed and rational explanation of wu-wei from the *Huai Nan Tzu*: "What I call *wu-wei* means that selfish motives cannot be allowed to disturb public business; wild wishes cannot be allowed to destroy right principle;...(*Wu-wei*) doesn't mean that one should have no reaction to feelings, or no response to pressure. If one wants to boil away a well, or to irrigate a mountain by the Huai River, these are stubbornly against nature, hence they are called 'taking action' (*yu-wei*). If you take a boat when you come upon water, or take a special cart when you walk in the desert or take a special sledge when you move on mud, or take a basket when you are on a mountain, or if you form a hill to make use of a high place, or make a pool to make use of low-lying land, these are not what is called 'Doing' (*wei*)."[36] This represents a completely new definition of wu-wei (no action) and yu-wei (taking action). Yu-wei becomes a derogatory term that indicates that morally wrong behavior stems from selfish motives and unreasonable efforts against natural law. Previously, yu-wei had meant any common behavior, and it was not considered wrong or undesirable. With this development it is no longer something positive.

Furthermore, the concept of wu-wei begins to mean doing everything according to objective conditions without yielding to selfish motives and wild desires. This rational attitude in the *Huai Nan Tzu* was inspired by Han Fei Tzu and other previous scholars and provides Taoism with a solid defense against criticism. However, in general, the theories in the *Huai Nan Tzu* are complicated, and much effort is still required to understand the Huang Lao school comprehensively. Generally speaking, the Chuang Tzu school represents individual and spiritual Taoism, whereas the Huang Lao school represents social and political Taoism, although both reflect the fundamental spirit of the *Lao Tzu.*

The Origins of Taoist Religion

The Roots of Thought in Taoist Religion

Religious Taoism started with traditional Chinese ideas and religious practices. According to oracle bone inscriptions of the Shang dynasty (seventeenth to eleventh century B.C.E.), by the second millennium B.C.E. the Chinese had begun to believe in a Heaven that was like a powerful God, and in other gods with lesser powers as well. They also worshiped ghosts and ancestors and believed that the ghosts of their ancestors could communicate with them through religious ceremonies and influence their happiness. At the same time, the art of divination by oracle bone developed. In the West Chou dynasty (eleventh to eighth century B.C.E.), in the early first millennium B.C.E., there were officers in charge of sacrificial offerings to three systems of gods: heaven gods, such as the sun, moon, wind, stars, thunder, and rain; earth gods, such as the land, grain, rivers, and mountains; and human ghosts, such as ancestors and sages. All of these gods and ghosts were sources of Taoist polytheism.

Religious Taoism featured belief in physical immortality, which developed from the east coast of China after the fourth century B.C.E., in the middle Warring States period. There, people called *fang-shih* ("prescription-masters") were active in the occult sciences and propagated theories about how to reach and realize immortality. Some of them worked their way into the inner circle of kings or emperors—for example, the first emperor of Ch'in, who ruled from 246 to 210 B.C.E., and the Emperor Wu, who ruled from 140 to 87 B.C.E., in the former Han dynasty. Kings or emperors sent these fang-shih sailing to find immortal isles in the sea. According to the *Historical Records,* the first emperor of Ch'in sent an expedition composed of fang-shih and three thousand boys and girls to search for immortals. The explorers could not find the immortal isles and did not return to China for fear of punishment. Some contemporary Chinese and Japanese scholars still argue that some Japanese are descendants of the boys and girls of that expedition.

In addition, a school of sorts, *ch'en wei* (or *ch'an wei*, Prognostication and Apocrypha), exerted much influence on Taoism. *Ch'en* means prognostic and enigmatic words or texts, being translated as "prognostication." *Wei* is the weft, the threads that cross the warp in weaving. In Chinese, the word for warp is *ching*, meaning both "classics" and "warp," hence the word *wei* was used to indicate a kind of enigmatic interpretation and commentary on Confucianist classics, being translated as "apocrypha." Ch'en wei indicated the prognostic and enigmatic words used in the reexplanation of both Confucianism classics and works about them. According to the *Historical Records*, some prognostic and enigmatic words appeared in the sixth century B.C.E.

It was also said that the First Emperor Ch'in, who ruled from 246 to 210 B.C.E., received a ch'en that said his dynasty would be wiped out by "Hu." Nobody knew what was indicated by the character "Hu." Because the character could have meant "barbarian," the emperor thought it might be referring to the barbarians of the north (Hsiung-nu), and therefore sent three hundred thousand troops to build up the Great Wall to prevent being attacked by Hsiung-nu. It was not until Ch'in's son, "Hu Hai," had come to the throne and the Ch'in dynasty was destroyed by rebellions that people realized "Hu" indicated his son. Both Wang Mang, who usurped the throne of the former Han dynasty, and Liu Hsiu, the first emperor of the latter Han dynasty, took advantage of prognostic words to spread propaganda in support of their usurping the throne. In the first century B.C.E., prognostic explanations of seven Confucian classics were produced, and in 56 B.C.E. they were declared essential books of official Confucianism. Thus ch'en wei—"prognostication and apocrypha"—became more and more important. Although ch'en wei was prohibited after the second century, its belief in gods influenced the formation of Taoist religion.

The emergence of the religious worship of Lao Tzu was decisive in the development of religious Taoism. In the early former Han dynasty (206 B.C.E.–8 C.E.), the Huang Lao school doctrines were political and philosophical, but in the latter Han dynasty (25–220 C.E.), Lao Tzu and Huang Ti, together with the Buddha, became the objects of common offerings in temples. Thus the Huang Lao school became the Way of Huang Lao (*Huang Lao Tao*), which prevailed in the provinces and was a predecessor of religious Taoism. In addition to the king of Ch'u, a brother of Emperor Ming, who made offerings to Lao Tzu, Huang Ti, and the Buddha, the emperor Huan, who ruled from 147 to 167, twice ordered that rituals be performed at the reputed birthplace of Lao Tzu in 165. The next year Huan went in person to an imperial palace to offer up a sacrifice to Lao Tzu. These were early signs that Lao Tzu would become a religious founder just like Buddha.

The Way of Great Peace

The *Classic of Great Peace* (*T'ai P'ing Ching*) had a long history before its importance was recognized. According to the *Han History*, the early version of the text with twelve volumes was compiled by Kan Chung-k'o, who said he received the book from a god, and it was presented to Emperor Ch'eng, who ruled from 32 to 7 B.C.E. Because it was inferred from the book that the fate of the Han dynasty would change, Kan was sent to jail and died. One century later, another version with one hundred and seventy volumes, compiled by Yü Chi, was presented to Emperor Shun, who ruled from 125 to 144 C.E.; and later again, it was presented to Emperor Huan. Few rulers liked the book, and it was more or less connected to the Yellow Turban Rebellion led by Chang Chiao (or Chüeh) in 184 C.E., who was said to have circulated many copies of it.

The title, *Classic of Great Peace*, expressed the social ideal of the Chinese. The word *t'ai p'ing*, as the opposite of struggle, war, and chaos, literally means "the highest peace." It has been an expression of the common values of the Chinese people, including Confucianists, Legalists, Buddhists, and Taoists, as well as rulers and the populace, from ancient times. According to the authors, the characters *t'ai* indicate "big," "huge," or "great"; *p'ing* indicates not only "peace" but also "equality," "justice," and "fairness."[37] The authors of this work clearly adopted some essential ideas from Confucianism. They believed that a peaceful world demanded sagacious sovereigns, virtuous subjects, and a yielding populace. The sovereigns, who were born from heaven, should follow its nature and establish a moral and humane government. The subjects were born from the earth, and the populace from human beings. They should be honest and pliable, and they should not only obey laws, but also help rulers to avoid and correct mistakes.

Unlike Chuang Tzu's way of indifference toward life and death, the *Classic of Great Peace* declared that between heaven and earth longevity is of the most value, and it is possible for everyone to reach immortality. It argued that among slaves and servant girls the wiser can become good people, among good people those who like to study can become virtuous people, among virtuous people those who study ceaselessly can become sages, and among sages those who study ceaselessly can recognize the door of the Way of Heaven. If after entering the Way they still study ceaselessly, they become immortals; if they continue, they reach the truth; if they continue further, they become gods; and if they continue still further, they can share the same shape as the Emperor of Heaven. Here immortals with a perfect combination of human body and soul are lower than gods, much higher than humans, and live in heaven. A soul that has left the human body is called a "ghost" and will descend to the "yellow spring"; namely, hell. Unlike an immortal who often helps people turn ill luck to good, the ghosts are often sent by gods to bring people disaster as punishment for their sins.

In order to achieve the realization of longevity and immortality, the authors analyzed the existing conditions of life. They developed a theory of life from early Taoist philosophy and emphasized that the human life force comes from a combination of *shen* and *ch'i*, or "spirit" and "material force." For a human life, spiritual movement rides on material force, and the existence of material force depends on the spirit. If people maintain their material force, then they have spirit, and if in turn they retain spirit, then they have material force. If they lose either spirit or material force they will die. Thus, the way to conserve life is through "meditation on the One" (*shou-i*), or, keeping spirit and material force in harmony. "The One" indicates heart, mind, and will, and "meditation on the One" means focusing the mind on one's spirit to avoid its dissipation. "Meditation on the One" is an important concept in Taoist religion, but its meaning and method vary widely among Taoist classics. In addition, other approaches to longevity are given in the book, such as *shou ch'i* ("meditation on material force"), *shih ch'i* ("eating material force"), *t'ai hsi* ("breathe like a fetus"), as well as the art of acupuncture and other medical knowledge.

Another important theory of Taoist religion is that of retribution or judgment, which is distinct from other philosophical schools or religions. Taoist philosophy disagrees with theories of judgment, because it maintains that under the influence of the Tao everything develops spontaneously, and that misfortunes and accidents really mean nothing for people. Confucianists declare that Heaven will punish or warn the sovereigns by disasters or monstrosities if they do something wrong, whereas Buddhists believe that people will receive retribution eventually through rebirth. The theories of Taoist religion, however, claim that retribution either affects peoples' life spans or is passed on to their descendants. The *Classic of Great Peace* says that Heaven sends gods to record a person's behavior and keeps itself well informed of the person's every fault, trivial or serious. Every day, every month, and every year, gods calculate each person's sins or merit. If a person has some merit, his or her life span will be extended, but otherwise it will be shortened.[38] However, if someone who has done many good works dies earlier than one who has done evil, it is because she bears the faults of her ancestors; and the one who has done evil lives longer, it is because his ancestors left him great merit. Merit and sins will influence five generations.[39]

This is so-called *ch'eng fu*, an important theory of Taoist religion. *Ch'eng* means literally "receiving," *fu* means "owing." Thus ch'eng fu suggests that one undergoes the consequences of the behavior of one's parents and passes on the consequences of one's own conduct to one's children. Theoretically, ch'eng fu is just transmission of burdens, either merits or demerits, transmitted from ancestors to descendants; however, practically, it emphasizes the transmission of guilt to warn people to behave themselves. Thus ch'eng fu may be translated either as "transmission of burdens" or "inherited guilt." This theory is in contrast to the Buddhist concept of karma and rebirth; that is, in ch'eng fu, the merits and demerits accrued by an individual are manifested not in future lives but are passed on to descendants.[40]

It was said that the ideas of the *Classic of Great Peace* precipitated a great religious movement in eastern China, under the leadership of Chang Chiao (d. 184 C.E.) and his brothers. Chang Chiao named himself the "Master of Great Wisdom and Virtue" and taught many disciples. By letting people kneel to confess and using magic formulas and incantations, he cured many people and thus had many followers. Chang sent eight disciples to carry out his commissions. In more than a decade, he had some hundred thousand believers in eight provinces, who were divided into thirty-six troops, each of which was headed by a general. In 184, which was the first year of a sixty-year cycle according to traditional Chinese chronology, the Yellow Turban Rebellion broke out, so called because the rebels wore yellow turbans to mark their declaration that the "blue heaven" was to be replaced by a "yellow heaven." "Blue heaven" indicates the throne of the Han dynasty, and "yellow heaven" is a symbol of their own power in the future. Chang and his younger brothers called themselves, respectively, the "General of Heaven," the "General of Earth," and the "General of Humanity," which were culled from the theory in the *Classic of Great Peace* about the harmony of heaven, earth, and human beings. Chang's religion was called the Way of Great Peace, as well as the Way of Huang Lao, and was in fact a military-religious organization. The main force of the rebellion was crushed in nine months, but its remains and related rebellions persisted for more than twenty years.

The Yellow Turban is the largest among many rebellions at the end of the Han dynasty, most of which involved religious sects similar to Taoism. Although they were eventually defeated by the imperial forces, such revolutionary religious movements with some Taoist ideological elements remained a persistent feature of medieval Chinese history. From the third to the fifth century, there are official records of eight rebellions under the name of Li Hung, who was said to be Lao Tzu incarnate. All of these movements are important aspects of the development of religious Taoism, but we cannot trace them in detail, because their literature was prohibited and is not available today.

The Way of Five Pecks of Rice

In addition to the Yellow Turban Rebellion on the east coast of Han China, an important Taoist movement was the Way of Five Pecks of Rice (*wu-tou-mi tao*), which developed in the southwest in 191. The founder of the sect, Chang Ling (34–156), also called Chang Tao-ling, was considered the father of Taoist religion. Converts had to contribute five Chinese pecks of rice, from which the religion received its nickname. Its formal name is the Way of the Celestial Masters (*T'ien-shih Tao*), because the protagonist of Taoist religion is a celestial master according to the *Classic of Great Peace*. Later it was also called the Orthodox and Unity Way (*Cheng-i Tao*) because Chang Tao-ling was said to have received the "Orthodox and Unity Way of the Authority and Covenant" (*cheng-i meng-wei chi tao*). The name means that the movement, under the leadership of Chang Tao-ling, was the formal beginning of the Taoist religion.

It was said that Chang Tao-ling was a Confucianist and had read the five classics of Confucianism when he was young, but he found that they were not useful for longevity and so began to study the art of longevity. For a better environment he moved to Shu (present Ssu-ch'uan Province) and lived on a mountain. He explored Taoist theories and wrote Taoist classics. One day Lord Lao the Most High (T'ai Shang Lao Chün, the deified Lao Tzu) came down to teach him the Orthodox and Unity Way, and after that he could treat illness. Thereafter people regarded him as a master, and soon he had disciples numbering tens of thousands of families. Chang Tao-ling believed that people died or fell sick because they carried guilt or because the paths they followed were obstructed. He thus asked people to confess or to repair a road to eliminate guilt or cure their sickness. If this did not work, he would use spells and talismans. For example, he wrote three documents for "three officials"—the god of heaven, the god of earth, and the god of water—and asked them to drive the ghost out of the ill body. He believed virtue was important for longevity: the most virtuous would become immortal, the less virtuous would only double their life spans, and those lower in virtue would in some lesser sense prolong life.

After he died, his son and grandson continued the movement. In 191 his grandson Chang Lu was sent as a general to attack and occupy the Han-chung commandary. Chang Lu established an independent religio-political organization with authority throughout the district, combining temporal and spiritual powers. For ceremonial and administrative needs, the realm was divided into twenty-four parishes (*chih*). Each of them was headed by a libationer (*chi-chiu*) as both priest and chief, and each had an oratory, or "chamber of purity" (*ching shih*). Chang also advocated the establishment of communal facilities providing free food for the needy. Pedestrians were free to take food, but anyone who took too much would be made ill by ghosts. He undertook all kinds of public works for the good of the commonwealth. People who violated laws would be forgiven three times and then punished. It was said that all people there willingly accepted the government.

In 215 a general, Ts'ao Ts'ao of the Han dynasty, attacked Chang Lu with a troop of one hundred thousand soldiers. Not long after his brother was killed in battle, Chang surrendered and Ts'ao conferred the title of general and marquis upon him. This resulted in official recognition of the sect by contemporary and later dynasties. To control Chang Lu's power, Ts'ao asked him to move to central China. The Way of the Celestial Masters thus spread and became more influential.

Though The Way of the Celestial Masters shared religious ideas with the *Classic of Great Peace,* the celestial masters had their own scripture: *Lao Tzu Hsiang Erh Chu* (a commentary on Lao Tzu by Hsiang Erh), which was said to have been written by Chang Tao-ling or Chang Lu. The book gave a different interpretation of Lao Tzu from a religious perspective. While Lao Tzu exalted the Tao (the "Way") from which oneness is born, the religion treats Lao Tzu himself as a god, and thus the commentary declares that Lao Tzu is the very Tao or the Way. It argues that the Tao is just oneness, and oneness becomes ch'i (material force) when it disappears, and in turn becomes Lord Lao the Most High when it is built up.[41] Hence the "Way" is sometimes impersonal, as in early Taoist philosophy, and sometimes it is a personal god for religious worship. The book also gives a new interpretation of "meditation on the One." Unlike the *Classic of Great Peace,* "meditation on the One" does not indicate a personal cultivation, but obedience to the Taoist commandments. The author insists on the importance of religious discipline. Both immortals and laypeople hate death and prefer life, but their reactions are different. Immortals believe in Taoism and keep the commandments, while laypeople don't follow the Way and do evil. Hence the Way uses death to punish people who do evil and life to reward people who obey Taoist principles.

The author claimed that not only ordinary Taoists but sovereigns as well should practice the Way. The Way is preference for life and goodness and is against war. If a sovereign believes in the Way and gives up force, subjects will be spontaneously loyal and the populace will practice filial piety honestly, and thus great peace and immortal life will be realized. It is clear that the author wishes to engage in both the political and the religious, the sacred and the secular. This is a key feature of Taoist religion manifested in most Taoist scriptures.

The Way of Great Peace and the Way of Five Pecks of Rice were the earliest Taoist movements that indicated the appearance of the Taoist church outside of folk society. After Chang Lu surrendered to Ts'ao Ts'ao, his sect began to be accepted by the ruling class. Folk Taoist religious movements are very important in Taoist history, but based on available literature, the history of Taoist religion basically indicates that it was prevalent in the middle or upper strata.

Ko Hung and Taoist Religious Theories

Ko Hung (283–363?),[42] who gave more attention to research than to serving as a priest, played a key role in the maturing of religious Taoism from a folk religion into a sect favored by the higher classes. Ko Hung called himself the Master Who Embraces Simplicity (*Pao P'u Tzu*). He is remembered for two books: one, known as the Outer Chapters, is about Confucianism; the other, the Inner Chapters, deals with his theories about religious Taoism.

Ko Hung was a son of a senior official, but because his father died when he was thirteen years old, he had a difficult youth. He said that he had to cut firewood for paper and writing brushes and write by the firelight. Because of this lack of paper, he wrote more than once on a piece of paper, thus creating difficulties for those reading it. He read many kinds of books, including Confucian classics, but only books about how to attain immortality interested him. He studied the secret of alchemy from a senior Taoist master, Cheng Yin. Once he took part in a battle to crush a rebellion and was offered a commission as a general because of his achievement. He refused the offer because he recognized that merit, wealth, and privilege are like guests who stay with you for a short time and then leave, that they cannot be kept forever. Just like the flowers that flourish in the spring and soon wither, so many illustrious heroes have died, and so many celebrated families have gone. People suffer from worrying about gaining and losing, from likes and dislikes. Ko Hung wanted to withdraw from society and focus on the art of longevity. Hence "the trace of his carriage never passed by the field of aristocracy, and a piece of his writing was never sent to an official's home."[43] Thus he became an independent and important Taoist thinker.

Ko claimed that the greatest nature of heaven and earth is the begetting of life, because it embodies love for creation. Therefore, of all that religious Taoists revere in highest secrecy, nothing is more important than the way to attain longevity.[44] However, as few people had actually seen an immortal, he was asked whether it was practical to believe that gods and immortals really existed. He argued that even with the best of eyes it is impossible to see every material object, and that even with the best of hearing not every sound can be heard. Even with long feet, the land we tread would never be as vast as the untrodden. Even if we possess all the learning of the wisest of people, what we know would never equal the bulk of our ignorance. What is there that does not exist somewhere in the multiplicity of creation? Why, then, should the immortals, whose life histories fill books, not exist? Why should there be no divine process leading to immortality?[45] Ko was wise to point out the limitations of human knowledge, and to remind us that people are wrong to believe that only what they see is true. Such a reminder, however, is of course not sufficient to prove that immortals exist.

Ko was also asked: Whatever begins is sure to end; whatever exists is sure to perish. Therefore, even sages like the Three Kings, the Five Emperors, Confucius, and the Duke of Chou died.[46] The best artisan could not sharpen a tile or stone into a needle, and the best metal-worker could not cast lead or tin into a good sword. Even ghosts and gods cannot do the impossible; even heaven and earth cannot achieve the unachievable. So where in our world could a miraculous recipe be found for restoring youth to the old or life to the dying?[47]

Ko replied: To be sure, life, death, beginning, and ending do form the grand framework, but there are differences and variations. What one man affirms, another will have reason to deny. In the myriad of changes and transformations of creation, marvels may occur without limitation. What any individual thing seems to be, its activity may belie; the roots of a thing may be well balanced, but its branches may be deviant. We cannot treat all things the same way. The majority of people claim that all that begins must also end, but one does not derive universal principles by lumping all the facts together and giving them equal weight. It is said that in summer there is sure to be growth, but this is just when shepherd's-purse and wheat wither. It is said that in winter plants are sure to fade, yet this is the time when bamboos and cypresses flourish. It is said that beginnings must have endings, but heaven and earth never perish. It is said that all the living must die, but the tortoise and crane enjoy a long life.[48] Ko's arguments were based on the variety and complexity of the universe: As common phenomena always have their opposites, varied creations cannot be judged by one standard.

Ko believed that by appropriate treatment something can become strong and durable. For example, muddied earth quickly loses its shape, but when fashioned into tiles it can last as long as all nature. Oak decays easily, but when it has been roasted into charcoal it will last for thousands upon thousands of years.[49] Also, some common medicines and the paltry arts of physicians can cure illness and even raise those who have just died. If this is true, why should the superior medicines not be able to make the living immortal?

Ko concluded that people's deaths result from desires, old age, illness, poisons, miasmas, and chills and, therefore, if they can avoid these baneful things, they will realize longevity, and if they find the divine process, they will be able to become immortal. He asserted that even food is effective for keeping people alive. As long as people get it, they live; when it is cut off, they die. Think then what the situation is in regard to the highest quality of divine medicine! Wouldn't its benefit to humans be thousands of times greater than that of food? Cinnabar preparations are such that the longer they are heated, the more marvelous the changes they undergo. Even after a hundred firings, gold does not melt away, nor does it decay, no matter how long it is buried. By taking these two substances, we refine our bodies, so that we neither grow old nor die. Ko believed that people acquire the nature of what they have eaten and therefore must seek external substances to fortify themselves.[50]

Ko, an encyclopedic Taoist scholar, offered many ways to longevity and immortality. First, he declared that those desiring longevity must strive to "accumulate goodness" (*li kung te*), win merit, be kind and affectionate to others, and practice the Golden Rule.[51] These Taoist injunctions originated in Confucianism and traditional morality, yet were used as a means of practicing longevity. Like other Taoist thinkers, Ko also connected morality and life span. He said that according to Taoist classics, doing good stands in first place; eschewing one's faults comes next. Followers of the divine process feel that among the highest acts are saving people in trouble so that they can avoid disaster and protecting others from illness so that they will not die before their time. Those who wish to seek immortality should treat loyalty, filial piety, friendliness, obedience, benevolence, and trustworthiness as basic principles. If they do not perform meritorious acts but solely pursue esoteric techniques, they will never attain longevity. For the person who commits a wrong of great enormity, the Director of Fates will deduct a period of three hundred days; for lesser wrongs, a reckoning of three days. Deductions vary according to the degree of the transgression.[52] Clearly, accumulating goodness was considered necessary by Ko to attain longevity, yet was insufficient on its own.

Like the *Classic of Great Peace,* Ko also emphasized the "meditation on the One" (shou-i), but the meaning of "the One" is altered. For Ko, "the One" is the internal god. He quoted the immortal classic: "Wish to enjoy immortality, Meditation on the One must be rife. Meditate on the One till famine, One will provide nourishment. Meditate on the One till drought, One will provide the refreshing beverage."[53] According to Ko, the One possesses names, shapes, and colors. In the male, the One is 0.9 inch long; in the female, 0.6. Sometimes it is 2.4 inches below the navel, in the lower field (*hsia tan t'ien*); at other times, it is below the heart, in the central field (*chung tan t'ien*). In the upper field, it is three inches behind the space between the eyebrows. This mysterious One can form yin (feminine) and beget yang (masculine), bring on the cold and the heat. Through the One there is sprouting in spring, growing in summer, harvesting in autumn, and storing in winter. Space is no analogy for its magnitude; nor is a hair or sprout an analogy for its minuteness.[54] If people can meditate on the One, the One will also preserve them. In this way harmful things find no place in them that will admit entrance to their evil, in defeat it is possible to be victorious, and in positions of peril to feel only security.[55]

Through "circulation of the breath" (*hsing-ch'i*), Ko believed that illnesses could be cured, snakes and tigers charmed, bleeding from wounds halted, that one can stay under water or walk on it, and that it can protract one's years. Its most important part is simply to "breathe like a fetus" (t'ai hsi). Those who succeed in doing this will do their breathing as though in the womb, without using nose or mouth, and for them the divine process has been achieved. Ko gave some instructions about how to practice such breathing. For example, when first learning to circulate the breath, one inhales through the nose and refrains from exhaling. After holding it quietly while counting to one hundred and twenty, it is expelled in tiny quantities through the mouth. During the exhalations and inhalations one should not hear the sound of one's own breathing, and one should always exhale less than one inhales. A goose feather held before the nose and mouth during exhalation should not move. After some practice the number counted in mind may be increased very gradually to one thousand before the breath is released. Once this is achieved, the aged will become one day younger every day.[56]

Religious Taoism emphasizes the importance of appropriate sexual intercourse in the theory of longevity. This is *fang chung shu*, which means literally the "art of the bedchamber" and may be translated as the art of sexual intercourse. Its purpose is to improve health and pursue longevity, which is a key point of difference from modern studies of sexual relations. Ko believed that one who wants to prolong life must know the art of sexual intercourse, otherwise energy will be frequently lost and breathing exercises won't reach peak effectiveness. According to historical records, there were several books on this subject in ancient China, but few survived. Through Ko, however, we have some general information. According to him, at least ten authors wrote on the methods of correct sexual intercourse. Some claim that they could show how to replenish losses, cure illnesses, gather more yin (feminine) to increase the yang (masculine), or increase years and protract longevity. An essential concept in the art of the bedchamber is *ching*, a word meaning cream, essence, or sperm. The ancient Chinese believed that sperm is a kind of life essence, thus the principle of the art of the bedchamber is to save and preserve ching, the essence of life, in sexual intercourse. In this way, it is believed, essence of life could be retained to nourish the brain (*huan ching pu nao*), so it is good for health and life span.

Obviously, according to Ko, the art of the bedchamber is necessary for realizing longevity and immortality. Even if one were to take all the famous medicines, without knowledge of how to save the essence of life in sexual intercourse, it would be impossible to attain longevity. People should not give up sexual intercourse entirely, otherwise they will contract melancholia through inactivity and die prematurely through the many illnesses resulting from depression and celibacy. On the other hand, overindulgence diminished one's life, and it is only by harmonizing the two extremes that damage could be avoided. However, it is difficult to know the details about the practices of the art of the bedchamber, because "true men" have transmitted this method orally without any writing, and unless the oral directions are available, not one person in ten thousand will avoid injury by attempting to practice this art.[57] Although Ko did not leave us any details, we can form some general idea through other available books. The art of the bedchamber contains mysterious instructions: For example, intercourse at different times or facing different directions would cause corresponding effects on health; one should have sexual relations with different young virgins to receive fresh essence of life; and one should avoid ejaculation in sexual intercourse to save the essence of life. Apparently the art of the bedchamber is easily misunderstood as a guide to enjoying sex and has sometimes led to obscenity and promiscuousness. However, it is originally about health and longevity, and neither about asceticism nor giving way to lust.

As to immortality, the most important and difficult practice is alchemy, namely, using gold and cinnabar. According to Ko, at the top of the immortal pharmacopoeia stands cinnabar. Second comes gold; third, silver; fourth, glossy ganoderma (*Ganoderma lucidum*); fifth, the jades; sixth, mica; seventh, pearls; eighth, realgar (a kind of mineral); and ninth, brown hematite, as well as various traditional medicinal herbs and minerals.[58] Ko asserted, "The volumes I have studied as I examined writings on the nurturing of life and collected recipes for acquiring everlasting vision must number in the thousands; yet there was not one amongst them that did not insist that 'reverted cinnabar and liquefied gold' (*huan tan chin yeh*) were the things of highest importance. These two, it seems, mark the peak of the divine process leading to immortality. If taking them does not make one an immortal, then immortals have never existed."[59] By doing the breathing exercises (*hu hsi*), doing calisthenics, and taking herbal medicines one may extend one's years but cannot prevent ultimate death. Taking the divine elixir, however, will produce an eternal longevity and make one coeval with sky and earth; it allows one to travel up and down in Paradise, riding clouds or driving dragons. Furthermore, one's whole household, rather than just oneself alone, will become immortal.

Certainly alchemy was not easy to learn. It was said that the preparation should be carried out in an uninhabited place on a famous mountain. One shall have not more than three companions. Previously, one should have undergone rites of purification for one hundred days and washed one's body and hair in fragrance to attain a state of cleanliness. One must not approach anything that soils, nor associate with common people. No disbelievers may know of your plan, for if they blaspheme the divine medicine, successful preparation will be prevented.[60] Because the practice of alchemy was so difficult and its cost high, Ko advised that people should be very careful in practicing it and admitted that he himself had not succeeded in mastering the art of gold and cinnabar. However, he made great contributions to Chinese chemical history.

The Transformation of Taoist Religion

K'ou Ch'ien-chih and the Taoist Reformation in Northern China

In addition to Ko Hung's theoretical contribution to the formulation of orthodox Taoist religion, K'ou Ch'ien-chih (365–448) played an important role in the process of Taoist religion's institutionalization. At the time when China was divided into northern and southern parts by dynasties, K'ou lived mainly in the early Northern Wei (386–534), which was governed by a minority, To-pa's family. The court hoped to be supported by the majority (Han nationality) and yet feared the majority would be so influential as to threaten its power, an anxiety that determined the sovereigns' complicated attitude toward the indigenous tradition of Taoism.

K'ou was born into a traditionally Taoist gentry family in Shang-ku, near present Beijing, and moved to Feng-i, present-day Shensi (Shaanxi). According to the *History of Wei*,[61] at an early age he developed an intense interest in the way to immortality and aspired to withdraw from worldly life. He studied and practiced the doctrine of Chang Lu and took transcendental herbs, but he experienced no results from all his efforts. Once he visited his aunt and met one of her manservants, Ch'eng-kung Hsing, who seemed extraordinary and never felt tired even when he worked very hard. K'ou therefore took Ch'eng-kung home to be a servant in his family. One day K'ou could not solve a mathematical problem and felt frustrated. Ch'eng-kung asked what the problem was and solved it immediately; as a result, K'ou wanted to be his disciple. Strangely, Ch'eng-kung insisted that he should be K'ou's student, although actually he would teach K'ou. Then Ch'eng-kung took K'ou into seclusion, first on the western sacred peak of Mount Hua, Shensi, and then on the central sacred peak, Mount Sung, Honan. After practicing Taoism together for some years, Ch'eng-kung observed that K'ou might not become an immortal, but rather a "master of the sovereign." Ch'eng-kung died after seven years, and K'ou continued his cultivation of Taoist arts alone on the mountain.

It was said that in 415, K'ou was rewarded with a visitation from the Great Super Lord Lao, the deified Lao Tzu (*t'ai-shang lao-chün*). Lord Lao told K'ou that there had not been a celestial master since the death of Chang Tao-ling, the first celestial master. People who wanted to practice Taoist belief could not find a master, and since K'ou's behavior conformed to Taoist principles, he was qualified to be the master. Thus Lord Lao bestowed on K'ou the title of celestial master. At the same time, Lord Lao delivered to him a scripture entitled the *New Code to Be Chanted to Yün-chung Musical*

Notation (*Yün-chung yin-sung hsin-k'o chih chieh*), parts of which are believed to be the *Lao Tzu Commandment with Musical Notation* (*lao-chün yin-sung chieh-ching*) in the present Taoist canon and can be taken as K'ou's doctrine. At the same time, Lord Lao revealed certain secret breathing and calisthenic techniques to K'ou, and then K'ou learned *p'i-ku* (avoiding food of grain) and felt full of vim and vigor with a lightened body and younger features. Eight years later, K'ou was visited again by another divine being, Li P'u-wen, who identified himself as Lao Tzu's great-great grandson and presented K'ou with the *True Scripture of Talismanic Designs* (*Lu-t'u chen ching*), which is not available in today's canon. Li ordered K'ou to assist the Northern Perfect Ruler of Great Peace (*pei-fang t'ai-p'ing chen-chün*), the emperor in Northern Wei, and take the responsibility of supervising both earthly and divine affairs.

To realize his ambition to reform the Taoist religious community and assist the emperor, K'ou required support from the government. He met an important minister, Ts'ui Hao, a scion of an old Chinese gentry family, who believed in Taoism. It is Ts'ui Hao who persuaded the emperor to support K'ou. Otherwise few officials were interested in his scripture. Thus an alliance of secular and sacred authorities was formed. K'ou was given the title of Celestial Master by the Emperor T'ai Wu, and in turn the emperor received the title of "Perfect Ruler of Great Peace," as well as talismanic designs and registers from K'ou. This period proved a unique era of Taoist ascendancy in Chinese political history.

According to Lord Lao, K'ou's mission was to purify and reorganize the Taoist community by clearing out false regulations and the practice of the three Changs (Chang Tao-ling, his son, and grandson), which had emerged after the founding of the sect by Chang Tao-ling in the late second century. The Changs' religious offices were transmitted within their own families, and in the name of Lord Lao, K'ou criticized the custom. He argued that hereditary transmission of religious offices might allow foolish persons to practice religious power and corrupt the Taoist practices, and that therefore they should be given to people who are honest and wise. K'ou, who was not a scion of the Celestial Master Chang's family, was "honest and wise" and so could be a new celestial master.

K'ou also insisted that the rice and money contributions imposed on the faithful, which tended to create subgovernmental enclaves within the state, should be prohibited. This was directed against the religio-political power established by Chang Lu, mentioned previously. K'ou was an apologist not only for religion, but also for earthly official power, and gave the Taoist religion a strong political color. For K'ou, the most important things were rites and morality, emphases drawn from Confucianism, although K'ou does not specifically mention it. Both the taking of medicine and cultivation were not as important for him as for other Taoists. His reformation of Taoism focuses on the point that religion should assist in maintaining the political system and social order and was no longer to be used by rebels or enclaves. He strongly attacked rebellions in the name of Taoism or Lord Lao. He scolded rebels for not being humane as fathers, for knowing nothing about filial piety as children, and for not being loyal as subjects. He said that they were fools, offenders, and sinners. His radical political stand was the reason that his new Taoism was accepted by the Wei court.

K'ou attacked the sexual practices, known as the "art of the bed-chamber" (fang chung shu) or the "union of vital forces" (*ho-ch'i*), which was the traditional art of health and longevity. As mentioned previously, the ritual taught people to save and preserve essence of life in sexual intercourse but was easily distorted and became a means of letting people indulge in sensual pleasures, even licentious sexual intercourse. K'ou said that some Taoist priests instructed wife and husband how to make love in such a way that public morals were threatened, and that therefore the "art of the bed-chamber" should be prohibited.

The most important contribution to Taoist religion in K'ou's reformation was the institutionalization of commandments and rites, which drew on Buddhism in form and Confucianism in substance. K'ou's commandments included loyalty to the royal court, filial piety, humanity, and righteousness, as well as prohibitions against rebellion, betrayal, and disobedience to parents or masters. K'ou also developed Taoist rites: For example, one who wanted to be initiated as a Taoist disciple should ask a Taoist priest to hold a rite in which the disciple prostrates him- or herself eight times before the *Scripture of Commandment with Musical Notation* and then stands up reverently before the scripture. Priests and other Taoist friends are to carry the commandment in both hands and chant it along with certain music. The disciple then lies face down on the ground and recites the commandment, after which he or she prostrates him- or herself eight times before the *Scripture of Commandment.*

In addition, K'ou defined the ceremonies for praying, funerals, confession, and dispelling evils. With official support K'ou reorganized and systematized Taoist commandments and rites, and thus Taoism began to become an orthodox and institutionalized religion. The new religious organization established by K'ou was historically called the Northern Celestial Master sect.

Lu Hsiu-ching and the Taoist Reformation in Southern China

Almost at the same time K'ou Ch'ien-chih was reforming Taoism in northern China, Lu Hsiu-ching (406–477), who lived in the Liu Sung dynasty (420–479) in southern China, was engaged in a similar reform. Both wanted to establish a new religion that could be accepted by sovereigns.

Born in a gentry family in present-day Che-kiang (Zhejiang) Province, Lu is said to have been fascinated by Taoist arts from childhood. He industriously studied Taoist classics and assiduously investigated mysterious principles of immortality. He left his family and lived on a mountain to study Taoist scriptures. One day he went down the mountain to seek a kind of herb and lived at home for a couple of days. Unexpectedly, his daughter fell seriously ill and was dying. His family earnestly begged him to save her, but he sighed and said: "I have already given up wife, children, and myself to the transcendental realm. Today I pass by a home which is like a hotel to me. How can I be caught by love again!" Hence he left with no hesitation. He traveled around to visit senior masters and renowned mountains to collect Taoist scriptures and to find traces of immortals. He thus became more and more famous and enjoyed close connections with the courts of several Liu Sung emperors. One emperor invited him to give lessons about Taoist principles, which he did without stopping even at night, and the emperor's mother treated him as her master. At the request of another emperor, Lu participated in public debates with learned Buddhists and Confucianists and won dramatic victories with his forceful arguments. Lu wrote more than thirty Taoist classics, but only a few have survived.

After the movement of the Five Pecks of Rice, which became the Celestial Master sect, two other important sects emerged, named after the scriptures they exalted. One revered the Supreme Purity (*shang ch'ing*) scriptures, which were traced to Yang Hsi (330–?) and Hsü Mi (303–373)[62] and emphasized the cultivation of inner spiritual peace and individual immortality. The other revered the Efficacious Treasure (*ling pao*) scriptures, which were composed in the late 390s by Ko Ch'ao-fu, a great-nephew of Ko Hung, and stressed salvation and the role of *fu-lu*. A *lu* is the register of the spirits' names and appearances, and the *fu* are secret charms and talismans for bringing them under the Taoists' power. Fu-lu may be translated as talismans and registers.[63] Master Lu was so erudite that he contributed to every major Taoist sect of his day. He reformed the Celestial Master sect, carried on Ko Hung's doctrine, and passed on the Three Sovereigns (*san huang*) scriptures, which went back to Pao Ch'ien in 301. He received and taught the Supreme Purity scriptures and was even praised as the seventh patriarch of the sect. He also wrote many important scriptures for the Spiritual Treasure sect. He referred to himself as "Disciple of the Three Caverns" (*san tung ti-tzu*) to show that he was not partial to only one sect and that his overall scholarship covered every branch of Taoism. The Chinese character *tung* literally means "cave" but, according to Taoist writers, here it has the same meaning as another tung that means penetrating or thorough comprehension.

Lu established the classification of the Taoist canon as "three caverns," although the expression did not originate with him. In 471 he finished the *Catalogue of the Scriptures of the Three Caverns,* which, with around 1,226 volumes, was the first comprehensive listing of all Taoist texts. Lu initiated the notion of a single canon common to the various early movements of the emerging tradition. *The Three Caverns* covered three distinct revelatory traditions: The *Tung-chen* section revolved around the *Supreme Purity* scriptures, the *Tung-hsüan* around the *Spiritual Treasure,* and the *Tung-shen* around the *Three Sovereigns.* In addition to the *Three Caverns,* in the present 5,485-volume Taoist canon, there are Four Supplements, which are known as the *T'ai-hsüan, T'ai-p'ing, T'ai-ch'ing,* and *Cheng-i* components of the canon. The first three have commonly been regarded as individual appendices to the *Three Caverns,* and the last one as a supplement to all of the *Three Caverns,* although the canon is not organized systematically.

To reform the Celestial Master sect, Lu emphasized the importance of the Three Meeting Days a year (*san hui jih*) and wanted to rebuild the system, which was established during the period of the Way of Five Pecks of Rice in the late second and early third centuries. The system required all "Taoist people" (*tao min*) to attend the three largest Taoist services in the parish on January 7, July 7, and October 5 every year[64] to report faults and merits, to get new orders and laws from the "Taoist officer" (*tao kuan*), and to report the change of the number of people in each family. This system had declined, and Lu was critical: "Now many people claim themselves to be Taoists but don't go to the meetings with the excuse of being too far away, or they flout their own masters and go to other parishes, and the worst is flaunting food, wine and spirits. Thus Taoist principles and disciplines are not proclaimed and explained, and religious practices and laws become null and void. Hence the whole religious and political organization is undermined."[65] Lu wanted to practice the Three Meeting Days strictly in order to strengthen the tie between the religious hierarchy and Taoist believers.

Another thing that Lu emphasized was household registration. According to the system in the Way of Five Pecks of Rice, Taoist people were required to register their family, including adults and children, males and females. Every year, usually on the Three Meeting Days, each family had to report any births, deaths, and marriages to update the register. Based on the registry, people paid their contributions and the religious authorities sent officers to protect families. As the system had declined when Lu began his reform, however, the registry was outdated. He pointed out someone who had registered as a single person and hadn't made any change even though he already had many grandchildren; someone who had become an old person with gray hair who hadn't registered yet; and someone who had died and his bones had decomposed but still had his name in the register.

Lu demanded that Taoists clear and update the family registers and strengthen the Taoist organization. The religion under the reformation inspired by Lu was called the Southern Celestial Master sect, which developed for a period and then declined when the Supreme Purity and the Efficacious Treasure sects became more popular.

Lu dedicated much of his career to writing, identifying, and editing the Efficacious Treasure scriptures. He formulated the role of liturgies, which restrain the "mind, mouth, and body" (*san yeh*) to prevent people sinning. He said: "A body might commit a crime such as murder, theft and licentiousness, hence performing a liturgy is necessary. From the mouth might come calumnies and blandishments, hence reciting scripture is necessary. The mind might have greed and anger, hence meditating upon gods is necessary. These three ways can purify one's mind and behavior, with the proper liturgy."[66] He believed Taoist rites could touch heaven and earth, reach gods, realize immortality, see the ultimate truth, remove the family of sins of generations, get rid of ill omen, calm down hatred of enemies, cultivate virtue, cure illness, and complete all affairs. Nothing for Lu was better than Taoist ritual. Taoist liturgies were the essential approach to the Way, and by following them everything would succeed.

Like most religions, the purpose of Taoist ritual is to reach gods to ensure happiness and prevent disasters. Drawing upon Confucianist morals and Buddhist ideas, Lu redefined and formulated new Taoist liturgies: nine rites and twelve practices (*ch'iu chai shih êrh fa*), which greatly expanded Taoist ritual by combining those of different sects such as the Celestial Master, the Supreme Purity, and the Efficacious Treasure. Few of his books of Taoist ritual have survived. However, according to other ritual classics, Taoist rites generally include building the altar, displaying the offering, burning incense, using talismans, proclaiming commandments, chanting scriptures, praising in hymns accompanied by candle lanterns, ritual music, and imitating the steps of Yü, a legendary king in ancient times (*Yü pu*). Master Lu's works made the Taoist church more institutionalized. Even fifteen centuries later, in modern China, some Taoist priests claim that the liturgies they perform extend back to Master Lu.

T'ao Hung-ching and the Further Development of Early Taoist Religion

T'ao Hung-ching (456–536) was an encyclopedic scholar of Taoism and the founder of the Mount Mao sect (*Mao-shan tsung*). He was born in a renowned landowning family in the modern province of Chiangsu (Jiangsu) in the Liu Sung dynasty (420–479) and became famous in the Ch'i (497–502) and Liang (502–557) dynasties. He was said to have enjoyed studying ever since childhood. When he was ten years old, he got a copy of the *Lives of the Immortals* (*shen-hsien chuan*) written by Ko Hung, read it constantly, and as a result was inspired to seek the way to longevity. He studied Taoism with Sun Yu-yüeh, a student of Lu Hsiu-ching, and served as a kind of adviser of princes for more than ten years. In 490, he was appointed as an adviser in the royal court but was not satisfied and resigned two years later. "As to an official career," he said, "one must be a minister at about forty years old, or head an important county. . . . I am thirty-six and just an advisor. Thus I should leave as soon as possible avoiding shame and exhaustion."[67] He withdrew to Mount Mao and gave himself a title, the "Hermit of Hua-yang."

T'ao received much more fame after his resignation and was even called the "Premier on the Mountains," a title that was due to his prominent scholarship as well as his political concerns. He presented a favorable prognostic picture, or forecast, and wrote to encourage Emperor Wu of the Liang dynasty to take over power when he was hesitant. Again, when Emperor Wu and his advisers could not decide on a name for the new dynasty, T'ao offered a prognostic picture, or forecast, showing that the new dynasty should be named Liang for good fortune. Although he refused to return to office, he was often consulted on state affairs by Emperor Wu. He continued to enjoy favored treatment from the court, even after the emperor officially converted to Buddhism and forbade Taoism in 504. When T'ao needed materials for alchemical experiments, the emperor sent him gold, cinnabar, realgar, and other things.

T'ao formulated new arguments regarding Taoist theories of immortality. He believed that the combination of essence and shape is no more than that of the spirit and the body. There is a person or thing if the spirit and the body are kept together; there is a soul or ghost if they are separated. Buddhism holds that the spirit and the body are neither combined nor separated, but the immortal school of Taoism believes that either combined or separated, both may exist. If one wants to have a long life or be an immortal, one should keep the spirit and body together by practicing Taoist cultivation and exercises. T'ao gave an analogy: A piece of semifinished pottery is earth but different from earth. It will collapse when it is in water before it is baked, although it is already dry. If it is not well baked, it will not endure. If it is fired well and becomes thoroughly strong, it will not disappear even if the mountain and the river should be destroyed. Similarly, people who want immortality take drugs and elixirs to make the body strong, take natural spirits to develop their own souls, breathe in fresh air, and terminate disputes with virtue. Thus all of these practices benefit each other without conflict. Then if the spirit and the body are kept together, as a senior immortal, one can ride clouds and drive a dragon; if the spirit and the body are separated, as a junior immortal, one can leave the old shape and get a new body.

To sum up Taoist immortal theories, T'ao wrote the *Records of Preserving Nature and Prolonging Life* (*yang-shin yen-ming lu*), which collected many accounts and doctrines of longevity and quoted more than thirty classics. T'ao differed from Chuang Tzu, who believed that human life is made by nature or Heaven, and stressed that our destiny depends on ourselves and not on Heaven. The reason people die early is not because of fate, but because of the way their living hurts their spirits or bodies. The Way of Heaven is spontaneous, but the way of human beings is decided by themselves.

To preserve spirit and body, T'ao emphasized the significance of moderation in desires and emotion. It is impossible for average persons to have no desires or to do nothing, but they can keep the mind in a state of harmony and have less concern. The "seven kinds of emotion" (*ch'i ching*) (anger, anxiety, thinking, sorrow, fear, aversion, and astonishment) and the "six desires" (*liu yü*) (for life, death, of the eyes, ears, mouth, and nose) are all harmful to spirit and should be controlled. Properly chosen meals and a proper life-style are also important for longevity. T'ao believed that the harm caused by bad eating habits is more serious than that of lust, because people repeat it daily, and he urged restraint in taking food. For health, T'ao claimed, less food is better than being overly full; to walk after meals is more helpful than lying down; and physical labor is preferable to an easy life. T'ao also renewed the significance of some traditional Taoist arts, such as the "circulation of the breath" (hsing-ch'i), "guiding the breath" (*Tao-yin*), a kind of gymnastics or calisthenics, the "art of the bedchamber," and alchemy.

In addition to compiling and writing many traditional medical classics, such as the *Collected Commentaries on Medicinal Herbs* (*pen-ts'ao chi-chu*), T'ao Hung-ching dedicated twenty years to alchemy and wrote many books about it, most of which, unfortunately, are lost. However, his *Collected Commentaries on Medicinal Herbs*, which contains sixty-seven inorganic substances, gives us some sense of his scientific attitude and some accounts of his alchemical experiments. Although he presented elixirs to Emperor Wu of Liang at some time between 502 and 519, no one was able to reach immortality by alchemy—on the contrary, a young disciple of T'ao's left the world by alchemical suicide. Therefore, along with general Taoist developments, the belief that immortality could be attained by alchemy and elixirs was gradually replaced by the doctrine and teachings of the Inner Alchemy (*nei-tan*). This doctrine compares the melting pot of alchemy to the human body, in which essence and life force are fashioned into a sacred embryo with the help of the mind. The former then became known as the Outer Alchemy (*wai-tan*).

The longer the Taoist religion developed, the greater was the number of deities that became part of its polytheistic system. The Way of Great Peace and the Way of Five Pecks of Rice created some gods and adopted many deities from traditional beliefs, and the Supreme Purity and the Efficacious

Treasure sects invented more gods. By the time of T'ao, there were many Taoist gods, all in disorder: heaven gods, earth deities, human ghosts and immortals, old and new, senior and junior. To organize the Taoist deities, T'ao wrote the *Picture of True Deities in Positions* (*chen-ling wei-yeh tu*). He put more than four hundred Taoist deities into seven gradations, each gradation having one main god with many gods in right, left, or other positions. According to him, the first divine class exalts the Prime Heaven God (*yüen shih t'ien-tsun*), the second, the Mystic Emperor Great Way Lord (*Hsüen huang ta-tao chün*), the third, the Great Ultimate Golden Palace Lord (*t'ai-chi chin-ch'üeh ti chün*), and the fourth, the Great Super Old Lord (*t'ai-shang lao-chün*). The seventh is the North Feminine Great God (*pei yin ta ti*), who is in charge of ghosts and souls. In this, T'ao was trying to systematize Taoist belief according to hierarchies in the world. In T'ao's book, the first four gods prefigure the later formal Three Purity Gods (*san-ch'ing*); that is, the Prime Heaven God (*yüan shih t'ien-tsun*), the representative of the Supreme Purity sect; the Efficacious Treasure Heaven God (*ling pao t'ien-tsun*), the representative of the Efficacious Treasure sect; and the Tao Te Heaven God (*tao te t'ien-tsun*), the representative of the Celestial Master sect.

T'ao's tremendous influence on the development of Taoism also derives from his contribution to the Supreme Purity sect and the foundation of the Mount Mao sect. He was in the direct line of the founder of the sect and received the scriptures of the Supreme Purity from a student of Lu Hsiu-ching. He personally visited many sacred mountains and famous masters and collected more than ten volumes of scriptures in Yang Hsi and Hsü Mi's own handwriting. Then he composed the *True Declarations* (*chen-kao*), which provided a definitive collection of the scriptures and a detailed account of their revelation and subsequent diffusion. With T'ao's scholarship and influence, the Mount Mao sect grew to be the most important school of Taoism during the T'ang dynasty (618–907).

In the *Declarations*, T'ao praised highly the *Supreme Purity* scriptures. He even believed that if one read the scriptures ten thousand times, one would become immortal even without taking elixirs. At the same time, T'ao insisted that the "three doctrines" (*san chiao*)—Taoism, Confucianism, and Buddhism—are all good and should be kept in harmony. The ultimate criterion of belief is goodness instead of sectarian prejudice. Hence, he quoted Confucianist classics to explain Taoist theory and emphasized the significance of loyalty to royalty and filial piety. He also adopted Buddhist doctrine to develop Taoist theology and attained the full status of a Buddhist monk. According to the *Declarations*, in the southern and northern dynasties, quite a few Taoist masters had both Taoist and Buddhist disciples. T'ao himself also had students who studied Buddhism, and his shroud was both Taoist and Buddhist. His thoughts on religion opened up a path for the development of new Taoist sects.

Wang Che and the Establishment of Ch'üan Chen Taoism

After the northern and southern dynasties, Taoism matured into an institutionalized religion. Under the T'ang dynasty (618–907) it enjoyed the patronage of the ruling house, because the emperors shared the same family name with Lao Tzu and revered him as their dynastic ancestor. Some emperors in both the northern and the southern Sung dynasty (960–1279) were also enthusiastic believers and patrons of Taoism. New schools and texts developed, and some scholars—for example, Cheng Hsüan-ying (middle seventh century), Ssu-ma Ch'eng-chen (655-735), Tu Kuang-t'ing (850–933), and Chang Po-tuan (987–1082)—contributed to Taoist literature from the seventh to the thirteenth centuries. However, the most important school in late Taoist history was Ch'üan Chen Taoism, which was founded by Wang Che (1113–1169).

Wang Che, also known by his clerical name, Ch'ung-yang Tzu or Wang Ch'ung-yang, was the son of a great landowner from Hsien-yang in Shensi (Shaanxi) Province. During his youth, the Sung dynasties were fighting against the Chin dynasty (1115–1234), which was ruled by the Jurchen (*Juchen*), ancestors of the Manchus from northeastern China. Eventually the Sung surrendered, and Shensi became a part of the Chin dynasty. Wang reluctantly accepted the reality that the Chinese majority were ruled by barbarians. He tried to take the civil service examination, and later took the less prestigious military examination. However, he failed to advance in rank and eventually resolved to abandon both his military office and his family for a religious career at the age of forty-seven. He claimed to have met Taoist sages who taught him the secret oral teachings. Thereafter he left home for a life of seclusion on Mount Chung-nan. While digging a hole two meters deep in which to meditate, Wang named his austere cell "the grave of a living corpse" and practiced an ascetic life. Eight years later he burned his hermitage and journeyed alone to Shantung Province, where he formally established the Ch'üan Chen (Completing Truth) religion and received seven disciples, who were later called the Seven Perfected Ones of Ch'üan Chen Taoism.

After Wang's death, his seven leading disciples continued their self-cultivation and did successful missionary work in Shensi, Hopei, Shantung, and Honan Provinces. It was the youngest among them, however—Ch'iu Ch'u-chi, also known as Ch'iu Ch'ang-ch'un (1148–1227)—who was crucial in bringing about the great popularity of Ch'üan Chen Taoism. Along with the decline of the Chin and southern Sung dynasties, Chinggis Khan was fighting and killing for the establishment of the Mongol Empire. In 1219 when Ch'iu was seventy-one, he refused invitations brought to him by envoys of the Chin and southern Sung emperors but responded to Chinggis

Khan's call readily and trekked more than ten thousand miles with eighteen disciples to visit him in central Asia. Chinggis was interested in the secret of longevity, but Ch'iu taught him the basic principles of Taoist philosophy, such as nonaction and nonkilling. Perhaps for political considerations, Chinggis Khan respected Ch'iu. He referred to him as "Immortal Ch'iu" and put him in charge of monks and nuns all over the country. This meeting was significant in Taoist history. When Ch'iu returned to China in 1224, he did so armed with decrees granting tax and labor exemption to all Ch'üan Chen Taoists. The Ch'üan Chen sect therefore had the best opportunity to gain popularity and prevail. When Ch'iu died, an abbey was renamed the Ch'ang-Ch'un Kuan (the Abbey of Eternal Spring) in Ch'iu's honor. It is the present White Cloud Temple in Peking (Beijing).

Monasticism, asceticism, and self-cultivation characterize Ch'üan Chen Taoism. It is the Ch'üan Chen sect that began to base itself in monasteries, although the practice of celibacy to maintain and purify one's powers had been embraced by some adepts earlier. The sect claims that the love between husband and wife is the golden shackle and that the family is prison. Ch'iu Ch'u-chi taught that men have the attribute of fire, while women have the attribute of water. Because femininity can destroy masculinity, as water can extinguish fire, those who want to practice the Way must first avoid sexual desire and activity.

All of the early Ch'üan Chen masters led lives that differed from the lives of average people. On one occasion, Wang Che was said to have slept on ice; at another time he meditated in a hole for a couple of years; then he built a small hermitage. In his "Fifteen Statements on the Establishment of (Ch'üan Chen) Religion," the first statement emphasizes the importance of "living in a hermitage" that accommodates only one person. In the fifth item he maintains that a thatched cell to protect the body from exposure is enough, and big buildings with huge halls are not the way that Taoist people should live. It is also said that Ch'iu Ch'u-chi lived in a hole and traveled in a straw rain cape without even a gourd for begging food. Ma yü, a disciple of Wang, begged for only one bowl of food a day, never wore shoes, and neither wanted drink in summer, nor sought warmth in winter. Hao Ta-t'ung, another follower of Wang, sat still below a bridge without a word and did not move for six years. Later Taoist priests modified many of the conventions of asceticism, especially after the sect had flourished and become widely popular. Although great Ch'üan Chen monasteries and other elaborate properties were constructed, the essential spirit of Ch'üan Chen Taoism still resides in the practice of a simple life.

Ch'üan Chen Taoism emphasizes self-cultivation, focusing on realization of "true nature" (*chen hsing*) in mind (*hsin*). The sect teaches that only nature can be true and eternal, while the body, like earth, water, fire, and wind, is false and transient. Hence they criticize conventional theories of physical immortality. Claiming that their own way of cultivation is the "Supreme Way," they belittle other Taoist approaches to immortality as "small arts of longevity." Ch'iu Ch'u-chi said: "The reason for our school rarely talking about immortality is not that we are not able to reach it, but that we are beyond it." Ch'üan Chen Taoism bases its theories on the separation of mind and body. For example, one goal of self-cultivation is "leaving the ordinary world," which means, however, a state of mind rather than a physical act. "The body is like a lotus root," according to Wang Che, "the mind is like the lotus blossom. The root is in the mud, but the blossom is in the air. People who attain the Way are physically in the ordinary world but mentally in the realm of sages. People today who want to avoid death forever and leave the ordinary world are imbeciles who do not understand the principle of the Way."[68] Taoist immortality theories were thus revised, and spiritual immortality instead of physical immortality was sought.

To realize one's true nature, one has to keep one's mind tranquil and refined. Whatever people do, they should always strive to be empty of all perceptions, cognitions, and feelings, and then they will have no afflictions. Wang Che said, "If the mind is always calm and still, dark and silent, not seeing anything, indefinable, not inside or outside, without a trace of thought, this is the settled mind, and is not to be overcome. If the mind gets excited at objects, falling all over itself looking for heads and tails, this is the disturbed mind, and should quickly be cut away."[69] A way to reach tranquillity and a purified mind is by sitting still. This does not mean physically sitting still with the eyes closed. True sitting requires shutting off the four gates—eyes, ears, mouth, and nose—and not letting external things get inside. According to Wang Che, the mind should be as unstirred as a mountain at all times, in the midst of action and in repose. In addition, one must not even harbor the slightest thought of motion or stillness.

In fact, the way of self-cultivation in Ch'üan Chen Taoism developed from theories of inner alchemy (nei-tan), which were said to be founded by Chung-li Chüan and Lü Tung-pin, who lived around the late T'ang dynasty or the Five Dynasties (907–960). Theories and practices of inner alchemy vary among schools and individual Taoists. Generally speaking, however, inner alchemy is based on Taoist cosmology. The Way produced the One, the One produced the two, the two produced the three, and the three produced the myriad things. Conversely, in the practice of inner alchemy, creatures return to the three, to the two, to the One, and thus reach the Way, and realize the eternal state along with the Way. The three in the human body include vitality (or essence, ching), life energy (ch'i), and spirit (shen), which are the inherent materials for immortal elixir. In the practice of inner alchemy, the eternal sublimation and combination of vitality, energy, and spirit is brought about by taming and sublimating the thought processes of the mind.

The practitioners of inner alchemy believe that natural processes resulting in the death of human beings can be reversed by self-cultivation; namely, by concentrating and purifying the life energies within the body. In the inner alchemy theory, nature (*hsing*) and life (*ming*) are the two basic concepts. Some earlier Taoists, for example, Chang Po-tuan, claimed that cultivation of life (ming) precedes that of nature (hsing). However, Ch'üan Chen Taoists insisted that the cultivation of one's nature is more important than that of life. They even asserted that by the cultivation of one's nature—purifying the mind and returning to nothingness—one can directly reach immortality. This is the reason that Wang Che said: "Those who can sit quietly in the real sense may be physically present in the material world, but their names are already in the ranks of the immortals. It is not necessary for them to call on others, for the century of work of the saints and sages in the body is fulfilled, and they shed the shell to climb to reality; a pill of elixir is made, and the spirit roams throughout the universe."[70]

Just as Ch'an Buddhism developed in the T'ang dynasty and Neo-Confucianism appeared in the Sung dynasty, the emergence of Ch'üan Chen Taoism was also a result of the interaction and mutual influence of the so-called Three Teachings—Taoism, Buddhism, and Confucianism. These three main trends of Chinese traditional culture have influenced and struggled with each other as long as they have existed in history. However, there have never been religious wars as such in the long history of China. A few conflicts among the three traditions were intensified and solved by political power, but the main relationship between the three systems has been mutual influence and absorption. Ch'an Buddhism and Neo-Confucianism, as well as Ch'üan Chen Taoism, are the outcome of this primary interaction.

Ch'üan Chen Taoists not only advocated the integration of Taoism, Buddhism, and Confucianism but also practiced them in combination, and moved further than their predecessors, such as the previously mentioned Lu Hsiu-ching and T'ao Hung-ching. Wang Che was successful in organizing five Taoist societies in the northern coastal area of Shantung Province, and each of them was named after the Three Teachings (*san chiao*): for example, the Golden Lotus Society of the Three Teachings (*San-chiao Chin-lien Hui*), the Society of Equality of the Three Teachings (*San-chiao P'ing-teng Hui*), the Three Rays Society of the Three Teachings (*San-chiao San-kuang Hui*). Wang Che said that Super Lord Lao is the ancestor, Śākyamuni is the forbearer, and Confucius is the sage and held that the three teachings are not separated from the true Way but are like three branches of a tree. Ch'iu Ch'u-chi said that the religious ancestors of the three teachings of Confucianism, Buddhism, and Taoism are of the same origin from antiquity through to the present. Another Taoist said that in the final analysis the three teachings return to the One, so that ultimately it is not necessary to refer to the distinctions between Taoism and Ch'an Buddhism.

Wang asked every new disciple who wanted to convert to Taoism to read the Confucianist *Hsiao Ching* (the *Classic of Filial Piety*), and the Buddhist *Pojo Polomito Hsin Ching* (*Prajñāpāramitāhṛdayasūtra*), in addition to the *Tao Te Ching* and other Taoist classics. It is said that Wang Che made friends without distinction with Taoists, Buddhists, and Confucianists. He chatted about Buddhism when meeting Buddhists, Confucianism when meeting Confucianists, and talked Taoism with Taoists.

Although it is possible that Taoists emphasized the importance of the harmony and integration of the three teachings to prevent Taoist conflict with Buddhism, Ch'üan Chen Taoism actually drew upon elements from Buddhism in its doctrine and practice. Among these elements were celibacy, monasticism, cultivation of mind and nature, clerical itinerancy, nonreliance on the scriptures, and the ideas of rebirth and karma. The sect adopted both the language and ideas of Buddhism and Confucianism, as in its doctrine of *ming-hsin chien-hsin* (purify the mind and reach nature). Clearly, Ch'üan Chen Taoism is representative of the trend to integrate the three traditions, which has existed since Buddhism was introduced into China. In a certain sense, the sect is a fusion of Taoism, Buddhism, and Confucianism, although it continued to stress modified versions of Taoist traditions, such as belief in spiritual immortality, the art of inner alchemy, and the Taoist genealogies.

The other two new Taoist sects, the *T'ai-i* (Grand Unity) sect and the *Ta-tao Chiao* (the Religion of the Great Way), were established earlier than Ch'üan Chen Taoism. The former gained favor for a time at the Chin court because of the promise of divine healing, while the latter advocated asceticism and ethical doctrines. Both sects were led by a succession of patriarchs for about two hundred years, but failed to survive to the end of the Yüan dynasty (1279–1368).

The Way of Celestial Masters (*T'ien-shih Tao*), founded by Chang Taoling, has survived through Chang's descendants. It was said that the Celestial Master of the thirty-fifth generation had prophesied to Khubilai's envoy that he would unify China in twenty years. After the establishment of the Yüan dynasty, therefore, because the Celestial Master of the thirty-fifth generation had died, Khubilai Khan put his son, Chang Tsung-yen, in charge of the talismans and registers of the three mountains—the Mount Ko-Tsao, the Mount Lung-Hu, and the Mount Mao. Later, in 1304, the next emperor conferred the title of *Cheng-i Chiao-chu* (the Lord of the Orthodox and Unity Way) on Chang Yü-ts'ai, the thirty-eighth descendant of the Celestial Master, and appointed him to supervise other Taoist sects of talismans and registers, which then combined together under the name of *Cheng-i Tao* (the Orthodox and Unity Way). Hence, the Cheng-i and the Ch'üan Chen sects have composed two main branches of Taoist religion that have survived until today.

In the Ming dynasty (1368–1662) and Ch'ing dynasty (1662–1911), official Taoism developed slowly and gradually declined. Although some Taoist priests—for example, Chang San-feng (early fifteenth century) and Chang Yü-ch'u (?–1410)—were well known in Taoist history, there were few new breakthroughs in Taoist doctrine and few new movements. However, Taoism's great influence over Chinese society has penetrated into folklore and folk religious movements. Today, as part of folk belief, social custom, and traditional culture, Taoism has greater and deeper influence over the Chinese populace than Buddhism, although the Taoist monastery system is smaller than that of Buddhism.

Conclusion: How Taoism Works and Its Contribution to the Study of Religion

Taoism, either philosophical or religious, has had great influence over both Chinese society in general and individual lives in particular. Chinese civilization and the Chinese character would have been utterly different if the books *Lao Tzu* and *Chuang Tzu* had never been written. Even Confucianism, the dominant system in Chinese history and thought, as well as Buddhism, the influential foreign religion, would not have been the same. Confucianism and Buddhism have never escaped Taoist influence in the course of their development. For example, Buddhism found its point of departure and inspiration for the creation of Ch'an Buddhism (Zen) in Taoism, and Neo-Confucianism established its theory of cosmic structure on the mode of Taoism. No one can hope to understand Chinese philosophy, religion, government, art, or medicine without a real appreciation of Taoism.[71]

Having surveyed the history and forms of Taoism, we discuss two points in conclusion: how Taoism works, and what are the unique contributions of Taoism to the general study of religion. First we will deal with the influence of Taoist philosophy on society and then with the practice and doctrines of Taoist religion.

Taoist Philosophy

Taoist philosophy has influenced Chinese culture deeply and broadly, but its essential importance may lie in its presentation of values and in its ways of thinking and living that differ from Confucianism. Confucianism emphasizes that everyone has and should accept social duty and responsibility. It was said of Confucius that he is one who does what he should do even when he knows that it is impossible. This spirit was reflected, for example, in Tso Ch'iu-ming's firm resolution to compile the first Chinese chronicle, *Tso Chuan* (Tso's Commentary on the *Spring and Autumn Annals*) after he had become blind, and Ssu-ma Ch'ien's completion of the first biographical history *Shih-chi* (*Historical Records*) after he was castrated by the imperial court as a punishment. Another example is Ch'ü Yüan, a great poet in the Ch'u State during the middle Warring States period, who threw himself into the Mi-lo river because he wanted to save the state from treacherous court officials but had failed to elicit trust and support in the king. He is commemorated in China even today. These examples give a sense of what Confucianism considered the ideal Chinese individual to be and how such an individual should behave.

However, not all people can endure humiliation in order to carry out an important mission or choose to die because they have failed to realize their ideals. Human beings require diversion from social and psychological pressure, and Chinese people found it in Taoist philosophy. Taoism teaches people to view human strife from the perspective of the whole universe. For example, there is a fable about the position of human beings in the *Chuang Tzu*. The Lord of the Yellow River believed that all beauty in the world belonged to him alone, because one hundred streams made the yellow river so broad that it was impossible to distinguish a horse from a cow when looking from bank to bank. However, when he journeyed east until he finally reached the North Sea and saw its unfathomable vastness, he recognized that he was so small he would be laughed at.[72] Then the God of the North Sea told him, "Of all the waters of the world, none is as great as the sea. It is so much greater than the streams of the Yangtze or the Yellow river that it is impossible to measure the difference. But I have never for this reason prided myself on it because I sit here between heaven and earth as a little stone or a little tree sits on a huge mountain. Compare the four seas with all the area between heaven and earth—is it not like one little anthill in a vast marsh? Compare the whole country with the area within the four seas—is it not like one tiny grain in a great storehouse? When we refer to the things of creation, we speak of them as numbering ten thousand—and man is only one of them. Compared to the ten thousand things, is man not like one little hair on the body of a horse? What the Five Emperors passed along, what the Three Kings fought over, what the benevolent man grieves about, what the responsible man labors over—none is more than this!"[73]

In other words, people should not take the difference between gain and loss, glory and humiliation, success and failure, too seriously. In comparing human affairs with the boundless universe, it becomes clear that nothing is worth fighting over or grieving for. Clearly, following Taoist philosophy, people were able to withdraw from endless struggle and conflict and comfort themselves when suffering spiritually.

This kind of comparative self-comfort is still prevalent even though many Chinese intellectuals have criticized it as "self-deception." For example, during the Great Cultural Revolution, everyone suffered considerably. If someone complained that he was put in prison for ten years for no reason, another might reply, "Well, you indeed lost a lot in your life, but compared to former President Liu Shao-ch'i who died while illegally imprisoned, what you suffered is not so much. Please think of how lucky you are because you are still alive and have your family." Because there is always something worse or better to compare your lot with, this kind of comfort is always available. Taoist philosophy leads people to open their minds and to widen their perspectives, and so can help relax people's tensions. Thus Taoism works by providing an appropriate philosophy for physical and psychological adjustments necessary for healthy living and by emphasizing the value of restraint.

The distinctive contribution of Taoist philosophy is the concept of wu-wei. What is its significance? Try to think of a car. It has a brake as well as an engine. No one wants to drive a car without a brake. In fact, all movement needs something like a brake system. But what about human motivation and social movement? Can people pursue what they want without limitation? Can social movements, even if they are believed to be beneficial for human beings, develop directly toward a chosen goal without restriction? Certainly not. Human motivation and social movements also need something working as a brake, which may adjust and limit human behavior to protect human society. What is that brake of human society? A possible one is the concept of wu-wei, one of the celebrated concepts of Taoist philosophy.

Taoist Religion

Ch'üan Chen Taoism works basically through self-cultivation according to inner alchemy theories, which explain how something common may be transformed into something precious. The most dramatic and interesting elements of Taoist religious activity are the liturgical traditions of Cheng-i Taoism, which were popular before 1949 and are still alive in Taiwan, Hong Kong, and other overseas Chinese communities today. Taoist priests perform a vast array of ceremonies, such as the rituals of inauguration of temples, the ordination of priests and the birthdays of deities. Many rites are also practiced for laypeople; for example, funerals, weddings, exorcisms, and healings for individuals. Community sacrifices are also undertaken for thanksgiving, for petition, for general blessings, and for preventing calamities. In fact, the purpose of Taoist ritual is threefold. For the adept, it leads to mystical union and immortality. For the men and women of the villages, it brings blessing and renewal. For the souls of the departed in the underworld, it brings salvation and release from the punishments of hell.[74] Taoism basically works through various rituals, which it is believed not only bring specific blessings but also renew the unity and vitality of the community.

Taoist rituals are much more complicated than they are generally believed to be. Many rituals last a couple of days, a week, some even sixty days. Few people can imagine the multitude of names of Taoist rites. According to a Taoist priest in southern Taiwan, the K'o-i rites of meditative union, a kind of ritual of Taoism (*chiao*), have thirty-one items and last for three days. For example, the first day is devoted to lighting the temple lamps (*pai-shen teng*), publishing the memorial (*fa-tsou*), inviting the spirits (*ch'ing-shen*), purifying the sacred area (*chin-t'an*), reciting the Jade Pivot Canon (*Yü-shu Ching*), making the noon offering (*wu-hsien*), litanies of repentance (*ch'ao-t'ien pao-ch'an*), lighting lamps to the three pure ones (*fen-teng chüan-lien, ming-chung*), and the ritual of the ling-pao five talismans (*Su-ch'i*). The second and third days, in addition to the recitation of quite a few new canons, are devoted to reinviting the spirits (*ch'ung-pai*), floating the lanterns (*fang shui teng*), publishing the grand documents (*teng-t'ai chin-piao*), feeding the hungry spirits (*p'u tu*), and thanking and seeing off the spirits (*hsieh shen, sung shen*).[75] Because it is too complicated to perform strictly, simplified versions of the chiao are more popular in northern Taiwan and overseas Chinese communities.

In Taoist rituals, fu-lu (talismans and registers) plays an important role. There are thousands of Taoist fu-lu for specific purposes among various Taoist sects. For example, there are talismans to protect life, to protect status and salary, for seeking employment, to protect the body from evil, to protect all six kinds of domestic animals, to protect against ghosts, to destroy evil influences and noxious spirits, and to protect the body in mountainous regions; to prolong life, to purify the body, to vitalize the five viscera, to vitalize the tongue, the kidneys, the eyes, the brain, the blood and the lungs, to improve vision, to remove deafness, and to comfort the unborn child in the womb; to scatter clouds, to stop fog, to stop rain, to raise wind, to raise thunder, and to raise hail. There are also charms of the North, South, East, and West, of the Planet Mercury, of the Planet Venus, of the Planet Jupiter, of the armor of earth, and of the heavenly messenger. On the following page are two simple samples from the Taoist canon: a talisman to scatter clouds and a talisman to stop rain. Most talismans are more complicated than these.

They look very easy to draw, but in fact their execution is quite difficult. According to a Taoist priest, to draw a talisman he needs first to bathe, fast, to keep his mind empty and tranquil, and to prepare the writing brush, inkstone, block of ink, paper, and water. He then chants incantations while making the ink and taking up the writing brush. Then he draws points of the three purity spirits with a certain incantation, invites the relevant spirits

Figure 1
A Talisman to Scatter Clouds

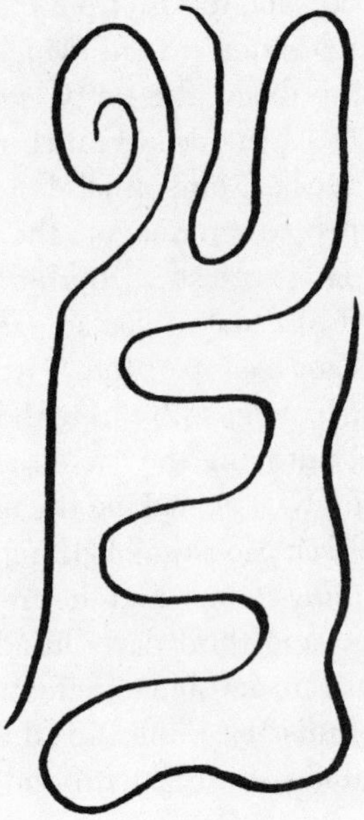

Figure 2
A Talisman to Stop Rain

to enter the talisman, and asks the heavenly generals to protect it. He finishes every part and holds it above three pieces of incense turning three circles, as well as chanting certain incantations. The efficacy of a talisman depends on the priest's mind: If he is totally focused on the talisman it is efficacious, otherwise it is not.

A distinct contribution of Taoist religion is the belief in physical immortality and hope for longevity. The two essential ideals of Taoist religion are individual longevity or immortality, and social harmony and peace. The dream of immortality can be traced back to the fourth century B.C.E., which is much earlier than the beginnings of Taoist religion. Some kings in the middle Warring States period, the first emperor of Ch'in, as well as the emperor Wu in early Han, sent many fang-shih (prescription masters) on voyages to find immortal herbs. The *Classic of Great Peace* (*T'ai P'ing Ching*) claims that longevity is the most valuable goal within the sphere between heaven and earth, and that it is possible for everyone to realize immortality. Ko Hung insisted that nothing in all that religious Taoists revere in highest secrecy is more important than the way of attaining longevity, and he wrote chapters about the arts of longevity and the possibility of being immortal. From his youth, Lu Hsiu-ching investigated mysterious principles of immortality. T'ao Hung-ching wrote the *Records of Preserving Nature and Prolonging Life* and declared that the human life span is determined by people themselves instead of by Heaven. The Ch'üan Chen Taoists pursue longevity and spiritual immortality, although they have given up the idea of physical immortality.

In the realm of Chinese thought, some aspects of Taoist religion are unique. Theoretically speaking, Buddhism wants to escape from human life and Taoist philosophy is indifferent to human life, whereas Taoist religion seeks to prolong it. While Confucianism emphasizes social interests, Taoist religion prizes the values of individual life. The two core topics of Taoist religion, longevity and immortality, reflect its optimism toward human life. In this sense, we might say that Taoist religion is more concerned with human life than other religious traditions. As an indigenous and organized religion in China, Taoism differs from other religious traditions. It insists that human life is the highest value, a worthy goal for people to pursue forever, rather than that human beings are born with sin, or that human society is full of untold suffering. Taoism believes that human beings can control their lives through self-exercise and moral behavior, instead of waiting to be delivered by God. The spiritual immortality of Ch'üan Chen Taoism is distinct from the Platonic belief that the soul is immortal, as Taoists believe that achieving immortality requires great effort on the part of human beings.

To realize their ideal, Taoists have developed many ways to pursue longevity: inner alchemy, *fu-ch'i* (inhaling), *hsing-ch'i* (circulation of life force), *tao-yin* (a kind of freestanding exercise), *shou-i* (meditation on the one), *nei-kuan* (inner viewing), *shou-ching* (maintaining tranquillity), *ts'un-ssu* (focusing mind), *t'ai-hsi* (fetus breath), *pi-ku* (avoiding eating grain), and *fu-shih* (taking herbs and medicine). Taoist arts of longevity combine the practice and doctrines of Chinese medicine, hygiene, and physical culture. A new form of tranquillity-cultivation is ch'i-kung, which covers varied forms of exercise. It is attracting more and more adherents, and quite a few people discover special gifts through practicing it, although scientists are not yet satisfied with their explanations.

Although no one has actually realized physical immortality, Taoism has developed many ingenious resources for ensuring longevity over a period of two thousand years. These still prove useful and attract adherents in the modern world. Given the preponderance in most religions of belief in spiritual immortality, one of Taoism's most significant contributions to the study of religion is its down-to-earth emphasis on physical well-being and long vital life and the consequent salvific revalorization of the body.

The contribution of Taoism to the modern world is now being increasingly recognized. Its appeal has extended beyond academic circles into popular Western culture. For instance, Taoist thought has gone public, as it were, in such cartoon books as *Lao Tzu Speaks* and *Zhuangzi (Chuang Tzu)*

Speaks, which enjoy a large readership. Even children's books such as *The Tao of Pooh* and *The Te of Piglet* have become popular vehicles of Taoist ideas and major best-sellers. Thus, some Taoist concepts are becoming more and more widespread, at least in a diluted form, because of the immense appeal of Taoism's earth-centered attuning-to-nature perspective and the natural appeal of its classics.

Recommended Reading

Farzeen Baldrian (tr. Charles Le Blanc), John Lagerway, Judith Magee Boltz, and T. H. Barrett. "Taoism." In *The Encyclopedia of Religion*, edited by Mircea Eliade. New York: Macmillan, 1987. A compact and comprehensive survey of several aspects of Taoism such as history, doctrine, practice, literature, and community.

Wing-tsit Chan, trans. *The Way of Lao Tzu.* Indianapolis: Bobbs-Merrill Company, 1963. A good translation of *Lao Tzu* with an introductory essay, comments, and notes. Also available in *A Source Book in Chinese Philosophy*, Princeton: Princeton University Press, 1963, by the same author.

Chung-yuan Chang. *Creativity and Taoism: A Study of Chinese Philosophy, Art, and Poetry.* New York: Julian Press, 1963. An examination of the influence of Taoism on Chinese life, including the potentialities of creativity, identification of reality and appearance, and self-realization.

A. C. Graham, trans. *Chuang-tzu, The Seven Inner Chapters and Other Writings from the Book Chuang-tzu.* London: George Allen & Unwin, 1981. A painstaking translation and a reorganized *Chuang Tzu*. Good for specialists.

Livia Kohn, ed. *Taoist Meditation and Longevity Techniques.* Ann Arbor: Center for Chinese Studies, the University of Michigan, 1989. The latest study on Taoist arts of longevity for nonspecialists by American, European, and Japanese scholars.

D. C. Lau, trans. *Tao Te Ching.* Hong Kong: Chinese University Press, 1982. A popular translation of *Lao Tzu*, including Wang Pi's version and the Ma-wang-tui silk manuscripts.

Michael Saso. *The Teachings of Taoist Master Chuang.* New Haven and London: Yale University Press, 1978. A brief account of Taoist history and teachings from a descendant of thirty-five generations of Taoist priests. Discusses practical ritual of Cheng-i Taoism in modern Taiwan.

James R. Ware, trans. *Alchemy, Medicine, Religion in the China of* A.D. *320: The Nei P'ien of Ko Hung (Pao-p'u tzu).* Cambridge, MA: M.I.T. Press, 1966. A translation of Ko Hung's book, the basic theoretical work of early Taoist religion.

Burton Watson, trans. *The Complete Works of Chuang Tzu.* New York and London: Columbia University Press, 1968. A popular translation of *Chuang Tzu*. For beginners, his *Chuang Tzu, Basic Writings* may be a better choice.

Holmes Welch. *Taoism, the Parting of the Way*. Boston: Beacon Press, 1966. An academic introduction to Taoism with some textual analyses.

H. Welch and A. Seidel, eds. *Facets of Taoism*. New Haven and London: Yale University Press, 1979. Basically consists of papers from the second international Taoism conference and covers such topics as *T'ai-p'ing Ching*, K'ou Ch'ien-chih, T'ao Hung-ching, and the Taoist canon.

Eva Wong, trans. *Seven Taoist Masters: A Folk Novel of China*. Boston: Shambhala, 1990. A novel about correct thought and action in Ch'üan Chen Taoism. A combination of history and legend, entertaining and instructive at the same time.

Notes

1. Donald E. MacInnis, *Religion in China Today—Policy and Practice* (Maryknoll, NY: Orbis Books, 1989), 205.
2. Wm. Theodore de Bary, ed., *Sources of Chinese Tradition* (New York and London: Columbia University Press, 1960), 50.
3. See MacInnis, *Religion in China Today*, 206.
4. Li Yangcheng, *Tao-chiao Chi-pen Chih-shih* (Peking: Association of Taoist Religion in China, 1988), 189.
5. MacInnis, *Religion in China Today*, 204.
6. MacInnis, *Religion in China Today*, 204.
7. MacInnis, *Religion in China Today*, 213.
8. MacInnis, *Religion in China Today*, 208.
9. MacInnis, *Religion in China Today*, 206.
10. MacInnis, *Religion in China Today*, 206.
11. H. Welch and A. Seidel, *Facets of Taoism* (New Haven: Yale University Press, 1979), 287.
12. Chao Chia-chuo, *Tao-chiao Tong-ch'üan* (Taiwan: Hua-gang Press, 1973), 108–109.
13. D. C. Yu, "Taoism," in *Dictionary of World Religions*, ed. Keith Crim (San Francisco: Harper & Row, 1989), 738.
14. *Lao Tzu*, chap. 14, translation modified from D. C. Lau, trans., *Chinese Classics: Tao Te Ching* (Hong Kong: Chinese University Press, 1982).
15. Burton Watson, *The Complete Works of Chuang Tzu* (New York and London: Columbia University Press, 1968), 78, 80.
16. *Pao Pu Tzu Nei-P'ien Chiao-Shih* (Peking: Chung-hua Shu-chü, 1985), chap. 3, p. 53.
17. See Liu Xiaogan, "Afterword," in *Classifying the Chuang Tzu Chapters*, to be published soon by the Center for Chinese Studies at the University of Michigan.
18. All quotations from *Lao Tzu* altered from translations of Wing-tsit Chan or D. C. Lau. See Wing-tsit Chan, *A Source Book in Chinese Philosophy* (Princeton: Princeton University Press, 1963); and Lau, *Chinese Classics*.

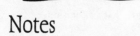

19. This is Ma Hsu-lun's opinion. Other scholars generally concur, as Ssu-ma Ch'ien wrote that Chuang Tzu lived at the same time as King Hui of Liang (369–319 B.C.E.) and King Hsüan of Ch'i (319–301 B.C.E.). The dates are thus not very controversial.
20. See Fung Yu-lan, *A Short History of Chinese Philosophy* (New York: Macmillan, 1948), 104.
21. See Liu Xiaogan, *Classifying the Chuang Tzu Chapters*, or *Chuang Tzu Che-Hsueh Chi-Ch'i Yan-Pien (Chuang Tzu's Philosophy and Its Development)* (Peking: China Social Science Press, 1988), chaps. 1, 2.
22. Translation of *Chuang Tzu* altered from Burton Watson and A. C. Graham. See Watson, *The Complete Works of Chuang Tzu*, and A. C. Graham, *Chuang-Tzu: The Seven Inner Chapters and Other Writings from the Book Chuang Tzu* (London: George Allen & Unwin, 1981).
23. See Watson, *The Complete Works of Chuang Tzu*, 61.
24. Watson, *The Complete Works of Chuang Tzu*, 192, with alteration.
25. Watson, *The Complete Works of Chuang Tzu*, 49.
26. Watson, *The Complete Works of Chuang Tzu*, 39–40.
27. See Liu Xiaogan, *Classifying the Chuang Tzu Chapters*, chap. 3.
28. By the no-sovereignists among Chuang Tzu's followers are meant the authors of chapters 8 through 10, 11 (section 1), chapters 28, 29, and chapter 31. See Liu Xiaogan, *Classifying the Chuang Tzu Chapters*.
29. Liu Xiaogan, *Classifying the Chuang Tzu Chapters*, chaps. 3 and 9.
30. Ssu-ma Ch'ien, *Shih Chi (Historical Records)* (Peking: Ch'ung-hua Shu-chü, 1973), vol. 10, p. 3289.
31. Liu Xiaogan, *Classifying the Chuang Tzu Chapters*, chap. 13 (Tian-tao). See Graham, *Chuang-Tzu*, 261–262.
32. Ssu-ma Ch'ien, *Shih Chi*, vol. 10, p. 3289.
33. Liu Xiaogan, *Classifying the Chuang Tzu Chapters*, chap. 14 (Tian Yun).
34. *Huai Nan Tzu*, chap. 14. Only a few chapters of this classic are presently available in English translation.
35. *Huai Nan Tzu*, chap. 14.
36. *Huai Nan Tzu*, chap. 19. The translation adopts the textual analysis of Wang Nien-sun (1744–1832) in the Ch'ing dynasty.
37. Wang Ming, *T'ai P'ing Ching Ho Chiao* (Beijing: Chung-hua Shu-chü, 1982), chap. 48, p. 148.
38. Wang Ming, *T'ai P'ing Ching Ho Chiao*, 525–526.
39. Wang Ming, *T'ai P'ing Ching Ho Chiao*, 22.
40. Kenneth Ch'en, *Buddhism in China: A Historical Survey* (Princeton: Princeton University Press, 1973), 476.
41. Jao Tsung-i, *Lao-tzu Hsiang-erh Chu Chiao-chien* (Hong Kong: Tong Nam Publishers, 1956), 13.
42. Another historical record gives 343 as the year of Ko's death. Either one is questionable.
43. *Pao-p'u-tzu Wai-p'ien*, chap. 50, "autobiography." A literal translation is available by Jay Sailey, *The Master Who Embraces Simplicity: A Study of the Philosopher Ko Hung*, A.D. 283–343 (San Francisco: Chinese Materials Center, 1978), 262.
44. Wang Ming, *Pao P'u Tzu He-chiao* (Peking: Ch'ung-hua Shu-chü, 1960), chap. 14. Translation altered from James R. Ware, *Alchemy, Medicine, Religion in the*

China of A.D. *320: The Nei P'ien of Ko Hung (Pao-P'u Tzu)* (Cambridge, MA: M.I.T Press, 1966), 226.

45. Ibid., chap. 2, p. 33.
46. Ibid.
47. Ibid., 35.
48. Ibid., 36.
49. Ibid., chap. 14, p. 101.
50. I adopt Sun Hsing-yen's textual analysis and omit the word "gold" before "cinnabar." See Wang Ming, *Pao P'u Tzu He-chiao*, 71, and Ware, *Alchemy*, 71.
51. Ibid., 116.
52. Ibid., 66.
53. Ibid., 302.
54. Ibid.
55. Ibid., 304–305.
56. Ibid., chap. 8, pp. 138–139.
57. Ibid., 140.
58. Ibid., chap. 11, p. 178.
59. Ibid., chap. 4, p. 68.
60. Ibid., vol. 4, p. 75.
61. *Wei Shu*, Shih Lao Chih (Peking: Chung-hua Shuh-chü), vol. 8, pp. 3049–3051. Some translations altered from Richard B. Mather, "K'ou Ch'ien-chih," in *The Encyclopedia of Religion*, ed. Mircea Eliade (New York: Macmillan, 1987), vol. 8, pp. 337–339.
62. An early Taoist text attributed the Supreme Purity scriptures to Mrs. Wei Hua-ts'un, who lived in the second century. Also see Michael Saso, *The Teachings of Taoist Master Chuang* (New Haven and London: Yale University Press, 1978), 37.
63. Saso, *The Teachings of Taoist Master Chang*, 219, 308, 311.
64. There were different records about the dates of the Three Meeting Days.
65. *Lu Hsien-shen Tao-men K'e-lüeh: Cheng-tong Taoist Canon* (Taipei: Yi-wen yin-shu-kuan, 1977), vol. 41, p. 33120.
66. *Tung-hsüan Ling-pao-chai Sho-kuan-chu Chieh-fa-teng Chu-yüan-yi*, vol. 16, p. 12717.
67. *Hua-yang Yin-chü Hsien-shen Pen-ch'i-lu*, vol. 38, p. 30234.
68. Thomas Cleary, trans. and ed., *Vitality Energy Spirit: A Taoist Sourcebook* (Boston and London: Shambhala Publications, 1991), 135.
69. Cleary, *Vitality Energy Spirit*, 133.
70. Cleary, *Vitality Energy Spirit*, 133.
71. Wing-tsit Chan, *A Source Book in Chinese Philosophy*, 136.
72. Modified from Watson, *The Complete Works of Chuang Tzu*, 175.
73. Watson, *The Complete Works of Chuang Tzu*, 176–177, with modification.
74. Saso, *The Teachings of Taoist Master Chuang*, 193.
75. Saso, *The Teachings of Taoist Master Chuang*, 208–210.

CHAPTER 5

Judaism

Jacob Neusner

Defining Judaism

About 5.5 million Jews live in North America, perhaps 13 million in the world—not so many that their religion demands as much attention as it gets. But if you read the papers, you know that "Jews is news"—and among religions, so is Judaism. A list of the well-known Jews of our time would include Henry Kissinger and Albert Einstein, Jonas Salk and Hyman Rickover—not to mention Mr. Goldberg from the corner delicatessen, and Mrs. Cohen, who works at Internal Revenue. Overseas live many more Jews, nearly 5 million of them in the State of Israel. All of them think being Jewish defines a critical part of their being; many of them believe that Judaism tells them the meaning of life. And Israeli Jews maintain that being Jewish requires them to create a political entity, a nation-state. Moreover because the Hebrew Bible, the Torah—which, according to the great sages, defines Judaism—is affirmed by Christianity and Islam as God's revelation, Judaism is news to most of the world as well.

Exactly how many Jews are in the world, and where are they located? Knowing the number of Jews in a given place does not tell us what it means to be Jewish, but it is the starting point for the description of the religion. Professor Calvin Goldscheider has estimated that as of 1985, there were 13 million Jews in the world.[1] The largest concentration of Jewish population is in the United States, where an estimated 5.7 million Jews live. In the State of Israel, the only country where the Jewish population makes up a numerical majority, there are 4.4 million; the former Soviet Union has an estimated 1.6 million. Together, these three countries contain more than 80 percent of all world Jewry. There are more than 1 million Jews in Western Europe: in France 530,000; Great Britain 350,000; Canada 308,000; Argentina 233,000; South Africa 120,000; and Brazil 130,000. These nine countries account for 95 percent of the world Jewish population. There are small Jewish communities in a wider range of countries within Europe (East and West), Asia, and North and South America. And if we consider that the Jewish population in the United States, as true of Jews in other countries, is not evenly spread throughout its regions, states, and cities,[2] then it becomes clear that Jews are highly concentrated in a few but very diverse societies.

In America, most Jews live in cities; indeed, they live in the largest metropolitan areas. We can get some idea of what this means by comparing the distribution of Jewish and non-Jewish populations in America. Consider this: 54 percent of American Jews live in the Northeast, whereas only a quarter of non-Jews live there. By contrast, about the same percentage of Jews and non-Jews live in the western region of the United States (17 percent of each group), and Jews are significantly underrepresented in the South (17 percent of Jews compared to 34 percent of non-Jews) and in the north central region (12 percent of Jews compared to 26 percent of non-Jews). Indeed, Jews have a population size of more than 100,000 in only ten states, and together these account for 87 percent of all U.S. Jewry. Canadian Jewry is similarly concentrated in Toronto and Montreal (there is a sizable community in Winnipeg, too).

Who Is a Jew?

But what does it mean to be a Jew? Does it mean belonging to a religion? Well, no, because there are Jews who are atheists and Jews who are Orthodox, and many in-between. Does it mean belonging to an ethnic group? Not really, because if you convert to some religion other than Judaism, you generally are thought to have dropped out of the ethnic group. Does it mean fulfilling certain conditions? That is, what does Judaism demand of Jews, as individuals, and of all of us, as a group? If it is to keep dietary taboos, not to eat pork or lobster or mix dairy products with meat, then many Jews—perhaps 90 percent of them—are excluded. And if it is to "love your neighbor as yourself" (Lev. 19:18), then while everybody tries, few succeed. Indeed, although one person who practices Judaism thinks that religious practices are vital, another, who also practices Judaism, does not.

Why these uncertainties, these contradictions in defining Jews and Judaism? Behind them lie two fundamental problems in Judaism. The first comprises the complex and at times almost oppositional relationship between ethnic and religious definitions of Judaism. All branches of Judaism select Jews along ethnic lines according to their birth. For instance, Orthodox and Conservative Judaism (terms explained below) define the Jew as a person born of a Jewish mother, and Reform Judaism, as a person born of a Jewish mother or father. But Judaism speaks of "Israel," meaning the Jewish people, as Christianity speaks of "the Church." That is, religious criteria operate too. The line between the supernatural social entity, called into being by God in God's service, and the this-worldly social group, formed by people of common background and culture, is a very fine one. In Judaism it is difficult to make out.

The second problem is a by-product of this conflict between religious and ethnic definitions of Judaism: Jews do not agree on what Judaism is. Since being Jewish also makes a person automatically part of "Israel," meaning God's holy people (counterpart to the Church as the Mystical Body of Christ), the opinions of individual Jews are often considered authoritative and even representative of Judaism. That explains why we have so many forms of Judaism. In the United States and Canada, and overseas as well, there are at least four organized forms of Judaism or, as we shall term them, four Judaisms: Orthodox, Reform, Conservative, Reconstructionist.

Orthodox Judaism believes in a literal way that God gave the Torah, both written (that is, the "Old" Testament, as Christianity knows it) and oral (that is, the traditions written down after 70 C.E. and the final destruction of the Temple by the rabbis who evolved to replace the priests). It keeps the law as God-given. *Reform Judaism* emphasizes change. It considers the Torah a statement of eternal principles in historical language and terms, and consequently believes that it can be changed to respond to new conditions. Indeed, it abandons much of the original Torah as no longer relevant. *Conservative Judaism*, by contrast, affirms the God-given standing of the Torah but accommodates change. As for *Reconstructionist Judaism*, it sees the faith as the historical religious civilization of the Jews and identifies God in naturalist, rather than supernatural terms. That is, the more recent Judaisms have moved further and further from the notion of Torah as their divinely inspired, authoritative text.

Moreover, although in the State of Israel only Orthodoxy is recognized by the state, Israel's Orthodox Jews are divided among themselves. So we have to take the classification "Orthodox Judaism" and subdivide that too. In its place stand Orthodox Judaisms—many, diverse, and fiercely competitive. All Orthodox Judaisms affirm the God-given authority of the Torah (and are therefore "Orthodox"), but they differ among themselves on how to interpret the Torah—and even on who should interpret and apply its law—as vigorously as they disagree with Reform Judaism, for instance.

So all Jews and each Jew constitutes "Israel," and what one "Israel" says is as much Judaism as what another "Israel" says—very complicated. Let us now turn to some this-worldly facts to sort out theological formulations of Judaism. We begin with the ethnic question.

Jewish Ethnicity

What makes anyone think that the Jews form an ethnic group? The reason is that all over the world Jews do exhibit traits that indicate their social continuity and corporate cohesion in the context of their various homelands. The great sociologist and demographer Calvin Goldscheider, among others, has shown that the Jews do form a distinctive social group, and that the indicators of their difference are sharply etched and well framed. Professor Goldscheider writes: "A detailed examination of family, marriage, childbearing, social class, residence, occupation and education among Jews and non-Jews leads to the unmistakable conclusion that Jews are different. Their distinctiveness as a community is further reinforced by religious and ethnic forms of cohesiveness."[3]

Professor Goldscheider's point is that although difference is defined in different ways in different places, everywhere the sense of being different, of being "unique," characterizes Jews. Of course, since difference is defined differently in different places, what makes a Jew different in one place will not mark him or her and not be recognized as a difference somewhere else. For instance, in America people think that bagels are a Jewish bread, or that corned beef is a Jewish dish, but to outsiders, American Jews appear to be Jewish Americans—and more American than Jewish. Similarly, in Morocco and Algeria, some forms of wheat used to be prepared in a way that Moroccans and Algerians considered specific to Jews and therefore Jewish, but in America we recognize no specifically Jewish way to prepare wheat. And although in Italy there is an artichoke dish that is called "Jewish artichoke," to some Americans, one Italian dish seems the same as any other—when they get past the garlic.

But as I have suggested, wherever you go you find there are traits that mark the local Jews as different from the rest of the people, even if those same traits would not distinguish them for outsiders. Although the specific traits vary across the world, all over the world that fact of Jewish difference persists, and that fact defines the principal concern of Judaism, as we shall see.

What kind of traits differentiate the group from others in one context and another? Family, stratification of Jewish society, and diverse characteristics of ethnicity all identify the Jews as a group distinctive in their larger social setting. Professor Goldscheider writes:

> The distinctive features of American Jewish life imply bonds and linkages among Jews which form the multiple bases of communal continuity. These ties are structural as well as cultural; they reflect deeply embedded forms of family, educational, job and residence patterns, reinforced by religious and ethnic-communal behavior, cemented by shared lifestyles and values.[4]

That is, Jewish difference is distributed across socioeconomic patterns. It appears in the form of marriage, type of family, place of residence, degree of mobility a Jew enjoys in that society. That is, we see it in a Jew's occupation, education, and economic status—the social class with its communal affiliation and identification and behavior. When we consider these phenomena, we see that Jews do exhibit qualities in common. For instance, they live together, forming Jewish neighborhoods; they work in a few specific types of occupations; they marry within the group. As a result, Americans think, for example, that psychiatry is a Jewish profession while professional football is not. By contrast, in the State of Israel, Jews are identified (as was the case in biblical times) as farmers and soldiers. None of these are inherently Jewish occupations, of course, any more than they are Norwegian. But in specific contexts they indeed indicate a person's

Jewishness. And thus they justify describing the Jews as a socioethnic group, not merely as individuals who happen to believe the same things and so have the same religion.

The Geographical Demography of Judaism

Now what about the demography of Judaism? Realizing that there are various Judaisms in the world, we ask what characterizes the practice of Judaism in various places where Jews form ethnic groups or communities. On this matter, Professor Goldscheider observes, "The extent and variation of contemporary Judaism—the religiosity and religious commitments of Jews—defy simple definition and classification." For most Jews there is limited evidence on the degree of Jewish identification, religious practice, ritual observance, or other indicators of Judaism. This is true despite the highly organized character, for example, congregational, institutional, of Jewish communities and synagogue and rabbinical associations.

An examination of some rough indicators of Judaism reveals the following profile for the largest communities in the United States. National American data show that about 85 percent of the adult Jewish population in the United States identify themselves with one of the three major denominations—Orthodox, Conservative, or Reform (which are generally ranked from higher to lower in intensity of religious observance). Overall, about 11 percent identify with the Orthodox, 42 percent with Conservative Judaism, and 33 percent with Reform Judaism.[5]

Goldscheider points out, further, that variation in this identification and practice of Judaism is also reflected in ritual practices and synagogue attendance. Nationally, data from a 1970–1971 survey showed that about 30 percent of the Jews observed the dietary rules, 13 percent attended synagogue frequently, 24 percent were members of two or more Jewish organizations. Data from New York (1981) show that about 90 percent of adult Jews attend a Passover Seder, 80 percent observe the December festival of Hanukkah, 70 percent have a *mezuzah* (an amulet) on the doorpost of their houses as Scripture requires, 67 percent fast on Yom Kippur (the Day of Atonement), 36 percent buy only kosher meats, and 30 percent keep two sets of dishes, one for meat and the other for dairy, as the Talmud requires. Few Jews attend services weekly (14 percent of the men in New York); most attend a few times a year. About 30 percent of the men never attend. Again, Jews in other American communities, particularly in the west, show lower levels of ritual observance and synagogue attendance.[6] Canadian Jewry is much like American Jewry; Orthodoxy competes with strong Reform and Conservative Judaisms there too. In Great Britain, much of Latin America, Australia and South Africa, and continental Europe, by contrast, most of the formal and centralized institutions are nominally Orthodox, but most of the population tends to be secular in orientation. The category "non-observant Orthodox" covers the bulk of these Jews.

What about Judaism in the State of Israel? Goldscheider observes, "The State of Israel is also a secular society and religious observances tend to parallel the patterns found in the United States. But religious divisions in Israel follow a broader pattern than 'Orthodox,' 'Conservative' or 'Reform.' They cannot be deduced from synagogue membership. National data in Israel show that between 10 and 15 percent of the state's Jews define themselves as 'very religious'"; almost half are "religious" or "traditional"; 36 percent define themselves as not religious and an additional 9 percent are totally secular. Although about 47 percent of Israel's Jews keep separate meat and dairy dishes, synagogue attendance there is as low as in New York—about 26 percent never attend and most attend only a few times a year.

The Jews who come from Mediterranean, North African, and Middle Eastern countries, and who now form a majority of Israel's Jewish population, tend to begin as more traditional than Jews from Europe and North America, but rapidly become secularized. Moreover, despite the large proportion of secular Jews in Israel (about one-third the adult Jewish population), most of the six to eight thousand synagogues in Israel are Orthodox. Only about forty congregations in Israel with a total membership of two thousand families are affiliated with Reform or Conservative Judaism. This undoubtedly reflects the association between politics and religion in Israeli society and the power of various Orthodox political parties within the government coalition.

In the former Soviet Union, until very recently, there have been constraints on religious observance and practice among Jews. Overriding the Soviet Constitution (as well as the now-defunct USSR's adherence to the Helsinki agreement), the Soviet government has not allowed the free exercise of Judaism. As a result, there are no communal Jewish organizations except for approximately sixty synagogues, half of which are located in the Caucasus and Asiatic Republics. With the demise of the USSR, Jews have found the freedom to organize synagogues, schools, cultural institutions, and communal bodies and have done so. Hundreds of thousands have emigrated to the State of Israel, tens of thousands to the West. The future of Judaism in Russia and the other successor-states of the USSR is unclear at this time, but it certainly is brighter than at any time under the militantly atheist, repressive Communist rule.

But what we can claim with some certainty is that diversity characterizes the religious practices, political circumstances, and cultural characteristics of Jews. Jews are divided, for example, into those who live in a Jewish state and those who do not; those who practice (any) Judaism and those who practice none; those who practice Judaism in one way, those who practice it in another. So the problem of studying Judaism is to deal with diversity, and our task is to make sense of the confusion of a variety of categories—the ethnic and the religious—and also of a variety of Judaisms. But then we may capture in one problem the urgent question that all Judaisms address, and that all accounts of the Jews, whether secular or religious, must take up: who is a Jew and why does it matter? When we understand that question, we can grasp all together and all at once the nature of Judaism(s) and the complexity of the Jews as a social entity. Putting together the ethnic and the religious, we get Judaism.

The Relationship of the Ethnic and the Religious in Judaism

There Is No Presbyterian Nation, but There Is a Jewish State

No one ever called the Methodists a people, but there is a Jewish state. And since the state calls itself "Israel," which, in the Holy Scriptures and the liturgy of Judaism always means God's people, wherever they live, the very name "Israel" for the State of Israel makes us wonder how secular that state can be. But the State of Israel is not the Jewish equivalent of the Vatican or even, more broadly, "the Church." So the distinction that we have made between the ethnic and the religious works better in theory than in fact.

But the issue remains not only chronic but sometimes urgent—partly because of the confusion of religion and ethnic identification outside of the State of Israel, and partly because of the confusion of religion and nationality in the State of Israel. When, as one of its first pieces of business, the Israeli parliament (the Knesset) defined who might become an Israeli citizen in the "law of return," it declared that any Jew in the world may become an Israeli citizen for the asking. The qualification for citizenship was simply belonging to the ethnic group. But who belongs to the ethnic group? That issue is not so simple. This is clear when we consider converts to Judaism. They must become not only Judaists, but Jews. They must join an ethnic as well as a religious group.

The State and the Church in Judaism in the State of Israel

The crucial question here is, then, who is a valid convert for the purposes of being declared an Israeli citizen? That is, who is a Jew as well as a Judaist? Repeatedly, Orthodox Judaisms of the State of Israel have asked the government to declare as a Jew by conversion only someone converted "in accord with the law"—by which the Orthodox Judaic leadership means that, among converts, only a convert to Orthodox Judaism is a Jew. Converts to Judaism in the Reform or Conservative or Reconstructionist formulations, who in the United States are accepted as full members of the Jewish people and of course as Judaists, are not considered validly converted. Indeed, Orthodox Judaisms in Israel have consolidated themselves into political parties and thus gained considerable power in the Knesset just to control legislation on this question, to define membership in the ethnic group solely by religious criteria.

We see, therefore, that the theoretical distinction between the ethnic and the religious does not work. The issues are confused with one another in practice. But the reason is that the ethnic life of the Jewish people is deeply shaped by the theological convictions of Israel, the holy people of God in Judaism. It has been said, by no means entirely as a joke, that though ethnic Jews do not believe in God, they nonetheless are sure that Jews are God's chosen people. What we see in the politics of the State of Israel is a working out of the theological confrontation that has marked Judaism over the past two hundred years: whether there can be any Judaism other than an Orthodox one (or any Judaism other than my particular, and Orthodox, one). Initially all Orthodoxies condemned Reform Judaism. Today there are so many Judaisms that the only thing all Orthodox Judaisms agree about is the illegitimacy of all other-than-Orthodox Judaisms.

Still, people who think Jews are secular because they are not religious in the way in which Protestants or Catholics are religious have now to rethink the matter. Indeed, in studying religion we must always make space for different definitions of what we mean by religiosity or piety. Specifically, in the State of Israel's political concern over "who is a Jew," we see an intensity of engagement with religion in its most religious formulation—who is holy, and who is not—because "who is a Jew" defines "who is Israel," meaning not state or ethnic group but holy people—a religious category.

The Classical Tension Between the Ethnic and the Religious in Judaism

The contemporary debates in Jerusalem, harsh and fresh though they appear, actually continue age-old and important arguments that reach back far beyond the last two centuries. From the formation of the Pentateuch in the aftermath of the return to Zion (after the exile to Babylon), people within the Jewish world have proposed through debates on "who is a Jew" to say who is in and who is out, who is Israel and who is other. Consider the reflection on the heritage of Abraham, Isaac, and Jacob in the Five Books of Moses formed by Ezra in 450 B.C.E.; the exclusivist doctrine, "we're all of Israel that there is," of the Essene community at Qumran on the shores of the Dead Sea, which saw itself as the only "Israel" in the world; the Apostle Paul's troubled assessment of the old Israel and the new; and the Talmudic rabbis' insistence on the sanctity and the sanctification of *all* Israel. The question of who is Israel remains one and the same.

The very name of the Jewish state—the State of Israel—tells the story of the union of the ethnic and this-worldly with the religious and the theological. It was David Ben Gurion's profound understanding that led him to name the new state, formed in the Land of Israel by the people of Israel in 1948, the State of Israel. The relationship between Zionism (national and ethnic) and Judaism (religious) forms the centerpiece of contemporary Judaic theology as well as of Jewish thought today. In debating issues as now formulated—with the Israeli legislature passing laws on who is a Jew, and with issues of the definition of peoplehood, state, land, and exile forming the center of public discourse—Jews carry forward in a perfectly straight line the exquisitely theological discussions that have characterized their shared existence from remote beginnings.

How so? Every Judaism defines not only "Judaism" but also "Israel," that is, the social entity that embodies that Judaism and forms the holy people envisioned within the given Judaic system. Accordingly, in calling that state simply "Israel," people deliver a profound statement upon who is Israel, what is (an) Israel, who is the true Israel, and similar, long-vexed dilemmas of religious thinkers in Judaism, past and present, and secular Jewish thinkers today.

Among the many definitions of who is Israel and who is a Jew, the view of "Israel" as the holy people of God, as the children of Abraham, Isaac, and Jacob, remains central to the liturgy of Judaism, on the one side, and its sacred scripture, on the other. That is a compendious definition, but it also is a distinctively religious one, for at prayer and study, "Israel" stands for, refers to, the entire Jewish people, wherever they live: "God who keeps Israel does not slumber or sleep," is everywhere and so watches over Israel everywhere, including Israel in the Land of Israel. Thus, Ben Gurion's daring utilization of "Israel" in an exclusive and land-centered framework offers a direct challenge to liturgy and scripture.

Do these issues have anything to do with the study of Judaism as a religion? Yes indeed. If the Israelis declare that a Jew is either one born of a Jewish mother or one converted to Judaism by an Orthodox Judaic authority, then they declare an outsider (in this context) as one born of a Jewish father but not a Jewish mother or one converted by a rabbi who is Conservative, Reconstructionist, or Reform. And that removes legitimacy, within Israeli state law, from all Judaisms other than the Orthodox ones that predominate in the State of Israel.

That fact explains why the issue of who is a Jew is not narrowly political and appears beyond the Israeli context, why it is central in the formation of Judaism in America too. It is in our own country that matters prove subject to debate. The political-religious parties of Israeli Orthodoxies concur in wishing to offend and insult non-Orthodox Judaisms overseas. That will not persuade diaspora Jews that they are not authentic. That fact explains why much of mainstream Orthodoxy in North America rejects the initiative to delegitimate all non-Orthodox Judaisms by an act of the State of Israel.

To make sense of the Jewish world likely to be familiar in North America, we have to remember that each religion defines not only itself but also what it means by "religion." In the case of Judaism, there are matters of intense meaning that, in the case of Christianity, are not deemed religious at all. For example, Protestant Christianity never recognized dietary matters as expressions of religion, whereas to many Judaisms, not eating pork is an act in service of God. Conversely, Christianity in its Protestant forms regards personal prayer, an individual's communion with and address to God, as critical in the religious life. But (like other religions) many Judaisms place heavier emphasis on the recitation of prescribed liturgy and less on the personal intentionality that is supposed to accompany prayer. And finally, although Christianity assuredly formed the theory of the Christian state, no Christianity identified itself with a particular state in a particular location in the way in which Judaism(s) have identified the State of Israel, located in the Land of Israel (also known as Palestine), as critical to sanctity. Thus, many Jews are religious in ways that Christians do not recognize as religious at all, and they are not religious in ways that Christians take for granted that piety requires.

As we have seen, such differences pertain within Judaism also. Though some Jews are Reform or Orthodox, Conservative or Reconstructionist, still other Jews are not at all religious in any sense American Christians can understand. And since outsiders generally assume that "Judaism is the religion of the Jewish people," we then identify the ethnic group we know with the religion(s), Judaism(s). So avoiding forbidden foods in Judaism is deemed religious, not (merely) ethnic. (And, to complicate matters, there are secular Jews who do not eat pork.) In addition, since all religions can be distinguished in affirming the existence of God (or an absolute, ultimate reality), whereas modes of secularity ordinarily are characterized by atheism, the fact that there exist Jews who in no way are religious further calls into question the ethnic definition of Judaism as "the religion of the Jewish people."

In fact, many Jews are apt to appear less engaged by the praying and by the pious life of the synagogue than their counterparts in Christianity and Islam are by the church and the mosque, respectively. So one wonders whether Judaism is a religion at all. But what makes one doubt that Judaism falls into the same class as Christianity and Islam is what should be kept distinct. It is the ethnic group, the Jews, and the religion, Judaism. The ethnic group, the Jews, encompasses everybody who is rightly regarded as Jewish. But not everybody in that ethnic group believes in or practices a particular Judaism. Some people think that Jews' views add up to Judaism. But that is not so, since Judaism is a religion, and not all Jews are religious. So we have to distinguish the ethnic group, the Jews or the Jewish people, from the religious group that is encompassed by the ethnic group, that is, the Judaists, practitioners of Judaism, who also happen to be Jews. Then we may fairly say that what (some) Judaists believe does add up to a Judaism, and that permits us to define a Judaism. The interplay of the ethnic and the religious is one of the studies of religion that Judaism makes possible, perhaps more accessibly than other religions.

To state the problem very simply: If you convert to the Roman Catholic religion, you do not automatically become Spanish, Italian, or Brazilian (to name three Roman Catholic nations), and if you become Episcopalian, you do not automatically get a British passport (or an English accent). But if you convert to Judaism, you automatically become a Jew, a member of the ethnic group. And, to flip the coin, as I have suggested, no one ever called the Methodists a people, and there is no Presbyterian state, yet the Jews are called a people, there is a Jewish state, and the people and state identify the religion as their own.

It follows that once we distinguish between the ethnic and the religious and realize that not all Jews are Judaists—practitioners of Judaism—the confusion between the often contradictory opinions held by persons who call themselves Jews and the religion Judaism is readily sorted out. Thus:

1. Judaism is a religion (or, as we already recognize, a set of religions), and the Jews are an ethnic group.
2. If a person is a Judaist, or a practitioner of Judaism, he or she also is automatically a member of the ethnic group, the Jews.
3. For a long time, that is, through nearly the whole of recorded history, everyone who was a Jew also was a Judaist.

The upshot is simple. If we know "what the Jews believe," for example, their opinions, obtained through public opinion polling, about various questions (whether religious or political or cultural), we do not necessarily know anything about Judaism. If we can find out what the Judaists among the Jews believe, we do. What makes matters complicated, of course, is that the distinction between the ethnic and the religious among people who are both is not so readily drawn. But we can, at least, avoid some obvious errors by identifying up front the sources of possible confusion.

The Problem of Diversity and Defining Judaism

Locating Judaism Among Religions

Judaism, the religion deriving from God's revelation to Moses at Sinai, is a monotheist religion, as are Islam and Christianity, which affirm that same revelation (to Christians, it is the Old Testament, to Moslems, the Tawrat). Distinguished from polytheist and nonmonotheistic religions, all three maintain that God is one and unique, transcendent, not subject to the rules of nature but wholly other. Judaism differs from Christianity in recognizing as God's revelation the Hebrew Scriptures, but not the New Testament. It differs from Islam in holding Moses to be unique among prophets and in recognizing no prophecy beyond the scriptural record.

The Diversity of Judaisms

Differentiating Judaism from Christianity and Islam is easier than defining Judaism because, as we already noted, the word *Judaism* applies to a variety of closely related religions, past and present. These share a number of traits. For example, all of them revere the Torah (literally: "revelation," often mistranslated, "the Law") revealed by God to Moses at Sinai—even if they do so to different degrees. But they also differ among themselves in important ways. So to define Judaism as a unitary and uniform religion, unfolding in a single continuous history from beginning to present, is simply not possible. The world today knows a number of Judaisms, and times past witnessed diversity as well.

To give a familiar example, Reform Jews do not keep the biblical laws about food or strictly observe the Sabbath day. Scripture says not to eat pork; they eat pork. Scripture interpreted by later tradition says one is not to work or perform secular activity on the Sabbath (Saturday); Reform Jews do. They will play golf or go to the movies or go to their office. By contrast, Orthodox Jews keep dietary laws, eating only *kosher*, or suitable, food; they will not go to their offices on Saturday, instead devoting the day to relaxing, worshiping, studying the Torah, and enjoying themselves. In these concrete ways, the patterns of religious observance and belief that characterize Reform Jews and those that mark Orthodox Jews bear little in common. How can God want me not to eat pork and not to perform mundane labor on the Sabbath, as Orthodox Judaism maintains on the strength of Scripture, and at the same time not care what I do at the table and on specified holy days, as Reform Judaism maintains, appealing to the same Scripture (if in different aspects)? Rather than try to harmonize clearly distinct Judaisms, whether two thousand years ago or today, we do better to recognize difference and deal with it.

It is the simple fact that we cannot treat as single, unitary, and harmonious the quite diverse versions or systems of Judaism that have flourished in time. The conception people commonly hold is that there is such a thing as a religious tradition that is continuous, has a history, and unfolds in a linear continuity. But in reality everyone takes for granted there are many "forms of" Christianity, and anyone who sees all Christianities as a single Christianity ignores the profound differences in belief and behavior among Roman Catholics, on the one side, Methodists and Baptists, on the second, Coptic Christians on the third, and the Church of Jesus Christ of Latter-Day Saints, and many other contemporary Christianities, on the multitude of other sides. But how shall we deal with the diversity of religions, all of which form a single religious species? The differences among Christianities are many; but all call themselves, and are rightly regarded as, Christianity. Can we make sense of diversity without ignoring difference? The case of Judaism shows us how we can.

Those who believe that Judaism is played out over time believe also that there is only one Judaism at a time—one Judaism for all time. They do not recognize other Judaisms or a Judaic system. They claim that Judaism develops in incremental steps, yielding at its zenith Judaism as "we" know "it." But who is that "we"? The answer must always be theological: The we of course is that group of Jews that identifies "it"—its particular system—not as a choice but as "Judaism pure and simple." We assume that the Judaism we participate in is both the epitome and the norm. Thus, the Reform rabbi near at hand, the Orthodox *rebbe* of a Hasidic sect in Bnai Braq in the State of Israel, the Chief Rabbi of this town in the State of Israel, the Chief Rabbi of the Judaism(s) of European origin in the State of Israel, each considers his Judaism the true religion. Indeed, the followers of the Lebovitcher rebbe, a Hasidic group in Brooklyn, believe that their leader is the Messiah. No other Judaism concurs. But as their separate assumptions indicate, there is not now, and there never has been a single Judaism that (speaking descriptively) dominated to the exclusion of all others. In modern times, we all recognize that a variety of Judaisms exist. Indeed, each Judaism, that is, each system, begins on its own and then—only then—goes back to the received documents in search of texts and proof-texts that can validate its role as "the Judaism."

So all Judaisms see themselves as incremental developments, the final and logical outcome of *The* History of Judaism. And every Judaism traces its origins retrospectively in a canon of relevant historical facts or holy books that it selects to support its reality—and that believers imagine constitute an a priori justification for their Judaism. All Judaisms, therefore, testify to humanity's power of creative genius, its ability to make something out of nothing more than hope—or God's intervention. Each creates and defines itself. Every Judaism in modern times alleges that it is the natural, or historical Judaism, but that allegation always denies the obvious fact. Each Judaism begins in its own time and place and then goes in search of a useful past. Every system serves to suit a purpose, to solve a problem, in our context, to answer through a self-evidently right doctrine a question that none can escape or ignore. Orthodoxy, no less than Reform, takes up fresh positions and presents stunningly original and relevant innovations. It is in the nature of theology to follow this pattern, and from the perspective of the theologian, I can imagine no other.

Defining Religion

Before we can define any religion, we had best start with a simple statement of what we mean by a religion. Religion is something people do together to face urgent problems and to resolve them by appealing to truths that seem self-evident to them. Indeed, if we want to know the relationship between religious ideas and the circumstances of the society that holds them, we do well to consider the example of Judaism. Religion—so we learn from Judaism—is a decisive fact of social reality, not merely a set of beliefs on questions viewed in an abstract and ahistorical setting. When we ask about the relationship between context and contents, we discover that while Judaisms respond to the questions of the social world around them, *they also shape that world.* In fact, already constituted Judaisms answer questions forced upon Israel, the Jewish people,[7] by important shifts in political circumstances.

So religion defines the social world that people make together. Indeed, it reshapes the everyday in accord with its own pattern, its own selection and interpretation of events and facts. Of course, people often think the opposite. Many suppose that the social world recapitulates religion, not that religion recapitulates that data—the given of society, economy, politics—let alone an imaginative or emotional reality. How does Judaism show the opposite? The study of Judaism shows us that, because of the paradigmatic, structuring power of a single generative experience, the experience from which it draws its origin, the religion, Judaism, has shaped and today defines the world in which Jews locate themselves. That is how religion shapes the world, not the world, religion. When we grasp that it is the Jews' religion, Judaism, that has formed their world and framed their realities, and not the world of politics, culture, and society that has made their religion, we understand the power of religion from a single important case.

Let me then repeat our major conclusions to this point:

1. A religion is diverse and encompasses a variety of subdivisions;
2. Religions take up urgent questions and answer them in a manner that believers find self-evidently valid;
3. Religion shapes the world.

To state the matter in a simple way, a religion shapes the world of its believers by identifying the questions that need answers and providing answers that people "know" to be true. In the nature of things, those who find those answers true, beyond the need for any argument or discussion, form a social entity and define the world of that community within the limits set by the compelling questions and the persuasive answers of the faith. When we know what questions a religion asks and answers, and can say who deems those questions the ones that must be answered, we can define a religion.

Defining a Judaism

Dealing with the diversity of Judaisms within Judaism proves somewhat easier if we simply alter our terms and thus our expectations. So from here on, we will speak not of a "religion" but of a "religious system." A religious system comprises three components:

A *worldview.* This worldview explains who the people it encounters are, where they come from, what they must do. In general, what a Judaism defines as "the Torah" will contain that worldview.

A *way of life.* This way of life expresses in concrete deeds the religious system's worldview. It thereby links the life of the individual to the community. For each Judaism, its way of life comprises what it sets forth as the things someone must do. (Thus the Judaism of the dual Torah foregrounds *halakhah,* the law.)

A *particular social group.* This is the group to whom the worldview and way of life refer. For a Judaic system, obviously, that group is "Israel" or, more specifically, the group it considers to constitute Israel—beginning with itself.

So a Judaic system or (in shorthand) a Judaism comprises a worldview, a way of life, and a group of Jews who hold the one and live by the other.

How do we tell when all three are present and thus define a social group, a Judaism? We look for the emergence of a striking and also distinctive symbol, something that expresses the whole all together and at once, a symbol—whether visual or verbal, gestured, sung, danced, or precipitated in the cultural formation (like a redefinition of the role of woman)—that captures the whole and proclaims its special message: its way of life, its worldview, its conception of Israel. For a Judaism, such a generative symbol may be "Torah," God's revelation to Moses at Sinai. Or it may be "Israel," God's holy people. Or, of course, the generative symbol may come to concrete expression in the conception of God.

Through the history of the Jewish people, diverse Judaisms have won the allegiance of groups of Jews here and there, each system specifying the things it regards as urgent both in belief and in behavior. Yet all systems in common allege that they represent the true and authentic Judaism, or Torah, or will of God for Israel, and that their devotees *are* Israel. And each Judaism ordinarily situates itself in a single historical line—hence, a linear history—from the entirety of the past. Commonly a Judaism sees itself as the natural outgrowth, the increment of time and change. These traits of historical or even supernatural origin characterize nearly all Judaisms. How then do we distinguish one Judaism from another? We can do so when we identify the principal symbol to which a given system on its own appeals, when we uncover its urgent question, define the answer it considers "natural."

The Formation of Judaism

Urgent Questions, Self-Evident Answers

All Judaisms, wherever formed, whatever type of question they have deemed urgent, must face up to the same persistent social facts that all Jews for all time have confronted. Jews are few in number, divided among themselves on many important questions, participants in different cultural and political systems, yet convinced that they form an ethnic group and that what happens to all of them matters to each one. Now when we identify these facts, we can explain the urgent questions that all Judaisms address. But, however diverse the answers, which to different groups of Jews appear to be self-evident, the questions form variations on a single question, the answers on one uniform pattern. That is why we may see Judaism as one family of closely related religious systems, different from all other families of religious systems.

The Pentateuch and Judaism(s)

If we ask what all Judaisms identify in common, we home in on the Pentateuch, or the Five Books of Moses ("the Torah").[8] The Torah comes "in the beginning," and so explains "where it all began" (or, "where *they* all started"). It is important because, as a matter of fact, it forms a critical component of the holy writings of every Judaism ever known. The key issue is what problem does the Pentateuchal authorship—the people who put it all together as we now have it—find urgent? And can we translate that problem into terms that are socially relevant wherever Jews have lived, from then to now? If we can, then we can account for *any* Judaism and *every* Judaism.

The Generative Event

Judaism finds its origins in two sequential happenings, which together form a single event.

1. In 586 B.C.E. the Temple of Jerusalem was destroyed. In addition, the political classes of the Jewish state and the persons of economic worth, the craftsmen and artisans—anybody who counted—were taken away to the homeland of the conquering empire. They were settled in Babylonia, where the Tigris and Euphrates rivers come close to one another (a province of antiquity now encompassed by the nation Iraq). And, similarly to mix the populations of the polyglot empire, the Babylonians brought other populations to the Land of Israel. These mixed with the Israelites who had not been taken away into exile. It was, as we realize, simply good public policy to form heterogeneous populations. The Babylonians divided and conquered.

2. Around "three generations later," toward the end of the sixth century B.C.E., the Babylonian Empire fell to the Iranian one led by the Persians. The Persian emperor, Cyrus, as a matter of public policy sought to win the loyalty of his diverse empire by returning to their homelands those peoples removed by the Babylonians. Consequently, the Jews of Babylonia were given the right to return to the Land of Israel. At that time, only very small numbers of them took the opportunity. Those Jews made a start at rebuilding the Temple. And some time later, in the middle of the fifth century (ca. 450 B.C.E.), a successor of Cyrus allowed a Jewish high court official, Nehemiah, together with a top bureaucrat and civil servant, Ezra, to go back to Jerusalem and with the support of the state to rebuild the Temple and establish a Jewish government in the surrounding region.

These two events come together as "exile and return," and are framed in terms as mythic and transcendent in their context, as rich and intense in their human messages, as "the Holocaust and Redemption" of contemporary Judaism. But, in making that comparison, we turn matters on their head. For, as we shall now see, the historical events of 586 and 450 are transformed in the Pentateuch's picture of the history and destiny of Israel into that generative myth of exile and return that characterizes every Judaism, then to now.

Event and Paradigm: The Secret of Persistence

To grasp the Pentateuch's main point, the vital concern that its compilers dealt with, we have first to understand how it took shape. The Five Books of Moses (Genesis, Exodus, Leviticus, Numbers, and Deuteronomy) speak of the creation of the world and God's identification of the children of Abraham, Isaac, and Jacob (who also was called "Israel") as God's people. That people, as you know, is portrayed as taking shape in the land of Canaan, which was promised to Abraham and his seed and would be called the Land of Israel. It is portrayed as then going down to Egypt, being freed of the bondage of Egypt by Moses, who led the people to Sinai, being given the Torah by God. The Torah is described as comprising rules that were to govern Israel's holy community and Israelites' service to God in the cult and in the temple that would be built in time to come. It also comprised the message that when Israel kept the covenant, the contract made with God by the patriarchs and given substance at Sinai, then God would favor Israel, but when Israel did not comply, then God would punish it.

This thumbnail sketch of the Torah suggests that the narrative is uniform and comes from the time of the events themselves. But the Pentateuch is made up of a variety of discrete writings, each marked by its own style and viewpoint. For example, the writings that speak of the caste system—priests, Levites, Israelites—and of the Temple cult—the special tasks and duties and rights of the priests—are ascribed to a priestly authorship; these writers produced the book of Leviticus and most of the book of Numbers, as well as passages in the book of Exodus that deal with the tabernacle. The entire book of Deuteronomy, attributed to Moses as he looked back and narrated the story of the formation of Israel, represents an altogether different authorship, with its own points of interest. One difference, for instance, is that the priestly writers in Leviticus take for granted that sacrifice to the Lord may take place in any appropriate holy place, while the authorship of the book of Deuteronomy insists that sacrifice may take place only in the place that God will designate, by which it means Jerusalem's temple. These striking differences alert us to the question, Where and when did the whole get put together as we now have it?

The answer to that question is important, because if you read the Torah as one sustained narrative, you are receiving the message as a whole, in the composition, proportion, order, and sense which that *final* group of authors, editors, and compilers imparted. The Pentateuch as we now have it is the work of an authorship of a particular period. So the message of the Pentateuch, encompassing diverse prior viewpoints and messages to be sure, is one that addresses the social world of the ultimate authorship, which has put everything together to say that one thing. To understand the Pentateuch, therefore, we require one further set of facts: what happened before the age of formation and conclusion of the Torah, and what problems pressed upon the authorship of the Torah.

The facts are simple. The ancient Israelites settled the Land before 1000 B.C.E. and lived there for five centuries. The details of their history, culture, and religion need not detain us, because they do not define the history of Judaism. Only as these details were *reshaped* after a world-shaking event and formed into the Torah (and certain other writings) does the life of Israel from the conquest of the Land to that utter break—a caesura in time—matter to Judaism.

Now we may return to the issue addressed by Judaic systems from the Pentateuch onward. Each Judaism responded to events within the pattern laid out by Scripture in the original encounter with the destruction of the Temple in 586 and the return to Jerusalem in the beginning of the fifth century. That event was, to begin with, interpreted as a paradigm of death and resurrection. The destruction of the Temple and the subsequent exile symbolized death, while the return from exile with the rebuilding of Jerusalem and reinstitution of the Temple cult constituted resurrection. It answered the question, Who is Israel?, by defining the rules that govern what it means to be Israel:

1. the formation of Israel and its covenant with God, time and again insisting on the holiness of Israel and its separateness from the other peoples, and
2. the conditional possession of the Land as the mark of the covenant.

The people has the Land not as a given but as a gift. So long as the people accords with the covenant, the Land will be his or hers and each will prosper in it. If the people violates the Torah, the conditions of the covenant, each will lose his or her Land. The key chapters are Leviticus 26 and Deuteronomy 32. But if you review the narrative of Genesis, with its account of how the people took shape and got the Land, you see that the relationship of Israel to the Land is the theme throughout. Everything else depends on it. When you get to the Land, you build the temple. When you get to the Land, you obey these laws. When you get to the Land, you form a godly society and carry out the Torah. So the condition of the people dictates his or her right to the Land, and in losing the Land, the people is warned to keep the Torah and the conditions that it sets forth. What that means, of course, is that in recovering the Land, the people enjoys a redemption that is conditional: not a given but a gift.

Difference and Destiny: Resentment Provoked and Appeased

The Torah stresses the distinctive rules that govern Israel, the unique character of Israel among the nations. If we may translate those points of stress into secular and neutral language, we may see a chronic concern for defining Israel—for discovering (if we may here slip into contemporary political language) "who is a Jew." Wherever they lived, in one way or another, Israel, the Jewish people, sought a means of declaring itself a group distinct from its neighbors. One reason that the concern with difference persists is that the Jews, wherever located, are simply a very small group surrounded by others that are larger, more powerful, and more important. If a small group under diverse circumstances wishes to sustain itself, it does so by underlining the points of difference between itself and everyone else. It will furthermore place a high value on these points of difference, going against the more common impulse of a minority to denigrate points of difference and so identify with the majority.

Throughout the Torah's narrative—in Genesis, where the patriarchs go "home" to Babylonia to obtain their wives; in Leviticus, with its exclusion of the Canaanites whom "the land vomited out" because of their wickedness; in Deuteronomy, with its command to wipe out some groups and to proscribe marriage with others—the stress is the same: Form high walls between Israel and its nearest neighbors. The stress on exclusion of the neighbors from the group, and of the group from the neighbors, runs contrary to the situation of ancient Israel, which, with its unmarked frontiers of culture, participated in the constant giving and receiving among diverse groups characteristic of ancient times.

The persistent stress on differentiation, yielding a preoccupation with self-definition, also contradicts the facts of the matter. In the time of the formation of the Pentateuch, the people Israel was deeply affected by the shifts and changes in social, cultural, and political life and institutions. When, a century and a half after the formation of the Pentateuch under Ezra and Nehemiah, the Greeks under Alexander the Great conquered the entire Middle East (ca. 320 B.C.E.) and incorporated the Land of Israel into the international Hellenistic culture, the problem of self-definition came up again. And when the war of independence fought by the Jews under the leadership of the Maccabees (ca. 160 B.C.E.) produced an independent state for a brief period, that state found itself under the government of a court that accommodated itself to the international style of politics and culture. So what was different, what made Israel separate and secure on its land and in its national identity? In that protracted moment of confusion and change, the heritage of the Five Books of Moses came to closure. And the same situation persisted that had marked the age in which the Pentateuch had delivered its message, answering with self-evident responses the urgent question of the nation's existence. That situation, briefly stated, constitutes the formative chapter in the history of all Judaisms: exile and return as the history of Judaism. Let us examine this point from the beginning, with the Pentateuchal reading of events and their meaning (framed post-586).

Formation of a Religion: Do Events Define Systems, or Do Systems Select Events?

Now we may address a question important in the study of any religion: Where does it all start? Do things happen, which people then interpret? Or do people start with a system and then select events to form the structure of the social world that, to begin with, they comprise? The case of Judaism strongly suggests that events come after the fact, and that the social requirements of a system dictate the criteria by which people identify the events to which, later on, they attribute the origin of their system.

The principal givens of the Pentateuchal Torah's model, namely, Israel's heightened sense of its own social reality, its status as an elected people standing in a contractual or covenantal relationship with God, inhere in the system. They express *its* logic, not a logic intrinsic in events, even in events selected and reworked; they apply *its* premises, not the data of Israel's common life in either Babylonia or the Land of Israel. This is particularly evident in that the system not only selected the events it would deem consequential, but also from the perspective of a vast population of Israel, of Jews who remained in the Land, of Jews who never left Babylonia, it spoke of events that simply had never happened.

Consider the Jews who remained in the Land after 586, or those who remained in Babylonia after Cyrus's decree permitting the return to Zion. To these people who never left, or who left and never came back, since they each belonged to a distinct generation that knew only one mode of living—in exile or out of it—*there was no alienation, and also, consequently, no reconciliation.* That is, the normative—the "right" and "true"—was not complicated by change. It corresponded to the way things were—and things were only one way. In effect, to be Israel meant to live like any other people, wherever it happened to locate itself.

By contrast, for the exile who returned, exile and return were normative. Further, this doubled normalcy imparted to the exile the critical and definitive position. It marked Israel as special, elect, subject to the rules of the covenant and its stipulations.

But as we now realize, for much of Israel—those who never left, and those who never returned—some system other than the system of the normative alienation constructed by the Judaism of the Torah necessarily appeared self-evident. Obviously, for example, to those who stayed put, the urgent question of exile and return, with its self-evident response of election and covenant, bore slight relevance. Exile did not constitute a problem, so return was not a question worth asking, and such a question could provide no answers worth believing.

Still, there are few more powerful examples of a religious system creating a society than we find in the operations of the Pentateuch's conception of Israel, since it tells people not only the meaning of what had happened but also details what had happened, creating for Israelite society a picture of what it must be—and what therefore it had been. (We should credit here not only the Pentateuch but also associated post-586 B.C.E. writings.)

Exile and Return as the Structure of All *Judaism(s)*

What happened in 586 and after, and what the pattern fabricated out of what happened, do not correspond. Scripture said, in both the Torah and the prophetic-historical books, that Israel suffered through exile, atoned, attained reconciliation, and renewed the covenant with God (as signified by the return to Zion and the rebuilding of the Temple). The Judaic system of the Torah made normative that experience of alienation and reconciliation. But only a minority of "Israel" in fact had undergone those experiences. Thus the Judaic system expressed by the Five Books of Moses, as well as by some of the prophetic books, did two things. First, it precipitated resentment, a sense of insecurity and unease, by selecting as events only a narrow sample of what had happened (exile). Second, it appeased the same resentment by its formula of how to resolve the tensions of events of dislocation and alienation (return). That is, Judaism in its initial model not only guaranteed its own persistence by creating resentment at how things were but also provided a remedy for that anger. It was this power both to create a problem and to solve it that made this early Judaism into Judaism's initial, originating model, a paradigm, or pattern, for time to come.

Consider:

1. The paradigm (pattern) began as a paradigm, not as a set of actual events transformed into a normative pattern.

2. The conclusions generated by the paradigm, it must follow, derived not from reflection on things that happened but from the logic of the paradigm—there alone.
3. That same paradigm created expectations that could not be met, and so renewed the resentment encapsulated in the myth of exile. But at the same time it set the conditions for remission of resentment, so resolving the crisis of exile with the promise of return.
4. This self-generating, self-renewing paradigm formed that self-fulfilling prophecy that all Judaisms have offered as the generative tension and critical symbolic structure of their systems.

Clearly, the paradigm that has imprinted itself on the history of this period did not emerge from, was not generated by, the events of the age. First came the system, its worldview and way of life—formed whole we know not where or by whom. Then came the selection, by the system, of consequential events, and their patterning into systemic propositions. And finally, at a third stage (of indeterminate length) came the formation and composition of the holy writings that would express the logic of the system and state those "events" that the system would select or invent for its own expression. Since chief among the propositions of the system as the Torah of Moses defined it is the notion of the election of Israel effected in the covenant, we may say that, systemically speaking, Israel—the Israel of the Torah and historical-prophetic books of the sixth and fifth centuries—selected itself.

At the very foundations of the original and generative Judaic paradigm, the account of the events from 586 (when the Israelites were exiled to Babylonia) to ca. 450 (when they had returned to Zion and rebuilt the Temple), we find history systemically selected. That is, by definition it is invented, not described. This would make slight difference—everyone understands the mythopoeic (myth-creating) power of belief—except for one thing. We err if we think that a particular experience, going into exile and returning home again, was subjected to interpretation, that is, was transformed by a religious system into a paradigm of the life of the social group. What really happened is that the particular experience—exile, return—itself happened, to begin with, in the minds and imaginations of the *authors* of Scripture. No one who left Jerusalem in 586 came home in 450,[9] so as a totality, the Pentateuch's narrative was not an experience interpreted, but invented; and once people imagined things in that way rather than in some other, they also found in real, everyday experiences examples of the same experience of exile and return that, to begin with, they were predisposed to find by the lessons of the faith.

But as to its restoration and reconstruction, people clearly differed—the incessant complaints of the postexilic prophets about the neglected condition of the altar attest to this fact. No one denied that some of Israel had stayed home, some had gone into exile. But as to the exclusion of those who had stayed home and not undergone the normative experience of alienation and return, opinion surely differed, since it was only by force that the dissolution of families was effected.

The same is so for a long list of systemic givens, none of them, as a matter of fact, "given" and self-evident except to those to whom they were self-evident. It follows that it is Scripture—and Scripture alone—that says that what happened was that Israel died and was reborn, was punished through exile and then forgiven, and that therefore—and this is critical—to be *Israel* is in a genealogical sense (since no individual can have lived that long) to have gone into exile and returned to Zion. But the very normative standing of that experience forms what was at issue in the time of Ezra and Nehemiah, who imposed upon the Judean society of the fifth century the norm of exile and return, that is to say, of death and resurrection.

What emerges therefore is a striking paradox. What happened to people does not correspond to what people were told had happened. The paradigm imparted to events that meaning that was expressed in narrative and law alike; the paradigm, not events, generated meaning. Most people after 586 stayed in Babylonia but called it exile. A few migrated to Jerusalem, where they found themselves a tiny minority among a larger group of Israelites whose ways they found improper—but told themselves they had come "home," had "returned to Zion." Call it what you will, by their own word they did not find much familiar about this "home" of theirs, since most of the people who lived there followed rules they declared alien. So on both sides, the "exiles" and those who had come "home," the systemic paradigm transformed what was happening into something else.

The Persistence of the Paradigm: Why All Judaisms Rehearse the Pentateuchal Judaism

But why did the system persist as paradigmatic? Why did its structure prove definitive long after the political facts had shifted dramatically, indeed, had ceased to pertain at all? As long as the Torah continued to be authoritative for Israel, the experience to which it originally constituted a profound and systematic response was recapitulated, age after age. Reading and authoritative exegesis of the original Scripture that preserved and portrayed the system perpetuated it as paradigmatic. Jews repeated: "Your descendants will be aliens living in a land that is not theirs . . . but I will punish that nation whose slaves they are, and after that they shall come out with great possessions" (Gen. 15:13–14).

The long-term reason for the persistence of the priests' Judaism as the self-evident explanation of Israel's life derives from two facts. First, as I have suggested, the Scriptures themselves retained their authority. But that begs the question. Why should the Scriptures remain authoritative? Another answer is that the priests' system in its basic structure addressed, *but also created*, a continuing and chronic social fact of Israel's life.

Of course, so long as the people perceived the world in such a way as to make urgent the question that Scripture framed and answered, Scripture appeared authoritative beyond all need for argument. It enjoyed (self-evidently) the status of God's will revealed to Israel. And the people perceived the world in this way for a very long time. Yet Scripture gained its own authority, too, independent of the circumstance of society. The priests' paradigm therefore imposed itself even in situations in which its fundamental premises hardly pertained. Thus, although when the world imposed upon Jewry questions of a different order, Jews went in search of more answers and even different answers, a great many Jews continued to envision the world through that original perspective created in the aftermath of destruction and restoration; that is, to see the world as a gift instead of a given, themselves as chosen for a life of special suffering but also of special reward. And the Judaism of Holocaust and Redemption—destruction of the Jews of Europe linked as a cause for the formation of the Jewish state, the State of Israel—fits quite neatly into the Pentateuchal paradigm. Indeed, it fits more comfortably than other Judaisms of a more classical character, for here we have exile in its most brutal form, mass murder, followed by restoration in its most concrete and real form in all of the history of the Jews, an actual return to the Land of Israel and rebuilding of the State of Israel. Ironically, then, although in any age but this one the power of the paradigm might be subject to dispute, in the twentieth century it enjoys the status of self-evident truth. It seems an indisputable fact.

I therefore see two reasons for the perennial power of the priests' system and perspective. One is that the generative tension precipitated by the interpretation of the Jews' life as exile and return, and that had formed the critical center of the Torah of Moses, persisted. Therefore the urgent question answered by the Torah retained its original character and definition; and the self-evident answer, read in the synagogue every Sabbath morning as well as on Monday and on Thursday, retained its relevance. With the persistent problem renewing, generation after generation, that same resentment, the product of a memory of loss and restoration joined to the recognition, in the here and now, of the danger of a further loss, the priests' authoritative answer would lose its power to persist and to persuade. But the other reason is that people saw what was not always there, because through the Torah of Moses they were taught to.

The second of the two reasons—the one explaining the long-term power of the Judaic system of the priests to shape the worldview and way of life of the Israel addressed by that Judaism—is the more important: The question answered by the Five Books of Moses persisted at the center of the national life and remained, if chronic, also urgent. The answer provided by the Pentateuch therefore retained its self-evident importance. The question persisted, to be sure, because Scripture kept reminding people to ask that question, to see the world as the world was described, in Scripture's mythic terms, out of the perception of the experience of exile and return. To those troubled by the question of exile and return, that is, the chronic allegation that Israel's group-life did not constitute a given but formed a gift accorded on conditions and stipulations, then, the answer enjoyed the status of (mere) fact.

The human condition takes on heightened intensity when God cares what you eat for lunch, on the one side, but will reward you for having a boiled egg, on the other. For a small, uncertain people, captured by a vision of distant horizons, behind and ahead, a mere speck on the crowded plain of humanity, such a message bore its powerful and immediate message as a map of meaning. Israel's death and resurrection—as the Torah portrayed matters—therefore left nothing as it had been and changed everything for all time. But the matter—central to the history of Judaism—demands yet another angle of analysis. We have to ask what was at stake and try to penetrate into the deepest layers of the structure to state the issues at their most abstract and general. For the sacred persistence in the end rested on judgments found self-evident in circumstances remote from the original world subject to those judgments.

Why then does the paradigm of exile and return characterize all later Judaisms? Because the problems addressed and solved by the Judaism of the Five Books of Moses remained chronic long after the period of its formation, from the seventh century onward down to its final editing in the time of Ezra and Nehemiah. Since that question would remain a perplexity continuing to trouble Israelites for a long time, it is not surprising that the categorical structure of the Torah's answer to it, so profound and fundamental in its character, should for its part have continued to define systems that would attract and impress people.

The Torah encapsulated, as normative and recurrent, the experience of the loss and recovery of the Land and of political sovereignty. Israel, because of its (in its mind) amazing experience, had attained a self-consciousness that continuous existence in a single place under a long-term government denied others (and had denied Israel before 586). There was nothing given, nothing to be merely celebrated, or at least taken for granted, in the life of a nation that had ceased to be a nation on its own land and then once more had regained that (once-normal, now abnormal) condition. Judaism took shape as the system that accounted for the death and resurrection of Israel, the Jewish people, and pointed for the source of renewed life toward sanctification now, and salvation at the end of time.

But Judaism as it flourished from antiquity to our own day appeals not only to the Pentateuch or even to the entire Hebrew Scriptures. Its canon encompasses a range of holy books that speak of the Pentateuch as "the written Torah" and calls into being a Torah that is not written but formulated and preserved in memory, a part of the one whole Torah revealed by God to Moses at Sinai that is called "the oral Torah." Hence, we know the formative history of Judaism does not close with the Pentateuch. But on the basis of what we have already observed, we also anticipate that a principal event will be selected by a nascent system to account for its origin, and to that event we shall now turn.

The Judaism of the Dual Torah

A Simple Definition

Let me begin with a clear definition of the particular Judaism that predominated from postbiblical times to our own day, the one that appeals to the myth that the Torah was revealed to Moses at Sinai through two media, oral and written (hence "dual Torah"). This Judaism of the dual Torah that came to full expression in the writings of the sages of the Land of Israel ("the Holy Land," "Palestine") during the later fourth and fifth centuries C.E. takes a position separate from all prior Judaisms, as well as from those that follow it (C.E.: Common Era. This Jewish denomination of time parallels years A.D.). What distinguishes this Judaism is precisely its doctrine of the dual media by which God's will for Israel, contained in the Torah revealed at Sinai, came down from ancient times. Specifically, this Judaism maintains that when God revealed the Torah at Sinai, God[10] transmitted the Torah through writing and memory. That is, there were effectively two Torahs, a written one and a Torah transmitted orally and memorized by great prophets, then by sages, down to the time of this particular Judaism's sages represented in their holy books, transcriptions of the originally oral Torah of Sinai.

This orally formulated and orally transmitted Torah—this memorized Torah—derives from this Judaism and no other, for we find the substance of the memorized Torah, that is, the oral Torah, in the writings of the rabbis of late antiquity who wrote their books from about 200 to 640 C.E. while referring to an oral tradition they claimed began at Sinai. The first document of this oral Torah was the Mishnah, a philosophical law code that reached its final form about the year 200 C.E. Further writings that fall into the classification of (oral) Torah include the Tosefta (a collection of supplements to the Mishnah's laws), a commentary on the Mishnah composed in the Land of Israel and called the Talmud of the Land of Israel (ca. 400 C.E.), a second such commentary produced in the Jewish communities of Babylonia and called the Talmud of Babylonia (ca. 600 C.E.), and commentaries on the written Torah by the sages of the age (e.g., Sifra based on Leviticus, Sifré based on Numbers, another Sifré, this one based on Deuteronomy, Genesis Rabbah, Leviticus Rabbah, and the like). All of these other documents, but especially the Mishnah and its two great Talmuds, contain the teachings of sages in late antiquity from the first through the sixth centuries of the Common Era. All together they form that other oral Torah that God revealed to Moses at Sinai—now apparently written down.

While the Judaism that reached its first formulation in writing began in 200 with the Mishnah (itself drawing upon statements formulated over the preceding century or so), it is only in the Talmud of the Land of Israel (ca. 400) and its closely allied documents, Genesis Rabbah and Leviticus Rabbah, that this Judaism's principal and indicative doctrines, symbols, and beliefs came to full and complete expression. The Mishnah shows us a version of the Judaism of the dual Torah that reached a fixed form before Christianity made an impact on the Judaic sages, while the Talmud of the Land of Israel and its associates show us the changes that occurred through its encounter with Christianity as that religion triumphed in the Roman state.[11] The Talmud evolved at the end of that critical century which began with the Roman Emperor Constantine's declaring Christianity licit, continued with his declaring it favored, and ended with the Empire's declaring it the state religion. Thus the first full statement of that Judaism of the dual Torah is contained in the Talmud of the Land of Israel and in complementary materials in other documents of the same age.

Precisely how the Judaism of the dual Torah responded to the crisis at hand remains to be seen. Most important is that the Judaism that took shape in the Land of Israel in the fourth century (attested by documents brought to closure in the fifth) responded to that Christianity and in particular to its challenge to the Israel of that place and time in such a way that it flourished, in Israel, the Jewish people, so long as the West was Christian. That, sum and substance, is the story of the most important Judaic system of all times. Now let us turn back and follow the story from its beginnings.

The Crisis of 70 and the Formation of Rabbinic Judaism

The Temple of Jerusalem, where sacrifices were offered to God, constituted the focus of Pentateuchal Judaism. Indeed, the cycle of holy time was marked by sacrifice. Thus the lives of the patriarchs repeatedly drew them into relationship with the sacrificial cult in various holy places, but especially in Jerusalem, and the laws of the Torah dealt in detail with the sacrifices, the priests, the maintenance of the priestly caste, and other cultic matters. So the power of the Torah composed in this time lay in its focus on the Temple.

This central Temple cult, with its total exclusion of the non-Israelite, raised high those walls of separation we have talked about between Jew and "other." They underlined such distinctiveness as already existed. What made Israel Israel was the center, the altar; the life of Israel flowed from the altar. But in 70 C.E., in the course of a war fought by Jews against Roman rule in the Land of Israel, Jerusalem fell and the Temple, except for the western wall of the platform on which it stood, was destroyed.

Over the next six hundred years, a variety of writings attest to the formation of a system of Judaism deriving from the Pentateuch but autonomous of it—a Judaism without a temple. In the case of the principal Judaism that emerged, the Judaism of the dual Torah, written (the Hebrew Scriptures) and oral (now preserved in writings on the authority of sages of the age [rabbis]), the new Judaism addressed the change in the cultic realities of Israel as well as in their political context. Moreover, since during this same time, a variety of Christian systems took shape, drawing upon the Hebrew Scriptures (which they designated in due course "the Old Testament") yet autonomous of them, the new Judaism addressed the critical issues raised by nascent Christianity. And this Judaism predominated from late antiquity to our own day precisely because of its success in addressing the following two critical problems that arose from political changes in the Jews' condition: their loss of standing as a political entity and the triumph of Christianity in the Roman Empire. As long as political subordination and religious disappointment and resentment persisted, in other words, for long centuries, the Jews drew upon the writings of this period. Only when the world in which they lived found its definitions elsewhere than in Christianity, only when their political circumstances were vastly changed from those that prevailed until the formation of the nation-state within the capitalist world, did new Judaisms emerge—each, as we might expect, asking its urgent question and offering its "self-evident" answer.

The Urgent Question and Self-Evident Answer of the Judaic System of the Dual Torah, Oral and Written

The principal question formulated by the sages who produced writings beyond 70—writings that ultimately were portrayed as the oral part of the one whole Torah of Moses, "our lord," our *rabbenu*—centered upon the sanctification of Israel now that the Temple, the locus of holiness, lay in ruins and the cult was no more. The Judaism of the dual Torah set forth a twin ideal: *sanctification* of the everyday life in the here and now, which when fully realized would lead to *salvation* of all Israel in the age to come. But what remained to be sanctified, as the Temple had been sanctified through its cult, now that the Temple was gone? One locus of sanctification endured beyond 70: the holy people itself. That people's life would be made holy—in the Holy Land at first, but later, as this Judaism spread across the world through exile in the Diaspora, everywhere the people lived. Holy, of course, meant separate and distinct from the ordinary, and the chronic question of who is a Jew and what is Israel would find its self-evident response in the same categories as the Pentateuchal system had defined for itself.

The stress of the Judaism of the dual Torah, of the post-Temple sages or rabbis who constructed it, on the sanctification of the home and the paradigmatic power of the Temple for the home points to a more extreme position within the priestly paradigm than that of the priests who wrote parts of Exodus, Leviticus, and Numbers. What the priests wanted for the Temple, the dual Torah's sages wanted for the community, Israel, at large. The premise of the written Torah, we recall, rested on a simple allegation: If Israel observes the terms of the covenant, leading a sanctified life, Israel will enjoy prosperity in a serene land, a national life outside of history. The traumatic event of annihilation and rebirth, of death and resurrection of the nation (as manifested in the reworking of ancient Israelite writings into the Pentateuch) brought about yearning for one thing above all: no more. The picture of what had happened presented solace—that is why people wanted to accept the portrait of their world. The restoration gave Israel a second chance at life, but Israel also could rely on its knowledge of the rules that governed its national life, those of the Torah and its repeated allegations of an agreement, or covenant, between Israel and God, to make certain there would be no more experiences of exile and alienation (whether or not followed by reconciliation and restoration). This same paradigm governed in the framing of the Judaism of the dual Torah. What shifted was the redefinition of salvation from the here and now to the end of time. And that change, of course, was not only plausible, it also was necessary in light of the destruction of the Temple in 70.

The reason for the transfer of the hope for salvation from now to the end of time derives from a political event that in some ways bore greater weight than the destruction of the Temple in 70. That event was the failure to recover the city and rebuild the Temple through war three generations later. Had the war been successful, it could have replicated the events that began in 586 and ended in 450. That is, it could have restored the people to the Land and the government and temple to Jerusalem. Indeed, when the war broke out in 132, the Jews evidently expected that after three generations, God would call an end to the punishment as God had done by restoring the Temple some "seventy years" after its first destruction (586). But that did not happen. Israel again suffered defeat—a defeat worse than before. The Temple lay in permanent ruins; Jerusalem became a forbidden city for Jews. So Israel, the Jewish people, necessarily set out to assimilate enduring defeat.

The Mishnah's Judaism of Sanctification Without the Temple

The Mishnah manifests the Judaism that took shape in the aftermath of the Jews' defeat in this Second War against Rome. (This is Ben Kosiba's ["Bar Kokhba's"] revolt. It was fought from 132 through 135.) Although later considered the written manifestation of the oral tradition that formed part of the Torah received by Moses at Sinai, and accorded proportionate status, the Mishnah was in fact a philosophical system in the form of a law code that responded to problems arising from the destruction of the Temple and Bar Kokhba's subsequent defeat. When in the aftermath of the destruction in 70 C.E. and the still more disheartening defeat of 135 the Mishnah's sages worked out a Judaism without a Temple and a cult, they produced in the Mishnah a system of sanctification focused on the holiness of the priesthood, the cultic festivals, the Temple and its sacrifices, and on the rules for protecting that holiness from levitical uncleanness. Four of the six divisions of the Mishnah expound on this single theme.

In an act of supererogatory imagination, defying the facts of the circumstance of a defeated nation, the Mishnah's system-builders composed a world at rest, perfect and complete, made holy because it is complete and perfect. In mythic terms, the Mishnah reaches back to creation to interpret the world of destruction round about. The system of the Mishnah confronts the fall from Eden with Eden, the world in time beyond the closure of Jerusalem to Israel with the timeless world on the eve of the Sabbath of Creation: "Thus the heavens and the earth were finished and all the host of them. And on the seventh day God finished his work which he had done, and he rested on the seventh day from all his work which he had done. So God blessed the seventh day and hallowed it, because on it God rested from all his work which he had done in creation" (Gen. 2:1–3).

The Mishnah's framers posited an economy embedded in a social system awaiting the seventh day, and that day's divine act of sanctification which, as at the creation of the world, would set the seal of holy rest upon an again-complete creation. That would be a creation that was well ordered, with all things called by their rightful names, in their proper classification, from the least to the greatest, and from the many to the One. There is no place for action and actors when what is besought is no action whatsoever, but only unchanging perfection. There is room only for a description of how things are, for the present tense, for a sequence of completed statements and static problems. All the action lies within, in how these statements are made. Once they stand fully expressed, when nothing remains to be said, nothing remains to be done. There is no need for actors, whether political entities such as king, scribes, priests, or economic entities, householders.

That is why the Mishnah's framers invented a utopia, one that exists nowhere in particular, a fantasy related to whom it may concern. The politics of Judaism began in the imagination of a generation of intellectuals who, in the aftermath of the Jerusalem government's and Temple's destruction (70) and the military defeat Jews suffered three generations later (132–135), had witnessed the end of the political system and structure that the Jews had known for the preceding millennium. The political theory of Judaism laid out political institutions and described how they should work. In that way these intellectuals, who enjoyed no documented access to power of any kind and who certainly were unable to coerce many people to do very much, sorted out issues of power. They took account, in mind at least, of the issues of legitimate coercion within Israel, the holy people, which they considered more than a voluntary association, more than a community formed around a cult.[12]

The Judaism shaped by the Mishnah consists of a coherent worldview and comprehensive way of living. It is a worldview that speaks of transcendent things, a way of life in response to the supernatural meaning of what is done, a heightened and deepened perception of the sanctification of Israel in deed and in deliberation. Sanctification means two things: First, it distinguishes Israel in all its dimensions from the world in all its ways; second, it establishes the stability, order, regularity, predictability, and reliability of Israel at moments and in contexts of danger. Danger means instability, disorder, irregularity, uncertainty, and betrayal. Each topic of the system as a whole takes up a critical and indispensable moment or context of social being. Each orders what is disorderly and dangerous. Through what is said in regard to each of the Mishnah's principal topics, what the system as a whole wishes to declare is fully expressed. Yet if the parts severally and jointly give the message of the whole, the whole cannot exist without all of the parts, so well-joined and carefully crafted are they all.

That brings us to a detailed account of the six components of the Mishnah's complete system. The critical issue in the economic life, which means in farming, is in two parts, revealed in the first division. First, Israel, as tenant on God's Holy Land, maintains the property in the ways God requires, keeping the rules that mark the Land and its crops as holy. Next, the hour at which the sanctification of the Land comes to form a critical mass, namely, in the ripened crops, is the moment ponderous with danger and heightened holiness. Israel's will so affects the crops as to mark a part of them as holy, the rest of them as available for common use. The human will is determinative in the process of sanctification.

Second, in the second division, what happens in the Land at certain times, at appointed times, marks off spaces of the Land as holy in yet another way. The center of the Land and the focus of its sanctification is the Temple. There the produce of the Land is received and given back to God, the one who created and sanctified the Land. At these unusual moments of sanctification, the inhabitants of the Land in their social being in villages enter a state of spatial sanctification. That is to say, the village boundaries mark off holy space, within which one must remain during the holy time. This is expressed in two ways. First, the Temple itself observes and expresses the special, recurring holy time. Second, the villages of the Land are brought into alignment with the Temple, forming a complement and completion to the Temple's sacred being. The advent of the appointed times precipitates a spatial reordering of the Land, so that the boundaries of the sacred are matched and mirrored in village and in Temple. At the heightened holiness marked by these moments of appointed times, therefore, the occasion for an affective sanctification is worked out. Like the harvest, the advent of an appointed time, a pilgrim festival, also a sacred season, is made to express that regular, orderly, and predictable sort of sanctification for Israel that the system as a whole seeks.

If for a moment we now leap over the next two divisions, the third and fourth, we come to the fifth and sixth divisions, namely holy things and purities, those which deal with the everyday and the ordinary, as against the special moments of harvest, on the one side, and special time or season, on the other. These form the counterpart of the divisions of agriculture and appointed times.

The fifth division is about the Temple on ordinary days. The Temple, the locus of sanctification, is conducted in a wholly routine and trustworthy, punctilious manner. The one thing that may unsettle matters is the intention and will of the human actor. This is subjected to carefully prescribed limitations and remedies. The division of holy things generates its companion, the sixth division, the one on cultic cleanness, purities. The relationship between the two is like that between agriculture and appointed times, the former locative, the latter utopian, the former dealing with the fields, the latter with the interplay between fields and altar.

Here too, in the sixth division, once we speak of the one place of the Temple, we address, too, the cleanness that pertains to every place. A system of cleanness, taking into account what imparts uncleanness and how this is done, what is subject to uncleanness, and how that state is overcome—that system is fully expressed, once more, in response to the participation of the human will. Without the wish and act of a human being, the system does not function. It is inert. Sources of uncleanness, which come naturally and not by volition, and modes of purification, which work naturally, and not by human intervention, remain inert until human will has imparted susceptibility to uncleanness, that is, introduced into the system, that food and drink, bed, pot, chair, and pan, which to begin with form the focus of the system. The movement from sanctification to uncleanness takes place when human will and work precipitate it.

This now brings us back to the middle divisions, the third and fourth, on women and damages. They take their place in the structure of the whole by showing the congruence, within the larger framework of regularity and order, of human concerns of family and farm, politics and workaday transactions among ordinary people. For without attending to these matters, the Mishnah's system does not encompass what, at its foundations, it is meant to comprehend and order. So what is at issue is fully cogent with the rest. In the case of women, the third division, attention focuses upon the point of disorder marked by the transfer of that disordering anomaly, woman, from the regular status provided by one man, to the equally trustworthy status provided by another. That is the point at which the Mishnah's interests are aroused: once more, predictably, the moment of disorder.

In the case of damages, the fourth division, there are two important concerns. First, there is the paramount interest in preventing, so far as possible, the disorderly rise of one person and fall of another, and in sustaining the status quo of the economy, the house and household, of Israel, the holy society in eternal stasis. Second, there is the necessary concomitant in the provision of a system of political institutions to carry out the laws that preserve the balance and steady state of persons.

The two divisions that take up topics of concrete and material concern, the formation and dissolution of families and the transfer of property in that connection, the transactions, both through torts and through commerce, which lead to exchanges of property and the potential dislocation of the state of families in society, are both locative and utopian. They deal with the concrete locations in which people make their lives, household and street and field, the sexual and commercial exchanges of a given village. But they pertain to the life of all Israel, both in the Land and otherwise. These two divisions, together with the household ones of appointed times, constitute the sole opening outward toward the life of utopian Israel, that diaspora in the far reaches of the ancient world, in the endless span of time. This community from the Mishnah's perspective is not only in exile but unaccounted for, outside the system, for the Mishnah declines to recognize and take it into account. Israelites who dwell in the land of (unclean) death instead of in the Holy Land simply fall outside of the range of (holy) life. Priests, who must remain cultically clean, may not leave the Land—and neither may most of the Mishnah.

The Mishnah's principal message, which makes the Judaism of this document and of its social components distinctive and cogent, is that man[13] is at the center of creation, the head of all creatures upon earth, corresponding to God in heaven, in whose image man is made. The way in which the Mishnah makes this simple and fundamental statement is to impute power to man to inaugurate and initiate those corresponding processes, sanctification and uncleanness, which play so critical a role in the Mishnah's account of reality. The will of man, expressed through the deed of man, is the active power in the world. Will and deed constitute those actors of creation which work upon neutral realms, subject to either sanctification or uncleanness: the Temple and table, the field and family, the altar and hearth, woman, time, space, transactions in the material world and in the world above as well. An object, a substance, a transaction, even a phrase or a sentence is inert but may be made holy, when the interplay of the will and deed of man arouses or generates its potential to be sanctified. Each may be treated as ordinary or (where relevant) made unclean by the neglect of the will and inattentive act of man. Just as the entire system of uncleanness and holiness awaits the intervention of man, which imparts the capacity to become unclean upon what was formerly inert, or which removes the capacity to impart cleanness from what was formerly in its natural and puissant condition, so in the other ranges of reality, man is at the center on earth, just as is God in heaven. Man is counterpart and partner and creation, in that, like God he has power over the status and condition of creation, through his intentionality putting everything in its proper place, through the exercise of his will calling everything by its rightful name. The goal then was the restoration of creation to its original perfection. Then it was that God ceased from labor, blessed creation, and sanctified it.

The Mishnah enjoyed two centuries of study and amplification. Indeed, a massive system deriving from and connecting with the Mishnah's but essentially distinct from it emerged in the Talmud of the Land of Israel (closed ca. 400, as mentioned previously). The urgent question that predominates in that enormous document, and that takes the form of an extended elaboration of the Mishnah, is salvation: When and why will it come, and, above all, how long must it be postponed? The urgency of the issue derived from two events that we have already touched upon. In 312 Constantine legalized Christianity, and in the course of the next three generations, the state became officially Christian. In the course of suppressing paganism, the Christian state adopted rules that for the first time since the Maccabees, in the second century B.C., denied the licit practice of Judaism. That trauma was intensified by a brief moment of relief, when one of the heirs of Constantine, Julian, left Christianity, reaffirmed paganism, and, in 361, proposed to discredit Christianity by permitting the Jews to rebuild the Temple in Jerusalem. Unfortunately, he died soon afterward and nothing came of the project.

The Talmuds' Judaism of Sanctification and Salvation

The urgency with which the Jews pursued the question of salvation is hardly a surprise. Consider that from their own political triumph and the Jews' deep disappointment by Julian's failed scheme, the Christians claimed that the political shifts in the standing of Christianity and Judaism confirmed the truth of Christianity and underlined the falsity of Judaism. In particular, Christianity stressed the falsity of the Jews' hope for a coming messiah. It argued that the Jews had been saved in the time of the return to Zion (450 B.C.E.). That return, Christians claimed, fulfilled the Old Testament prophecies of Israel's salvation. But from that moment, by rejecting the messiahship of Jesus, Jews had lost all further standing in the divine scheme for saving humanity. So the question of salvation turned from a chronic concern to an acute crisis for the Jews—in positive and negative ways. And predictably, it was addressed by the sages who revised the Mishnah by setting forth the Talmud of the Land of Israel.

Two hundred years after that Talmud took shape (ca. 400), a second one, the Talmud of Babylonia, recast matters in a permanent and authoritative form (ca. 600). From then to the present, "the Talmud," meaning the Talmud of Babylonia, together with its commentaries, codes of laws deriving from it, and institutions of autonomous administration resting on it, has defined the life of most Jews and the Judaic system that prevailed as normative. Its successful definition of the essentials of Judaism for Jews living in the Christian and Muslim worlds depends on the compelling power of its account of who is a Jew, what it means to be Israel, and how the holy people must work out its life in the here and now so as to attain salvation at the end of time. This was, then, a Judaism intersecting with, but essentially asymmetrical with, the Mishnah's Judaism. It was a system for salvation focused on the salvific power of the sanctification of the holy people.

And this brings us back to the method, for studying a religion, of asking what question a religious system proposes to answer. Reading the statements of a system as answers to urgent questions, we reconstruct the issues that engaged its framers. And when we listen to the silences of the Mishnah, as well as to its points of stress, we hear a single, strong message. It is the message of a Judaism that answered one encompassing question concerning the enduring sanctification of Israel, the people, the Land, the way of life. What, in the aftermath of the destruction of the holy place and holy cult, remained of the sanctity of the holy caste, the priesthood, the Holy Land, and, above all, the holy people and its holy way of life? The answer: Sanctity persists, indelibly, in *Israel, the people,* in its way of life, in its Land, in its priesthood, in its food, in its mode of sustaining life, in its manner of procreating and so sustaining the nation. That holiness would endure. And the Mishnah then laid out the structures of sanctification. It detailed what it means to live a holy life. But that answer found itself absorbed, in time to come, within a successor system, with its own points of stress and emphasis. That successor system, both continuous and asymmetrical with the Mishnah, would take over the Mishnah and turn it into the one whole Torah of Moses, our rabbi, that became Judaism.

What the Judaism of the dual Torah as portrayed in the two Talmuds did was shift the focus from the Temple and its supernatural history to the people Israel and its natural, this-worldly history. Once Israel, holy Israel, had come to form the counterpart to the Temple and its supernatural life, that other history—Israel's—would stand at the center of things. Accordingly, a new sort of memorable event came to the fore in the Talmud of the Land of Israel. It was the story of Israel's suffering—remembrance of that suffering on the one side, and an effort to explain events of such tragedy on the other. And that story enjoyed the standing of self-evident, indeed self-validating truth because Jews found that it corresponded to and satisfactorily explained the powerless political situation they found themselves in.

The components of the historical theory of Israel's sufferings were manifold. First and foremost, history taught moral lessons. Historical events entered into the construction of a teleology for the Talmud of the Land of Israel's system of Judaism as a whole. What the law demanded reflected the consequences of wrongful action on the part of Israel. So, again, Israel's own deeds defined the events of history. Rome's dominance, like Assyria's and Babylonia's, in fact arose from Israel's provoking divine wrath—the empire's anger was surrogate for God's. So Israel had to learn the lesson of its history to take command of its own destiny. But this notion of determining one's own destiny should not be misunderstood. The framers of the Talmud of the Land of Israel were not telling the Jews to please God by complying with commandments to gain control of their own destiny. On the contrary. The paradox of the Talmud of the Land of Israel's system is that Israel can free itself of control by other nations by humbly agreeing to accept God's rule. The nations—Rome, in the present instance—rest on one side of the balance, while God rests on the other. Israel must choose between them. There is no such thing for Israel as freedom from both God and the nations, total autonomy and independence. There is only a choice of masters, a ruler on earth or a ruler in heaven. And until modern times all Jews, and in modern times a vast number of Jews, chose the dominion of God in heaven.

It is only when we come to the modern world no longer defined by Christian politics and culture that this classic Judaism ceases for many to address urgent questions, that new compositions of symbols and systems of ideas, invented in some measure out of the received writings of ancient times to be sure, arise in its place. The Judaism of the canon of the later fourth century and beyond, therefore, flourished when the world to which it spoke found persuasive not its answers alone, but its central questions. And that Judaism ceased to speak to Jews when its message failed to answer the questions Jews found they had to answer. The critical issue, therefore, was how far this Judaism fitted contemporary circumstances, not how obvious its answers appeared. And circumstance, to begin with, found salient traits in the conditions of politics, in people acting together in an organized way.

The History of Judaism: An Overview

The Four Periods of the History of Judaism

Because of the predominant position of the Judaism of the dual Torah from late antiquity to modern times, we may sum up the history of Judaism with a simple statement of fact. The norm-setting position of that Judaism was such that until the nineteenth century all heresies within Judaism, all schisms and fissures in the social fabric, defined themselves against it. And all secondary expansions, revisions, developments, and modes of renewal that came to expression adopted the mythic structure and much of the canonical writings of that same Judaism. Consequently, the history of Judaism from late antiquity to modern times proves cogent, since we can find a place for all later Judaic systems until the late nineteenth century either within, or by contrast to, that one Judaism and its system. Within this picture, we may then identify the following periods in the history of Judaism(s).

The histories of Judaisms are to be divided into four periods. First came *the age of the second Temple,* which we discussed in the section "The Formation of Judaism." This period stretched from the formation of the Hebrew Scriptures (ca. 586–450 B.C.E.) to the destruction of the second Temple (70 C.E.).[14] Second came *the formative age* (just described in the previous section). It stretched from 70 to the closure of the Talmud of Babylonia (ca. 600 C.E.). Third came *the classical age.* This age extended from late antiquity into the nineteenth century. Through this period, the original definition of Judaism dominated the lives of the Jewish people nearly everywhere they lived. This brings us to *the modern age,* which began in the nineteenth century and extends into our own day. During this period, an essentially religious understanding of what it means to be Israel, the Jewish people, came into competition with other views and other symbolic expressions of those views.

Since we have discussed the first two periods extensively in the two preceding sections, we now turn to the third.

THE CLASSICAL PERIOD OF JUDAISM (640–1789)

When shortly after the closure of the Talmud of Babylonia, Islam swept across the Middle East and North Africa (640 C.E.), the Christian ocean evaporated. Vast groups that had been Christian for half a millennium accepted Islam. But the small pools of Judaism scarcely receded—they ran deep. Whereas Christianity, which had triumphed by the sword of Constantine, fell before the sword of Muḥammad, the Judaic system that accounted for and made tolerable Judaic subordination in the here and now explained this new event and sustained the Jews. Whereas lands from Syria and Palestine to Egypt, North Africa, and Spain, which had been Christian for many centuries, turned Muslim in a few decades, this consolidated Judaic system persisted into the nineteenth century in Eastern Europe, and into the mid-twentieth century in Muslim countries. Indeed, it flourished, which is to say, it remained the self-evident answer to the urgent question.

The rise of Islam thus marks the end of the formative period for the Judaism that would prove normative. It marks the onset of the classical period, during which a single Judaism, the one teaching the dual Torah of Sinai, came to full definition and predominated. The year 1787 marks the end of this period. In that year, by explicitly espousing religious freedom and cultural pluralism, the American Constitution at last inaugurated a new political and cultural setting for the Jews in Europe and America. (European readers will justifiably prefer the date of 1789, the French Revolution.)

During that time, whatever important ideas or issues developed, Jews worked them out within the categories of the Judaism of the dual Torah. Thus, for example, a variety of mystical ideas and practices entered the world of Judaism and were assimilated through the Torah. And as the Moslem philosophical schools transmitted Greek modes of thought represented by Aristotle and Plato to the West, Judaism restated the truths of the Torah in these terms. In the mystical tradition, the great work was the Zohar, written toward the end of the thirteenth century in Spain. In the philosophical tradition, the most important figure was Maimonides (1135–1204). He restated the whole of Judaic law and theology in a systematic and profoundly philosophical way. Each mode of thought found an ample place well within the received canon, to which each made a massive contribution of new and authoritative writings. And each mode of thought, the mystical and the philosophical, transformed "the one whole Torah of Moses, our rabbi." In the first instance, it was transformed into an intensely felt and profound doctrine of the true nature of God's being; in the second instance it became an intellectually rich and rational statement of the Torah as truth.

This power of the one whole Torah, oral and written, to encompass and make its own essentially new ways of thought and life testifies to the classical character of this Judaism, everywhere definitive. So mysticism and philosophy alike made their contribution to the altar of the Judaism of the dual Torah.

THE MODERN AND CONTEMPORARY SCENE (1789–)

In modern times, the diversity characteristic of the period of origins has come, once again, to prevail.[15] Now the symbolic system and structure of the Judaism of the dual Torah has come to compete for Jews' attention both with other Judaic systems and with a wildly diverse range of symbols of other-than-Jewish origin and meaning. In this time, what has become of the Judaism of the dual Torah, its relation with the life of Israel, the Jewish people? (Israel is still not to be identified solely with the contemporary state, which came into being in 1948.) That Judaism endured, and it flourishes today as the religion of a small group of people.

However, from 1800 to 1900, as I have hinted, a number of other Judaic systems—other worldviews and ways of life addressed to an "Israel"—came into being. These included Reform Judaism, the first and most important of the Judaisms of modern times. Reform took shape in the first quarter of the nineteenth century. The changes it deemed "reforms" at first involved liturgy, then doctrine. Reform took seriously the political changes that accorded to Jews the rights of citizens and demanded that Jews conform, in important ways, to the common practices of their countries of citizenship.

Some decades later, in the middle of the century, Orthodoxy too admitted that one may observe the law and also enter into the civilization of the West. Affirming the divine origin of the Torah, Orthodoxy effected a selective piety. For example, it affirmed secular education in addition to study of the Torah.

This general weakening of the Judaism of the dual Torah and the development of competing Judaisms is epitomized in the Judaism of Holocaust and Redemption, which we met at the outset. That Judaism in no important way appeals to the dual Torah, or even to the Torah at all. It is formed out of a different canon of writing—and a different experience as well. Yet it addresses an urgent question and for its devotees—they are many and include this writer—it of course answers that question in a self-evident way.

The Judaisms That in Modern Times Competed with the Judaism of the Dual Torah

We return to our starting point, the dissolution of the union of the ethnic and the religious, the development of the possibility of a secular Jewish system, distinct from the religious Judaic ones. The formation of a secular ethnic identification as an alternative to a religious one forms part of the chapter on secularization in the history of religion in the West. Redefining the political civilization of the West, a vast process of secularization removed Christianity, first in the Protestant West, then in the Roman Catholic center and south, and finally in the Christian Orthodox (Greek, Russian) east, of Europe, from its established position as the definitive force. Through the nineteenth century important political movements, appealing to the nation-state and to man as the measure of all things, rather than to the Kingdom of God and to heaven's will, set forth a new politics. That program of secularization raised a fresh set of questions also for Israel, the Jewish people. In the nature of things, these had nothing whatever to do with Israel's supernatural standing in God's plan for creation and the history of humanity. Posed by political changes—just as the original questions had taken political form—the new set of urgent concerns engaged many Jews, at first particularly in Western European countries, but later on in Eastern European countries and in their extension in America, in a new set of inquiries. These inquiries produced a fresh program of self-evident answers, and those answers in the nineteenth century constituted a new set of Judaisms.

Although continuous with the received system of the dual Torah, these new Judaisms broke from that system. All of them took as their principal concern the definition and justification of change. For two hundred years all new Judaisms began by defining the character and meaning of their departure from the old, received one. The generative issue faced by each new Judaic system had to do with the secular standing and status of Jews, seen as individuals and (at least ideally) as citizens like all other citizens. That is, they took up a critical issue wholly outside the imagination of the received Judaism. Consider the slogan, "To the Jews as citizens, everything, to the Jews as a nation, nothing," which found in Israel the counterpart: "A Jew at home, a man outside."[16] That formulation violated the language rules of the Judaism of the dual Torah, for the appropriate subject of any verb was not *a Jew* but *Israel*, understood always to refer to the holy people. The received Judaism of the dual Torah did not (and did not have to) deal with the possibility that Jews could ever be individual, let alone secular, that is to say, anything other than holy Israel, all together, all at once. It made no provision for Jews to be something else unless they ceased, of course, to be Jews at all. The Judaism of the Torah could not imagine the Jews ever to be something in addition, over and above Israel. But all Judaisms of the nineteenth century sought to explain that *something else* that Jews could and should become.

Taking that same political form that the received system had adopted, the new Judaisms explained where, how, and why Jews could find a place in a new classification in addition to the category, Israel, namely, the classification of citizens of diverse countries not solely (or not mainly) members of a holy, supernatural nation of their own. In exploring the premise that

Jews could be also German or American or British or French, the Judaisms of the nineteenth century, first Reform, then Orthodox, finally Conservative, provided self-evident answers to their adherents. Concurring that Jews would continue to be Israel, all three Judaisms redefined the category, Israel, that formed the centerpiece of any Judaism. All three moreover reworked the worldview contained within the canon of the Judaism of the dual Torah and reconsidered the way of life required by it. They reread the Torah in light of the intellectual principles of the new age, and they all affirmed that Jews could live in modern society and also in accord with the Torah. Orthodoxy to be sure made fewer compromises, Reform more, but the upshot was the same. And, finally, addressing the condition of secularity in which, Jews imagined, they would find for themselves a place within the nation-states then coming into existence, the three Judaisms derived from the Judaism of the dual Torah further assumed that the secular stood distinct from the religious. Thus, in answering the question, how to be both Israel and something in addition, they posited that Judaism is, therefore always had been, a religion.

The political changes that framed the urgent question for nineteenth-century Judaisms generated quite different issues from those which people had anticipated. Jews (and not they alone) imagined that they had to find a way of being both Jewish and something else. But their enemies wanted to find a way for Jews to stop *being* altogether. And they very nearly succeeded. They began their work in the late nineteenth century, writing a chapter in the history of imperialism and racism that encompasses in a single history most of Europe, Africa, and Asia, as well as the Western Hemisphere. Part of that long and dismal story, modern anti-Semitism culminating in the Holocaust (but still a powerful force in today's world), forced upon the Jews a question they never before had had to answer. The generally benign, and only intermittently malign, settlement of Christendom and Islam ordinarily promised the Jews (at least) their lives, so the critical question facing them previously had involved merely their dignity and self-respect, of which they themselves could take charge. The new situation, by contrast, changed the Jews' existence no less drastically than had the destruction of the second Temple in Jerusalem in the year 70, and far more decisively than had the rise of Christianity to political dominance in the fourth century.

The impact of the Holocaust on Judaism began long before the advent of Hitler. During the late nineteenth century, economic changes dislocated those long-term structures that for centuries had sustained the peoples of Eastern Europe, including the Jews. While Jews identified as the critical issue the question of change—both political and religious—the world, as it happened, changed in other ways. The stakes proved those of life or death, in economics but also in politics. On the one hand, large numbers of Jews faced a condition of underemployment and near-starvation, as they did in Eastern Europe under the general changes accompanying the modernization of the economy of the region. On the other hand, anti-Semitism identified the Jews as the source of all misfortune.

Indeed, for the Judaisms of the twentieth century, the new age began in 1897, when two great systems came to dominate—Zionism, a less popular Judaism until the Holocaust and the creation of the State of Israel, and Jewish Socialism (in the form of the Jewish union, the *Bund*), the most powerful Judaism of the first half of the twentieth century. Although both fell into the classification of secular and political movements, concentrating on organizing powerful institutions of political and economic change, each in its way framed a Judaic system, for the requirements of such a system—a worldview that answered the critical question, a way of life that expressed in concrete form the elements of the worldview, the two components coherent and explicitly addressed to a clearly defined Israel—were met by both. Zionism answered the political question with the (to its devotees) self-evident answer that the Jews constituted a people, one people, and should found the Jews' state. Jewish Socialism answered the economic question (which also was a political one) with the (to its adherents) obviously true answer that the Jews had to form their own union and to undertake economic action as the Jewish sector of the working class of the entire world, united effectively to reform the economic foundations of the West. Jewish Socialism further identified itself with the Yiddish language, and the ideology of Yiddishism (speaking the Yiddish language as a principal medium of Jewish ethnic identification) joined Jewish Socialism, so that Yiddishism formed the cultural and ideological statement—the worldview, in terms of the analytical categories used here—for that Judaism for which Jewish Socialism dictated the way of life. These Jewish but not Judaic systems maintained, as self-evident truths, the positions that the Jews form a political entity like other polities (Zionism) or constitute part of the international working class and must organize themselves as a distinct ethnic entity with its own language into effective unions for class interest (Jewish Socialism).

To place into context the Judaism we already have considered, we must examine one further Judaism of note produced by the twentieth century. Like the others, this one stresses political questions, but frames its own set of urgent questions and produces its distinctive, self-evident answers. It is what I have called here the Judaism of Holocaust and Redemption. This Judaism takes as its ineluctable question the meaning of Jewish existence after the systematic murder of most of the Jews of Europe. It offers as its self-evident reply the proposition that the redemption constituted by the creation of the State of Israel serves as the other half of the whole story, bringing forth a whole experience and a meaning for it. The way of life of that distinctive Judaic system—flourishing side by side with the way of life of the continuator-Judaisms of the nineteenth century—lays emphasis upon activities in support of the State of Israel and other political causes closely related to Israeli concerns (e.g., the liberation of Soviet Jewry). Its worldview, a set of self-evident truths identified or discovered in response to this essentially political agenda, sees the Jews as beleaguered, without choices or alliances, facing a world of unremitting hostility, which, however, Jews can change to their own taste through political action.

The Two Judaisms of the Contemporary World

The Judaism of Holocaust and Redemption

The "Judaism of Holocaust and Redemption" focuses on Germany's destruction of most of Europe's Jews (1933–1945) and on the creation of the State of Israel (1948).[17] It transforms these events from secular, this-worldly occurrences into generative symbols of mythic proportions. This particular Judaism thus is communal, stressing public policy and practical action. It involves political issues, for example, policy toward the State of Israel, government assistance in helping Soviet Jews gain freedom, and matters of local politics for Canadian and American Jews (to name just two groups). Whereas the Judaism of the dual Torah proves compelling only on specific occasions (rites of passage such as puberty, marriage, death), the Judaism of Holocaust and Redemption enjoys a perpetual and nearly universal response. That is, for a great many Jews, this recent Judaism asks an urgent question and answers it with a self-evident and compelling response. This is because, although the question and answer refer to times past, the urgency derives from the here and the now. In politics, in history, in society, Jews in North America respond to the Judaism of the Holocaust and Redemption by imagining that they are someone else, living somewhere else, at another time and in another circumstance. The somewhere else is Poland in 1944, or the earthly Jerusalem of the State of Israel. Evidently, people define their everyday reality in terms of "Holocaust" and "redemption." So for this Judaism, the Holocaust defines the question, the State of Israel the answer, to the Jewish condition.

Precisely what urgent question does this Judaism address, and what are its self-evident answers? The Judaism of Holocaust and Redemption speaks of exclusion and bigotry, hatred and contempt; it asks Jews to imagine themselves in gas chambers. This provides a rationale for "being Jewish," for being essentially separate from others. Why so? The logic is that no Jew can imagine himself or herself to be utterly like "everyone else," because the beginning of being a Jew is, by definition, to be different because one is a Jew—whatever the difference may mean.

So the Judaism of Holocaust and Redemption addresses an experience that is common and—by definition—accessible to all Jews. As we shall see shortly, the Judaism of the dual Torah, by contrast, speaks of God and humanity in God's likeness, after God's image.

Is the Judaism of Holocaust and Redemption a religion? Of course it is, because it has the power to turn "being Jewish" into a mode of transcendent and mythic being. What that means is that things are not what they seem, and "we" are more than what "we" appear to be. Specifically, "we" were there in "Auschwitz," which stands for all of the centers for the murder of Jews, and "we" share, too, in the everyday life of that faraway place in which we do not live but should, the State of Israel. So the Judaism of Holocaust and Redemption turns things into something other than what they seem, teaches lessons that change the everyday into the remarkable. The Judaism of Holocaust and Redemption tells me that the everyday—the here and the now of home and family—ends not in a new Eden but in a cloud of poisonous gas, that salvation lives today, if I will it, but not here and not now. And it teaches me not to trouble to sanctify, but also not to trust, the present circumstance.

The Judaism of Holocaust and Redemption, like any other Judaism, changes the assembly of like-minded individuals into a group, an "Israel," and makes of occasions of assembly moments for the celebration of the group and the commemoration of its shared memories. Events defined, meetings called, moments such as the declaration of the independence of the State of Israel—all these define the Judaism of Holocaust and Redemption. Like the Judaism of the dual Torah, this Judaism too has a public event. These events draw people from home and family to collectivity and community. A mark of the importance of this other Judaism is that it has the capacity to draw more people into public activity than the synagogue and its Judaism. Most of the organized and collective life of the Jews as an ethnic group appeals to the myth and symbols of this Judaism of Holocaust and Redemption. That is why it is important.

As we have noticed, the power of the Judaism of Holocaust and Redemption lies in its capacity to answer the urgent question, How are Jews distinct? The Judaism of Holocaust and Redemption surfaced in the late 1960s, at the same time as blacks, native and ethnic Americans, women, and sexual minorities attained prominence. Paradoxically, that whole movement of rediscovery of difference resulted from the completion of America's work of assimilation. Once people spoke English without a foreign accent, once they had assimilated American civilization and its norms, they could think about learning Polish or Yiddish or Norwegian once more. It then became safe and charming. So just as black students got interested in ethnically characteristic food, Jewish students discovered they wanted kosher food. In that context the Judaism of Holocaust and Redemption came into sharp focus, with its answers to unavoidable questions deemed to relate to public policy. Let me frame the urgent questions as the participants do. They are these. Who are we? Why should we be Jewish? What does it mean to be Jewish? How do we relate to Jews in other times and places? What is "Israel," meaning the State of Israel, to us, and what are we to it? Who are we in American society? These and other questions form the agenda for the Judaism of Holocaust and Redemption. And the self-evident answers derive from the existence of the State of Israel as a final solution to the Jewish problem, the place where, if you have to go somewhere, they have to take you in. The very existence of the State of Israel allows Jews everywhere to live with a measure of watchful security.

Synagogues, except on specified occasions, appeal to few, but activities that express the competing Judaism of Holocaust and Redemption appeal to nearly everybody. That is, nearly all American Jews identify with the State of Israel and regard its welfare as more than a secular good, as a metaphysical necessity—the companion chapter to the Holocaust. Nearly all American Jews not only support the State of Israel, but they also regard their own "being Jewish" as inextricably bound up with the meaning they impute to the Jewish state. In many ways these Jews every day of their lives relive the terror-filled years in which European Jews were wiped out—*and every day they do something about it.* It is as if people spent their lives trying to live out a cosmic myth and, through rites of expiation and regeneration, accomplished the goal of purification and renewal. Access to the life of feeling and experience, to the way of life that made one distinctive without leaving the person terribly different from everybody else, is gained in the Judaic system of Holocaust and Redemption. It presents an immediately accessible message, cast in extreme emotions of terror and triumph, its round of endless activity demanding only spare time. That Judaism realizes in a poignant way the conflicting demands of Jewish Americans to be intensely Jewish, but only once in a while. It provides a means of expressing difference in public and in politics while not exacting much of a cost in meaningful everyday difference from others.

Private Judaism and Public Judaism: The Separation of the Family from the Corporate Community

We learn about the condition of religion in the contemporary world from the coexistence of a private and familial and conventionally religious

Judaism, and a public and political and (on the surface) more ethnic than religious Judaism. Why do these two distinct Judaisms persist, the one for home and family, the other for community and public life? It is because of what people call "the privatization" of religion. And this is how the Jews accommodate themselves to the definition of religion as something personal and individual and familial, not collective, communal, corporate, and social. For when it comes to home life, as we shall see later on, most Jews do observe the rites of passage—they require circumcision for male children, celebrate puberty through bar or bat mitzvah, marry and bury by the rites of Judaism. And of course, most Jews attend a Passover celebration ("Seder" or banquet). Indeed, a majority of Jews attend synagogue worship on holy days devoted to the individual's life and his or her conscience, the New Year and the Day of Atonement. At the same time, the public experience of politics, economics, and society that Jews share comes to expression in quite different ways altogether.

Two reasons stand behind the present state of affairs, which finds the Judaism of the dual Torah intensely active in the private life, the Judaism of Holocaust and Redemption paramount in public life. First, there is the prevailing attitude toward religion and its correct realm; that is, religion is personal and private. The second reason derives from how Jews interpret what has happened to them in the twentieth century—or rather, how they have not interpreted the history of their own time. When it came to making sense of anti-Semitism and the Holocaust, Jews viewed these as political events and did not invoke the theology of Judaism to explain them. Just so, when skinheads deface a synagogue, Jews do not assemble and say Psalms and conduct a day of fasting and prayer, as the Judaism of the dual Torah teaches; they go to the police and solve the problem through political means.

The worldview of the Judaism of Holocaust and Redemption evokes political, historical events—the destruction of the Jews in Europe, the creation of the State of Israel—events of a wholly political character. It treats these events as unique. It finds in them the ultimate meaning of the life of the Jews together as Israel. Therefore it defines an Israel for itself—the State of Israel in particular—just as the Judaism of the dual Torah found in Eden, in Sinai, and in the world to come the meaning of the life of Israel and so defined for itself the holy Israel, the social entity different in its very essence from all other social entities.

Judaism in the Protestant Model

Why the bifurcation between the personal and the familial? How do people know the difference between the Judaism of the dual Torah, perceived as religion, and the Judaism of Holocaust and Redemption, which is political, public, and civic? For the answer we have to ask what is happening to religion in the world today. But studying about Judaism teaches something about the world as it now is. We learn from Judaism to identify an important trait of religion in contemporary life. For here, the explanation lies in the definition of permissible difference in North America and the place of religion in that difference. Specifically, in North American society, defined as it is by Protestant conceptions, it is permissible to be different in religion, and religion is a matter of what is personal and private. Hence, Judaism as a religion is experienced as personal and familial.

The Jews as a political entity then put forth a separate system, one that defines their public and cultural life. Judaism in public policy produces political action in favor of the State of Israel, or Soviet Jewry, or other important matters of the corporate community. Judaism in private affects the individual and the family and is not supposed to play a role in politics at all. That pattern conforms to the Protestant model of religion, which separates not the institutions of church from the activities of the state, but the entire public polity from the inner life.

In Protestant North America, people commonly see religion as something personal and private. Prayer, for example, speaks for the individual. It is part of a larger perception that religion and rite speak to the heart of the particular person. What can be changed by rite then is first of all personal and private, not social, not an issue of culture, not effective in politics, not part of the public interest. What people do when they respond to religion, therefore, affects an interior world—a world with little bearing on the realities of public discourse: What—in general terms—should we do about nuclear weapons or, in terms of Judaism, how should we organize and imagine society? The transformations of religion do not involve the world, or even the self as representative of other selves, but mainly the individual at its most unique and unrepresentative. Religion—so people maintain—plays no public role. It is a matter not of public activity but of what people happen to believe or do in private—a matter mainly of the heart.

Summary

To summarize: A community joined by interest and experience, such as that made up by the Jews, will appeal to shared values that give expression to common experience. It will thus explain in a single way how diverse individuals and families find it possible to see things in so coherent a manner. The issue, therefore, is not whether a Judaism forms the center, but *which* Judaism—in this case, which one of our contemporary pair. What is important in understanding where and how Judaism is a religion and where it is not is this: The two Judaisms coexist, the one in private, the other in public. The Judaism of the dual Torah forms the counterpart to religion in the

Protestant model, affecting home and family and private life. The Judaism of Holocaust and Redemption presents the counterpart to religion in the civil framework, making an impact upon public life and policy within the distinctive Jewish community of North America. The relationships between the two Judaisms prove uneven, since the Judaism of home and family takes second place in the public life of Jewry—and public life is where the action is in that community. From contemporary Judaisms, let us look back upon the historical ones. For we have now seen what happens when two distinct Judaisms join together to deal with the personal and familial, on the one side, and the public and political on the other. But before modern times, Judaisms joined the individual and the corporate, the private life and the public interest.

What does a Judaism look like when it is single and cogent—and what characterizes all Judaisms, past and present, to justify our treating them as a single religion as we do? We now turn to these questions—questions of definition, but of a different sort from those that the contemporary world requires we address. To answer these questions, we now realize, we cannot deal with the Jews and Judaism in isolation from the world in which they live and to which they respond. The nurturing society beyond defines the issues that become urgent or chronic; the world outside the limits of the community imparts to one answer not mere plausibility but even self-evidence, and to another denies any hearing at all. We cannot explain why today two Judaisms flourish in the West if we do not know about what has happened to the West. That much is clear.

So if we wish to understand Judaism, whether today or a thousand years ago, we have to identify the definitive circumstance, the context in which the Jews determined those questions that urgently demanded attention and identified those answers that proved self-evident. So before we can speak of a Judaism that is cogent and an age in which religion and culture, politics, and the social world form a coherent whole, we have to determine the context in which any religion can encompass, also, the social world of its adherents.

How Judaism Works Today

The Religious World of Judaism

Up to now we have considered a Judaism as a religious system that shapes the social order of its participants, its particular Israel. It is time to ask how, within the familiar Judaism of today's world, the Judaism of the dual Torah, peoples' lives are shaped and changed; because, at some points, they choose to be not only Jewish but also Judaic.[18] In search of an answer, we will deal with two occasions of celebration (the Days of Awe, and the Passover), and one rite of passage (a wedding). I choose them because they are universal today not only among all Judaists (as we should assume) but also among most ethnic Jews, and because they exemplify the entire religious life of Judaism as it has been practiced through time.

To deal with the meaning of Judaism to the Jews who now practice that religion, we must revert to the simple distinction between the two Judaisms with which we began. Otherwise we cannot understand why people do widely practice certain rites within the received system but not others.

Here, we recall our starting point, the proposition that the rites of the actually practiced Judaism focus on the individual, inclusive of the family. The rites of the Judaism of the dual Torah that do not enjoy wide adherence outside of Orthodox Judaisms are the ones that speak to a whole society, or to civilization, to nation or people. For that purpose, the other Judaism of the age, that of Holocaust and Redemption, serves. In the Judaism of the dual Torah, Israel, the corporate community, doing things together and all at once, conducts worship, celebrates and commemorates events in the world of creation, revelation, and redemption. Sabbaths and festivals focus upon the corporate life of Israel, a social entity. The words that people say on these occasions do not speak to many Jews. These occasions do not find the synagogues filled to overflowing.

But as we made clear above, the individual rites of passage celebrating family, such as circumcision, and marriage, and the rites that focus on the individual and his or her existence, such as the Days of Awe—the New Year (*Rosh Hashanah*) and Day of Atonement (*Yom Kippur*)—retain enormous power to move people. What speaks to the family on Passover, the spring festival that celebrates the Exodus from Egypt, which is the home rite of the banquet, enjoys nearly universal response. In addition, the banquet symbol, *matzah*, will impose its spell, so that people who through the year and on Passover do not keep the dietary taboos do give up bread for the week and eat only matzah. At the same time, the synagogues on Passover contain plenty of empty seats. In this collective affirmation of the home and family within the one Judaism but denial of the public and the communal in that same Judaism, the "we" gives way in favor of the "I," and that is what accounts for what people do and also for what they ignore.

The Days of Awe

Judaism follows a lunar calendar that takes cognizance of the solar calendar, hence correlating full moons with the vernal and autumnal equinoxes. The key months are Nisan, which contains the first full moon after the vernal equinox, and Tishri, which contains the first full moon after the autumnal equinox. The key holy day of Nisan is Passover, beginning with the full moon of Nisan, and the key holy day of Tishri is Sukkot, the Festival of Tabernacles, with the full moon of Tishri.

Tishri is the holy month par excellence, a counterpart to Ramaḍān in Islam. Its holy days and festivals cover three weeks. The Days of Awe, a penitential season, begin with the New Year, which is marked by the new moon of the Hebrew month of Tishri. The Day of Atonement follows on the tenth day of that same lunar month, and reaches its climax at the full moon of Tishri, which also marks the beginning of Sukkot. Sukkot lasts for seven days and ends on the eighth day in solemn assembly, three weeks in all. So to understand how the rhythm of the year unfolds, we begin with the new moon of the month of Tishri, corresponding to September. That marks the New Year, Rosh Hashanah. Ten days later comes the Day of Atonement, Yom Kippur, commemorating the rite described in Leviticus 16, and marking God's judgment and forgiveness of humanity. Five days afterward, with the full moon, the festival of Tabernacles (Sukkot) begins. That festival lasts for eight days and ends with a day of solemn assembly, *Shemini Aseret*, and of rejoicing of the Torah, *Simhat Torah*. So nearly the whole month of Tishri is spent in celebration, in eating, drinking, praying and studying, in enjoying and celebrating God's sovereignty, creation, revelation, and redemption, as the themes of the festivals and solemn celebrations of the season work themselves out.

Let us listen with some care to the answers to the Jews' situation propounded through the Days of Awe (culminating in the Day of Atonement). From these we shall be able to derive the questions articulated by that larger social context that frames the whole. Thereby we can at last reach back to define that context itself.

The New Year (Rosh Hashanah), and the Day of Atonement (Yom Kippur), together constitute days of solemn penitence, at the start of the autumn festival season. Their prayers indicate the solemnity of the times. The words of the liturgy, specifically, create a world of personal introspection, individual judgment. So the turning of the year is a time for looking backward. It is melancholy, like the falling leaves, but hopeful.

The answer propounded through the Days of Awe concerns life and death. Here, these take mythic form as affirmations of God's rule and judgment. On the one hand, the words create a world aborning, the old now gone, the new just now arriving. For instance, the New Year, Rosh Hashanah, celebrates the creation of the world: *Today the world was born.* Yet the time of new beginnings also marks endings: *On the New Year the decree is issued: Who will live and who will die?* At the New Year—so the words state—humanity is inscribed for life or death in the heavenly books for the coming year, and on the Day of Atonement the books are sealed. The world comes out to hear these words. The season is rich in celebration.

The synagogues on the New Year are filled—whether with penitents or people who merely wish to be there hardly matters. The New Year is a day of remembrance on which the deeds of all creatures are reviewed. The words invoke creation, and God's rule over creation; revelation, and God's rule in the Torah for the created world; redemption, God's ultimate plan for the world.

Thus on the birthday of the world God made, God asserts sovereignty. Consider the New Year Prayer:

> Our God and God of our Fathers, Rule over the whole world in Your honor...and appear in Your glorious might to all those who dwell in the civilization of Your world, so that everything made will know that You made it, and every creature discern that You have created him, so that all in whose nostrils is breath may say, "The Lord, the God of Israel is king, and His kingdom extends over all."[19]

These liturgical words concerning divine sovereignty, divine memory, and divine disclosure call up the themes of creation, revelation, and redemption. For example, sovereignty is established by creation of the world, and judgment depends upon law. The liturgy runs: "From the beginning You made this, Your purpose known...." That is, since people have been told what God requires of them, they are judged:

> On this day sentence is passed upon countries, which to the sword and which to peace, which to famine and which to plenty, and each creature is judged today for life or death. Who is not judged on this day? For the remembrance of every creature comes before You, each man's deeds and destiny, words and way....

The call for inner contemplation inheres in the mythic words. That contemplation comes to fore on the Day of Atonement, Yom Kippur, the Sabbath of Sabbaths. This is the most personal, solemn, and moving of the Days of Awe. It is marked by fasting and continuous prayer. On it, people make confession:

> Our God and God of our fathers, may our prayer come before You. Do not hide yourself from our supplication, for we are not so arrogant or stiff-necked as to say before You...We are righteous and have not sinned. But we have sinned.
>
> We are guilt laden, we have been faithless, we have robbed.... We have committed iniquity, caused unrighteousness, have been presumptuous....
>
> We have counseled evil, scoffed, revolted, blasphemed....[20]

This confession is built upon an alphabetical acrostic (effective, obviously, only in the original Hebrew). Perhaps the hope is that if every letter is represented, God, who knows human secrets, will combine them into appropriate words. That is, the very alphabet bears witness against us before God.

In these circumstances, the introspective response is the following:

> What shall we say before You who dwell on high? What shall we tell You who live in heaven? Do You not know all things, both the hidden and the revealed? You know the secrets of eternity, the most hidden mysteries of life. You search the innermost recesses, testing men's feelings and heart. Nothing is concealed from You or hidden from Your eyes. May it therefore be Your will to forgive us our sins, to pardon us for our iniquities, to grant remission for our transgressions.

Interestingly, however, as a further list of sins follows, again on alphabetical lines, the prayers to be spoken by the congregation all fall into the plural. Thus we read: "For the sin which we have sinned against You with the utterance of the lips . . . For the sin which we have sinned before You openly and secretly . . ." That is, the sins confessed are mostly against society, against one's fellowmen, and the community takes upon itself responsibility for what is done in it. All Israel is part of one community, one body, and all are responsible for the acts of each. But at the end comes this final word:

> O my God, before I was formed, I was nothing. Now that I have been formed, it is as though I had not been formed, for I am dust in my life, more so after death. Behold I am before You like a vessel filled with shame and confusion. May it be Your will . . . that I may no more sin, and forgive the sins I have already committed in Your abundant compassion.

So while much of the liturgy speaks of "we," the individual focus dominates, beginning to end. The Days of Awe speak to the heart of the individual, telling a story of judgment and atonement. The individual Jew stands before God, possessing no merits yet hopeful of God's love and compassion. If that is the answer, can there be any doubt about the question? I think not. The power of the Days of Awe derives from the sentiments and emotions aroused by the theme of those days. And that theme runs: What is happening to me? Where am I going?

The Passover Seder

The single most widely practiced rite of Judaism in North America—the Passover Seder, or ritual meal—requires family and friends to sit down for supper. How is so secular an act as a supper party transformed into a highly charged occasion, rich in deeply felt meanings? This meal, consumed with ceremony, turns people into something other than they think they are, and it sets them down right in the flow of an onrushing history. Symbols, both visual and verbal, transform family and friends into an Israel redeemed from Egypt.

Gathered around their tables, Jewish families retell the story of the Exodus from Egypt. With unleavened bread and sanctified wine, they celebrate the liberation of slaves from Pharaoh's bondage. And through their ritual, the "we" of the family becomes the "we" of Israel, the eternal and perpetual coming of spring is channeled to signify a singular act, one moment in the sequence of linear time. One formula expresses this complex, ritual conflation of time and space. It runs:

> For ever after, in every generation, *every Israelite must think of himself or herself as having gone forth from Egypt* [italics added].

Yet it is one thing to tell Jews to think of themselves in one way, rather than in some other—to "think of himself or herself as having gone forth from Egypt." It is quite a different thing to explain why Jews respond to the demand—and they do respond. For our purposes, it is essential to explain this response.

Let me suggest, here, that when we (in this case, the Jews) see the everyday as metaphor, it is because we perceive that deeper layer of meaning that permits us to treat as obvious and self-evident the transforming power of comparison, of simile applied to oneself. That is, when things appear to us to have meaning beyond their superficial reference, it is because we have already concluded that beyond the here and now there must be a something else. That is how metaphor does its work.

We can see this for the Jews in their Passover liturgy. There, one theme stands out: We, here and now, are really living then and there. Consider the following examples:

> *We* were slaves of Pharaoh in Egypt and the Lord our God brought us forth from there with a mighty hand and an outstretched arm. And if the Holy One, blessed be he, had not brought our fathers forth from Egypt, then we and our descendants would still be slaves to Pharaoh in Egypt. And so, even if all of us were full of wisdom, understanding, sages and well informed in the Torah, we should still be obligated to repeat again the story of the Exodus from Egypt; and whoever treats as an important matter the story of the Exodus from Egypt is praiseworthy.
>
> This is the bread of affliction which our ancestors ate in the land of Egypt. Let all who are hungry come and eat with us, let all who are needy come and celebrate the Passover with us this year here, next year in the Land of Israel; this year slave, next year free people.
>
> This is the promise which has stood by our forefathers and stands by us. For neither once, nor twice, nor three times was our destruction planned; in every generation they rise against us, and in every generation God delivers us from their hands into freedom, out of anguish

into joy, out of mourning into festivity, out of darkness into light, out of bondage into redemption.[21]

For ever after, in every generation, *every Israelite must think of himself or herself as having gone forth from Egypt* [italics added]. For we read in the Torah: "In that day thou shall teach thy son, saying: All this is because of what God did for me when I went forth from Egypt." It was not only our forefathers that the Holy One, blessed be He, redeemed; us too, the living, He redeemed together with them, as we learn from the verse in the Torah: "And He brought us out from thence, so that He might bring us home, and give us the land which he pledged to our forefathers."[22]

If we ask, therefore, what experience in the here and now is taken up and transformed by enchantment into the then and the there, we move from the rite to the reality. That progress tells us what troubles these people and makes play-acting plausible as they turn their lives into metaphor, themselves into actors, the everyday into pretense and drama. The question takes on urgency when we remind ourselves that we confront the single most popular and widely observed rite of Judaism. What speaks so ubiquitously, with such power, that pretty much everybody who wishes joins in? In my view, the message penetrates to the heart of people who remember the Holocaust—the murder, in the near-past, of six million Jews—and who know that they too are a minority and at risk, if not on a global scale, then on a personal one.

We have not moved far from the situation addressed by Ezra and the Pentateuchal Judaism in its way. The Jews are a minority. But their small number is offset by their visibility. So far as they differ from "the others"—and, of course, these "others" constitute a fantasized majority for Jews, a group of (mere) Gentiles considered alike in all respects because not Jewish—Jews confront not a critical but a chronic discomfort. Being different—whatever the difference—requires explanation; it provokes resentment; it creates tension demanding resolution and pain requiring remission. For the young, difference is deadly. For the middle aged, difference demands explanation and compensation, and it may well exact the cost of diminished opportunity. For the individual may not be different from other individuals, but families always do retain that mark of difference from other families, and that in the very nature of their existence.

Passover, celebrated by the families of Israel, celebrates the family of Israel. With its rhetoric of rejoicing for freedom, it plays out in a minor key the song of liberation: today "slaves," next year, "free"; today here, next year in "Jerusalem" (that is, not the real Jerusalem but the imagined, heavenly one). These contemporary families, then, find a principal side to their existence so troubling that they invoke it, deny it, celebrate its end in ancient times—and fervently ask that it come to a conclusion once again.

Passover is popular now because it speaks to a generation that knows what the Gentiles can do, having seen what they did to the Jews of Europe. Indeed, Passover today speaks not of history alone but also to personal biography. It joins together history with the experience of the individual, because the individual as a post-Nazi member of a minority finds self-evident—relevant, true, urgent—a rite that reaches into the everyday and the here and now and turns that common world into a metaphor for the reality of Israel, enslaved but also redeemed. Whether or not twentieth-century Jews see themselves as having gone forth from Egypt I cannot say, but I know that they see themselves as slaves in Egypt. And that is what draws them to the Seder: It explains what, in the everyday, things mean beyond the four walls of the private person's world. It shows the individual that the everyday stands for something beyond, the here and now represent the everywhere and all the time: "In every generation they rise against us." And it shows that God saves. Who would not be glad to have supper to celebrate that truth?

A Rite of Passage: The Marriage Ceremony

It is uncommon indeed for one Jew to marry another only in a civil, secular rite. Nearly all marriages between a Jewish man and a Jewish woman are conducted under the bridal canopy, or *huppah*, in accord with "the laws of Moses and Israel." This is because the rite that accomplishes the public union of two private persons calls upon encompassing eternity. Marriage for Jews links the participants in the here and now to Eden past and Zion redeemed at the end of time; that is, the rite of passage into marriage transforms the space, time, action, and community of the groom and the bride. Marriage invokes creation; a new Eden arises. In the two *I*'s becoming one *we*, the couple enters a paradigm of humanity set by Adam and Eve. Adam is the first man, Eve, the first woman. The groom stands for Adam, the bride, for Eve, and creation begins anew with this union. So the huppah, the marriage-canopy, contains space representing heaven. And in that space, the time is "now," in the beginning. When else could it be?

According to Rashi, the great medieval Bible-interpreter (1040–1105), in this way the snake's prophecy in Eden is realized. When the snake says, . . . *but God knows that as soon as you eat of it, your eyes will be opened and you will be like God* . . . (Gen. 3:5), Rashi maintains, the meaning is that humankind will become "creators of worlds." Thus in marriage, the woman becomes Eve, the man Adam. The rite begins a new world: a family, a social entity, humanity.

The climax of the rite of Adam and Eve, of "you and me" as "us," Israel in Jerusalem beyond time, comes in the recitation of Seven Blessings (*sheva berakhot*) over a cup of wine. Among them is the following, invoking the world of Eden:

> Praised are You, O Lord our God, King of the universe, who created all things for Your glory.
>
> Praised are You, O Lord our God, King of the universe, Creator of Adam.
>
> Praised are You, O Lord our God, King of the universe, who created man and woman in his image, fashioning woman from man as his mate, that together they might perpetuate life. Praised are You, O Lord, Creator of man.

The sequence of three is perfectly realized. First comes creation of all things, then creation of Man, then creation of man and woman in his image. These words of the sanctification of wine for bride and groom invoke a world for which the occasion at hand serves as metaphor. "We now are like them then"—that is what is at stake.

Israel's history begins with creation—and creation is for God's glory. First comes the creation of the vine, symbol of the natural world. All things speak to nature, to the physical as much as the spiritual, for all things were made by God. And above all creation stands Adam—in Hebrew, the blessings end, "who formed the *Adam*." The theme of ancient paradise is introduced by this simple choice of the word *Adam*, so heavy with meaning. Then the myth of man's creation is rehearsed: man and woman are in God's image, together complete and whole, creators of life, "life God." Woman was fashioned from man together with him to perpetuate life. So again, "blessed is the creator of Adam." We have moved, therefore, from the natural world to the archetypal realm of paradise. Before us we see not merely a man and a woman, but Adam and Eve.

But then comes the following:

> May Zion rejoice as her children are restored to her in joy. Praised are You, O Lord, who causes Zion to rejoice at her children's return.

This is a jarring intrusion. No one has mentioned Zion to now. It comes uninvited. But Zion has been present metaphorically. And, given the standing of Zion as a metaphor for the resolution both of Israel's exile and of the suffering human condition, its appearance seems logical at this point.

And this Adam and Eve also are Israel, children of Zion the mother, as expressed in the fifth blessing. Zion lies in ruins; her children are scattered. So Adam and Eve cannot celebrate together without thought to the condition of the mother, Jerusalem. The children will one day come home. The mood is hopeful yet sad, as it was meant to be, for archaic Israel mourns as it rejoices and rejoices as it mourns. Quickly then, back to the happy occasion, for we do not let mourning lead to melancholy: "Grant perfect joy to the loving companions," for they are creators of a new line in humankind—the new Adam, the new Eve—and their home: May it be the garden of Eden. And if joy is there, then "praised are you for the joy of bride and groom."

The joy of the moment gives a foretaste of the joy of restoration, redemption, return. Now the two roles become one in that same joy, first Adam and Eve, groom and bride—Eden then, the marriage canopy now:

> Grant perfect joy to these loving companions, as You did to the first man and woman in the Garden of Eden. Praised are You, O Lord, who grants the joy of bride and groom.

That same joy comes, second, in the metaphors of Zion the bride and Israel the groom. But this is made very specific, for the words in italics *allude to the vision* of Jeremiah, when all seemed lost, that Jerusalem, about to fall and lose its people, will one day ring with the shouts not of the slaughtered and the enslaved, but of the returned and redeemed. That is why the concluding blessing returns to the theme of Jerusalem. This time it evokes the tragic hour of Jerusalem's first destruction. When everyone had given up hope, supposing that with the end of Jerusalem had come the end of time, only Jeremiah counseled renewed hope. With the enemy at the gate, he sang of coming gladness:

Thus says the Lord:

> *In this place of which you say, "It is a waste, without man or beast," in the cities of Judah and the streets of Jerusalem that are desolate, without man or inhabitant or beast,*
> *There shall be heard again the voice of mirth and the voice of gladness, the voice of the bridegroom and the voice of the bride, the voice of those who sing as they bring thank-offerings to the house of the Lord....*
> *For I shall restore the fortunes of the land as at first, says the Lord.*
>
> Jeremiah 33:10–11

The joy is not in two but in three moments: Eden then, marriage party now, and Zion in the coming age:

> Praised are You, O Lord our God, King of the universe, who created joy and gladness, bride and groom, mirth, song, delight and rejoicing, love and harmony, peace and companionship. O Lord our God, may there ever be heard in the cities of Judah and in the streets of Jerusalem voices of joy and gladness, voices of bride and groom, the jubilant voices of those joined in marriage under the bridal canopy, the voices of young people feasting and singing.

The closing blessing is not merely a literary artifice or a learned allusion to the ancient prophet. It defines the exultant, jubilant climax of this acted-out myth: Just as here and now there stand before us Adam and Eve, so here and now in this wedding, the old sorrow having been rehearsed, we listen to the voice of gladness that is coming. The joy of this new creation prefigures the joy of the Messiah's coming, hope for which is very present in this hour. And when he comes, the joy then will echo the joy of bride and groom before us. Zion the bride, Israel the groom, united now as they will be reunited by the compassionate stand under the marriage canopy.

To state the significance of this in secular terms, the fundamental condition of "being Jewish"—that is, the ethnic identification—so far as people identify "being Jewish" with the received Judaism of the dual Torah in the West, is that it involves individual and family but imparts in social experience no knowledge of what it means to live in corporate community. For corporate experience is identified with the destruction of the Jews in Europe and the creation and maintenance of the State of Israel. The Judaism of the dual Torah defines the categories of time, space, action, and community when individual imagination participates. That same Judaism makes slight impact when the experience of the individual in family as part of a larger social entity can be invoked: *as if* depends on *is*.

The Power of Judaism and Its Success

The power of all Judaisms to precipitate and then assuage resentment offers a useful point at which to conclude, because it suggests a theory of the nature of religion that can be tested in the study of other religions. Judaism must be classified as a living and highly vital religion, because its adherents frame the world in its terms and form a social entity in its definition. Why is that the case? The reason is that the generative paradigm, formed in the Torah of Moses or the Pentateuch, asks a question and answers it, creates a problem and solves it, and that question and problem correspond to the social world people perceive or are taught to perceive. That is, Jews see their life together not as a given but as a gift, stipulated and subject to conditions. That creates a measure of anxiety or resentment, and these translate that discomfort with being different, which any minority group feels, into spiritual terms. But then, the Torah teaches, the Jews' difference is destiny: Holiness is in the here and now, salvation comes at the end of time. So the anxiety or discomfort on account of difference is turned into a good and hopeful feeling: Things have deep meaning now, and we will matter even more in time to come.

In psychological terms, what "religion recapitulates resentment" means is that a generation that reaches the decision to change (or to accept or to recognize the legitimacy of change) expresses resentment of its immediate setting and therefore its past, its parents, as much as it proposes to commit itself to something better, the future it proposes to manufacture. In political terms, the meaning of "religion recapitulates resentment" is that each Judaism addresses a political problem not taken up by any other and proposes to solve that problem. Accordingly, resentment—whether at home or in the public polity—produces resolution. The two, when joined, form a religious system, in this context, a Judaism.

At issue when we study religion, therefore, is how religious ideas relate to the political circumstances of the people who hold those ideas. Religion as a fact of the practical life of politics constitutes a principal force in the shaping of society and imagination alike, while politics for its part profoundly affects the conditions of religious belief and behavior. So one thing we should want to know when we study a religion, as we have seen in our study of Judaism(s), is how stunning shifts in the political circumstance of a religion affect that religion's thought about perennial questions. When we understand the interplay between this world and our aspirations to transcend this world, we know what, within the limits of human knowledge, we can find out about religion.

The power of Judaism forms a striking contrast with the pathos of the Jewish condition. From the formation of the Pentateuch in 450 B.C.E. to the present day, the Jews have been scattered, few in number, lacking a clear definition for themselves. They are not joined by a common language, though Hebrew serves in synagogues everywhere. They do not share a common set of ethnic or social or economic or political traits, though Scripture imputes to them a common identity. They assuredly do not derive from a single, unitary history, though through Scripture they contemplate in common a single past and future. So Judaism describes what reality does not present, which is one people, with one land, one language, one faith, one destiny. In the contrast between Judaism's perspective and the Jews' everyday circumstances, we grasp what Judaism accomplishes for the Jews. It is to make them see not what is but what ought to be, to shape their vision so that the facts of the everyday, whatever they are, conform to the structure of the faith, everywhere. Judaism makes Jews see things that no one else sees, and to see them in a way that only they find self-evident.

The Jews, diverse and scattered, called themselves "Israel" and saw themselves as the people to whom God speaks in the Torah. Weak and subordinated, disliked because they were unlike and sometimes abused and even murdered because of the difference, they rejoiced in who and what they were and wanted to continue to be different and to form a distinct and important people in the world. And they always had the choice, except in the Holocaust, to be or not be a Jew, and they always chose to be Israel. Had they not made that decision in every generation, "Israel" the holy people—counterpart to the Church, the mystical body of Christ—as well as the Jews, the this-worldly ethnic group, would have disappeared from humanity. But the Jews remain a visible presence in many parts of the world, and holy Israel and its Torah—that is, Judaism—endures as a vital religion as well. That simple fact shows the amazing power of what we call Judaism and what Judaism calls "the Torah" to exalt the humble, to strengthen the weak, to give joy to the disappointed and hope to the disheartened, to make ordinary life holy and sacred and significant for people who, in the end, are not much different from everybody else, except that believing has made them so. To take the full measure of the success of Judaism, you have to realize that, when it comes to religion, Jews really do like being Jewish and do not want to be anything else.[23]

Recommended Reading

Lucy S. Dawidowicz, ed. *A Holocaust Reader.* New York: Behrman House, 1975. Powerful documents of the Holocaust.

Edward Flannery. *The Anguish of the Jews.* New York: Macmillan, 1965. An explanation of the Christian and pagan sources of anti-Semitism.

Malcolm Hay. *Europe and the Jews* (also published as *The Foot of Pride*). Boston: Beacon, 1960. A history of anti-Semitism in Europe.

Abraham J. Heschel. *God in Search of Man: A Philosophy of Judaism.* New York: Farrar, Straus and Giroux, 1976.

Raul Hilberg. *The Destruction of the European Jews.* Chicago: Quadrangle, 1961. The best account of the facts of the Holocaust.

James Michener. *The Source.* New York: Random House, 1965. A fictionalized version of the history of the Jews, rich in information and insight.

Jacob Neusner. *The Doubleday Anchor Reference Library Introduction to Rabbinic Literature.* New York: Doubleday, forthcoming.

———. *The Doubleday Anchor Reference Library, Rabbinic Judaism: A Historical Introduction.* New York: Doubleday, forthcoming.

Howard M. Sachar. *The Course of Modern Jewish History.* New York: World Publishing Co., 1958. An eloquent and systematic history of the Jews in modern times.

Robert Seltzer. *Jewish People, Jewish Thought: The Jewish Experience in History.* New York: Macmillan and Collier, 1980. A systematic account of the history of the Jews.

Richard Siegel, Michael Strassfeld, and Sharon Strassfeld. *The Jewish Catalog.* 2 vols. Philadelphia: Jewish Publication Society, 1975. A fine introduction to the practice of Judaism in contemporary America.

Herman Wouk. *This Is My God.* New York: Doubleday, 1959. An elegant account, by a practicing Jew who is a great writer, of what it means to live by the religion, Judaism.

Notes

1. Calvin Goldscheider, *Jewish Continuity and Change: Emerging Patterns in America* (Bloomington: Indiana University Press, 1986), 170.
2. The largest five Jewish population sizes by state are:
   - New York: 1,870,000
   - California: 790,000
   - Florida: 479,000
   - New Jersey: 425,000
   - Pennsylvania: 408,000

   Within states, Jews are heavily concentrated in the largest cities (Goldscheider, personal letter, April 15, 1988).
3. Goldscheider, *Jewish Continuity and Change,* 170.
4. Goldscheider, *Jewish Continuity and Change,* 171.
5. There is, of course, variation in denominational identification within the United States. In 1981, for example, the distribution in New York, the largest Jewish community in the world, was 13 percent Orthodox, 35 percent Conservative, and 29 percent Reform. About one-fourth of New York Jews define themselves denominationally as either "other" or "none." In St. Louis, there were fewer Conservative Jews but more Reform Jews. In the western states the proportion Reform and "other-none" tends to be higher.
6. For further discussion, see this writer's *Fortress Introduction to American Judaism: What the Books Say, What the People Do* (Minneapolis: Fortress Press, 1993).
7. Not merely the Jewish state, the State of Israel. The usage in the liturgy and theology of all Judaisms is uniform: "Israel" always means the holy people, children of Abraham, Isaac, and Jacob, as well as those who have converted to Judaism. It is a native religious category of Judaism. We return to the questions, Who is a Jew? and What is Israel?, in the next part of this chapter.
8. This section reviews the thesis of this writer's *Self-Fulfilling Prophecy: Exile and Return in the History of Judaism* (Boston: Beacon Press, 1987; second printing: Atlanta: Scholars Press for South Florida Studies in the History of Judaism, 1990, with a new introduction).
9. Cf. Ezra 3:12. The scholarly consensus sees the return as beginning right after the Persian overthrow of Babylon, 540–520 B.C.E., so it is conceivable that someone taken into exile to Babylon in 586 could have returned forty or fifty years later; but the notion that the story of exile and return applies to a large number of individuals is unlikely.
10. Since we cannot refer to God as "He," any more or less than as "She," it is best simply to repeat the substantive.
11. See this writer's *Judaism without Christianity: An Introduction to the Religious System of the Mishnah in Historical Context* (Hoboken: Ktav Publishing House, 1991).
12. The power exercised by Gentiles, e.g., the Roman government, never entered the picture, since it was not a legitimate politics at all. Gentiles play no systemic role in the history of Rabbinic Judaism.

13. Man, not woman, who in the Mishnah is sometimes person, sometimes chattel, but rarely a being of autonomous will.
14. Since the initial document of (any) Judaism is the Pentateuch, which reached closure after 586, the period in ancient Israel's history before the destruction of the Temple in 586 has no bearing upon Judaism and its history, except as, after 586, the received materials were reworked and revised by the Judaism taking shape in, and through, the Pentateuch. The actual history of ancient Israel from remote antiquity to the formation of the Pentateuch has no bearing at all on the history of Judaism or on its theology. Judaism begins its history with the completed Pentateuch, and it is the ongoing history of the interpretation of the Hebrew Scriptures ("the Written Torah" = "the Old Testament") that contains the history of Judaism.
15. This section goes over the writer's *Death and Birth of Judaism: The Impact of Christianity, Secularism, and the Holocaust on Jewish Faith* (New York: Basic Books, 1987; second printing: Atlanta: Scholars Press for South Florida Studies in the History of Judaism, 1993).
16. The role and standing of women in the history of the formation of Judaic systems in modern times form a subject awaiting systematic study. In general the new Judaisms redefined, also, the theory of the woman. Reform Judaism was first to ordain women as rabbis, but that took place only in the 1970s. Much earlier, by contrast, both Jewish Socialism and Zionism in theory accorded to women equal responsibilities and rights. But in practice this has not amounted to much (e.g., in the kibbutz movement in the beginning women still washed the dishes and took care of the children). One of the many topics within the intersecting fields of women's studies and the study of the history of Judaism is provided by the present problem.
17. This section reviews the writer's *Stranger at Home: Zionism, "The Holocaust," and American Judaism* (Chicago: University of Chicago Press, 1980; paperback edition, 1985. Second printing, 1985. Third printing, 1988).
18. This section goes over this writer's *The Enchantments of Judaism: Rites of Transformation from Birth through Death* (New York: Basic Books, 1987; Judaic Book Club selection, September, 1987. Jewish Book Club selection, October, 1987. Second printing: Atlanta: Scholars Press for University of South Florida Studies in the History of Judaism, 1991. Edition on tape: Princeton, 1992: Recording for the Blind).
19. Translation by Jules Harlow, ed., *Mahzor for Rosh Hashanah and Yom Kippur: A Prayerbook for the Days of Awe* (New York: Rabbinical Assembly, 1972), 263.
20. Translation by Harlow, *Mahzor for Rosh Hashanah and Yom Kippur,* 377.
21. Maurice Samuel, trans., *Haggadah of Passover* (New York: Hebrew Publishing Co., 1942), 26.
22. Samuel, *Haggadah of Passover,* 27.
23. The author thanks Professor Caroline McCracken-Flesher, University of Wyoming, who edited the fourth draft of this chapter and made numerous important improvements; and Professor William Scott Green, University of Rochester, who read and criticized all five drafts.

CHAPTER 6

Christianity

Harvey Cox

What Is "Christian"?

Christianity in the World Today

In many Christian churches today an annual memorial service is held to recall the life of Archbishop Oscar Romero, of El Salvador. He was shot through the heart in 1980 while celebrating mass at a hospital chapel. Romero was murdered because he refused to remain silent about the killing and torturing that were tearing at the vitals of his poor country and was willing to risk his own life to protest it. But his was only one of many such deaths that have occurred in a land named—ironically—for "the Savior," Jesus Christ. In November 1989, newspapers and TV programs around the world carried the grisly account of the assassination in the same country of six Jesuit priests, their housekeeper, and her daughter, by a "death squad." Earlier four North American women church workers and countless peasants, students, and others had also been killed.

To many people these murders seemed like a strange modern reenactment of Jesus' own last days—midnight arrests, hasty interrogations, cruel torture, and ugly executions with bodies left shamefully exposed to public view. It appeared that some Christians, in some places in the world, were continuing to die under circumstances strikingly similar to those under which Jesus himself had died nearly two millennia earlier. Is this what it means to be a Christian today?

Even the most alert readers of the world press had reason to be confused, for in the same newspapers that reported these martyrdoms, press accounts also told of people who called themselves "Christian militia" firing mortars into Muslim sections of Beirut, the capital of Lebanon, and then shooting members of rival "Christian" factions. A few weeks earlier a well-known American TV evangelist was packed off to a long prison term for cheating many of his elderly followers out of hundreds of thousands of dollars they had planned to use in retirement. Americans in particular had good reason to puzzle about what it means to be a Christian in our times. In 1988 two prominent Christian ministers had become candidates for their parties' nominations for president. But the platforms of Jesse Jackson and Pat Robertson represented opposite ends of the political spectrum. Meanwhile, on questions like officially sanctioned prayers in public schools, abortion, and the morality of making or using nuclear weapons, people who called themselves "Christian" not only took diametrically opposed positions but also claimed that those opinions grew directly out of their Christian faith. What does the word *Christian* really mean?

The proverbial visitor from Mars walking the streets of America today could become mightily perplexed in trying to find an answer to this question.

In most American cities he (or she or it, depending on whether such distinctions exist on Mars) would find dozens or even hundreds of buildings called "churches" in which people who call themselves "Christian" gather periodically to pray, sing, eat potluck dinners, get married, prepare the dead for burial, drink gallons of coffee, instruct each other about a book called the Bible and the beliefs they derive from it, shake each others' hands, and listen to sermons and homilies delivered by men and women dressed in clothing never seen on other occasions. In most of these buildings, often—though not always—marked by a cross and surmounted by a tower, the people would sometimes swallow small quantities of bread or wafer and sip tiny amounts of wine, and at other times they would sprinkle small children and babies with water or immerse adults or teenagers completely in a special pool. Some of these buildings would be enormous, and even an extraterrestrial visitor might be awed by their stained glass spaciousness. Others would be smaller and much more severe in decor. Still others would be tiny rooms that were once butcher shops or fish markets. In some of these church edifices people would kneel, in some they would prostrate themselves in front of pictures, in others they would sit in neat rows, while in still others they might dance in the aisles and leap for joy with their hands extended over their heads. In some, huge pipe organs would fill the space with Bach and Schubert and Mozart. In others people would shout and clap their hands to guitars, trapdrums, and cymbals. In a few, they would sit in utter silence, with no musical instruments at all, and speak only occasionally.

If the galactic observer was puzzled and began to ask the people who gather in these buildings to explain it all, he or she might at first fall into an even deeper bewilderment. In America alone there are estimated to be nearly five hundred separate and distinct forms of Christianity. Some groups, like the Catholics and the Baptists and the Pentecostals, are quite large and encompass millions of people each. Others are somewhat smaller with a few million or a few hundred thousand members. Many more are quite tiny, with memberships ranging from a few hundred to a few thousand. There are also local Christian churches that are completely independent of any larger body whatever. If our mythical visitor trudged from church to church, trying to find out what "Christian" means, he or she would be met by a wide variety of answers. Some respondents would emphasize prayer and praise. Others might talk about how participating in a church helped them live from day to day. Still others might stare at the Martian and throw up their hands in dismay as though anyone who did not catch the meaning of what was going on would hardly profit from hearing an explanation.

At first the confusion and contradiction might appear to be total. But gradually the alert visitor would begin to piece together some bedrock elements on which all who call themselves "Christian" do agree. Most importantly, the visitor would constantly hear a *name* and would discover that all these people, despite their dramatic differences, claim to base their faith on an otherwise obscure Jewish teacher and prophet who lived for only about thirty-three years in a remote outpost of the Roman Empire nearly two thousand years ago. Some hold that this Jesus of Nazareth was—and is—the Son of God or the actual "incarnation" of the Creator of the universe. Others believe that he is the principal bearer of the gospel, the message about the coming of God's reign of justice and peace, to humankind. Still others see in him the prime exemplar of God's will for all people, a model of what human life is meant to be and what it might become. Persisting in his inquiry, the investigator would also find that there is a widespread agreement among Christians that this Jesus should have considerable significance—some would say the greatest significance—for how they lead their lives and make their moral decisions. So, if the visitor stuck with this daunting task, the core of it all would finally begin to emerge. The outside visitor would find that although they may differ about virtually everything else, all Christians agree that Jesus Christ is pivotal and indispensable to Christianity.

But this discovery, although crucial and fundamental, would not in itself answer the question, What is Christianity? It is true that all Christians agree on the centrality of Jesus Christ. But there is also widespread disagreement on who Jesus was and is, and on just how the moral significance of his life is supposed to be brought to bear. Some try to follow his way of life as disciples. Others look to his principal teachings such as the Golden Rule and the Sermon on the Mount. Still others believe his death was a sacrificial offering to God that atoned for human wrongdoings and that his resurrection from the dead makes a new kind of human life possible. Most Christians, in fact, probably hold to a mixture of all of these interpretations. Still, all Christians agree that without Jesus Christ the faith they identify themselves with would not exist. All worship, revere, honor, follow, admire, or try to emulate him in some way. And this provides an essential clue to anyone who is interested in what Christianity is but is puzzled about its seemingly endless variety and complexity: We must begin with Jesus.

Who Was Jesus?

How do we know about Jesus? Even to this straightforward question Christians offer many different answers. Many would insist that the only fully reliable evidence of who he was and what he means is to be found in the New Testament, a collection of letters, interpretive histories, prophecies, and accounts of Jesus' life. These were assembled from hundreds of similar documents written during the century after his death by the movement that evolved from his original band of followers and that we know today first as the "Jesus movement" and eventually as "the church." Others claim, however, that although these early records are indispensable, the only authentic way to *know* Jesus, as distinct from simply knowing *about* him, is to encounter him in a personal, experiential way. Knowing this living Jesus in a direct or mystical manner is possible, Christians say, because God did not permit death to retain its hold on him but raised him from the grave in an event celebrated every year at Easter. Some Christians would put this conviction in a slightly different way. They would say that the powerful assurance his followers had—and still have—that Jesus was in some way still with them even after his death on the cross gave rise to the belief that he was alive again, and that therefore God must have raised him from the dead. However this crucial event at the outset of Christianity is explained, the *experience* of a living Christ and the joyous *belief* in the Resurrection arose together. Their belief in Jesus' resurrection from the dead represents the way the earliest disciples compressed into a single reality both their vivid memories of the prophet and teacher they had journeyed and eaten with, and their personal certainty that he was still with them.

The gap between the pre-Easter and the post-Easter Jesus, which much later came to be called the tension between the "historical Jesus" and the "Christ of faith," goes as far back as St. Paul. One of the most influential figures in the shaping of early Christianity, Paul insisted that he had never even seen Jesus during his earthly life. Rather, he had met the Risen Christ on the road to Damascus in an encounter that was so incandescent it left him temporarily blind and reversed his whole life course, so that instead of continuing to persecute the early followers of Jesus, he joined them, and carried the gospel message throughout the Roman Empire.

But we should not overdraw the contrast between the various ways of knowing, or knowing about, Jesus. Most Christians combine them and are further informed by what the various churches have taught about him over the years. Consequently, the answer anyone gives to the question of who Jesus was and what he means for us today will inevitably include a mixture of historical judgment, religious and cultural tradition, and personal faith.

During the centuries since Jesus taught and healed in ancient Palestine, the modes of interpreting him and the different ways of following or worshiping him have gradually crystallized into hundreds of churches and denominations. They are all in one manner or another examples of what we call "Christianity." The best analogy of their relationship to each other is that of a family with a large number of siblings. Some of the sisters and brothers get along with each other better than others. Some distrust each other. Some feel very close. Some despise others as black sheep. Sometimes, during a particularly acrimonious quarrel, one may tell another that he or she does not belong in the family at all. But usually they accept each other, with various degrees of willingness or reluctance, as members of the same extended family. Also as in families, the various members of the Christian family share common memories and celebrate certain special events. Some of these events, especially the ones that mark key episodes in the life of Jesus, they all celebrate, albeit in quite different ways. This is why Christmas, the holiday on which the birth of Jesus is remembered; Good Friday, the day of his crucifixion by the Romans; and Easter, the occasion of his resurrection, are observed by almost all Christians, even though some do it on different days. Many other holidays, however, such as the Feast of the Immaculate Conception, which honors Mary the mother of Jesus, or Reformation Sunday, which recalls the beginnings of many of the Protestant denominations in the early sixteenth century, are marked by one branch of the family and not by the others.

To make matters even more complicated, some of the main disagreements among Christians have not followed these denominational divisions at all, but have arisen—often within the same church—between Christians whose lives as persons of different classes or races or gender groups have led them to interpretations of the gospel that are at variance with those of their fellows in the same denomination. Thus both Jesse Jackson and Pat Robertson, the two ministers mentioned earlier who tried to be nominated for president, are Baptists. But this did not prevent their disagreement on most public policy issues. The sharp disagreements between Roman Catholic leaders in Rome on the one hand and some Latin American and North American theologians on the other also represent different ways of reading the same gospel within the same church tradition. But since, even in these cases, all parties agree that they base their views on Jesus Christ, let us go back to the beginning and try to uncover what Christians agree to about Jesus and where the most serious disagreements lie.

The Gospels and the Gospel

According to one of the accounts of the life of Jesus in the New Testament, which are also called "Gospels," he himself once posed to his immediate followers the question of who people thought he was and how they interpreted what he was doing and saying. "Who do people say that I am?" he asked them at a place called Caesarea Philippi (Mark 8:27). The followers offered several answers. Some people, they reported, thought he was another Elijah, the Jewish prophet who was expected to return to earth just before the end of the world. Others thought he was some other prophet. Then Peter, one of the disciples, when asked to give his own answer to the question, told Jesus he was the "Messiah," the ambiguously defined figure most of his fellow Jews were hoping would soon appear and help them to overcome the national captivity and religious persecution they were suffering under the Roman Empire.

Jesus told Peter he was right. But the next lines in the story suggest that Peter's answer, far from solving the question of Jesus' identity, instead deepened it. For Jesus went on to state that he would soon have to go to Jerusalem, the religious and political capital of his captive nation, and that there he would meet his death. At this point Peter disagreed with his master and rabbi. There was no place in his thinking or in that of most of his contemporaries, for a Messiah who would be defeated and die. It was a contradictory scenario. One could fail and die, and thus obviously *not* be the Messiah, or one could triumph and therefore manifestly *be* the long-awaited one. But the combination seemed bizarre.

Virtually every interpretive issue that has troubled Christians in the subsequent centuries is found in this famous passage. Jesus and his disciples were all Jews. What relation does his message and the movement that grew out of it bear to the centuries of ancient Judaism that went before it and—even more urgently perhaps—to the two millennia of Judaism that have continued since? What does the defeat and death of Jesus by the elites of Jerusalem say about the way God is present in human history? Since the word *Messiah* means one who is sent or anointed by God, for what purpose did God send him? What was Jesus' own purpose? What was he actually trying to do, and what should those who claim to follow him be trying to do today?

Christians hold many different beliefs on all these questions. Some of the disagreement is amicable, but some of it is quite acrimonious. One possible way to search for an answer is to examine another richly informative incident in Jesus' life. In this one, instead of asking other people who they thought he was, Jesus defines his own program and life purpose. The episode is recorded in the fourth chapter of the Gospel of Luke (verses 14–30). It represents Jesus as returning to his home town of Nazareth near the beginning of his public ministry in Galilee. Apparently reports of his eloquence as a teacher and his gifts as a healer had already reached the home folks and there was considerable curiosity about him. In Nazareth Jesus attended the weekly synagogue service "as his custom was." After some of the traditional prayers, the attendant handed him a scroll of the prophet Isaiah and Jesus began to read from it to the assembled congregation. This is not itself surprising, since it was the custom in the synagogues of Jesus' day to invite distinguished guests to read and comment on Scripture.

Apparently Jesus himself selected the passage he read, and the scene itself has a certain charm. Here is a local boy who shows real promise and who knows where to find a particular passage in the Bible. But the text Jesus selected also tells us something very important about him and about what he saw his purpose in life to be. This is what he read:

> *The Spirit of the Lord is upon me,*
> *because he has anointed me to*
> *preach good news to the poor.*
> *He has sent me to proclaim release*
> *to the captives*
> *and recovering of sight to the blind,*
> *to set at liberty those who are oppressed,*
> *to proclaim the acceptable year of the Lord.*
> (Luke 4:18–19)

This is a text that would have been quite familiar to his hearers. It is drawn from Isaiah, the great prophet-poet of the Jewish exile. It announces not only what God intended to do to deliver these captives from their bondage but also what the same God promised to do for them on a continuing basis. Nonetheless, for those who were listening to Jesus, the coming of this Reign of God to which the prophet was pointing was still something very much in the future, something to be prayed for and anticipated. But in his interpretation of the passage, Jesus took a dramatic new turn. He told his hearers that this long-anticipated Reign of God was no longer merely something to look forward to: It was taking place in the here and now. While they sat there, he said, it was already happening.

It is important to notice that up to this point in Jesus' interpretation of the prophet, no one seemed unduly disturbed. They continued to purr with appreciation about this local kid who spoke with such authority. But then something unexpected happened, and understanding it helps us grasp just how much Jesus identified with the Jewish faith of his day and just where he began to extend and reinterpret it. Continuing to interpret the passage, he used two illustrations, also drawn from the Jewish Scriptures, of incidents in the past in which God had bestowed particular favor on foreigners, on non-Jews, even at the expense of Jews. To make matters more graphic, Jesus became specific. He spoke of a woman of Sidon who was a widow, and about a Syrian leper. These illustrations, according to Luke, aroused such a fury in this formerly receptive and admiring congregation that they actually rose up and chased Jesus out of town. Few sermons in history have begun so promisingly and ended so unpropitiously. What had happened?

The answer to this question underscores the fact that Jesus did not want to abolish the traditional faith of his own people. He wanted to intensify it and give it an urgent present reality. The Jewish prophets had constantly foretold the coming of a Reign of God. John the Baptist, Jesus' immediate forerunner, had said it was imminent. But Jesus himself said it was present, now *occurring* in and around his hearers. Still, what probably made the congregation in Nazareth especially upset was Jesus' insistence that this divine reign would now include those who were frequently excluded from its benefits, the poor and sick and ritually impure and foreigners. It was not that Jesus had invented anything entirely new with which his hearers would not have been familiar. He simply made it unavoidably present in a way that disturbed them. It has continued to disturb millions of people ever since.

The incident at Caesarea Philippi and the one at Nazareth are informative because they both show that from the very outset of his career people *disagreed* about who Jesus was and what he was up to. This fundamental disagreement reminds us that in asking the question, Who was Jesus?, we must expect different answers because only part of the response can come from history. The other part comes from the heart of the person answering the question. The query is both historical and personal, so the answers will be both as well.

Given the complexity of the question about who Jesus was and is, we must face a second and possibly even more fundamental question: *How* do we go about answering such questions? How do we know what Jesus means, and whom can we trust to tell us? Do we focus exclusively on the Bible? Do we also take church teachings into consideration? What about archaeology or secular history? How much weight should one attach to one's own personal experience? These questions all add up to what is sometimes called the "question of authority." It has often divided Christians as much as the more substantive issues mentioned earlier. But here also there is an important area of consensus: the Bible.

Most Christians accept in one form or another the New Testament, and the traditional Jewish scriptures (which Christians call the "Old Testament" in the sense that it antedated the new one), as authoritative in matters of faith. The Bible supplies both the most indispensable resource and also the most nettlesome problem. Not even the most skeptical historians doubt that the documents collated in the New Testament constitute the oldest and most reliable testimony to the life of Jesus and to what he meant to those who followed him and to the first few generations of Christians. But the nature of the documents is such that the reader must approach them with some awareness of how they arose and what they were first intended to do.

For example, the parts of the New Testament that were written first are not the four Gospels (Matthew, Mark, Luke, and John) but the letters (Epistles) of St. Paul. We have no idea how many letters St. Paul wrote, but reliable scholarship suggests that the first of the seven or eight that are preserved in the New Testament (the authorship of some is contested) dates from about A.D. 52, only about twelve years after Jesus' death. The four Gospels themselves were written down later, probably between A.D. 70 and A.D. 100, but they undoubtedly draw on much earlier oral and written sources, some of these going back to the period of Jesus' own lifetime. The other books of the New Testament, the so-called "Pastoral Epistles," the book of Revelation, and the Acts of the Apostles document the turmoil of the early Jesus movement and the emerging church.

All this suggests that these New Testament sources must be read with an eye to their diversity and the variety of purposes for which they were originally written. Since the New Testament in the form in which we now have it did not receive acceptance in the churches until the fifth century, it is well to remember that for nearly three hundred years Christians did not have it but considered the Old Testament their only scripture.

Scholars love to analyze and classify the various genres of literature one finds in the New Testament. There are letters and parables, miracle stories and songs, extensive quotations from the Old Testament, advice and counsel, descriptions of healings by Jesus himself, and later by his apostles, accounts of Jesus' own actions and teachings. Still, through all the variety, a clear profile of who Jesus was and what he intended to do emerges. Having already mentioned two incidents in Jesus' life—his questioning of the disciples about his identity and his first sermon in Nazareth—it might be useful to sketch briefly what most scholars now accept as the overall trajectory of Jesus' life.

From Nazareth to Jerusalem

Jesus was born into the family of a carpenter in Galilee, the northern province of the Roman colony of Palestine whose residents were often looked upon with condescension by their more sophisticated cousins who lived closer to the big city—Jerusalem. He was born under circumstances that suggest his parents were not married at the time the pregnancy was discovered. With the exception of one incident ascribed to him at the age of twelve, the Gospel writers pick up his story only when he was about thirty and appeared on the stage as a disciple of a radical desert prophet named John the Baptist who called his fellow Jews to repentance and declared that the harsh judgment of God was about to fall on them. John was later executed by King Herod, who considered John a threat to the political stability of his reign.

Jesus apparently spent only a relatively short time with John's movement. Soon he began to proclaim an even more radical version of John's warning. According to Jesus, the promised coming of the Reign of God was not just imminent, it was "at hand." In fact it was already making itself felt in the world in his own words and actions. But the nature of the Reign of God Jesus proclaimed and demonstrated was somewhat different from what most people had been led to expect. He surprised and angered some of the religious leaders of his day, according to the Gospel accounts, by insisting that the favored recipients of this coming—indeed arriving—reign were to be the most despised and disinherited people of the day, the "sinners," those who, according to some of his contemporaries, had little chance of benefiting from God's favor. To make his point even clearer Jesus sometimes violated one or another of the most cherished customs of his time by keeping company and even sharing meals with prostitutes and tax-collectors, the most socially despised and politically suspect people in his society. In his healing and teaching, he insisted that his primary mission was to the poor, prisoners, the mentally and physically sick and disabled, and those who suffered other forms of oppression. He did not hesitate, on some occasions, to criticize both the political and the religious leadership elites of his day whenever he believed they were dealing unjustly with these "little ones."

Throughout Jesus' life the expressive form he used to convey his message was that of the parable. He used it so often and so effectively that it has now become almost synonymous with his teaching. A parable is a story that draws the listener's attention to the normal events of ordinary life, but then introduces an unexpected twist, a surprise inversion that undercuts the audience's normal expectations and pushes them into looking at life in a new way. Jesus told dozens of parables. The best known are the ones about the "Good Samaritan" and the "Prodigal Son."

The first is about a mugging. It tells of a traveler who is set upon by bandits who beat and rob him, leaving him severely injured. Distinguished representatives of the upper social strata, including a priest and a lawyer, come upon him but offer him no help. Instead he is eventually assisted by a Samaritan, the representative of an ethnic and religious minority that was viewed by many people in Jesus' audience with scorn.

The other parable recounts the saga of a brash young man who demands his inheritance before his father's death, squanders it all in wild parties, then returns home anxiously only to have his father hurry out to welcome him even before he arrives.

In both of these anecdotes, as in many others, Jesus led his hearers on and then assaulted their sensibilities with a startling reversal. It was the respected members of the community, not an outcast, who should have been expected to help the wounded man. The son should have crawled on his knees to his father and begged forgiveness instead of finding that his father had rushed out the door to embrace him. Sometimes Jesus' parables have been compared to Zen koans, the Buddhist stories that leave the listener shocked and perplexed, the taken-for-granted world turned upside-down. The difference is that while koans subvert reality as such, Jesus' parables overturn social and religious conventions.

Not only did Jesus speak in parables, he often enacted parables as well. The Gospels brim with stories of Jesus doing things that upset the predilections of his society, especially those of its more privileged echelons. He violated certain norms of behavior, dined with unacceptable people, conversed with disreputable characters, and staged a nonviolent march into Jerusalem that was the first-century equivalent of street theater, a comic caricature of the pompous Roman entrance processions. It has frequently been observed about Jesus that his words and his deeds meshed to an unusual degree, that he taught both by what he said and by what he did. It is possible to look at Jesus' whole life as an extended parable, as God's way of making clear the divine message by drawing people into a story and then pulling the rug out from under them so that they are snapped into perceiving the world and themselves in an entirely new way.

But what was the *content* of the message Jesus was proclaiming and enacting? He summed it up in the phrase, "Repent, for the Kingdom of God is at hand." In more contemporary terms this might mean, "Now is the time to change the way you live because the transforming activity of God is already present here and now." Jesus also made clear what he meant by "Kingdom of God." It was a time in which the poor and the oppressed would be vindicated, the outcasts and rejects would be brought into the covenant community, and the peace of God would also bring harmony between human beings and nature. It was not, however, a divine reign that could be observed from the outside or viewed with detachment. It was something that required a radical change in the way people lived.

As long as Jesus remained in Galilee, at some distance from the center of religious and political power, even though he was increasingly unpopular with the establishment, he was still not considered a serious threat. Naturally his message about a new kingdom sounded subversive to those who served the Roman emperor and to the toadies around the puppet King Herod. Still, it was only when he decided to lead his band of followers into Jerusalem that these ruling groups began to see Jesus as a genuine danger to their privileges. From then on, he was in real jeopardy.

Palestine was a Roman colony, but the empire ruled through a network of local elites constituted largely by the representatives of priestly families that had been installed by the legions. These ruling cliques knew they had little popular support, so they were understandably apprehensive about what Jesus was up to and about the growing following he was gathering. By proclaiming a Reign of God that was coming even now, he was undercutting the symbolic basis of their own authority. They were also worried that the Romans might interpret his grass-roots movement as a threat to the empire, and they had reason to be concerned, since only a few decades earlier another popular preacher had actually led an armed uprising against Rome.

(Also, though they could not have foreseen it exactly as it happened, only forty years after Jesus' death, a popular revolt against both the Romans and their puppets did take place in Jerusalem, with calamitous consequences.) So they watched with deepening uneasiness as Jesus and his followers entered Jerusalem and elements of the local populace, along with some of the pilgrims who had arrived for the Jewish holidays, welcomed him as a deliverer.

The situation was tense. But it came to a head only when Jesus, accompanied by his followers, entered the outer court of the temple and created a disturbance. All four Gospels record this famous incident, although with slightly different emphases. According to the Gospel of Mark, the earliest and sometimes the most historically accurate, Jesus and his disciples actually took over a part of the temple and prevented anyone from entering or leaving it for a time. The other Gospels restrict themselves to a description of Jesus' driving the money-changers out and overturning their tables. Whatever actually happened, the rulers saw this action of Jesus as a provocation.

Now the die was cast. The nervous local puppets decided that rather than risk a possibly bloody Roman crackdown, they themselves would have to take action. Jesus was arrested and turned over to the Roman authorities who, after some indecision, executed him by torture in the manner reserved for those found to be subversive to the imperial order. Jesus was crucified. His followers scattered and fled. A minor incident in the long saga of Rome seemed to be over.

But the entire meaning of Christianity hangs on the belief that this was *not* the end of the story, or of Jesus. Two days later, again according to the Gospel accounts, some of the women who were closest to Jesus walked out to the tomb where he had been buried to anoint his body and found it missing. Through a series of events and encounters they and the other disciples, and later increasing numbers of people, became utterly convinced that Jesus was alive, albeit present in the world in a very different manner than he had been before. They took this victory over death as God's vindication of what Jesus had been teaching and demonstrating in the years they had been with him.

Now, from a dispirited and fearful remnant this tiny group of followers became an exuberant and energetic movement. "He is risen!" they announced and fanned out to announce this "good news" (the meaning of the word *gospel*). At once the Jesus movement began to multiply, first in Palestine, then in neighboring regions, then in every part of the Roman Empire and eventually throughout the entire world. As the world edged toward the two thousandth anniversary of the birth of Jesus, demographers estimated that there are now something over one billion Christians. This makes Christianity numerically the largest religion in the world. Slightly more than half these Christians are Roman Catholics. The remainder is made up of

Protestants, Orthodox Christians found mainly in Greece, Russia and Eastern Europe, and the various branches of Pentecostalism, which is the fastest-growing Christian movement anywhere in the world today. How did this growth from one man and twelve disciples to more than a billion people happen? To answer this question will require us to take a fast spin through twenty centuries of history.

Early Christianity

Peter and Paul

The transition from the Palestinian "Jesus Movement" of what Christians now call the "first century A.D." (Anno Domini meaning "in the year of our Lord") to the early Christian church was wracked by hardship and internal tensions. First there were persecutions of the Jews who joined the Jesus movement by some of their leaders who saw it as a dangerous heresy. Then came the awful destruction of Jerusalem as the Roman army pounced on the Jewish revolutionaries (possibly including some Christians who were not yet seen as a separate faith) who had temporarily liberated the city from the empire. The Romans razed Jerusalem and destroyed the temple. All the citizens of the city, including the Christians, were forced to flee, and this inadvertently sowed the seeds of the new Christian movement in other areas. Thus the disaster of the destruction of Jerusalem had a vastly important side effect. It pushed the young Christian movement out into the wider world and forced it to become a truly universal faith.

The transition Christianity had to make from Jewish sect to world faith was not an easy one. There was considerable internal strife among the leaders of the nascent movement. Present-day Christians who innocently believe there was once a serene and unified period of church history before arguments and divisions set in must ignore abundant evidence in the New Testament itself. The four Gospels, for example, although they agree on the large outline of Jesus' life trajectory, disagree on certain details. Many of Paul's letters are devoted to refuting other teachers and leaders in the early church with whom he disagreed on fundamental issues. A heated dispute quickly arose between the Peter, who had known Jesus before his crucifixion, and the Paul who, as we have seen, emphasized that he had never seen Jesus in the flesh but had met him only after the Resurrection. This bitter quarrel centered on whether those Gentiles who responded to the gospel message were required, in effect, to become Jews before they could become members of the church. Did they need to be circumcised, for example, or to observe the Jewish dietary laws? Peter argued at first that they did, but Paul insisted they did not. Paul contended that God had not abandoned his first chosen people but that in Jesus Christ the original covenant had now been widened to include those who had not been admitted before. God had done "a new thing" and the outsiders were now to be welcomed into God's family. The dispute rankled but was finally settled by a council of the church (described in the Acts of the Apostles) that met in Jerusalem and decided that Paul was correct. Gentiles could become Christians without becoming Jewish converts first.

It was a momentous decision, perhaps the most far-reaching ever made by a church council. It meant that the door of the Christian movement was now wide open to anyone who wanted to affirm the gospel message and become a part of the new community. Thousands swarmed in, and this brought with it a momentous change. In the beginning all Christians had been Jewish, but now hardly any of the newcomers were. Within a century of its founding, Christianity had become a predominantly gentile movement with a small Jewish Christian minority within it. From this moment on we must speak of two religions, or two faith traditions, Christianity and Judaism, each springing from the same original sources but each developing in its own characteristic way.

There is little doubt that in this formative period of Christianity, the Apostle Paul played an enormously influential role in shaping what the newborn movement was to become. But three points have to be underscored about this influence. First, Paul was not the only theologian in the first decades of Christianity. There were other leaders who taught different views of Christian life and faith. One of these non-Pauline ways of being Christian was that of the so-called "gnostic Christians," who held some views analogous to what is currently called "New Age" religion. Their beliefs have been clarified recently with the discovery of ancient manuscripts that exemplify the rich variety present in early Christianity.

Also, in at least one respect, Paul may not have been wholly responsible for the breakthrough of the Christian movement into the gentile world. Historians now know that many non-Jews had been drawn to the worship and teaching of the Jewish synagogues all over the Roman Empire before Paul appeared, but he provided the coherent theological basis for what was to become the new religion's most daring move—the welcoming of the outsiders into the covenant that God had made earlier with the Jews.

St. Paul did, however, create one very important precedent. Since he had never met Jesus before the Crucifixion but claimed to have encountered the Risen Christ in a powerful experience on the road to Damascus, he set an example for the direct relationship to the Risen Christ that was to become an important dimension of Christianity. His "Damascus Road experience" made it possible for succeeding generations of individuals to accept the reality of a personal, sometimes mystical, encounter with Jesus Christ that did not depend either on having met him in the flesh or on authoritative reports about him handed down by succeeding generations of church authorities. Thus, ironically, the same St. Paul who is often cited so favorably by ecclesial authorities also helped give rise to the mystical/experiential strain in Christian history that has so often caused such problems for these very authorities. Understandably, the people who manage religious hierarchies and try to regularize and channel human contacts with God often fret about mystics or anyone else who claims a direct and unmediated contact with the divine. But St. Paul was just such a "mystic."

St. Paul is not well understood today and is often maligned as someone who distorted the earlier and simpler teachings of Jesus. Actually the difference between Jesus and Paul is that between *the* central figure (Jesus) and *one* of his interpreters for a particular time and place (Paul). It is very unlikely that when Paul was writing his letters to the various tiny Christian communities in Corinth, Ephesus, and Rome during the decades immediately following Jesus' death that he foresaw their use as scripture in churches two thousand years later. Nonetheless, Christians rightly hold these Epistles to be invaluable, since they set an example for what could be a different interpretation for other times and other places.

Still, the core elements (not the specific details) of Paul's letters remain central to much of Christianity today. Of these, three in particular should be mentioned. First, by basing his interpretation of Christ so firmly on the Resurrection, Paul boldly addressed the age-old religious and moral problem of the apparent contradiction between love and power. He did so by emphasizing what he called the "righteousness of God" within which these two elements are united. It was, and remains, a daring assertion; namely, that although love and goodness and compassion (such as they were exemplified in the life of Jesus) may be defeated and destroyed in the short run, they will *ultimately* triumph. Jesus may be tortured and murdered by the selfish elites of his time, but God *vindicates* what Jesus has done by raising him from the dead. God thereby makes "righteousness"—which for Paul had none of its current prudish connotations but meant justice within the human community—possible. In Jesus, for Paul, the ultimate unity of love and power have been demonstrated once and for all.

Second, Paul left in his writings an assurance that all human beings are capable of discerning right from wrong. This idea, sometimes called "natural law," has remained integral to many parts of Christianity ever since. Paul did not invent the concept. It was a part of his cultural and religious heritage. But he used it to argue that it did not really matter in the final analysis whether one were a Jew who had the advantage of knowing God's revealed law, or a non-Jew who did not. The fact was that all human beings—himself included—did not live up to the full potential of human life or the purpose for which God had created them. Therefore the real question, for Paul, was not How do we *know* the good? but, rather, How can we *live* the good we already know? This is another powerful insight, and it is one that flies in the face of much of the history of moral philosophy. Paul was not concerned about the endless arguments around questions of what one *should* do in this or that situation. He believed the real moral dilemma of human beings was how to have the courage actually to *do* what we know to be the good. Thus Paul's analysis of the human moral situation serves as a useful corrective to the more conceptual and cognitive theories of morality that continue to appear in history.

Paul's third most basic religious category—and the answer to his own moral question, How do we actually *do* the good we know?—is the concept of "grace." Shorn of all its theological overlay, "grace" simply means that God—who is both love and power—enables human beings to do what they cannot do entirely on their own. Grace need not be something exotic or esoteric. It includes all the ways God, who is present in all of life, nurtures and supports that which is life-giving and that which is moving toward justice and human community. Grace is what makes righteousness—full human life in community—possible. Paul was eventually imprisoned by the Romans and probably died as a martyr during the fierce persecution of Christians instituted by the Roman emperor Nero who reigned from A.D. 54–68. As someone has rightly pointed out, although Nero had Paul killed, today we name our dogs for Nero and our sons for Paul.

Christ and Caesar

The Roman Empire in the first and second centuries A.D. was seething with contending religious movements. Not only was there the ancient Roman pantheon but there was also the cult of the "great mother" Cybele, whose devotees worshiped her with ecstatic dancing and singing. There was also Mithraism, in which the central liturgical act was the sacrifice of a bull, and which taught a severely ascetical code of ethics. It was restricted exclusively to men, won great popularity among the Roman legions, and was more widespread than Christianity during the second century. There was also the religion of Isis, the nature goddess, which had originated in Egypt and featured the annual celebration of the death and resurrection of her consort, Osiris. There was also Judaism, and, most important, there was the symbolically powerful cult of the Roman emperor who was presented as a semidivine being whom all Roman citizens were expected to worship and revere. At the time the young Christian movement made the leap from being a sect within Palestinian Judaism and became one of these many contending religions of the Roman Empire, it would have been hard for anyone to foresee its future: that within less than three centuries it would not only become the predominant faith of that empire but also would eventually succeed it and become the cultural structure that united Europe for more than one thousand years. How did it happen?

Scholars have debated this question for centuries, and there is no real consensus. Two things are clear, however. One is that the presence of Jewish synagogues in virtually all the major cities of the empire provided the religious space within which the young Christian faith could get a hearing. There can be little doubt that the people to whom the gospel first appealed were mainly those who were already drawn to Judaism but who did not want to undergo the demanding process of converting, which would have required, among other things, circumcision. The other is that the most forceful rival Christianity faced was not the mystery cults we have mentioned above, but the cult of the emperor. As far as this imperial cult's administrators were concerned, one could belong to any of the religions so long as one performed the proper ritual obeisance to the divine emperor, and the adherents of the other religions (except for Judaism) willingly did so. But this the Christians would not do. They insisted that one had to choose between Christ and Caesar. They were willing to pray *for* the emperor, but not *to* him. They believed that the "kingdoms of this world" had been created by God and should, within limits, be obeyed. But they also claimed that the Risen Jesus was the true sovereign of the universe and that all earthly kings, including the mighty Caesar, were subject to him.

The intransigence of the early Christians on this point brought them much suffering and also much notoriety. In the year 180, for example, seven men and five women were executed at Scillium in Roman North Africa because the Roman officials interpreted their claim that Jesus was "King of kings" as an affront to the emperor and an act of subversion. Their stubborn attitude was often puzzling to the generally tolerant imperial officers. With obvious frustration, one of them asked a Christian named Polycarp of Smyrna, "What harm is there in saying 'Caesar is Lord'?" One can understand his bewilderment. But to do so would have meant, for Christians, denying that Jesus was Lord (*kyrios*) and would have been a betrayal of their faith. So Polycarp, and thousands like him, refused. Consequently, they were driven underground and kept their faith secret whenever they could. But when they were discovered and put to the test of placing the "pinch of incense" on the imperial altar, they refused. Many were found out and then cruelly executed. Some were killed by gladiators or lions in the public arenas for the entertainment of the masses.

Why then, under such adverse circumstances, did the church continue to grow so rapidly? For one thing, the persecution, though severe, was sporadic, especially in areas distant from Rome. Also, as history has shown on other occasions, "the blood of the martyrs is the seed of the church." People who witnessed or heard about the persecution of Christians came to admire their courage. Their obvious assurance in the rightness of their cause and the truth of their message, for which they were willing to die, startled and impressed people who lived among the confusion of contending gods and skeptical cynicism. People also apparently joined one of the many local congregations of the new faith because they found something attractive and satisfying both about the message of salvation they proclaimed and about the quality of life they found within the fellowship.

Although not exclusively, many of the people who were drawn to Christianity came from the lower social strata, especially in the cities. Women and slaves and ordinary workers were touched by the equalitarian ethos these tiny clusters of Christians exhibited, at least in the early years. They would meet regularly in one of the member's homes, usually on Sunday, to pray and sing and talk, to read letters from other congregations, to care for the needs of the poor among them, to hear readings from the Old Testament Scripture (the New Testament was still being written), and to share bread and wine, not just ceremonially but as part of a full meal. Using the Greek word for "love," a central concept in Jesus' teachings, they called it an "agape feast." The church also grew because Christians worked very hard to win people to their faith. They preached and taught and testified. Those who showed an interest were instructed, sometimes for as much as two years, in what was called the catechumenate. Eventually they were baptized, usually by immersion in water, on Easter Sunday.

As more and more people embraced Christianity, it gradually became clear that, since Judaism did not make much effort to recruit converts, only two real religious options were open to most people. There was either the emperor cult, which increasingly melded the other religions into itself in a comprehensive syncretism, or there was faith in the Risen Christ. Then came an event, however, that no one could have anticipated, which fundamentally altered the future course of Christianity. Sometime early in the fourth century—no one is sure exactly when—the Roman emperor, whom Christians had steadfastly refused to worship, himself became a Christian.

Constantine and the Councils

The "conversion" of the Emperor Constantine I to Christianity is a blurry affair. It can hardly be doubted that he started as a pagan and ended his life calling himself as a Christian. How serious or "sincere" he was, of course, no one knows. It seems that on the eve of a particularly critical battle the emperor had a dream in which he was told to order his soldiers to mark their shields with the Chi-Rho sign that had come to be associated with

Christianity. Later, in a flattering biography of Constantine written by one of his admirers, the Christian historian named Eusebius said the sign had appeared in the heavens. Whatever really happened, Constantine did attach a Christian symbol of some sort to his soldiers' weapons. And he did win a decisive victory. After the battle, duly impressed, he returned to Rome and erected a statue of himself on which he had inscribed, in Latin, "By this saving sign, the true test of bravery, I saved and freed your city from the yoke of the tyrant, and restored the senate and the Roman people, freed, to their ancient fame and splendor." It was one of history's most dizzying reverses. The unarmed Galilean who three hundred years earlier had been crucified as a threat to Roman imperial order had now become the patron of Roman military power. How did it happen?

What transpired in Constantine's soul is not for us to fathom. In any case, he not only began to refer to himself as a Christian but also took an active, indeed overweening, part in the affairs of the church. The results, though perhaps not always in the best interests of Christianity, have left a major imprint on it for all the centuries since. Constantine's most important action, after becoming a Christian, was to convoke the first "ecumenical council," a meeting of the leaders of the whole Christian church. He did so for both religious and political reasons. He wanted to settle some internal disputes that had arisen among various Christian factions so that Christianity would be a unifying and not a divisive force within the empire. Fittingly, the council met in Bithynia in a city called Nicaea, named after the Roman goddess of Victory ("Nike").

There were many rifts in the young church. For one thing, women, who had exercised a wide range of leadership positions in the earliest days, were barred from many ministries and sometimes ordered to keep silent. Those Christians (later called "gnostics") who held to certain mystical interpretations of Christianity that some others deemed heretical were often driven out. (Some of these people, when they were ordered to burn their texts, secretly buried them at a place called Nag Hammadi in Egypt where they were found only a few decades ago.) But the main dispute that had appeared among the congregations and their leaders, who were called "bishops" or "elders," focused on this question: What exactly was the relationship between the God these Christians were sure they had met in the Risen Christ and the God who had created the world? Was Jesus fully at one with that supreme God? Or was he something else, perhaps a demigod? This was the controversy the emperor and the bishops tried to settle once and for all at Nicaea, but with mixed success.

Various opinions flourished among the Christians of the time (as they do today) about how Jesus Christ represents God, and about the nature of the inner bond between God and Christ. These different ideas all coexisted within the same church. But Constantine, and many of the bishops as well, wanted nothing less than unanimity. After much rancorous discussion the council finally declared that Jesus was "one in being (*homoousios*) with the father." This in itself was an important theological decision, and although many Christians continued to hold different views of the link between Jesus and God—and still do today—this formulation became the "orthodox teaching." It was enshrined in the Nicene Creed, which members of many churches repeat in worship services to this day, and was ratified by several subsequent councils during the following centuries.

These later councils also elaborated in much more detail a doctrine that has become central to most, though not all, Christian churches—the idea of God as a "Trinity." Though this notion has sometimes been presented as a strange paradox or an unfathomable riddle, the intention of those who formulated it is not so hard to grasp. They were trying to affirm the various different actions of God they had experienced—as the Creator of the universe, as the One who called the people of Israel to their special task, as the loving power they had met in Jesus, and as the continuing spiritual presence that deepened and sustained their lives—and at the same time insist that these were all manifestations of the *same* God. They wanted to assure themselves, and the world, that there is a divine unity underlying the genuine diversity of divine appearances. So they said that God is one, but consists of three "persons," not in the sense of three individuals, but rather as three different "persona" (the Latin word for the masks worn by actors in the theater who sometimes played different characters in the same drama). The divine unity, in other words, can be encountered in a number of different ways but is still fundamentally one.

The decisions of the Council of Nicaea were immensely influential for the future of Christianity. But possibly even more important than the decisions themselves was that, due to the emperor's leadership, Nicaea's conclusions became the law not only for the church but also for the empire. Constantine had personally presided over several meetings of the council and had made several speeches. Then, after it closed, he issued an imperial edict that prohibited the Christians who disagreed with Nicaea from meeting and confiscated their places of worship. This action set an ominous precedent. Unlike Judaism, which has often encouraged a wide range of acceptable opinions on important religious questions, or Hinduism, which seems to flourish on heterogeneity and variety, the leaders of at least that part of Christianity which accepted the council injected into the Christian faith the idea that in key matters of doctrinal controversy, there is one and only one valid position. This insistence on doctrinal conformity also gave birth to the counternotion of "heresy," of holding the mistaken or "unorthodox" position. One can only speculate on how differently the history of Christianity might have unfolded if the bishops who met at Nicaea had not been under pressure from the emperor to come to a single mind, if they had declared instead, for example, that so long as Christians tried to love and follow Christ they could hold any one of a variety of different opinions about his inner relationship to God. But they did not. Consequently, the habit of defining Christianity in terms of belief rather than of behavior took hold, and with it the acute sensitivity to allegedly wrong beliefs that has so often marred and disrupted Christian history.

Constantine did indeed mark a turning point. Within a few short years after his reign, the Christian movement that had started out as the victim of accusations of blasphemy and subversion, and that had been hounded by a crushing combination of religious and political authority, was itself now seeking out "heretics" and using the sword of Caesar to enforce its will on them.

Rome and Constantinople

So far we have traced the history of Christianity in something like a straight line. At this point, however, that is no longer possible. Again, the Emperor Constantine I marks the boundary. Before him, Christianity had been one of a number of sometimes persecuted sects and cults within the Roman Empire. After him, though there were certain setbacks, it gradually became not only the one fully tolerated religion in the empire but also the unifying culture and the sacred ideology of that empire. Before Constantine, although there were many groups that were not wholly satisfied with the increasingly hierarchical and sometimes authoritarian rule of the bishops, after him there were whole movements and regions that tried to distance themselves from the emerging "catholic" church structure, centered in Rome and wielding imperial power. Previously, while Christians had still been subject to persecution, one had to think very carefully before taking the risk of joining this suspect movement. Now it became easier, and some people converted for more opportunistic reasons. After all, might it not prove advantageous to hold to the same faith the emperor did?

But again, it was Constantine himself who made what turned out to be one of the biggest changes. He did it by building a "new Rome" five hundred miles to the east (which with his characteristic lack of modesty he named "Constantinople"). He then abandoned the old city to immigrants from northern Europe, the "barbarians" who were already entering in large numbers, establishing in his new capital an institutional pattern that integrated religion and politics, church and empire in a manner that eventually differed markedly from that of Rome and the west.

For many centuries after the death of Constantine, "Catholic Rome" and "Orthodox Constantinople" symbolized the two major strands of Christianity, the Latin and the Greek branches. But as they grew apart from each other, eventually splitting officially in A.D. 1054, largely over the issue of papal authority, Christianity was spreading throughout Europe, Africa, parts of Asia, and the Middle East. It was assuming such a variety of expressions that at this point it is no longer useful to try to answer the question—What is Christianity?—by tracing a linear history. Rather we will now seek to respond to the question by introducing some of the exemplary individuals who have personified Christianity during its complex history, and whose life stories will remind us that it is largely through his continuing impact on actual people that the reality of Jesus continues to be felt in the world.

Christian Lives

Christianity is a religion of incarnation. It is not unique among the religions of the world in making its message known principally through the lives of actual people rather than through law codes or systems of doctrine (though both these have played important roles as well). Still, there is a high degree of congruity between the *essence* of Christian faith, which centers after all in a *person*—Jesus Christ—and its reliance on exemplary figures to convey its inner meaning. These people are sometimes called "saints," and an extraterrestrial visitor would be bound to notice that Christians often name their local churches after them. It will be useful to catalog a few of the most widely recognized of these representative personalities to suggest the variety of life-styles that can accurately be called "Christian." I will first describe three such saints, drawn from different historical periods. All three enjoy a real popularity and acceptance in virtually all branches of Christianity. I will then mention several other exemplary Christians, including some from our own period. This will in no way exhaust the varieties of Christian lives, but it will dramatize the diversity that is possible when one seeks to answer the question, What does it mean to be Christian?

Mary, the Mother of Christ

Jesus was, of course, a man. But from the outset women have played an extraordinarily important role in Christianity. It was Jesus' women followers who discovered the empty tomb on the first Easter and who raced to tell his other friends, thus becoming the first messengers of the gospel. Women preached and taught and healed in the early decades of Christian history, until men leaders, accommodating Christianity to its patriarchal social environment, restricted them and eventually established an exclusively male hierarchy. But even after that, and throughout all the centuries, Christian women have headed monasteries, instructed popes and kings, healed and taught. They also did the quiet work of feeding the poor, caring for the sick, and burying the dead.

The first woman in Christian history, the one who both preceded and survived the earthly life of Christ, and the one who remains in some ways the model for all subsequent Christians, male and female, is the young Jewish peasant who bore Jesus in a cold stable, nurtured him in his youth, tried—not always successfully—to understand his dangerous life work, and tearfully witnessed his final suffering and death. But what do we really know about this Galilean woman who, for many Christians, remains second only to Christ himself as the one who embodies the inner meaning of Christianity?

The truth is that, historically speaking, we do not know very much about Mary. Two of the Gospels—Luke and Matthew—state that she was still a virgin and not yet married to Joseph when she agreed to become pregnant through the Holy Spirit and thus to provide the body within which God, as Christianity teaches, became a human being. Not all Christians hold to the literal truth of the "Virgin Birth" of Christ, but the fact that God actually "became flesh" and joined the human race in all its pain, finitude, and mortality is central to virtually all Christian views of God. Thus, by accepting God's will (she might have refused since she was free to do so), Mary in effect *made possible* the event without which Christianity would not exist: God "became flesh and dwelt among us." Whatever else this "yes" of Mary means, it suggests that by her utter confidence in God's love and her willingness to accept the social stigma that would inevitably attach to bearing a child outside of wedlock, Mary played an indispensable role in the drama of salvation.

It is important to notice that Jesus Christ did not, like the divine figures in some religious myths, descend directly from heaven. Nor was he born full grown from a god's or a goddess's brow. Rather, Jesus began as a fetus, as we all do, and entered the world drenched in blood and urine as every baby does. And Mary made it possible. By doing something very normal—having a baby—she demonstrated that God chooses to be present in the most everyday and "ordinary" facets of life. For this, all Christians are grateful.

But beyond this gratitude and affection there is as much, possibly more, disagreement among Christians about Mary than there is about Jesus. Was her own conception shielded from any taint of sin as the idea of the "Immaculate Conception" suggests? Can or should one pray to her to intercede with God? Did she remain a virgin the rest of her life, work miracles, enter heaven without dying as the belief in her Assumption teaches? Roman Catholics and many other Christians would answer yes to these questions. Most Protestants would either say no or would suggest that they can find no evidence in the Bible itself for such claims. Yet, despite these doctrinal disagreements about her, Mary remains an immensely popular and venerated figure among almost all Christians. She is a favorite subject for artists (think of the hundreds of Italian Renaissance madonnas) and a central figure in popular devotions. In wood, stone, plastic, and cement she stands serenely, with or without the infant Jesus in her arms, on automobile dashboards and mantelpieces, and in gardens, front yards, and grottoes all over the world. Some people believe she continues to appear in places like Lourdes and Fatima (and more recently in Medjugorje in Yugoslavia) to inspire, encourage, and instruct those who will listen. Next to the "Lord's Prayer," which Jesus taught his disciples, the "Ave Maria" ("Hail, Mary") is probably the most frequently uttered prayer in the Christian world.

But just what does this powerfully attractive figure actually tell us about what it means to be a Christian? Responses are mixed. Some women today claim she combines values that are mutually irreconcilable—chastity *and* motherhood—and is therefore not a practical role model in the real world. Others say the qualities often ascribed to her—humility, receptivity, gaining her life meaning by giving birth—are not the ones women should emulate today. Still others, however, find in her a clear example of the prophetic voice of Christianity. They point to the most substantive utterance attributed to Mary in the Bible—found in the Gospel of Luke (1:46–55)—which foretells the radical impact Jesus would have on the world.

> *And Mary said,*
> *"My soul magnifies the Lord,*
> *and my spirit rejoices in God my Savior,*
> *for he has regarded the low estate*
> *of his handmaiden.*
> *For behold, henceforth all*
> *generations will call me blessed;*
> *for he who is mighty has done great things for me,*
> *and holy is his name.*
> *And his mercy is on those who fear him*
> *from generation to generation.*
> *He has shown strength with his arm,*
> *he has scattered the proud in the*
> *imagination of their hearts,*
> *he has put down the mighty from their thrones,*
> *and exalted those of low degree;*
> *he has filled the hungry with good things,*
> *and the rich he has sent empty away.*
> *He has helped his servant Israel,*

in remembrance of his mercy,
as he spoke to our fathers,
to Abraham and to his posterity for ever."
Luke 1:46–55 RSV

This song, called "the Magnificat," hardly celebrates the values of submission or resignation. Here Mary sings of scattering the proud and putting down imperial rulers, feeding the hungry and sending the rich away empty-handed. No wonder Mary has at times inspired movements of social insurrection. The troops of the Mexican rural revolutionary Emiliano Zapata, for example, rode into Mexico City wearing pictures of Our Lady of Guadalupe, one of the apparitions of Mary, tucked into the bands of their sombreros.

There are other forms of appreciation of Mary as well. Some see in her persona as the Queen of Heaven a valuable link between Christianity and those religions that venerate goddesses. Still others feel she discloses the "feminine face" of a God who might otherwise appear entirely masculine. The psychologist Carl Gustav Jung once wrote that the proclamation of the doctrine of the Assumption in 1950 was the most important event in the Christian world since the Reformation because it raised the feminine to a secure place within the Christian godhead.

Not all Christians would agree with Jung. But whatever they may think or feel about Mary, her continued prominence in popular spirituality is irrefutable. Despite the theological battles over her significance she somehow continues to cut through it all, to touch human hearts and to represent one perennial answer—or perhaps several different answers—to the question, What does it mean to be Christian?

St. Francis of Assisi

Sometimes called "the most Christ-like man who ever lived," Francis was born in 1182 into a rich Italian cloth merchant's family. He was such a winsome person during his brief forty-four years that he drew admirers and followers in large numbers while he lived. After his death, he became the person who, with the exception of Mary, is undoubtedly the most beloved of all Christian saints. Francis hardly started out to be a saint. If anything, in his early years he was known as an antic playboy, an ebullient but irresponsible gamester who reveled in troubadours and parties. Indeed, St. Francis never lost some of these qualities, thus demonstrating that religious conversion often intensifies and transmutes characteristics that were already present in an individual's life rather than obliterating them. Always the songster, even when things went badly, St. Francis is sometimes known as "God's troubadour," and few doubt that he would have been pleased with the appellation.

The young Francis was raised by his family in the full expectation that he would move comfortably into its prosperous cloth business. But it did not work out that way. As a teenager he was drawn to poor people, some of whom he met while attending his father's store and to whom, so it is reported, he often handed out doublets and capes free without his parents' approval. Francis was not a particularly religious youth, but one day in church he heard the priest reading the portion of the Gospel in which Jesus tells a rich young man to sell all that he has and give it to the poor. Francis was fascinated. He decided at once that this was exactly what he wanted to do. As might be expected, his parents were not enthusiastic about the idea and tried in every way they could to dissuade him, even locking him for a time in a cell. But Francis insisted. For him, getting rid of money and fine clothes and belongings did not seem to be a deprivation at all but a liberation. It was an unburdening, a robust break with the social expectations that hemmed him in. It was a chance, as he put it, "nakedly to follow the naked Christ." It was a way to make himself open and receptive to anything the future would bring, to savor the full impact of all its pain and joy.

Francis began to beg for a living and to gather about him a gaggle of like-minded youths. They wore coarse garments and tied them around the waist with a rope rather than an expensive leather belt. Francis shaped these companions, mainly young men from middle-class families, into what was soon to become the Order of the Friars Minor (younger brothers), known now as the Franciscans. His organization was a controversial one, especially since the simple life-style of the Franciscans implied a certain criticism and even rejection of the wealth and power of the institutional church. But Francis was a loyal churchman, as well as a canny person, so he went to Rome and persuaded the pope to grant a charter to this unlikely new movement. Still, the relationship with the papacy was never a smooth one, and within a century of Francis's death, some Franciscans had become so critical of the church's opulence and secular power that they were burned as heretics.

Francis, taking another mandate of Jesus seriously, also became a peacemaker. He began by helping to negotiate settlements between warring Italian city-states. Then, in what must have appeared a nearly insane gesture, he sailed to Syria in 1219 during the Fifth Crusade to try to persuade the sultan of the Turkish forces to stop the bloodshed. The leaders of the crusader armies were skeptical about Francis, but they did not prevent him from trying. Surprisingly, he was allowed through the lines by the Muslim troops and spent three days as the sultan's personal guest. We do not know exactly what went on between this ragamuffin preacher and the Muslim commander, only that the sultan seems to have agreed to conditions for a truce. Francis was elated, but when he returned through the lines and presented the agreement to the crusaders, they rejected it. Crestfallen, he sailed back to Italy and told his friends that what was really needed was not the defeat of the infidels but the conversion of the Christians.

Despite some distorted portraits of him, St. Francis was not a dour or morbid figure. No one in Christian history had a more celebrative attitude toward nature, which he praised with canticles to the sun and the moon. He made friends with the birds and the wolves. He rejected wealth not for self-punitive reasons but to follow Christ unencumbered by baggage and property. What he opposed, in himself and in others, was the need to possess and accumulate, whether it be money or education or power. He even warned his followers against owning books. Francis wanted to share the life of Christ as fully as he could, "to feel," as he said in a famous prayer, "the sorrow of your passion." Legend says that this request was finally granted, at least in some degree, and that one day the marks of the nails that had pierced Christ's hands and feet also appeared on Francis' own body. But perhaps his real crucifixion was the pain he endured as he watched with growing frustration as his followers, in connivance with church and secular authorities, gradually transformed his order from the band of brothers he had assembled into a tightly disciplined order, something quite different from what he had intended. He died a disappointed man, still full of inner serenity, but brokenhearted by the fossilization of the movement he founded.

St. Francis means different things to different people. Some see him as a predecessor of Luther, angered by the church's worldly pomp and privilege and hungering for a direct mystical relationship with God. Others view him as the inspiration for the first of a long series of movements, especially among youth, that rebel against the stifling confines of bourgeois, mercantile society, and seek to return to nature and the simple life. Socially radical Christians find in St. Francis the prototype of those who seek God's presence among the poor and the outcast. Still others see in him a link between Christianity and such Asian religions as Buddhism and Hinduism, which also value the simplicity and voluntary poverty that is epitomized by the wandering monk. In any case, God's troubadour, the "poverello" of Assisi—the sparrows perched on his shoulder, the wolf nuzzling his hand—embodies one powerful way of being Christian, a way that has exerted a continuing attraction for centuries.

St. Joan of Arc

About the year 1425 a pious young girl living in a small village in Lorraine announced to her astonished parents that the voices of saints and angels had instructed her to go to the Dauphin of France, Charles VI, and to lead his dispirited French armies in raising the English siege of Orleans. The riveting story of this bold woman's life, her successes and failures, and her eventual torture and execution by the Inquisition have made her one of the most attractive and popular saints in Christian history. Her audacity, her physical courage, her persistent belief in her "inner voices," her tragic death, and her eventual sanctification all combine to make her a model of Christian spirituality for those who believe that a woman's place is not only in the kitchen or in the nursery. How did this improbable but true story occur?

It is a mark of the desperation of the Dauphin, French claimant to the throne, and his military leaders that they would even agree to meet with this strange young peasant dressed in men's clothing. To put her to the test the Dauphin concealed himself among his many courtiers, but Joan was not fooled. She walked directly to him to announce that she was ready to cast the English out of France so that he could be properly crowned in the Cathedral at Reims. At the amazed Dauphin's request, she was then interrogated by ecclesiastical authorities who recommended, since the situation was indeed grave, that the Dauphin would be foolish not to make some use of this possibly crazy girl and her most unusual offer.

In late April of 1429 the French troops were mustered near Orleans, and in a series of attacks, some of which Joan herself led, the English were in fact driven from the town. Joan then left immediately to meet the Dauphin and urge him to hurry to Reims for his coronation. His advisers, however, wanted to see a more decisive victory over the English, so Joan continued to lead the French forces in a series of brilliant battles. Ultimately Charles did go to Reims and was consecrated king on July 17, 1429, with Joan standing—banner in hand—next to the altar. Immediately after the ceremony she knelt before Charles and addressed him as king for the first time. Then she took off her sword and told the archbishop of Reims that she would now like to go back to her parents' home and once again tend her flocks.

But Joan had become too much of a national asset. More military campaigns followed, in one of which she was wounded. Eventually she was captured by a contingent of French soldiers who were not loyal to Charles, and through the intervention of the Bishop of Beauvais, she was turned over to the English for ten thousand francs. She was imprisoned in the Castle of Bouvreuil, and it was announced that she would be brought to trial before a court concerned with faith and morals. Her judges were to be the same bishop who had paid for her person and John Le Meistre, the Vice-Inquisitor of France.

The trial of Joan of Arc began in January 1431. For the next month, she was interrogated several times. Between sessions she was locked in a cell and bound by iron chains. She was guarded day and night by English soldiers, some of whom remained inside the cell with her. Although she requested permission to attend Mass, her interrogators refused to allow her.

Joan's accusers insisted that her whole attitude and behavior demonstrated "blasphemous presumption." They taunted her for claiming divine authority for her voices, for saying that the saints spoke to her in French and not in English, for claiming that she knew what would happen in the future, and for wearing men's clothing. The most serious charge was that she put credence in direct commands from God above what church authorities taught.

Joan responded that she was a faithful daughter of the church, but that she had to make herself responsible first of all to God. The authorities threatened her with torture, but she persisted, saying that even if they tortured her to death, she would not reply differently. Exasperated, her tormentors then warned her that if she persisted in her error she would be turned over to the secular arm for execution. She persisted and was burned at the stake on May 30, 1431. As the flames consumed her, Joan asked the Dominican priest who had accompanied her to hold a crucifix before her eyes and to shout out assurances of salvation so loud that she could hear them above the crackle and roar. Until the last she maintained that her voices were sent by God and had not deceived her. It was not until five hundred years later that Pope Benedict XV canonized her and declared that her feast should be celebrated on May 30.

St. Joan of Arc is a favorite of poets, artists, filmmakers, and playwrights. With her short hair, armor, sword held high, and her stout determination to do what her inner voices told her, she continues to be an inspiration for all those who place direct contact with God above the authority of religious institutions.

In his play "St. Joan," George Bernard Shaw depicts two characters arguing about whether Joan was the first "protestant," since she protested ecclesial authority in the name of individual conviction, or the first "nationalist," because she identified the will of God with the liberation of a particular nation. Joan may have been something of both of these. But she was also much, much more. She is particularly loved by French Christians, but that affection is also shared very widely by those who see in her the model of a plucky young woman who refused to bow before the will of overbearing political and ecclesial authorities. She had a sense of humor, perseverance, bravery, and a certain stubbornness, which continue to make her highly appealing. She represents a gritty and venturesome answer to the question, What does it mean to be Christian?

Saints, Large and Small

These three figures, though drawn from different centuries and regions, do not begin to exhaust the vast range of Christian lives. There are numberless others. Past ages have produced St. Augustine of Hippo (354–430), who constructed such an imposing intellectual edifice for Christian theology in his *City of God* that it has lasted fifteen hundred years. His life work reminds us that Christianity, unlike Shinto and some other religions, lays a heavy stress on the importance of ideas, doctrine, and theology. Christians believe one serves God with one's mind as well as with the other organs. But Christianity is also affective and emotional. One of the greatest exemplars of this aspect of the faith is St. Teresa of Avila (1515–1582), a Spanish Carmelite nun who has grown more influential with every passing century. "St. Teresa of Jesus," as she was also known, managed to combine an active life—organizing convents and friaries and reforming the church—with a nearly uncanny power to penetrate to the inmost recesses of the spiritual life. Her book *Interior Castle,* with its depth, humor, and common sense, is often described as the chief mystical classic of Christianity.

Another mystic, the Italian St. Catherine of Siena (1347–1380), proved in her life that a profound devotional piety could be combined with a passion to care for the sick and the poor. She also exerted herself in public life, and as the pope's ambassador to Florence she helped negotiate a peace treaty between that city-state and the Holy See. St. Catherine, for all her spiritual achievements, never learned to write but dictated hundreds of letters. Like St. Francis she is said to have received the stigmata, the wound marks of Christ, on her own body. No one combined love for God and for humanity in one unified life vision better than this unusual woman.

The roll call goes on, and it includes both officially canonized saints and many who never got such ecclesial recognition. Giotto and Leonardo da Vinci sang God's praise in painted canvas and carved stone. Nameless carpenters, masons, and glaziers crafted cathedrals at Chartres and Salisbury. Priests like Thomas Becket faced down the despotism of kings even when it led to death. Theologians like Thomas Aquinas and Bonaventure built bridges between faith and human understanding. Reformers like Martin Luther and John Calvin tried to restore a church they believed had departed from its original gospel while Ignatius Loyola sought to purify the church from within. Madame de Stael organized a theological study circle, although women were not supposed to do that sort of thing. Intrepid apostles and missionaries like Francis Xavier and Adoniram Judson planted Christian communities in India and Asia, and as the spread of the Western empire threatened to stifle indigenous peoples, Bartolomeo de las Casas championed the rights of the local peoples of the Indies. Sor Joanna, a Catholic nun, ignored the warnings of her male superiors to become the first real Latin-American poet. Anne Hutchinson defied the Puritan magistrates of Boston in order to interpret the Bible from a woman's perspective. Many Christians disgraced themselves by profiting from the slave trade, but others like Henry Ward Beecher and Harriet Beecher Stowe opposed it from without while African-American Christians like Sojourner Truth helped lead slaves to freedom and black preachers like Nat Turner and Denmark Vesey led rebellions against the evil system.

But to point out only the widely known among the saints is to distort the picture. The host of Christians who have quietly followed Jesus at home and at work and have tried to love God and their neighbors in ordinary, day-to-day ways far exceeds those few who are known beyond their small circle. This may be why some Christian groups are reluctant to single out particular individuals as "saints," but instead apply the term to even the most anonymous believers. Still, sainthood, whether focused on extraordinary people or not, reminds us that Christianity, though it is a religion with cathedrals and doctrines, liturgies and sacraments, has as its main dwelling place the human heart and the actions of those who try to put into practice Jesus' command to "follow me."

Contemporary Saints

Do the saints of bygone ages provide usable answers to the question, What does it mean to be Christian?, in *our* time? The answer is probably yes and no. Certain features of their characters—courage, simplicity, perseverance, inner joy—continue to tell us something important about Christian existence. But for many Christians today there is also something missing in these classical figures. They lived so long ago that much of what they did and said does not connect so easily to today's radically altered world. Whatever their merits, they did not have to cope with an age of secularization in which, for many people, God seems to be so entirely absent that living a Christian or any other religious life appears virtually impossible. For this reason we will now turn to some more recent lived exemplars of Christianity to arrive at a more synchronic range of responses to the question of what "Christian" means. Though drawn from different denominations and cultures, these Christian men and women all share the common experience of having lived and died in our own waning twentieth century.

The first contemporary we turn to is Dietrich Bonhoeffer, the German pastor and theologian, a twentieth-century man par excellence. The elegant, brilliant—perhaps even somewhat conceited—scion of a notable aristocratic family in Berlin, Bonhoeffer was a world traveler, a lover of the arts, a connoisseur of vintage wines and string quartets. He wore tailored suits and played a crack game of tennis. An admirer of Gandhi, Bonhoeffer nevertheless was able to sacrifice his philosophical pacifism in order to join the plot to assassinate Hitler. He was arrested by the Gestapo, imprisoned, and finally hanged in Flossenbürg concentration camp in April 1945, hours before the camp was reached by the advancing American army.

Bonhoeffer provides a particularly good example of a twentieth-century Christian life because his story is so unapologetically contemporary. He harbored no hankering for bygone eras. His *Letters and Papers from Prison* sketches, though in barest outline, the dream of a gospel freed at last from the remnants of obsolete metaphysics and constrictive pietism. Bonhoeffer tried until his dying day, although never successfully, to find a spirituality that would enable him to live in a world in which, as he put it, God had allowed himself to be edged out, but Christ could be met "at the center" where earthly life is thickest and most worldly. Bonhoeffer provides a model of Christian faith for those of us who, as he said, need to "live before God as though God did not exist"—which is what it must mean in part to be a Christian in the late twentieth century when serious forms of atheism are simply part of the air we breathe. His ideas of "anonymous Christianity" and "secret discipline," his reliance on a cadre of compatriots, and his adamant refusal to let God be used to make up for human weakness or ignorance all provide us with essential clues to the mystery of what it means to be Christian today.

The second example of an authentically modern Christian saint is the eccentric and stubbornly indigestible Frenchwoman Simone Weil. Roughly the contemporary of Bonhoeffer, Weil grew up in an educated if not a privileged family. Like him she was also raised on the classics but came later to yearn for nothing more than to serve God among the godless. As it happened, Weil's entry into the "godless world" was different from Bonhoeffer's and took her to a different kind of incarceration—working in a noisy Renault automobile factory. But while on the assembly line she learned, as he did in the cellblock at Tegel, about affliction, courage, and cowardice, and the tiny but infinitely valuable joys fellow prisoners and co-workers can share with one another. Like Bonhoeffer, Simone Weil hated the boundary the church had erected between believers and nonbelievers. Bonhoeffer dismantled the wall by insisting that the "true church" is nothing else than the world, claimed by God and inhabited by Christ. But Simone was born Jewish, raised a pagan, and became a quasi-Marxist. She did not really have to go anywhere to be in the godless world; she was already there. Consequently, for Simone Weil, it was her reluctance to be baptized into the church she believed in that signified her conviction that the Christ she loved dwelt also among scoffers and sinners.

Bonhoeffer and Weil share a connection with nearly all exemplars of postmodern Christian saintliness—they demonstrate that to encounter the holy today one must move deeper into the "godless" world, not away from it. For all of them the narrow road to the Kingdom of God leads through the terrestrial city, not away from it. The Bible scholar Amos Wilder, in an essay on what he calls the "lay mystery," says:

> Is it not true that Christianity has a need of recurrent baptism in the secular, in the human, to renew itself... to be saved over and over again from a spurious and phantom Christ?... Theology and witness today will be impoverished unless they take account of the secular man in all his dynamics; of the lay mystery that gives evidence of itself precisely in a desacralized world.

Dietrich Bonhoeffer and Simone Weil perished within a year of each other. Neither ever read these words. But both dramatize how right they are. Both represent the rebaptism of the holy in the secular, a dawning awareness of the mystery that evidences itself in the desacralized world. Their paths into the mystery were different. Bonhoeffer's took him into the dark demiworld of conspiracy and espionage, and eventually to the gallows. Weil's took her into the often petty and acrimonious world of French intellectuals, and then to an early death in England caused in part by her refusal, though she was ill, to eat more than was permitted to her compatriots in occupied France. Both, however, died determined to share fully in whatever it means to embrace life in a century that believes it has left God behind, yet feels a hunger for a holiness that no churchly provision seems to feed. Both, from different sides, refused to allow the church wall to cut them off from a world where they believed Christ is present even among the godless.

Other contemporary models help us in the way they lived their days to discern some answer to the question, What is Christian? For many today that catalog would include the founder of the Catholic Worker movement, Dorothy Day. A pacifist and anarchist, Dorothy started life as a politically radical journalist. Always drawn to the down-and-outers, she began purposely getting arrested in New York City on Saturday nights so that she could share the tank with the prostitutes. Later she organized shelters and soup kitchens for the homeless and hungry unemployed. She got herself in jail again at the height of the Cold War by calmly refusing to crawl into an air-raid shelter during a test alert. Her final brush with the authorities came when, already in her eighties, she sat serenely on a picket line with Mexican-American farm workers in California and sweetly refused to move when ordered. Many Christians today, both Catholics and Protestants and others, firmly believe that whether or not the church ever gets around to canonizing her, Dorothy Day is surely a twentieth-century saint.

On the other side of the violence/nonviolence spectrum, for many Latin Americans, the modern calendar of saints includes Father Camilo Torres-Restrepo. Torres is the Colombian priest who tried to organize a democratic united people's political movement in his country in the 1960s. When it failed, he finally abandoned the effort in order to join a band of armed guerrillas in the hills. He was killed a few weeks afterward in a skirmish with the army.

His body was never recovered. The authorities no doubt wanted to prevent a cult from growing up around his remains. Their caution was probably justified, for already a popular Latin American song declares that "where Camilo Torres fell, there sprung up a cross, not of wood but of light."

It might seem strange at first to include both Dorothy Day the pacifist and Camilo Torres the guerrilla in a single list of exemplars of present-day Christian spirituality. But it should not be. After all, the calendar already includes Francis of Assisi and Joan of Arc. What Dorothy and Camilo share, in addition to a certain personal quality of intensity, modulated by irony, is the recognition that the world has taken the place of the wilderness as the classical testing ground for sanctity and purification. Though they would certainly not have approved of each other's methods, and though they came from different social strata (Torres-Restrepo remains one of Colombia's most aristocratic families), there is still a strange similarity that links them. Both had a strong commitment to the struggle for bread, spiced by a winning tolerance for the weaknesses of the flesh, even in themselves. Both broke from the cloying custom of identifying piety with moralism. Both felt that personal holiness is a wrestling match with the powers of evil in high places, and that this duel must be fought today eye to eye with monstrous corporate forces. Their conflict-ridden lives give us an indispensable insight into what any genuinely contemporary Christianity must incorporate.

One could add more names to the list of present-day saints. Mother Teresa, a Portuguese Roman Catholic nun who works among the sick and dying people of Benares in India and also has founded shelters and hospitals in several other countries may, at this writing, be the best known Christian in the world. Martin Luther King has been idolized too soon by many (his birthday is now a legal holiday in most states) and discredited too quickly by others. But those who were stirred by his eloquent preaching and his indomitable physical courage, and who followed him willingly through the streets and into the jails, know that he represents a robust example of being fully Christian and fully immersed in the fever and the insensibility of the urban world. Other politically committed Christians come to mind, such as Bishops Desmond Tutu of South Africa and Helder Câmara of Brazil. But for most Americans, black or white, King still seems closer and more credible. And his assassination at the age of thirty-nine reminds everyone that serious Christian discipleship still exacts its price.

The Kings and Weils and Bonhoeffers and Days and the others provide luminous answers to the question, What is a Christian today?, for more than one reason. First they were not simple shepherds, fisherfolk, or unlettered peasants. They were urban, sophisticated people. They knew about Darwin, Freud, Marx, contraception, imperialism, and ennui. Their lives span not some idealized past, but our own fractured times. They carried all the alleged handicaps to belief that we do, yet they still managed to be incandescent Christians in very different ways. Not only do their answers to our questions come to us clearly, but also the temporal proximity of their lives to ours makes these answers more credible.

Still, it is important to realize that their lived answers are neither perfect nor complete. To learn from them we do not need to emulate them. We do not even need always to agree with them. Bonhoeffer, for example, often seems never to have shed his aristocratic hauteur, even in prison. Simone Weil occasionally let her spirited criticisms of the history of Israel veer toward something close to anti-Semitism. Dorothy Day and Martin Luther King had their various failings. They were not stained glass saints but human beings. It may be their very failings that make them more credible. Also, we ought to remember that each of these twentieth-century disciples had a singular style. We learn from each of them individually, not as mere representatives of a vague construct such as "contemporary Christianity." Still, when one examines their lives and writings with care, some common threads do emerge, and these, when considered along with comparable elements in the lives of the earlier exemplars we have discussed, do help us in our effort to say and show what it means to be Christian.

Contours of Christian Existence

Are there any irreducible elements or indispensable ingredients to living a life that can reasonably be called Christian? If we consider our sampling of saints from past ages, we can uncover three such components, though they assumed diverse forms and carried different weights in the lives of different people. First, they were all touched and shaped in some formative way by the teachings of Christianity, its core *ideas*. The second is that each was a part of the Christian *community*, the church, in one or another of its expressions. Third, each had a relationship, however mediated or indirect, to the *person* of Jesus Christ. It is clear that all our classical exemplars, though they put more emphasis on one or another of these, combined all three. Can the same be said for our contemporary models? Or are we evolving today a type of Christian spirituality that does not necessarily need all three classical dimensions?

The evidence is mixed. Some Christians today seem to be able to get along without one or more of the three. There are some, for example, who seem to thrive on ideas alone. They read the works of St. Augustine, or Bonhoeffer, or C. S. Lewis, or even the Bible, depending on their tastes, but they seem to need Christian fellowship or personal prayer only in very minor ways. Their worship is often confined to Christmas Eve and Easter Sunday plus periodic feast days and *rites of passage*. Their Christianity is individual and intellectual, not communal or liturgical. Such people probably constitute a small minority within Christianity but it would be wrong to read them out because their temperaments do not attune them to other avenues of Christian expression. Jesus, after all, was a teacher, and Christianity's ideas have attracted thoughtful people throughout its history.

Another species of contemporary Christian relies mainly on the liturgy or the fellowship of the congregation but seems generally untroubled by the question of what message this medium is conveying. Such Christians seem genuinely uninterested in the idea of Christianity except in the most conventional terms. These are the people who can lose themselves in the Mass, soar with fervor into Bach anthems or traditional prayers, or give of themselves unsparingly in social-action projects, but whose eyes glaze over when asked to tell anyone what Christianity teaches. They should not be excluded either. There are times in the history of any religion, and this may be such a time, when the teaching may seem confused and opaque but the community of worship and concern goes on, sharing the uncertainty but sharing nonetheless. Such piety, based in liturgy or on works of love, is sometimes viewed with contempt by the more content-oriented Christians. But it should not be. Especially in an era so starved for friendship, the fact that many people subsist on Christian fellowship without much theological content must be expected. They are part of the body of Christ and represent a perfectly legitimate way of being Christian.

Finally, there are those Christians who survive without much help from teachings or congregations but rely almost entirely on a one-to-one relationship with God. This type of Christianity is less familiar than the other two because it is, by its very nature, less institutionalized and therefore less visible. Still many people today who call themselves Christians lead lives in which they try to follow Christ but have little to do with the institutional church and could probably not pass an exam on Christian doctrine. They should not be excluded, however, from the totality of the people who make up the company of saints, the people who can reasonably be called "Christian."

Still, something seems missing in the Christians who incorporate only one or two of the three classical ingredients of Christian existence. If the contemporary figures we have introduced tell us anything about being Christian, it is that all three elements are found in the most credible saints.

Let us look first at how each of them related to Christian *community*. No one who ever read Dorothy Day's column "On Pilgrimage," which appeared regularly in *The Catholic Worker*, can have missed noticing that it read almost like a combination travel diary and address book. It is studded, as are all her books, with the names of people, living and dead, and places, near and far. For Dorothy Day the mystical body of Christ was not ethereal at all. It was not just the church, and not even "The Catholic Worker" as an organization. It was the Joes and Marcias she visited, ate with, traveled with, and prayed for. Dorothy Day's spirituality was utterly dependent on the Christian community. Without it, her life and witness would have been unimaginable.

The same centrality of the community holds for Bonhoeffer. During the early years of Hitler's rule, Bonhoeffer was deprived by the Nazis of any opportunity to teach or preach legally; so he organized an underground seminary. But, unlike a university theological school, Bonhoeffer's seminary-in-exile in Finkenwalde was a closely knit household where students and professors lived together and shared everything, including the constant danger of a Gestapo raid (which eventually came, causing the closing of the school). After the dispersal of the Finkenwalde brotherhood, Bonhoeffer spent long hours composing letters by the dozen to his students and colleagues who had been drafted into the army. But he did not find such companionship again until his brother-in-law, Hans von Dohnanyi, initiated him into the clandestine group that was planning to kill Adolf Hitler. Bonhoeffer's arrest on another charge in April 1943 deprived him of these friends too. It was then that, much to his own surprise, he began to discover a new community among the political prisoners and the common offenders with whom he shared the gray routine of incarceration. In his *Life Together,* based on the Finkenwalde years, Bonhoeffer writes explicitly about the indispensability of a disciplined supportive circle. Though he is sometimes seen as a lonely and isolated man—which he often was—Bonhoeffer's spirituality could have emerged only from this life together.

Martin Luther King grew up in the warm vigorous atmosphere of the African-American Baptist church. Later, his Southern Christian Leadership Conference multiplied local branches during the 1960s and provided a web of confidantes and phone numbers for hundreds of civil-rights activists at a time when official church bodies often looked askance at pickets and demonstrators. It also supplied a community for King himself.

Only Simone Weil, among our models, seems at first to be the exception. Although powerfully attracted to the Catholic church, she resisted joining it. In fact she seems to have harbored a strong aversion to joining anything. This suspicion of organizations is not an expression of Weil's rejection of the idea of community, however, but rather a mark of the earnestness with which she sought it. In her book *The Mysticism of Simone Weil,* Marie-Magdeleine Davy attributes the striking lack of any corporate quality in Weil's spirituality to her sometimes overly zealous pursuit of self-denial and solitude. Weil often consciously deprived herself of just what she wanted most, not to gain some other goal but to let the suffering of humankind touch her own soul as sharply as possible. Her rejection of organizations was a self-discipline, but it was also a criticism of the thinness and artificiality of the fellowship they proffered. "She rejected [the collective]," Davy writes, "with a violence which is only explicable through the purity and intransigence of her search for the holy. . . .” She was such a perfectionist that she never found the friendship she so obviously longed for.

What do our contemporary saints teach us about the importance of Christian *teaching?* The most striking thing is that they all took it very seriously. They all had personal theologies that could appear a bit old-fashioned in light of modern Christian theology’s dominant interest in modernizing and accommodating. Bonhoeffer, for example, was often considered a maverick by his scholarly colleagues. Like Karl Barth, the leading “neo-orthodox” theologian of his time, whom Bonhoeffer admired—though with reservations—he rejected most of the liberal German theologians’ efforts to accommodate Christianity to modern culture. In one of his better-known letters, Bonhoeffer sharply criticized Rudolf Bultmann, a fellow theologian, for the “typical liberal reduction process” he used in interpreting the New Testament. Bonhoeffer insisted that “. . . the full content, including the mythological concepts, must be maintained.” The New Testament “is not a mythological garbing of the universal truth; this mythology (resurrection and so on) is the thing itself—but the concepts must be interpreted in such a way as not to make religion a precondition of faith. . . . Not until that is achieved,” Bonhoeffer concludes, “will, in my opinion, liberal theology be overcome.”

Although Bonhoeffer often seems to be criticizing his colleagues for being too timid, what he really was striving for was a devastating rejection of all “conventional” Christianity, a rejection based on a bold reappropriation of the idea of the Incarnation. His point was that since God had already joined the human race irrevocably in Christ, no further accommodation is needed. The ultimate accommodation, so to speak, has already taken place. Bonhoeffer’s intransigence on this teaching made him a radical among the liberals.

Exactly the same can be said, in their own ways, for both Dorothy Day and Simone Weil. Dorothy Day was uncomfortable with some aspects of the Vatican II “*aggiornamento*.” She never advocated women priests, a vernacular Mass, or even a rethinking of papal infallibility. She described herself as an angry but loyal daughter of the church, and she was able to coax so many people toward a more radical social stance in part because she remained so conservative in other respects. Like Bonhoeffer and Simone Weil, who was also no modernist, Dorothy Day demonstrates how a theology that takes the core of the gospel seriously can provide a more cutting, critical perspective on the world than a grossly accommodated one. The other exemplars discovered the same thing. Even Martin Luther King, who came closer to being a liberal theologian in some of his writings than the others do, was at his best when his preaching and protest were grounded in the Hebrew prophets and the biblical tradition of the black Baptist church.

Finally, all our immediate forerunners had a strong sense of the *personal presence of Christ,* either immediate or mediated through friends and mentors. Dorothy Day considered her pacifism and her determination to share life with the slum-dwellers and losers to be following Jesus in the life he had demonstrated. Bonhoeffer wrote in his letters that he had learned to encounter and listen to Christ in and through "the nearest other person at hand." Simone Weil continued to pray intensely even when the largest doubts assailed her. Martin Luther King told friends that late one night, as he sat alone and discouraged over a cup of coffee in his kitchen, when his wife and children had been threatened with death by racists and he was ready to quit, Jesus spoke to him, saying he should continue the fight and promising to be with him and "never to leave me alone."

Where does this leave us in our attempt not only to answer the question, What is Christian?, but also to answer the more pressing one, What does it mean to be Christian *today*? "If we are to have any transcendence today," writes Amos Wilder, in the essay on the lay mystery quoted above, ". . . it must be in and through the secular. . . . If we are to find any grace it is to be found in the world and not overhead. . . ." Wilder is right. Christians today are forging a "worldly" form of spirituality; but it is one that includes, in one way or another, all the contours that have been there in the past. This means it will incorporate a group of actual flesh-and-blood human beings who will nourish them, a teaching that makes sense not of some special religious realm but of the actual day-to-day world, and a personal connection to the one in whom it all started.

Christian Prayer and Practice

The proverbial visitor from another planet who stumbles into a Christian church on, let us say, a Sunday morning, might be puzzled about what exactly was going on. The people sing, share tiny portions of food and wine, contribute money, and seem to be speaking *to* someone who is not visibly present. In some churches the people may shout in joy, extend their arms in ecstatic praise, weep, or listen while passages are read from books. Then if the visitor were to follow one of the participants when the meeting ends, he might eventually find that person in his or her own home engaging in similar activities alone or with others. If he persisted, and asked enough questions, the visitor might even find the same people who assembled in the church building doing all sorts of things from feeding the hungry to marching off to do battle, all in response—they say—to the One to whom they had been speaking in the meeting. How could we assist the perplexed planetary traveler to comprehend what was going on?

It might help to begin by explaining that Christians think of themselves, despite their many differences, as a single "people of God," who are grateful for what God has done for them and all people, and who feel compelled to express that gratitude in various ways. This expression takes the form of praising and thanking God, celebrating God's gifts, serving and helping other people, doing what they believe God wants them to do, and making known the good news of who God is and what God is doing in the world. So this people of God can be thought of as living in alternating phases. One is the "gathered phase" in which they come together for the kind of activities that might be observed on any given Sunday morning. But the other is the equally important "scattered phase" in which they go out to become what Jesus asked them to be, the "salt of the earth" whose function it is to bring out the natural flavor of the whole. In this section we will describe these alternating moments of Christian life, showing not only how the gathered one undergirds the scattered one, but also how the joys and concerns of the scattered phase enrich and inform the gathering.

The Liturgical Year

The spinal column of the gathered phase of Christian life is the liturgical year or "church year." Although as we shall see it differs to some extent from one church to another, there are several common features, and the fact that it is not the same as the regular calendar year reminds Christians that they live, as it were, in two different but overlapping times, two histories. As human beings they live through the cycles of seasons and the holidays and special occasions their own nations and cultures celebrate. But as Christians they also live according to a calendar of events and celebrations the rest of the world does not share. What is this special Christian calendar?

The Christian year starts just as the secular year, as reckoned by most of the rest of the world, is about to end. It begins on the Sunday closest to November 30 with the season known as "Advent." The word is an important one. It means "the coming" and it refers to the most central of all Christian beliefs, that God "comes" to the world. Although Advent refers principally to the coming of God to the world in Jesus of Nazareth, it also carries a more inclusive meaning. It suggests that God does not hold aloof from the created world, does not dwell in some distant or inaccessible region, but chooses to be present in the ordinary world of animals and plants and to share the pains and aspirations of ordinary mortals. Perhaps the most appropriate title for God as envisioned in the season of Advent is "Emmanuel" or "God with us."

Indeed the most familiar song sung by Christians during this season is entitled "O Come, O Come Emmanuel." The Advent season is one of waiting and preparation, of looking forward to that which is to come.

Christmas with its joyous feasting and caroling, its nearly universal spirit of peace and goodwill, brings the Advent season to a close. The One whose coming has been awaited comes. Christmas is also known as "The Feast of the Nativity of Our Lord and Savior Jesus Christ." It recalls the birth of Jesus in Bethlehem, in the poverty of a stable, surrounded by the cows and sheep, greeted by the humble shepherds, sought by the cruel king, his beleaguered parents forced to flee for their lives—and his—from their native land into exile. It is a moving story to which nearly everyone, whether Christian or not, can respond in some manner.

Although Christmas was not one of the most important holidays in the earliest years of Christianity, it soon became one and is now the occasion Christians share with more non-Christians than any other holiday. But the popularity of Christmas in the secular culture at large, especially but not exclusively in the Western world, is a mixed blessing. Fed by the enormous sales efforts of those who wish to make use of its spirit to sell commodities, this merchandising of Christmas causes serious problems both for Christians and for their non-Christian neighbors. Those who see the day as marking the birth of Jesus are resentful that for many people Santa Claus, a secularized version of a fourth-century Christian bishop (St. Nicholas), rather than Jesus Christ has become the main symbol of Christmas. Non-Christians, on the other hand, resent being forced to listen to carols on loudspeakers in the streets proclaiming the birth of a messiah they do not accept. Also the commercialization of Christmas has produced a singular irony. The season that marks the birth of one who cast his lot with the poor and warned against the temptation of riches is misused to tout materialistic values and to make money. Aware of how much of their annual profits they must take in during this frenetic period, some businesses try to extend the time by decking their stores with Christmas decorations earlier and earlier in the year. This obvious distortion of the Christian meaning of Christmas puts Christians into a dilemma. On the one hand they want to share the glad tidings of God's coming to the world in Jesus. But they often fear that the deluge of elves and reindeer obscures and trivializes the essential message.

On the church calendar the Christmas season ends on January 6 with the holiday known as Epiphany. The word itself means "manifestation," usually, but not always, of a divine power. In literature, for example, an epiphany occurs when there is a sudden or sharp revelation of one of the characters or some element of the plot. For most Christians this revelatory event, or epiphany, took place first when the legendary three wise men or kings from the East arrived, bearing their gifts, at the stable where Jesus had been born. Indeed in Latin cultures the holiday is often known as the "day of the three kings." The scene is a familiar one. The three figures, usually depicted to represent the various races of humankind, kneel with their precious gifts at the manger. But the inner meaning of the familiar story, which is sometimes obscured by its familiarity, is that an epiphany of God has occurred. The wise men are not Jews. They represent all the nations of the earth. Their arrival symbolizes the fact that in this unlikely event, the birth of yet another seemingly insignificant child to an impoverished peasant family in a remote province, something of immeasurable importance for the whole world has taken place. It is therefore an "epiphany," a manifestation of the meaning of this child and of the story in which he is to be the main actor. In many parts of the Christian world, especially in the realm of the Eastern Orthodox church, this day and not December 25 is the one on which children receive gifts, reminiscent of the gifts of the mysterious visitors.

After Epiphany the next major holiday of the Christian year is Easter, the celebration of the Resurrection of Jesus Christ from the dead. But Easter is preceded by forty days of self-examination, penitence, and preparation called "Lent." It is during these weeks that Christians are expected to think seriously about their own lives in the light of the life and death of Jesus. Lent begins on Ash Wednesday, a day on which, in some Christian churches, it is customary to distribute ashes, a symbol of penitence and of human mortality, and some believers wear these ashes on their foreheads for the day. Since Lent is a time of sobriety and restraint, it has become a custom in some places to eat and drink and celebrate on the day before Lent begins as a kind of last blast before the forty days of solemnity and fasting. Thus the Tuesday preceding Ash Wednesday is sometimes called Mardi Gras ("Fat Tuesday") and is marked with bacchanalian festivity, especially in Latin cultures.

The Sunday just before Easter is known as Palm Sunday. It initiates Holy Week and recalls the entrance of Jesus into Jerusalem a few days before his crucifixion. Since according to the Gospel accounts Jesus was welcomed with palm branches on that day, in many churches small palm leaves are given out and those receiving them often wear them or carry them home. There is a note of joy about Palm Sunday but also a hint of sadness. For we know how the events of this crowded week will end.

Maundy Thursday is the Thursday of Holy Week. The word comes from the Latin for the directive Jesus gave his disciples when he met with them in the upper room on the last Thursday of his life. He told them they should not lord it over people but should think of themselves as servants and should symbolize this attitude by humbly washing each others' feet, a service which in his time was usually carried out by servants. Maundy Thursday also marks the institution of the Lord's Supper or Holy Communion because it was on that night that Jesus broke bread and shared wine with his disciples, telling them that this food and drink signified his death, in which they might be asked to share. It was after this "last supper," a favorite subject for artists, that one of Jesus' disciples, Judas, betrayed him to those who wanted to get rid of him, and it was on the same night that Jesus was apprehended and taken in for the interrogations that led to his crucifixion by the Romans as a threat to the empire.

Good Friday, the most solemn day of the Christian year, recalls the actual Crucifixion. Many churches hold services during the hours that Jesus hung on the cross. Some of these include ritual reenactments of the crucifixion, the singing of the great music of passion week such as Johann Sebastian Bach's "St. Matthew Passion," and sometimes sermons or homilies on the "seven last words of Christ."

Easter Sunday is a peal of joy after the sadness of Good Friday. In Eastern Orthodox Christian churches, where the celebration begins on a solemn and doleful note on Saturday night, suddenly at midnight the whole atmosphere changes. The priest sings out, 'Christ is Risen!" and the congregation responds, "Risen indeed!" Many Protestant churches like to celebrate Easter at the crack of dawn, outside, with so-called Easter sunrise services. Roman Catholics are expected to take communion on Easter Sunday. In every Christian church, it is a day for feasting and expressing the joy of people who believe that, in the resurrection of Jesus, not only had God vindicated the work of his whole life but also that death itself, the oldest enemy of human life, had been defeated. The most characteristic single word associated with Easter in the Christian vocabulary is *alleluia*, a glad shout.

Fifty days after Easter comes the Feast of Pentecost. It marks the occasion described in the Acts of the Apostles in which the disciples and followers of Jesus, dispirited by the crucifixion but cheered by Jesus' resurrection appearances, were gathered in an upper room to pray. Suddenly, so the biblical account continues, there was a sound like rushing wind, and tongues of fire appeared over their heads. More importantly, although they were all speaking in different languages, they understood each other. Christians believe this event marks the coming of the Holy Spirit who, along with God the Creator and Jesus, is worshiped as God. It is also celebrated as the "birthday of the church," the moment at which the body of believers that was to continue his work and presence in the world was constituted. As we shall see below, those Christians who put special emphasis on the "gifts of the Spirit" and on the immediate experience of God in the Spirit frequently call themselves "Pentecostalists."

After Pentecost comes that long stretch in the church year which is referred to in Catholic language as "ordinary time." Other than saints' days, religious holidays peculiar to one national culture or denomination and—among many Protestants—Reformation Sunday, which marks the anniversary of the beginning of Luther's reform, there are no other special occasions. But "ordinary time" is not without religious significance. It reminds Christians that life is not made up completely of red-letter days, or even of preparing for them and recovering from them. It also consists of seemingly drab, everyday parts, but God is present in them too. After ordinary time comes Advent again, and the whole cycle starts over.

The Sacraments or Ordinances

If the church year provides the course of the yearly pilgrimage through time, the sacraments (which some Christian churches also call "ordinances") supply the symbolic nourishment for the journey. Thus the extraplanetary visitor, as we have noted, would observe Christians ritually eating and drinking bread and wine together, pouring water on babies or immersing adults in pools or rivers, exchanging rings, anointing sick people with oils, laying hands on the heads of specially designated persons and engaging in other activities that, as even a casual onlooker might guess, refer to something beyond themselves. What is going on?

"Sacrament" is classically defined as "the outward and visible sign of an inward and invisible reality." Christians differ somewhat among themselves about how many sacraments there are, with Roman Catholics and some others teaching that there are seven while most Protestant denominations hold that there are two. Also, some Christian groups prefer the word *ordinances* to suggest that these are actions specifically ordered by Jesus Christ himself. Nonetheless, as we shall see, even the churches that do not count seven sacraments tend to develop analogous practices, so this will enable us to describe the sacraments in order, as they might occur through an individual's life, while noting how the various branches of the Christian family differ somewhat in their interpretations of them.

We begin with baptism because it symbolizes entrance into the community of the church, which is why in some church buildings the baptismal font often stands near the door. The word *baptism* comes from the Greek word meaning to submerge in water, and water is the visible means used for baptism. In those churches that baptize children by sprinkling, the water suggests cleansing. In those that baptize adults, usually by complete immersion, it takes on the significance of being buried and raised to new life. The churches that baptize children recognize that the child is not ready to express his or her own faith at such an early age, so usually the parents and those who have come to be known as "godparents" take that responsibility and promise they will educate and nurture the child to be a Christian. Some churches hold, however, that such a momentous decision should only be made by the person himself or herself, so they do not administer baptism until the child has reached the age of consent, usually the early teens. In these churches, however, there is often a custom whereby the parents "dedicate" a child to God and promise in the presence of the congregation to raise the child as a Christian. Jesus himself, it should be noted, was baptized by John the Baptist, when he, Jesus, was a young man of about thirty, and the New Testament clearly indicates that he told his disciples to baptize those who wished to follow him. It should not be surprising, therefore, that practicing some form of baptism, however different the interpretations, is virtually universal among Christians.

In those churches that baptize infants, the sacrament of confirmation enables young people to "confirm" or make their own the profession of faith that had already been made for them at the time of their baptism. In some churches this confirmation must be done by a bishop, often by laying hands on the head of the young confirmee. After such confirmation, the person is a full member of the church, so in some traditions is now permitted to receive communion for the first time.

Communion, sometimes referred to as the Eucharist or the Lord's Supper, is another sacrament/ordinance that is shared by virtually all Christian churches. It stems from the famous "last supper" Jesus ate with his disciples in Jerusalem on the night in which he was betrayed by Judas Iscariot and arrested on the Mount of Olives. It is important to recall that Jesus had come to Jerusalem to celebrate the Jewish holiday of Passover, and the meal he was eating that night was probably a "seder," the same one Jews continue to celebrate today. The seder commemorates God's delivery of the Jews from their captivity in Egypt, and Jesus appears to have been marking that same event while also giving it a new dimension—emancipation not only from earthly oppression but from death as well. In any case, while partaking of the bread and wine with his disciples he referred to these elements as his body and his blood, and he instructed his followers to continue to break bread and drink wine in the same way in remembrance of him.

Sadly, although again nearly all Christians celebrate the Lord's Supper in one way or another, it is the Christian practice about which there have been more disputes than about almost anything else. Roman Catholics hold that in the hands of a duly ordained priest the bread and the wine of the communion, through what is called "transubstantiation," become the actual body and blood of Christ. Lutherans teach that Christ is present "in, with and under" these elements but do not agree with the idea of transubstantiation. Anglicans (called "Episcopalians" in the United States) also hold that Christ is present in the communion but differ with each other on how this happens, and in this respect they are similar to Orthodox churches. Most other Christian churches hold that the bread and wine symbolize Christ and his sacrificial death.

The manner in which communion is observed also varies widely from church to church and also from congregation to congregation within the same church. At one end of the spectrum can be found the High Mass such as the one the pope celebrates in Rome on Christmas Eve, which is often televised around the world. The pageantry is rich and colorful, the ceremony within which the bread and wine are consecrated is solemn and elaborate. But at its heart, even a pontifical High Mass is a communion service. At the opposite end one could think of a handful of people grouped around a rough table passing a coarse loaf to each other and sipping from a common cup in memory of Jesus. Nonetheless, in all examples of communion the same underlying truths become explicit. Christians remember the life and death of Jesus. They are reminded that God is present in the homely events of life: eating and drinking. They take the story of Jesus' life and the meaning of his death into their own bodies. Also, in a real sense, communion is like a family meal, the gathering of old and young, sick and well, around a common table and reminds all those who participate that the goods of the earth should be shared, not hoarded. All in all, Holy Communion is a powerful sacrament, and it is not surprising that Christians of nearly every variety practice it with impressive regularity.

Marriage is included as a sacrament in some churches. In the Roman Catholic church it is administered by the bride and groom to each other, with the priest as a witness. In the Orthodox family of churches, the priest actually marries the couple. In most Protestant churches, although marriage is held in very high esteem, it is not considered to be a sacrament, but a deeply serious and binding commitment, which God blesses. Must Christian marriages always be monogamous (e.g., involving one man and one woman)? Although this has been the normal practice in the past, in recent years questions have been raised, especially in Africa, about whether men who are already married to more than one woman when they become Christians should be permitted to keep their wives. The Anglican church has recently decided that such polygamous marriages should be allowed to stand but that once a man, or presumably a woman, becomes a Christian, he or she should not add further spouses or, if single, should marry only one.

Because attending a wedding is often one of the few times people in a religiously pluralistic society get a taste of someone else's tradition, the marriage vows exchanged by the bride and groom at a Christian wedding service have become somewhat familiar to almost everyone. The minister or priest first asks both the man and the woman if they freely take each other as husband and wife. If they answer in the affirmative they then proceed to make their vows or promises to each other, often using the words "for better, for worse; for richer, for poorer; in sickness and in health; to love and to cherish, so long as we both shall live." They then usually exchange rings, the presiding minister or priest asks God to bless their union, and then declares that they are husband and wife. Customarily the bride and groom then kiss each other as the first act of their married life.

Ordination is an important ritual activity in those Christian churches and groups (not all of them) that have an ordained clergy. To become an ordained minister or priest it is usually believed that a person must have a "call" to this particular form of Christian service, although this does not mean that other Christians are not called to their ministries. This call usually comes as a strong internal conviction that God wants this person in this position. The various churches have their different ways of ascertaining whether this has been a genuine call, but it is widely agreed that neither personal talents or tastes or education suffice to make a person eligible for ordination. A "call" is essential. Then, in some churches a long period of training is required in which the candidate studies the Bible, Christian history and theology, the arts of ministry such as preaching and pastoral care, and sometimes subjects like ethics, the psychology and philosophy of religion, and comparative religion. It is only after having completed this arduous preparation that the candidate can be ordained. In other churches, more emphasis is placed on the gifts the person exhibits, like the ability to preach, counsel, and lead, which count more than the official academic preparation. In most cases the actual ordination service itself includes a moment when previously ordained persons place their hands on the head of the candidate, asking the spirit of God to bless him or her in this vocation.

Him or *her?* Herein lies a troublesome division among the various branches of Christianity. Some churches ordain both men and women, others only ordain men. Neither the Roman Catholic nor the Orthodox churches ordain women, though both insist that men and women have an equal—if different—importance in the eyes of God. In some churches, such as the Anglican one, the question is an especially vexing one, because some of its constituent churches do and others do not ordain women. Meanwhile, in many of the Protestant churches of the United States an increasing number of women are becoming ministers and in some of them women will account for half the ministers by A.D. 2000.

Confession, sometimes known as the sacrament of Penance or Reconciliation, is practiced in a variety of ways in different churches, but its inner meaning is similar in each. It provides an occasion for the Christian to face frankly the actions and attitudes that separate him or her from God and from other people. Sometimes this is done through a conversation with an individual priest, sometimes as the expression of a whole group. However it is done, the act of confession recognizes that human sin and frailty undermine the loving community God intended for the human family but that God stands ready to forgive, to reconcile, and to make a new beginning possible.

Finally, for some Christian groups there is a sacrament, sometimes called "Extreme Unction," in which the person is anointed with oils while special prayers are said. Among Roman Catholics this sacrament has sometimes been known as "the Last Rites" because the ritual took place when there was reason to believe that the person was dying. In more recent Catholic theology, however, it is seen more as a visible symbol of God's capacity to heal human ills both of the body and of the spirit.

Taken together, the various sacraments of the churches—however many there are and however they are practiced—add up to a view of the world that calls attention repeatedly to the presence of the unseen God in the midst of the visible events and artifacts of the world. But the sacraments or ordinances have another purpose as well. They constantly remind Christians that God has a purpose for them as a people in the world. In some churches as the prayer and praise in the church building end and the people prepare to leave the sanctuary to resume their lives in the workaday world, the minister says, "now the *service* begins." It is a fitting reminder that the coming of God's reign in its fullness is the ultimate goal of every prayer, not just the Lord's Prayer. Christian worship is never an end in itself. It is one means by which this ultimate purpose will, in God's time, be accomplished.

What Next for Christianity?

As the world speeds toward the two thousandth anniversary of the birth of Christ four major impulses that could shape Christianity during the next millennium are underway. One is the worldwide emergence of a form of Christian life based on a direct experience of the Holy Spirit, often accompanied by what adherents claim are "gifts of the Spirit" such as healing and speaking or praying in unknown tongues. This "Pentecostal" movement is named for the dramatic account in Acts 2 of the descent of the Holy Spirit that took place on the Jewish feast of Pentecost shortly after Jesus' resurrection. The movement began about 1900 in the United States, springing mainly from both black and poor white circles of Christians. It spread quickly among the less-privileged strata of the society, moved out into other countries, and is now the fastest-growing segment of Christianity. So quickly are Pentecostal churches multiplying that by the third decade of the next millennium their numbers could well equal those of all Protestants put together.

The second trend is the appearance all over the Christian world, but especially among the more marginalized population, of various "theologies of liberation." Cutting across Protestant, Catholic, and Pentecostal lines, liberation theology emphasizes the presence of the living Christ today among the poor and the powerless and insists that God is not neutral, but takes the side of these suffering ones in their struggles for freedom, dignity, and a just share of the necessities of life. Beginning in Latin America in the 1960s, liberation theology soon spread to South Africa, Korea, the Philippines—anywhere Christians find themselves victimized by unjust social structures, economic oppression, or racial prejudice.

The third major current enlivening Christianity at the close of the second millennium is the emergence of women into unprecedented roles in church leaderships, theology, and Christian life in general. Of course women have always played a prominent role in Christian history, beginning with the women who discovered the empty tomb and became the first to proclaim the news of Christ's resurrection. But women have more often than not been barred from theological study, ordination, and other expressions of leadership. Today that is changing very rapidly in many churches.

The fourth major trend is a deepening sense of dialogue and reciprocity that is developing, at least in some places, between Christians and members of the other major religious groups in the world. I will now describe in somewhat more detail the possible implications of these currents for the future of Christianity.

The Pentecostalism Explosion

In April of 1906 in the black section of Los Angeles, an event occurred that was to have enormous implications for the Christian world. At a small mission church, attended mainly by domestic workers and led by a black Holiness minister named William Joseph Seymour, people began to experience the presence of God in a particularly intense way and to pray and sing in what sounded to many of them like foreign languages. Soon crowds—both black and white—from all over the city began to attend. The meetings went on day after day, for three years, and Seymour told the people he believed that their experience signaled nothing less than the onset of the "Last Days" mentioned in the Bible, a time during which God would once again lavish gifts enabling Christians to heal and to pray in unknown tongues.

> And in the last days it shall be, God declares, that I will pour out my Spirit upon all flesh, and your sons and your daughters shall prophesy, and your young men shall see visions and your old men shall dream dreams. (Acts 2:17)

Actually there had been scattered instances of ecstatic speech throughout Christian history, so the Los Angeles experience was not unique. But for many people the "Azusa Street revival" marks the beginning of the Pentecostal movement which, under Seymour's leadership, suddenly began to grow and spread until it reached around the world. By the outbreak of World

War I in 1914, Pentecostalism had reached across America and then abroad. It has often splintered and subdivided, but it has been gaining members steadily and now claims four hundred million worldwide.

The symbolism of the birth and early history of Pentecostalism is striking. It sprang to life not in one of the great centers of learning but among poor and marginated people. William Seymour, according to John T. Nichol in his book *Pentecostalism*, was described by a contemporary as "... a colored man, very plain, spiritual and humble... He was blind in one eye." Although it eventually reached out to include middle-class people as well, Pentecostalism traces its infancy to a one-eyed black man and has continued to appeal disproportionally to women, minorities, and disabled people ever since. Very often Pentecostalists were spurned and taunted by people of the more established churches as "holy rollers" (because of their emotionally explicit and sometimes ecstatic forms of worship). But their movement persisted and grew and has sometimes been characterized as a religious revolution comparable in importance with the original Church of the Apostles or with the Protestant Reformation. In recent years the growth of Pentecostalism has been especially dramatic in the "Third World," with some observers predicting that whole countries in Latin America could have Pentecostal majorities by A.D. 2020.

What are we to make of this startling explosion? And how are we to judge the claims of at least some Pentecostalists that we are living in the "last days" of human history and that God is providing to some people the capacity to heal sickness and to speak in other tongues? As for the healing, there can be little doubt that although some of those who claim to be cured soon relapse to their previous state, much of it is also real and lasting. This has been carefully documented by medical specialists. Pentecostalism is not alone in making its claim—increasingly accepted by many doctors—that there is a wide variety of different forms of healing that go beyond the parameters of modern scientific medicine. Historically most religions have linked faith with healing. In Christianity there have always been shrines such as those at St. Anne in Quebec and Lourdes in France where people travel to pray for healing. Christian Scientists have always insisted that healing is principally a spiritual rather than a merely physical matter. Virtually all Christians believe it is efficacious to pray for the sick. Pentecostalists are not alone, and now that such previously suspect modes of healing as acupuncture and meditation are more widely accepted, Pentecostal healing should perhaps be seen as merely a somewhat more dramatic variant of this more general phenomenon.

The claim to be speaking in what are actually languages the individual does not know is harder to understand, and indeed today many Pentecostalists do not claim to be doing so. They say rather that God's Spirit enables them to leave behind the constraints of ordinary speech (and thus of conventional discourse) and to express their love for God and each other in a more direct and unencumbered way. They may be practicing at a popular level what others do when they participate in so-called "primal scream therapy" or invent neologisms (new words) as James Joyce did in his novels. All these are ways to protest the limits of existing speech patterns. In any case, "speaking in tongues" (or "glossolalia" as it is called by outsiders) obviously provides some people with a joyous and life-enhancing mode of communication that seems to free them from the rigidity of more formal and linguistically conventional modes of worship.

Some critics have contended that Pentecostalism leads to a kind of social irresponsibility, directing people's religious energy toward individual transport and otherworldliness rather than toward seeking solutions to the actual problems of the world. The fact is, however, that all religions contain a mixture of this-worldly and otherworldly elements—and of mystical and rational dimensions. Pentecostalism is no exception. Further, in recent years Pentecostalists have become increasingly concerned with the social outreach of faith. They have done extraordinary work in combating drugs and corruption and have even begun in some places (Latin America and South Africa) to construct their own types of liberation theology. This latter development should really not come as a complete surprise, since both Pentecostalism and liberation theology function as correctives against the "overspiritualization" of Christianity. Both stress that the *material*, whether in bodily health or in political and economic well-being, is also a channel of God's grace.

There is a final observation to be made about Pentecostalism as a prominent trend within Christianity in the third millennium. Because it focuses on the Spirit, it opens up more possibilities of interaction with other religions than its founding fathers and mothers might have anticipated. Pentecostal practices have begun to appear in other Protestant churches and even in the Roman Catholic church. This so-called "charismatic movement" has become a significant stream in these churches. Most Christians have claimed for years to believe in Father, Son, and Holy Spirit, but the full potential of this third person of the Trinity has never been developed or even imagined. The Spirit is notoriously resistant to channeling and control, and the possible links of this Holy Spirit with the Spirit present in other faiths has never been fully probed. Observers of Third World Pentecostalism, especially among indigenous peoples such as tribal groups in South America, note that its open style of praise sometimes allows them to reclaim elements of their pre-Christian heritage that were excluded by more traditional Catholic and Protestant modes of worship. Other scholars believe Pentecostalism can be understood as the Christian wing of a more comprehensive worldwide change in religion, one that signals a move toward more emotional, imaginative, and pragmatic (immediately useful) forms of religiosity. If this is true, Pentecostalism, much to the surprise of those who mistakenly view it as a variant of biblical fundamentalism, could be in the vanguard of Christianity's new and more reciprocal ways of interacting with other faiths. Whatever happens, this vigorous movement of the Spirit, coming like Jesus himself from a scorned quarter and a despised people, will surely be one of the principal actors in twenty-first-century Christianity.

Liberation Theologies

For many centuries Christian churches have existed in Ethiopia, in some parts of Asia, and, since the European invasion of the sixteenth century, in Latin America as well. But as the twentieth century neared its end a seismic shift in the global composition of Christianity became evident. Now the majority of Christians no longer lived within the old borders of European "Christendom" and its North American extension but in the postcolonial "Third World" of the Southern Hemisphere. As this change took place it was to be expected that new Christian theologies would emerge from these areas that had for so long been viewed as peripheral by "northern" Christians. The most significant of these new theologies by far is called the "theology of liberation" and it first appeared in the late 1960s in Latin America. Although it had existed before, it was given its name in a book called *The Theology of Liberation* written by a Peruvian Catholic priest named Gustavo Gutierrez in 1970. During the next three decades this vital theology (or theolog*ies*, since there are many variants) radiated into all parts of the world, stimulating comparable currents in other religions such as Judaism and Buddhism. What then are the main characteristics of the liberation theologies?

When the Roman Catholic bishops of Latin America met in 1968 in Medellin, Colombia, to consider what the Second Vatican Council would mean for the hungry and downtrodden people of their continent, they agreed on one basic point: Their church would have to forego the role of arbiter between the oppressed and the oppressors and to place itself on the side of the desperate, the wounded, and the marginated peoples. This decision came to be known as the "preferential option for the poor," a phrase that became the new theology's watchword and ensign as Christians tried to understand Christ's message from the perspective of the most disprivileged people in the society.

It was a momentous change, not in the *content* of Christian teaching but in both the *method applied* to the interpretation of the Bible and in the *kinds of people* who did the interpreting. For centuries the power to interpret had rested almost exclusively in the hands of certain privileged elites of the educated strata, usually men. Now, however, it was recognized that poor people, persecuted racial minorities, women, and other dispossessed persons could correct the distortion this elitist interpretive minority had inevitably perpetuated. The liberation theologies arose from voices that had been silenced or ignored for centuries. Although they differed with each other from region to region, these theologies all had a single basic element in common. They all read the Bible as an assurance that the same God who had delivered the Israelites from their slavery in Egypt still sides with the weak and the disinherited today. And they reasoned that if Jesus Christ, who was himself part of the tyrannized people, had demonstrated a consistent "preferential option" for the impoverished crowds, despised lepers, subjugated women, and religious outcasts of his day, then he must have that same position today. Taken together these insights inspired countless people living in what appeared to be hopeless conditions to cast off despair and claim the liberating promise of God's Word. Within a few decades the theology of liberation had become the most energetic and vital—and controversial—of any in contemporary Christianity.

The key for understanding liberation theologies is to see them as *wholistic*. They teach a Christianity that is not restricted to the interior or the personal but that encompasses society as well as the individual, this life as well as the next, and the material as well as the spiritual. Liberation theologies do not address themselves mainly to nonbelievers of their cultures (as almost all modern and many earlier theologies did), but to those Gutierrez refers to as the "nonpersons," the people whom the prevailing values in a society denigrate as somehow less than fully human.

It is important to note that although trained theologians write about and interpret liberation theologies, they did not invent them. In Latin America and in the rest of the postcolonial world, these theologies grew out of small, grass-roots communities of faith often called "Christian Base Communities." These "CEBs" (so-named for the Portuguese "communidades ecclesiales de base" because they first started in Brazil) bring together handfuls of people from the lower social reaches to sing, pray, study the Bible, share daily experiences, and devise ways to tackle the pervasive injustice that warps their lives. Many CEBs were first organized by trained church leaders, but most are now led by laypeople, a significant proportion by women. The members of CEBs do not think of themselves as "leaving the church" but as having found a new way "to *be* the church." These CEBs provide the soil from which liberation theologies, seeded by biblical scholarship and trained leaders, grow to fruition.

As might be expected, neither the CEBs nor the liberation theologies have escaped opposition, even persecution. Both within the churches and among the ruling groups of the regions in which they have sprung up, they have often been criticized and attacked for allegedly posing a threat to the ecclesial and societal powers-that-be. Sometimes this opposition to liberation theology has turned violent. Archbishop Oscar Romero and most of the priests, sisters, and lay church leaders who have been killed in Central America in recent years were advocates of liberation theology and base communities.

What is the future of base communities and liberation theology? It has already spread to Asia and Africa and has influenced movements in the United States aimed toward the liberation of those who also have been persecuted for reasons of race, gender, or sexual preference. Still, as the center of gravity in Christianity shifts from the largely more prosperous "north" to the poorer and more populous "south" of the globe, the process some Latin Americans call the "de-northification of theology" will inevitably continue. This radical rethinking of Christianity from the perspective of the former "outsiders and down-siders" will inevitably produce more liberation theologies. However, even as they multiply, these theologies are changing. Once sometimes exhilarated by the hope for a relatively rapid change in their condition, the people in the CEBs are now viewing the process of liberation as a much larger and longer one. In many places they are also digging into their local cultures and customs more seriously in an effort to implant the gospel more firmly. Still other CEBs have begun to adopt some of the more vibrant and emotionally expressive modes of worship introduced by Pentecostalists. Indeed if, in the next century—as some observers foresee—a certain creative synthesis of liberation theology and Pentecostal spirituality emerges as the dominant form of Christianity, it will constitute a powerful new vehicle for the message of Jesus in the third millennium after his birth.

The New Role of Women

On February 11, 1989, the Reverend Barbara Harris, an Episcopal priest, was consecrated a bishop of her church in the diocese of Massachusetts. Thousands of people gathered in Boston for the colorful and festive event, to which three choirs, a long winding procession, and multicolored, deep-dyed liturgical vestments lent an air of grandeur and solemnity. During the ceremony, at the moment when she was invested with the cope and mitre, ancient symbols of the bishop's office, a gasp seemed to rise from the congregation. The reason was not hard to fathom, for there before the eyes of those in attendance now stood a person who had broken a centuries-long taboo. The Episcopal (Anglican) church represents one of the "catholic" traditions. It puts considerable emphasis on the long unbroken line of continuity, the "apostolic succession" that—it is believed—links its current bishops to Christ's own disciples. But not in all these twenty centuries or among these thousands of bishops had a woman stood before the altar and taken vows to be a bishop and faithful shepherd of God's people.

It was a major turning point in Christian history. Women had held leadership posts before, and some non-Catholic denominations had been ordaining them as ministers for many years. The Episcopal church itself had begun ordaining women priests fifteen years earlier. In Africa, where new Christian movements are growing rapidly in the form of "Independent" churches, women often assume significant roles in leadership, and in thousands of storefront and small unaffiliated congregations women have preached and led for many years. Still, this was the first woman to become a bishop, a successor to the apostles, in a church that claimed to be Catholic.

As with most symbolic events the repercussions of this consecration went far beyond its immediate meaning. It brought into public awareness a dramatic change that was occurring throughout most of Christianity: Women were beginning to exercise all the gifts of the Spirit, not just the ones men thought appropriate, and they were claiming an equal place in an institution that had kept them as second-class Christians for centuries. Even in the Roman Catholic church, which does not yet permit them to be ordained, women were teaching and writing theology, serving as chaplains, leading Christian base communities, and exercising many other leadership roles.

But the consecration of Bishop Harris also symbolized more than that. Just as in the various liberation theologies, those who had once been excluded from the opportunity to shape and interpret Christianity were now beginning to do so, women were also subtly changing the way both men and women understand the reality of God. In the more liturgical traditions of Christianity, the priest who celebrates communion to some extent symbolizes God. In the document in which he rejected the possibility that women could be ordained as priests in the Roman Catholic church, Pope John Paul II declared that a priest must bear a "natural resemblance" to Jesus Christ. But some Christians read this resemblance another way. If God transcends sex and gender differences, then there was no need for priests always to be male. An all-male priesthood, they contended, falsified the reality of the divine. Now, as women priests and a woman bishop began serving at the altar it began to become clear to thousands of worshipers that their pictures of God had been too restricted, that God encompasses qualities we have usually associated with both man and woman. Therefore, having both men and women priests seemed a more, not less, adequate symbolization of God.

As women began serving in larger numbers as priests and ministers, an analogous evolution was underway in the field of Christian theological scholarship. In biblical studies, ethics, theology, and other branches of the discipline, women were beginning to overturn centuries of male domination and to raise sharp questions about distortions and misreadings that monopoly had perpetrated. Women scholars pointed out that many references in both the Old and the New Testament permit us to think of God as both a mother and a father. This means that those efforts in many churches to develop "inclusive language" prayers and hymns that refer to God with both masculine and feminine adjectives and pronouns has a solidly biblical basis. Women studying the early Christian period have shown that some of the so-called "gnostic" Gospels that were excluded from the New Testament by a male hierarchy contain more references to women among Jesus' followers, especially to Mary Magdalene, and also picture God as having more of the qualities that are sometimes thought of as feminine. When they turn to later Christian history, women scholars find that men have often downplayed the contributions of women who headed convents, penned mystical treatises, organized dissenting Christian movements, and in many other ways shared with men in the shaping of that history.

The feminist revolution in contemporary Christian life has left little unchanged or unchallenged. The prayers we pray, the hymns we sing, the physical appearance of those who lead us in worship, the insights and imagination of those who write our theological books are all changing. For some people, both men and women, the change has happened too quickly. It has jarred long-standing patterns and upset established sensibilities. For others, again both men and women, the changes are long overdue and have opened whole new vistas in our understanding of who God is and what Jesus intends us to do and to be.

Will Christianity ever shed its patriarchal shell and rid itself of the predominantly masculine categories that have narrowed and restricted it in the past? If the unanticipated changes of the past two decades are any indication, a Christianity cleansed of sexist distortion may not be as far away as it once seemed.

Christians and People of Other Faiths

Christians have always lived in the presence of people of other religious faiths. Jesus himself was a religious Jew and continued to practice his own religion throughout his life, albeit giving it his own distinctive stamp and interpretation. The earliest Christians lived as a minority in a predominantly Jewish culture. Later Christianity became one of the many "new religions" in the declining days of the Roman Empire. During the medieval period when Christianity was centered mainly—but not exclusively—in Europe, many Christians were aware that some of their neighbors (Jews or in some regions Muslims) did not share their faith. For centuries Christians,

Jews, and Muslims lived together on the Iberian peninsula sometimes harmoniously, sometimes fighting, but always borrowing architectural features and spiritual practices from each other. St. John of the Cross, for example, the Spanish Catholic mystic, may well have derived some of his images of the "dark night of the soul" from Muslim Sufi sources. But except for a rare Marco Polo, Europeans knew virtually nothing about the Asian religions.

With the coming of the Renaissance and the period of European explorations, all that changed. Christians now became aware for the first time that there were whole nations of peoples who were neither Christians nor Jews nor Muslims. What were they to make of the Buddhists they met in Southeast Asia, the Hindus in India, and the Mayans and Aztecs of South America? How did these people who did not share faith in Jesus Christ and had neither the Old Testament nor the Qur'ān fit into the overall providence of God?

There has never been a clear consensus about the answer to this question. Some Christians have insisted that the gospel mandate requires that every human being be confronted with the message of Christ and that ideally every person in the entire world should become a Christian. A second and much larger group has accepted the plurality of religions as part of reality, if not part of God's plan, and has not attempted to incorporate people of other religious traditions within the church. A third position, the one that is probably held by most people, falls somewhere in between. It suggests that on the one hand God's love and mercy shown through Jesus Christ belongs to everyone in the world without exception and that the gospel message of God's reconciliation is not just for Westerners or for people born and raised in Christian cultures. On the other hand, people who hold this position also affirm that God can also be present in the other religious traditions, and that Christians have a responsibility not only to respect people of other faiths but also to learn from them, and to give thanks together with them that all people are created by a single God.

As Christianity neared the completion of two thousand years of history, one of the most important changes going on within the church was in Christian attitudes toward men and women of other religious faiths. In many local communities interfaith councils and meetings for dialogue among adherents of varying religious traditions were organized. At the national level in the United States, Christians and Jews, Muslims and Hindus, and people representing other religious persuasions were meeting together to try to understand each other better and to minimize the danger of prejudice and intolerance. At the global level the World Council of Churches, which represents mainly Protestant and Orthodox Christian bodies, had spawned an ambitious program in interfaith dialogue. The Vatican had established official secretariats to encourage conversation between Roman Catholics and people of non-Christian faiths. There was room for genuine hope that, in some areas at least, religious distrust and animosity might be waning.

But there was another side to the picture as well. Not only in Christianity but also in some other religions, a so-called "fundamentalist" wing characterized by vehement opposition to such interfaith dialogue had sprung up. This antidialogical tendency was growing stronger not only in some Christian groups but also among Muslims, Hindus, and Jews. The result of these two antagonistic currents was somewhat paradoxical. It seemed that within each religious tradition there was more openness to fruitful interaction with those of other faiths and at the same time a growing recalcitrance and opposition to such conversation. Sometimes the tensions between the dialogical and the antidialogical wings within a particular religion such as Christianity became more severe than any tensions between Christianity and its sister faiths.

As Christians encounter people from other religions they have learned to begin to differentiate among them. Christians, for example, will always have a special tie with Judaism that makes the Jewish-Christian relationship different from the interaction of Christians with any of the other faiths. Christianity was born in the milieu of Judaism. Jesus and the disciples were Jews. Christians accept the entire Jewish Scripture as the Old Testament and therefore as an integral part of their Bible. It is a fundamental conviction among Christians that the same God who created the world, who delivered the Israelites from Egyptian captivity, sent the prophets, and gave human beings the Ten Commandments has continued to be present in Jesus Christ, extending and widening the divine initiative so that those who previously had been excluded—namely, the Gentiles—could now become a part of the covenant people. At the same time it is also recognized by an increasing number of Christians that God's original covenant with the Jewish people has never been abrogated but remains in full effect. It is, as St. Paul says in Romans 11:29, "irrevocable."

Indeed a new respect for postbiblical Judaism has developed among Christians in recent decades. In part it is because of the painful realization, on the part of at least some Christians, that centuries of Christian anti-Judaism may have contributed to an atmosphere that made Auschwitz and the Jewish Holocaust possible. For this reason it seemed increasingly clear to many Christians in the twentieth century that it was wrong for Christians to expect Jews to accept Christianity. Rather, learning how to live together as two children of the same mother seemed a more fitting form of relationship.

On the other hand, the relationship of Christianity to Islam is perhaps the most vexing and problematical of all the interreligious relations. There are a number of reasons for this. One is that Islam began six hundred years after the birth of Christianity and incorporated into its teachings much that Christians had already taught. Islam honors the Old Testament prophets and Jesus of Nazareth. In much Islamic literature and poetry Jesus is celebrated and praised. Christians, on the other hand, have generally held a very negative attitude toward Muḥammad. In a famous passage in Dante's *Inferno,* this prophet and founder of Islam is pictured suffering in one of the lower circles of hell. The relationship between Christianity and Islam was further damaged by the Muslim expansion into southern and eastern Europe and by the Christian attempt to wrench parts of the Middle East out of Muslim control during the Crusades. The wounds and the animosity of these painful collisions remain in the collective memories of both people, but they are especially strong among Muslims who have now smarted for a century under the humiliation of Western occupation and colonial control.

Still, there are signs of hope recently that after centuries of unmitigated suspicion, a genuine Christian-Muslim dialogue has begun. The Qur'ān, the holy book of Islam, teaches that Christians and Jews are "people of the book" and therefore have a special relation to Muslims. Some Christians have begun to speak of the "three Abrahamic faiths," meaning Christianity, Judaism, and Islam—all of which trace their origins back to the patriarch, Abraham. The diaspora of Muslim peoples in the Western world has enhanced the opportunity for interaction between Muslims and people of other faiths, including Christians. At the same time the rise of both Christian and Muslim fundamentalism has often dampened the appetite for such conversation. Still, the situation continues to appear more hopeful, and many observers think that a settlement of the antagonism between the state of Israel and its Arab neighbors might well lay the groundwork for more fruitful relations among these three faiths in the future. Others note that better relations between these three faiths might contribute to such a settlement.

What will be the significance of Christianity's "special relationship" to Judaism for its interaction with the other, historically more distinct faiths, like Buddhism and Hinduism? Some believe that because of the insistent monotheism and sense of exclusivity Christians share with Jews, the special link could make that larger dialogue more difficult. But the opposite is probably more likely. As Christians begin to recognize that God made a special covenant with the Jews at Sinai and that the same God also revealed himself in Jesus Christ without annulling the earlier bond, it seems consistent to believe this same God could also reveal himself to Buddhists, Hindus, and others. What seems required of Christians is a measure of humility and a sharp awareness of the magnitude and mystery of God. In the eleventh chapter of his Epistle to the Romans, St. Paul quotes the ancient Jewish prophet Isaiah's words:

For who has known the mind of the Lord,
or who has been his counselor?
(Rom. 11:34)

St. Paul himself comments in a kind of exclamation about God's power and reach:

O the depth of the riches and
wisdom and knowledge of God! How
unsearchable are his judgements and
how inscrutable his ways!
(Rom. 11:33)

By thus drawing on the genius of Judaism, not ignoring or minimizing it, and by underlining the vast wisdom of God, Paul challenges those Christians who insist—with considerable pretentiousness and against the evidence—that God could not or would not also reveal himself among Buddhists and Muslims. He exposes the real danger of second-guessing God, of Christians claiming to decide what God can and cannot do.

Recognizing that the biblical God could reveal himself elsewhere does not, however, solve all the questions. What remains is the difficult issue of *how* Christians integrate their faith in the Risen Christ with the facets of God's "unsearchable and inscrutable" reality that are reflected in other religious traditions. But this is a task that, given a humble recognition of the infinite scope of God's mercy, can and should be undertaken with joy and confidence. In fact it is already well underway. Christians have been exploring the intriguing similarities and differences between the Buddhist notion of divine "emptiness" and the Christian sense of God's mystery. Catholic priests are practicing Zen meditation. At the same time other Christians are trying to grasp the inner meaning of what at first appear to be strange Hindu devotional practices by patiently listening, watching, and entering into them in whatever way they can. Some Christians claim that in these rites they discover hints of the feminine energy of the divine and of the spiritual significance of the erotic that they had not found as clearly in biblical faith. The same "dialogue" is unfolding with followers of Shintō, with Sikhs, with people who practice local Spirit-centered religions (such as Native Americans), and with many others. Most Christians who have participated in such dialogues, and have shared prayer and made efforts at mutual understanding, testify that instead of weakening their Christian faith these ventures have matured it. Some say that the Holy Spirit, the third person of the traditional Christian Trinity, provides a secure Christian basis for expecting to find God in religious practices other than our own. For as Jesus himself said, "the Spirit blows where it will..." and as mere human beings we do not have the wisdom to make judgments on "whence it comes or whither it goes."

Religions, including Christianity, grow and change through the centuries. Those that do not grow wither and die. Religions also live *within* world history, they do not dwell in a realm set apart. In our time jet travel, electronic communication, migration, and high mobility are shrinking the globe daily. We are all neighbors, if not always good ones.

It is daunting to think that for the first time in all of human history, not only Christianity but all religions are beginning to share a common religious history. The interaction of the faiths, whether rancorous or sympathetic, open or dismissive, is now becoming an integral part of the history of *each* faith, and of *all* of them. The traditional religious groupings, furthermore, are no longer conveniently centered in somewhat isolated geographical terrains—Buddhists in Southeast Asia, Muslims in the Middle East, and Hindus in India. Now there are adherents of all these traditions on all the continents. The cities of the Northern Hemisphere have become multicolored collages of religious diversity. "Interfaith dialogue," once a very specialized activity carried on by experts, is now required of ordinary people, including Christians, on a day-to-day basis. These tidal changes in both the secular and the common religious milieu in which Christians live are no longer simply part of the external history of Christianity. They are now part of its internal story, an integral dimension of its own identity. Even the answer to the most fundamental question we have pursued throughout this chapter, What does it mean to be Christian?, can no longer be answered without listening carefully to what God is doing and saying among those who do not call themselves Christians.

Last Things

How does the Christian story end? The earliest Christians believed it would wind up quickly, with the imminent consummation of world history and the visible establishment on earth of the Reign of God that Jesus had initiated. But now, nearly two thousand years later, not many Christians anticipate this grand finale in the near future. It is true that some people, as we have seen, believe we are now literally living in the "last days." But even among fast-growing Pentecostals these remain a minority. Still, those Christians such as Catholics, Anglicans, and Lutherans who belong to creedal churches regularly confess during worship services that one day Jesus will "come again in glory"; and most Christians (along with Jews and Muslims) believe that human history is neither infinite nor cyclical—as some other religions teach—but that it is moving in a particular direction like an arrow in flight. It has a goal, and it will eventually end. But how and when will this culmination come? This question, having to do with what theologians call "eschatology" (teachings about the "last things"), is not something about which Christians share a widespread agreement.

Whatever the "second coming" of Christ might have meant to his first followers, many Christians today foresee no dramatic change in the way Jesus is now present in the world. For these Christians, the Reign of God that Jesus announced is already operative, albeit hidden. It is available here and now to anyone who, with the eyes of faith, can discern it amid the sin and tragedy of history. Perceiving it requires a change of heart, a new way of seeing and acting, but it is nonetheless a reality for those who embrace it and open themselves to it.

Another group of Christians holds that although the believer can savor certain anticipatory hints of God's Kingdom here on earth, one drinks its full blessedness only after death. In this pattern of belief, although Christ will one day return to transform the world into the Kingdom, that could be a long time hence, and in the meantime those who die in the faith will enjoy the benefits of the Kingdom in a heaven where God's love rules supreme.

Throughout Christian history there has also been a small but sometimes vociferous minority of Christians who believe they can detect signs and portents of the last days in contemporary events and who sternly insist that the end is surely near. They are called "millennialists," from the Latin word for a "thousand years" referring to the symbolic length of God's reign mentioned in the New Testament book of Revelation. They usually warn that because the cosmic climax is so near, it is a matter of great urgency for everyone to repent and prepare now for the divine judgment that will accompany it.

On the opposite wing there are also Christians who take a very long view of the course of human history. Reasoning that God is not constrained by human time limitations, they suggest that we are not near the end but only at the beginning of a vast and sweeping evolutionary process that, although it has been underway for billions of years, could spiral into millions or billions more. Some of these long-view exponents believe that the whole cosmos, with human life playing a key role, will eventually become divinized or at least drawn completely into God's own life. The twentieth-century French Catholic theologian and paleontologist Pierre Teilhard de Chardin described this eschatological vision in lyrical terms, with Jesus as the preliminary revelation of a final "Christification" toward which all life and all matter are heading. Some readers believe Teilhard's schema comports better with the available scientific data on the age and extent of the universe than do the more millennial views. Others think his ideas are more poetic than scientific. Still, Teilhard and others like him have helped some Christians to rethink the eschatological aspect of their faith in the light of contemporary physics, geology, and astronomy.

Each of these views of the ending, and others as well, can be found among present-day Christians. Most probably hold to some mixture of them, and many rarely think about the subject at all. Still, the eschatological dimension of Christianity—the belief that history is going somewhere—remains an important one. Millions of poor and dispossessed people are buoyed up by the conviction that their suffering is not endless and is not imposed by Providence or by fate, but that God supports their efforts to actualize the reign of justice the gospel message proclaims. Those who mourn the loss of friends and family members or who contemplate their own mortality take comfort in the belief that in the death and resurrection of Jesus Christ, God has opened the doors of life in the Kingdom to all people. Those who find existence empty or meaningless can look forward to a time when, as St. Paul put it, we no longer look "through a glass darkly, but see face to face."

Still, nothing strains and tests human language more than the attempt to articulate or explain the culminating vision of what God has in store for human beings. The reality of God's ultimate reign is at once the most important thing Christians believe and at the same time the most resistant to expression. It is the point at which it seems most natural to turn to poetry. Perhaps the greatest Christian poet of all time, Dante Alighieri, may have put it better than anyone else has. In his classic, *The Divine Comedy*, he tells of his slow ascent from hell through purgatory to heaven itself. As he draws near the highest celestial sphere there falls on his ears, he says, a sound he had never heard before. Stopping to listen, he writes (in the Italian original) "me sembiana un riso del universo." It sounded "like the laughter of the universe."

Laughter in heaven?

Why the hilarity? Could it be that God laughs because God knows how it all turns out in the end, and finally the whole universe will know too? Maybe so. Even on earth, laughter can be a gift of grace, the fragile human spirit's last defense against banality and despair. Clowns, as much as prophets, may be God's emissaries. Rightly grasped, the comic spirit transcends tragedy. Dante knows that genuine laughter is strangely close to faith. It allows people to set aside the merely empirical and to catch a fleeting glimpse of what might be, or even of what finally will be.

The living Christ remains the Alpha and Omega of Christianity, the point where the laughter of the universe—so often muffled by cries and sobbing—becomes unmistakably audible. It may sometimes fade, but once one has heard it, even quite dimly, one knows it is there, and always will be.

Recommended Reading

Sidney Ahlstrom. *Religious History of the American People.* New Haven: Yale University Press, 1972. Prizewinning and comprehensive account of the history of religion, and Christianity in particular, in the United States. Encyclopedic in scope, describing the sources and characteristics of the different denominations.

Saint Augustine. *Confessions.* Catholic University Press, 1953 (Fathers of the Church Series, vol. 21). The key text and deeply personal testimony of perhaps the single most influential thinker in all of Christian history, a classic for over a millennium.

Roland Bainton. *Christianity.* American Heritage, 1986. Lively, accurate single-volume history of Christianity from its beginnings to the present. A useful reference that also reads well.

John Dominic Crossan. *The Historical Jesus: The Life of a Mediterranean Jewish Peasant.* Harper, 1991. A skillful and comprehensive reconstruction of the historical Jesus based on the latest findings in archaeology, manuscript analysis, sociology, and textual criticism.

Mary Daly. *Beyond God the Father.* Boston: Beacon Press, 1985. Sharpest and most widely read radical feminist critique of Christianity. An influential book to which most subsequent feminist theologians refer.

Eldon Epp and George W. MacRae, eds. *The New Testament and Its Modern Interpreters.* Minneapolis: Augsburg/Fortress, 1987. A clear and judicious description and brief interpretation of each of the books of the New Testament, placed in its historical setting.

Gustavo Gutierrez. A *Theology of Liberation.* Orbis Books, 1988, 1973. The *magna carta* of all the various liberation theologies by the respected Peruvian founding father, a Catholic priest who exemplifies the preferential option for the poor.

Roger Hudleston, ed. *Little Flowers of St. Francis.* Templegate, 1988. The enduring and deeply appealing spirituality of the most beloved of all postbiblical Christian saints comes across endearingly in these legends.

Paul Knitter. *No Other Name? A Critical Survey of Christian Attitudes Toward World Religions.* Orbis Books, 1985. An eloquent and comprehensive description of the various contending ideas within Christianity of its proper relationship to other religious traditions.

C. S. Lewis. *Mere Christianity.* Collier/Macmillan, 1986. Perhaps the most widely read sustained argument—simple but lucid—for the credibility of Christianity. By a talented writer and critic who is a special favorite of evangelical Christians.

Martin Luther. *Christian Liberty.* Minneapolis: Augsburg/Fortress, 1943. Here the clarion voice of the pioneer of the Reformation and the ancestor of all Protestant Christians sounds forth his historic call for freedom under God.

Jaroslav Jan Pelikan. *Jesus Through the Centuries: His Place in the History of Culture.* New Haven: Yale University Press, 1985. Traces the images and portraits of Christ in theology, literature, and the arts over the nearly two thousand years since his life.

Saint Teresa. *The Interior Castle.* 2 vols., American Classical College Press, 1984. The capstone spiritual classic of Western Christianity by a woman who combined energetic activity in the world with profound inwardness. Unmatched for its subtle insights into the labyrinth of the soul.

Marina Warner. *Alone of All Her Sex: The Myth and Cult of the Virgin Mary.* New York: Random House, 1983. A theological and historical description of the continuing power and appeal of the woman who lived closer to Jesus than any other mortal, his mother.

CHAPTER 7

Islam

Seyyed Hossein Nasr

What Is Islam?

The Significance of the Study of Islam Today

These days, the reality of Islam penetrates into the consciousness of contemporary Western people from nearly every direction. Whether it be consequences of the decades-old Middle Eastern conflict between Arabs and Jews, the aftershocks of the upheavals of the Iranian Revolution, the civil war in Yugoslavia where Muslim Bosnians are caught between feuding Orthodox Serbs and Catholic Croats, the breakup of the Soviet Union and the sudden appearance of the significance of the Muslim Republics, or the ever more frequent use of Muslim names in the pages of American newspapers, it seems that the name and reality of Islam has come to constitute an important dimension of the life of humanity today even in America and Europe. And yet there is no major religion that is more distorted in its study in the West than Islam, which is too close to be considered as an exotic religion and yet distinct enough from Christianity to pose as the "other," as it has in fact done for the West for well over a millennium.

The study of Islam as a religion and as the "presiding idea" and dominating principle of a major world civilization is of great significance not only because it makes better known the worldview of more than a billion people ranging from blue-eyed Slavs and Berbers to blacks, from Arabs to Malays, and from Turks and Persians to Chinese. It is also significant because Islam and its civilization have played a far greater role than usually admitted in the genesis and development of European (and including American) civilization. Today Islam constitutes the second largest religious community in Europe and has a population of almost the same size as Judaism in America. But most of all, the study of Islam is significant because it concerns a message from God revealed within that very Abrahamic world from which Judaism and Christianity have issued forth. The Islamic revelation is the third and final revelation of the Abrahamic monotheistic cycle and constitutes a major branch of the tree of monotheism. It is, therefore, a religion without whose study the knowledge of the whole religious family to which Jews and Christians belong would be incomplete.

Islam as the Final Revelation and Return to the Primordial Religion

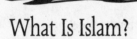

Islam considers itself as the final plenary revelation in the history of present humanity and believes that there will be no other revelation after it until the end of human history and the coming of the eschatological events described so eloquently in the final chapters of the Qur'ān, which is the verbatim Word of God in Islam. That is why the Prophet of Islam is called "the Seal of Prophets" (*khātam al-anbiyā'*). Islam sees itself as the final link in a long chain of prophecy that goes back to Adam, who was not only the father of humankind (*abu'l-bashar*) but also the first prophet. There is in fact but a single religion, that of Divine Unity (*al-tawḥīd*), which has constituted the heart of all messages from heaven and which Islam has come to assert in its final form.

The Islamic message is, therefore, none other than the acceptance of God as the One (*al-Aḥad*) and submission to Him (*taslīm*), which results in peace (*salām*); hence the name of Islam, which means simply surrender to the Will of the One God, called Allah in Arabic. To become a Muslim, it is sufficient to bear testimony before two Muslim witnesses that "There is no god but God" (*lā ilāha illa'Llāh*) and that "Muḥammad[1] is the Messenger of God" (*Muḥammad^{un} rasūl Allāh*). These two testimonies (*shahādah*) contain the alpha and omega of the Islamic message. One asserts the unity of the Divine Principle and the other the reception of the message of unity from the person whom God chose as His final prophet. The Qur'ān emphasizes continuously the doctrine of Unity and the Oneness of God, and it can be said that the very raison d'être of Islam is to assert in a final and categorical manner the Oneness of God and the nothingness of all before the majesty of that One. As the chapter on unity (*sūrat al-tawḥīd*) in the Qur'ān asserts: "Say He is God, the One! God the eternally Besought of all! He begetteth not nor was He begotten. And there is none like unto Him" (CXII,1-4).[2]

The term Allah used in this and other verses of the Qur'ān refers not to a tribal or ethnic god but to the supreme Divine Principle in the Arabic language. It is therefore translatable as God, provided this term is made to include the Godhead and is not identified solely with the triune doctrines of an especially Christian nature. Islam, in asserting over and over again the oneness and omnipotence, as well as mercy and generosity of God as the One, puts the seal of finality upon what it considers to be the religious message as such. It crystallizes human reality before the Divine Presence. That is why, according to the Qur'ān, even before the creation of the world, God asked man: "Am I not your Lord?" and not one man but the whole of humanity, both male and female, answered: "Yea, verily we bear witness" (Qur'ān; VII,172). As the final religion of humanity, Islam is the last divinely orchestrated response of yea to the pre-eternal divine question, the response that constitutes the very definition of being human.

By virtue of its insistence upon Divine Unity and pre-eternal response of humanity to the lordship of the One, Islam signifies also the return to the primordial religion and calls itself as such (*dīn al-fiṭrah*, or the religion that is in the nature of things, or *dīn al-ḥanīf*, the religion of primordial unity). Islam is not based on a particular historical event or an ethnic group but on a universal and primordial truth, which has therefore always been and will always be. It sees itself as a return to that truth which stands above and beyond all historical contingencies. The Qur'ān, in fact, refers to Abraham, who lived long before the historic manifestation of Islam, as *muslim* as well as *ḥanīf*; that is, belonging to that primordial monotheism that survived among a few, despite the fall of the majority of men and women of later Arab society, preceding the rise of Islam, into a crass form of idolatry and polytheism that Muslims identify with the age of ignorance (*al-jāhiliyyah*). Islam is a return not only to the religion of Abraham but even of Adam, restoring primordial monotheism without identifying it with a single people, as is seen in the case of Judaism, or a single event of human history, as one observes in the prevalent purely historical view of the incarnation in Christian theology.

The Prophet asserted that he brought nothing new but simply reaffirmed the truth that always was. This primordial character of the Islamic message is reflected not only in its essentiality, universality, and simplicity but also in its inclusive attitude toward the religions and forms of wisdom that preceded it. Islam has always claimed the older prophets of the Abrahamic world and even before Abraham going back to Noah and Adam as its own, to the extent that these spiritual and religious poles play a more important role in everyday Islamic piety than they do in the Christian. Also as a result of this characteristic, Islam has been able to preserve something of the ambience of the Abrahamic world in what survives of traditional Islamic life to the extent that the journey to traditional Muslim areas even today usually reminds Westerners of the world of Hebrew prophets and of Christ himself.

It was not, however, only the Abrahamic world that became included in Islam's understanding of itself as at once the final and primordial religion. As Islam encountered non-Semitic religions later on in Persia, India, and elsewhere, the same principle of the universality of revelation was applied. The result was that many of the philosophies and schools of thought of the ancient world became fairly easily integrated into the Islamic intellectual perspective, as long as they conformed to or affirmed the principle of unity. In this case they were usually considered as remnants of the teachings of old prophets, constituting part of that vast family which brought the message of God's Oneness to every people and race, as the Qur'ān asserts. One of the results of this primordial character of Islam, therefore, was the formation and development of the Islamic intellectual tradition as the repository for much of the wisdom of the ancient world ranging from the Graeco-Alexandrian to the Indian.

As every veritable omega is also the alpha, Islam as the terminal religion of humanity is also a return to the primordial religion. In its categorical and final formulation of the doctrine of Unity, it returns to that primordial message which bound Adam to God and which defines religion as such. The universality of Islam may be said to issue from this return to the primordial religion, whereas its particularity may be said to be related to its finality, which has provided the distinctive form for one of the world's major religions.

Unity and Diversity within the Islamic Tradition (Sunnism and Shi'ism)

Unity cannot manifest itself without entering into the world of multiplicity while remaining the means whereby humanity is led from multiplicity to unity. The great emphasis of Islam upon unity, therefore, could not prevent diversity on the formal level nor could Islam have integrated a vast segment of humanity with diverse ethnic, linguistic, and cultural backgrounds without making possible diverse interpretations of its teachings. These teachings, nevertheless, lead to that unity residing at the heart of the Islamic message as long as the interpreters of the Islamic message remain within the framework of Islamic orthopraxy and orthodoxy considered in its widest and most universal sense. The Islamic religion, therefore, is composed of diverse schools and interpretations that are deeply rooted and united in the principles of the Islamic revelation.

The most important elements among those that unite the vast spectrum of schools comprising Islam in its orthodox manifestations, this term being understood in a metaphysical and not only theological and juridical manner, are the two testimonies (*shahādahs*) themselves. By virtue of the first *shahādah,* that is, "There is no god but God," all Muslims confirm the unity of the Divine Principle and the reliance of all things upon Him. Through the second *shahādah,* "Muḥammad is the messenger of God," they accept the prophethood of the Prophet and therefore become specifically Muslims. Moreover, all Muslims agree that the Qur'ān is the verbatim revelation of God. They also agree about its text and content; that is, no variant texts are found among any of the schools, although the exegetical meaning can, of course, differ from one school to another. Muslims also agree concerning the reality of the afterlife, although again there are various types and levels of interpretation and meaning of the teachings of the Qur'ān and the *Ḥadīth* concerning eschatological matters. Muslims are also united in the main rituals performed, ranging from the daily prayers to fasting to making the pilgrimage, although here again there are certain small differences in ritual details among the various schools of law.

Finally, one must mention the spirit emanating from the Qur'ānic revelation and the grace (*barakah*) of the Prophet, issuing both from his *Sunnah,* or wonts, and resulting from the very fact that Islam is a living religion with its channels to heaven open here and now, not only in a moment of past history. These less definable factors are nevertheless powerful elements that unify Islam and the Islamic world. They also possess more concrete manifestations, especially in Sufism, which in the form of Sufi orders covers the whole of the Islamic world and provides a powerful yet hidden force for the unity of that world. Nevertheless, the presence of these factors is ubiquitous and can hardly be denied even externally. Their effect is to be seen all the way from the manner in which the Qur'ānic chanting in Arabic transforms the soul of Muslims everywhere, whether they be Arabs or Bengalis, to the architecture and urban planning of Islamic cities, whether they be in Morocco or Persia, all the way from the way in which traditional Muslim men dress to the way people take off their shoes when entering a traditional Muslim house, whether it be in Senegal or Malaysia.

Within this unity, which is perceptible even to an outsider, diversity exists on various levels, including the exegetical, legal, theological, social, and political. In fact the Prophet has said, "The difference of view among the scholars (*'ulamā'*) of my community is a blessing from God." Throughout the history of Islam there have existed diverse interpretations of the Qur'ān and *Ḥadīth*, different schools of law, many theological and philosophical interpretations, and political claims on the basis of the interpretation of religious texts. These differences have sometimes led to not only fierce religious rivalries but also wars, a phenomenon that is, however, not unique to Islam. Differences, however, have never been able to destroy the unity of Islam either as a religion or as a civilization. It was in reference to the danger of excessive theological and religious dispute that the Prophet said that the Islamic community would divide after him into seventy-three schools, of which only one would be completely true. In this saying he predicted not only the contention of the various schools that would appear but also the persistence of the truth, which could not in its most universal sense be other than that of the *shahādah.* Nor could the Prophet be referring to the vertical and hierarchical dimensions of Islam and levels of interpretation of its truths, which do not represent diversity and opposition in the same sense and to which we shall turn later in this chapter.

All Muslims belong to one of three groups: Sunnis, Shi'ites, and Kharijites. This last group comprises those who opposed the claim of both 'Alī and Mu'āwiyyah to the caliphate, which will be discussed later. Kharijites have always been numerically very small and today remain confined to Oman and southern Algeria. The most important division within Islam is between Sunnism and Shi'ism. The vast majority of Muslims, that is, about 87 to 88 percent, are Sunnis, the term coming from *ahl al-sunnah wa'l-jamā'ah,* that is, followers of the *sunnah* of the Prophet and the majority. About 12 to 13 percent of Muslims are Shi'ites, from *shī'at 'Alī,* the partisans of 'Alī. They in turn are divided into Twelve-Imām Shi'ites, Ismā'īlīs, and

Zaydīs. The Twelve-Imām, or Ithnā-'asharī, Shi'ites are by far the most numerous, comprising some 130 million people living mostly in present-day Iran, Iraq, Lebanon, the Persian Gulf, eastern Saudi Arabia, Afghanistan, Adharbaijan, Pakistan, and India. Iran, Iraq, Adharbaijan, and Bahrain have majority Twelve-Imām Shi'ite populations while in Lebanon the Shi'ites constitute the largest single religious body.

The Ismā'īlīs played an important role in Islamic history and established their own caliphate in Egypt during the Fāṭimid period in the fourth/tenth and fifth/eleventh centuries.[3] Today they are scattered in various communities mostly in Pakistan and India but also with important concentrations in East Africa, Syria, and the Pamir and Hindu Kush regions of Afghanistan, Pakistan, and Tajikistan. They also have an important community in Canada, consisting mostly of emigrants from East Africa and the Indian world. Ismā'īlīs are divided into two branches, one with its center in India and the other under the direction of the Agha Khan, whose followers consider him as their Imām (or spiritual and temporal leader). It is difficult to give an exact figure for the members of this community but altogether the Ismā'īlīs are estimated to be a few million in number. As for the Zaydīs, who among various schools of Shi'ism are theologically the closest to Sunnism, there are about three to four million of them residing almost completely in the Yemen.

The Shi'ites separated from the Sunnis upon the death of the Prophet when the question of succession became vital. The majority of the community chose Abū Bakr, the venerable friend of the Prophet, as the first caliph (from the Arabic *khalīfah* meaning, in this context, the vicegerent of the Prophet of God) while a small number believed that 'Alī, the cousin and son-in-law of the Prophet, should have become caliph. The problem was, however, more profound than one of personalities. It also concerned the function of the person who was to succeed the Prophet. The Sunnis believed that the function of such a person should be to protect the Divine Law, act as judge, and rule over the community, preserving public order and the borders of the Islamic world. The Shi'ites believed that such a person should also be able to interpret the Qur'ān and the Law and in fact possess inward knowledge. Therefore, he had to be chosen by God and the Prophet and not the community. Such a figure was called *imām*.[4] Although such a person did not share in the Prophet's prophetic function (*nubuwwah*), he did receive the inner spiritual power of the Prophet (*walāyah*). Moreover, the Shi'ites identified this person with 'Alī ibn Abī Ṭālib, whom they believed the Prophet chose as his successor before his death. Shi'ism is, therefore, very much related to the family of the Prophet (*ahl al-bayt*), the later Imāms being all descendants of 'Alī and Fāṭimah, the daughter of the Prophet.

The Shi'ite Imām is also considered as the only legitimate ruler of the Islamic community, hence the rejection by Shi'ites of the first three caliphs as well as the later Sunni caliphates. Twelve-Imām Shi'ites, with whom this analysis is mostly concerned, therefore rejected all political authority ever since the short-lived caliphate of 'Alī came to an end abruptly with his assassination. They believe that the twelfth Imām is in occultation (*ghaybah*), that is, not outwardly present in this world and yet alive. All legitimate political power must derive from him, and he will appear one day to bring justice and peace to the world as part of eschatological events that will bring human history to a close. Since 1979 and the Iranian Revolution—as a result of which Shi'ite religious authorities rule directly in Iran—new interpretations of the relation between religious and governmental authority have been made, but the significance and role of the hidden Imām or the Mahdī remains unchanged.

Shi'ism became consolidated particularly with the death of the third Imām, Ḥusayn ibn 'Alī, who was killed in the first/seventh century along with most of the members of his, and therefore the Prophet's, immediate family by the army of the Umayyad caliph, Yazīd, in Karbalā' in Iraq. His body is buried there, but his head was brought to Cairo to be interred in a mosque, which remains the heart of that city to this day. Henceforth, Shi'ism continued as a protest movement of increasing political significance but did not gain complete political power over any extensive area of the Islamic world until the Safavids conquered Persia in 922/1501 and established Twelve-Imām Shi'ism as the official state religion. Ismā'īlism had major political manifestations earlier in Islamic history, especially with the establishment of the Fāṭimids, who ruled over a vast area from Tunisia to Syria with their base in Egypt from 297/909 to 567/1171. Turning to Zaydīsm, its power base remained in the Yemen, where its followers ruled until the invasion by Egypt in 1962.

Shi'ism, however, must not be considered simply as a political movement. Rather, Shi'ism developed its own schools of law, theology, philosophy, and other religious sciences, including methods of Qur'ānic exegesis. There also continued to exist debates and sometimes confrontations in various religious sciences with Sunnism, dialogues that played no small role in the development of religious thought in both worlds. However, despite periods of Sunni–Shi'ite political, and sometimes military, confrontation and the exploitation of these differences by Western powers that began to colonize the Islamic world since the twelfth/eighteenth century and even before, Sunnis and Shi'ites have also lived in peace in many climes and times. Especially during the past century their religious scholars have sought to create accord on the basis of the many elements that unite them within the embrace of the totality of the Islamic tradition.

Besides Sunnism and Shi'ism, other diversities of a much less significant nature need to be mentioned. For example, there are theological and philosophical differences among various schools mentioned in the class of writings with the title *milal wa'l-niḥal,* literally religious groups and schools of thought. Many of these can be compared to, let us say, the Bonaventurian and Thomistic interpretations of medieval Christian theology, but others developed into what one can call a veritable sect in contrast to Sunnism and Shi'ism. These two—Sunnism and Shi'ism—compose Islamic orthodoxy and should not be referred to as sects. The sects within the Islamic world include some like the 'Alawīs or Nuṣayrīs of Syria, who remain in some way related to the Islamic religion. Others like the Druze of Lebanon and adjacent areas or the Bahā'īs, originally of Persia but now spread in many lands, broke away from Islam and became independent religious communities, which are, nevertheless, related historically to Islam. In any case these sects and groups compose a part of the tapestry of certain parts of the Islamic world and contribute to the diversity to be found within Islamic society, although their nature and teachings are in most cases very different.

The Islamic People (al-Ummah) and Ethnic and Cultural Groups within the Ummah

One of the key concepts in Islam is that of the *ummah* or the totality of the people who are Muslims and compose the Islamic world. Islam sees history itself in religious terms and refers to other people not primarily through their linguistic or ethnic affiliations but through their religious identity, hence the reference to the *ummah* of Moses or Jesus found so often in Islamic texts when reference is made to Judaism and Christianity. The Islamic *ummah* is one, bound by solidarity to the Qur'ānic message of Divine Oneness and Sovereignty and acceptance of the Divine Law (*al-Sharī'ah*). Muslims are united by the strong bond of brotherhood, and also sisterhood, a bond that is felt strongly to this day despite all the turmoils that have pitted and continue to pit Muslims against each other and against which God has warned in the verse: "And hold fast, all of you together, to the cable of God and do not separate" (Qur'ān; III,103). One cannot understand Islam without gaining a sense of the significance of the concept of *ummah* and the reality of that community which, although no longer politically united, is nevertheless a single religious community characterized by that sense of brotherhood (*ukhuwwah*) so much emphasized by the Qur'ān and the Prophet.

The *ummah* is not, however, composed of a single ethnic, racial, or cultural group. Islam was, from the beginning, a religion that addressed the whole of humanity and strongly opposed all forms of racism and tribalism as the following famous Qur'ānic verse bears out so clearly: "O mankind! Lo! We have created you male and female, and have made you nations and tribes that ye may know one another! Lo! the noblest of you, in the sight of God, is the most righteous" (Qur'ān; XLIX,13). The later history of Islam was to bear out its global destiny. Over the centuries Arabs and Persians, Turks and Indians, blacks and Malays, Chinese and even some Tibetans, Mongolians, and Slavs became part of the *ummah*, and during the last few decades Islam has even been spreading in Europe and America and, to some extent, in Australia. There is hardly any ethnic and racial group in the world that does not have some members belonging to the Islamic *ummah*. This can be seen physically in the annual pilgrimage to Makkah, where people from every corner of the globe assemble to worship at the house built by Abraham in honor of God who is One.

The Islamic World

The Spread and Demographic Growth of Islam

Islam did begin in Arabia, where the revelation was first received, but then spread rapidly among the Persians and black Africans, and soon thereafter among Turks and some of the Chinese, Indians, and many other ethnic groups. The spread of Islam occurred in waves. In less than a century, the Arab armies conquered a land stretching from the Indus River to France and brought with them Islam, which, contrary to popular Western conceptions, was not forced upon the people by the sword. In some places, such as Persia, it took several centuries for the majority of people to embrace Islam, long after Arab military power had ceased. Later, Islam spread peacefully among the Turks of central Asia, even before their migration to the western regions of central Asia, and finally westward through northern Persia to Anatolia. It also spread peacefully mostly through Sufis throughout the Indian subcontinent from the fifth/eleventh century onward and throughout Java, Sumatra, and Malaya from the eighth/fourteenth century on. From about the twelfth/eighteenth century, Islam has been also spreading ever farther into the African continent, moving both southward and inland. During the Ottoman occupation of the Balkans, Islamic communities were established especially in Albania and Bosnia, some of these communities being five hundred years old. It is generally believed that Islam is the fastest-growing religion in the world today.

These phases of the spread of Islam brought peoples of many different ethnic and cultural backgrounds into the single *ummah*, introducing a type of diversity that complements what has been mentioned previously. Yet, like the types of diversity already mentioned, this ethnic diversity has not at all destroyed but rather enriched the unity of the *ummah,* for unity is not uniformity. In fact it stands diametrically opposed to uniformity. When one looks at the Islamic world today, one sees several major ethnic and cultural zones with their own subdivisions but unified in their attachment to the Islamic tradition and composing in their totality the Islamic *ummah.*

The Global Distribution of Muslims and Zones of Islamic Civilization

Most people in the West automatically identify Muslims with Arabs. Today, however, Arabs compose less than a fifth of the world Muslim population. But they remain of central importance in the *ummah* because of their historical role in the Islamic world, their language—which is that of the Qur'ān—and the significance for all Muslims of the sacred sites of Islam that lie within the Arab world, especially the cities of Makkah and Madinah in the Hejaz in present-day Saudi Arabia. Today about 200 million Muslim Arabs are living from Mauritania to Iraq, identified as Arabs not ethnically but linguistically; that is, a person is considered as an Arab whose mother tongue is Arabic. The vast majority of Arabs are, of course, Muslims, although in certain Arab countries such as Lebanon, Egypt, and Syria, as well as among the Palestinians, there is a sizable Christian population; and before the partition of Palestine, highly culturally Arabized Jewish communities also existed in most Arab countries. There are many subcultures within the Arab world, but the main division is between the eastern and the western Arabs, the line of demarcation being somewhere in Libya. Each part, while profoundly Islamic and Arabic, has its local cultural color and traits, which can be seen in the literature, architecture, and cuisine of the two areas.

The second oldest ethnic and cultural zone of the Islamic world is the Persian, comprising not only the people of present-day Iran but also those of similar ethnic and linguistic stock including the Kurds, the people of Afghanistan, Tajikistan, and parts of Uzbekistan and Pakistan. Together they number about a hundred million people and are of particular historic and cultural importance, because it was the Persians who, along with the Arabs, built classical Islamic civilization, and Persia has always been one of the most important artistic and intellectual centers of the Islamic world. Furthermore, the Persian language is, after Arabic, the second most important language of Islamic civilization and the only other classical language spoken and written beyond the land of its native speakers. For more than a millennium it was the primary literary medium used by people from Iraq to China.

Closely related ethnically to the various Iranian groups and the world of Persian culture and, like the Persians, of Indo-European stock are the Muslims of the Indian subcontinent. They constitute the largest single group of the followers of Islam, consisting of some 350 million people in Pakistan and Bangladesh, which are predominantly Muslim, as well as in India, Śrī Laṅkā, and Nepal, where they are in a minority. India in fact has well over 100 million Muslims, the largest single minority in the world. The predominant language of this area is Urdu, related closely to both Sanskrit and Persian, although many other Indian languages such as Punjabi, Sindhi, Gujarati, and Tamil are also used by Muslims. Bengali must be considered, along with Urdu, as the other major literary Islamic language of the subcontinent.

After the Arabs and Persians, the next important group, in terms of its participation in Islamic civilization and its role in Islamic history, are the Turkic people, spread from the Balkans to eastern Siberia. The Turks have played a major role in the political life of Islam during the past millennium and created the powerful Ottoman Empire, which lasted about seven centuries until World War I. But the Turkic people are not limited to the Turks of the Ottoman world and present-day Turkey. Several of the now independent republics of Caucasia and central Asia are ethnically and linguistically Turkic, although some are culturally very close to the Persian world. There are also people of Turkic stock within Russia itself. There are perhaps more than 150 million people belonging to this ethnic group, with languages that are neither Semitic like Arabic nor Indo-European like Persian but Altaic. They represent a distinct zone within Islamic civilization that has been in constant interaction with the Arabic and Persian worlds over the centuries.

Islam spread over areas of black Africa very early in its career, and African black Muslims have played an important role in Islamic history; the caller to prayer (*mu'adhdhin*) of the Prophet, Bilāl, was himself a black. Black African Muslims had established thriving empires in sub-Saharan Africa by the seventh/thirteenth century, and Islam in Africa has been and continues to be a vital and vibrant force even during the period of European colonization. Today more than 100 million black African Muslims, as distinct from the Arab and Berber North Africans, compose a notable zone of Islamic civilization. Black Africans speak many different languages, such as Fulani, Hausa, and Swahili, and constitute many subcultures. But the main division in this part of the Islamic world is between East and West Africa, although, again, a strong bond of unity exists between the two areas. They are bridged by numerous links, including the Sufi orders, which have had a major role in the spread of Islam in Africa and are still very active in most regions of Muslim black Africa.

Islam spread into the Malay world later than in the areas already mentioned. Today this world includes the most populated of all Islamic countries, Indonesia, and a rich Islamic culture embracing, in addition to

Indonesia, Malaysia, Brunei, the southern Philippines, and certain areas of Thailand and Kampuchia as well as a part of Singapore. This zone is characterized by its use of Malay as its main literary tongue and the adaptation of Islam to a particular natural and cultural environment very different from what one finds in the cradle of classical Islamic civilization in the Middle East. More than 180 million Muslims are scattered in this vast area, which includes thousands of islands as well as the Malay Peninsula.

Less is known about Chinese Muslims than any other group in the Islamic world. Their number is estimated anywhere from 30 to 100 million, and they are scattered all over China, with the main concentration being in the western province of Sinkiang. They are an old community, there being records of Muslims in Canton in the first/seventh century, and they have created a distinct Chinese Islamic culture of their own, including their own distinct style of Arabic calligraphy. There is also a corpus of Chinese Islamic literature, most of which remains unknown to the outside world. But Muslims remain an important minority in China as they do in certain other countries, from Burma in South Asia to Finland in northern Europe.

It is of some significance to mention the parts of the *ummah* living in Europe and America, although their number is relatively small. About 10 million Muslims live in various European countries. Some, including the Bosnians, are of Slavic stock, and the Albanians of Albania and Kosovo belong to communities that are centuries old, as are small communities of Turkish and even Bulgar origin. The rest are predominantly emigrants who have come to Europe since World War II, consisting mostly of North Africans in France; Indians, Pakistanis, and Bangladeshis in Great Britain; and Turks in Germany. The Muslims now constitute important communities in many areas and have even posed cultural and social challenges in some countries such as France.

There is no doubt that many of the slaves brought over from Africa to America were originally Muslims, but their religion was gradually forgotten. Since the 1930s, however, Islam has been spreading among African Americans and today represents a notable religious voice in America. Today, from four to five million Muslims live in North America, consisting not only of African Americans but also numerous Arabs and Persians, and also some Turks and people of the Indian subcontinent who have migrated to America during the past few decades. A number of Americans and Canadians of European stock also have embraced Islam. Thus, the Islamic community continues to grow in North America as well as in Central and South America, where in Brazil, Argentina, Trinidad, and several other areas sizable Muslim populations exist.

The Islamic *ummah* therefore comprises many ethnic, linguistic, and cultural elements: Semites, Indo-Iranians, Turks, blacks, Malays, Chinese, and others speaking numerous languages—especially Arabic, which is a

Semitic tongue, but also Indo-European, Altaic, and African languages. Although concentrated in Asia and Africa, the members of the *ummah* also are scattered over the other five continents and constitute important minorities in many lands and nations. They possess their own languages and cultures and yet participate in that greater whole which is the *ummah* and the Islamic civilization of which they are all members. Islam is like a vast tapestry into which all these local cultural modes and vanities are woven like arabesques into a larger pattern that reflects the unity of the Divine Principle.

Islam as Religion (Al-Dīn)

The Islamic Understanding of the Role of Religion in Human Life

The term that corresponds most closely to "religion" in Arabic is *al-dīn*. Whereas religion comes from the root *religare,* meaning that which binds and therefore by implication binds us to God, *al-dīn* is said by some grammarians of Arabic and Qur'ānic commentators to derive from *al-dayn,* which means debt. *Al-dīn,* therefore, is the repaying of our debt to God and involves the whole of our life, because we are indebted to God not only for this or that gift but also for existence itself. For the Muslim mind it is the most obvious of facts and greatest of certitudes that we are nothing and God is everything, that we own nothing by ourselves and that all belongs to God according to the Qur'ānic verse: "God is the rich (*ghaniy*) and ye are the poor (*fuqarā'*)" (XLVII,38). We are poor in our very essence; we are poor not only in an economic, social, or even physical sense but in an ontological one. Therefore, all that we are and all that we have belongs to God for which we are indebted to Him and for whose gifts we must give thanks (*shukr*). Religion or *al-dīn,* which is inseparable from the sense of the reality of this "debt," therefore, embraces the whole of life and is inseparable from life itself.

In the Islamic perspective, religion is not seen as a part of life or a special kind of activity along with art, thought, commerce, social discourse, politics, and the like. Rather, it is the matrix and worldview within which these and all other human activities, efforts, creations, and thoughts take place or should take place. It is the very sap of the tree of life. As has been said so often, Islam is not only a religion, in the modern sense of the term, redefined in a secularized world in which the religious life occupies at best a small part of the daily activities of most people. Rather, Islam is religion as a total way of life. Islam does not even accept the validity of a domain outside of the realm of religion and refuses to accord any reality to the dichotomy between the sacred and the profane or secular or the spiritual and temporal. Such terms as secular and profane cannot even be translated exactly into the Islamic languages in their classical form, and current terms used to render them into these languages are recently coined words usually derived from the idea of worldliness, which is not the same as secular or profane. The Qur'ān often refers to this-worldliness, which is contrasted with the abiding realities of the other world (*al-dunyā* and *al-ākhirah*), but this dichotomy must not be confused with the division between the sacred and secular or profane. One can be worldly in a completely religious universe in which worldliness itself has a religious meaning, but one cannot be secular in such a universe unless one claims the independence for a particular realm of life from religion. Islam asserts that there is no extraterritoriality in religion and that nothing can be legitimately outside of the realm of tradition in the sense of religion and the application of its principles over the space and temporal history of a particular human collectivity. Moreover, Islam claims this all-encompassing quality not only for itself but also for religion as such.

Religion, then, must embrace the whole of life. Every human thought and action must be related ultimately to the Divine Principle, which is the source of all that is. Both the existence of the cosmic order, including the human world, and all the qualities to be found in the cosmos come from God and are therefore inseparable from His Will and the theophanies of His other Names and Qualities. Religion is there to remind forgetful human beings of this metaphysical reality and, on the more practical level, to provide concrete guidance so that men and women can live according to the Will of God and at the highest level gain or rather regain the knowledge of His Oneness and the manner in which all multiplicity is ultimately related to the One. Every act that a man or woman performs, every thought he or she nurtures in his or her mind, and every object that he or she makes must be related to God, if he or she is to remain faithful to the very nature of things and of himself or herself. Religion is that reality which makes this nexus between the human world in all of its aspects and God possible. Therefore, its role in human life is central. It can even be said from the Islamic point of view that religion in its most universal and essential sense is life itself.

The Private Aspects of Religion

Although Islam has this all-embracing concept of religion, it does divide the injunctions and teachings of religion into what concerns private life and what is related to the public domain, without these two aspects being totally distinct. On the contrary, their interrelatedness is constantly emphasized. The private aspects deal primarily with all that concerns the inner rapport of men and women with God. They involve prayer in all its modes from individual supplication (*al-du'ā*) to the canonical prayers (*al-ṣalāh*) to the invocation of the Names of God (*al-dhikr*), which is quintessential prayer, practiced especially by the Sufis and identified at the highest level with the prayer of the heart. The other major rites such as fasting and pilgrimage, all of which will be treated later, also pertain to the private aspects of life. Yet these rites also have a strong public aspect, as do the canonical prayers, which are often performed in community with other Muslims. Of course, the canonical prayers can always be performed alone and in private—except for the congregational prayers of Friday, which naturally involve the public whether it be of a small or large number.

Islam also governs human actions as they pertain to private life. First, a human being's treatment of his or her own body is governed by the Divine Law (*al-Sharī'ah*). This includes not only hygienic and dietary regulations of religious importance, but also the religious duty to take care of the body, religious injunctions concerning all sexual practices, and religious prohibition of harming the body including, of course, suicide, which is forbidden by Islamic Law and considered a great sin. Many of these elements are of course found in other religions, a fact to which Islam points as support for the view that religion is inseparable from the life of normal humanity.

As far as dietary regulations are concerned, Islam, like Judaism, considers them to be of religious significance and a means of sacralizing everyday life. Muslims are forbidden (*ḥarām*) to eat pork and all its derivatives, drink alcoholic beverages, or consume certain other types of meat, such as those of carnivorous animals. The animals whose meat is permitted to be consumed (*ḥalāl*) must be sacrificed in the Name of God. There is thus a full awareness of the religious conditions that alone permit the slaughtering of animals. This sacrificial view has, needless to say, the deepest effect upon the relation between man and the animal world.

Other private aspects of life, such as one's relation with one's parents, wife, children and other relatives, and friends and neighbors, are also governed by religious laws. All of these domains have both legal and moral injunctions of a religious character. For example, the Qur'ān exhorts children to be kind and to respect their parents. This is a moral injunction based on religious authority. Laws also exist concerning the distribution of a person's inheritance among various members of the family. This is a legal injunction, again, based on religious authority. Altogether, so far as the private sector of life is concerned, the teachings of Islam emphasize men and women's duties toward their own bodies and souls in relation to God as well as close bonds within the family, with the result that the family constitutes a very strong institution in Islamic society.

It is important to emphasize here that the attitude so prevalent in the modern world, according to which a person's body and life are his or her own to do with as he or she wants, is totally absent in Islam. Our bodies and lives are not our own; they are God's. We did not create either our bodies or our lives. They belong to God, and we must treat them with this truth in mind and with a sense of duty and responsibility in the light of God's injunctions as revealed in the Qur'ān and explained by the Prophet. There is no such thing as human rights without human responsibility. All human rights derive from the fulfillment of responsibilities to the Giver of human life.

The most private aspect of life is of course the inner, spiritual life wherein men and women approach God to an ever greater extent according to the degree of their inwardness; one of the Names of God mentioned in the Qur'ān is the Inward (*al-Bāṭin*). The Islamic revelation contains elaborate teachings pertaining to this most private, in the sense of inner, aspect of human life, teachings that have been formulated and elaborated over the centuries by Islamic masters of the path toward inwardness, the vast majority of whom have been Sufis. But even this most inward dimension of religion has its public and outward complement, as God Himself is not only the Inward but also the Outward (*al-Ẓāhir*) according to the Qur'ānic verse: "He is the First (*al-Awwal*) and the last (*al-Ākhir*) and the Outward (*al-Ẓāhir*) and the Inward (*al-Bāṭin*) and He knows infinitely all things" (Qur'ān; LVII,3).

The Public Aspects of Religion

As a religion that emphasizes equilibrium in all things and aspects of human life, Islam also accentuates the outward and the public aspects of religion to complement the inward and the private. According to Islam, religion is not only a matter of private conscience, although it certainly includes this dimension, but it also is concerned with the public domain, with humans' social, economic, and even political lives. There is no division between the Kingdom of God and the kingdom of Caesar in the Islamic perspective. Rather, all belongs to God and must therefore be regulated by Divine Law and moral injunctions that come from Him and are religious in nature.

The public aspects of Islam concern every aspect of the community *qua* community, stretching from the local social unit all the way to the *ummah* itself and even the whole of humanity and creation. There are no relations between human beings that do not possess a religious significance, starting with the relations between members of the most concrete community, which is that of the family and the neighborhood, village, or tribe, and leading to greater and less palpable units such as a province or state, in the traditional Islamic sense of the term, and finally to *dār al-islām* or the Abode of

Islam itself and Muslim minorities in non-Islamic lands. Islamic injunctions also embrace non-Muslims whose treatment is covered by Islamic Law. These relations include social transactions and interactions ranging from duties and responsibilities to one's neighbors and friends to orphans and the destitute, stranger Muslims, and non-Muslims. Some of the teachings of Islam in this domain are general moral institutions such as being charitable or just in all situations and toward all people and even other creatures of God. Others are formulated in concrete laws that have governed Islamic social behavior over the centuries, including the personal laws concerning such matters as marriage, divorce, and inheritance, which belong to the private as well the public domain.

One important public aspect of Islam concerns economic activity. In contrast to Christianity, which, in its early history, displayed a disdain for mercantile activity and in which there are no explicit economic injunctions as far as its revealed sources are concerned, the Qur'ān and the *Ḥadīth* contain explicit economic teachings. These teachings form the foundation of what has come to be known more recently as Islamic economics, although it might be mentioned here that the economic views of St. Thomas Aquinas resemble Islamic teachings in many ways. There are Islamic injunctions relating to how transactions should be carried out, the hoarding of wealth as well as its distribution, religious taxation, endowment (*awqāf*), economic treatment of the poor, the prohibition of usury, and many other injunctions that became institutionalized over the centuries in various Islamic establishments and laws.

The bazaar has always played an important religious role in Islamic society and continues to do so to this day. The guilds that have been responsible for the making of objects, from rugs to pottery, and the carrying out of projects of public economic significance, from the digging of underground waterways (*qanāt*) to roads, have always had a direct religious aspect and have been usually associated with the Sufi orders. According to the Islamic perspective, there is no such thing as economics considered in and of itself. What is called economics today has always been considered in Islam in relation to ethics, and religious injunctions have been promulgated to curtail, or at least to check and limit, human greed, selfishness, and avarice, preventing them from destroying completely the sense of justice that is so strongly emphasized in Islam.

The public aspects of religion in Islam are also concerned with military and political life, which is not to say that every Muslim ruler or military leader has followed the Islamic injunctions fully. There is an elaborate code of conduct in war based primarily on the defense of *dār al-islām* rather than aggression, fair treatment of the enemy including prisoners of war, prohibition of killing innocent civilians, and the like. Islam is said to be the first civilization to have developed a fully codified international law that takes such matters into consideration. Likewise, there are extensive Islamic teachings concerning political rule, although in contrast to the case of the social and economic activities, the Qur'ān and *Ḥadīth* are less explicit about the actual form that government should take and much more explicit about the general nature of good governments and rulers. It was only later in Islamic history that the classical theories of Islamic government were developed, a subject to which we shall turn later.

What Does Islam Teach Us about Religion?

Islam teaches that religion is in the nature of man. To be human is to be concerned with religion; to stand erect as men and women do is to seek transcendence. Human beings have received the imprint of God upon the very substance of their souls and cannot evade religion any more than they can avoid breathing. Individuals here and there may reject religion or a society can turn against its God-given religion for a short time, but even those events possess a religious significance. Men and women are created in the "image" (*ṣūrah*) of God, according to the famous Prophetic *Ḥadīth*. Here ṣūrah means the reflection of God's Names and Qualities, for otherwise God is formless and imageless. Also God breathed into man His Spirit according to the verse: "I have made him and have breathed into him My Spirit" (Qur'ān; XV,29). To be human is to carry this Spirit at the depth of one's being and therefore to be concerned with religion and the author of all religion Who has breathed His Spirit into us.

According to Islam, as in all traditional teachings, men and women did not ascend from lower forms of life but have descended from on high from a divine prototype. Therefore, humanity has always been humanity and has always had religion. The first man, Adam, was also the first prophet. Religion did not evolve gradually during the history of humanity but has always been there, in different forms but always containing the eternal message of Divine Unity until, as a result of forgetfulness, its teachings were neglected and corrupted, only to be renewed by a new message from heaven. Monotheism has not evolved from polytheism. Rather, polytheism is a decadence of monotheism necessitating ever newer revelations that have characterized human history.

It is religion alone that can bestow meaning upon human life, because it and it alone issues directly and in an objective manner from the same Source as that of human life itself. Religion alone can actualize the potentialities within human beings and enable them to be fully themselves. It is only with the help of heaven that we can become what we are eternally in the Divine Presence. Religion provides that supreme knowledge which is the highest goal of intelligence and reveals the nature of that Reality which is also supreme love and the ultimate goal of the will. Religion is the source of all ethics and values, providing the objective criteria for the worth of human actions and deeds. It is also the source of veritable knowledge of both the Divine Principle and the created order as well as the bearer of those principles which constitute the science of beauty and of forms in a traditional civilization.

Islam cannot accept a human world in which religion would be irrelevant. It can understand perfectly what it means to rebel against God and His prophets and has a fully developed doctrine concerning the nature of evil, the trials and tribulations of the life of faith, the dangers of unbelief, and the consequences of being responsible, as a being endowed with freedom to choose, before God. But the idea of humanity without religion and a world in which the being or nonbeing of God are irrelevant and inconsequential are totally rejected by Islam, which sees religion as the sine qua non of human life. Indeed, it is a human being's relation to the Absolute, whatever that relation might be, that determines his or her relation to the relative. The loss of religion for the individual can only mean separation from both inner beatitude and the beatitude of the Beyond and, for a society as a whole, a sure sign of the falling apart of that society as a viable human collectivity.

The Foundations of Islam

The Qur'ān—Its Significance and Structure

The Qur'ān is the central theophany of Islam, the verbatim Word of God revealed to the Prophet by the archangel Gabriel and transmitted by him in turn to his companions who both memorized and recorded it. It was later assembled in its present order under the instruction of the Prophet and written down in several manuscripts during the caliphate of 'Uthmān a few years after the death of the Prophet. Only one version of the text of the Qur'ān is agreed upon by all schools of Islam, a text whose entirety is considered to be divine not only in meaning but also in form.

The name of the sacred scripture of Islam by which it has become famous, especially in the West, is the Qur'ān, or Koran, from the Arabic *al-Qur'ān,* which means "The Reading." But the sacred text has many other names, each referring to an aspect of it. It is also known as *al-Furqān,* "The Discernment," for it contains the principles for both intellectual and moral discernment. Another of its well-known names is *Umm al-kitāb,* "The

Mother of Books," for it is the ultimate source of all knowledge and the prototype of the "book" as container of knowledge. It is also known as *al-Hudā*, "The Guide," for it is the supreme guide for people's journey through life. In traditional Islamic languages, it is usually referred to as the Noble Qur'ān (*al-Qur'ān al-majīd*) and is treated with the utmost respect as a sacred reality that surrounds and defines the life of the Muslim from the cradle to the grave. The verses of the Qur'ān are the very first sounds heard by the newly born child and the last the dying person hears on his or her way to the encounter with God.

In a sense, the soul of the Muslim is woven of verses and expressions drawn from the Qur'ān. Such expressions as *inshā' Allāh*, "if God wills"; *al-ḥamdᵘ li'Llāh*, "thanks be to God"; *bismⁱ'Llāh*, "in the Name of God," all used by Arab as well as non-Arab Muslims alike, punctuate the whole of life and determine the texture of the soul of the Muslim. Every action is begun with a *bismⁱ'Llāh* and ends with an *al ḥamdᵘ li'Llāh*, while the attitude toward the future is always conditioned by the awareness of *inshā' Allāh*, for all depends upon the Divine Will. These and many other formulas drawn from the Qur'ān determine the attitude toward the past, the present, and the future and cover the whole of life. The daily prayers that punctuate the Muslim's entire life, from the age of puberty until death, are constituted of verses and chapters from the Qur'ān while Islamic Law has its root in the sacred text. Likewise, all branches of knowledge that can be legitimately called Islamic have their root in the Qur'ān, which has served over the centuries as both the fountainhead and the guiding principle for the whole of the Islamic intellectual tradition.

The Qur'ān was at first a sonoral revelation before becoming written in book form. The Prophet first *heard* the Word of God and then uttered it to his companions, who memorized the verses and wrote it on parchments, camel bones, and skin. According to the Islamic tradition, the Prophet was unlettered (*al-ummī*), which on the highest level means that his soul was pure and virginal, undefiled by human knowledge and worthy of receiving the Divine Word. When the archangel Gabriel first appeared to the Prophet, the sound of the first verse of the Qur'ān reverberated throughout the space around him. This aspect of the reality of the Qur'ān remains very much alive to this day. Not only is the Qur'ān a book written often in the most beautiful calligraphy and read throughout one's life, but it is also a world of sacred sound heard constantly in Islamic cities and towns. Its sounds reverberate throughout the spaces within which men and women move and act in their everyday lives, and there are many who have memorized the text and recite it constantly without reference to the written word. The art of chanting the Qur'ān, which goes back to the Prophet, is the supreme sacred art of Islam in its sonoral form and moves Muslims to tears whether they be Arabs or Malays.

As for the written text, it was the response of the soul of the Muslims to the Qur'ānic revelation that created the art of calligraphy, which was closely associated with the text of the Qur'ān from the beginning and which constitutes, along with architecture, the supreme sacred art of Islam in its plastic form. Architecture itself is a sacred art because it grows from and finds its highest expression in the architecture of the mosque, whose very spaces are defined by the reverberations of the recitation and chanting of the Qur'ān.

The text of the Qur'ān consists of 114 chapters (*sūrāhs*) divided into the Makkan and the Madinan, that is, those revealed to the Prophet when he was in Makkah or after he migrated to Madinah. The very first verses revealed are those of the chapter entitled Bloodclot (*al-'Alaq*), which open chapter XCVI of the Qur'ān. These verses are as follows:

> *In the Name of Allah, the Beneficent, the Merciful*
> *Recite in the name of thy Lord who created!*
> *He createth man from a clot of blood.*
> *Recite; and thy Lord is the Most Bountiful,*
> *He who hath taught by the pen,*
> *taught man what he knew not.*[5]

The first chapter of the Qur'ān is, however, *ṣūrat al-fāṭihah*, "chapter of the opening," which consists of seven verses (*āyāt*). It is without doubt the most often recited chapter of the Qur'ān, because it constitutes the heart of the daily canonical prayers and contains, in a synoptic fashion, the message of the whole of the Qur'ān:

> *In the Name of Allah, the Beneficent, the Merciful*
> *Praise be to God, the Lord of the worlds,*
> *The Infinitely Good, the all-Merciful,*
> *Master of the day of judgement.*
> *Thee we worship, and in Thee we seek help.*
> *Guide us upon the straight path,*
> *the path of those on whom Thy grace is,*
> *not those on whom Thy anger is,*
> *nor those who are astray.*[6]

The other chapters of the Qur'ān are not based on the chronological order of their revelation but on an order given by the Prophet, although it may be said in general that the longer chapters precede the shorter ones.

The content of the Qur'ān varies greatly and covers many subjects from ethics to metaphysics. It might be said that the Qur'ān contains first the roots, or the principles, of knowledge pertaining to both the domain of action and that of intellection and contemplation. It contains ethical and legal teachings as well as metaphysical ones pertaining to the nature of God, cosmological ones related to the nature of His creation, and psychological ones concerning the human soul. It also bears a knowledge that pertains to the inner, spiritual life and eschatological realities that concern both the final ends of the individual and of human and cosmic history. The Qur'ān also contains a sacred history, much of which it shares with the Bible without being derived from the latter historically. The function of sacred history in the Qur'ān is not so much to describe the outward history of the prophets of old, but rather to render vivid the reality of the ever present battle within the soul of human beings between the forces of good and evil, between knowledge and ignorance. The Qur'ān also possesses a spiritual presence, an impalpable sacred reality that transforms the soul and is like a divine net cast into the world of multiplicity to lead us back to the world of Unity.

For Muslims, everything about the Qur'ān is sacred—its sounds, the very words of the Arabic language chosen by God to express His message, the letters in which it is written, and even the parchment and paper that constitute the physical aspect of the sacred text. Muslims carry the Qur'ān with full awareness of its sacred reality and usually do not touch it unless they have made their ablutions and are ritually clean. They kiss it and pass under it when going on a journey, and many carry small copies of it with them at all times for protection. The Qur'ān is that central sacred presence which determines all aspects of Muslim life and the source and fountainhead of all that can be authentically called Islamic.

The Qur'ānic Sciences and Commentaries upon the Qur'ān

Many traditional sciences are associated with the Qur'ān. There is first the art and science of recitation of the Qur'ān, which is based on strict traditional sources that have been preserved and transmitted over the centuries. One cannot recite and chant the Qur'ān in any way that one wills. The very pauses and intonations are determined according to traditions going back to the Prophet. And then there is the science of studying the conditions under which particular verses were revealed (*sha'n al-nuzūl*) in order to understand better the intention of the text. There are also philological sciences concerned with the study of the language of the Qur'ān, which is so significant that it has determined the characteristics of classical Arabic for the past fourteen centuries. Classical Arabic is often taught quite rightly as Qur'ānic Arabic in many Western universities. The serious study of the Arabic language and grammar is inseparable from the philological study of the Qur'ān, which gave rise historically to a large extent to the codification and systematization of Arabic grammar.

Perhaps the most important aspect of Qur'ānic studies, however, concerns the deciphering of its meaning or what is traditionally called *tafsīr* and *ta'wīl,* the first referring to the outward meaning of the text and the second to its inner meaning. The science of Qur'ānic commentary is one of the most important of the religious disciplines taught to this day in the traditional Islamic schools. Qur'ānic commentaries range from those concerned primarily with the language and grammar of the Qur'ān, such as that of al-Zamakhsharī, to those concerned mostly with sacred history, including the *tafsīr* of al-Ṭabarī, to primarily theological commentaries such as the immense *tafsīr* of Fakhr al-Dīn al-Rāzī. Practically every category of Islamic savants has written commentaries upon the Qur'ān, including some of the most famous Islamic philosophers such as Ibn Sīnā and Mullā Ṣadrā. Moreover, the tradition of writing Qur'ānic commentaries has continued unabated into the present century with such notable *tafsīrs* as those of Mawlānā Abu'l-Kalām Āzād, Mawlānā Mawdūdī, Sayyid Quṭb, and 'Allāmah Ṭabāṭabā'ī, all of which deal not only with traditional questions but also with many of the challenges and problems of the modern world in light of the teachings of the Qur'ān.

There is also a category of Qur'ānic commentaries that deals with the inner or esoteric meaning of the Qur'ān and is properly speaking *ta'wīl* as this term is understood by Sufis and Shi'ites. These commentaries were written mostly by Sufis and also by Shi'ites and go back to the famous commentary of Imām Ja'far al-Ṣādiq, both a pole of Sufism and the sixth Shi'ite Imām. Over the centuries numerous Sufis have provided such commentaries from al-Tustarī in the fourth/tenth century to Ibn 'Arabī in the seventh/thirteenth century and up to the present period and also including many works in Persian such as the vast commentary of Mībudī. Such a celebrated work of Sufism as the *Mathnawī* of Rūmī is in reality an esoteric commentary upon the Qur'ān as specified by the author himself. These commentaries deal with the inner meaning of various verses and even letters of the Qur'ān, which have their own symbolic significance and are of prime importance in the development of Islamic metaphysics and cosmology. As for the Shi'ite commentaries, they too have been concerned with the inner meaning of the sacred text in relation to the reality of the Imām, who is for them the interpreter par excellence of the inner dimension of the Word of God. In the climate of Shi'ism, some of the most important commentaries, such as that of al-Ṭabarsī, have been written by the *'ulamā'* or official religious scholars, but many others have been written by those who were also philosophers and theosophers. The extensive commentaries of Mullā Ṣadrā are the prime example of this latter category.

The text of the Qur'ān has been rendered often into English and numerous other European and non-European languages, although in its total reality the Qur'ān is untranslatable. Some of the translations have succeeded in conveying something of the poetic power of the original Arabic and others some of the external meanings. But no translation has been able or will be able to render the full meaning and "presence" of the text, which has many levels of interpretation and symbolic significance associated with the sound and structure of the words in the Arabic language and often the very form of Arabic letters. The commentaries could be a guide for the understanding of at least some aspects of these hidden and symbolic meanings, but very few of them have been rendered so far into English or other European languages.

The Prophet—His Significance, Life, and Wonts (Sunnah)

The Prophet does not play the same role in Islam as does Christ in Christianity. He is not God incarnate or the God-man. Rather, he is human (*al-bashar*) as asserted explicitly by the Qur'ān but unlike ordinary humans for he possesses the most perfect of natures, being, as a famous Arabic poem asserts, like a jewel among stones. The Prophet is seen by Muslims as the most perfect of all of God's creatures, the perfect man par excellence (*al-insān al-kāmil*) and the beloved of God (*ḥabīb Allāh*), whom the Qur'ān calls the perfect model (*uswah ḥasanah*) to emulate. He represents perfect surrender to God combined with proximity (*qurb*) to Him, which makes him the best interpreter of God's message as well as its faithful transmitter. He is the person to whom God gave the most perfect character and embellished his soul with the virtues of humility, generosity or nobility, and sincerity in the highest degree, virtues that characterize all Islamic spirituality as it has become realized in the souls of Muslim men and women over the centuries.

Islam is based on the Absolute, Allah, and not on the messenger. Yet, the love of the Prophet lies at the heart of Islamic piety, for humans can only love God if God loves them, and God only loves the person who loves His Prophet. The Qur'ān itself orders humans to venerate the Prophet in the verse: "Lo! Allah and His angels shower blessings upon the Prophet. O ye who believe! Ask blessings upon him (*ṣall^u*) and salute him (*sallim^u*) with a worthy salutation" (XXXIII,56). This is the only act whose performance human beings share with God and the angels. Traditional Muslims therefore revere the Prophet in an inviolable manner and always ask for blessings (*ṣalāh*) and salutations (*salām*) upon him. In Muslim eyes, the love and respect for the Prophet is inseparable from the love for the Word of God, the Qur'ān, and of course ultimately God Himself. There is something of the soul of the Prophet present in the Qur'ān, and in one of his famous sayings uttered before his death, the Prophet asserted that after him he was leaving two things behind for his community: the Qur'ān and his family, which represents a prolongation of his being in the Islamic community.

In Sufism and many schools of Islamic philosophical thought, the inner reality of the Prophet, the "Muḥammadan Reality" (*al-Ḥaqīqat al-muḥammadiyyah*) is identified with the Logos, God's first creation, which is the ontological principle of creation as well as the archetype of all prophecy. The Sufis assert that the inner reality of the Prophet was the first link in the prophetic chain while his outward and historical reality came at the end of the prophetic cycle to bring it to a close. It was in reference to this inner reality that the Prophet asserted, "I was a prophet when Adam was between water and clay."

The love of the Prophet embraces all dimensions of Islam, affecting both those who follow the *Sharī'ah* and those who walk upon the spiritual path, the *Ṭarīqah*, of which he is the founder and guide. This love helps individual Muslims to emulate his wonts and example, which constitute, along with the Qur'ān, the foundation of Islamic Law. It also helps them to exert their effort (*jihād*) with greater fervor to embellish their souls with the virtues and perfections that are to be found in their fullness in the person of the Prophet whose life remains a model for every generation of Muslims.

The Prophet, who has many names and titles including Muḥammad, Aḥmad, Muṣṭafā, and Abu'l-Qāsim,[7] was born in the full light of history in the city of Makkah in Arabia in 570 C.E. in the powerful tribe of Quraysh and the branch of Banū Hāshim. Makkah was at that time a major center and at the same time the religious heart of Arabia, for it was here that the various Arab tribes that had fallen into idolatry kept their idols at the Ka'bah built by Abraham to commemorate the One God. Arabia lived at that time in the "Age of Ignorance" (*al-jāhiliyyah*), having forgotten the message of Unity associated with the father of monotheism, Abraham, who had visited Makkah and who is the father of the Arabs through his son Ismā'īl (Ishmael). Yet, a number of monotheists who preserved the primordial monotheism survived, the people to whom the Qur'ān refers as the *ḥunafā'* (followers of the primordial religion). The young Muḥammad never practiced idolatry but was faithful to the One God until he was chosen as prophet.

He lost both parents at an early age and was brought up by his grandfather 'Abd al-Muṭṭalib and uncle Abū Talīb who was the father of 'Alī. He also spent some time among the bedouins in the desert outside of the city environment of Makkah. He soon gained the respect of everyone because of his great trustworthiness and came to be known as al-Amīn, the trusted one. At the age of twenty-five he married Khadījah, a rich widow, some fifteen years older than him, who trusted him with her caravans that he would guide through the desert up to Syria. Khadījah, his first wife, bore him several children including Fāṭimah, who married 'Alī and who is the mother of all the descendants of the Prophet. The Prophet had a happy family life with Khadījah and did not marry any other woman as long as she was alive. She was to provide great comfort and support for him especially when he received the call of prophecy and was confronted with the very harsh treatment and enmity of the Makkans, including members of his own tribe.

The great event of revelation came to the Prophet when he was forty years of age. He had always been a contemplative and would often retreat into the desert to fast and pray. Once, when performing one of these retreats in the cave of al-Ḥirā' outside of Makkah, the archangel Gabriel appeared to him, bringing him the first verses of the revelation that changed his life drastically for the next twenty-three years until his death.

The verses of the Qur'ān descended upon the Prophet at different times and conditions until the revelation was completed shortly before his death. At first he doubted the reality of his experience, but soon the true nature of what he had received became evident. His first converts were his wife Khadījah, his revered friend Abū Bakr, and his young cousin 'Alī. Gradually his circle of followers expanded to include his uncle Ḥamzah and some of the most eminent personages of Makkah such as 'Umar ibn al-Khaṭṭāb. This success in turn increased the pressure of the Quraysh against him, for the new message implied nothing less than a complete change of their way of life, including the destruction of idols and idol-worship upon which their power rested. They finally decided to kill the Prophet, but God had planned otherwise. A delegation from a city to the north named Yathrib had invited the Prophet to migrate (*al-hijrah*) to their city and to become their ruler. The Prophet accepted their invitation and set out for that city in June 622. This date is so important that it marks the beginning of the Islamic calendar. For it was in this city soon to be named *Madīnat al-nabī*, "the city of the Prophet," or simply Madinah, that Islam was to become for the first time a social and political order soon to expand into one of the major civilizations of the world.

In Madinah, the Prophet became the ruler of a community, at once statesman, judge, and military leader as well as the Prophet of God. The newly founded community was threatened by the Makkans, who attacked it on several occasions in battles of crucial significance for Islamic history. These battles, such as those of Badr, Uḥud, Khandaq, and Khaybar, were all won by the Muslims despite their being greatly outnumbered (except Uḥud in which the Makkans left the field thinking that the Muslims had been defeated). Thus, the survival of the new community became a certainty. Meanwhile, gradually tribes from all over Arabia came to pay allegiance to the Prophet and accept the new religion until finally the Makkans themselves could no longer resist. The Prophet marched into Makkah triumphantly in the year 8/630, forgiving all his enemies with great nobility and magnanimity. This episode marked, in a sense, the highlight of his earthly life when even his most ardent enemies embraced Islam. The Qur'ān refers to this occasion in chapter CX:

> *In the Name of Allah, the Beneficent, the Merciful*
> *When Allah's succour, and triumph cometh and thou seest mankind entering the religion of Allah in troops, Then hymn the praise of Thy Lord, and seek forgiveness of Him. Lo! He is ever ready to show mercy.*

The Prophet returned to Madinah from which he completed the Islamization of Arabia to the north. In the tenth year of the migration, he returned to Makkah to make the completely Islamic greater pilgrimage (*al-ḥajj*), instituting the rites of *ḥajj* that continue to this day. That was also to be his farewell pilgrimage, for upon returning to Madinah he soon fell ill and after three days of illness died on the thirteenth of Rabī'al-Awwal of the year 10/632. He was buried in the apartment of 'Ā'ishah, one of his wives whom he loved dearly, next to the mosque that was the first to be built in Islam. To this day his tomb stands at the center of the vast "mosque of the Prophet," and Madinah remains the second holiest city of Islam after Makkah.

In a twenty-three-year period, the Prophet succeeded in not only uniting Arabia under the banner of Islam but also establishing a religious community of global extent for which he remains always the ideal model of human behavior and action, and his biography (*al-Sīrah*) has remained a spiritual and religious guide for Muslims throughout the centuries. His extraordinary life included almost every possible human experience that he was able to sanctify and integrate into the Islamic perspective. He experienced poverty, oppression, and cruelty as well as power and dominion. He tasted great love as well as the tragedy of the death of his only son. He lived in great simplicity yet ruled over a whole cosmic sector. He lived with a single wife much older than him until the age of fifty and then contracted many marriages at a much older age, which proves precisely that his multiple marriages had nothing to do with passions of the flesh. In fact most of them were for political reasons, to unite various tribes together. They also represent the sacred character of sexuality in Islam and a perspective upon sexuality very different from the one that identifies it with original sin.

The supreme inner experience of the Prophet occurred in Makkah when one night he was taken miraculously by the archangel Gabriel to Jerusalem and from there to heaven in that nocturnal Ascension which is called *al-mi'rāj*. This experience, mentioned in the Qur'ān, constitutes the inner reality of the daily prayers and the model for all spiritual ascent in Islam. When we think of the life of the Prophet in its totality, we must not only think of him as the leader of a human community, or a father and head of family, a man who married several wives and who participated in battles or social and political decisions for the preservation of Islam. We must also meditate upon his inner life of prayer, vigil, and fasting and especially the *mi'rāj*, for the Prophet and with him Islam came into the world to create a balance between the outward and the inward, the physical and the spiritual, and to establish an equilibrium on the basis of which humans are able to realize the Unity, or *al-tawḥīd*, that is the goal of human life.

In the realization of this unity, the model of the Prophet plays a basic role. That is why his actions and wonts, known in Arabic as *al-Sunnah*, are so central to the whole of Islam. The way he dressed and ate, the manner in which he treated his family and neighbors, his actions of a juridical and political nature, and even treatment of animals and plants constitute elements of his *Sunnah*, which are the most important source of Islam after the Qur'ān. The *Sunnah* has been transmitted both orally and in written form over the centuries, and countless Muslims over the ages have sought to live and act in emulation of it. Its most direct expression is the *Ḥadīth* or collection of sayings of the Prophet, which embrace practically every aspect of human life and thought.

The Ḥadīth and Its Codification

Since the *Ḥadīth* forms a major pillar of Islam, it is only natural that a great deal of attention should have been devoted to it from the beginning. The earliest traces of written texts of the *Ḥadīth* are found in the edicts, letters, and treatises dictated by the Prophet himself, followed by his sayings recorded in the "pages" (*ṣaḥīfah*) of his Companions and the next generation, usually known as the Followers or *tābi'ūn*. This genre was followed by the class of texts known as "Documents" (*al-Musnad*) of such scholars as Abū Dā'ūd al-Ṭayālisī, but the most famous of this genre is that associated with the name of Imām Aḥmad ibn Ḥanbal, the founder of one of the four schools of Sunni Law, who was born in the second/eighth century. One needs to mention here also the celebrated *al-Muwaṭṭā'* of Imām Mālik ibn Anas, the founder of another of the major schools of Sunni Law, who lived shortly after Imām Aḥmad ibn Ḥanbal, and whose work many consider as the first major collection of *Ḥadīth*, although the treatise deals primarily with jurisprudence (*al-fiqh*) and with *Ḥadīth* in relation to it.

All of these works as well as numerous other categories of writings were integrated into the major books of *Ḥadīth*, which appeared in the Sunni world in the third/ninth century. These great compendia, which are usually known as the "Six Correct Books" (*al-Ṣiḥāḥ al-sittah*) and comprise the canonical and orthodox sources of *Ḥadīth* in the Sunni world, include the *Jāmi' al-ṣaḥīḥ* of Abū 'Abd Allāh al-Bukhārī, the *Ṣaḥīḥ* of Abu'l-Ḥusayn ibn Muslim al-Nayshābūrī, the *Sunan* of Abū Dā'ūd al-Sijistānī, the *Jāmi'* of Abū 'Īsā al-Tirmidhī, the *Sunan* of Abū Muḥammad al-Dārimī, and the *Sunan* of

Abū ʿAbd Allāh ibn Mājah. There have been other important compilations, but they never gained the authority of these six works.

The great scholars of *Ḥadīth* examined carefully all the chains of transmission (*isnād*) of each saying and many other religious sciences to sift the authentic sayings from those of dubious authority and both from sayings attributed to the Prophet but without any historical basis. Al-Bukhārī is said to have traveled widely from city to city and to have consulted more than a thousand authorities on *Ḥadīth*. Muslim scholarship had already created detailed criteria for evaluating the authenticity of each *ḥadīth* more than a millennium before Western orientalists appeared upon the scene to deny the authenticity of the whole corpus of *Ḥadīth*, which if denied would destroy the structure of the Islamic tradition itself. Needless to say, the so-called historical criticism of such Western scholars is not taken seriously by traditional Muslim scholars, especially since many of the formers' arguments have been negated by the discovery of later historical evidence, while their whole position is implicitly based upon the negation of the reality of the Islamic revelation.

In the Shiʿite world, the corpus of *Ḥadīth* was collected and classified a century later than in the Sunni world and was based on the Shiʿites' own chain of transmission centered mostly upon the Family of the Prophet (*ahl al-bayt*), although most of the *ḥadīths* are the same. The Shiʿite canonical collections consist of "The Four Books" (*al-Kutub al-arbaʿah*): the *Uṣūl al-kāfī* of Muḥammad ibn Yaʿqūb al-Kulaynī; the *Man lā yaḥḍuruh^{u}'l-faqīh* of Muḥammad ibn Bābūyah al-Qummī; and the *Kitāb al-istibṣār* and *Kitāb al-tahdhīb*, both by Muḥammad al-Ṭūsī. It is important to point out that whereas in the Sunni world the term *ḥadīth* refers exclusively to a saying of the Prophet and a book of *Ḥadīth*, a collection of such sayings, in the Shiʿite world a distinction is made between a "Prophetic saying" (*al-ḥadīth al-nabawī*) and a "saying of one of the Imāms" (*al-ḥadīth al-walawī*), which is also highly prized and considered as a kind of extension of the Prophetic *Ḥadīth*.

The *Ḥadīth* deals with nearly every question from details of legal significance to the most exalted moral and spiritual teachings. One *ḥadīth* asserts: "God is beautiful and He loves beauty," and another: "Verily there are heavenly rewards for any act of kindness to animals." Some *ḥadīths* deal with spiritual virtues and moral attitudes such as: "Charity that is concealed appeaseth the wrath of God" and "God loveth those who are content." Much of the *Ḥadīth* deals with self-control, such as: "The most excellent *jihād* [usually translated as holy war but literally exertion] is that of the conquest of self" or "Whoever suppresseth his anger, when he hath in his power to show it, God will bestow upon him a great reward." Many other *ḥadīths* deal with duty toward others, such as "When the bier of anyone passeth by thee, whether Jew, Christian or Muslim, rise to thy feet" and "Abuse no one, and if a man abuse thee, and lay open a vice which he knoweth in thee; then do not disclose one which thou knowest in him."[8]

Altogether the *Ḥadīth* is a vast body of sayings concerning both the outer and inner dimensions of existence, the plane of action and that of contemplation, all of human life and every aspect of thought inasmuch as they pertain to the Islamic universe. The *Ḥadīth* reveals both the grandeur of the soul of the Prophet and his function as the supreme interpreter of God's Word and the prime exemplar for every Muslim. The *Ḥadīth* is a key for the comprehension of the attitudes and tendencies of the Muslim soul and the indispensable guide for the understanding of God's Word as contained in the Qur'ān.

Among the thousands of *ḥadīths* of the Prophet are a small number that are called "sacred sayings" (*al-aḥādīth al-qudsiyyah*), in which God speaks in the first person through the Prophet without these sayings being part of the Qur'ān. This category of *ḥadīths* refers exclusively to the inner life and constitutes a very important source of Sufism. The definition of Sufism as the attainment of inner virtue (*iḥsān*) is in fact contained in one of the most famous of these sacred sayings, which is as follows: "*Iḥsān* is that thou adorest God as though Thou didst see Him, and if thou seest Him not, He nonetheless seeth Thee." These sayings deal with the most inward and intimate aspects of the spiritual life and therefore have echoed over the centuries within the works of numerous Sufis who have meditated and commented upon them. They issue directly from God and concern the inner aspects of the teachings of Islam. They, therefore, constitute an indispensable source of that inner dimension of Islam which crystallized and became known as Sufism.

The Doctrines and Beliefs of Islam

God

The central doctrine of Islam concerns God in Himself as well as in His Names and Qualities. The plenary doctrine of the nature of the Divinity as at once the Absolute, the Infinite, and the Perfect Good lies at the heart of the teachings of Islam. The Supreme Reality or Allah is at once God, the Person, and suprapersonal Reality. Allah is not only Pure Being but the Beyond-Being about which nothing can be said without delimiting His Infinite and Absolute Essence, which is beyond all determination. That is why the *shahādah, Lā ilāha illa'Llāh,* which contains the full Islamic doctrine of the nature of God, begins with the negative prefix *lā*, for to assert anything of the Divine Essence or God in His or Its Supreme Reality is to limit it by that very assertion. Hence the Qur'ānic verse: "There is nothing whatsoever like unto Him" (XXXXII,2).

Allah is the Absolute, the One, totally transcendent and beyond every limitation and boundary, every concept and idea. And yet, He is also the Immanent for according to the Qur'ānic verse: "He is the First and the Last and the Outward and the Inward and He knows infinitely all things" (Qur'ān; LVII,3). God is the First (*al-Awwal*), for He is the Origin, the alpha, of all things. He is the Last (*al-Ākhir*), for it is to Him that all things, not only human souls but the whole of the cosmos, return. He is the Outward (*al-Ẓāhir*), for manifestation is ultimately nothing other than the theophany of His Names and Qualities upon the tablet of "nothingness," and all existence is ultimately a ray of His Being. But He is also the Inward (*al-Bāṭin*), for He is immanent in all things. Only the sage is able to understand and know in the full plenitude of the sense of this term that God is the Immanent and to grasp fully the sense of the verse: "Whithersoever ye turn, there is the Face of God" (II,115). Moreover, he or she can gain this understanding only by virtue of his or her having realized the Divine Transcendence (*ta'ālī*), for the Divine reveals itself as the Immanent only by virtue of having been first known and experienced as the Transcendent.

God possesses an Essence (*al-Dhāt*) that is beyond all categories and definitions like that darkness which is dark because of the intensity of its luminosity, the black light to which certain Sufis have referred. Although beyond all duality and gender, the Divine Essence is often referred to in the feminine form and *al-Dhāt* is of feminine gender in Arabic. In its aspect of infinitude it is, metaphysically speaking, the supreme principle of femininity, standing above and beyond the aspect of the Divinity as Creator. Yet, the Essence reveals Itself in the Divine Names and Qualities that constitute the very principles of cosmic manifestation and are the ultimate archetypes of all that exists, both macrocosmically and microcosmically. The Qur'ān asserts: "to God belong the most beautiful Names; call Him by these Names" (VII,180). The science of the Divine Names lies at the heart of all Islamic intellectual and religious disciplines and plays a central role in metaphysics as well as cosmology, theology as well as ethics, not to mention the practical aspect of religion in which the invocation and recitation of the Divine Names occupy a central role, particularly in Sufism.

The Names of God in Islam were revealed and sanctified by God Himself through the Qur'ānic revelation; hence their power to aid man to return to his Origin. The Supreme Name is Allah Itself, which refers to both the Divine Essence and the Divine Qualities and which contains all the Names. There are traditionally ninety-nine Names of God, hence the ninety-nine beads of the Muslim rosary. These are all Names in Arabic used by God as

He has revealed Himself in Islam. They are made known to Muslims through the Qur'ān and *Ḥadīth*. These Names are divided into the Names of Majesty (*asmā' al-jalāl*) and the Names of Mercy (*asmā' al-jamāl*), which are, respectively, the principles of the masculine and the feminine as manifested throughout the cosmic order. God is both merciful and just. He is *al-Raḥmān* (the Most Merciful), *al-Raḥīm* (the Most Compassionate), *al-Karīm* (the Generous), *al-Ghafūr* (the Forgiver), and so on. But He is also *al-Qahhār* (the Victorious), *al-'Ādil* (the Just), and *al-Mumīt* (the Giver of Death). The universe and all that is in it are woven of the theophanies and reflections of these Names, which as already mentioned play a central role in both Islamic thought and piety. Together, they reveal one of the most complete doctrines of the nature of the Supreme Divinity in any religion. It seems that through them the One God of Abraham finally revealed the fullness of His Face.

Prophecy and Revelation

Islam asserts that after the doctrine of Divine Oneness or the doctrine concerning the nature of God (*al-tawḥīd*), the most important doctrine is that of prophecy (*nubuwwah*). According to the Islamic understanding of prophecy, God has made it the central reality of human history, which began with the prophecy of Adam, while the cycle of prophecy was brought to a close with the Qur'ānic revelation. There are, moreover, 124,000 prophets sent to every nation and people, and God has never left a people without revelation as the Qur'ān asserts explicitly: "Verily to every people there is a messenger" (X,48).

A prophet is chosen by God and by Him alone. There are classes of prophets (*anbiyā'*) ranging from those who bring some news from God (*nabī*) to messengers (*rasūl*) who bring major messages to the possessors of determination (*ūlu'l-'azm*) who, like Moses, Christ, and the Prophet of Islam, establish major new religions. In all cases, the prophet receives his message from God; his words and deeds are not the result of his own genius or historical borrowings. A prophet owes nothing to anyone. He brings a message that has the freshness and perfume of veritable originality because his message comes from the Origin, a message vis-à-vis which he remains the passive receiver and transmitter. Revelation (*al-waḥy*) in Islam is understood in the precise sense of receiving a message from heaven through the angelic instrument of revelation and without interference of the human substance of the receiver of the message who is the prophet. It needs to be added, however, that the message is always revealed in forms that are in accordance with the world for which it is intended and with the earthly receptacle chosen by God for His particular message. Understood in this sense, revelation is clearly distinguished from inspiration (*al-ilhām*), which is a possibility for all human beings by virtue of their being human but which is usually actualized only within the being of those who prepare the mind and soul through spiritual practice for the reception of true inspiration. Of course, the "Spirit bloweth where it listeth" and inspiration on various levels can occur in cases and circumstances that cannot always be understood by judging only the external conditions and causes in question.

The Angelic World

The Qur'ān refers constantly to the angels (*al-malā'ikah*), and belief in their existence is part of the definition of faith (*al-īmān*). Angels play a major role in the Islamic universe, in bringing revelation as was done by Jibra'īl (Gabriel) or in taking the soul of men and women at the moment of death as is done by Isrā'īl. There is a vast hierarchy of angels from those who surround and support the Divine Throne (*al-'arsh*) to those who carry out the command of God during everyday life in the world of nature. The angels are of course luminous and forces for the good, totally immersed in the beatitude of the Divine Presence and subservient to His Will. And yet the Devil, al-Iblīs, was also originally an angel who fell from grace and became the personification of evil because of his refusal to prostrate himself before Adam.

The angels play a basic role in Islamic cosmology as well as philosophy, where some of them are identified as instruments of knowledge and illumination. They also play an important role in everyday religious life, where they are experienced as very real parts of the cosmos within which Muslims live. One can say that the angels have not as yet been banished from the religious cosmos of Muslims as they were from the seventeenth century to an ever greater degree in Western Christianity. Angels must, however, be distinguished from the *jinn*, also mentioned in the Qur'ān, who are psychic rather than spiritual forces but who also inhabit the Islamic cosmos and play a role in the total economy of that cosmos.

The Human State

Islam considers man, that is, the human being in both the male and female forms, in himself and in his suchness as standing directly before God and being at once His servant (*al-'abd*) and vicegerent (*al-khalīfah*) on earth. God created the first man (Adam) from clay and breathed His Spirit unto him. He taught Adam the name of all things and ordered all the angels to prostrate before him, which they all did save Satan. To quote the Qur'ānic verse: "And when we said unto the angels: Prostrate yourselves before

Adam, they fell prostrate, all save Iblīs. He demurred through pride, and so became a disbeliever" (II,34). God created Eve from Adam and made her his companion and complement, and the two resided in paradise until the pair disobeyed God's command by eating of the fruit of the forbidden tree. Henceforth they fell (*al-hubūṭ*) from paradisal perfection on earth and became tainted with the forgetfulness (*al-ghaflah*) which characterizes fallen human beings; but they did not commit the original sin in the Christian sense, which would radically distort human nature. Furthermore, Adam and Eve were jointly responsible for their fall, and it was not Eve who tempted Adam to eat of the forbidden fruit.

According to the Islamic perspective, men and women still carry deep within their soul that primordial nature (*al-fiṭrah*) which attests to Divine Unity and which Islam essentially addresses. For Islam, man is an intelligence, which by nature confirms al-tawḥīd, and to this intelligence is added the will, which needs to be guided by revelation. The function of religion is to remove the veil of the passions, which prevents the intelligence from functioning correctly. Religion is essentially the means for men and women to recollect who they are and to return to their inner and primordial natures that they still carry within themselves.

Humans must be perfectly passive toward heaven, hence the servant or slave of God (*'abd Allāh*), and active toward the world around them as God's vicegerents on earth. To be truly human is to receive in perfect submission from God and to give to creation as the central channel of grace for the created order. Islam rejects completely the Promethean and Titanic conception of human beings in rebellion against heaven, a conception that came to dominate almost completely the Western conception of humans since the Renaissance in the West. In the Islamic perspective, the grandeur of people is not in themselves but in their submission to God, and human grandeur is always judged by the degree of servitude toward God and His Will. Even the power given to human beings to both know and dominate over things is legitimate only on the condition of humans remembering their theomorphic nature according to the *ḥadīth* "God created man upon His form" and continuing to remain subservient to that blinding Divine Reality which is the human beings' ontological principle and ultimate goal of return. All human grandeur causes the Muslim soul to remember that *Allāh^{u} akbar*, "God is greater," and that all grandeur belongs ultimately to Him.

Islam also sees human nature in its permanent reality as standing before God and reflecting like a mirror all of His Names and Qualities while all other creatures reflect only one or some of His Names. Adam has not evolved into man as we know him now. Man has always been man and will always be so, and no evolution of the human state is possible. Man is like the center of the circle of terrestrial existence. Once one is at the center of the circle, one cannot evolve or move any closer toward the center. During human history, the Divine Truth has shone or become eclipsed to various degrees, but man has always remained man, the being whom God addresses directly in the Qur'ān, making every Muslim, male and even female, like a priest who stands directly before God and communicates with Him without the aid of any intermediary.

Man and Woman

Many Qur'ānic verses address men and women distinctly as separate sexes while others refer to the human species. The injunctions of Islam are meant for both men and women, both of whom have immortal souls and are held responsible for their actions in this world and will be judged accordingly in the hereafter. The gates of both heaven and hell as well as the intermediate purgatorial states are open to members of both sexes, and the injunctions of religion pertain to both men and women.

As far as the social and economic aspects of life are concerned, Islam sees the role of the two sexes in their complementarity rather than competition. The role of women is seen as being more in the preservation of the family and upbringing of children and that of men as providing economically for the family. Both men and women have, however, complete economic independence according to Islamic Law, and a woman can do with her wealth as she wills independent of her husband's will. What is especially emphasized is the central role of the family, which remains very strong to this day despite the fact that divorce is not forbidden in Islamic Law. According to a saying of the Prophet, of all the things permitted by God that which He dislikes most is divorce.

Sexuality in Islam is considered as being sacred in itself; therefore, marriage is not a sacrament but a contract made between the two sides. Polygamy is permitted under certain conditions, including consent of all the parties concerned and just behavior toward the wives, but all sexual promiscuity is strictly forbidden and strongly punishable according to Islamic Law, although the punishment of adultery can only take place if there are four witnesses to the act. Most families in the Islamic world are monogamous, and the practice of polygamy is dictated usually by economic factors and also the insistence of Islam to integrate all members of society into a family structure. When practiced according to Islamic teachings, polygamy is not so much legalized promiscuity, as some modern critics claim, but the placing of responsibility upon the shoulders of men who must bear all economic and social responsibility for all their wives and their offspring.

The Islamic conception of the complementarity of men and women and the sacred character of sexuality is also reflected in the separation of men and women in social situations and the meaning of the wearing of the veil. The latter is not unique to Islam and has been practiced over the millennia by the Jewish and Christian populations of the East as well. Yet, since it is emphasized by Islam, it is often identified in the Western mind with that religion. Islam demands modesty of dress for women and their preventing their "ornaments," which has been usually interpreted as their hair and their bodies, from being displayed before strangers. The veiling of the face was an ancient practice of the sedentary centers of the East adopted by many Muslim women and is still not practiced by either nomadic or peasant women in smaller villages. The covering of women is also directly related to the interiorization that the female represents vis-à-vis the male. If one takes the total Islamic doctrine of the two sexes into consideration, one can say that the rapport between them is that of equality, superiority of the male over the female, and the superiority of the female over the male, depending on whether one considers the metacosmic, cosmic, or the terrestrially human aspects of this relationship and duality. It has its roots in the complementarity of the Divine Names and even beyond that domain in the nature of God as both absolute and infinite.

The Cosmos

The Qur'ān refers constantly to the world of nature as well as to the human order. The sky and the mountains, the trees and animals in a sense participate in the Islamic revelation through which the sacred quality of the cosmos and the natural order is reaffirmed. The Qur'ān refers to the phenomena of nature as *āyāt* (i.e., signs or portents), the same term that is used for the verses of the Qur'ān and the signs that appear within the soul of man according to the famous verse: "We shall show them our portents (*āyāt*) upon the horizons and within themselves, until it be manifest unto them that it is the Truth" (XLI,53). Natural phenomena are not only phenomena in the current understanding of this term. They are signs that reveal a meaning beyond themselves. Nature is a book whose *āyāt* are to be read like the *āyāt* of the Qur'ān and in fact can only be read thanks to the latter, for only revelation can unveil the inner meaning of the cosmic text. Certain Muslim thinkers have referred to the cosmos as the "the Qur'ān of creation or cosmic Qur'ān" (*al-Qur'ān al-takwīnī*), whereas the Qur'ān that is read everyday by Muslims is called "the recorded Qur'ān" (*al-Qur'ān al-tadwīnī*). The cosmos is a primordial revelation whose message is still written on the face of every mountain and tree leaf and is reflected from the light that shines from the sun, the moon, and the stars. But as far as Muslims are concerned, this message can be read only thanks to the message revealed by the Qur'ān.

In the light of this perspective, Islam does not make a clear distinction between the natural and the supernatural. The Divine grace, or *barakah*, flows both from the sacred rites and in the arteries of the universe, and natural elements play a major role in the Muslims' religious life. The Muslim rites have an astronomical and cosmic dimension. The times of the daily prayers are determined by the actual movement of the sun as are the moments of the beginning and end of the fast. The earth itself is the primordial mosque and spaces of human-made mosques are themselves emulations and recapitulations of the space of virgin nature. Muslims have always lived traditionally in harmony with nature and in equilibrium with the natural environment, which is seen clearly in the urban design of traditional Islamic cities. Humans have always been seen as God's vicegerents, who can dominate over nature only under the condition of being aware of their vicegerency, which brings with it responsibility toward all of God's creation.

The ecological and environmental disasters to be seen in many parts of the Islamic world today, especially in the big cities, must not be seen as being the result of Islamic teachings any more than can the terrible pollution in many parts of Japan be considered as the consequence of Zen Buddhism or Shintō teachings about nature. The traditional Islamic view of the cosmos and the natural order did not cause such disasters but created for more than a millennium a civilization that lived in peace with nature. Islam also developed a vast metaphysics and theology of nature and also a traditional art in which nature as God's creation and reflection of His wisdom and power plays a central role without the art ever becoming naturalistic. It is important to note in this connection that the Islamic paradise is not composed only of crystals but also is populated by plants and animals, many of which reflect even here below paradisal qualities.

Eschatology

Much of the Qur'ān and many of the *ḥadīths* of the Prophet are concerned with eschatological realities, both microcosmic and macrocosmic. As far as the individual is concerned, he or she is considered by Islam to enter a state upon death in conformity with his or her faith and actions in this life, although there are always imponderable dimensions of Divine Mercy. The Qur'ān and *Ḥadīth* describe vividly both paradise and hell and also point to the purgatories or intermediate states that have been described more fully in the inspired traditional commentaries. The language that is used, especially in the Qur'ān, is vivid, concrete, and also symbolic and must not be understood only in its literal sense. The depiction of posthumous states and eschatological realities, which are beyond the ken of human imagination, can only be expressed symbolically. The true meaning of these descriptions must be sought in the inspired commentaries and the sapiential writings of such figures as Ibn 'Arabī and Ṣadr al-Dīn Shīrāzī.

Islam also possesses an elaborate teaching concerning eschatological events on the macrocosmic level. For Islam, human and cosmic history have an end as they have a beginning. The end of human history will be marked by the advent of the coming of a person named the Mahdī, who will defeat the enemies of religion and reestablish peace and justice on earth. The Sunnis believe the Mahdī to be a member of the tribe of the Prophet and bearing the name Muḥammad while the Shi'ites identify him with the Twelfth Imām Muḥammad al-Mahdī. In any case, both branches of Islam believe that the rule of the Mahdī will be followed, after a period known exactly only to God, by the return of Christ to Jerusalem, which will bring human history to a close and lead to the Last Day of Judgment. Christ plays a central role in Islamic eschatology not only as the Christian Christ but also as a major figure in the chain of Abrahamic prophets. The belief in the coming of the Mahdī is so great that throughout Islamic history, especially during periods of oppression and turmoil, it has led to various millennialist movements, and many charismatic figures have appeared over the centuries who have claimed to be the Mahdī. Some of them have left an important mark upon various regions of the Islamic world, as one sees in the case of the thirteenth/nineteenth-century Mahdī of the Sudan. In any case, belief in the coming of the Mahdī remains strong throughout the Islamic world, and the acceptance of the eschatological realities connected to the Last Day of Judgment is part and parcel of the Islamic credo and remains a living reality for a Muslim throughout his or her life here on earth, which is but a preparation for the meeting with God and the hereafter.

The Dimensions of Islam

The Divine Law (al-Sharī'ah)—Its Content and Codification—The Schools of Law (al-madhāhib)

The *Sharī'ah,* or Divine Law of Islam, is not only central to the religion but also is what comprises Islam itself in its ritual, legal, and social aspects. Muslims consider the *Sharī'ah* to contain the concrete embodiment of the Will of God, what God wants them to do in this life to gain happiness in this world and felicity in the hereafter. A Muslim can fail to practice the injunctions of the *Sharī'ah* and still remain a Muslim, although not a practicing and upright one, but if he or she no longer considers the *Sharī'ah* to be valid, then he or she ceases to be a Muslim. The life of the Muslim from the cradle to the grave is governed by the *Sharī'ah,* which sanctifies every aspect of life, creates equilibrium in human society, and provides the means for humans to live virtuously and fulfill their functions as God's creatures placed on earth to submit themselves to His Will and live according to His laws. A Muslim may go beyond the outer meaning of the *Sharī'ah* and through the Path, or the *Ṭarīqah*, reach the Truth, or *Ḥaqīqah*, which resides within the sacred forms and injunctions of the Law, but he or she must start with the *Sharī'ah* and follow it to the best of his or her ability. The *Sharī'ah* is like the circumference of a circle, each point of which represents a Muslim who stands on that circumference. Each radius that connects every point on the circumference to the center symbolizes the *Ṭarīqah*, and the center is the *Haqīqah*, which generates both the radii and the circumference. The whole circle with its center, circumference, and radii may be said to represent the totality of the Islamic tradition. But it must be remembered that one can follow one of the radii to the center only on the condition of standing on the circumference—hence, the great significance of the *Sharī'ah*, without which no spiritual journey would be possible and the religion itself could not be practiced.

The word *Sharī'ah* comes from the root *shr'*, which means road, for the *Sharī'ah* is the road that men and women must follow in this life. Since Islam is a complete way of life, the *Sharī'ah* is all-embracing and includes all of life from rites of worship to economic transactions. Usually, however, it is divided for the sake of clarification and to facilitate learning its injunctions into *'ibādāt* (what pertains to worship) and *mu'āmalāt* (what pertains to transactions). In the first category, all the injunctions pertain to Islamic rites, both the obligatory and the recommended, such as prayer and fasting, while the second category includes every kind of transaction whether it be social, economic, or political and concerned with one's neighbor or the whole of society.

The *Sharī'ah* divides all acts into five categories: those which are obligatory (*wājib*); those which are recommended (*mandūb*); acts toward which the Divine Law is indifferent (*mubāḥ*); acts that are reprehensible (*makrūh*); and those which are forbidden (*ḥarām*). An example of the first would be the daily prayers (*ṣalāh*); of the second giving money to the poor; of the third the kind of vegetable one eats or exercise one performs; the fourth divorce; and the fifth murder, adultery, and theft as well as certain dietary prohibitions such as pork and its derivatives or alcoholic beverages, whose consumption is forbidden. The Muslim lives a life woven of actions whose evaluation is known to him or her on the basis of the *Sharī'ah*. That does not mean that Muslims have no freedom, for freedom is defined in Islam not simply as individual rebellion against all authority but participation in that freedom, which in its fullness belongs to God alone. A Muslim gains freedom and not confinement by conforming to the Divine Law, because the very boundaries of his or her being are expanded through such conformity. By surrendering to the Will of God, Muslims are able to transcend the imprisonment of their own egos and the stifling confinement of their passionate selves.

The root of the *Sharīʻah* is found in the Qur'ān, and God is considered as the ultimate legislator (*al-Shāriʻ*). The *Ḥadīth* and *Sunnah*, however, complement the Qur'ān as the second major source of the *Sharīʻah*, for the Prophet was the interpreter par excellence of the meaning of God's Word. From the very beginning in the Medinan community, the *Sharīʻah* began to be promulgated through the actual practices of the Prophet and the community and the judgments handed down by the Prophet as the judge of the newly founded Islamic society. On the basis of this early practice and the twin sources of the Qur'ān and *Sunnah*—and also the use of such principles as *ijmāʻ*, or consensus of the community, and *qiyās*, or analogy—later generations continued to apply and codify the Law until the second/eighth century when the great founders of the schools of Law (*al-madhāhib*), which have continued to this day, appeared on the scene. In the Sunni world these include Imām Mālik ibn Anas, Imām Aḥmad ibn Ḥanbal, Imām Abū Ḥanīfah, and Imām Muḥammad al-Shāfiʻī, after whom the Mālikī, Ḥanbalī, Ḥanafī, and Shāfiʻī schools are named. Among these figures, Imām Shāfiʻī is especially remembered for developing the method of jurisprudence related to the four principles of the Qur'ān, *Sunnah*, *ijmāʻ*, and *qiyās*, not all of which are accepted by all the schools of Law.

Today the vast majority of Sunnis continue to follow these schools, the North Africans being almost completely Mālikī; the Egyptians, Malays, and Indonesians almost all Shāfiʻīs; the Turks and the Sunnis of the Indo-Pakistani subcontinent mostly Ḥanafī; and the Saudis and many Syrians Ḥanbalī. As for Twelve-Imām Shiʻism, its school of Law is called Jaʻfarī, named after Imām Jaʻfar al-Ṣādiq, who was the sixth Shiʻite Imām and also the teacher of Imām Abū Ḥanīfah. Together these five schools compose the major *madhāhib* of the *Sharīʻah*. There are, however, a few smaller schools such as that of the Zaydī and Ismāʻīlī Shiʻites and that of the ʻIbādīs of Oman and southern Algeria. There were also other schools of Sunni Law that gradually died out and have no followers today.

These schools of the *Sharīʻah* represent different interpretations of the Law on the basis of the basic sources, but their differences are minor. Even between the four Sunni schools and Jaʻfarī Law, there are no major differences save for the fact the Jaʻfarī Law permits temporary marriage, which is forbidden in the four schools of Sunni Law, and emphasizes inheritance more in the line of the descendants, rather than the siblings, of a person. As for the basic rites, the differences between Sunnis and Shiʻites hardly exceed those between the various schools of Sunni Law.

The great jurists (*fuqahāʼ*, pl. of *faqīh*) who codified the schools of Law practiced the giving of fresh opinion based on the basic sources or what is called *ijtihād*. In the Sunni world the gate of *ijtihād* was closed in the fourth/tenth century, and many authorities have been seeking to open it since the end of the last century. In the Shi'ite world, the gate of *ijtihād* has always been open, and it is considered essential that in each generation those who have the qualifications to practice *ijtihād*, and who are called *mujtahids*, go back to the Qur'ān and the *Sunnah* and *Ḥadīth* (which for Shi'ites includes the sayings of the Shi'ite Imāms) and reformulate in a fresh manner the body of the Law.

The *Sharī'ah* has immutable principles but also contains the possibility of growth and application to whatever situation Muslims face. It must, however, be remembered that in the Islamic perspective law is not simply a human-made system created for convenience in a particular social context. Law is of divine origin and must create society according to its norms and not simply change itself according to changes in society vis-à-vis which human beings are expected to remain passive. To the assertion often made by modern Western critics of Islam that Islamic Law must keep up with the times, Islam answers that if this be so then what must the times keep up with, what it is that orders and forces the times to change as they do? Islam believes that the factor which must itself make the times and coordinate human society must be the *Sharī'ah*. Human beings must seek to live according to the Will of God as embodied in the *Sharī'ah* and not change the Law of God according to the changing patterns of a society based on the impermanence of human nature.

The Spiritual Path (al-Ṭarīqah)—The Sufi Orders, and the Doctrinal and Practical Teachings of Sufism

The inner or esoteric (*al-bāṭin*) dimension of Islam became crystallized for the most part in Sufism, although elements of this esoterism can also be found in Shi'ism. Sufism, a word derived from the name *al-taṣawwuf*, is nothing but the teachings and practices related to the path toward God (*al-ṭarīqah ila'Llāh*). According to a *ḥadīth*, there are as many paths to God as there are children of Adam, and although, needless to say, an indefinite number of paths did not come into being, over time a large number of *ṭuruq* (pl. of *ṭarīqah*) did develop, which were and are able to cater to different spiritual and psychological human types. Usually called Sufi orders, these paths have protected and promulgated the esoteric teachings of Islam to this day and still constitute a vital element in Islamic society.

Sufism is like the heart of the body of Islam, invisible from the outside but providing nourishment for the whole organism. It is the inner spirit that inbreathes the outward forms of the religion and makes possible the passage from the world of the outward to the inward paradise—a paradise we carry at the center of our being in our heart but remain for the most part unaware of because of the hardening of the heart associated by Islam with the sin of forgetfulness (*al-ghaflah*). Sufism provides the cure for this malady in the balm of invocation (*al-dhikr*), which is at once remembrance, mention, and invocation, the quintessential prayer that becomes finally united with the heart, which according to Islam is the "Throne of the Compassionate" (*'arsh al-raḥmān*). The whole of Sufism is based, on the one hand, on *al-dhikr*, the means of meditation, and action to facilitate the *dhikr*. On the other, it is based on the exposition of a knowledge of reality, which at once prepares humans for the journey to God and the mind and soul for *dhikr* and is the fruit of the path in the form of realized knowledge (*al-ma'rifah* or *'irfān*). In this path to God, humans begin with the sense of reverence and fear of God (*al-makhāfah*) in accordance with the *ḥadīth*: "The beginning of wisdom is the fear of God." He is then led to the love of God (*al-maḥabbah*), concerning which the Qur'ān asserts: "a people whom He loves and they love Him" (V,57). And the path is crowned by that illuminating knowledge or gnosis (*al-ma'rifah*) which in Sufism is never separated from love.

The prototype of the life of the Sufis is the life of the Prophet, and no group throughout Islamic history has loved him as intensely and has sought to emulate his wonts with such fervor as have the Sufis. The virtues that the Sufis extol and with which they seek to embellish their souls are those of the Prophet whose nocturnal ascent, as already mentioned, is the prototype of all spiritual ascent in Sufism. The esoteric teachings of Islam were transmitted after him to a few of his companions. Foremost among them was 'Alī, who is the link between the Prophet and almost all the Sufi orders in that initiatic chain (*al-silsilah*) which relates every Sufi from one generation to another back to the Prophet. A few of the other companions such as Abū Bakr and Salmān al-Fārsī, the first Persian to embrace Islam, also played an important role in the early history of this esoteric teaching, which began to be called *al-taṣawwuf* in the second/eighth century. The most important figure after this early generation, who connects its members to the Sufis of the second/eighth century, was the great patriarch of Basra, Ḥasan al-Baṣrī, who had many students, including the famous woman Sufi saint and poet from Jerusalem, Rābi'ah al-'Adawiyyah.

Gradually two distinct schools of Sufism developed following the period of the Mesopotamian ascetics and Sufis following immediately in the wake of Ḥasan. These schools were associated with Baghdad and Khurasan, each of which produced many illustrious Sufis, the first being known more for its "sobriety" and the second for its "drunkenness." At this time Sufis gathered around individual masters and their organization was quite loose and informal. The most famous circle of this kind in the third/ninth century was that of Junayd of Baghdad, who had numerous disciples, including the celebrated Manṣūr al-Ḥallāj, who was put to death as a result of political intrigue but on the specific charge of religious heresy for having uttered in public: "I am the Truth" (*ana'l-Ḥaqq*), *al-Ḥaqq* being one of the Names of God. Khurasan also produced numerous masters whose fame has continued to this day including the great saint Bāyazīd al-Basṭāmī. It was also from here that the intellectual defense of Sufism vis-à-vis the jurists, exoteric scholars, and theologians was to be carried out in the fifth/eleventh century by the famous Persian theologian and Sufi, Muḥammad Abū Ḥāmid al-Ghazzālī. It was also the land from which Persian Sufi literature—a literature that changed the spiritual and religious landscape of much of Asia—was to rise, reaching its peak with Jalāl al-Dīn Rūmī in the seventh/thirteenth century.

From the fifth/eleventh century onward Sufism became more organized, and the Sufi orders, or *ṭuruq* as we know them today, appeared upon the scene. The earliest ones, the Qādiriyyah and the Rifā'iyyah, still exist today. The orders were and are usually named after their founder, who is able to establish a new order with its own regulations and practices on the basis of his God-given authority. Some of these orders such as the Mawlawiyyah founded by Rūmī, the Shādhiliyyah by Shaykh Abu'l-Ḥasan al-Shādhilī, and the Naqshbandiyyah by Shaykh Bahā' al-Dīn Naqshband, all in the sixth/thirteenth and seventh/fourteenth centuries, have or have had a geographically widespread following. Others, such as the Aḥmadiyyah order in Egypt or the Ni'matullahī order in Persia, have been confined to a particular land until at least recently even if they have a vast following in that area.

The Sufi order consists of a hierarchy at the head of which resides the spiritual master usually known as *shaykh* or *pīr* (in Persian and many Eastern languages used by Muslims). He, or she, has representatives of various ranks who run the affairs of the orders and in some cases provide spiritual advice and even have the permission to initiate people into the order. Then there are the disciples, usually called *murīd* (the person who has the will to follow the spiritual path), *faqīr* (literally the poor, meaning the person who realizes that he or she is poor and all richness belongs to God), or *darwīsh* (a Persian term meaning humble or lowly). Sufis usually do not call themselves by such a term in Arabic or Persian, the term *ṣūfī* being reserved for those who have already reached the end of the path. The adept is initiated by the *shaykh* or one of his or her authorized representatives according to a rite that goes back to the Prophet. Henceforth the disciple follows upon the spiritual path under the direction of the guide with the goal of reaching God, becoming effaced (*al-fanā'*) in His Infinite Reality and gaining subsistence (*al-baqā'*) in Him.

The path may be said to consist of three elements: a doctrine concerning the nature of Reality; a method to reach the Real; and a science or alchemy of the soul dealing with embellishing the soul with virtue and removing from it all the imperfections or veils that prevent it from becoming wed to the Spirit; or to use another Sufi symbol, removing the veils that prevent the "eye of the heart" (*'ayn al-qalb* or *chism-i dil*) from seeing God and viewing everything as a theophany of God rather than opacity and veil. The doctrine is ultimately always a commentary on the two *shahādahs*, although in later Islamic history it became elaborated into a vast metaphysical edifice, especially in the hands of the seventh/thirteenth-century master of Islamic gnosis, Muḥyī al-Dīn ibn 'Arabī. Over the centuries the Sufis have provided the profoundest metaphysics, cosmology, angelology, psychology, and eschatology to be found in the Islamic tradition and one of the most complete metaphysical expositions found in any religious tradition. In the expounding of these doctrines, they have drawn at times from the formulations of Neoplatonism, Hermeticism, ancient Iranian, and, in some cases, Indian teachings, but the central truth of their doctrine has remained the doctrine of Unity (*al-tawḥīd*) and the teachings of the Qur'ān, whose inner meaning they have expounded in their many works.

As for method, the central means of attachment to the Real is the dhikr. Each order has its own particular methods of meditation and litanies devised by the master of the order according to the need of the adepts. As far as the science of the soul and the cultivation of the virtues are concerned, all Sufi orders emphasize this element, and in its more popular aspect Sufism is nothing other than the cultivation of spiritualized virtues. In a sense the metaphysical knowledge and the method belong to God. The adept's contribution is his or her attainment of the virtues and the use of his or her will to combat constantly the negative and passionate tendencies of the soul, until, with the help of the method and the "Muḥammadan grace" (*al-barakat al-muḥammadiyyah*), the lead of the soul becomes transmuted into gold, and the heavy substance of the carnal soul, which, left to itself, falls down like a rock, becomes transformed into an eagle that flies upward toward the supernal sun.

Sufism has played and continues to play a central role in the Islamic tradition. It has played a major role in the intellectual life of Islam and has interacted with both theology and philosophy in numerous ways over the centuries. It has been a fountainhead for Islamic art, and much of the greatest masterpieces of this art have been the creation of the Sufis, especially in the domain of music and poetry. It has also played a major role in the social life of Islam. Not only has Sufism revived Islamic ethics over the centuries but the *ṭuruq* have played a direct role in the economic life of the community through their relation with the various guilds (*aṣnāf* and *futuwwāt*). Sufism has also played a considerable political role, and from time to time Sufi orders have established whole dynasties, as in the case of the Safavids in Persia and the Idrisids in Libya. Finally, it is important to recall that the spread of Islam outside of the Arab and Persian worlds up to the present day has been mostly through Sufism.

Islām, Īmān, Iḥsān

To understand the hierarchic structure of the Islamic tradition better, it is important to turn to the ternary *islām, īmān, iḥsān,* all of which are used in the text in the Qur'ān. The first means surrender, the second faith, and the third virtue or beauty. All those who accept the Qur'ānic revelation are *muslim,* that is, they possess *islām.* But then there are those who possess intensity of faith in God and the hereafter and who are often referred to in the Qur'ān as *mu'min,* that is, the person possessing faith or *īmān.* Not every muslim is *mu'min,* and to this day in the Islamic world this distinction is kept clearly in mind. And then there are those whom the Qur'ān calls *muḥsin,* that is, those who possess *iḥsān,* which, as mentioned already, implies a high level of spiritual perfection, the attainment of which allows humans to live constantly with the awareness of being in God's presence, *iḥsān* being none other than that spiritual teaching which has been preserved, transmitted, and promulgated in Sufism.

A famous *ḥadīth* known as the *ḥadīth* of Gabriel gives a definition of all these terms. The *ḥadīth,* as transmitted by 'Umar, is as follows: "One day when we were sitting with the Messenger of God there came unto us a man whose clothes were of exceeding whiteness and whose hair was of exceeding blackness, nor were there any signs of travel upon him, although none of us knew him. He sat down knee unto knee opposite the Prophet, upon whose thighs he placed the palms of his hands saying: 'O Muḥammad, tell me what is the surrender (*islām*)'. The Messenger of God answered him saying: 'The surrender is to testify that there is no god but God and that Muḥammad is God's Messenger, to perform the prayer, bestow the alms, fast Ramaḍān and make, if thou canst, the pilgrimage to the Holy House.' He said: 'Thou hast spoken truly,' and we were amazed that having questioned him he should corroborate him. Then he said: 'Tell me what is faith (*īmān*).' He answered: 'To believe in God and His Angels and His Books and His Messengers and the Last Day, and to believe that no good or evil cometh but by His Providence.' 'Thou hast spoken truly,' he said, and then: 'Tell me what is excellence (*iḥsān*)'. He answered: 'To worship God as if thou sawest Him, for if thou seest Him not, yet seeth He thee.' 'Thou hast spoken truly,' he said, and then: 'Tell me of the Hour.' He answered: 'The questioned thereof knoweth no better than the questioner.' He said: 'Then tell me of its signs.' He answered: 'That the slave-girl shall give birth to her mistress; and that those who were but barefoot naked needy herdsmen shall build buildings ever higher and higher.' Then the stranger went away, and I stayed a while after he had gone; and the Prophet said to me: 'O 'Umar, knowest thou the questioner, who he was?' I said: 'God and His Messenger know best.' He said: 'It was Gabriel. He came unto you to teach you your religion.'"[9]

When one thinks of Islam as the term is used in the English language to denote the whole tradition, one must think not only of *islām* but also of *īmān, and iḥsān.* The teachings of Islam have levels of meaning, and the religion consists of a hierarchy that, destined to become the religion of a whole humanity, had to cater to the spiritual and intellectual needs of the simplest peasant and the most astute philosopher, the warrior and the lover, the jurist and the mystic. Islam achieved this goal by making the teachings of religion accessible on various levels from the most outward to the most inward. But it preserved unity by insisting that all of the members of its community share in the Sacred Law and the central doctrine of *al-tawḥīd* summarized in *Lā ilāha illa'Llāh.* Their degree of penetration into the meaning of unity depended and continues to depend on the intensity of their faith and the beauty of their soul. But in submission to the One (*al-islām*), all Muslims stood and stand in the same manner before God in a single community governed by the bond of brotherhood and amity. Paradoxically, the more inner dimensions of the religion do not destroy this unity but in fact only strengthen it, because these inner and higher modes of participation in the religion bring the worshiper even closer to the One and cannot but strengthen unity, even in the more outward aspects of human life that all Muslims share together, whatever their degree of participation might be in the understanding and practice of Islam.

Islamic Practices and Institutions

The Pillars (arkān)—Prayer, Fasting, Pilgrimage, Alms-giving, and Exertion in the Path of God (jihād)

The basic rites of Islam revealed to the Prophet and institutionalized by him are sometimes called the *arkān*, or pillars of the religion, for upon them rests the whole practical structure of the religion. These rites include the canonical prayers (*ṣalāh* in Arabic or *namāz* in Persian), fasting (*ṣawm*), pilgrimage (*ḥajj*), and the paying of tithe or religious tax (*zakāh*). To these *arkān* is generally added the very important act of *jihād*, usually mistranslated into English as holy war but meaning literally exertion in the way of God. This act or rite must be seen, however, not only as a separate pillar, but as an element that must be present in the whole of life and especially in the performance of the rites and acts of worship.

The canonical prayers—*ṣalāh*—are the most central rite of Islam. They are incumbent upon all Muslims, both male and female, from the age of adolescence until death. They punctuate the Muslim's daily life and place him or her directly and without any intermediary before God. The prayers must be performed in the direction of the Ka'bah in Makkah, five times a day: in the early morning, between dawn and sunrise; at noon; in the afternoon; at sunset; and at night before midnight. They are preceded by the call to prayer (*adhān*) and ritual ablution (*wuḍū'*) and can be performed on any ritually clean ground whether outdoors or indoors as long as one has the permission of the owner. The units (*rak'ah*) of prayer differ on each occasion, being two in the morning, four at noon, four in the afternoon, three in the evening, and four at night. All the movements, postures, and words follow the model established by the Prophet. In the *ṣalāh,* men and women pray to God in the name of the whole of creation and as God's vicegerents on earth. The *ṣalāh* makes possible the integration of the worshiper's whole being in the state of perfect servitude to God. For the people of *īmān* and *iḥsān,* it is the very means of ascent to the Throne of God according to the saying: "The *ṣalāh* is the spiritual ascent of the faithful" (*al-ṣalāh mi'rāj al-mu'min*). The ascent refers to the nocturnal ascent or *mi'rāj* of the Prophet.

The daily *ṣalāh* is often performed at home or in the fields but can be and is, of course, also often performed in mosques (the term mosque being derived from the Arabic word *masjid,* meaning the place of prostration, which is the ultimate movement in the *ṣalāh* designating submission to God). In addition to the *ṣalāh,* there are the Friday congregational prayers. These prayers are almost always performed in mosques and in their absence in open fields or the desert. They bring the members of the community together and have an important social, economic, and even political dimension as well as a purely religious one. During these prayers a sermon is given by the leader of the prayers (imām). Throughout Islamic history the name of the ruler mentioned in such sermons has had a great deal to do with the legitimacy of rule. Most of the sermon is, however, spent on ethical and moral issues, and after the prayers money is usually given to the poor. There are also special canonical prayers associated with the end of Ramaḍān and the end of the rite of pilgrimage. There are also *ṣalāh* offered at times of great fear or need to beseech God for help.

In addition to the *ṣalāh,* individual prayers (*du'ā*) are performed after the *ṣalāh* or at other times during the day. Some of these *du'as* are more formal in that they are repetitions of prayers formulated by great saints and religious authorities of old. Others are simply prayers of the individual recited in his or her own mother tongue. The *ṣalāh,* however, is always performed in Arabic for it is a sacred rite whose form is sacred and beyond the individual, providing a Divine Norm in which men and women take refuge from the withering effects of the storm of life and the transient conditions of temporality.

The obligatory fast in Islam—*ṣawm*—consists of complete abstention from all food and drink from the first moment of dawn to sunset during the holy month of Ramaḍān. It also requires abstention from all sexual activity and all illicit acts as designated by the *Sharī'ah*. Moreover, the fast requires keeping one's mind and tongue away from evil thoughts and words and being especially considerate to the destitute. The fast is required of all Muslims, male and female, from the age of adolescence until one possesses the physical strength to undertake it. The sick and those on a journey are not required to fast but must try to make up the days lost when possible. Also women do not fast, just as they do not perform the *ṣalāh*, during their menstrual period and also in the case of the fast when a mother is breast feeding. The month of Ramaḍān is when the Qur'ān first descended upon the soul of the Prophet, during the night that is called the "Night of Power" (*laylat al-qadr*). It is therefore a very blessed month during which much time is given to prayer and also to the recitation of the Qur'ān. The month ends with the greatest Muslim religious holiday, the *'īd al-fiṭr*, which is celebrated for several days in most countries. The formal ending of the month of fasting comes with the congregational prayers of the *'īd*, after which usually a sum of money equal to the expense for all the meals not eaten by oneself and one's family during the month is given to the poor.

Ḥajj is the supreme pilgrimage form of Islam and is made to the House of God in Makkah. This rite, instituted by Abraham and revived by the Prophet of Islam, involves circumambulation around the *Ka'bah* and certain movements, prayers, and also sacrifice of an animal in Makkah and adjoining areas according to the norms established by the Prophet. The *ḥajj* signifies a return both to the spatial center of the Islamic universe and to the temporal origin of the human state itself. Muslims believe that God forgives a human being's sins if he or she performs the *ḥajj* with devotion and sincerity. The *ḥajj* is performed during the Islamic lunar month of Dhu'l-ḥijjah and is obligatory for all men and women who have the financial means to accomplish it. In the last few years, some two million people from the Philippines to Morocco and Russia to South Africa, including American and European Muslims, have made the *ḥajj* into a rite unique in its grandeur.

In addition to the great pilgrimage, it is also possible to make the lesser ḥajj, or *ḥajj al-'umrah*, to Makkah at any time during the year. Muslims also make pilgrimage to Madinah and, when they could, to Jerusalem. There are also many local sites of pilgrimage in nearly every Muslim land from Moulay Idrīs in Morocco to Ra's al-Ḥusayn in Cairo and the site of the remains of Imām Ḥusayn in Karbalā', to the tomb of Imām Riḍā in Mashhad, to the tomb of Dādā Ganjbakhsh in Lahore and that of Shaykh Mu'īn al-Dīn Chishtī in Ajmer—all of which attract hundreds of thousands of pilgrims every year. To this day pilgrimage remains a major part of the religious and devotional life of Muslims.

The term *zakāh* in Arabic is related to the word for purity. *Zakāh* is the religious tax stipulated by the *Sharī'ah* to be paid by all Muslims who have enough income to do so to purify their wealth and make it legitimate (*ḥalāl*) in the eyes of God. The tax collected in this way is to be kept in the "public treasury" (*bayt al-māl*) and spent for public and religious services and works including feeding the poor and the needy. In addition, other religious taxes have been devised to bring about a more just distribution of wealth and prevent hoarding and excessive amassing of wealth by one individual or group.

In the West, Islam is often associated with holy war, despite the fact that the Crusades were ordered by the Cluny monks and the Pope and not some Muslim ruler or religious authority. This deeply ingrained distortion of the image of Islam going back to these events has caused the Arabic term *jihād* to be translated as holy war, but it means simply exertion in the way of God. Of course, one meaning of it is to protect Islam and its borders, but the term has much wider usage and meaning for Muslims. First, every religious act, such as performing the *ṣalāh* regularly day in and day out for a whole lifetime or fasting for fourteen hours in a hot climate, requires *jihād*; in fact, the whole of life may be said to be a constant *jihād* between our carnal and passionate soul and the demands of the immortal spirit within us. It was in reference to this profounder meaning of *jihād* that the Prophet said to his companions after a major battle in which the very existence of the early Islamic community was at stake, "Verily ye have returned from the smaller *jihād* to the greater *jihād*." And when one of the companions asked what is the greater *jihād*, he answered, "to battle against your passionate soul (*nafs*)." Islam, therefore, sees *jihād* as vigilance against all that distracts us from God and exertion to do His Will within ourselves as well as preserving and reestablishing the order and harmony that He has willed for Islamic society and the world about us.

Specifically Shi'ite Practices

In addition to all the rites mentioned above, which are performed by all Muslims, Shi'ites perform certain specific rites and religious practices that need to be mentioned here. There is first the mourning associated with the killing of the grandson of the Prophet, Ḥusayn ibn 'Alī, in Karbalā' in Iraq by the army of Yazīd, the Umayyad caliph. This event, which took place during the month of Muḥarram in the year 61/680, is remembered for forty days beginning with the first of that month which also coincides with the commencement of the Islamic lunar year. During Muḥarram there are vast religious processions sometimes accompanied by beating of one's chest (*sīnah-zanī*); gatherings in which the tragedy of Karbalā' is recounted (*rawḍah-khānī*); and also passion plays (*ta'ziyah*), which represent the only religious theater of consequence in the Islamic world. Some of these events in Iran, Iraq, the Lebanon, Pakistan, and India reach monumental dimensions and are among the most moving religious events in the Islamic world.

The Shi'ites also emphasize the importance of pilgrimage to the tombs of the Imāms in addition to Makkah, Madinah, and Jerusalem. Pilgrimage to such places as Najaf, where the tomb of 'Alī is located, Karbalā', the site of the tomb of his son Ḥusayn, Kāẓimayn of the seventh and ninth Imāms, Samarra' of the tenth and eleventh Imāms, and Mashhad of the eighth Imām—as well as to the tombs of the descendants of the Imāms such as the mausoleum of Qum, where the sister of Imām Riḍā is buried—are among the most notable features of the religious life of Shi'ites. The Shi'ites recite many litanies and prayers inherited from the Imāms, especially during Ramaḍān and Muḥarram, in addition to the Qur'ān, which they recite regularly as do Sunni Muslims.

Islamic Ethics

The whole life of Muslims is impregnated by ethical consideration in that Islam does not accept the legitimacy of any domain—whether it be social, political, or economic—as falling outside ethical consideration. The principles of all Islamic ethics are to be found in the Qur'ān and *Ḥadīth*, which direct Muslims to exhort human beings to perform what is good and to refrain from what is evil. The ultimate criterion of what constitutes good and evil resides in revelation, although over the centuries an important debate has existed between various schools of Islamic theology concerning the role of intelligence, as a God-given gift to humans, in distinguishing between good and evil. Some have asserted that God has given humans *al-'aql* (which means both intellect and reason), with which they can discern good from evil precisely because this gift is given by God, who is the source of all goodness. Others have insisted that whatever God has willed as good is good and as evil is evil and that the *'aql* has no power to make such a distinction by itself. Whatever the theological position, however, Islam has avoided the kind of humanistic ethics that claims to know good and evil and to guide humans to act ethically independently of God. Even the rational ethics of Islamic philosophers is grounded in the reality that the good comes from God and has an ontological reality related to the Divine Nature.

There are many theological and philosophical treatments of ethics and, especially, the question of good and evil, in Islamic thought. Few major questions in this realm as treated by Western thinkers over the centuries have not been dealt with amply in Islamic sources. Islamic thought, however, never accepted the divorce between ethics and religion, which was one of the results of the development of postmedieval humanism in the West. Nor has the question of theodicy, that is, the problem of God who is good creating a world in which there is evil, ever led in the Islamic world to that flight from the world of faith that one sees in the West during the past five centuries.

It is important to emphasize the practical aspect of ethics as lived and practiced in Islamic society in addition to the theological and philosophical dimensions of the issue. On the practical level ethics is embodied in the *Sharī'ah*, which, as Divine Law, weds all legal matters to ethical concerns. Whether it be in the question of work ethics, social ethics in general, or the ethics of individual behavior, the *Sharī'ah* remains the guide for Muslim behavior. It is also necessary to note that throughout Islamic history, Sufis have sought to interiorize the ethical teachings of the *Sharī'ah* and breathe new spirit into Islamic ethics and ethical behavior by living virtuously in the highest sense of this term and guiding others toward living according to ethical norms seen in their inward dimension. The most influential works of Islamic ethics over the centuries have in fact been treatises written by Sufis, of which the most important, as far as its far-reaching impact is concerned, is the *Iḥyā' 'ulūm al-dīn* ("The Revivification of the Sciences of Religion") by Abū Ḥāmid al-Ghazzālī, the great Sufi and theologian of the fifth/eleventh century, who wrote this monumental work in Arabic and then summarized it himself in Persian in his *Kīmiyā-yi sa'ādat* ("Alchemy of Happiness").

The Family

The society envisaged by Islam and dominated by Islamic ethical norms is an organic whole in which various institutions and units are intertwined. Of these institutions, which range from the state to the most local social unit, none is more important than the family, whose bonds are so much emphasized in Islam. The Qur'ān extols Muslims to respect their parents, and many *ḥadīths* emphasize how pleasing it is in the eyes of God to preserve the bonds of family and especially to respect and honor one's mother and father. The strength of the family in Islamic society is so great that it alone, among all the major social institutions of Islam, has remained practically intact even through the major dislocations to which much of the Islamic world has been witness during the past century.

The Muslim family does not consist only of the parents and their children as one observes in the atomized family of modern urban society in the West. Rather, the Muslim family is still, for the most part, the extended family, consisting of grandparents, uncles and aunts, cousins, and in-laws as well as the parents and their children. The father is like the imām of the family, representing religious authority and responsible for both the economic welfare of the members of the family and the preservation of the teachings of religion among them. But the actual religious instruction often depends on the mother, especially in the earlier stages, and Muslim women play a dominant role in every other aspect of home life as well as in the education of the children.

Although the Muslim male dominates in economic and social activity outside the home, it is the wife who reigns completely in the home, where the husband is like a guest. It is the wife who is central to family life and who provides most of the social bonding among members of the family. Women exert a much greater influence through the family within the whole of society than an outward study of what appears to be a patriarchal religious structure would indicate. The most important concrete reality in the life of a Muslim after God, the Prophet, and the spiritual and religious figures, who are in a sense an extension of the being of the Prophet, is the family; the most important figures who preserve the organic bonds within the family are the women, who as wives, mothers, and mothers-in-law usually wield great power and influence over the whole family.

All the family relations, whether they be between husband and wife, the parents and the children, or other members of the family, are governed by religious injunctions. The family is seen by the Muslim as not only a biological and social unit but also as a religious unit that protects the individual member in a thousand ways, which nourishes, nurtures, and trains him or her, which is the immediate social reality in which the first lessons of religion are taught and also the "world" in which religious injunctions must be constantly applied and practiced. The Muslim lives between two powerful social realities: the *ummah*, or the whole of the Islamic community, whose total reality he or she cannot grasp but with which he or she identifies her- or himself ideally; and the family, which for the Muslim constitutes the most real part of his or her world. All other institutions, whether they be economic or political, although of some importance, occupy a secondary rank in comparison with them. And between the two, the family remains the most immediately palpable and therefore constitutes the most basic unit in the fabric of Islamic society.

Nomadic and Sedentary Life

While emphasizing family bonds within the context of Islam, the teachings of Islam sought to combat from the beginning the tribal bonds that were so strong in the world into which Islam was born. Throughout its history, Islamic civilization has been witness to the confrontation and complementarity between nomadic life based on tribal structures and sedentary life. The Arabia of the Prophet was dominated by various tribes, and allegiance to the tribe was of paramount importance in the life of the Arabs. Islam sought to break this tribal bond in favor of the bond that unites all Muslims in one *ummah.* Despite great success, which did create a single Islamic people, tribal bonds continued to persist to some extent, especially among those who preserved the nomadic way of life. They have not totally died out even today when so many have been forced to settle in towns.

Besides the Arabs, the Turks and Mongols who invaded the eastern lands of Islam were also nomads, and in many countries from Persia to Morocco there existed over the centuries and continues to exist to some extent today an interplay of the greatest significance between nomadic and sedentary life. The nomad gave to the sedentary centers a new blood, simplicity of life and mores, discipline, and religious intensity and fervor. The sedentary population provided finesse and cultivation of knowledge and the arts, but its culture also led to excessive luxury and moral decadence, which needed periodic rejuvenation by the nomadic element. A rhythm was thereby created between the two major constitutive elements of Islamic society, a rhythm whose understanding is basic to a better grasp of the dynamics of Islamic civilization. It was the great Tunisian historian Ibn Khaldūn who, in the eighth/fourteenth century, analyzed this rhythm so masterfully in his *Muqaddimah* ("Prolegomena") and who revealed its significance as well as the power of the forces that held tribes and various ethnic units together over the centuries. To this day tribal bonds inherited from nomadic life of earlier periods remain of much significance in many parts of Islamic society and intertwine, in many cases, with the bonds and structures of the extended family to which they are obviously related.

Economic Activity and the Craft Guilds

Economics as a distinct discipline and field is a modern invention, but economic activity has, of course, been an integral part of every human culture. Islam, therefore, sought to integrate all that would be called economics today into its unitary and religious perspective. There are many Qur'ānic injunctions and *ḥadīths* that bear directly on economic life, such as the ban on usury (*ribā'*), which is considered to be strictly forbidden (*ḥarām*) by Islamic Law, and the excessive amassing of wealth in private hands. Islam also consigns many forms of wealth, such as forests and certain types of water resources, to the public sector while emphasizing the right of private property as long as the religious conditions are fulfilled. In reality, from the Islamic point of view, all possessions belong ultimately to God, but God has given the right of private property to human beings as long as they remain aware that it is a trust from Him. They must therefore pay the required religious taxes, follow licit means of gaining wealth, and help the poor to the extent that they can. There is a strong relation between economic activity and religious values in traditional Islamic society and throughout Islamic history, and up to now, there has always been a close link between the class of merchants and the religious scholars (*'ulamā'*). To this day the bazaars of Islamic cities, that is, the locus of traditional economic activity, have remained also centers of intense religious activity, and the traditional merchants are among the most pious members of Islamic society.

One of the most important economic institutions through which religious values and attitudes have been propagated in Islamic society are the guilds (*aṣnāf* or *futuwwāt*), some of which still survive in parts of the Islamic world. *Futuwwah* (*jawānmardī* in Persian), which can be rendered as spiritual chivalry, was originally connected more with the military class rather than the craft guilds and merchants. Toward the end of the Abbasid caliphate in the seventh/thirteenth century, it became more associated with the crafts and has remained so during the past seven centuries. *Futuwwah*—which means the combination of the virtues of courage, nobility, and selflessness—was associated from the beginning of Islamic history with the name of 'Alī, who is considered the master of *futuwwah* and in a sense the "patron saint" of the guilds. Some guilds, however, are considered by their members to have been founded at the beginning of human history by the son of Adam, Seth. The qualities associated with *futuwwah* became gradually incorporated into the guilds, which were often linked to Sufi orders and in which the art of making and producing objects from cloth to buildings was combined with religious and spiritual considerations.

The guilds are usually headed by a master (*ustādh*) who teaches the disciple not only the techniques of the art and craft in question but also inculcates moral and spiritual discipline in the student. The process of production of objects, which then enter the market, is thus combined with religious and spiritual training. The profoundly religious character of Islamic art, from the central sacred arts of calligraphy and architecture to the art of creating objects of everyday usage such as carpets, textiles, or utensils for the home, is related to the structure and nature of the guilds, which over the centuries have produced most of the objects of Islamic art. In Islam, art is considered not as a luxury but as practically life itself, and everything has its special art (*fann*) by virtue of which it can be made correctly. Through the guilds, Islam was able to endue its arts and crafts, which are inseparable from the arts, with the deepest values of the Islamic religion and thereby to Islamicize completely the ambience in which the traditional Muslim lived and functioned. Without doubt, the guilds are among the most important of Islamic economic institutions, responsible for linking the production of objects to the deepest ethos of Islam. If Islamic art reflects what lies at the heart of the Islamic message, it is because this art issues from the inner dimension of the Islamic tradition and is executed and produced, thanks to the guilds, by those for whom the process and technique of making things has remained inseparable from that supreme art, which is the perfecting of the soul and drawing it nigh unto God—a goal that constitutes the heart of the Islamic message.

Religious Endowments (waqf)

Another major Islamic institution that has played and continues to play an important economic and social role is that of *waqf,* or religious endowment. The Arabic term means literally "arresting" a sum of money or assets. This is done by establishing an endowment for purposes and by means of an administration determined by the person who makes the endowment. Any purpose that is in accordance with the *Sharī'ah* and is not illicit can be chosen, ranging from establishing schools to water fountains. Throughout Islamic history wealthy patrons have created *waqfs* with either monetary assets, land, or other forms of wealth. These *waqfs* have created and maintained mosques, Sufi centers, hospitals, homes for the elderly, sanatoriums, roads and bridges, wells and water fountains, hospices for pilgrims, and many other works related to public service.

The most important function, however, after the purely religious associated with the construction and maintenance of mosques and similar buildings, has been probably educational. In Islamic civilization, education has been always in private hands and not a governmental responsibility. Nor is there a church in Islam, as one finds in Christianity, that could direct education activity as is seen in the West. Throughout the Islamic world, various educational institutions from the simple Qur'ānic schools in mosques to the *madrasahs,* which are the models of medieval Western universities, were sustained until modern times mostly by private contributions, income from religious taxes, and *waqfs* and continue to be supported in this manner to this day, although government-run educational institutions now complement and in some places replace the traditional schools. In traditional Islamic civilization, even when schools were established by government authorities such as kings or ministers, this act was performed by them *qua* individuals and not as agents of the government. The best example is the famous university system called the Niẓāmiyyah founded by the Persian prime minister of the Seljūqs, Khwājah Niẓām al-Mulk, in the sixth/twelfth century with centers in Baghdad, Nayshapur, and elsewhere. The whole system was supported by a *waqf* established by Khwājah Niẓām al-Mulk himself and not in his function as prime minister. In modern times, in most Islamic countries, the institution of *waqf*, along with the immense assets that the *waqfs* possess in each country, has been taken over by governments and administered by ministries usually bearing the name of *awqāf* (plural of *waqf*). But even under such conditions, the *waqf* remains an important religious institution to further religious and charitable causes within society, and wealthy Muslims continue to establish new *waqfs* along the lines that have been followed throughout Islamic history.

Political Institutions

Islam has never separated religion from politics in the sense of dividing the kingdoms of God and Caesar. The Prophet himself was at once the religious and political leader of the first Islamic community established in Madinah, and since that ideal Islamic society every period of Islamic history has been witness to the interplay between religion (as the term is currently understood) and politics. And yet, neither the Qur'ān nor the *Ḥadīth* provide clear instructions as to what political institution or models should be established. What they do establish is the principles that can be summarized by stating that God is the ultimate ruler of Islamic society from whom descends all power and legitimacy and that His Law should be the law of any Islamic society. One should therefore say, strictly speaking, that Islam believes in nomocracy, that is, the rule of Divine Law, rather than theocracy, which is usually understood as the rule of the priesthood or the church.

After the death of the Prophet, the most important of all Islamic political institutions, namely the caliphate (from the Arabic *khilāfah*), developed and survived in one form or another until the seventh/thirteenth century, despite the opposition of various Shi'ite groups and elements. The caliph was considered as the vicegerent (*khalīfah*) of the Prophet whose function it was to promulgate the Divine Law, preserve internal order and the borders of *dār al-islām*, and appoint judges to officiate over *Shari'ite* courts. The caliph was not expected to possess knowledge of the inner meaning of the Divine Law or even be an authority (in the sense of *mujtahid*) in the Law as was claimed by Shi'ites, who therefore opposed the selection of the caliph by consultation but insisted that he had to be appointed by the previous legitimate ruler (for them the Imām), hence going back to the Prophet, and also confirmed by Divine decree.

Gradually the actual military power of the caliphs diminished, and local kings gained real military and political power while retaining the nominal authority of the caliph. Under these conditions, a new religious theory of political authority was developed by the Sunni jurists (*fuqahā'*) in which the caliph remained as the symbol of the unity of the Islamic community and the rule of the *Sharī'ah,* while actual military and political power resided in the hands of the king or *sulṭān* whose duty it was to preserve public order and protect the borders of the Islamic world. This theory, which received its most famous formulations in the hands of such famous religious authorities as al-Māwardī and al-Ghazzālī in the fifth/eleventh century, lasted in a sense into the present century until the downfall of the Ottoman caliphate (which many considered to be a sultanate and not a real caliphate) and still survives among many Sunni Muslims. Historically, the Shi'ites rejected the institution of the Sunni caliphate and in the case of the Twelve-Imām Shi'ites expect the coming of the Mahdī, but they accepted the monarchy as the most suitable form of government in the imperfect conditions of the world deprived of the direct presence of the Imām. With the Iranian Revolution of 1979 this traditional view was challenged and rejected by Ayatollah Khomeini, who substituted for it the theory of the "vicarage of the jurisprudent" (*wilāyat-i faqīh*).

It is important to understand the role of the traditional '*ulamā'*, or scholars in various Islamic political theories as well as in practice. By being the interpreters and guardians of the *Sharī'ah,* the '*ulamā'* have always wielded great political power in the Islamic world, although they never ruled directly anywhere until the Iranian Revolution of 1979. In this context it needs also to be emphasized that the Shi'ite '*ulamā'* have usually been more closely organized and politically and economically more powerful than their Sunni counterparts.

The relation between Islam and political life is a very complex one. Throughout its history, Islam created political institutions such as the caliphate and sultanate, which came to be challenged by the advent of modernism and the colonial domination of much of the Islamic world by a West in which the traditional ideas of political rule had been seriously challenged by several revolutions. Among these, the French Revolution had the greatest impact upon the Islamic world. The result of the weakening or destruction of these traditional Islamic political institutions is seen in the political turmoil that has encompassed much of the Islamic world during this century. But whatever the crises and the forces involved in a particular situation, the nexus between Islam and political life remains and has not been severed. If Muslims were to accept in principle the separation of religion from the domain of public life (which would then become secularized as it has in the West to an ever greater degree since the Renaissance), they would have to abandon the doctrine of Unity that lies at the heart of the Islamic message. They would have to act against the *Sunnah* of the Prophet and fourteen centuries of the historical unfolding of the Islamic tradition.

The History of Islam

The Age of the Prophet and the Four Rightly Guided Caliphs

The history of Islam is inseparable from the history of Islamic society, institutions, and civilization in which the transhistorical realities of Islam have been manifested, although those realities are not themselves of purely historical origin. Moreover, Islamic history provides a temporal cadre within which one can situate the history of the religion itself even if the ebbs and flows and beginnings and ends of various modes and schools of Islamic thought are not always identical with the periods of Islamic history marked by dynastic and political changes.

The period of the migration of the Prophet, which marks the establishment of the first Islamic society in Madinah, to his death and the caliphate of the first four caliphs (i.e., the period from 1/622 to 40/661) constitute a unique period in Islamic history. It is like the apostolic age in Christianity, and it is an era to which Muslims have looked for guidance throughout their later history. The earthly career of the Prophet, already discussed, was followed by the caliphate of Abū Bakr from 11/632 to 13/634. He was the first of the four caliphs accepted by Sunni Muslims as the rightly guided caliphs (*khulafā' al-rāshidūn*) and considered to be men of great sanctity and piety, whose political rule was impregnated by profound religious considerations even if they might have committed occasional errors of political judgment. Abū Bakr, who ruled for only two years, was faced almost immediately with the centrifugal forces fanned by Arab tribalism, which threatened to break up the political unity of Arabia created by the Prophet. The greatest contribution of Abū Bakr was to put down these uprisings and to preserve the unity of the newly founded political entity with its capital in Madinah. The second caliph 'Umar, who ruled from 13/634 to 23/644, continued on the basis established by Abū Bakr, insisting on a strong center that could preserve the unity of the Islamic state that was beginning to expand. It was during his rule that Muslims captured Jerusalem, where 'Umar showed great respect for the houses of worship of Jews and Christians, and Islam spread into Syria, Persia, and North Africa. 'Umar lived a life of remarkable simplicity and austerity and like Abū Bakr was a paragon of piety. Most Sunnis consider his rule as being the most successful, from a practical point of view, among the rule of all the rightly guided caliphs, a rule that was witness to the establishment of many administrative practices and institutions that became permanent features of later Islamic society.

'Umar was succeeded by 'Uthmān, who was chosen, like all the *rāshidūn*, by consensus of the elders of the community. His rule from 23/644 to 35/656 was witness to the pouring of wealth into Madinah and the rest of Arabia from conquests in the provinces with resulting tensions, including tribal uprisings. Many also criticized 'Uthmān for the practice of nepotism, especially in appointing Mu'āwiyah from his own family to the governorship of Syria. The opposition to 'Uthmān finally led to an uprising against him led by the son of Abū Bakr and resulted in the killing of 'Uthmān, an event of grave consequence for later Islamic history, for it was to avenge the death of his uncle 'Uthmān that Mu'āwiyah moved against 'Uthmān's successor, 'Alī, and precipitated the division in the body politic that has persisted to this day.

'Alī, who ruled from 35/656 to 40/661, was faced with civil strife and even war on many fronts, including between his followers (*shī'ah*) and some of the Quraysh and against the companions of the Prophet Ṭalḥah and Zubayr, joined by the wife of the Prophet 'Ā'ishah, in the battle of the Camel in both of which 'Alī was victorious. With the center of his supporters in Iraq, 'Alī moved the capital of Islam to Kufa and from there set out to confront the Syrian garrisons of Mu'āwiyah, who had refused to pay allegiance to 'Alī. The two sides fought the crucial battle of Ṣiffīn in 36/657 in which 'Alī was victorious, but at the moment of victory Mu'āwiyah had his army come to the battlefield with Qur'āns on their lances, asking for the Qur'ān to arbitrate between the two sides. To avoid the desecration of the sacred book, 'Alī accepted arbitration in which his side lost to the much more astute representatives of Mu'āwiyah. 'Alī returned to Kufa, where, in 40/661, a member of a group that opposed arbitration in principle and considered both sides of the battle to have deviated from the earlier norms of Islam killed 'Alī and brought to an end the rule of the *rāshidūn*. One can say that from the battle of Ṣiffīn, the distinction between the Sunnis, the Shi'ites, and the third group called the Khawārij (literally those who stand outside) became marked, only to be accentuated by later events, especially the death of 'Alī's son Ḥusayn in Karbalā'. Also, with 'Alī's moving of the capital to Kufa, the political and cultural center of the Islamic world moved outside of Arabia while the religious center remained and continues to remain in the Hejaz.

The Classical Caliphates (Umayyad and Abbasid)

The Umayyads (40/661–132/750)

With 'Alī removed from the scene Mu'āwiyah became the ruler and caliph of the Islamic world, although for a few months 'Alī's son, al-Ḥasan, continued to claim the caliphate in Madinah. Mu'āwiyah, who was a very competent and calculating ruler, was able to establish a vast empire with Damascus at its center but at the cost of converting the caliphate of the *rāshidūn* to a hereditary sultanate. The Umayyads were able to rule from central Asia to Spain and France, establishing a system of communication, administration, and legal and military institutions, much of which survived over the centuries. They were faced with attempts to restore the power of the aristocracy of Makkah and to gain the freedom of the bedouins from central authority, as well as Shi'ite dissent. 'Abd al-Malik (65/685–86/705) succeeded in securing the unity of the empire, but to an ever greater degree religious principles were seen by the pious to be sacrificed for worldly ends, although one of the caliphs, 'Umar ibn 'Abd al-'Azīz, who sought to reform the existing economic system, was a model of piety and highly revered by not only the Sunni faithful but even the Shi'ites, whom he treated with kindness.

The Umayyads strengthened the administrative and military foundations of the empire and Arabized coinage and the chancelleries. They completed the early conquests and permitted Islamic culture to establish itself from the Oxus to the Pyrenees. And yet they began to lose the support of many Muslims and their "legitimacy." Many considered them to be Arab rather than Islamic rulers, and resentment grew against them, especially among the *mawālī*, that is, the non-Arabs who had embraced Islam in an ever greater number, chief among them being the Persians. Much of this protest took place under the banner of Shi'ism and centered in Iraq, especially after the killing of Ḥusayn ibn 'Alī during the caliphate of Yazīd. The opposition was kept at bay by strong governors, but it gradually spread farther east until in Khurasan, under the leadership of the charismatic Persian general Abū Muslim, an uprising began with the purpose of returning the caliphate to its religious origin and the family of the Prophet. The movement succeeded and the Banū 'Abbās, descendants of the uncle of the Prophet, defeated the Umayyads and captured Damascus with the help of their Persian supporters, bringing the rule of the Umayyads to an end. The only exception was Muslim Spain, where one of the Umayyads, who had been able to flee from Damascus, established himself as ruler and inaugurated the golden age of Muslim rule in that land.

The Abbasids (132/750–656/1258)

The Abbasid rule marks the period in which what is usually called "classical Islamic civilization" reached its apogee. The early Abbasids continued the work of the Umayyads in strengthening the Islamic Empire, preserving its unity, Islamicizing various institutions, and spreading further the use of Arabic as the *lingua franca* of the empire. It was also during their rule that Persian developed and became the second *lingua franca* of the Islamic world. While reasserting the sacred character of the caliphate, the Abbasids began to emulate Persian models of rule and administration to an ever greater degree. The capital was moved eastward toward Persia with Baghdad being built in 145/762 by al-Manṣūr near the ancient Sassanid capital of Ctesiphon and near the heartland of the Persian world. Persians also became much more active in affairs of state, and many of them served as chief ministers to the caliphs.

Baghdad soon became the greatest cultural center of the Islamic world and perhaps of the whole of the world in the third/ninth and fourth/tenth centuries. The famous Abbasid caliphs such as Hārūn al-Rashīd and al-Ma'mūn were great patrons of the arts and sciences, and it was at this time that both Islamic philosophy and science began to flourish. But the early Abbasid period was also the era when the crystallization of the *Sharī'ite* codes, begun during the Umayyad period, were finalized and the traditional schools of Law as they subsist to this day were established. Almost certainly the most important religious achievement of this period was the establishment of the definitive and canonical collections of *Ḥadīth* by Bukhārī and others, an achievement that was, again, the culmination of the process begun from the time of the *rāshidūn* and continued in the Umayyad period. Likewise, the early Abbasid period coincides with the rise of the classical schools of Sufism in both Baghdad and Khurasan.

Gradually, however, the power of the Abbasid caliphate began to wane. Caught amid rivalries between Arabs and Persians, the caliphs sought to surround themselves with Turkish guards, thus opening the center of the Islamic world to the third major ethnic group, after the Arabs and Persians, which was to play an ever greater role in the politicosocial life of the central regions of the caliphate. Soon the caliphs became pawns in the hands of their own Turkish generals. Caught between the tension of the agrarian population and city dwellers, the military and civil administrations, problems of land and taxation, and ethnic rivalries, the center finally ceased to be able to hold the vast Islamic Empire together. Regional rulers gained power to the extent that the Persian Būyids captured Iraq itself in 334/945 and made the caliph their instrument of rule to legitimize the power that was actually in their hand. Henceforth, local dynasties wielded actual political power while the caliphate became the symbol of the unity of the Islamic world and the rule of the *Sharī'ah* as well as the source of legitimacy for various kings or sultans who ruled not only in Persia but also in many Arab lands.

Local Dynasties up to the Mongol Invasion

PERSIA, CENTRAL ASIA, AND TRANSOXIANA

Already in the third/ninth century, local governors in the eastern provinces of Persia were beginning to assert their independence of the central authority of the caliphate in Baghdad and soon established the first independent Persian dynasties such as the Ṣaffāvids and Sāmānids. The latter, who ruled in Khurasan and central Asia into the fourth/tenth century, are especially important from a cultural point of view, because they were the great patrons of the Persian language, which soon became a basic factor in the cultural and also political independence that the Persians were asserting vis-à-vis Arab domination. Semi-independent dynasties also began to appear in northern and western areas of Persia, resulting finally in the appearance of the Būyids, who conquered not only Persia but Iraq as well during the fourth/tenth century and ruled as Shi'ites supported by strong Persian national sentiments.

The advance of tribes of Turkic stock changed the political and even ethnic landscape of the territory governed by the Sāmānids, especially central Asia. The Ghaznavids, who were of Turkic origin, defeated the Sāmānids and established a powerful kingdom in eastern Persia, extending their realm to Sindh and the Punjab. Their rule set the background for the appearance of a number of dynasties of Turkic stock who began to dominate the political scene not only in central Asia and Persia but in Arab lands and Anatolia as well.

THE SELJŪQS

The most important of these Turkic dynasties was the Seljūqs, who ruled for more than two centuries from about 426/1035 to 656/1258. The Seljūqs conquered nearly all of western Asia, including Baghdad itself, which fell into the hands of Toghrïl Beg in 447/1055. They reunified western Asia, once again preserving the Abbasid caliphate, but only as a symbol of Sunni rule, which they avidly supported. They opposed the power of local Shi'ite rulers and in fact suppressed Shi'ism to a large extent. They also began the Turkish conquest of Anatolia, which was to result in the establishment of Osmanli and later Ottoman rule. The Seljūqs also supported Islamic theology (*kalām*) against the attacks of the philosophers and sought to strengthen Sunni orthodoxy through the establishment of the traditional university (madrasah) system associated so much with the name of their most famous prime minister, Khwājah Niẓām al-Mulk. Although of Turkic stock, they were great patrons of Persian culture. During their rule, Persian prose literature reached its peak of perfection, and Persian poetry produced some of its greatest masters.

EGYPT AND SYRIA

The destinies of Egypt and Syria, along with the lands in between such as Palestine, were often intertwined in the Islamic period. Already in the third/ninth century the Abbasid governor of Egypt, Ibn Ṭūlūn, who built the magnificent mosque in Cairo that still bears his name, began to assert his independence and extended his authority to Syria. In the fourth/tenth century, the Ismā'īlī Fāṭimids began their conquest of nearly the whole of North Africa from al-Ifīqiyyah (present-day Tunisia) and in 358/969 conquered Egypt, claiming the caliphate in the name of their Imām. They are the founders of Cairo, which they made their capital. They further extended their rule over Jerusalem, Makkah, Madinah, and Damascus, where they defeated the Ḥamdānids and even threatened Baghdad. The Fāṭimid caliphate became a rival to the Abbasids and ushered in a period during which the arts and sciences flourished greatly, especially in Cairo. Threatened by the Seljūqs and later the Crusaders, the Fāṭimids were weakened and finally defeated by Saladin, who also defeated the Crusaders and expelled them from Jerusalem in 583/1187.

Saladin, or Ṣalāḥ al-Dīn al-Ayyūbī, as he is known to Muslims, was a Kurdish general from Aleppo who established the Ayyūbid dynasty, which united Egypt, Palestine, and Syria under Sunni rule, revived the economic life of the region after the long struggle of the Crusades, and set the background for the Mamlūks, originally their slaves, who gained ascendancy and finally established their own powerful dynasty. It was the Mamlūks who finally stopped the onslaught of the Mongols and defeated the Mongol armies in southern Palestine in 658/1260.

NORTH AFRICA AND SPAIN

The Abbasids did not control the western provinces of the Islamic world, which pursued a separate political history. In Morocco, a descendant of Ḥasan, the grandson of the Prophet, established his own rule among the Berbers with his capital in Fez, which has remained ever since the heart of North African Islam. In Algeria, 'Abd al-Raḥmān ibn Rustam established another Berber kingdom called the Rustamid, based on the 'Ibādiyyah school that was the inheritor of the perspectives of the Khārijites. As for Tunis, it was ruled by the Aghlābids, who accepted the authority of the caliphate in principle but who were for all practical purposes independent.

In Spain, or al-Andalus, as the Muslims have known it, the Umayyad prince, 'Abd al-Raḥmān I, established the Spanish Umayyad dynasty in 138/756 with its capital in Cordova, which soon became the largest and most cosmopolitan city in Europe. Thus began a rule of two and a half centuries during which Spain was witness to an incredible cultural achievement in nearly every field and the creation of a social climate in which Muslims, Jews, and Christians lived in peace and harmony to a degree rarely seen in human history. Muslim Spain was witness to not only a flowering of Islamic culture but also to one of the major flowerings of Jewish culture, which remained in close relation with the Islamic as seen by the number of works written by Jewish thinkers, including the most famous among them, Maimonides, in Arabic. Spain also became the most important center from where Islamic learning in the sciences, philosophy, and the arts was transmitted to the Christian West, the city of Toledo playing a particularly central role in this transmission, which had such a profound effect upon later European history.

In the fifth/eleventh century, Umayyad power waned. Spain became divided into small principalities ruled by local princes (called *mulūk al-ṭawā'if* in Arabic), making it an easy target for the Berbers of North Africa, especially the puritanical Almoravids and Almohads who conquered much of Spain in the fifth/eleventh and sixth/twelfth centuries. But these victories were short-lived. With the power of Muslims considerably weakened, the reconquest by Christians began, marked by the fatal defeat of Muslims in the Battle of Las Navas de Tolosa in 608/1212. Muslims survived only in the mountainous regions of the south where the Naṣrids ruled, building one of the greatest masterpieces of Islamic art in Granada in the seventh/thirteenth century. Formal Muslim rule over the Iberian Peninsula came to an end in 897/1492 with the conquest of Granada by the Christian rulers Isabelle and Ferdinand. After that event, the Muslims who remained were persecuted as *Moriscos* until they disappeared outwardly from the scene in the eleventh/seventeenth century, although the influence of Islam and its culture persists in Spain to this day.

In North Africa itself, after the assertion of Fāṭimid rule, tribal battles continued between those who paid allegiance to the Fāṭimid caliphate and those who remained faithful to the Abbasids. In the fifth/eleventh century the Sanhaja Berbers, who had spread Islam from Mauritania to the mouth of the Senegal River, united to form the al-Murābiṭūn (which has come to be known as Almoravids in the West) with their capital in Marrakesh and united much of North Africa and Spain. They were succeeded by the al-Muwaḥḥidūn (the Almohads), a dynasty founded by a disciple of the famous Persian theologian and Sufi al-Ghazzālī. This puritanical movement spread as far east as Tripolitania and survived into the seventh/thirteenth century.

With the weakening of the Almohads, local dynasties asserted themselves once again, the Marīnids in Morocco and the Ḥafṣids in Algeria and Tunisia. By the tenth/sixteenth century, North Africa fell into the hands of the Ottomans, except for Morocco, which has been ruled since the tenth/sixteenth century by the *sharīfs,* or descendants of the Prophet, who founded the 'Alawid dynasty. All of the Maghrib or the western lands of the Arab world fell into the hands of the French in the thirteenth/nineteenth century and did not gain their independence until the decades of the 1950s and 1960s.

THE MONGOL INVASION

Although the western lands of Islam were unaffected by the onslaught of the Mongols, the eastern lands were devastated by the descendants of Chinggis Khan who captured first central Asia, then Persia, Iraq, Syria, and Palestine, and were only stopped by the Mamlūks after destroying much of the eastern lands of the Islamic world. The Mongols also put an end to the Abbasid caliphate, thereby bringing about a major change in the political landscape of the Islamic world. With their conquest of Baghdad and death of the last Abbasid caliph in 656/1258, the Islamic world entered a new phase of its history. After a period of turbulence, several new empires appeared on the scene and dominated over much of the Islamic world until the expansion of Western colonialism and the subjugation of most of the Islamic countries.

The Aftermath of the Mongol Invasion

THE OTTOMANS, SAFAVIDS, MOGULS, AND THEIR SUCCESSORS AND THE OUTER REACHES OF THE ISLAMIC WORLD

Turmoil followed in both the economic and political domains in the wake of the Mongol invasion of the eastern lands of Islam. The descendants of Hülagü, who had captured these lands, began to rule, promulgating at the beginning their own Mongolian laws and customs. But soon these rulers, known as the Īl-khānids, embraced Islam, especially when their king, Öljeitü, accepted Islam and became Sultan Muḥammad Khudābandah. It is interesting to note that he embraced Islam in its Twelve-Imām Shi'ite form, and this period from the seventh/thirteenth to the eighth/fourteenth century was witness to the spread of Shi'ism in Persia, setting the background for the establishment of Shi'ite rule in the Safavid period.

The Īl-khānid period, marked by local powers vying with each other, was terminated toward the end of the eighth/fourteenth century by Tamerlane, who conquered all of Persia, Iraq, Syria, Anatolia, southern Russia, and central Asia—where he established his capital in Samarqand, which became a great center of Persian art. Although his vast empire perished with him in 807/1405 when he died on his way to China, his descendants, the Tīmūrids, reigned in Persia and central Asia into the tenth/sixteenth century, making such cities as Shiraz, Tabriz, and Herat great centers of culture and art, especially the art of Persian miniature and calligraphy. Moreover, it was one of Timūr's descendants, Bābar, who came to India from Afghanistan to establish the Mogul dynasty in the subcontinent.

Meanwhile in Egypt, which had repelled the Mongol invasion, the old order continued, and the Mamlūks were able to establish a powerful, stable state, which usually included Palestine and Syria. The state lasted for over two centuries from 648/1250 to 923/1517, when it was integrated into the Ottoman Empire. The Mamlūks were Sunni Muslims and emphasized their Sunni affiliation. They were great patrons of the arts, producing some of the finest examples of Islamic architecture, which adorn Cairo to this day, as well as some of the greatest masterpieces of Qur'ānic calligraphy that the Islamic world has ever known. They left their indelible mark upon Egypt, and their influence in the arts can still be felt in Cairo.

THE OTTOMANS

The most powerful Islamic state of recent centuries was established in Anatolia by Turkic tribes who had migrated westward from central Asia through Persia. Although the earlier Turkic dynasty of the Seljūqs was defeated by the Mongols, after a short period, Turkish power rose again around Konya in southern Anatolia and further west with various tribes ruling over small municipalities. Soon the "sons of 'Uthmān" or Osmanlis gained the upper hand and by 726/1326 conquered much of Anatolia, making Bursa their capital. Now known as the Ottomans, they began their conquest of the Balkans in 758/1357 while in 792/1390–1391 Bāyezīd Yildirim defeated the other small municipalities and claimed rule over all of Anatolia.

Although defeated by Tamerlane, the Ottomans soon regained their strength and in 857/1453 under Mehmet II conquered Constantinople, henceforth known as Istanbul, putting an end to the Byzantine Empire. In 923/1517, Sultan Selim annexed Syria and Egypt while the famous Ottoman ruler Sulayman the Magnificent invaded Hungary in 932/1526 and made the whole of the Balkans a part of the Ottoman Empire. The vast empire that spread from Algeria through the rest of North Africa, the Arab Near East, and Anatolia to the Balkans lasted for several centuries, and, despite being attacked by European powers in the thirteenth/nineteenth century, survived until World War I when its Arab provinces were divided between the English and the French, its Balkan territories gained independence, and the Turkish heartland of the Empire became modern Turkey.

The Ottomans claimed to be caliphs who succeeded the Umayyads and the Abbasids, although they were not technically caliphs but sultans. Nevertheless, they created a political order that functioned in many ways like the other caliphates. They were staunch defenders of Sunni Islam while their culture was highly influenced by Persian elements as seen in both Turkish poetry and painting. They also supported Sufism, which flourished under their rule, with some of the orders such as the Mawlawiyyah and Baktāshiyyah playing an important political as well as spiritual role in the Ottoman world, particularly in Turkey itself. The Ottomans were great builders and created major architectural edifices, which one can still see in Istanbul and elsewhere. They created the last powerful Islamic Empire, which stood up to the West until the present century and prevented European expansion from following the overland route in its attempt to conquer India and the Far East. The Arab Near East as well as Turkey are heirs to some six centuries of Ottoman rule, as are pockets of Muslims in the Balkans in such areas as Albania and Bosnia-Herzegovina.

THE SAFAVIDS AND THE LATER PERSIAN DYNASTIES

From the segmentation of political rule in Persia following the Mongol invasion, a powerful religiopolitical movement grew in western Persia under the banner of the Ṣafawī Sufi order and Twelve-Imām Shi'ism. Supported by Turkic-speaking tribes, the Safavids conquered Tabriz in 905/1499 and soon established their rule over the whole of Persia, which included not only present-day Iran, but also much of Caucasia, the whole of Baluchistan, Afghanistan, and much of central Asia. They thus established a powerful empire on the eastern flank of the Ottomans and sought to protect themselves from Ottoman domination by appealing to Shi'ism as the state religion, as the Ottomans emphasized their support of Sunnism. In a sense the Safavids reestablished the Persian national state after some nine centuries and laid the basis for the modern state of Iran.

They made Isfahan their capital and turned it into one of the most beautiful cities in the Islamic world. Their artistic creations, whether it was in architecture, tile work, rugs, or miniatures, mark some of the major peaks of Islamic art. Also, despite the migration of many Persian Sunni scholars and thinkers to India, the Safavid period was witness to a major revival of Islamic philosophy. The dynasty, which had been originally a Sufi order, however, turned against Sufism and conflict arose between Shi'ite *'ulamā'* and the Sufis. Weakened by both internal rivalries and frictions and external pressures, the Safavids were finally defeated by the Afghan invasion of 1135/1722, which put an end to the Safavid dynasty.

For a while Persia was threatened by both the Ottomans and the Russians, who were expanding southward. But in 1142/1729 Nādir, who had been a Safavid general, rose to power and expelled the Afghans and Ottomans out of Persia, regaining also Georgia, Shirwan, and Armenia. He established himself as king, founded the Afshār dynasty, and became the last Oriental conqueror, capturing Delhi in 1150/1738 and gaining possession of northern India. But his rule terminated with his murder by his entourage. After him, the Zands established themselves in southern Persia while Aḥmad Shah Durrānī declared autonomy in Afghanistan, leading finally to the formal separation of Afghanistan from Persia in the middle of the thirteenth/nineteenth century.

In 1193/1779 the Turkman leader Āqā Muḥammad Khān Qājār seized Tehran and from there the rest of Persia, establishing the Qājār dynasty that lasted until 1343/1924. Threatened by both Russia in the north and the British in the south, the Qājārs sought to tread a fine line to preserve Persia's autonomy at least nominally. Much of the territory of Persia was lost, however, at this time to Russia and the British, but at least the formal independence of Persia was preserved. However, because of the weakness of the central government, foreign interference and machinations were rampant. Several attempts at reform failed, but the Constitutional Revolution of 1323/1906, which created a constitutional monarchy and the first elected parliament in the Islamic world, did succeed, at least formally, although the struggle for power between the shahs and the religious authorities continued in one way or another until the coming of Reza Shah and the founding of the Pahlavi dynasty. Persia now began a new phase of its life, a period of national assertion combined with modernization. The old struggles, however, between the power of the state and the Shi'ite *'ulamā'* had obviously not disappeared but took a new form, leading finally to the Islamic Revolution of 1979.

THE MOGULS

Islam had begun to spread into the heartland of India from the sixth/twelfth and seventh/thirteenth centuries mostly through Sufi orders such as the Chishtiyyah. Gradually, local Muslim rule became established, especially during the period known as the Delhi Sultanate. There were also notable small Muslim municipalities in Kashmir and Bengal as well as in the south, especially in the Deccan. In the tenth/sixteenth century, Bābar and his army established their rule over northern India and founded the Mogul Empire, which ruled over most of that land from 932/1526 to 1274/1858. The great early emperors such as Akbar, Humāyūn, Jahāngīr, and Shah Jahān created one of the most culturally vibrant and wealthy empires in the world.

Dominated at first by the Persian administrative system and Persian language and art, the Moguls allowed a creative interaction between Islam and the local culture of India to take place, which resulted in the creation of some of the finest works of architecture ever built, such as the Taj Mahal in Agra, as well as the flowering of Sufi poetry and music, the poetry being not only in Persian but also in the local languages. This was also the period that gave birth to Urdu, a language that came into its own in the twelfth/eighteenth and thirteenth/nineteenth centuries as a major vehicle for the expression of Islamic thought and sensibility in India and is now one of the major Islamic languages.

After Aurangzeb, the power of the Moguls began to wane as they were confronted with not only external invasions by Nādir Shah Afshār and

Aḥmad Shah Durrānī but also with the rise of local Hindu rulers and most of all the British, who, after the death of Aurangzeb in 1118/1707, extended their colonial rule over India and annexed the whole of India as part of the British Empire. After the Muslim uprising of 1273/1857, even the nominal rule of the Moguls (also known as Mughals) came to an end, and Muslim as well as Hindu India became a full-fledged colony until the independence and partition of India in 1947.

Islam in Other Areas

BLACK AFRICA

The history of Islam in black Africa begins with the time of the Prophet, when a number of his companions took refuge in Abyssinia. The eastern coast of Africa became integrated into the Islamic world very rapidly, but Islam remained bound to the coastal line until the thirteenth/nineteenth century when communication into the jungle areas, which come close to the sea in that region, made the penetration of Islam into the inner regions of Africa from the east possible. It was from the western region of Africa that Islam spread into the hinterlands, mostly in the savannah that separates the Sahara, inhabited by Berbers and Arabs, from the jungles, which, like the savannah, were inhabited by black Africans. Already in the fifth/eleventh century, Muslim historians described the Muslim quarters of the capital of Ghana, which was later conquered by the Almoravids to be succeeded by local dynasties. By the sixth/twelfth century, most of Ghana had embraced Islam.

There are also records of Muslims in Mali, whose king converted to Islam. Referred to by Arabs as Takrūr, which was in reality only part of Mali, the Muslims of Mali established a major kingdom with a thriving Islamic culture, which was in close contact with Muslim centers of North Africa. A city such as Timbuktu became a center of Islamic learning, and to this day the libraries of Mali contain rich collections of Arabic manuscripts. The greatest ruler of Mali was Mansa Mūsā, who lived in the seventh/thirteenth century and who captured Timbuktu as well as the Songhay in the middle of the Niger, which by the ninth/fifteenth century had eclipsed Mali as a Muslim kingdom. This kingdom had such famous rulers as Askiya Muḥammad, who, like many eminent Islamic leaders of West Africa, made the pilgrimage to Makkah, where he met the Berber *ʿālim* Muḥammad al-Maghīlī, who exercised a great influence in that region. Al-Maghīlī preached a form of puritanical Islam, opposed any mixing with local African religious practices, and emphasized the concept of *mujaddid* (which means the renewer of Islam at the beginning of each century)—a concept that has had an important role to play in Islam in black Africa to this day, being closely associated with the messianic ideas known as Mahdiism.

In the eighth/fourteenth century, the Hausa, who had lived in early isolation until then, became gradually converted to Islam, at first through the immigrants from Mandingo who converted the kings of Kano and Katsina to the faith. Later, Fulani *'ulamā'* brought Islamic education to the region and spread the influence of Islam considerably. By the tenth/sixteenth century, Islam was beginning to spread to Bagirmi and Waday, where again the Fulani *'ulamā'* played an important role. At this time also the Moroccan kingdom began to show greater interest in the Saharan salt mines and after several battles established its hegemony over much of this area, especially the land of the Songhay. But it soon lost interest and withdrew, leaving various pashas to rule over local municipalities. For a while the Bambara, who were not influenced to any appreciable degree by Islam, gained power, but at the same time other members of the Mande group who were Muslims began to disperse west and south to the Atlantic, spreading Islam to the upper Guinea and the Ivory Coast.

In the twelfth/eighteenth century, just preceding the European colonization of Africa, a number of major religious movements swept over West Africa, establishing Islamic states based on the appeal of charismatic leaders, some of whom claimed to be the Mahdi. The most famous of these figures was 'Uthmān dan Fadio, born in Gobir in 1167/1754, who soon conquered much of West Africa as both religious leader and ruler. He united many of the fractious tribes and established an order whose religious and political effect persists to this day. Another of these charismatic figures was al-Ḥājj 'Umar, who lived at the beginning of the thirteenth/nineteenth century. Originally from Futu Toro, he traveled as a young man to Makkah, Madinah, and Jerusalem and joined the Tijāniyyah Sufi order. He returned to Futa Jallon, where his religious and military followers began to increase, and then to Dinguiray, where in 1268/1852 he declared *jihād.* He fought many battles against both the Bambara and the French and encouraged the emigration of Muslims to avoid living under European colonial rule. He made long spiritual retreats even amid a most active life and was said by his followers to possess extraordinary powers. Killed in battle in 1281/1864, he also left a religious and political heritage that has not been forgotten to this day.

In Arabic the lands lying below the Berber and Arabic regions of North Africa are called *Bilād al-sūdān,* the land of Sudan, of which present-day Sudan occupies the eastern region. This latter area, known more technically as Nilotic Sudan, was penetrated by Islam later than West and Central Africa. Nubia, which lies north of this region and south of present-day Egypt, was the site of a very ancient civilization that later embraced Christianity and resisted Islamic penetration from Egypt for several centuries. Gradually, however, Arab tribes began to move south, and Nubia became more and more Muslimized until the eighth/fourteenth century, when it became completely Islamic and henceforth was closely related in its history to Egypt. The rest of Sudan, save its southern province, became ever more Arabized, especially from the tenth/sixteenth century onward when nomadic Arabs pushed into the grasslands of Nilotic Sudan. At the same time a non-Arab tribe, the Funj, pushed north, embracing Islam and completing the Islamization of Nubia and northern Sudan. The Funj were very devoted to Sufism, and during their hegemony, Sufi orders exercised great power, a power that continues in many areas to this day.

From the tenth/sixteenth century the Ottomans also exercised some influence over certain areas of the country now known as the Sudan. The Funj power finally declined in the twelfth/eighteenth century, and in the thirteenth/nineteenth century, Egypt sent a mission to dominate the country that is now known as the Sudan. The Turco-Egyptian domination of the Sudan was to last until the rise of British power in the region in the late thirteenth/nineteenth century. But the situation in the Sudan was such that British colonization was to meet major obstacles before its path. Islamic religious revival was observable everywhere, and in 1298/1881 a charismatic religious figure named Muḥammad Aḥmad proclaimed himself as the Mahdī, seeking to unite not only the Sudan but also the Islamic world in a new religious polity and opposing Westernization that was beginning to appear among certain classes. He united the tribes and fought against the Egyptian garrisons that were helped by the British. In 1302/1885 he defeated General Gordon and captured Khartoum, establishing a new Islamic state and a religious organization that is still of great significance in the Sudan.

As for the Horn of Africa, there are records of Muslim establishments along the east coast of Africa by the third/ninth century. Gradually, Muslim kingdoms were created that often paid tribute to the Christian Ethiopian emperors, but such towns as Zaylā' and Mogadishu were already deeply Arabized centuries ago. Although the culture and language were Swahili, contact with the Arab and also Persian world was very close, and the Somalis, who accepted Islam and spread it in that region, claimed Arab ancestry. In the tenth/sixteenth century both the Ottomans and the Portuguese gained power in the region, the latter burning the city of Zaylā'. Under these circumstances Aḥmad Grāñ, the first of many religious reformers in the area, arose seeking to assert Islamic rule in the region. But Grāñ was finally killed in battle, and Muslim power in the interior began to wane. Along the coast, Islamic Swahili culture thrived as both the Ottomans and 'Umānīs from the Arabian Sea were gaining greater power. By the thirteenth/nineteenth century, European colonial presence, particularly German and British followed later by Italian, destroyed Islamic rule over the region until the political independence of the area after World War II. But the religious authority of the Muslims on the coast remained strong inland and though their political power had diminished under colonial rule, Islam as a religion began to penetrate to an ever greater degree westward into the heart of

Africa, commencing a process that continues to this day. More and more African people became drawn into the Islamic setting represented by the Swahili culture of the coast, in contrast to western and central Africa, where Islam came as a result of the migration of foreign elements, namely Berbers and Arabs.

SOUTHEAST ASIA

Islam spread into the Malay world from the seventh/thirteenth century onward through Sufi teachers, pious merchants, and a number of men from the family of the Prophet and ruling classes of the Hadramaut and the Persian Gulf, who married members of Malay royal families and brought about conversion to Islam from above. The role of Sufis was, however, paramount, the Sufis coming from both the Indian subcontinent and Arabia. It was the Sufis who translated classics of Sufi literature from Arabic and Persian into Malay and transformed the Malay language into a major Islamic language. They also began to write original Islamic works in Malay as can be seen in the writings of such figures as the eleventh/seventeenth-century Ḥamzah Fanṣūrī.

Marco Polo had already detected an Islamic kingdom in Sumatra in Perlak upon returning from China to Persia in 691/1292, and Chinese records speak of an Islamic embassy being sent from Samudra to the Chinese emperor in 681/1282. Samudra soon grew into a powerful Muslim kingdom known as Pasai, which lasted until 927/1521 when it was conquered by the Portuguese. Islam gradually spread from northern Sumatra to Malacca, whose ruler Muḥammad Iskandar Shah became famous, although earlier Hindu and Buddhist practices continued to prevail for some time elsewhere in the Malay world. By the time of Sultan Muẓaffar Shah, around 855/1450, Malacca's conversion to Islam had become complete. From there, the religion spread throughout the Malay Peninsula from Trengganu to Kedah and Pahang and into eastern Sumatra itself. In 917/1511 Malacca was conquered by the Portuguese, who thus put an end to its Islamic political power, but the spread of the religion continued unabated.

Soon Acheh rose to become the preeminent center of Muslim power. In 930/1524 'Alī Mughayat Shah captured Pasai from the Portuguese and laid the ground for the political rise of Acheh. The kingdom of Acheh survived into the eleventh/seventeenth century, reaching its peak with Sultan Iskandar Mūdā, who ruled from 1015/1606 to 1046/1637. After him the kingdom declined and gradually fell apart by the end of the century, but Islam itself became ever more entrenched in Sumatra.

During the tenth/sixteenth century, Arab traders and pious men journeying from Malacca to the Philippines brought Islam to Brunei, the Sulu Archipelago, and Mindanao, where there were Muslim sultanates when the

Portuguese and the Spaniards arrived. The Islamic communities that are found in these areas today are remnants of these thriving Islamic kingdoms whose populations have survived despite the great repression against them, especially by the Spaniards in the Philippines, where the Muslims came to be known as the Moros. In Java there are records of the presence of Muslims in the ninth/fifteenth century, although many of these Muslims were not indigenous but Chinese Muslims, who left a profound effect on eastern Java. There is also a tomb in Java of a Muslim preacher, probably a Persian merchant and pious man by the name of Malik Ibrāhīm, dated from 822/1419, bearing witness to the presence of Islam at that time. Gradually, the power of the Mahapahit Hindu kingdom waned, and more people began to embrace Islam. This process was accelerated by the arrival of a number of Islamic preachers who were Sufis from India and who played a major role in the spread of Islam into much of Java. As the Muslims gained greater power, they sought to drive the Portuguese from Malacca but were defeated. They then turned their attention to western Java, which had not yet embraced Islam, and many local battles ensued. Islam penetrated peacefully into the south of central Java through the effort of figures such as Kigede Pandan-Arang, whose lives are interwoven with accounts of miracles and supernatural events and whose tombs are sites of pilgrimage to this day.

The process of Islamization continued in the ninth/fifteenth century eastward to the Moluccas, whose first real Muslim ruler, Zayn al-ʿĀbidīn (891/1486–905/1500), is famous. When the Portuguese arrived, they tried hard to replace Islam with Christianity (even Francis Xavier visited the islands), but they were not successful in weakening the hold of Islam in favor of Christianity in that land. Likewise, Islam spread into southern Borneo and the Celebes Islands where by the eleventh/seventeenth century Makasar had become a center of Islam, resisting for some time the encroaching power of the Dutch.

The eleventh/seventeenth century witnessed the gradual domination by the Dutch of much of what is now known as Indonesia. Even in Java, where the Mataram Empire had succeeded in conquering all the local kingdoms and establishing an empire over nearly the whole of Java, the power of the Dutch and the English increased constantly; battles also continued among various Muslim groups offering different interpretations of Islam. By the thirteenth/ninteenth century the whole of the Malay-speaking world was administratively ruled by the Dutch, the English, and the Spaniards with small groups of Malay Muslims located in Cambodia and Thailand being governed by the rulers of those lands.

Islam among the Malay people, who occupy the present-day countries of Indonesia, Malaysia, Brunei, and the southern Philippines with minorities in other adjacent lands, replaced both the Hindu and Buddhist religions (which began to weaken from the fourth/tenth and fifth/eleventh centuries onward) and local mystical religious practices. Malay became the dominant Islamic language, nourished profusely by Arabic and Persian sources but also drawing from the earlier literary and religious traditions of the Hindu and Buddhist past. Although Malay Muslims remained deeply attached to Islam and the center of Islam in Makkah and made pilgrimage (the *ḥajj*) very central to their religious lives, they integrated many aspects of their religious past into their Islamic culture. The shadow play, using themes of the Hindu epics, the *Rāmāyaṇa* and the *Mahābhārata*, which has even reached the popular art of Turkey, is an example of this synthesis. In the process of Islamicization, which still goes on in the faraway islands, Sufism played a major role from the beginning, and it is to Sufism that one must turn to understand the process whereby Malay was transformed into one of the major languages of the Islamic world.

ISLAM IN CHINA

The history of Islam in China is almost as old as Islam itself, for during the Umayyad period Muslims had reached the coast of China by sea as Arabs had done even before the rise of Islam. Gradually, Muslim communities were founded along the coast while Islam was also reaching China overland through Persian merchants who traveled over the Silk Route, bringing not only goods but also religious ideas with them. There were Islamic communities in many areas of China even during the T'ang period, which ended in the early fourth/tenth century. The Mongol invasion of both Persia and China increased contact between the two worlds, bringing even Islamic astronomy and mathematics to China. Khubilai Khan, the conqueror of China, also brought Persians into his military and civil service. Some of these men settled later in Yunnan, forming an Islamic community. Many important figures of state, including ministers, were Muslims. Gradually Islam spread throughout China, and an indigenous form of Islamic culture with its own distinct artistic and literary forms developed. It is unique in many of its features, having adopted numerous characteristics of the dominant Chinese culture. The degree of participation of Muslims in Chinese life can be seen in the career of the famous admiral of the Ming dynasty, Chang Ho, who carried out ambassadorial duties for the Chinese emperor and compiled a major survey of the Indian Ocean. For the most part, the Ming were lenient toward Muslims, and two of the emperors were even sympathetic to Islam. It was only with the advent of the Ch'ing in the eleventh/seventeenth century that strong opposition to Muslims became a state policy while Chinese armies sought to overrun Muslim lands in central Asia. It is interesting to note that the first Chinese work on Islam by a Chinese Muslim was not written until the eleventh/seventeenth century when Wang Tai-yü wrote an explanatory work on Islam using Confucian language.

His most famous successor, the twelfth/eighteenth-century Wang Liu Chih, continued the approach of seeking to create harmony between Islam and Confucianism while in the same century the Naqshbandi Sufi Ma Ming-hsin strongly opposed Confucianism as well as the Ch'ing dynasty.

During the thirteenth/nineteenth century, several Muslim uprisings took place throughout China, leading to the death of many Muslims and the complete destruction of a number of Islamic communities in such places as Kansu, Tsinghai, and Yunnan. Later during that century, in 1294/1877, China completed its invasion of eastern Turkestan, renaming it Sinkiang. Today the Muslim population of this area, mostly of Uighur and Turkoman origin, constitutes the largest concentration of Muslims in China. Also it is in this province that some of the old sites of Islamic civilization, such as Kashghar, continue as thriving communities, despite the persecution of religion during the Communist period.

The Islamic World in Contemporary History

If we were to look at the map of the Islamic world in the thirteenth/nineteenth century, we would see that aside from an ailing Ottoman world, a weak Persia, an unruly Afghanistan, and the heart of the Arabian Peninsula, the rest of the vast Islamic world was colonized in one form or another by various European powers and in the case of eastern Turkestan, the Chinese. The French ruled over North Africa, some of West and Central Africa, and after the breakup of the Ottoman Empire after World War I, over Syria and Lebanon. The British controlled most of Muslim Africa, Egypt, Muslim India, much of the Malay-speaking world, and after World War I, Iraq, Palestine, Jordan, Aden, and the Persian Gulf Emirates. The Dutch ruled over Java, Sumatra, and most of the other parts of present-day Indonesia with an iron hand. The Russians gradually extended their domination over Muslim areas such as Daghestan within what is considered as Russia today as well as lower Caucasia and central Asia. The Spaniards held on to parts of North Africa while they subdued the Muslims of the southern Philippines. The Portuguese lost their earlier vast holdings in the Indian Ocean and controlled colonies with only small Muslim populations. It was in this context that late in that century movements for the independence of Islamic countries began, incited both by the religious ethos of Islam and by nationalism, which had begun to penetrate the Islamic world to an ever greater degree, becoming even more powerful during the present century.

With the breakup of the Ottoman Empire at the end of World War I, present-day Turkey became an independent nation and the first and only state in the Islamic world to claim secularism as the basis of its state ideology. Its former European territories, many of which had gained independence earlier, all became independent while its Arab provinces to the south, as already mentioned, fell under direct French and British colonial rule. In the Arabian Peninsula the Saudi family, allied religiously to the Wahhābī scholars of Najd, unified Najd and Hejaz in 1926 and founded the Saudi Kingdom as it is known today. Only the rim of the Peninsula from the Arabian Sea to the southern shores of the Persian Gulf remained under the power of the British, who ruled with the help of local shaykhs and princes or *amīrs*. Egypt retained its sovereignty, although it also came under the influence of the British.

At the end of World War II, with the wave of anticolonialism sweeping the world, independence movements began throughout the Islamic world. Soon after the war, India was partitioned into Muslim Pakistan, then the biggest Muslim nation, and the predominantly Hindu India, where a sizable Muslim minority continued to live. Pakistan itself was partitioned in 1971 into Pakistan and Bangladesh. Also, soon after the war, after bloody battles, Indonesia gained its independence from the Dutch, followed by Malaysia. In Africa, the North African Islamic nations fought against French colonialism, gaining their independence in the 1950s, save for Algeria, where the fiercest battle for independence, resulting in the death of a million Algerians, took place. Algeria finally became independent in 1964. Likewise, the Islamic countries of black Africa gained their independence one after another from the British and the French, although the economic influence of the former colonizers continued and persists to this day.

By the 1970s nearly the whole of the Islamic world was at least nominally free save for the lands that were still contained within the Soviet Empire and eastern Turkestan. With the breakup of the Soviet Union in 1989, however, the Muslim lands of both Caucasia and central Asia have now become independent. Only Muslim areas captured by the Russians in the thirteenth/nineteenth century and considered as part of present-day Russia remain under external political domination, as do the Muslim areas within China and the Philippines.

The independence of Islamic countries in modern times has not meant, however, their veritable cultural, economic, and social independence. If anything, after political independence many parts of the Islamic world became culturally even more subjugated than before. Moreover, the very form of the nation-state imposed upon the Islamic world from the West is alien to the nature of Islamic society and is the cause of great internal tension in many areas. There is, on the one hand, the desire on the part of Muslims for Islamic unity vis-à-vis the segmentation of the *ummah* and the division of the Islamic world not only into ancient and well-defined units and zones but often ill-conceived and artificial new ones. There is, on the other hand, the strong desire to preserve the identity and character of the Islamic world before the onslaught of Western civilization, the invasion of whose values continues unabated. The contemporary history of the Islamic world is characterized by these and other tensions, such as that between tradition and modernism, whose very presence proves that not only Islam but also Islamic civilization is still alive. These tensions, often resulting in upheavals and unrest, indicate that, despite the weakening of this civilization because of both external and internal causes during the past two centuries, the Islamic world is a living reality with its own religious and cultural values, which remain very much alive for the more than one billion followers of Islam living in lands stretching from the East to the West.

Schools of Islamic Thought and Their History

Besides legal thought related to the *Sharīʿah* and the field of the principles of jurisprudence (*uṣūl al-fiqh*), which is closely related to the Sacred Law, Islamic religious thought has developed in three main channels or disciplines: *kalām*, usually translated as theology; metaphysics and gnosis (*maʿrifah* or *ʿirfān*); and philosophy and theosophy (*falsafah*, *ḥikmah*). Having discussed the *Sharīʿah* before, we shall leave aside Islamic legal thought, which remains of paramount importance, and deal in this section with the other three disciplines, which have confronted and also interacted with each other in numerous ways during the various epochs of Islamic history.

The Schools of Kalām

The term *kalām* literally means "word" and is said to have come from the Qur'ān itself, which is the "Word of God" (*kalām Allāh*). Its founder is traditionally said to have been ʿAlī ibn Abī Ṭālib, and its function was to provide rational arguments for the defense of the Islamic faith. Altogether, however, the role of *kalām* is not at all as central to Islam as theology is to Christianity, and many Muslim religious thinkers have been opposed to *kalām*, which is a distinct school of Islamic thought among several others. Not everything that would be called theological in Islam is to be found in the schools of *kalām*, and many Muslim intellectual figures who would be called theologians in English were not *mutakallimūn*, that is, scholars of *kalām*.

The earliest Islamic community was caught, like other religious communities, in the throes of disputes over such questions as whether man is saved by faith or works, whether there is free will or determinism, and questions concerning the nature of the sacred text as the Word of God. It was not, however, until the second/eighth century that there grew from the teaching circle of Ḥasan al-Baṣrī (d. 110/728), but in opposition to his teachings, the first distinct school of *kalām*, known as the Muʿtazilite. This school, which dominated the scene for several centuries and produced such famous figures as Abū Isḥāq al-Naẓẓām (d. 231/845) and Abu'l-Hudhayl al-ʿAllāf (d. 226/840), emphasized the use of reason in evaluating the teachings of religion. It has therefore sometimes been referred to as rationalistic, although this term is correct only if understood in the context of the Islamic universe within which the Muʿtazilites functioned.

The Muʿtazilites were known especially for their espousal of five principles: unity (*al-tawḥīd*); justice (*al-ʿadl*); the promise and the threat (*al-waʿd wa'l-waʿīd*); in-between position for a Muslim who is sinful (*al-manzil bayn al-manzilatayn*); and exhortation to perform the good and forbidding to do evil (*al-amr bi'l-maʿrūf wa'l-nahy ʿan al-munkar*). The first two of these principles concern God, whose Attributes of oneness and justice the Muʿtazilites emphasized above all else. The next principle concerns the relation between good and evil actions and the promise of reward and punishment for them in the next world. The fourth principle reflects the Muʿtazilites' way of taking an intermediate position between those who claimed that if a Muslim were to commit any sin, he or she would not only be condemned to hell but could no longer be a member of the Islamic community and those who asserted that if a Muslim had faith, he or she would remain a member of the community even if he or she were to commit sin. The last principle, which is emphasized by many other Islamic schools, asserts that a Muslim must not only follow the teachings of the religion him or herself but also seek to encourage others to perform good acts and prevent them from committing evil.

The Muʿtazilites sought to guard Divine Transcendence in a rational manner, thereby turning God into an abstract unity shorn of His Divine Attributes, whose meaning they refused to discuss for fear of falling into anthropomorphism. Therefore, where the Qur'ān asserts that God is the Hearer and the Seer, the Muʿtazilites claimed that hearing and seeing in this case had nothing to do with what we understand by these Attributes; otherwise we would have an anthropomorphic image of God. Having denied reality to the Divine Attributes independent of the Divine Essence, the Muʿtazilites then denied the eternity of the Qur'ān, which, being the Word of God, is obviously inseparable from the reality of the Divine Names and Attributes. The Muʿtazilites also applied their rational methods to natural philosophy and developed the characteristic doctrine of atomism for which Islamic *kalām* is well known. They also developed a "rational ethics" for which they became famous.

Supported by the early Abbasid caliphs while being strongly opposed by many jurists and scholars of *Ḥadīth,* the Muʿtazilites gradually fell out of favor with even the caliphate in the latter part of the third/ninth century. They practically disappeared from Baghdad by the fourth/tenth century, although they survived for another century or two, as is seen in the monumental Muʿtazilite encyclopedia *al-Mughnī* ("The Satisfying") of the Persian scholar Qāḍī ʿAbd al-Jabbār, who lived in the fifth/eleventh century. But this was like the swan song of Muʿtazilism, which disappeared as a distinct school of thought save in the Yemen, where its tenets were adopted by the Zaydī Shiʿites who continue to live in that land to this day.

It was from this background that there arose the second major school of Sunni *kalām,* called the Ashʿarite, named after its founder Abū'l-Ḥasan al-Ashʿarī (d. 330/941), who originally had been a Muʿtazilite. After a dream of the Prophet, however, al-Ashʿarī turned against the Muʿtazilite theses and sought to curtail the practice of reason in matters of faith. However, he did not oppose the use of reason completely as had been advocated by Imām Aḥmad ibn Ḥanbal and the Ḥanbalites, who to this day stand opposed to all *kalām.* Al-Ashʿarī sought to charter an intermediate course between the extreme positions of groups like the Ḥanbalites and the Muʿtazilites. He asserted the reality of Divine Attributes but insisted that they were not like human attributes. He insisted that the reality of the Qur'ān was uncreated and eternal but that its ink and paper, individual letters and words were created. He also emphasized the possibility of Divine forgiveness of human sins and the possibility of the Prophet interceding for sinners in the other world with the permission of God. Altogether he sought to chart a course between transcendence (*tanzīh*) and immanence (*tashbīh*) and Divine Justice or Rigor and Divine Mercy.

Al-Ashʿarī wrote a number of important works. The most famous as far as *kalām* is concerned are the *Kitāb al-lumaʿ* ("The Book of Light") and *al-Ibānah ʿan uṣūl al-diyānah* ("Elucidation Concerning the Principles of Religion"). His thought gained acceptance rapidly, and such students as Abū Bakr al-Bāqillānī made it well known in Baghdad. Soon it gained the support of the caliphate and the Seljūq Sultanate and spread over much of the Islamic world. In the sixth/twelfth century, the later school of Ashʿarism, which was more philosophical, arose in Khurasan with Imām al-Ḥaramayn al-Juwaynī, the author of *Kitāb al-irshād* ("The Book of Guidance") and his student Abū Ḥāmid Muḥammad al-Ghazzālī, the most famous of all Ashʿarite theologians and the author of numerous famous works on theology, ethics, and Sufism. In the seventh/thirteenth and eighth/fourteenth centuries the major compendia of Ashʿarite *kalām* were composed by such men as Fakhr al-Dīn al-Rāzī, Mīr Sayyid Sharīf al-Jurjānī, ʿAḍud al-Dīn al-Ījī, and Saʿd al-Dīn al-Taftāzānī. The works of these men are taught to this day in Islamic *madrasahs* in the Sunni world along with later recensions and summaries. Since the last century, however, an attempt has been made to renovate and reformulate *kalām* by such men as the Egyptian Muḥammad 'Abduh, and certain Mu'tazilite theses and greater emphasis on the use of reason have come to the fore once again.

As for Shi'ite *kalām*, it has always been closer to *falsafah* and emphasizes greater use of reason. Ismā'īlī *kalām* developed earlier than Twelve-Imām Shi'ite *kalām*, and many of the greatest of the early Ismā'īlī thinkers, to whom we shall turn soon, were at once theologians and philosophers. Twelve-Imām Shi'ite *kalām* received its first explicit formulation in the hands of Khwājah Nasīr al-Dīn al-Ṭūsī (d. 672/1273), whose *Kitāb tajrīd al-i'tiqād* ("The Book of the Catharsis of Doctrines") is both the first and the most important systematic work of Shi'ite *kalām*. Many of the greatest later scholars of Shi'ite *kalām*, such as 'Allāmah Jamāl al-Dīn al-Ḥillī, were its commentators. This school of *kalām* continued to flourish into the Safavid period and is still taught in Shi'ite *madrasahs* in Persia, Iraq, Pakistan, India, and elsewhere.

Schools of Metaphysics and Gnosis (al-Ma'rifah)

A crucial and central dimension of Islamic religious thought, which in fact transcends the formal and external aspects of religion, is metaphysics and gnosis, or what is known in Arabic as *al-ma'rifah* and in Persian as *'irfān*. Metaphysics, as used here, however, means not a branch of philosophy as it has been understood in modern Western philosophy but the supreme science (*al-'ilm al-a'lā*) of the Real. Gnosis must not be confused with the sectarian movement known in Christianity as Gnosticism. Rather, it is a knowledge that illuminates and delivers humans from all bonds of limitation, which is accompanied in Islam with the love of God (*al-maḥabbah*) and is based on the foundation of the fear of God (*al-makhāfah*). This knowledge, which is related to the inner dimension of the Islamic revelation, has its origin in the Qur'ān and the inner teachings of the Prophet and is ultimately none other than the *Ḥaqīqah*, or Truth, alluded to previously. Although in the early centuries of Islam this knowledge was transmitted mostly orally and alluded to in the sayings of the Sufis as well as the Shi'ite Imāms and certain other authorities, gradually it came to be expounded and formulated more openly and systematically. From the seventh/thirteenth century, it came to constitute a distinct intellectual dimension in the Islamic world.

The first Sufis who wrote doctrinal treatises and began to expound metaphysics and gnosis in a more crystallized form were Abū Hāmid Muhammad al-Ghazzālī and 'Ayn al-Quḍāt Hamadānī, both of whom lived in the fifth/eleventh century. In some of his late works, especially the *Mishkāt al-anwār* ("The Niche of Lights"), al-Ghazzālī laid the foundation for Sufi metaphysical treatises. 'Ayn al-Quḍāt's *Tamhīdāt* ("Dispositions") and *Zubdat al-ḥaqā'iq* ("The Best of Truths") represent important texts of metaphysics and what one might call "mystical philosophy," which set the stage for the appearance of the grand expositor of Islamic gnosis and metaphysics, Muḥyī al-Dīn ibn 'Arabī.

Ibn 'Arabī, who is sometimes referred to as the greatest master (*al-Shaykh al-akbar*), hailed from Murcia but lived his later life in Damascus, where he died in 638/1240. And it was mostly in the eastern lands of Islam that his influence, as far as doctrinal Sufism is concerned, is seen most strongly over the centuries, though his spiritual influence can be detected throughout the Islamic world from Morocco to Malaysia. The most prolific of all Sufi authors, Ibn 'Arabī composed more than eight hundred works. The most monumental, *al-Futūḥāt al-makkiyyah* ("The Meccan Revelation or Illuminations"), consists of some 560 chapters dealing with all the Islamic esoteric sciences and the inner meaning of the Islamic rites. But it is his best-known masterpiece, *Fuṣūṣ al-ḥikam* ("Bezels of Wisdom"), that is like the bible of Islamic metaphysics and gnosis. Consisting of twenty-seven chapters, each dedicated to a prophet or aspect of the Universal Logos, the book is considered in Sufi circles to have been inspired by the Prophet of Islam, as claimed by the author. Over the centuries, more than 120 commentaries expounding the many levels of its meaning have been written on it.

The grand expositor of the doctrinal teachings of Ibn 'Arabī, who in fact left his own imprint upon the later interpretations of the master in the east, was his stepson Ṣadr al-Dīn al-Qūnawī who was the first commentator on the *Fuṣūṣ*. Later authorities in Islamic gnosis—such as Mu'ayyid al-Dīn al-Jandī, 'Abd al-Razzāq Kāshānī, Dā'ūd al-Qayṣarī, 'Abd al-Raḥmān Jāmī, Ismā'īl Ḥaqqī, 'Abd al-Salām al-Nabulusī, and others from the seventh/thirteenth to the twelfth/eighteenth century—were to write other well-known commentaries, a tradition that has continued to our own day. Also Sufi and philosophical figures such as Mullā Ṣadrā and Mullā Muḥsin Fayḍ Kāshānī in eleventh/seventeenth-century Persia, and Shaykh Aḥmad Sirhindī and Shah Walī Allāh of Delhi, who lived in India during the tenth/sixteenth and twelfth/eighteenth centuries, respectively, continued to add to the body of works dealing with Islamic gnosis, even though they were not all simple followers of Ibn 'Arabī; some, like Sirhindī, wrote against certain theses associated with the Ibn 'Arabian school.

Nevertheless, Ibn 'Arabī is the central figure in the intellectual and doctrinal exposition of Islamic metaphysics and gnosis. Over the centuries, and especially during the second half of Islamic history, this dimension of Islamic religious thought has been of great importance. It has been, in fact, the dominant element in Islamic religious thought in such lands as Muslim India and even the Malay world, where the greatest Sufi thinker and writer of that area, Ḥamzah Fanṣūrī, was the inheritor and expositor of Ibn 'Arabian teachings. This dimension of Islamic religious thought, singularly neglected by Western scholarship until recently, is at last receiving the attention it deserves in the West while it continues as an important aspect of Islamic intellectual life even today.

The major fields dealt with by this type of Islamic religious thought are primarily metaphysics but also cosmology, psychology, and what one might call traditional anthropology. Treatises of the authors mentioned and numerous others deal primarily with the nature of Reality, which they considered to be One. Most of them were followers of the school of "the transcendent unity of being" (*waḥdat al-wujūd*), which claims that these cannot ultimately be but one Being and one Reality, multiplicity constituting the many "mirrors of nothingness" in which that one Reality is reflected. However, a number of Sufi metaphysicians, such as 'Alā' al-Dawlah Simnānī and Sirhindī, did not accept this formulation and spoke of the "unity of consciousness" (*waḥdat al-shuhūd*) while preserving a clear distinction between the Being of the Creator and the being of the created. The school of gnosis also deals extensively with the cosmos as the theater of theophanies, with the levels of human consciousness, and the structure of the psyche in relation to the Spirit. It also considered man in his cosmic and even metacosmic reality or as the universal man (*al-insān al-kāmil*). This doctrine was formulated in perhaps its most famous version by 'Abd al-Karīm al-Jīlī, the eighth/fourteenth-century Sufi who was the author of the most famous treatise bearing this title. No wonder then that Islamic metaphysics and gnosis reacted on numerous levels with other modes of Islamic thought, such as theology and philosophy, while providing in itself the highest form of knowledge concerning the nature of things and, above all, of that Reality which is the Origin and End of all that exists.

Schools of Islamic Philosophy and Theosophy

Islamic philosophy (*al-falsafah*) was born as a result of the meditation of those who lived in the intellectual universe dominated by the reality of the Qur'ānic revelation upon the philosophical ideas of the Hellenic and Hellenistic worlds and to some extent the philosophical heritage of India and pre-Islamic Persia. Islamic philosophy is not simply the conduit of Greek philosophy for the West, although it performed an important role in this respect in the fifth/eleventh and sixth/twelfth centuries. Nor is it simply Aristotle in Arabic. Islamic philosophy is essentially "prophetic philosophy," that is, a kind of philosophy that is based on a worldview in which revelation is a living reality and a source, or rather the supreme source, of knowledge and certitude. It is a philosophy born of the synthesis of Abrahamic monotheism and Greek philosophy, giving rise to a type of philosophical thought that was to wield great influence in both the Jewish and Christian worlds. Although opposed by proponents of *kalām*, Islamic philosophy must be considered as a major type of Islamic religious thought, and one can no more deny its significance for Islamic thought than one can negate the importance of Maimonides for Jewish thought or St. Thomas Aquinas for Christian thought. In contrast to the view held by so many Western students of Islamic philosophy, this philosophy is part and parcel of the totality of the Islamic intellectual universe without which one cannot gain full understanding of that universe.

Activity in Islamic philosophy began in the third/ninth century in Baghdad as more and more Greek and Syriac philosophical texts, especially those belonging to the school of Aristotle and his Neoplatonic commentators, became available in Arabic, transforming Arabic into one of the major philosophical languages and a repository for a great deal of the philosophy and science of the Graeco-Alexandrian antiquity. The first outstanding Islamic philosopher, Abū Ya'qūb al-Kindī (d. ca. 260/873), sought to create a synthesis between Islamic teachings and Aristotelian and also Neoplatonic philosophy, laying the foundation for the *mashshā'ī*, or Islamic Peripatetic School, which is therefore not purely Aristotelian as the name might indicate.

It remained for the second great figure of this school, Abū Naṣr al-Fārābī (d. 339/950) from Khurasan, to complete the synthesis that al-Kindī was aiming to achieve. Al-Fārābī not only commented upon the logical works of Aristotle and Porphyry but also attempted to unify the political ideas of Plato with Islamic political ideas and harmonize the views of Plato and Aristotle, who for Muslims "included" Plotinus, whose *Enneads* the Muslims thought was written by Aristotle and which they referred to as *The Theology of Aristotle*. Many consider al-Fārābī, who was called the Second Teacher after Aristotle, and whom the Muslims called the First Teacher, to be the founder not only of Islamic political philosophy but of Islamic philosophy itself.

It was, however, Ibn Sīnā (d. 428/1037), the most influential of all Islamic philosophers within the Islamic world, who brought the *mashshā'ī* school to its peak of maturity and perfection. His *magnum opus*, the *Kitāb al-shifā'* ("The Book of Healing"), is a monumental encyclopedia of both philosophy and the natural and mathematical sciences, which exerted vast influence in the Islamic world and even among Jewish and Christian thinkers. There, as well as in shorter works, Ibn Sīnā develops ontology as the foundation of philosophy and has been called by some modern scholars the first "philosopher of being" who left his indelible mark upon all medieval philosophy. It was he who first formulated the distinction between necessity and contingency, equating the Necessary Being with God and contingency with all of creation. The themes of the relationship between faith and reason, creation and emanation, spiritual and physical resurrection, rational and revealed knowledge—and numerous other subjects of religious philosophy created by the confrontation between the two worldviews of Semitic monotheism and Greek philosophical speculation—were treated by Ibn Sīnā. He did this in a manner that was to exercise a great influence on many types of Islamic religious thought, including *kalām*, whose proponents such as al-Ghazzālī and Fakhr al-Dīn al-Rāzī singled out Ibn Sīnā in their criticism of *mashshā'ī* philosophy.

Toward the end of his life, Ibn Sīnā wrote of "The Oriental Philosophy" (*al-ḥikmat al-mashriqiyyah*), which he considered to be for the "intellectual elite" while the *mashshā'ī* philosophy was for the common public. This "Oriental Philosophy," of which only fragments survive, is based more upon intellection than ratiocination and views philosophy as a means of transcending the limits of our human condition rather than providing a scheme of things that is rationally satisfying. This dimension of Ibn Sīnā's philosophy was pursued two centuries later by Suhrawardī, the founder of the School of Illumination (*ishrāq*), and had a profound influence on the later history of Islamic philosophy.

Parallel with the rise of Islamic Peripatetic philosophy was the gradual growth and development of a more "esoteric" school of philosophy associated with Ismā'īlism. As far as various schools of pre-Islamic philosophy are concerned, the Ismā'īlī school of philosophy was more interested in Hermeticism, Pythagoreanism, and certain strands of older Iranian philosophical and cosmological thought than in Aristotelianism. Starting with the enigmatic and anonymous *Umm al-Kitāb* ("The Mother of Books"), this philosophy grew rapidly in the third/ninth and fourth/tenth centuries with the appearance of such figures as Abū Ḥātam al-Rāzī, Ḥamīd al-Dīn al-Kirmānī, the Brethren of Purity, and Nāsir-i Khrusraw, the fifth/eleventh-century poet and thinker, who was perhaps the greatest of the Ismā'īlī philosophers. The school continued up to the Mongol invasion, when it went more or less underground in Persia, while it flourished in Yemen and during the last few centuries, in the Indian subcontinent.

Ismā'īlī philosophy, based on the principle of *ta'wīl*, or spiritual hermeneutics, saw authentic philosophy as being identical with the inner teachings of revealed religion, which is transmitted by the imām, and was especially attracted to the esoteric dimensions of the thought of antiquity. It was one of the Islamic schools of thought most receptive to philosophical speculation and, although refuted by Sunni theologians as well as the Twelve-Imām Shi'ites, it played an important intellectual role in early Islamic history, especially during the Fāṭimid period.

Meanwhile, in the eastern lands of Islam, following the domination of the Seljūqs, the attack against *falsafah*, particularly the Peripatetic school, by scholars of *kalām* increased. It was during this period that the celebrated criticisms of *mashshā'ī* philosophy were made by al-Shahristānī, al-Ghazzālī, and Fakhr al-Dīn al-Rāzī. Among these, the attack of al-Ghazzālī—contained in several of his works, especially his *Tahāfut al-falāsifah* ("The Incoherence of Philosophers")—is the best known, although the critique by al-Rāzī of Ibn

Sīnā's *al-Ishārāt wa'l-tanbīhāt* ("The Book of Directives and Remarks") had greater influence on later Islamic philosophy in Persia and other eastern lands of Islam. Al-Ghazzālī criticized the Peripatetics on several accounts, especially what appeared to be their denial of the created nature of the world, God's knowledge of particulars, and bodily resurrection. His powerful pen was able to silence the school of *falsafah* in the eastern lands of Islam for a century and a half during which Islamic philosophy flourished in Spain.

The fourth/tenth to the sixth/twelfth centuries mark the golden age of Islamic philosophy in Spain, where the first major figure was the rather enigmatic philosopher Ibn Masarrah (d. 319/931), who was interested in both philosophy and Sufism. The wedding between philosophy and mysticism characterizes many of the later figures of Spain, such as Ibn Ḥazm (d. 454/1063), one of the greatest of Muslim Spanish intellectual figures who was at once theologian and philosopher; Ibn al-Sīd of Badajoz (d. 521/1127), who was interested in Pythagorean numerical symbolism; Ibn Bājjah (d. 533/1138), the first full-fledged Spanish *mashshā'ī* philosopher, whose *Tadbīr al-mutawaḥḥid* ("Regimen of the Solitary") is outwardly a work of political philosophy and inwardly a treatise on the perfection of the soul; and Ibn Ṭufayl (d. 580/1185), the author of the famous *Ḥayy ibn Yaqẓān* ("Living Son of the Awake")—known extensively in the West as *Philosophus autodidactus*—which deals with the question of the ability of the inner intellect to reach ultimate knowledge.

The most famous and influential of Muslim philosophers of Spain, however, was Abu'l-Walīd ibn Rushd (d. 595/1198), known in the West as Averroes, whose influence on Western intellectual life was even greater than on later Islamic thought. At once chief religious authority in Islamic Law and judge (*qāḍī*) in Cordova and a highly respected physician, Ibn Rushd was also the purest of the Muslim Peripatetics as far as following the doctrines of Aristotle is concerned. He wrote numerous commentaries on the works of the Stagirite and became known in the West as "*the* Commentator" to whom even Dante refers in the *Divine Comedy*. He also wrote on Islamic political philosophy and the question of the relation between faith and reason, while seeking to answer al-Ghazzālī's criticism of Islamic philosophy in his *Tahāfut al-tahāfut* ("Incoherence of the Incoherence").

Although Ibn Rushd's ideas, as interpreted in another way than can be seen in the original Arabic, set the intellectual scene ablaze in Western Europe, he did not have a great following in the Islamic world. With rapid political changes in the western lands of Islam, Islamic philosophy began to wane as a distinct school of thought in that area, becoming merged into the seas of either *kalām* or *ma'rifah*, so that only a handful of notable philosophers, such as the mystical philosopher Ibn Sab'īn and the great philosopher of history Ibn Khaldūn, arose in the Maghrib or western lands of Islam during the period following the death of Ibn Rushd. As for the east, philosophy was resurrected by Suhrawardī, Naṣīr al-Dīn al-Ṭusī, and other figures on the basis of the teachings of Ibn Sīnā rather than the more rationalistic and Aristotelian Ibn Rushd.

During the lifetime of Ibn Rushd, a remarkable intellectual figure named Shihāb al-Dīn Suhrawardī (d. 587/1191) arose in Persia. Although he was killed at a young age in Aleppo on the accusation of heresy (but in reality because of entanglement in the politicoreligious struggles of Syria at that time), before his death, he founded a new school of philosophy called *al-ishrāq*, or illumination. Based not only on ratiocination but also on illumination or intellectual vision, this school sought to integrate the wisdom of ancient Persia as well as Greece within the bosom of Islamic gnosis and on the basis of the earlier philosophy of Ibn Sīnā, which Suhrawardī considered to be necessary for the training of the mind but not sufficient, since authentic philosophy also requires the purification of the mind and the heart, making possible the receiving of illumination. Suhrawardī returned philosophy to the status it has always had in Oriental civilizations, namely, a wisdom that is intimately related to virtue and the manner in which one lives. His masterpiece, the *Ḥikmat al-ishrāq* ("The Theosophy of the Orient of Light"), is like the bible of the school of *ishrāq*, which means at once illumination and the light that shines from the Orient, which, in the symbolic geography of Suhrawardī, is not the geographical Orient but the Orient or Origin of the world of existence itself. Suhrawardī, who wedded philosophy to mystical vision and intellectual intuition, created what came to be known as *al-ḥikmat al-ilāhiyyah* (literally *theo-sophia* or theosophy), which exercised the deepest influence on later Islamic thought in both Persia and the Indian subcontinent, not to speak of the effect it had on certain schools of Jewish and Christian thought. The school of *ishrāq* remains a living reality to this day wherever Islamic philosophy and theosophy survive and flourish and has witnessed a revival during the past few decades.

In the seventh/thirteenth century, Naṣīr al-Dīn Ṭūsī (d. 672/1273) responded to the attacks of Fakhr al-Dīn al-Rāzī and revived the philosophy of Ibn Sīnā. During the next few centuries the four schools of *mashshā'ī* philosophy, *ishrāqī* theosophy, *kalām*, and Ibn 'Arabian metaphysics, or *ma'rifah*, reacted in various ways with each other, producing many notable figures who sought to synthesize the tenets of some of these schools. It was on the basis of this movement toward synthesis that the School of Isfahan was established by Mīr Dāmād in the tenth/sixteenth century in Persia. The student of the founder, Ṣadr al-Dīn Shīrāzī (d. 1050/1640), brought this school to its peak of perfection and created still another intellectual perspective in Islam called "the transcendent theosophy" (*al-ḥikmat al-muta'āliyah*). In his numerous works, especially his monumental *Al-Asfār al-arba'ah* ("The Four Journeys"), he created a masterly synthesis of the four schools mentioned previously. He emphasized that the three major paths open to humans to attain knowledge—namely, revelation, illumination, and ratiocination—lead ultimately to the same goal, and he created a synthesis based on all three methods of knowing. He gave perhaps what became the most satisfying response to the question of the relation between faith and reason in Islamic philosophical thought and produced the most important Qur'ānic commentaries ever written by any Islamic philosopher.

Mullā Ṣadrā became well known in both Persia and India. In his own homeland his teachings were resurrected in the thirteenth/nineteenth century by such philosophers as Mullā 'Alī Nūrī and Ḥājjī Mullā Hādī Sabziwārī and are still very much alive in both Persia and Iraq. As for the Indian subcontinent, many figures in the twelfth/eighteenth and thirteenth/nineteenth centuries, such as Shah Walī Allāh of Delhi and Mawlānā Maḥmūd Jawnpūrī, were deeply influenced by him. He remains very much of a living intellectual figure as Islamic philosophy continues its traditional life in the eastern lands of Islam and becomes resurrected in certain parts of the Arab world, especially Egypt, where Islamic philosophy was revived in the last century by Jamāl al-Dīn Astrābādī, known usually as al-Afghānī, who was a follower of the School of Mullā Ṣadrā before his migration from Persia to the Ottoman world.

In studying the Islamic religion, it is important to remember the long history, diversity of perspectives, and continuous vitality of the various schools of Islamic thought. Far from having died out in what the West calls the Middle Ages, these schools have had a continuous life to this day, although a particular school may have died out in a particular region during a certain period. To understand the total reality of Islam as religion and also the interactions of Islam with the modern world, it is necessary to be aware of this rich intellectual tradition of a religious character that is over a millennium old and contains some of the most profound meditations upon God, the universe, and human beings in their existential situation, in a universe in which human beings are condemned to seek meaning by virtue of being human.

Islam in the Contemporary World

Traditional Islam Today

Studies made of Islam in the contemporary world usually concentrate on various types of modernism or revivalism, whereas the majority of Muslims continue to live in the traditional Islamic world despite all the attacks made against the traditional point of view in modern times. To understand

Islam today, it is first important to realize that the histories of different religions do not all follow the same trajectory. Christianity had its Protestant Reformation in the sixteenth century and the *aggiornamento* in the Catholic church in the 1960s. Judaism has also been witness to the rise of both the Reform and Conservative schools, at least in the West. Islam, however, has not undergone nor is it likely to undergo in any appreciable degree the same kinds of transformation either juridically or theologically. Its religious life and thought remain for the most part within the framework of orthodoxy and tradition. The modernism and so-called fundamentalism that are evident in certain sectors of Islamic society and in certain lands have caused traditional Islamic life to wither but have been unable to create any appreciable theological worldview that could challenge the traditional one.

The vast majority of Muslims still practice the traditional rites described previously, and the rhythm of their lives is punctuated by events related to Islam as traditionally understood. Moreover, the traditional Islamic sciences of Qur'ānic commentary, *Ḥadīth*, jurisprudence, and the like continue as they have done over the centuries despite the devastations brought upon the traditional Islamic education system (the *madrasahs*) in many lands. The '*ulamā'*, or religious scholars, continue to wield their authority in the realm of religion and in some lands over political life as well. Likewise, despite being forbidden or circumscribed in certain areas, the Ṣufi orders continue in strength in many parts of the Islamic world. During the thirteenth/nineteenth century, when certain elements of Islamic society were emphasizing the importance of modernism, it was primarily the Sufis who opposed modernism avidly. And the events of the past half century have only confirmed their diagnosis of the nature of the modern world. If anything, they are stronger now than they were at the beginning of this century, especially among the educated in many lands, such as Egypt.

Until a few decades ago, however, the various contemporary strands of traditional Islam—ranging from law to theology, philosophy to art, and literature to Sufism—continued to be expressed in a traditional manner, which became less and less comprehensible to those Muslims who were products of Western educational institutions either within the Islamic world or in the West itself. Western scholarship almost completely neglected contemporary traditional Islamic modes of thought, concentrating its studies on the so-called reformers and modernists. In recent decades, however, the scene has begun to change. Traditional Islam has begun to express itself not only in the contemporary medium of Arabic, Persian, Turkish, and other Islamic languages—to be more accessible to the modern educated classes—but also in European languages, especially English and French, which have become the main languages of intellectual discourse for many Muslims themselves from lands such as Pakistan, Bangladesh, and North Africa, lands which had experienced a long period of colonial rule. Western scholars have also begun to pay greater attention to traditional Islam despite the still-prevalent confusion in the West between traditional Islam and what Westerners have come to call "Islamic fundamentalism."

Traditional Islam is like the mountain on whose slopes various geological processes, such as weathering and sedimentation created by streams, take place. It is these processes that can be compared to modernism, "fundamentalism," and the like and that are usually studied by scholars accustomed to the study of change and oblivious to the vast, permanent mountain on whose slopes these changes are taking place. To understand Islam fully in the contemporary world, it is first necessary to comprehend the living nature of traditional Islam, to consider the powerful hold of the worldview of the Qur'ān on the souls and minds of the vast majority of Muslims, and to grasp the truth that the majority still believes in the immutability of the Qur'ān as the Word of God, in the reality of the perfect model of the Prophet to be emulated in one's life, in the validity of the *Sharī'ah*, and for those who follow the path of inwardness, the efficacy of the permanent and ever renewed teachings of the *Ṭarīqah* or Sufism.

Moreover, in many domains ranging from law to the natural sciences, and from abstract philosophical and theological thought to art and architecture, there is an attempt throughout the Islamic world to revive and resuscitate the traditional teachings, to live and think more fully Islamically rather than emulate foreign models. This deep yearning also manifests itself on the sociopolitical level and relates traditional Islam on this domain to certain forms of revivalism and so-called fundamentalism, although traditional Islam never condones the use of foreign ideological means to bring about such an end or to reduce religion to ideology. Traditional Islam, while remaining the central religious reality within the Islamic world, is in fact engaged in a battle not only against modernism but also against those forms of revivalism that employ completely non-Islamic categories of thought and action in the name of Islam and make use of distinctly non-Islamic means to justify what they consider to be Islamic ends.

Millennialism

Although the principle of millennialism is part of traditional Islam, its manifestation in history in its specifically Islamic form as Mahdiism has usually stood against traditional institutions; later on its effects have been integrated in most cases into the traditional structure. In the early thirteenth/nineteenth century when, following the Napoleonic invasion of Egypt, the heartland of the Islamic world became fully aware of the dominating power of the West, a number of millennialist movements took place from Muslim West Africa to India. Such famous charismatic leaders as Ismā'īl dan

Fadio in West Africa, 'Abd al-Karīm in the Atlas mountains of North Africa, and the grand Sanūsī in Cyrenaica had a millennialist dimension to their mission, and the Mahdī of the Sudan, mentioned earlier, claimed directly to be the promised Mahdī. Religious movements such as those of Sayyid Muḥammad and Bahā' Allāh in Persia and Ghulām Aḥmad in what is today Pakistan, movements that broke away from Islamic orthodoxy, were also of Mahdiist origin.

This wave gradually died out in the late thirteenth/nineteenth century to rise again during the past two decades following the political independence of Muslim nations without corresponding cultural independence. The very subjugation of Islam, despite outward political independence, which had raised many people's hopes, led to an atmosphere of expectation of divine intervention in human history. This eschatological atmosphere which characterizes Islamic millennialism, or Mahdiism, was present during the Iranian Revolution of 1979. It was the determining factor in 1979 in the capturing of the grand mosque in Makkah by a group of Saudis whose leader claimed to be the Mahdī. It also manifested itself in a strong Mahdiist movement in Northern Nigeria. Nor has this atmosphere of expectation of eschatological events associated with the coming of the Mahdī disappeared. On the contrary, it is one of the important aspects of the reality of Islam in the contemporary world, as it is of Judaism, Christianity, and Hinduism, not to speak of the primal religions of the North American continent.

Revivalism and "Fundamentalism"

The past few years have also been witness to a great upsurge of Islam upon the political plane, which can be seen in the Iranian Revolution of 1979; the rise of Islamic activism in Lebanon and among the Palestinians; the strengthening of revivalist movements in Egypt and Algeria; the increase of power of Islamic parties in Pakistan, Malaysia, and Indonesia; and the ever-increasing strength of Islamic forces, even in the outwardly secular state that is Turkey. Due to a great misunderstanding of these movements in the West, they have usually been grouped together under the name of fundamentalism, a word originally taken from an American Protestant context and applied to Islam and even to other religions.

As far as Islam is concerned, there are many varying types of religious activity, with very different natures, that, unfortunately, are usually assembled under the category bearing the name of "fundamentalism." We use the term here only because it has now become so prevalent. There exists in the Islamic world the widely prevalent desire, shared by the great majority of Muslims, to preserve their religious and cultural identity, to reapply the Divine Law that was replaced by European legal codes during the colonial period in many Islamic lands, to draw the various parts of the Islamic world and the Islamic people (*al-ummah*) closer together, and to reassert the intellectual and artistic traditions of Islam. These widely held wishes and the impulse to implement them must not be identified purely and simply as "fundamentalism." Rather, most people who share these ideals are traditional Muslims.

Then there is an older puritanical and often rationalistic reform movement, or rather set of movements, that seek to return to a strict application of the *Sharīʿah* while opposing both Western encroachment and the intellectual, artistic, and mystical traditions of Islam itself, in the name of an early puritan Islam considered to have been lost by later generations. To this category belongs the Wahhābī movement, which, in alliance with the Saudi family, finally captured Arabia during this century and which remains dominant in that land today. Such movements as the Salafiyyah of Syria and Egypt and the Muḥammadiyyah of Indonesia are related in their perspectives to Wahhābism and need to be mentioned here. One can also include in this type of fundamentalism the Ikhwān al-muslimīn founded in Egypt in the 1920s by Ḥasan al-Bannā', a movement that is still strong in many Islamic countries, especially Egypt and the Sudan, and the Jamāʿat-i islāmī of Pakistan founded by Mawlānā Mawdūdī after the partition of the Indian subcontinent. The latter continues to be a strong religiopolitical force to be reckoned with in Pakistan as well as through its offshoots in Bangladesh and among the Muslims of India. All of these movements share in their desire to re-Islamicize society and to apply the *Sharīʿah* fully but have usually been peaceful in their methods of achieving this, except in the case of Wahhābism during its earlier history, when it came to power as a result of its political union with the Saudi family in the Najd.

Another type of fundamentalism of a very different nature, which has come to the fore during the past two decades and especially since the Iranian Revolution of 1979, is more activist, revolutionary, and radical than the type associated with Wahhābism. This type of revolutionary movement, with which the very notion of "fundamentalism" is mostly associated in the West today, is seen not only in Iran, where it came to power through the revolution guided by Ayatollah Khomeini, but also among various Islamic groups in the Lebanon and among Palestinians, in certain radical circles in Egypt, in the Sudan, and in small circles in many other Islamic countries. Although strongly opposed to the West, this type of "fundamentalism" often incorporates certain theses of nineteenth- and twentieth-century European political thought, including the very notion of revolution. It politicizes Islam not in the traditional sense but in a way that is an innovation in Islamic history. Also, in contrast to the earlier form of fundamentalism, which was opposed not only to Western culture but also to Western technology, this more revolutionary "fundamentalism" is favorable to the adoption of Western science and technology and seeks to gain access to power by whatever means possible. Fed by resentment of Western domination over the Islamic world, which continues in the economic and cultural fields despite the nominal political independence of Islamic countries, this type of "fundamentalism" hopes to provide a solution for the problems of Islamic society by a return to Islamic norms and practices. In doing so, however, it often adopts certain Western theses and value judgments against which it has rebelled. Its power is a reality in the Islamic world, but it is not as great as portrayed in most Western media, where all attempts to retain or return to Islamic principles and teachings are banded together as revolutionary and violent "fundamentalism."

Modernist Tendencies

Nearly every activity in the Islamic world during the past century and a half that has had a modernizing character is in some way related to the modernist tendencies in Islam under consideration here. These range from the introduction of Western-inspired nationalism to the adoption of Western technology and the introduction of the Western type of education into various Islamic countries. It is not possible to deal with such subjects here, but their religious implications must not be forgotten. Here, we can only say a few words about modernist tendencies directly related to Islam as a religion.

Already in the thirteenth/nineteenth century, when the impact of European domination began to be felt in the heartland of the Islamic world, there appeared those who believed that the survival of Islam depended upon its modernization. In the Ottoman Empire, edicts were passed to modernize the Islamic Law of the land, and similar measures soon took place in Persia as well as in lands under European colonial rule. In such a central land as Egypt, a number of thinkers such as Muḥammad ʿAbduh sought to modernize Islamic theology through greater introduction of the use of reason while ʿAbduh's teacher, Jamāl al-Dīn Astrābādī (known as al-Afghānī), fought against traditional Islamic political institutions in an attempt to unify the Islamic world. In India, the project to modernize Islamic education was begun by Sayyid Aḥmad Khān, and in Persia, European political ideas finally led to the Constitutional Revolution of 1323/1906 and the establishment of the first parliament in the Islamic world that had the power to pass laws but, at least in principle, with the consent of the religious authorities, or *ʿulamā'*.

During this century the modernist tendencies have continued along lines established in the thirteenth/nineteenth century but with many new developments. In Turkey, Zia Gökalp became the intellectual defender of the secularism proposed by Ataturk when he put an end to the Ottoman caliphate in 1922. In Muslim India, Muḥammad Iqbāl, perhaps the most gifted of the so-called Islamic reformers of this century, not only proposed the foundation of an Islamic homeland, leading to the formation of Pakistan, but also espoused the cause of Islamic revival through his moving poetry written mostly in Persian but also in Urdu. His prose works, however, reveal much more than his poetry how deeply he was influenced by Western philosophy, especially nineteenth-century German thought.

After World War II, a number of modernists in the Islamic world, particularly in Persia and the Arab world, turned to Marxism. Both Islamic and Arab socialism came into vogue and continued until the downfall of the Soviet Union. Also, a number of Muslim scholars who had studied in the West fell under the sway of Western orientalism and began to criticize traditional Islamic scholarship concerning Qur'ānic commentary, *Ḥadīth*, the *Sharī'ah*, and other basic Islamic disciplines. Movements grew up in such countries as Pakistan to repudiate the authenticity of the *Ḥadīth* and in the Sudan to reinterpret Islam according to only the Makkan period of revelation. A number of Muslim modernists have also sought to criticize traditional Islamic thought on the basis of structuralism, existentialism, and other prevalent schools of Western thought, whereas others have attempted to "synthesize" Islam with Marxism.

Although these modern tendencies were strong and continue to be present despite their relative eclipse during the past few years, they have not had any appreciable impact on Islamic religious thought as such and have not brought about the "protestant" movement within Islam that so many Western scholars had predicted and wished for. The modernist impact on the Islamic world has come much more through the introduction of modern modes of living and thinking, which penetrate the Islamic world through a thousand channels from modern educational institutions to films.

Modernist tendencies have been confronted during the past few decades not only by the so-called fundamentalism, which often seems to be of less intellectual substance than the thought processes and works of the modernists, but also by the revival of traditional Islamic thought by those who are as well versed with the modern world as the modernists themselves. Islam in the contemporary world presents, therefore, a picture of a powerful living faith with its still-living intellectual and spiritual tradition confronted with challenges of a materially more powerful secular world, which inhabits not only the land outside its borders but its own living space. Various forces are at play in a living reality that is not monolithic but that is still dominated, to a far greater degree than is the case in the contemporary West, in all of its schools and tendencies by the message of revelation and religion. Islam today is a living reality faced with multiple problems and challenges but still deeply anchored in the Islamic tradition and the truths that have guided its destiny since the descent of the Qur'ānic revelation more than fourteen centuries ago.

Islam and Other Religions

The Historical Encounter of Islam and Other Religions

Islam is the only religion that has had direct historical contact before modern times with nearly all other families of religions. Born in Arabia and destined to occupy the middle belt of the world from the western Mediterranean to Southeast Asia, Islam encountered Judaism and Christianity in its birthplace and has had continuous contact with these other members of the Abrahamic tradition throughout its history. Islam even came face to face with smaller religious groups belonging to the Semitic world, such as the Sabaeans or Mandaeans who survive to this day in southern Iraq and Persia. Likewise, it came into direct contact with such syncretic religions as those of the Harraneans, who had combined certain elements of the ancient Babylonian religion with the more esoteric elements of Greek religion as well as Hermeticism and Gnosticism.

In spreading into Persia, Islam met all the Iranian religions from Zoroastrianism and Manichaeism to Zurvanism and Mazdakism, including Mithraism. Early Islamic texts contain many translations from these religions, to the extent that Arabic remains to this day an important source for the study of the religions of the Sassanid period. As Zoroastrianism, Manichaeism, and even Mazdakism survived for centuries in a Persia that was already Islamic, many Islamic religious movements occurred with elements taken from these more ancient religions, while polemic against Manichaeism remained a main concern of many Muslim theologians for several centuries in the same way that it became central to the interests of many early Christian theologians, especially St. Augustine.

Islam also encountered the Indian religions in Persia itself as well as in Sindh and other provinces of India proper. It must be remembered that there were many Buddhists in the eastern provinces of the Sassanid Empire, which can be seen in the fact that Buddhism reached China through these provinces and that to this day major Buddhist sites survive in Afghanistan. Some historians have even claimed that the famous Persian family of Barmakids, who were ministers to the Abbasids, was originally Buddhist and not Zoroastrian. As for Hinduism, some of its teachings were to be found in Jundishapur in present-day Khuzistan in southern Persia while Muslims naturally encountered Hindus in their spread through

Sindh. In the fourth/tenth century, al-Bīrūnī provided some of the most important documentations on medieval Hinduism in his *India* and translated the *Patañjali Yoga* into Arabic, and popular stories of Hindu and Buddhist origin had become common among Muslims. Many Muslim commentators of the Qur'ān, in fact, have written that the Prophet *Dhu'l-kifl* referred to in the Qur'ān is the Buddha. The Arabic version of the tale of animals, *Pañcatantra,* known to Muslims as *al-Kalīlah wa'l-Dimnah,* had become very popular in Arabic-speaking lands and through its later translation into Persian in Persia itself. It was from the Pahlavi version of this tale that the original Arabic translation had been made in the seventh/eighth century. It is also noteworthy to mention that from the seventh/thirteenth century onward, many of the Hindu classics were translated into Persian and that the West came to know of the *Upaniṣads* for the first time early in the nineteenth century through the Latin translation of A. Anquetil Dupérron, made from the Persian translation of the *Upaniṣads* and not directly from the Sanskrit.

Islam also encountered Shamanism, both Turkic and Mongolian, north of its border and the Chinese religions not only in China but also within its own eastern lands as a result of the transmission of ideas as well as merchandise along the Silk Route. Of course it was mostly after the Mongol invasion that knowledge of matters Chinese increased dramatically in Persia. Of the major areas of the Far Eastern world only Japan and Korea remained a *terra incognita* for Muslims until modern times, although even these areas were known to Chinese Muslims without this knowledge having any appreciable influence on the central lands of the Islamic world.

Finally, we must mention the contact of Muslims with the primal African religions south of the Sahara, with local religions of Java and Sumatra and other archaic forms of religion that were still alive when Islam spread into their area. Religious ideas and images from such sources penetrated into the consciousness of Muslims through travelogues, folk tales, and stories, although the teachings of such religions were not usually confronted intellectually and theologically, as we see in the case of the Semitic, Iranian, or Indian religions.

Altogether it can be said that except for the religions of the natives of the American continent and Australia, there were few living forms of religion that Islam did not meet during its historical development in the Eurasian landmass and Africa. Thus, the idea of functioning in a world with many religions of diverse natures and forms became part and parcel of the classical worldview of Islam. In contrast to Western Christianity, Islam did not have to await the advent of modernism to discover the incredible diversity of religious life and thought among various nations and peoples.

Islamic Metaphysical and Theological Views Concerning the Diversity of Religions and Their Relationship

The Qur'ān always refers to religion in a universal sense. Even the term *islām* is used to mean general surrender to God and the acceptance of Divine Unity and not only the historical message of the Qur'ānic revelation; hence, the reference in the Qur'ān to Abraham as *muslim*. Likewise, the Islamic attestation of faith (*īmān*) is in God, His angels, and His *prophets* and *books* not prophet and book, therefore confirming the plurality of religions, which Islam sees in terms of prophets and revealed books. Numerous verses of the Qur'ān refer to this reality, as when it asserts: "Mankind were one community, and Allah sent (unto them) Prophets as bearers of good tidings and as warners..." (II,213). A Prophetic saying (*ḥadīth*) asserts that there are 124,000 prophets, of whom the Prophet of Islam is the last, whereas, as already mentioned, the Qur'ān says: "Verily, for every nation there is a messenger" (X,48). The first prophet was also the first man, Adam, so that religion in the Qur'ānic perspective is always seen in its universal reality and not as being simply limited to Islam in the more particular sense of the term.

Not all Muslim thinkers and schools, however, considered the full consequences of the Qur'ānic doctrine of the universality of revelation, and many works were written by theologians and jurists in the refutation of other religions or at least most other religions. It was primarily the Sufis and Islamic metaphysicians who drew the full consequences of the doctrine of the universality of revelation and the unity of the inner message of religions beyond the world of forms. The poetry of such Sufi masters as Ibn 'Arabī and Rūmī is replete with references to this doctrine, as the following poem by Rūmī referring to his inner religious and spiritual state exemplifies:

> I am neither eastern nor western, neither heavenly nor earthly,
> I am neither of the natural elements nor of the rotating spheres.
> I am neither from India nor China, from neither Bulgaria nor Tabriz,
> From neither the country of Iraq nor the land of Khurasan.
> My sign is without sign, my locus is without locus,
> It is neither body nor soul for I am myself the Soul of souls.
> Since I expelled all duality, I see the two worlds as one.
> I see the One, I seek the One, I know the One, I call upon the One.[10]

This doctrine has been formulated in modern times in an explicit fashion by the traditional authors and has come to be known as the "transcendent unity of religions," following the title of the well-known work of F. Schuon.

The theologians (*mutakallimūn*) also studied other religions in a series of texts known as *al-Milal wa'l-niḥal,* which have been considered, along with al-Bīrūnī's *India,* as the first works of comparative religion. The Andalusian theologian Ibn Ḥazm, who wrote one of the most extensive of such works, is often called the first scholar of comparative religion, although others bestow this title upon al-Bīrūnī himself. In such works both Islamic schools of thought and Jewish, Christian, and Zoroastrian ones are described. Occasionally there are also references to Manichaeism, Sabeanism, and other religious groups. Some of the works also include theological evaluations and rebuttals against views held by non-Islamic schools of thought or by Islamic ones that are other than those held by the author.

Descriptions of other religions are also found in works of Islamic philosophers and historians, not only in the texts of the theologians. When all these works are considered together, one discovers that there developed within the classical schools of Islamic thought not only a great deal of information about other religions but also theories of comparative religion ranging from the purely metaphysical to the philosophical, theological, and even anthropological—not to speak of the juridical discussion that was of great significance, since it bore upon the practical life of religious minorities within the Islamic world.

The Juridical View of Non-Islamic Religions and Religious Minorities

According to Islamic Law, all "people of the book" (*ahl al-kitāb*) are to be protected in Islamic society, and their laws are to be respected by the rest of the community. Although Islamic history has been witness to many transgressions against various non-Islamic religious communities by this or that ruler or group, the record of Islamic civilization as a whole in its treatment of religious minorities is better than many other civilizations. To this day the seat of the Orthodox Church remains in Istanbul, and the most authentic form of the Christian mass in Aramaic can only be found in Iraq and Persia. The Jewish thinkers in Spain wrote much of their work in Arabic but hardly ever in Latin, and, when they were expelled from Spain in 1492 upon the termination of Muslim power, many took refuge in the Islamic world, where they have preserved their religious heritage to this day. The conflict over land in Palestine between Jews and Arabs has made many people in the West impervious to the long period of accord and harmony between the two communities of Muslims and Jews in Spain, Turkey, Egypt, Persia, and elsewhere. One could also mention many instances of harmonious coexistence between Muslims and Hindus in India outside the Abrahamic world, where there was naturally greater conflict between two diverse interpretations on the formal level of the meaning of religion.

The "people of the book" within the Islamic world, where Islam is a majority, are called *dhimmīs* and are asked to pay a religious tax. In exchange, the Muslim authorities must protect the boarders from attack and keep public order for them as well as for others in the community who are to pay other types of specifically Islamic taxes. The ruler, whether caliph, sultan, or someone else, is responsible for the protection of the life and property of the religious minorities, once they have been accepted juridically as "people of the book."

As to who would be accepted as "people of the book," the Qur'ān mentions explicitly the Christians, Jews, and Sabaeans. But as Islam spread outside of Arabia, first Zoroastrians and later even Buddhists and Hindus came to be considered, at least by a number of jurists, as *ahl al-kitāb* with all that this categorization implies juridically. This includes permission for Muslims to carry out business transactions and even marriage with them as long as the male side is Muslim; that is, a Muslim male may marry a woman of the *ahl al-kitāb* but not vice versa. The dynamics of the relation between the Muslim majority and religious minorities living in its midst is complicated, affected by many historical causes and factors, and not all the instances have been governed by strictly Islamic teachings. Nevertheless, by and large, other religious groups have received protection in Islamic society as witnessed not only by the survival of their most authentic religious and artistic traditions over the centuries but also their economic status, even though they have not been able to exercise the same political and military power as the Muslim majority.

The Contemporary Encounter of Islam and Other Religions in Both East and West

In the contemporary period Islam continues to encounter other religions both within its borders in lands where it is a majority and in lands where Muslims constitute a minority. As far as the Islamic world itself is concerned, Muslims continue to have contact with Christians in the Arab world, Persia, Turkey, Southeast Asia, and Islamic Africa. In some lands, this encounter is for the most part friendly, based on centuries of social and cultural exchange as one sees in Egypt, Syria, Persia, and Iraq. In other lands Christian missionary activity of Western origin is active, which has brought about a much more confrontational attitude on behalf of Muslims vis-à-vis Christianity as one sees in Indonesia and Nigeria, where Muslims view Christianity not only as another religion in competition with Islam but also as an extension of Western civilization, supplied not only with the Gospels but also with bags of rice, hospitals, and specialists in animal husbandry. It is, in fact, necessary to distinguish between the attitude of Muslims to eastern Christians, such as the Orthodox, the Assyrians, and Armenians, and the Christianity brought by European and American missionaries during the colonialist period, which continues to this day. Although the Islamic attitude to the first group is, for the most part, friendly, the attitude to the second is hostile because it threatens the fabric of Islamic society itself.

There are also areas in the world where Muslim-Christian relations have become out-and-out confrontational when strong political and economic factors have been added to the religious. One instance is the Lebanon, which has been laid waste by a tragic civil war. Another is the Philippines, where the Muslims continue to battle for their cultural and religious independence. With the breakup of the Soviet Empire, such cases have increased in both the former Soviet Union and Eastern Europe, the most tragic cases being those of Bosnia-Herzegovina and the revival of old rivalries between the Azerbaijanis and Armenians, not to speak of the attempt of numerous Muslim peoples within Russia itself to assert their sovereignty.

As far as Judaism is considered, relations with Oriental Jews continued on the basis of a long-established equilibrium until the establishment of the State of Israel. Since then the relation has become strained to an ever greater degree, although at the beginning of the conflict, the battle was fought in terms of Israelis and Arabs rather than Jews and Muslims. As the struggle continued, however, non-Arab Muslims became more involved, although the Arab element remains central, and in fact the Palestinian reaction to the occupation of their land is shared by Muslim and Christian Palestinians alike. During the past two decades, while in the bitter existing atmosphere the struggle draws more and more Islamic elements and forces into its orbit, a dialogue has also begun between Muslims and Jews, both within Israel and outside its borders. There is no doubt, however, that all religious dialogue between Islam and Judaism is colored by the paramount problem of Palestine and Israel.

As for Hinduism, the Muslims of the subcontinent took two different roads upon the partition of India in 1947. Those who separated to create Pakistan followed for the most part an attitude of opposition and confrontation vis-à-vis Hinduism; those who remained within India took the path of accommodation and accord. It seems that the two communities followed the destinies of the two Mogul princes, Dārā Shukūh, who translated Hindu texts into Persian, and Aurangzeb, who became emperor and who emphasized the distinctions and differences between Hinduism and Islam. In recent years, however, with the rise of the Hindu Raj and what is called "Hindu fundamentalism," even within India, Hindu-Muslim relations have reached a difficult impasse on the political level. On the human level, however, there is still a great deal of friendship and accord between Hindus and Muslims, wherever the modern fire of partisanship has not destroyed the older traditional order.

The only lands where Muslims have an appreciable direct relation with Buddhists are Malaysia or where Muslims are a small minority, such as in Śrī Lankā, Thailand, Indo-China, and Burma, the case of China itself being an exception because of the Communist order that still dominates over it. In Malaysia, relations are relatively friendly despite occasional communal conflicts that are usually caused by economic questions that become combined with religious identity. In Śrī Lankā, the Muslims have suffered along with the Hindus and Buddhists through the turmoil of the past few years; before the present conflict, they enjoyed a harmonious relation with all the other religious communities. In Indo-China, many of the Muslim groups were destroyed because of the wars of the past decades and are only now trying to rebuild their communities. Muslims live at peace with the Buddhist community in Thailand, whereas in neighboring Burma there is open conflict between Muslims and the central government, which is trying to wipe them out, causing many to flee to Thailand. This conflict is not at all between Islam and Buddhism but rather between a secular government and tribes at its borders that it is trying to dominate.

Many Muslims also are living as minorities in Europe and America, where there is increasing dialogue with Jews, Christians, and other religious communities. Though there has been an anti-Islamic wave since the late 1970s, fanned by the media and certain vested interests, religious harmony prevails for the most part between Muslims and Christians and to some extent Jews in the West and especially in America. However, in certain European countries such as France recent extreme political movements opposed to immigration of foreigners have directed their rhetoric especially against Muslim workers and the "bugbear" of an all-pervasive Islamic "fundamentalism." The main Christian bodies, such as the Vatican and the World Council of Churches, however, have been pursuing a program of creating better understanding with Muslims. As for Muslims, although many fear a new wave of Western cultural domination, there is interest in dialogue and better understanding between Islam and other religions. They are interested as long as such a dialogue does not lead to that kind of ecumenism which reduces religions to the least common denominator and sacrifices Divine institutions and doctrines in the name of peace but ultimately for a banal humanism that can never lead to that peace which "passeth all understanding."

The Significance of the Study of Islam for Religious Studies Today

If the study of Islam is taken seriously, it challenges many of the presumptions of current methods and theories for religious studies in the West. That is why the discipline that is called comparative religion, the history of religions or *Religionswissenschaft* (these terms being far from having the same meaning), has made so little contribution to Islamic studies to this date. If taken seriously as a religion, Islam challenges the "evolutionary" concept of religion by its very presence. Since the nineteenth century, most Western scholars studied religions as evolving to an ever higher level and culminating in Christianity. In such a perspective Islam cannot be but an embarrassing postscript. In reaction to this historicism, the phenomenological approach, which is especially interested in myth and symbol, developed. Again, this approach has found it difficult to fit into its scheme of things a religion such as Islam with its emphasis upon the Divine Law and a metaphysics expressed for the most part in a nonmythological form. The result has been that the greatest practitioners of the phenomenological method in the field of religion, such as M. Eliade, have made their least noteworthy contributions to the field of Islamic studies.

The presence of Islam and its later intellectual tradition also poses a problem for that type of Eurocentric intellectual history, going back to the Encyclopedists and Hegel, that sees all earlier theological and religious thought as stages in the development of European thought. Islam poses the problem of a religion and civilization that is rooted, like that of the West, in the Abrahamic world and that also drew from the philosophical heritage of the ancient Mediterranean world and yet followed another course of development. To take Islamic studies seriously is to cast doubt about the absoluteness of the Eurocentric view of intellectual and religious history, which is a dominant element in Western scholarly and intellectual circles. All of these factors indicate that Islamic studies poses major challenges to the enterprise of religious studies as it is carried out in Western academic circles today.

Islamic studies is also significant for religious studies in that, as a member of the Abrahamic family of religions, Islam has meditated upon the multiplicity of religions for centuries and outside of the framework provided by the secularized modern ambience in which this question is now debated and pondered by scholars of religion and theologians in the West. It was Islam that first crossed the boundary between the world of Abrahamic religions and that of India while taking religion itself seriously as religion and not reducing it to philosophy, history, or anthropology. It is also important for the discipline of religious studies as a whole to mention that much of the formulation of the doctrine of the "transcendent unity of religions" and the perennial philosophy with which it is associated has issued from the Islamic tradition or been closely related to that tradition. Islamic studies is, therefore, at once a challenge to religious studies in the West and a source that can enrich this field, both by expanding its horizons and making it more aware of the necessity of studying religion as religion and not through that reductionism which is so prevalent today and ends up losing the sense of the sacred that lies at the heart of religion.

The Spiritual and Religious Significance of Islam for Present-Day Humanity

The very presence of Islam in the contemporary world is first of all proof, if proof is needed, of the vitality of religion and its all-encompassing nature. Throughout the Islamic world, the faith of Muslims remains strong. The vast majority of Muslim men and women still turn five times a day to Makkah to perform their prayers, fast during Ramaḍān, and try to perform the pilgrimage at least once during their lifetime. Religion has not as yet become a Sunday morning affair nor has laxity set in as far as *praxis* is concerned. Moreover, Islam demonstrates the case of a world in which religion is related to the whole of life, to the economic and social spheres as well as to ethics, to art and thought as well as to private conscience. Although, because of its strength in society, Islam can and has been used by various political forces for their own ends, the very ubiquitousness of the religion prevents that withering secularization of art, thought, society, and the world of nature and the marginalization of religion to which the modern world has become witness and whose bitter fruits are now seen everywhere.

The significance of Islam for present-day humanity also consists in that this religion has been able to preserve to this day something of the spirituality of Abraham and the ancient patriarchs even beyond the confines of the ethnically and linguistically defined Semitic world; for the Prophet of Islam is the last representative of that chain but with a universal message whose content, based on the Oneness of God and obedience to His Law, Islam shares with other monotheistic religions, especially Judaism. Despite the ravages brought upon traditional Muslim life by the invasion of modernism, Islam has preserved to this day, across many cultural and ethnic boundaries, a world in which the transcendent is a living reality in everyday life and in which the Divine Law determines human life and punctuates its moments from beginning to end. Moreover, its Laws are such that they can be practiced in any ambience or social setting, each Muslim being a priest and Imām, and all members of the Islamic community can practice their religious duties whether or not they have access to mosques or other formal Islamic institutions.

The significance of Islam for present-day humanity lies also in the preservation to this day of its spiritual and sapiential dimension, of its methods of inward prayer and meditation, of the possibility of following a spiritual path that leads to God. In contrast to what happened in the Western world, the inner and sapiential dimension of Islam did not become eclipsed or marginalized. On the contrary, spiritual and initiatic guidance still remains available as does access to that sapiential and illuminative knowledge, or gnosis, combined with love, which is the ultimate goal of human existence from a spiritual point of view.

The Islamic intellectual tradition is also of great significance for contemporary humanity, which suffers so much from a divorce between faith and reason, or on another level religion and science. This tradition, while drawing from the same religious and philosophical sources as the West, developed in such a way that it always preserved the nexus between reason and the intellect, and rational thought, mystical intuition, and revelation. Intellectually this tradition occupies a world that is intermediate between the Mediterranean climate in which Western European thought was born and grew, and the banks of the Ganges dominated by the very different world of Hinduism, and in a certain sense Buddhism, at least at its beginning. The Islamic religious and intellectual tradition has a dimension akin to the world of Nāgārjuna and Śaṅkara and another that breathes in nearly the same world as that of St. Thomas Aquinas and Maimonides. And yet this intellectual tradition is not simply "medieval"; it is a living reality that has survived to this day.

In this age in which modern humans are busy destroying their home on earth, in the name of the absolute rights of a purely terrestrial humanity, and where certain scholars blame this prostitution of nature upon the Judeo-Christian tradition, Islam, as the third member of the Abrahamic family, presents a very significant message concerning humankind's relation with the natural world. It emphasizes that all natural phenomena are signs (*āyāt*) of God, that nature shares in the Qur'ānic revelation, and that humans, as God's vicegerents (*khalīfahs*) on earth, are responsible before God for not only themselves but all creatures with which they come into contact.

In fact, Islam emphasizes, in general, responsibility before rights. Human rights derive from the acceptance of human responsibility to both God and His creation. In leveling all creation before the Majesty of God, Islam also destroys the possibility of that agnostic humanism which places human beings at the center of existence, creating that purely earthly anthropomorphism which is now threatening the very life of the anthropos who has sought to take the place of the Divinity. In emphasizing the theocentric perspective, in placing God at the center of the life of both human beings and the world of nature, in emphasizing the rights of God above the rights of our earthly egos, in making possible obedience to a Divine Law that integrates the whole of human life into a pattern possessing ultimate meaning and presenting the possibility of salvation for men and women, and in providing the possibility of pursuing a spiritual path toward that

Ultimate Truth which is also the Supreme Good and Infinite Beauty, Islam displays its spiritual and religious significance not only for the more than a billion Muslims who follow its teachings, but also for all men and women whose minds and souls are touched by the truth and reality of authentic religion, in whatever form it might be.

Recommended Reading

A. J. Arberry. *The Koran Interpreted: A Translation.* New York: Macmillan, 1955. An elegant translation of the Qur'ān that captures better than other English renderings some of the inexhaustible beauty of the original Arabic text.

T. Burckhardt. *An Introduction to Sufism.* Wellingborough: Aquarian Press/Crucible, 1990. A condensed and intellectually precise introduction to the basic tenets of Sufism, written from the Sufi perspective.

V. Danner. *The Islamic Tradition: An Introduction.* New York: Amity House, 1988. An account of both the Islamic religion and the Islamic intellectual tradition from its origin to the present day written from the traditional point of view.

G. Eaton. *Islam and the Destiny of Man.* Albany: State University of New York Press, 1985. A lucid account of the different aspects of Islam by a British Muslim aware of the needs of the Western audience as well as the necessity of presenting the authentic Islamic perspective.

J. Esposito. *Islam, the Straight Path.* New York: Oxford University Press, 1988. An account of Islam and its contemporary development by a sympathetic Western scholar of Islam.

M. Lings. *Muhammad: His Life Based on the Earliest Sources.* London: Islamic Text Society, Allen & Unwin, 1988. A brilliantly written recitation of the life of the Prophet, based upon the traditional sources and making available for the first time for the English reader an account of the life of the Prophet as seen by Muslims.

S. Murata. *The Tao of Islam.* Albany: State University of New York Press, 1992. The most profound study in English of gender relations in Islam based not only on Islamic sources but also on certain tenets of Far Eastern thought related to gender complementarity.

S. H. Nasr. *Ideals and Realities of Islam.* London: Allen & Unwin, 1966. A work written from the perspective of traditional Islam and dealing with the Qur'ān, the Prophet, and other basic aspects of the religion, including the relation between Sunnism and Shi'ism.

———, ed. *Islamic Spirituality,* 2 vols. London: Routledge & Kegan Paul, 1987, 1991. A major reference work written by both Muslim scholars and Western scholars sympathetic to the Islamic point of view, it covers nearly every aspect of Islamic spirituality both in its foundation and in its historical and geographical unfolding.

F. Schuon. *Understanding Islam*. Translated by D. M. Matheson. London: Allen & Unwin, 1963. The most profound work written by a European on Islam, dealing primarily with the inner dimension of the religion with many references and comparisons to other traditions including Christianity and Hinduism.

Notes

1. In traditional Islamic sources the name of the Prophet of Islam is always followed by the formula "may blessings and peace be upon him" (*ṣalla'Llāh*[u] *'alayhī wa sallam*) while the name of other prophets is followed by "may peace be upon him" (*'alayhi's-salām*). Throughout this essay, whenever the word "Prophet" is used in a capitalized form, it is in reference to the Prophet of Islam. Traditional phrases of praise and respect concerning both God and the Prophet have been omitted.
2. The Qur'ānic translations throughout this essay are based on M. Pickthall and A. J. Arberry with modifications made whenever it has seemed necessary.
3. The date on the left side refers to the Islamic lunar calendar beginning with the migration of the Prophet from Makkah to Madinah in 622 C.E. and the date on the right to the Western calendar.
4. The term *imām*, literally "the person who stands before or in front," has many meanings in Islam. Its most ordinary meaning is in reference to the person who leads the prayers and by extension the person in a mosque who usually leads the congregational prayers. It also means one who is outstanding in a field of knowledge and as such it is an honorific title given to certain great Islamic scholars such as Imām Abū Ḥanīfah or Imām Ghazzālī. It can also be used as the title of the ruler in classical Sunni political theory, in which case it is equivalent to *khalīfah*. In Twelve-Imām Shi'ism, the term *imām* has been traditionally used in a much more restricted sense as referring to the person who carries the "Prophetic Light" (*al-nūr al-muḥammadī*) within himself and like the Prophet is inerrant (*ma'ṣūm*). The number of Imāms (henceforth capitalized in the case of the Shi'ite Imāms) is limited to twelve in Twelve-Imām Shi'ism, of whom the first is 'Alī, the second and third his sons Ḥasan and Ḥusayn, and the last the hidden Imām, Muḥammad al-Mahdī. For Ismā'īlīs there is a chain of living imāms going back to 'Alī and Fāṭimah and for Zaydīs, anyone who is able to gain power to protect the Divine Law and rule according to it is accepted as imām.
5. M. Lings, *Muhammad: His Life Based on the Earliest Sources* (London: Islamic Text Society, Allen & Unwin, 1988), 44.
6. Lings, *Muhammad*, 69.
7. These are just some, of more than a hundred, of the most famous names of the Prophet, which correspond to different aspects of his nature, function, and status. Muḥammad is derived from the root *ḥamd*, meaning praise, and means the praised one. Aḥmad is the more inward name of the Prophet related to the same

root whereas Muṣṭafā means the "chosen one." The litany of the names of the Prophet plays an important role in Islamic devotion and piety and especially in Sufism.

8. All these quotations are from Allama Sir Abdullah al-Ma'mun al-Suhrawardy, *The Sayings of Muhammad* (New York: Carol Publishing Group, 1990), with certain modifications.
9. Lings, *Muhammad,* 330–331.
10. From Jalāl al-Dīn Rūmī's *Dīwān-i-kabīr,* as translated by S. H. Nasr.

Conclusion

If the experience of the editor has any relevance to that of the reader, I felt like converting to the religious tradition I happened to be reading about—only some of them would not let me, at least not easily. So if you have felt similarly at the end of each chapter, do not get alarmed. It is not surprising that, as human beings, we might feel, at one time or another, an almost overpowering pull exerted by each of these varied expressions of human religiosity. When expressed by one who is at one with it, each tradition possesses its own unique appeal: Hinduism, with its calm reassurance that we live in a user-friendly universe; Buddhism, with its dynamic and liberative blend of wisdom and compassion; Confucianism, which reminds us that decency may be next to divinity if not one with it; Taoism, with its enchanting appreciation of life as integral with nature and having a loose, and preferably long, story-line; Judaism, as a compelling example of survival and then revival in the face of prolonged oppression; Christianity, gloriously endeavoring to emulate its founder as "fully human and fully divine"; and Islam, with the majestic simplicity, like that of a mosque, of its conviction of God's absolute supremacy. If these epigrammatic summations no longer appear enigmatic to the reader, then the authors of this book have achieved their goal. And the book also will have served its purpose if the reader lays it down with the conviction that there is something charming rather than alarming about religious plurality.

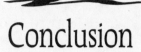

Notes on Contributors

Arvind Sharma was born in India and is Professor of Comparative Religion at McGill University, Montreal, Canada. He is the author of *The Hindu Gītā* (1986); *A Hindu Perspective on the Philosophy of Religion* (1990); the editor of a trilogy on women and religion: *Women in World Religions* (1987); *Religion and Women* (1993); and *Today's Woman in World Religions* (1993); and is presently engaged in compiling *A Source Book of Religious Tolerance.*

Masao Abe was born in Japan and is currently Visiting Professor in the Department of Philosophy at Purdue University. A leading interpreter of Buddhism, he is also a prominent participant in Christian-Buddhist dialogue. His key essay "Kenotic God and Dynamic Śūnyatā" appears in John B. Cobb, Jr., ed., *The Emptying God: A Buddhist-Jewish-Christian Conversation* (1990), and his book *Zen and Western Thought* (1985) won the American Academy of Religion Award for outstanding contribution to scholarship in religion.

Tu Wei-ming was born in China and taught Chinese intellectual history at Princeton University and the University of California at Berkeley before joining Harvard University as Professor of Chinese History and Philosophy in 1981. He has also lectured on Confucian Humanism at Peking University, Taiwan University, Chinese University in Hong Kong, and University of Paris. He is the author of *Neo-Confucian Thought in Action: Wang Yang-ming's Youth* (1976); *Centrality and Commonality* (1976); *Humanity and Self-Cultivation* (1979); *Confucian Thought: Selfhood as Creative Transformation* (1985); and *Way, Learning and Politics: Essays on the Confucian Intellectual* (1989). A member of the Committee on the Study of Religion at Harvard and a Fellow of the American Academy of Arts and Sciences, he is currently interpreting Confucian ethics as a spiritual resource for the emerging global community.

Liu Xiaogan was born in China. He obtained a Ph.D. in philosophy from Beijing University and taught there before coming to the United States. He is currently Visiting Scholar in the Department of Religion at Princeton University. Most of his publications are about Taoism. The first part of his book *Chuang-Tzu's Philosophy and Its Development* will soon appear in English translation under the title *Classifying the Chuang-Tzu Chapters.*

Jacob Neusner is Distinguished Research Professor of Religious Studies, University of South Florida, Tampa, and Life Member of Clare Hall, Cambridge University, England. He holds thirteen honorary degrees and has published five hundred books on Judaism. He has also served as president of the American Academy of Religion (1968–1969).

Harvey G. Cox is Victor S. Thomas Professor of Divinity at Harvard University. His best-known work is *The Secular City* (1965); *Many Mansions: A Christian's Encounter with Other Faiths* is the most recent. His other works include *The Feast of Fools* (1969); *The Seduction of the Spirit* (1973); and *Turning East* (1977). He is an ordained Baptist minister.

Seyyed Hossein Nasr was born in Iran. From 1958 to 1979 he was Professor of Philosophy at Tehran University. He became the Professor of Islamic Studies at Temple University in 1979 and is presently University Professor of Islamic Studies at George Washington University. He delivered the Gifford lectures in 1981, which have been published under the title *Knowledge and the Sacred.* His other works include *Ideals and Realities of Islam* (1966) and *Traditional Islam in the Modern World* (1987).